MARYVILLE UNIVERSITY
REF BX955 .P35 v.26
W9-BXB-991
3 0000 18309

DATE DUE

NO LONGER PROPERTY OF
MARYVILLE UNIVERSITY LIBRARY

GAYLORD PRINTED IN U.S.A.

HISTORY OF THE POPES

VOL. XXVI.

PASTOR'S HISTORY OF THE POPES

THE HISTORY OF THE POPES. Translated from the German of LUDWIG, FREIHERR VON PASTOR. Edited, as to Vols. I.–VI. by the late FREDERICK IGNATIUS ANTROBUS, and, as to Vols. VII.–XXIV. by RALPH FRANCIS KERR, of the London Oratory. In 26 Volumes.

Vols. I. and II.	A.D. 1305–1458
Vols. III. and IV.	A.D. 1458–1483
Vols. V. and VI.	A.D. 1484–1513
Vols. VII. and VIII.	A.D. 1513–1521
Vols. IX. and X.	A.D. 1522–1534
Vols. XI. and XII.	A.D. 1534–1549
Vols. XIII. and XIV.	A.D. 1550–1559
Vols. XV. and XVI.	A.D. 1559–1565
Vols. XVII. and XVIII.	A.D. 1566–1572
Vols. XIX. and XX.	A.D. 1572–1585
Vols. XXI. and XXII.	A.D. 1585–1591
Vols. XXIII. and XXIV.	A.D. 1592–1604
Vols. XXV. and XXVI.	A.D. 1605–1621

The original German text of the *History of the Popes* is published by Herder & Co., Freiburg (Baden).

THE
HISTORY OF THE POPES

FROM THE CLOSE OF THE MIDDLE AGES

DRAWN FROM THE SECRET ARCHIVES OF THE VATICAN AND OTHER ORIGINAL SOURCES

FROM THE GERMAN OF

LUDWIG, FREIHERR VON PASTOR

TRANSLATED AND EDITED BY

DOM ERNEST GRAF, O.S.B.

MONK OF BUCKFAST

VOLUME XXVI.

LEO XI. AND PAUL V. (1605–1621)

12069

B. HERDER BOOK CO.

17 SOUTH BROADWAY,

ST. LOUIS, MO.

1937.

Maryville College Library Saint Louis

Imprimi potest.
Subiaco, April 9, 1936.
Dom M. Etcheverry, Abbot General.

PRINTED IN GREAT BRITAIN

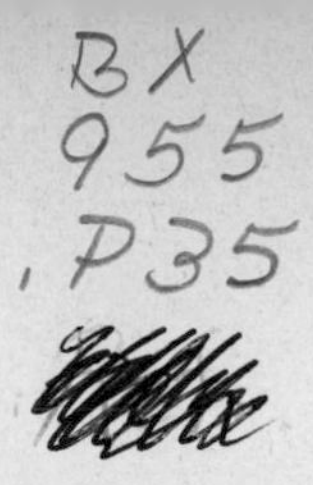
BX
955
.P35

CONTENTS OF VOLUME XXVI.

For Bibliography, see Volume XXV.

TABLE OF CONTENTS OF VOLUME XXVI.

CHAPTER I.

CATHOLIC REFORM AND RESTORATION IN FRANCE—BERULLE AND HIS ORATORY THE URSULINES AND THE VISITATION—FRANCIS DE SALES AND FRANCES DE CHANTAL—REVIVAL OF CATHOLICISM IN THE SPANISH NETHERLANDS.

CHAPTER II.

THE POSITION OF CATHOLICS IN THE GERMAN DIASPORA, IN THE REPUBLIC OF THE NETHERLANDS, AND IN GREAT BRITAIN AND IRELAND—THE GUNPOWDER PLOT AND THE OATH OF ALLEGIANCE—PAUL V. AND JAMES I.'S PLANS FOR A SPANISH MARRIAGE.

CHAPTER III.

RUSSIA AND POLAND—THE END OF THE FALSE DEMETRIUS — CATHOLIC RESTORATION UNDER SIGISMUND III., KING OF POLAND—THE UNION OF THE RUTHENIANS.

CHAPTER IV.

RELATION OF PAUL V. WITH THE EMPERORS RUDOLPH II., MATTHIAS AND FERDINAND II—GOOD RESULTS OF THE CATHOLIC RESTORATION IN GERMANY—THE BOHEMIAN REVOLUTION AND THE BEGINNING OF THE THIRTY YEARS' WAR.

CHAPTER V.

PAUL V. AS A PATRON OF THE ARTS—COMPLETION OF ST. PETER'S—THE PAULINE CHAPEL IN S. MARIA MAGGIORE—THE PALACE OF THE QUIRINAL—STREETS AND FOUNTAINS—THE BORGHESE PALACE AND VILLA—TRANSFORMATION OF THE ETERNAL CITY.

LIST OF UNPUBLISHED DOCUMENTS IN APPENDIX.

CHAPTER I.

CATHOLIC REFORM AND RESTORATION IN FRANCE—BERULLE AND HIS ORATORY—THE URSULINES AND THE VISITATION —FRANCIS DE SALES AND FRANCES DE CHANTAL—REVIVAL OF CATHOLICISM IN THE SPANISH NETHERLANDS.

ONE of the things which Paul V. had most at heart was to further the revival of Catholic life in France which followed Henry IV.'s reconciliation with the Church. An immense effort was required to undo the harm of the last thirty troublous years.[1] Rome was well aware of the fact, hence, when Paul V. confirmed Maffeo Barberini in his post of nuncio at the French Court to which Clement VIII. had appointed him at the close of 1604, he also confirmed the instructions which Barberini had then received. These were lucidly summarized in the instruction which Cardinal Aldobrandini drew up for the guidance of the papal representative and they are a remarkable statement of the aims of the policy for a Catholic restoration which the Holy See pursued in France.[2]

[1] In the " Drey Reisen nach Cistertz ", which the Cistercian, FR. JOH. KONRAD TACHLER made to the General Chapters, in 1605, 1609, 1615 (published at Bregenz, 1893), we find remarkable evidence of this state of things ; a dearth of sermons, neglect of the churches, desecration of the Sunday, and a light and frivolous tone. VINCENZO SCAMOZZI, in the journey he undertook in 1606, from Paris to Venice, saw with horror the desolation to which the Huguenots had reduced the churches ; see MORSOLIN, *Viaggio inedito di V. Scamozzi da Parigi a Venezia*, Venezia, 1881, 25.

[2] See the text from the original in the Barberini Library, Rome, in the appendix to Vol. XXXIII, No. 45. According to NICOLETTI (*Vita di Urbano VIII.*, t. I., l. 1, ch. 11 and 12) the question had been raised under Leo XI. as to whether Barberini should

The instruction rightly starts from the fundamental principle that the religious unity which France had at one time enjoyed, could only be restored by means of a complete reform of ecclesiastical conditions. This idea should guide the nuncio in his attitude towards the hierarchy as well as towards the Crown. For this reason the instruction enjoins the greatest circumspection and a due regard for the character of Henry IV. Personal experience obviously inspired the writer of the instruction when he warned the nuncio to give no credence to the shrewd Béarnais when he gave himself the air of understanding but little of the art of diplomacy, seeing that he was but a soldier; the exact opposite was the truth; the gifted and vivacious monarch was endowed with far greater knowledge even in those things than he deemed it expedient to display. Barberini was especially exhorted to be very cautious because Henry IV. was extremely suspicious as well as very elusive. Sharp measures would be out of place in his case, but this did not preclude frank remonstrances; but on no account must he be offended. In treating with him it was best to alternate the soft with the loud tone.

The task of the nuncio was both comprehensive and arduous. He was to try to induce the frivolous monarch not only to lead a religious and moral life in his own person, but to win him over, as a ruler, to the aims of the policy for a Catholic restoration. In this matter the nuncio must always bear in mind that Henry IV. was above all things a soldier and a politician. As a man of arms he had but little understanding of religious matters, hence he must be enlightened on the subject. As a politician, all he thought of was his own

be continued in France; Cardinal Arigoni secured his confirmation, "*da cui consigli servivasi Paolo V. i primi anni del pontificato" (Barb. 4730, Vatican Library). The *reports of Barberini on his French nunciature are in (Barb. 7834, 7867–7872, and papers belonging to them in Barb. 3622, specially pages 72 *seq.*, 177 *seq.*, being statistical and geographical details), Vatican Library, and *Nunziat. di Francia*, 50, Papal Secret Archives.

advantage, hence he must be made to see that his interests would best be served if he fell in with the plans of the Pope. To this end the nuncio was instructed to point out to the king how greatly it was in his interest, as king of France, to follow even in the religious sphere the tradition of a most Christian king and how greatly his political plans would benefit if he were to restore religious unity in his kingdom. The nuncio should not neglect to point out what the loss of this blessing meant for Germany.

Before all else Henry IV. must be prevented from granting further concessions to the Huguenots who had already derived far too many advantages from the Edict of Nantes.[1] Out of the many means by which the king could repress the Huguenots, the easiest and the least likely to provoke trouble would be to pursue the policy adopted in Poland, that is, not to give heretics any office in the State but, on the contrary, to favour those who returned to the Church. The Huguenots were the enemies of peace and order; no weapons should be put into their hands.

Besides these more negative means many others, of a positive kind, are also mentioned. In the first place, stress is rightly laid on the importance of episcopal appointments. Only worthy and blameless persons must be put forward as candidates for bishoprics; none other could hope to secure the approval of Rome. The misuse of the privileges conceded by the Concordate had been the real cause of every evil; it had led to soldiers and women obtaining bishoprics and abbeys; the Pope would no longer suffer such abuses. In regard to this matter the king himself had given Cardinal Medici promises for the future. Nor would the Holy See hear of any further extension of the concordatory privileges which the Instruction describes as excessive. Here the writer had chiefly in view the so-called royal prerogative in

[1] The truth of this opinion is confirmed by RANKE's remark (*Päpste*, II.[6], 279) that Henry IV. had, by the Edict of Nantes, "granted the Huguenots an independence such as to justify the question whether it was compatible with the idea of the State."

virtue of which the Crown took it on itself to appoint an administrator of every vacant diocese until the papal confirmation of the nominee to the See, and that official disposed of the revenues and the lower ecclesiastical offices as if he were a real bishop. This pretension the Instruction qualifies as intolerable. The nuncio should be no less careful to prevent any infringement of ecclesiastical jurisdiction on the part of the secular power. In this respect the nuncio Bufalo had already achieved a measure of success ; it was necessary to pursue this path, but by means of prudent discussion rather than with threats, otherwise the bishops would be unable to carry out the work of reform, a thing which was also of considerable importance. It was rightly thought in Rome that in order to bring about a reform of ecclesiastical conditions in France the best, nay the only means, was the publication of the decrees of the Council of Trent. The Instruction recalls the promises to this effect which Henry IV. had made on the occasion of his reconciliation with the Church. Let the nuncio strongly insist on their execution. Barberini was instructed to make strong representation on this point both to the king and to the ministers and the Parliament, and not to desist until he had achieved his purpose. In this respect Henry IV. had given the best assurances to Cardinals Medici and Aldobrandini ; to the latter the king had promised, on the occasion of his farewell audience, to carry the affair through within two months, and now years had gone by, notwithstanding the fact that the king had himself recognized the utility of the decrees. It was intolerable that France alone should resist the decrees of a General Council. The difficulties that were put forward could not stand inasmuch as the decrees dealt almost exclusively with the reform of the clergy and hardly touched the secular sphere. If the king was so minded he could easily bend Parliament to his will. The nuncio is further instructed to remove the prejudice that the decrees of the Council would injure the privileges enjoyed by France and to show how, on the contrary, the bettering of ecclesiastical conditions was closely linked to the preservation of the political order. The Pope had made up his mind to see this affair finally settled and he would never desist from his demands in this respect. Until the publication, the nuncio was to direct individual bishops to carry out the necessary reforms, to visit their dioceses, to erect seminaries and to hold diocesan and provincial synods. Among the indispensable reforms one was emphasized which was bound to give pleasure to Henry IV., namely a warning to preachers not to let their zeal carry them into the political sphere.

Besides these, the chief demands, the Instruction contained a number of special wishes of the Holy See. These were concerned with the position of the Jesuits, the problem of Calvinism in Château-Dauphin, near Monte Viso, the continued support of the Catholic restoration in Béarn, the neglect of the French bishops to come to Rome for the pallium and, lastly, military measures by Henry IV. against Geneva.

What was desired for the Jesuits had been happily obtained by Barberini whilst Clement VIII. was still alive.[1] The realization of his other plans, such as the execution of his extensive programme of reform, would have required a much longer term of office than that which was granted to Barberini. There was no lack of zeal on his part. He did not find it difficult to persuade Henry IV. to forbid the profession of Calvinism in Château-Dauphin, seeing that this prohibition had already been enforced by a royal edict of the year 1598.[2] In other ways also Barberini influenced the king

[1] *Cf.* our notes, Vol. XXIII, pp. 174 *seqq.*

[2] *Havevano in questo tempo gli heretici nel borgo di Chianale della valle di Castel Delfino sottoposta alla Corona di Francia e situata di qua dall'Alpi nella diocesi di Torino, introdotte le prediche et altri ministerii della lor setta contro un editto publicato da Enrigo l'anno 1598, nel quale si prohibisce di qua da monti ogni esercitio di heresia ; e ciò havevano fatto sotto finto pretesto d'haverne da lui ottenuta licenza ; di che dolendosi i Cattolici, i quali già altre volte si erano opposti a questi tentativi e ricorrendo per aiuto al Nuntio di Torino, fecero ch'egli si adoprasse con Maffeo, acciocchè dal Christianissimo s'impetrasse espresso comandamento per l'osservanza del suo editto. Abbracciò volentieri Maffeo tanto giusta protettione, e con vive ragioni dimostrate al re le fraudi, con le quali davano quegli heretici falsamente

against the Calvinists. Among other things he suggested measures against the publication of heretical writings. These proposals were under discussion at the time of his recall by Paul V. to Rome.[1] By means of friendly discussions Barberini also endeavoured, though unsuccessfully, to bring back to the Church the influential minister Sully and the learned philologist Isaac Casaubonus.[2] He was instrumental in securing the appointment of the devout Pierre de Berulle as tutor to the Dauphin.[3] Through Barberini also the see of Apt was given a good bishop to replace one who had been utterly unfit.[4] He took energetic action against an anti-papal pamphlet of Louis Servin, the advocate-general, whose opposition to the Jesuits was well known, as well as against those who spread forged papal indulgences.[5] To the efforts

ad intendere che Sua Maestà havesse acconsentito a quelle ingiuste dimande, lo indusse a comandar loro, che si astenessero per l'avvenire da tali esercitii, consolando in un tempo i Cattolici di quel contorno, e tenendo lontano dall'Italia il pericolo di così abominevole infettione. NICOLETTI, *Vita di Urbano*, VIII., t. I, in Barb. 4730, p. 102, Vatican Library.

[1] *Ibid.*, pp. 222 *seq.*

[2] See NICOLETTI, *loc. cit.*, p. 223. Paul V. also urged Sully's conversion; see the *Brief of October 3, 1605, in the *Epist.*, I., 229, Papal Secret Archives. *Cf. Goujet*, I., 26 *seq.*

[3] See NICOLETTI, *loc. cit.*, p. 225.

[4] The unworthy behaviour of the bishop of Apt, Pompey de Perille, and his removal through Barberini are described in more detail by NICOLETTI (*loc. cit.*, pp. 219–222).

[5] See NICOLETTI, *loc. cit.*, pp. 219 and 222: Et in quanto agli heretici sicome Maffeo mostrossi generalmente nimico della lor setta, nondimeno maggior odio mostrò verso di quelli, ch'esso chiamava libertini, persone non heretiche di nome, ma ne tampoco cattoliche, ond'erano li più perversi di ogni altra setta. Fra questi si teneva il principale il Servino altre volte nominato, al cui libro intitolato il Gallo Franco, che conteneva diversi errori, fece rispondere da Federico Salice; et egli medesimo con versi latini lo improbò, dove alludendo al nome di Servino, dicevasi ch'egli servilmente vendesse l'opera sua a quelli che erano contrarii al Papa et alla Sede Apostolica. For *Servin cf.* REUSCH, *Index*, II., 285, 345, 349, 359.

of the nuncio it was likewise due that the Sorbonne passed a censure on the opinions, as strange as they were dogmatically untenable, which Pierre Victor Calvert Palma Cayet, a convert, had propounded in an historical work.[1] Barberini exerted himself on behalf of the reform of the clergy especially in the assembly of the clergy of France which met in Paris towards the end of 1605 and which made the restoration of ecclesiastical discipline one of the chief points of its debates.[2] On this occasion the spokesman of the clergy paid tribute to the improvement in the appointment of bishops but he could not refrain from lamenting, with the utmost freedom, the fact that in this respect abuses were still of frequent occurrence. Henry IV. replied that the praise thus bestowed on him would encourage him to do even better in the future, but that as regards the removal of abuses, the higher clergy should make a beginning with their own body. With respect to this Barberini rightly pointed out that if the bishops were to take measures to bring about a reform, they must also possess the necessary authority; moreover it was imperative that the king should himself set a good example. Henry did not resent these frank remarks since they had been made both courteously and discreetly. So great was his regard for Barberini that he took steps for his elevation to the College of Cardinals.[3]

The nuncio's remark that the bishops must have the necessary authority if they were to reform the clergy, had for its aim the publication, in France, of the decrees of the Council of Trent, and to this end Barberini exerted himself to the utmost. It was he who determined Paul V. to press energetically for a solution of this weighty question by means of a series of Briefs. In the summer of 1605, papal Briefs, nicely adapted to the character and position of their

[1] See NICOLETTI, *loc. cit.*, p. 216, and SERBAT, *Assemblées*, 397 *seq.* This refers to CAYET's *Chronologie septennaire*, 1604; *cf.* REUSCH, *loc. cit.*, 191.

[2] *Cf.* SERBAT, *loc. cit.*, 317.

[3] The above from the detailed description of NICOLETTI, *loc. cit.*, pp. 266 *seqq.*, 280 *seq.*, 331–351.

respective recipients,[1] were addressed to Henry IV.[2] as well as to Cardinals Joyeuse, Gondi and Sourdis. To these princes of the Church the Pope wrote that he had called upon the French hierarchy to carry through a reform of the clergy; the best means to this end, as was seen in Spain and elsewhere, was the execution of the Tridentine decrees, and for this they should press the king and the bishops with all their power.[3] Through Barberini as his intermediary, the Pope also appealed in this affair to two of the most prominent members of the royal council, viz. Nicolas Brulart de Sillery [4] and Chancellor Pomponne de Bellièvre.[5] Previously to this the Pope had addressed an earnest appeal to all the French bishops urging them to work for the reform of the clergy, as this was one of Paul V.'s greatest anxieties.[6] At the same time Paul V. begged the king to assist him in this matter.[7] Repeatedly he urged him to take action against the Huguenots of the South of France.[8]

[1] See MARTIN, *Gallicanisme*, 334 *seq*.

[2] *Brief of August 18, 1605, *Epist.*, I., 132.

[3] See the *Briefs to Cardinal Joyeuse, Gondi, and Sourdis, August 18, 1605, which all agree as to their contents. In that to Joyeuse, it is stated: "Cogitamus assidue de reformatione istius cleri, quam etiam plerosque ex episcopis Gallicanis desiderare intelligimus. Ad hanc rem nihil utilius arbitramur quam introductionem constitutionum sacrosancti concilii Trid. Nam quantum profuerint correctioni ecclesiasticorum tum in Italia tum in Hispania, optime nosti. . . . Multae difficultates sese offerunt." By your influence, "multi ex ecclesiast. disponantur. Scripsimus de hac eadem re Henrico regi," on whom we count. *Epist.*, I., 133, 134, 135, Papal Secret Archives.

[4] *Brief of August 18, 1605, *ibid.*, 140.

[5] *Brief of August 18, 1605, *ibid.*, 138.

[6] *Brief July 15, 1605, *ibid.*, 72.

[7] *Brief of July 15, 1605, *ibid.*, 73.

[8] *Brief of June 19, 1605: "Haereticos habuisse conciliabula atque conventus in finibus comitatus Avinionensis; . . . inita ab eis fuisse consilia invadendi Aurangii oppidum; . . . petit, ut prudentia et auctoritate sua eorum consilia vana reddat; . . . Nuncius de his omnibus aget" (*Epist.*, I., 12). *Ibid.*, 149,

This time also resistance to the reform decrees of Trent proceeded from the cathedral chapters and more particularly from the various Parliaments. Against these Barberini deployed all the resources of his diplomatic skill. Above all he sought to influence the king himself through the Jesuit Père Coton. Fully aware as he was of the difficulties of the situation the nuncio was of opinion that it was enough, for the time being, to keep alive, before all else, the question of the publication of the Council. But Paul V. was anxious for an early decision and for the convocation of the clergy. However, the obstacles to these measures proved too strong. Henry IV. protested his good intentions but for the moment there was nothing to be done.[1] Thereupon Barberini drew up a plan according to which a Congregation of the Council was to be erected in Paris itself of which Cardinals de Joyeuse and Du Perron and some of the outstanding bishops were to be members.[2] He was not to see the realization of so original a plan inasmuch as in consequence of his elevation to the cardinalate, on September 11th, 1606, he had to leave France in order to take his place in the Sacred College.

As a successor to Barberini Paul V. chose his *Maestro di camera*, Robert Ubaldini, who was known to be a sincere friend of France.[3] The gifted and energetic Florentine was

*Brief of August 22, 1605 : " Curet ne oppidum Aurangii tradatur gubernatori haeretico (civitat. nostram Avinionem et comit. Venaysinum laedere possit)," Papal Secret Archives.

[1] See MARTIN, *Gallicanisme*, 335 *seqq*. *Cf*. SERBAT, *Assemblées*, 317.

[2] *Cf*. MARTIN, *loc. cit.*, 333 *seq.*, who draws special attention to the merit of Barberini in having seized the initiative in this important matter.

[3] *Cf*. DU PERRON, *Ambassades*, 305. As the ambassador of Mantua wrote from Rome, June 13, 1607, the nomination of Ubaldini was already fixed then (Gonzaga Archives, Mantua). Paul V. did not willingly give up his Maestro di camera. As to the statement of CARDELLA (VI., 177) that the nephews of the Pope urged him to send away Ubaldini, out of jealousy, there is no source for such an assertion. On the other hand we know

to hold the French nunciature for the space of nine years. Under Ubaldini the Hôtel Cluny, which had been the residence of the papal representative since 1601, became the heart of Catholic life in France: from this central point the nuncio kept up active relations with all convinced Catholics of some importance, thereby rendering the most signal services to the Holy See.[1] His influence over the queen-regent and the French clergy was as important as it was salutary. As regards

for certain that Ubaldini was chosen instead of Joseph Ferrier, whom Henry IV. had asked for, because he was the candidate who, failing the king's own choice, would have been the most welcome. See MARTIN, *Gallicanisme*, 352, note i. The *Briefs to Henry IV. and the Admiral of France concerning the nomination of Ubaldini are dated September 20, 1607. *Epist.*, III., 168, 187, Papal Secret Archives.

[1] The *reports of Ubaldini during the time of his nunciature, as interesting as they are important, addressed mostly to Cardinal Borghese, but also to other nuncios and princes, are in the original in the Papal Secret Archives, *Borghese*, II., 251, and *Francia*, 53, 54, 55; there are also copies in *Bolognetti*, 149–153. How much these reports were appreciated by his contemporaries is shown by the numerous copies extant. They are to be found, in Rome, in the Altieri Library, in 6 vols.; the Barberini Section, viz. 5873–9, 5898–5903; in the Chigi Library, M., I., 15 and 16; in the Corsini Library, *Cod.* 512–517 (= 33 G., 14–19) for the years 1608–1615 (*cf.* LÄMMER, *Zur Kirchengesch.*, 167 *seq.*), and finally, in the Bibliothèque Nationale in Paris (*cf.* MARSAND, I., 245 *seq.*). The *Instructions of Borghese to Ubaldini are in the Papal Secret Archives, *Borghese* I., 928, 929, 931, and *Francia*, 294, 295. *Cf.* also Barb. 5914–5915, Vatican Library, and *Cod.* S. 6, 7, and 8 of the Angelica Library, Rome (see NARDUCCI, *Bibl.*, 501 *seq.*; LÄMMER, *loc. cit.*, 76 *seq.*). Single excerpts of Ubaldini's reports were published by SIRI (*Mémorie*, I., *seq.*); many others by LÄMMER, *loc. cit.*, and MELET (*cf.* below, p. 14 *seq.*); RITTER, *Briefe und Akten*, II.; PERRENS, *Mariages espan.* and *L'Église et l'État*, I–II; PRAT, *Coton*; lastly, quite recently, by HILTEBRANDT in *Quellen u. Forsch. des Preuss. Instit.*, XV. and XVI., and in MARTIN, *loc. cit.*, 352 *seqq.* A critical edition of all the reports, in which those already published should be indexed, would be a most welcome piece of work.

the rôle played by him in the internal policy of the realm, we can only regret, in the interests of France, that his intervention could not go further because of the religious questions which absorbed the best part of the nuncio's energy.[1]

Ubaldini reached Paris towards the end of the autumn of 1607. He lost no time in establishing contact with such persons as stood highest in the consideration of Henry IV. Chief among these were the Chancellor Sillery, the Secretary of State Villeroi, President Jeannin, the Jesuit Coton and Cardinal Du Perron.[2] Ubaldini played a decisive part in the appointment, in 1608, of Coton as confessor to the King and tutor to the Dauphin [3]; on the other hand he failed in his attempt to set up the Inquisition in France [4]; even his efforts to get the reform decrees of the Council of Trent accepted proved in vain. For the moment, so he was compelled to report to Rome in August 19th, 1608, the thing was impossible.[5] On the other hand he was able to announce that Henry IV. favoured the return of the Calvinists to the Church.[6] In other respects also the king occasionally took measures favourable to the Catholic restoration [7] though he refused to adopt a definitely Catholic policy which would have arrayed against him the Protestant forces, both domestic and foreign, whose worth he had learned to

[1] Opinion of MARTIN (*loc. cit.*, 352).

[2] *Cf.* PERRENS, *L'Église et l'État*, I., 283 *seq.*

[3] See PRAT, III., 2 *seq.*, 17 *seq.*

[4] See the report of Ubaldini of January 20, 1608, used by PERRENS, I., 299.

[5] See Ubaldini's report of August 19, 1608, used as above, 299 *seq.*

[6] *Cf.* PERRENS, I., 301 *seq.*; PRAT, II., 566 *seq.*, 626 *seq.* *Cf.* Y. DE LA BRIÈRE in *Études*, XCIX., 57 *seq.*

[7] *Cf.* PHILIPPSON, in the *Hist. Zeitschr.*, XXXI., 125 *seq.* The edict of Henry IV. of December, 1606, on the non-collection of royalties from churches long exempt from them was vetoed by the Parliament; see PHILLIPPS, *Das Regalienrecht in Frankreich*, Halle, 1873, 130 *seqq.*

appreciate at an earlier period, when they were still at his service.[1]

Just as Henry IV. kept up his old relations with the foreign Protestant Powers, so was he unwilling to break with the French Huguenots and the Gallicans.[2] When in May, 1608, Ubaldini suggested to the king to deprive the Huguenots of their strongholds the answer he received was very unsatisfactory.[3] Henry took up a similar attitude towards the efforts which the Gallicans were renewing just then to bring about a separation, or at least an estrangement between the Pope and the Church of France. The focus of these endeavours was the Parliament of Paris whose first president, Achille de Harley, in conjunction with the Advocate-General Louis Servin and the Second President, Auguste de Thou, a friend of the Huguenots, formed a clique which together with prominent Calvinists such as Groslot de Lisle and Du Plessis Mornay, was filled with the same hatred for the papacy as that kindred spirit of theirs, Paolo Sarpi.[4] Gallican pamphlets and satirical writings against the Pope and the Jesuits, which originated in these circles, caused Ubaldini much

[1] See CORNELIUS, in the *Münchner Hist. Jahrb.* for 1866, 85 *seq.*

[2] *Cf.* MARIÉJOL, VI., 2, 100 ; PHILIPPSON, in the *Hist Zeitschr.*, XXXI., 128 *seq.* The transference of the Calvinist chapel to Charenton, near Paris, mentioned here, carried out in defiance of the Edict of Nantes, was still made a grievance against Henry IV., by Philip III., when writing to Paul V. in 1609 ; see the *king's letter to Aytona, November 30, 1609, Archives of the Spanish Embassy, Rome, I., 28.

[3] See PERRENS, I., 304.

[4] See PRAT, III., 122 *seq.* For the divergent opinion expressed by PERRENS in his work, *L'Église et l'État*, *cf.* the detailed criticism of H. DE L'EPINOIS in the *Rev. d. quest. hist.*, XV., 587 *seq.*, who remarks very appropriately, " Les doctrines gallicanes sont l'arche sainte à laquelle on ne peut toucher sans encourir le blâme de M. Perrens." Earlier, PHILIPPSON, in the *Hist. Zeitschr.*, XXXI., 97, note 2, took Perrens to task for " relying exclusively, in his characterization of Paul V., on the descriptions, often very contradictory, of such an intolerant Gallican as Brèves." *Cf.* also RANCÉ, in the *Rev. d. quest. hist.*, XXXVII. (1885), 608.

anxiety; his efforts to induce the government to intervene were as good as fruitless.[1] Besides his propagandist literature, the historical work of De Thou, who was as highly gifted as he was hostile to the papacy, was considered no less dangerous by the Roman authorities. When his first volume appeared in 1604, Bufalo, who was nuncio at the time, complained to Henry IV. and he did so not without success.[2] A decree of the Index of November, 1609, prohibited the book, as well as some other publications; among the latter was a discourse delivered in 1595, in which the attorney of the Paris university, Antoine Arnauld, bitterly attacked the Jesuits after the attempt by Chastel against Henry IV., as well as the parliamentary resolution then passed by which Chastel was condemned to death and the Jesuits, as his accomplices, to banishment.[3] The censure passed on this resolution was a mistake for, though it contained objectionable clauses which had already met with the disapproval of Clement VIII., it was nevertheless to be foreseen that evil-minded persons would interpret the censure as meaning that either Rome approved Chastel's attempt or disapproved his condemnation. As a matter of fact capital was made out of the incident in just this sense. Louis Servin moved in Parliament that the decree be burnt by the public executioner. Henry IV., on Ubaldini's representations, deferred indeed a decision in the matter, but he caused a protest to be lodged in Rome and demanded satisfaction. Paul V. at once refrained from further measures. In a fresh decree of January 30th, 1610, drawn up in accordance with Ubaldini's suggestions, there was no mention of Arnauld's discourse and the resolution of the Parliament

[1] See PERRENS, I., 317 *seq.*, 320 *seq.*; PRAT, III., 132. For Henry IV.'s action in the quarrel over James I.'s book, see below, Chapter II.

[2] *Cf. Lettres miss. Suppl.*, 902; PRAT, II., 471 *seq.*; *Rev. d. quest. hist.*, XXV., 671. For THOU and his work *cf.* the monographs of DUNTZER (Darmstadt, 1837) and HARISSE (Paris, 1905), see also J. RANCÉ, *De Thou, son hist. univ. et ses démêlés avec Rome*, Paris, 1881.

[3] *Cf.* present work, Vol. XXIII., 115 *seqq.*

of Paris, but the prohibition of De Thou's history was maintained.[1] Ubaldini made an unsuccessful attempt to induce Thou himself to revise his work. In Rome any such attempt was considered from the beginning as quite hopeless because, as Cardinal Borghese declared, the whole presentment of the facts was inadmissible.[2] As a matter of fact Thou's history is characterized by as much prevention and hostility towards the papacy as by consideration for, and sympathy with, the Huguenots. The danger of his work, which is not without many good qualities, was pointed out by the Jesuit Jean Machault in a refutation of Thou, published in 1614, which has for its motto the following quotation from St. Bernard: "A bad Catholic does far more harm than a declared heretic."[3]

Whilst Ubaldini had to deal with these internal agitations in France, the warlike policy of Henry IV., which was fraught with peril, increasingly claimed his attention.[4] When the violent death of the king abruptly ended all such plans, France was faced with an entirely new situation. Instead of a strong man, a weak and by no means gifted woman found herself at the head of the realm, and though her religion and her devotion to the Holy See were sincere, she was quite

[1] *Cf.* SIRI, II., 76 *seqq.*; GOUJET, I., 314 *seq.*; LÄMMER, *Melet.*, 273 *seq.*; REUSCH, II., 192 *seq.*, 284 *seq.*; MARTIN, *Gallicanisme*, 351.

[2] See the letter of Borghese to Ubaldini of February 2, 1610, in LÄMMER, *loc. cit.*, 278.

[3] "Longe plus nocet falsus catholicus, quam si verus appareret haereticus" (in I. A. THUANI, *Hist. libros notationes . . . auctore* Io. BAPT. GALLO Machault; [see SOMMERVOGEL, V., 256 *seq.*], Ingoldstadii, 1614). Thou, as FUETER also considers (*Historiographie*, 147), "entertained extreme Gallican opinions, and while he liked to attribute bad motives to the Guises, he treated the Protestants with undeniable leniency. The acts of violence and atrocity, of which the Catholics were guilty towards the Huguenots, are described in detail, not without ulterior purpose." *Cf.* too, DE MEAUX, *Réforme*, II., 121.

[4] *Cf.* above, vol. XXV., 402 *seq.*

unequal to the situation.[1] The parties began to stir at once, the Gallican politicans among them, under the leadership of Harley and Servin. These men hated the Jesuits quite as much as their friends the Huguenots did. They were not going to miss the chance of exploiting against the Society the attempt of Ravaillac; though the trial yielded not a shred of evidence of any conspiracy on the part of the Jesuits, and though Ravaillac himself both before, during and after torture persisted in his assertion that he had no accomplices and that he had not discussed his plan with anyone, not even in confession,[2] the Huguenots and their friends in Parliament, who still called themselves Catholics, would not desist from throwing the responsibility for the crime upon the Jesuits. The accusation was as unlikely as it was absurd since Henry had been a great benefactor to the Order; but the calumny was advanced with such assurance that it ended by obtaining credence. The Parliament based itself upon the work of the Spanish Jesuit Juan Mariana, published at Toledo in 1599, under the title: *On the King and the education of a King.* In the Middle Ages some theologians of repute had defended the thesis that it was a meritorious act to kill *a usurper* in order to liberate one's country, if no higher authority existed that could pass sentence on a tyrant. Mariana extended this doctrine so as to include even a *legitimate ruler* who grossly abused his position and thus brought ruin upon the State and who defied public law and religion. In the opinion of Mariana it was lawful for a private citizen to remove a sovereign of this kind, provided he was sure of the consent of the bulk of the people.[3] Mariana expressly stated that this opinion

[1] *Cf.* Martin, *loc. cit.*

[2] See "Procès de Ravaillac", in *Arch. curieuses*, XV., 113 *seq*,. new, English edition, *The Trial of Fr. Ravaillac*, ed. by E. Goldsmid, Edinburgh, 1885. *Cf.* too, vol. XXV., 414, n 2.

[3] Mariana, *De rege et regis institutione*, ed. 1599, 75 *seq.* *Cf.* Janssen-Pastor, V., 592 *seq.*, and Michael in the *Insbrucker Zeitschr. f. kath. Theol.*, XVI., 561. See also Pilatus, *Jesuitismus* (1905), 191 *seq.*, and *Archiv. f. Gesch. der Philos.*, XXI. (1908), 305 *seqq.*

on the murder of a tyrant was his own personal one.[1] When in 1599 the Superior of the French Province drew the attention of the General of the Order, Aquaviva, to this opinion of Mariana, which was assuredly worthy of condemnation even though its author had hedged it in with various restricting clauses, he expressed his sorrow that the visitor of the province of Toledo should have allowed such a book to be printed without his permission and he ordered the work to be destroyed.[2] The enemies of the Jesuits, who wielded great power in the Parliament of Paris, completely ignored the Jesuit General's disapproval of Mariana's theory. That body, which only two decades earlier had pronounced the deposition of Henry III. and had justified and approved the assassination of a tyrant, and in particular the removal of that king, now professed to see a great danger lurking in the theory of Mariana. It therefore instructed the Sorbonne to renew the condemnation it had pronounced in 1413 against the teaching of the Dominican Jean Petit on the subject of tyrannicide. When the Sorbonne had complied with their request, the Parliament included the book of Mariana in the decree of June 8th and ordered it to be burnt. With a view to exciting the French people still further they went so far as to order the parish priests to read the decree from the pulpit ![3]

On the initiative of Ubaldini the prelates then in Paris lodged a protest with the queen-regent, Marie de Medici, against a procedure of this kind. The queen demanded a modification of the decree. To this request the president of the Parliament demurred, alleging that the decree aimed

[1] See DUHR, *Jesuitenfabeln* [3], 689 *seq*. *Cf. ibid.* for the partially erroneous presentation of Mariana's teaching, by RANKE, *Zur Gesch. der polit. Theorien : Ges Werke*, XXIV., 236 *seq.*, 244. *Cf. Päpste*, II.[6], 124 *seq.* Nevertheless RANKE admits : "The doctrine of Mariana could not be regarded as that of his Order, still less as that of the Catholic Church."

[2] See BAYLE, *Dictionnaire*, 1924 *seq.*, and IUVENCIUS, V., 1, 12, n. 86–7. *Cf.* PRAT, III., 246.

[3] See PRAT, III., 249 ; FÉRET in the *Rev. d. quest. hist.*, LXVIII. (1900), 402 *seq.* ; FOUQUERAY, III., 242 *seq.*

solely at the welfare of the State. They justified their action by pointing to the great peril with which the teaching and practice of the Jesuits were fraught. Marie de Medici replied that the teaching of the Jesuits was none other than that of the Church and that their only aim was the salvation of souls; they could not make the Order pay in France for the writings of the Spaniard Mariana, seeing that it had always been loyal to the Crown and had enjoyed the particular esteem of the late king; if a member of Parliament were to transgress in any way it would not be fair to make the whole body suffer for his misdemeanour.[1]

Notwithstanding the reasonableness of such representations, Harley and his associates pursued their intrigues. The scandal which they had provoked was further intensified when some priests were found, such as the extravagant and restless Jean Dubois, who desecrated the pulpit by defamation of the Jesuits.[2] In order to cut short all further agitations, the General of the Jesuits, Aquaviva, in a circular of July 6th, 1610, forbade under pain of excommunication to all the members of the Order to maintain either in public or in private, either as teachers or as advisers, or in writing, that a private person, of whatsoever condition, could, on any

[1] See Ubaldini's report, translated by PRAT, III., 251 *seq.* *Cf.* FOUQUERAY, III., 244.

[2] *Cf.* PRAT, III., 256 *seq.* Recently, PERRENS, in *Rev. hist.*, LXXIV., 241 *seq.*, LXXV., 1 *seq.*, has treated in great detail but not impartially as regards Ubaldini, the adventures of that strange figure, Abbé Dubois. Ubaldini tried in vain to bring Dubois to better sentiments. Marie de Medici sent the recalcitrant Abbé to Rome, in September, 1611, ostensibly on business, in reality she wished him to be delivered to the Inquisition. As Dubois made challenging speeches against the Pope and Marie de Medici, as well as against religion, and as his private life was not blameless, he was sent to the prison of the Inquisition in November, 1611, and later to the Castle of S. Angelo. Only in 1621, under Gregory XV., was he allowed a certain liberty; he was eventually released, but not until the beginning of the reign of Urban VIII.

plea whatsoever of tyranny, either kill kings and princes or make an attempt on their life.[1] In a second circular of August 14th, 1610, Aquaviva strictly forbade all discussions, whether favourable or unfavourable, of Mariana's book.[2] Paul V. also expressly pronounced against the book in a conversation with de Brèves, the French ambassador, though the Pope at the same time insisted that it belonged to the ecclesiastical authorities to take steps against it and that the parish priests could not be compelled to read the decree of Parliament from the pulpit.[3]

The real purpose of these efforts of the enemies of the Jesuits was betrayed by the spiritual head of the Huguenots, Du Plessis Mornay, in a memorial he addressed at that time to the Parliament: the Order must be put into a condition of complete helplessness as regards any form of activity in France; in fact it must be banished once more.[4] The first step was to bring about the fall of Père Coton who was highly esteemed at court. This was the purpose of numerous pamphlets, especially an anonymous compilation entitled: "*Anti-Coton*, a book whose author endeavours to demonstrate that the Jesuits were guilty and were the instigators of the execrable murder which was perpetrated on the person of the most Christian King Henry IV. . . . of blessed memory." Every imaginable infamy, even the vilest, are here ascribed to the Jesuits without a shadow of proof.[5]

Ubaldini was well aware that the agitation of the Huguenots and their friends, who still styled themselves Catholics, was

[1] See IUVENCIUS, V., l. 12, n. 157; DUHR, *loc. cit.*, 387. *Cf.* SCORRAILLE, *Suarez*, II., 184.

[2] *Monum. Germaniae Paedag.*, IX., 48.

[3] Reports of Brèves of July 8 and 22, 1610, in PERRENS, I., 414 *seq.*, only in part, published in whole by GAILLARD, in the *Notices et extraits de la Bibl. du Roi* VII., 2, Paris, 1804, 331 *seqq.*

[4] See PRAT, III., 282 *seq.*

[5] See *ibid.*, 285 *seq.* The author of this libel has not yet been ascertained. See PERRENS, I., 448 *seq.* For the agitation against the Jesuits, *cf.* the report of Ubaldini of September 14, 1610, in LÄMMER, *Melet.*, 291, note 1.

ultimately directed against the Holy See: hence he did all in his power to protect the Jesuits.[1] The nuncio could only be strengthened in his conviction that the attack was directed against the Holy See when, notwithstanding all his efforts to the contrary, the Parliament accepted, on November 26th, a motion of Servin to forbid under pain of high treason a treatise of Cardinal Bellarmine on the Pope's power in temporal matters. In this work the Cardinal defended the opinions laid down by him in his *Controversies* as against the attacks of the Scottish jurist William Barclay, whose book was put on the Index as soon as it appeared in November, 1609. Whilst this work was allowed to circulate freely in France, the Parliament sought to prohibit the defence by a Cardinal who was famous throughout the world, for the reason—so it was boldly asserted—that the views propounded in its pages advocated the overthrow of the divinely appointed authority of the State and the revolt of the people against their Sovereign![2] In reality Bellarmine, basing himself on theologians of renown, had made a temperate statement of the relation between Church and State and, in opposition to many theologians, he claimed for the Pope not a direct, but only an indirect authority over the princes and peoples in regard to temporal affairs.[3] The blow which the Parliament dealt to one of the most deserving and most learned among the Cardinals, who on two occasions had very nearly obtained the tiara, was directly aimed at the Holy See.[4] Hence Ubaldini did not fail to protest with all his energy and even to threaten to leave France. On the nuncio's representations the regent, Marie de Medici, suspended the publication of the

[1] See PRAT, III., 292 *seq.*

[2] *Cf.* Ubaldini's report in LÄMMER, *loc. cit.*, 298, note 1; GOUJET, I., 331 *seq.*; PRAT, III., 310 *seq.*; REUSCH, *Index*, II., 331 *seq.*, 345.

[3] *Cf.* HERGENRÖTHER, *Kirche und Staat*, 421 *seq.*; J. DE LA SERVIÈRE, *La Théologie de Bellarmin*, Beauchesne, 1908.

[4] See BAZIN, *Hist. de France sous Louis XIII.*, I., 104. *Cf.* RANKE, *Franz Gesch.*, II., 177.

ordinance of the Parliament of Paris.[1] For this she received the thanks of Paul V. in a letter of December 22nd, 1610, though the Pope remarked that he had expected an even fuller satisfaction, namely the complete repeal of the decree and the suppression of Servin's speech.[2] Bellarmine himself wrote a dignified letter to the regent in which he pointed out that in his dissertation against Barclay he taught nothing that was not found in his *Controversies* which freely circulated everywhere, even in France, and that the Parliament attributed to him views which he had never maintained.[3] "If the French government," Cardinal Borghese wrote to Ubaldini on February 2nd, "does not soon put a stop to the licence of writers, as it has often promised, new difficulties will arise every day." The Cardinal then referred to two recently published books, one of which was directed against Cardinal Bellarmine and the other against the Jesuits. The Pope, the letter went on to say, would speak to the French ambassador, whilst the nuncio was to go on making representations to the queen-regent.[4] In a letter under the same date Cardinal Borghese demanded that steps should be taken against several priests who had abused the occasion of the Advent sermons in order to attack papal authority and to calumniate the Jesuits.[5] The lines had scarcely been written when Ubaldini saw himself obliged to protest against a new libellous pamphlet from the pen of the Huguenot Vigner, the title of which,—"Theatre of Antichrist,"—was a clear sign of what the writer felt he could offer to the Catholics of France. The nuncio represented to the regent that just as

[1] See Lämmer, *Melet.*, 293 *seq.*; Prat, III., 311 *seq.*; Perrens, I., 476 *seq.*; Döllinger-Reusch, *Moralstreitigkeiten*, II., 394 *seq.*; Martin, *Gallicanisme*, 355 *seq.*; Fouqueray, III., 259 *seq.*

[2] Lämmer, *loc. cit.*, 294 *seq.* Perrens (I., 507 *seq.*) and Martin, *loc. cit.*, 357 *seqq.*, show how the attempts to gain fuller satisfaction were unsuccessful.

[3] See Prat, III., 317 *seq.*

[4] See Lämmer, *loc. cit.*, 299.

[5] See *ibid.*, 299 *seq.*

the Pope would not tolerate in his States any attack on the king of France, so was he entitled to expect that the French Government would protect him from calumny. However, Marie de Medici was so intimidated by the Huguenots, who threatened to revolt, that for the time being she did not dare to do anything.[1] Paul V. complained to the French ambassador and instructed Ubaldini not to slacken in his remonstrances.[2] An attempt was made to pacify the Pope by proceeding against the Advent preachers.[3] The "Theatre of Antichrist" was not prohibited till May, and then only by word of mouth, and its author was not molested.[4] Such weakness and indecision made it possible for Du Plessis Mornay to publish in that same year a book entitled *The Mystery of Wickedness, or, A History of the Papacy,* in Latin and French, in which he attacked the Holy See in unprecedented fashion and practically described Paul V. as the beast of the Apocalypse. This work Du Plessis dedicated to the youthful Louis XIII ! Only when Ubaldini pointed out to the queen that if the Pope was antichrist, the legitimacy of her marriage might also be called in question, was the pamphlet submitted to the Sorbonne and condemned by it in the severest terms, on August 22nd, 1611.[5]

In March, 1611, Ubaldini had been able to report to Rome an occurrence which he considered as an important achievement; he had at last succeeded in bringing about the appointment of the president of the Parliament of Toulouse, Nicolas de Verdun, on whose Catholic attitude he thought he could rely, as first president of the Parliament of Paris instead of the Gallican Harley. Thereupon Harley's sympathizer, Thou, resigned in high dudgeon. Ubaldini hoped that Servin would take a similar course. "The determination which the Pope showed on the occasion of the decree against Bellarmine," the nuncio reported to Rome, "has now yielded

[1] See Perrens, II., 13 *seq.*

[2] See Lämmer, *loc. cit.*, 301 ; Perrens, II., 17 *seq.*

[3] See Lämmer, *loc. cit.*

[4] See Perrens, II., 18.

[5] *Cf.* Goujet, II., 27 *seq.* ; Perrens, II., 19 *seq.*

valuable results and we may look to the future with confidence."[1] However, Ubaldini was destined to be disappointed in his trust in Servin.[2] But even this disappointment did not discourage the indefatigable nuncio's ardour in the defence of Catholic interest. After the disappointment which he suffered in February, 1612, through the weak and unwise attitude of the Jesuits who trembled for their existence before the Parliament,[3] he achieved an important success in the autumn of the same year when he brought about the removal of Edmund Richer from the post of syndic of the Sorbonne, a position he had held since 1608, and of which he took advantage to spread anti-papal theories.

The son of poor country-people in Champagne, Richer[4] had gone through a course of studies in Paris under conditions of extreme difficulty. Grim determination and a strong constitution which had made it possible for him to do with only three hours' sleep, at last led him to his goal—in 1592 he became a doctor of the Sorbonne. He began as an ardent adherent of the League, but his attitude soon underwent a serious change and he ended by becoming a passionate

[1] See LÄMMER, *loc. cit.*, 302, note 1; PERRENS, I., 514 *seqq.*

[2] *Cf.* PERRENS, II., 27 *seq.*; PRAT, III., 369 *seq.*

[3] *Cf.* herewith the detailed account of FOUQUERAY (III., 289 *seq.*, 291 *seq.*), of the declaration given on February 22, 1612, by the French Provincial, Christoph. Baltazar, and six other Jesuits: "de se conformer à la doctrine de l'École de Sorbonne même en ce qui concernait la personne sacrée des rois, le maintien de leur autorité royale et les libertés gallicanes de tout temps gardées dans le royaume." Fouqueray remarks: "S'ils ne souscrivirent à aucune proposition contraire à la doctrine de l'Eglise, l'acte de condescendance auquel ils se soumirent n'en était pas moins opposé à la dignité du St. Siège et de la Compagnie." Fouqueray also adds the sharp reproof written by Aquaviva to Fr. Baltazar, after an interview with Paul V.; he was forbidden to make any declarations in future without the General's consent (FOUQUERAY, 291 *seq.*).

[4] *Cf.* PUYOL, *Edm. Richer. Étude sur la renovation du gallicanisme du XVIIe siècle*, 2 vols., Paris, 1876. *Cf.* the critical review in *Études*, 1877, I., 910 *seq.*

advocate of Gallicanism. Already Barberini, when nuncio, found himself in conflict with him,[1] and Ubaldini watched with ever-growing disquiet the ardour which Richer put into spreading his views and in combating the Jesuits.[2]

During the civil wars and the wars of religion, the Gallican theories had increasingly fallen into abeyance at the theological faculty of Paris and at the opening of the new century, thanks to the influence of Bellarmine and Maldonatus, the famous university seemed in a fair way towards a return to a sound, sincerely ecclesiastical teaching.[3] With a view to preventing such an evolution and in order to breathe fresh life into the Gallicanism of the faculty, Richer put forth all his energy and outstanding ability as well as the influence he had acquired as syndic of the Sorbonne.

What risky paths Richer was prepared to tread is shown by a dissertation, small in bulk but of grave import, which was published anonymously in Paris in 1611, though the author's name was soon detected.[4] In this pamphlet Richer maintained exceedingly dangerous propositions. According to him the Church's government has only the outward appearance of a monarchy; in reality it is aristocratic. Legislative power as well as infallibility are not the attributes of the Pope but belong to the hierarchy composed of the bishops and the priests, which functions in its totality at a general council. The Pope is absolutely subject to the council. The episcopate is an essential element of the constitution of the Church, the papacy only an accessory. Christ gave to His Church only spiritual means for the attainment of her object, Richer further taught, hence the Pope may only make use of spiritual means, but never of material force. Forcible

[1] *Cf.* Reusch, *Index*, II., 355.

[2] See Perrens, I., 410, 438, 458 *seq.*, II., 62 *seq.*; Prat, III., 365 *seq.*

[3] See Lassberg, in *Freib. Kirchenlexikon*, X., 1190 *seq.*

[4] *De potestate ecclesiastica et politica*, at first printed privately with only 300 copies for distribution, but reprinted in 1611, nominally at Paris, but really abroad and later reprinted several times; see Reusch, *Index*, II., 356.

means are the exclusive prerogative of the secular power. As the natural guardian of his domains the prince has both the right and the duty to decide whether the executive ministers of the Church proceed according to the Canons, and for such judgments he is responsible to God alone.[1]

Though Richer's dissertation had but slender scientific value, for it neither contained anything new nor produced any fresh arguments in support of the theories it asserted,[2] the daring with which the rights of the Pope were challenged did not fail to create a good deal of stir.[3] The joy of the Church's deadly enemies knew no bounds. Of this we have a proof in the correspondence of Sarpi with his French sympathizers.[4] But on the Catholic side a gratifying and determined resistance became apparent. Among the first to oppose Richer were his colleagues Durand and Duval. The latter's dissertation on "The Pope's supreme authority in the Church" was remarkable both for its learning and its moderation. Burning indignation characterized Pelletier's treatise on "The Monarchy of the Church". To these writings must be added refutations by the Jesuits Eudæmon Joannes, Gautier and Sirmond. Moreover, in the Sorbonne itself, in addition to Durand, Jean Filesac and Harley's own son pressed for the condemnation of Richer's theories since they were bound to provoke a schism in the Church. The Parliament, however, defended these opinions and forbade all further discussion of them by the Sorbonne.

The indignation with which these proceedings filled Paul V. appears from the reports of Brèves, the French ambassador, and from those of Cardinals Joyeuse and Rochefoucauld.

[1] See PUYOL, *Richer*, I., 234 *seq.*, 425 *seq.*; and LASSBERG, *loc. cit.*, 1191. *Cf.* BAUER, in the *Stimmen aus Maria-Laach*, IV., 22 *seq.*; and HERGENRÖTHER, III.[5], 721, 789, where a further bibliography is given. "Le livret (de Richer) reduisait la papauté à n'être plus dans l'Eglise qu'une sorte d'accessoire," says GOYAU most pertinently (*Hist. relig.*, 392).

[2] This is SCHULTE's opinion (III., 577).

[3] *Cf.* Ubaldini's report in LÄMMER, *Melet.*, 311, note 1.

[4] See PRAT, III., 420 *seq.*

The latter pointed out to Marie de Medici that Richer's attack on the monarchical power of the Pope was likewise a threat to that of the State.[1]

Ubaldini was particularly gratified by the prudence and determination with which Cardinal Du Perron dealt with Richer's treatise. To this prince of the Church, a splendid man in every respect, it was chiefly due that the French episcopate also took the field, although the Parliament of Paris did its utmost to prevent such a manifestation. In March, 1612, Cardinal Du Perron, as archbishop of Sens, convened a provincial council of his suffragans, the bishops of Paris, Auxerre, Meaux, Orléans, Troyes, Nevers and Chartres. This assembly condemned the opinions of Richer, without mentioning his name, since his book had appeared anonymously, declaring them to be erroneous, schismatical and heretical, "without prejudice to the rights of the King, the French crown and the immunities and liberties of the Gallican Church." The bishop had these condemnations read from the pulpits of all the churches. In May the archbishop of Aix, Hurault de L'Hôpital held a provincial council of his suffragans, viz. the bishops of Fréjus, Sisteron and Riez, in which the condemnation was repeated but without the clause which Sens had added to its decree out of consideration for the Parliament of Paris.[2] The Pope also would have been glad of the omission of so ambiguous an adjunct[3]; nevertheless in a Brief of May 2nd, 1612, he praised the suffragans of Sens for their condemnation of a book which was full of dangerous doctrines and erroneous assertions.[4] To this was

[1] See *Notices et extr. de la Bibl. du Roi*, VII., 2, Paris, 1804, 362 *seqq.*; PRAT, III., 373 *seq.*, 377 *seq.*; PUYOL, I., 289 *seq.*, 298 *seq.*, 326 *seq.* The Brief which Paul V. addressed to the prelates of France and to Marie de Medici, at the first news of Richer's book, on March 2, 1612, is printed in the *Hist. du syndicat de Richer*, II., 95.

[2] See PUYOL, I., 354 *seq.*, 366 *seq.*

[3] *Cf.* PERRENS, II., 152 *seq.*; PRAT, III., 380 *seq.*; FOUQUERAY, III., 299.

[4] See DU PLESSIS D'ARGENTRÉ, III., 2, 187; PUYOL, I., 364 *seq.*

added, in May, 1613, a condemnatory decree of the Congregation of the Index.[1]

Richer had appealed to the Paris Parliament against his condemnation by the bishops, urging that they had exceeded their authority, but Marie de Medici did not allow the appeal and forbade all proceedings against the bishops. She likewise stopped other measures contemplated by the Parliament, such as, for instance, the publication of the Acts of the schismatical council of Pisa. Both the queen-regent and Ubaldini were convinced that Parliament was heading for a schism.[2] For that reason Parliament tried to uphold Richer for as long as possible, though its efforts proved in vain. In September, 1612, Richer found himself compelled to lay aside his office of Syndic of the Sorbonne, a post he had so shamefully misused in order to lead the faculty into the path of schism and heresy. All his attempts to regain that important dignity were foiled by the counter-measures of the nuncio.[3]

After such a defeat, the enemies of the Holy See deemed it more prudent to concentrate their attacks once more on the Jesuits. In this resolve they were guided by the principle which their friend Sarpi had formulated with his wonted exaggeration: "The most important thing is to destroy the Jesuits; if they are defeated, Rome is lost and if they are out of the way, religion will 'reform' itself of its own accord."[4]

[1] See REUSCH, *Index*, II., 357.

[2] See Ubaldini's report of April 24, 1612, translated in PRAT, III., 383.

[3] See PUYOL, I., 390 *seq.*, 395 *seq.*, 404 *seq.*; FOUQUERAY, III., 299. Brief, praising the Prince of Condé and the Count of Soissons for their assistance in the deposition of Richer, dated September 26, 1612, are in DU PLESSIS D'ARGENTRÉ, III., 2, 188.

[4] See the letter of Sarpi to Groslot of July 5, 1611, in FONTANINI, *Storia arcana*, 366, quoted by PRAT, III., 413. For the further conflict with the Jesuits *cf.* especially PRAT, III., 577 *seq.*, 593 *seq.* A *Brief of Paul V. of January 20, 1612, to Marie de Medici, thanks her for all she has done for the protection of Catholics. *Epist.*, VIII., 228, Papal Secret Archives.

In the Paris Parliament Servin showed himself now as before both adroit and indefatigable in every kind of agitation and intrigue against the Jesuits. Thanks to the weakness of President Verdun he secured, in June, 1614, a decree in virtue of which the "Defence of the Catholic Faith against the errors of the Anglican Sect" written by the Jesuit, Francis Suarez, was to be burnt by the public executioner. The judgment of the Parliament was a crying injustice, as Bellarmine pointed out in a special report.[1] Doctrines antagonistic to the State could only be discovered in Suarez's book by taking out isolated sentences, as Servin had done, sentences that could only be rightly appraised when seen in their context.[2] Surely Suarez should have been the last man whom anyone would suspect of attempting to interfere with the sovereignty of monarchs and statesmen, for in that case a ruler so absolute and so extraordinarily jealous of his rights as Philip II. would certainly not have suffered him to occupy the chair of Coimbra. Philip III. also had given his full approval to Suarez's work. How far that divine was from any whittling down of the autonomy of the State is shown by the fact that in his classical work on Law published in 1612, he expressly states that "the Pope has not received from Christ any secular ruling power by right divine, neither over the whole world, nor over the whole of Christendom or any part of it".[3]

Paul V. had himself encouraged the publication of the *Defence of the Catholic Faith* of Suarez, the most noted theologian of the time,[4] which the Paris Parliament now took upon itself to condemn, and on September 10th, 1613, the Pope praised the book in a special laudatory brief. The

[1] See LE BACHELET, *Auct. Bellarm.*, 536 *seq.*

[2] *Cf.* PRAT, III., 578 *seq.*; SCORRAILLE, II., 176 *seq.*; FOUQUERAY, III., 305 *seq.*

[3] *De legibus ac Deo legislatore*, Coimbrae, 1612, l. 3, ch. 8, § 10. *Cf.* REICHMANN, *F. Suarez, ein Vertreter des Naturrechtes im 17. Jahrhundert*, in the *Stimmen der Zeit*, XCIV. (1917), 275 *seq.*

[4] *Cf.* WERNER, I., 90; SCHEEBEN, *Dogmatik*, I., § 1094, and the opinion of HURTER, *Nomenclator*, I., 139 *seq.* See also R. DE SCORRAILLE, *Fr. Suarez*, 2 vols., Paris, 1912.

decree of that secular body was a twofold provocation of the Pope. To this must be added that the resolution of the Parliament also implied a rejection of the indirect power of the Holy See in temporal matters. Small wonder, then, if Paul V. put up a strong resistance. Through Ubaldini he lodged a protest, insisting that whereas in France nothing was allowed to be published in defence of the Holy See, the grossest calumnies, such as those of Du Plessis Mornay, who had called the Pope antichrist,[1] went unpunished. However, the French government seemed at first more afraid of the anger of Parliament than of that of the Pope. Tension became so acute that at one time there was reason to fear an open breach between Paris and Rome. But Paul V. precipitated nothing. In the wearisome discussions that ensued, for all his insistence on his authority and his solicitude for the unjustly attacked Suarez, he showed, as even the French ambassador, the Marquis de Tresnel, had to admit, the utmost goodwill towards France. It was due to the Pope's moderation that the painful incident was at last got out of the way, for he declared himself satisfied with a simple suspension of the parliamentary decree.[2]

In the meantime the three Estates of the realm had assembled in Paris at the end of October, 1614. In this assembly the Church was splendidly represented; with absolute unanimity the French clergy pronounced for the

[1] See FOUQUERAY, III., 313 *seq.*

[2] *Cf.* the treatise of RANCE, *L'arrêt contre Suarez*, in the *Rev. d. quest. hist.*, XXXVII (1885), 597 *seq.*, and the detailed presentation of SCORRAILLE (II., 197 *seq.*, 209 *seq.*). Scorraille shows that when Suarez, in his work, discussed the question of tyrannicide, he did so against the prohibition of Aquaviva (*cf.* above, p. 17), but that no blame can be attached to him for this, as the decree had not been published in his province. Aquaviva renewed the veto on August 1, 1614, deploring that it had not been effective everywhere. The letter of Cardinal Borghese " in nome di Nostro Signore ", on this matter, addressed to Marie de Medici on July 30, 1614, is printed in LÄMMER, *Zur Kirchengesch.*, 88 *seq.* *Cf.*, too, *Melet.*, 328 *seq.*

acceptance of the decrees of Trent. This decision was all the more important inasmuch as a majority of the Third Estate, which included the wealthy burghers and the State officials, favoured the schismatical tendencies of the Parliament of Paris and put forward questions the discussion of which could only be disastrous.[1] This was clearly shown by the almost unanimous agreement with the proposal of the deputies of Paris, that in imitation of schismatical England, the assembly should lay it down as a fundamental law of the State that the king holds his crown from God alone and that for no reason whatsoever could any power of any kind, be it temporal or *spiritual*, have competence to depose him or to release his subjects from their oath of allegiance. All the Estates, and thereafter all officials and priests, were to swear, without reservation, that this proposition was a holy, inviolable law and one in accordance with the word of God. If anyone advanced a contrary opinion, especially the theory that the king may be murdered or deposed, he was to be punished as one guilty of high treason against the State and the king. An additional clause declared that all religious Orders in France were bound to combat, without regard to persons, and without equivocation, any opinion directly or indirectly opposed to this teaching, by whomsoever propounded; otherwise they rendered themselves liable to punishment as favouring the enemies of the State.[2]

Claude Le Prêtre, councillor to the Paris Parliament, was the author of this resolution of the Third Estate, the aim of which was disguised under the thin veil of seeming concern for the rights and the person of the king. Those who saw more clearly could be in no doubt as to what was intended, viz. approval of the schismatical ends which the Parliament of Paris had pursued for years, and proscription of all those who defended the rights of the Holy See, whether or no they

[1] See MARTIN, *Gallicanisme*, 365 *seq.*

[2] See FLORIMOND RAPINE, *Recueil . . . de tout ce qui s'est fait et passé . . . en l'Assemblée gén. des États tenus à Paris en l'année 1614*, Paris, 1651, 205 *seq.* *Cf.* PUYOL, I., ch. 9, and MARTIN, *loc. cit.*, 368 *seqq.*

belonged to the Society of Jesus.[1] This was made perfectly plain by Cardinal Du Perron when, on January 2nd, 1615, accompanied by a number of bishops and sixty representatives of the nobility, he presented himself in the assembly of the Third Estate. His brilliant speech of three hours duration was calculated to open the eyes of those deputies who had failed to realize the import of the proposed measure and who imagined that by assenting to it they were proving their loyalty to the king. The Cardinal began by questioning the competence of a lay assembly to pronounce on such purely ecclesiastical questions. Clearly, and with strict logic, he then examined each separate paragraph of the resolution. With regard to the independence of kings in temporal matters and any attempt on their lives, there could be no controversy at all; everybody would agree with the statements on the subject made by the Third Estate. But it was otherwise in a case thus stated by Du Perron: if it should happen that rulers, who themselves, or whose forbears, had promised on oath, to God or to their peoples, that they would live and die in the Catholic faith, break their oath, openly fall into apostasy, do violence to the consciences of their subjects and endeavour to introduce either Arianism or Mohamedanism in their States, may not their subjects in such circumstances be released from their oath of allegiance? And if so, who is qualified to declare them thus freed? The Cardinal emphasized the fact that the answer was not beyond dispute. It could not be made an article of faith; in things of this kind the Church alone had authority to decide, nor could the people be compelled to take an oath in the matter. Hence the clergy would undergo martyrdom rather than attack the Pope's authority or provoke a schism by giving their adhesion to the resolution put forward by the Third Estate.[2] Robert Miron, who acted as spokesman of the Third Estate and as representative of

[1] See PRAT, III., 624. *Cf.* DE MEAUX, *Réforme*, II., 127.

[2] See RAPINE, *loc. cit.*, 296 *seq.* *Cf.* DE MEAUX, *Réforme*, II., 128 *seq.*; HERGENRÖTHER, *Kirche u. Staat*, 446. See also LE BACHELET, *Auct. Bellarm.*, 680 *seq.*

Paris, sought to weaken the Cardinal's speech by denying the aims of the resolution which the latter had so clearly exposed. In his reply Du Perron once again emphatically declared that laymen had no right to decide ecclesiastical questions of this kind.

The surest proof that Du Perron had clearly discerned the true purpose of the resolution was provided by the Parliament of Paris when, on that same day, and on a motion of Servin's, it sanctioned once more all the measures which had been previously passed against the Jesuits and other defenders of the Holy See, and expressly declared that the Pope could neither excommunicate nor depose a king, even if he became a heretic. The next day the clergy protested against the pressure which it was sought to apply by these measures. Du Perron spoke once more: he roundly declared that the Pope had full and direct power in things spiritual and indirect power in things temporal; whosoever thought otherwise was a schismatic and a heretic. This applied also to the Parliament of Paris. Unless the king rejected its resolution, it would become necessary to excommunicate that body.[1]

In order to avoid giving their adversaries the slightest pretext for accusing the clergy or the Jesuits of condoning murderous attempts against kings, the representatives of the clergy confirmed anew the decree of the Council of Constance against the Dominican Petit; on the other hand it insisted on the repeal of the Parliamentary resolution. The government sought to smooth down difficulties by forbidding the continuation of the controversy and by reserving any decision to itself. This was all the more unacceptable to the clergy as the printed text of the resolution in dispute was already being circulated, as if there were no question of its legality. By their firmness—they threatened to suspend their deliberations—the clergy, who had the support of the majority of the nobility, succeeded in inducing the crown to punish the printer of the parliamentary decree, to repeal the decree itself and to order the resolution of the Third Estate to be expunged

[1] See Rapine, *loc. cit.*, 356 *seq.*

from the *Cahier*.[1] In this way a most important victory was won. The Pope, who had been exceedingly anxious about the issue, expressed his thanks to all who had contributed to this triumph and exhorted them to display a like constancy in the time to come.[2]

On the other hand all efforts of the French clergy proved fruitless in another matter, one to which Paul V. attached the greatest importance.[3] This was the solemn publication of the reform decrees of the Council of Trent. This time opposition seemed all the more out of place as in the memorial to the king it had been said, in as many words, that the act would take place as soon as the Pope should have given an assurance that such a publication would not curtail the rights of the crown, compromise the peace of the State, or infringe the liberties of the Gallican Church, and the privileges of the cathedral and collegiate churches and the clergy of France.[4]

Indefatigable, as always, Ubaldini gave of his best in this affair. He asked the Jesuit Coton to write a refutation of the various objections which had been raised against the publication of the decrees and to dedicate his work to the three Estates. The hostility of the Huguenots, Coton explained,

[1] See Prat, III., 629 *seq.*; Picot, *Hist. des États gén.*, III., 367 *seq.*; De Meaux, *Réforme*, II., 132 *seq.*

[2] *Cf.* the Briefs, dated *prid. cal. Febr.*, 1615, to the Cardinals and other members of the assembly of the clergy (see Vol. XXV, App. No. 4) to Cardinal Joyeuse (" expectavimus pacem et ecce turbatio "; he is to help); to Cardinal Sourdis (" tribulationes cordis Nostri multiplicatae sunt super numerum "; he praises him and continues to hope); to Cardinal Du Perron (" exacerbatur quotidie animi Nostri molestia; " heartfelt thanks for which no words suffice); to Cardinal Rochefoucauld (praises him); to Cardinal Bonsi (" novis semper atque gravioribus afflictionibus afficimur "), " Nobilibus viris ordinis nobilium regni Franciae in conciliis general. congreg." (he praises them). *Epist.*, X., 261–8, Papal Secret Archives.

[3] *Cf.* in the App. No. 5 the Brief to Louis XIII. of January 22, 1615, Papal Secret Archives. See also Martin, *Gallicanisme*, 371.

[4] See Philippson in the *Hist Zeitschr.*, XXXI., 114 *seq.*

was nothing to be wondered at, but surely in a matter of this kind, Catholics should not allow themselves to be led astray either by heretics or by false brethren whose schismatical dispositions and hostility to the Holy See were such that they refused to have anything to do with the Pope or with Rome.[1] Men of this type formed the majority in the assembly of the Third Estate. René Potier, bishop of Beauvais, preached to deaf ears when he earnestly represented to the assembly that even if the decrees were published they need have no fear that the Inquisition would be set up, or that the privileges of the king and those of the Gallican Church would be in any way curtailed.

Although the Third Estate had strongly insisted on the necessity of removing abuses in the Church, it nevertheless definitely rejected the only means to that end. It was ready to accept the dogmatic decrees, Robert Miron explained, but not the disciplinary ones ; no General Council had ever been published in France and no exception could be made for that of Trent. With biting sarcasm he added that the clergy might quite well carry out the decrees of the Council of their own accord by suppressing the pluralism of benefices and other abuses which had been condemned at Trent ![2]

Though the nobility sided with the clergy, the obstruction of the Third Estate proved insurmountable. In his famous speech of February 23rd, 1615, the bishop of Luçon, Richelieu, renewed the demand for publication and pointed in eloquent words to the example of the other Catholic States and to Henry IV's. own promise. However, for fear of internal disturbances, the government did not dare to do anything.[3] For the rest the French clergy took Miron at his word. Regardless of the agitation of the Gallicans and the Huguenots, they decreed in the assembly of July 7th, 1615, without prejudice to the liberties of the Gallican Church, the observance of the

[1] See PRAT, III., 645 *seq.* *Cf.* the letter of Ubaldini of December 18, 1614, in LÄMMER, *Melet.*, 303, note 1.

[2] See RAPINE, *Recueil*, 436 ; DE MEAUX, *Réforme*, II., 136.

[3] See MARIÉJOL, VI., 2, 309. *Cf.* MARTIN, *loc. cit.*, 375 *seq.*

reform decrees of Trent and their publication by provincial synods which were to be held in every diocese within the next six months. Forty-seven archbishops and bishops swore to obey this decision. The nuncio was jubilant; in Rome also joy was great. True, the royal assent was still wanting, but the leaders of the Church had spoken and all true Catholics in France now knew their duty. It goes without saying that bitter attacks on the part of the Gallicans were not wanting. Soon, however, universal attention was drawn elsewhere, for Condé's rising had taken place.[1] A section of the Huguenots also took to arms: but they could prevent neither the king's journey to the Spanish frontier nor his marriage. On November 25th, at Bordeaux, Louis XIII. led the Spanish princess, Anne of Austria, to the altar. A month later peace negotiations with Condé were initiated. The peace congress opened on February 10th, 1616. Among other stipulations arrived at was the confirmation of the decrees previously passed in favour of the Huguenots as well as some further concessions. The Third Estate also achieved a notable success when the government promised not to give effect to the demand of the clergy for the publication of the Tridentine decrees.[2]

At one moment there was real danger lest the proposal for a new constitution of the French State which, thanks to Du Perron's efforts, had been defeated in the General Assembly of the Estates, should be accepted. Ubaldini displayed as much ability as zeal in frustrating these designs. It was due to him that Marie de Medici pledged her royal word to the Pope that the question would never again come up for dis-

[1] *Cf.* PERRENS, II., 334; MARTIN, *loc. cit.*, 381; and PRUNEL, 14 *seq.*, where the reports of Ubaldini, especially the important ones of July 15 and August 11 and 27, and October 17, 1615, are used. SERBAT (*Assemblées*, 394 *seq.*) published Ubaldini's reports of August 10 and 16, 1615, *in extenso*. *Cf.*, too, the *Briefs to Du Perron and other French Cardinals, of April 8, 1616. *Epist.*, XI., 231, Papal Secret Archives.

[2] See PICOT, *Hist. des États gén.*, III., 468.

cussion.[1] By that time the indefatigable nuncio had been raised to the purple; the presentation by the king of the red biretta had taken place at the beginning of February, 1616,[2] but Ubaldini remained in France until the arrival of his successor. The prelate appointed by Paul V. was Guido Bentivoglio, of Ferrara, who had been nuncio at Brussels from 1607 until 1615.[3] The choice was arrived at about the middle of July, 1616,[4] but the Brief of nomination was not published until September 8th, 1616.[5] Repeated bouts of illness still further delayed the nuncio's departure and not until the end of November did Bentivoglio reach Lyons. On December 15th, 1616, he arrived in Paris. Eight days later Ubaldini left the capital.[6]

The task that awaited the new nuncio at the French court is thus summed up in his Instruction, viz. the consolidation of a good understanding between France and Spain; watchfulness with regard to the nomination of suitable bishops; the furthering of the Catholic reform by the convocation of provincial and diocesan synods and other similar measures; the abolition of the appeal to secular judges under pretext of abuse of the spiritual power; lastly the termination of the paper war against the Catholic faith and the papal

[1] See *Ubaldini's report of March 26, 1616, Papal Secret Archives, *loc. cit.* Although RANKE, *Französ. Gesch.*, II [2]., 198 *seq.*) had referred to this important document, PERRENS overlooked it completely.

[2] See *Ubaldini's report of February 9, 1616, Papal Secret Archives, *loc. cit.* The nomination of Cardinals had taken place on December 2, 1615; see Vol. XXV., 340 *seqq.*

[3] *Cf.* CAUCHIE-MAERE, *Instructions*, xxiv *seqq.* See also below, 85 *seq.*, 88 *seq.*

[4] See *Lettere del card. Bentivoglio*, ed. G. Biagioli, I., Napoli, 1833, 43.

[5] See the *Brief to Louis XIII., dated September 8, 1616, *Epist.*, XI., 128. *Ibid.*, 239, for the recall of Ubaldini. Papal Secret Archives.

[6] See *Lettere del card. Bentivoglio*, I., 45, 48, 59.

authority.[1] The Instruction exhorts Bentivoglio to adopt an attitude of the greatest friendliness towards the Sorbonne and, to this end, to give only private support to the plan of the Jesuits for the opening of courses at their Collège de Clermont, in Paris, and to advise the Fathers to put off the settlement of this question which, at present, would only create fresh enemies for them, until the king should have attained his majority.

In view of the prudence and moderation of Bentivoglio such admonitions fell on good soil. In this respect the new nuncio was the exact opposite of Ubaldini who was by nature a fighter. And since Rome too was anxious to avoid all conflicts as much as possible, Bentivoglio did not find it difficult to settle, by means of a compromise, the conflict provoked at the very beginning of his nunciature by the conduct of the unworthy bishop of Boulogne, Claude Dormy, who had got mixed up in the conspiracy of the Prince of Condé.[2] As for Louis Servin, who remained obstinate in his

[1] The Instruction for Cardinal Bentivoglio is in the Corsini Library, Rome, *Cod.* 468, p. 410 *seq.* Prat, as well as Perrens, would have judged differently of Bentivoglio if they had known the instructions given to him. H. DE L'ÉPINOIS, in the *Rev. d. quest. hist.*, XV. (1874), 588, has already shown how inadequate is Perrens' account of Bentivoglio. The edition of the French nunciature reports of the clever Bentivoglio, invaluable documents for the intimate history of the French court, was undertaken by L. SCARABELLI (*Lettere diplom. di G.B.*, 2 vols., Torino, 1852–3). It was based on a copy in the Municipal Library at Genoa. This edition, faulty in other respects also, is now out of date since that of L. DE STEFFANI, *La Nunciatura di Francia del card. G.B. Lettere a S. Borghese, tratte dagli originali*, Firenze, 1863. These are housed in the Archives of the Counts of Bentivoglio at Ferrara. De Steffani also gives the more important instructions of the Secretary of State. The *Lettere* of Bentivoglio of the period of his French nunciature are also in *Barb.*, 5880–5888, Vatican Library.

[2] See Bentivoglio's report of April 11, and Borghese's letter of May 9 and July 25, 1617. *Cf.* DE STEFFANI, *Nunziatura*, I., n. 171, 304, 528.

Gallican opinions, Bentivoglio sought to win him over by kindness[1] and he also encouraged the efforts of Cardinal Retz to bring Richer to better sentiments.[2]

Differences of character and other circumstances resulted in the relations of Bentivoglio with the Jesuit Coton, the king's confessor and the trusted collaborator of Ubaldini, becoming somewhat strained. This also led to the termination of the close relations which under Ubaldini had obtained between the nunciature and the Jesuits.[3] Happily the awkward situation developed no further. With the Jesuit, Jean Arnoux, who became confessor to Louis XIII. in the summer of 1617, in succession to Coton, Bentivoglio stood on excellent terms. When the Huguenots published a violent pamphlet in answer to the sharply anti-Calvinistic sermons of Jean Arnoux, and dedicated it to Louis XIII. with a prayer that God would open the king's eyes, Bentivoglio lodged so strong a protest with the government, that he obtained the suppression of the publication.[4] How highly the nuncio valued the work of the Jesuits in France was shown when at last, after immense difficulties had been surmounted, a royal decree of February, 1618, authorized the Jesuits to inaugurate courses of study in their Collegè de Clermont, in Paris. Bentivoglio at once sought an audience with Louis XIII. in order to express his thanks; in its course he spoke of the Jesuits in the highest terms. To Cardinal Borghese he suggested that a laudatory Brief be sent to the king, for, he added, our enemies themselves confess that the only reason why they oppose the Jesuits is that they are such keen supporters of the authority of the Holy See. The duke of Luynes also should receive a laudatory Brief, the nuncio thought, for the powerful support he had given to the Jesuits on this occasion.[5]

[1] See Bentivoglio's letter of July 5, 1617, *ibid.*, no. 407.

[2] See Bentivoglio's letter, *ibid.*, II., no. 678, 728, 831, 887.

[3] *Cf.* PRAT, III., 734 *seq.*, 756 *seq.* Instead of Coton, Bérulle became Bentivoglio's confidant; see *ibid.*, 752 *seq.*

[4] See PRAT, IV., 41 *seq.*, 49 *seq.*; *cf.* 297 *seq.*

[5] See Bentivoglio's letter of February 14, 1618, in DE STEFFANI, *loc. cit.*, II., no. 961.

It is characteristic of Paul V's. caution that he did not fall in with these suggestions. Bentivoglio received a formal command to observe the greatest caution in this affair and not to rouse the Sorbonne.[1]

A triumph was in store for Bentivoglio at the assembly of notables which opened at Rouen on December 4th, 1617. He shared Père Arnoux' fear lest the notables should allow themselves to be influenced by the ideas of the Paris Parliament and take up once more the dangerous motion concerning a new constitution[2] which the Third Estate had introduced in 1614.[3] However, nothing happened, but another danger arose instead. In view, without any doubt, of the understanding of the Huguenots with foreign Protestant princes, the government had proposed that all Frenchmen should be forbidden, under pain of severe punishment, to hold any intercourse whatsoever with the representatives of foreign powers. One section of the Assembly was for inserting the clause: "even with the nuncio of the Pope." But this was opposed by the clergy and a majority of the nobles who insisted that the Pope, as the Head of the Church and the Father of all the faithful, could not be regarded as a foreign prince. In consequence of the energetic protests of Bentivoglio, who threatened to take his departure, the attempt failed.[4]

A critical moment in Bentivoglio's nunciature arose when in August, 1619, the French ambassador in Rome, the Marquis de Cœuvres, came in conflict with the Roman police. The quarrel became so acute that at one time a rupture between Rome and Paris seemed imminent. When the satisfaction which Cœuvres demanded was denied him, he ceased to put in an appearance at the office of the Cardinal Secretary of State. Bentivoglio's position became all the more precarious

[1] See De Steffani, II., no. 1041.

[2] See the reports of October 11 and November 8, 1617, *ibid.*, no. 641, 722; *cf.* 830.

[3] *Cf.* above, p. 28 *seq.*

[4] See Bentivoglio's report of December 22, 1617, in De Steffani, II., no. 817.

as he took the Pope's part with the greatest determination. The nuncio had made up his mind to leave the court of Paris when Père Coton, who happened to be in Rome at the time (December, 1619) succeeded in finding a peaceful solution of the dispute.[1]

An event of importance, especially from the ecclesiastical point of view, was the union of Navarre and Béarn with the French crown which was effected in October, 1620, by Louis XIII. who had gone to Pau at the head of an army. By this act the Edict of Nantes became operative in those provinces also. The resistance of the Huguenots, who wished to be sole masters of Béarn, was broken by force and the re-establishment of Catholic worship and the restoration of property of which the Catholics had been robbed, were similarly enforced. Henry IV. had already pledged himself to do this on the occasion of his reconciliation with Clement VIII., but he had failed to keep his word to the full.[2] The measure taken by Louis XIII., with which Bentivoglio and Paul V. fully concurred, could not be called unfair, for the king merely restored to the Catholics that of which Jeanne d'Albret had unjustly deprived them. For the rest Louis XIII. indemnified the Huguenots by assigning to them, out of his own purse, the same revenues which until then they had derived from the Catholic Church property.[3] However,

[1] See PRAT, IV., 191 *seqq.* A brief to Louis XIII., referring to this quarrel, dated Tusculum, October 4, 1619, is in FILLON, 2454.

[2] *Cf.* our account, Vol. XXIII., p. 131 *seqq.*

[3] *Cf. Relatione del restabilimento de' vescovi e persone ecclesiastiche del Béarn ne' lor' honori, funtioni, carichi, e godimenti de' beneficii usurpati da gli heretici, et successo del felice viaggio in quel paese di S.M. Christianissima.* In Bologna, e ristampata in Viterbo, MDCXXI. ad instanza di Lodovico Dozza Bolognese (1621); DE MEAUX, 341 *seq.*; KLOPP, II., 31; HANOTAUX, in the *Rev. d. Deux Mondes*, January, 1902, p. 486 *seq.*; PUYOL, *Louis XIII. et le Béarn ou rétablissement du Catholicisme en Béarn et réunion du Béarn et de la Navarre à la France*, Paris, 1872. Paul V.'s contribution is said to have amounted to 200,000 scudi. See *Anal. iuris pontif.*, 1895, 80 (according to *Coppi*).

it soon became apparent that the followers of Calvin had no mind to cease from oppressing the Catholics and they were resolved to carry matters to the last extremity. In the face of the king's prohibition they met at La Rochelle, in October, for the purpose of organizing armed resistance. Bentivoglio gave it as his opinion that France would have no peace as long as the Huguenot party remained in existence.[1]

As a reward for his labours, the nuncio was raised to the purple on January 11th, 1621.[2] The letter of thanks which he addressed to Paul V. on January 31st,[3] no longer found the Pope among the living. The Cardinal set out at once for Rome, to attend the conclave, but by the time he got as far as the neighbourhood of Lyons news reached him of the election of Gregory XV.[4]

(2.)

Bentivoglio's French nunciature had coincided with a period of grave upheaval. It did not take him long to understand the great difference that existed between France and the Spanish Netherlands: "The first month of my stay in Brussels," he wrote at the time to a friend, "taught me all that I was to learn by experience during the next nine years of my nunciature. Here every day yields something fresh. In the Netherlands there is uniformity, in France constant change. If there they fail through slowness, they do so here by excessive ardour." [5]

However, though conditions in France, on which Bentivoglio's reports tell us so much that is of interest, were extremely unstable, the renewal of Catholic life was nevertheless steadily on the increase, both in extent and in depth, throughout the realm.

It was a matter of the greatest importance that the govern-

[1] *Lettere del card. Bentivoglio,* I., 173 *seq.*; *cf.* 193.
[2] *Cf.* Vol. XXV., p. 340.
[3] *Lettere del card. Bentivoglio,* I., 97 *seq.*
[4] See *ibid.,* 107, 109.
[5] *Ibid.,* 51.

ment favoured the Catholic effort. In this respect Catherine de Medici and Louis XIII. showed far more zeal than Henry IV.; they also allowed the papal nuncio to exercise a far wider influence. The rise of the duke of Luynes led to no change in this respect.[1]

Paul V. and his nuncio sought to stir the Catholic zeal of the queen regent by every possible means, even though they met with the opposition of counsellors who, from considerations of statecraft, deemed it necessary to show the greatest possible leniency to the Huguenots.[2] But however important a factor the favourable disposition of the government may have been, it would have availed nothing had it not been accompanied by the internal regeneration of the Church in France.[3] Paul V. kept in very close touch with the protagonists of this movement. The following incident is characteristic of this attitude: in the summer of 1607, Cardinal Joyeuse had reported to the Pope on the condition of religion in France, on its needs, and on the keenness with which the regent supported every effort for reform. Thereupon Ubaldini was instructed to thank the queen and to beg her and her advisers, Villeroi and Jeannin, to persevere in their efforts on behalf

[1] See MARIÉJOL, VI., 2, 204; DE MEAUX, *Réforme*, II., 79.

[2] *Cf.* the *report of Ubaldini to Cardinal Borghese, of October 29, 1610, in which he says: "Io mi ci affatigherò per ogni via, come è necessario, che S. Stà tenga spesso proposito con breve di questa materia, perchè egli spesso lo rappresenti qua, dove l'interesse della religione ha hora gran bisogno di chi li assista di continuo con zelo e con autorità, ancorchè nella materia della regina non sia da desiderare un'ottima mente e santissima e purissima intentione verso il servitio di Dio e l'augmento della religione cattolica, della quale è zelantissima; ma il male è che quelli, ai quali ella ragionevolmente è tenuta a credere, hanno per massima che bisogni per qualsivoglia mezzo procurare di tener gl'Ugonotti lontani dall'armi ed andarli comportando sino che dura la minorità del re: consiglio, che fu già dato et eseguito dalla fu già regina madre e con molto danno della religione." *Nunziat. div.*, 37, p. 208 *seq.*, Papal Secret Archives.

[3] RANKE (*Päpste*, II.[6], 282) also notes this.

of ecclesiastical discipline, but at the same time to take counsel with the leading spirits of the Catholic restoration. As such the following were singled out: the archbishops of Embrun and Aix, Honoré du Laurens and Paul Hurault; the bishops of Paris, Angers and Nantes, Henri de Gondi, Charles Miron and Charles de Bourgneuf, and lastly, Cardinal Du Perron.[1] Like Cardinals Joyeuse and La Rochefoucauld, Du Perron, who had become archbishop of Sens in 1606, laboured unceasingly on behalf of the Catholic restoration and reform. The death of this splendid Prince of the Church, which took place on September 5th, 1618, was a grievous loss to the movement for a Catholic revival. Bentivoglio styled the dead Cardinal the Augustine of France.[2]

In addition to the energetic action of Du Perron and Ubaldini, a strong contributory cause to the defeat of the anti-papal efforts of the Third Estate was the fact that the section of the nobility which had kept its Catholic faith had been steeled and refined by the fight it had been compelled to wage for its preservation.[3] Not a few among the bourgeoisie who toyed with heretical tendencies, did so simply because they failed to recognize their danger and not for a moment did they entertain the idea of a schism or of apostacy from the Church's teaching.[4] At that time instances of apostacy were extremely rare in France.[5] The great mass of the people,

[1] LÄMMER, *Melet.*, 303 *seq.*

[2] *Lettere del card. Bentivoglio*, 64.

[3] *Cf.* DE MEAUX, *Réforme*, II., 79.

[4] *Cf. ibid.*, 95.

[5] The Neapolitan, Giulio Cesare Vanini was condemned to death for heresy in February, 1619, by the Toulouse Parliament. The naturalistic poet Théophile de Vau, imprisoned by the Paris Parliament, only escaped the same fate through the intercession of powerful friends; see MARIÉJOL, VI., 2, 204; PRAT, IV., 470 *seq.*; DE MEAUX, *Réforme*, II., 40 *seq.* For Vanini, see TIRABOSCHI, VIII., 135 *seq.*; REUMONT, *Bibliografia*, 78; K. FISCHER, *Descartes*, I³., 106 *seq.*; CHRIESTIEN, in the *Engl. Hist. Review*, X., April issue; PALUMBO, in the *Riv. Stor. Salentina*, VI., Lecce, 1909, 9 *seq.*

above all the peasantry, were resolved to remain true to the ancient Church.[1] The immense majority of the French people clung firmly to the Catholic faith. In his report of 1605, the Venetian ambassador, Angelo Badoer, states that for a hundred Catholics there was one Calvinist and that since the restoration of peace the proportion was constantly growing in favour of the Catholics,[2] and it would be even more favourable if during the civil wars the people's instruction by sermon and catechism had not been grievously neglected. However, in this respect also, a sensible improvement was gradually taking place.

With a view to a thorough religious training of the lower classes, Jean Baptiste Romillion (died 1622) and César de Bus (died 1607) had founded the Congregation of the secular clerics of Christian Doctrine. Between 1599 and 1600, the female teaching Order of the Ursulines had also taken root in France.[3] The Jesuits, on their part, displayed a widespread and comprehensive activity on behalf of the education of the children of the nobility and the bourgeoisie, as well as for the religious needs of the upper classes. The war which the Parliament of Paris waged against the Order, only helped to strengthen its position. So happy a result the church in France owed to one man more than to any other, the same who prevailed on Henry IV. to recall the Jesuits to France—Pierre Coton.[4] A scion of a royalist family, this noble youth entered the Society of Jesus at Arona, in 1583, notwithstanding the

[1] See MARIÉJOL, *loc. cit.*

[2] See BAROZZI-BERCHET, *Francia*, I., 94. According to BENTIVOGLIO (*Relationi degli Ugonotti di Francia*, in *Relationi*, pubbl. da Erycio Puteano, Colonia, 1632, 183) the number of the Huguenots in 1619, only amounted to a million out of a total population of 15 millions. According to Boerot in 1611 the proportion had been less favourable (see GIODA, *Botero*, III., Milano, 1895, 277).

[3] *Cf.* p. 63 *seq.*

[4] For the following *cf.* the great work of PRAT (Paris, 1876), and also DE MEAUX' warm appreciation of Coton (*Réforme*, II., 25 *seq.*).

opposition of his father. He pursued his studies at Milan, where he assisted at the last Mass of the dying Carlo Borromeo, and at the Roman College in the Eternal City, where he was ordained priest in 1591. On his return to France, Coton displayed, at a difficult time, a fruitful activity as a preacher of mark, an able controversialist, a popular confessor and a wise administrator of a college. He succeeded in gaining the confidence of Henry IV. to such an extent as to be appointed confessor to the king and tutor to the Dauphin. In these difficult posts he remained what he had always been—a model religious who combined in wonderful fashion meekness with severity. He never failed to stand up manfully for the interests of the Church and his Order. The enemies of the Holy See knew why they made him the chief butt of their slanderous attacks.[1] "If the efforts to secure the removal of Coton from Court succeed," wrote Ubaldini to Aquaviva a few months after the death of Henry IV., "the Society of Jesus will succumb in France."[2] By good fortune Coton acted as confessor to Louis XIII. until 1617, and he was succeeded by another Jesuit, Père Arnoux. To this circumstance France chiefly owes it that the conduct of Henry IV.'s son was far more blameless than that of any ruler of France since the days of St. Louis.[3]

The spread of the Society of Jesus on French soil is shown by the fact that in 1616 it counted five Provinces with 1,676 members.[4] In the Province of France, the Jesuits had in Paris, besides the Collège de Clermont, a professed and a noviciate house, a residence at Pontoise and colleges at

[1] *Cf.* above, p. 18. BAYLE'S *Dictionnaire* (Loyole note C.) energetically refuted the slander against Coton.

[2] See PRAT, V., *Pièces justif.*, No. 92.

[3] See DE MEAUX, *Réforme*, II., 45 *seq.* For Louis XIII.'s favourable disposition towards the Jesuits *cf.* the essay of E. GRISELLE, in the *Rev. du monde catholique*, XXIII., 5. See also DUHR, *Jesuitenfabeln*[3], 632 *seq.*, and FOUQUERAY, III., 435 *seq.*

[4] See IUVENCIUS, V., 2, 354. In the French Provinces of the Order, as indeed in other places, the extent was not conterminous with political boundaries.

La Flèche, Bourges, Nevers, Eu, Moulin, Amiens, Caen and Rouen ; in the latter town they also had a noviciate house. In the Province of Aquitania they had a college and a house of probation at Bordeaux, and colleges at Agen, Perigueux, Limoges, Poitiers, Saintes and Rennes, and a residence at Saint-Macaire. The Province of Lyons possessed a college and noviciate both at Lyons and at Avignon ; there were likewise colleges at Tournon, Chambéry, Dôle, Besançon, Vienne, Embrun, Carpentras, Roanne, Vesoul and Sisteron. In the Province of Toulouse there was a college and a house of probation in the episcopal city : furthermore, there were colleges at Billom, Mauriac, Rodez, Auch, Le Puy, Véziers, Cahors, Aubenas, and Carcassone. In the Province of Champagne, the chief residence was at Nancy, with a college and a house of probation ; there were colleges at Reims, Verdun, Pont-à-Mousson, Dijon, Charleville, Autun, Châlons-sur-Marne and Bar-le-Duc.[1]

As everywhere else so in France, the Jesuits devoted themselves with particular ardour to the education of youth. Their teaching method proved itself in brilliant fashion, their success being due to the *Ratio Studiorum* of the year 1599, which Aquaviva had drawn up for general use, as well as to the efficiency of the teachers who devoted themselves wholeheartedly to their task.

The religious life was fostered by means of sodalities of the Blessed Virgin Mary. Coton, who had learnt the value of these associations during his stay in Rome, took particular

[1] There are good monographs on some of these foundations, thus, L. PUYSIEUX, *Les Jésuites à Caen* (since 1606), Caen, 1846 (*cf.* PRENTOUT, *L'université de Caen à la fin du 16e siècle. Contre-Réforme catholique et réformes parlementaires*, Caen, 1908) ; ED. DE BARTHÉLÉMY, *Origine du collège de Rheims* (1608) in the *Rev. de Champagne et Brie*, 1876, Avril ; DE CHARMASSE, *Les Jésuites au Collège d'Autun*, Autun, 1884 ; BOISSONADE ET BERNARD, *Hist. du Collège d'Angoulême*, *ibid.*, 1895 ; CHOSSAT, *Les Jésuites à Avignon*, Avignon, 1896 ; J. DELFOUR, *Les Jésuites à Poitiers*, Paris, 1901. A general account has now been compiled by FOUQUERAY (III., 96 *seq.*, 128 *seq.*, 363 *seq.*, 488 *seq.*).

care to spread them in France. The members, who were carefully selected from among the best students, did not limit their zeal to their own sanctification but worked for the moral uplifting of others also, by example, word and deed. Coton describes the fruits that came to maturity by this means in a book which he entitled: *A Spiritual Nosegay gathered in the Garden of the heavenly Queen of the Sodalists.*[1]

Out of the student sodalities, which were divided into greater and smaller ones according to school classes, grew the men's sodalities of the Blessed Virgin. The action of these associations proved a not inconsiderable factor in the Catholic restoration. Nor was the zeal of the Jesuits confined to the young. They were no less keen on the reform of relaxed Convents and on the holding of spiritual exercises for the secular clergy,[2] than on the practice of the works of mercy on behalf of the sick, the needy and those in prison. Above all they were active as confessors and preachers. This side of their work was no less decisive than their enterprise in the educational field. At Court and in monasteries, in big towns and in small ones, everywhere they displayed a spirit of self-sacrifice without parallel.[3]

When we consider the incredible energy which the Jesuits put into their pastoral work on behalf of Catholics, we cannot but wonder how they still found time to combat the Calvinists. This work was all the more imperative as the followers of the religious innovation were once more making a very active

[1] *Cf.* PRAT, I., 87 *seq.*, IV., 417 *seq.*, 420 *seq.* There are many details about the Congregations in *Litt. Annuae*, 1605 *seq.* As to their influence in spreading devotion to our Lady, which increased greatly in France at this time, see CH. FLACHAIRE, *La dévotion à la Vierge dans la littérature catholique du commencement du 17ème siècle*, in the *Rev. de l'hist. des réligions*, LXXII., Paris, 1915, 311 *seq.*

[2] *Cf. Litt. annuae*, 1607, 618; 1608, 268; 1609, 117.

[3] Numerous accounts are contained in *Litt. annuae, 1605 seq.*, in the bibliographies mentioned above, p. 45, note 1, dealing with the colleges of the Jesuits in France, and FOUQUERAY, III., 153 *seq.*, 386 *seq.*, 557 *seq.*

propaganda at the beginning of the seventeenth century, more particularly in the South of France.[1] However, their efforts met with the most determined opposition on the part of the Jesuits who, heedless of the fact that by so doing they were drawing on themselves the full weight of the hatred of the Protestant party, showed themselves in France also the staunchest champions of the Church and the papacy. They were also the most successful. The writings of such men as Jean Gontery, François Veron, Jean de Bordes, Fronton du Duc, and Louis Richeôme are among the best productions which French controversial literature of the period has to show.[2] Coton and Arnoux also distinguished themselves in this field. Like Du Perron at the celebrated conference of Fontainebleau, Coton and Gontery met outstanding Calvinist preachers in victorious disputations.[3] Coton's chief work, published in 1610, contains an exhaustive defence of Catholic doctrine and of every individual dogma against the attacks of the Huguenots. He subsequently published, in 1617, a larger work on the falsifications of Holy Writ in the Geneva Bible.[4]

These controversial publications and more particularly the public disputations led many souls to return to the Catholic faith.[5] The movement had begun in the last years of the reign of Clement VIII.; under Paul V. it gathered further strength. Among the numerous personages who, fully

[1] *Cf.* PRAT, I., 259.

[2] See besides, WERNER, *Gesch. der polem. Literatur*, IV., 585 *seq.*, 647 *seq.*, also PRAT, I., 517 *seq.*; II., 566 *seq.*, 569 *seq.*, 637 *seq.*; III., 727 *seq.*; IV., 53 *seq.* For Veron *cf.* P. FÉRÉT, *Un curé de Charenton au XVIIe. siècle*, Paris, 1881. For Richeôme, see H. BREMOND, *Hist. litt. du sentiment religieux en France*, I., Paris, 1916, 17 *seq.*, 23 *seq.*

[3] Further details in PRAT, I., 276 *seq.*, 280 *seq.*, 371 *seq.*, 407 *seq.*, 474 *seq.*, 525 *seq.*, 542 *seq.*; II., 601 *seq.*, 635 *seq.*, 646 *seq.*; III., 456 *seq.*, 517 *seq.*; IV., 103 *seq.* *Cf.* BREMOND, *loc. cit.*, II. (1916), 75 *seq.*

[4] See PRAT, II., 655 *seq.*; IV., 33 *seq.*

[5] *Cf.* PRAT, I., 621 *seq.*

convinced by reflection and instruction, came back to the bosom of the one, indivisible Church, from the Calvinistic heresy, besides savants such as Henri Sponde, to whom Paul V. assigned a post in Rome, and the orientalist Jean Morin, there were also statesmen such as Nicolas de Harley and Philippe de Fresne de Canaye, Henry IV's. ambassador at Venice. Calvinist preachers also returned to the Church in great numbers.[1] In order to follow their convictions many of these sacrificed their means of livelihood. For the purpose of providing for them the clergy of France started a fund which received the support of Paul V., Henry IV., and Marie de Medici. The annual sum set aside for this end was eventually raised to 30,000 livres.[2]

Several Capuchins likewise applied themselves to the defence of Catholic truth by means of controversial writings. Of their number mention may be made of Andeolus, Angelicus Tresulensis and Daniel of St. Severus.[3] Others sought to convert the Calvinists by their preaching, for instance, Edonard Mole, brother to the famous attorney general and known by his religious name of Athanasius. He did much to combat public immorality and founded a house where loose women could find a refuge on their conversion.[4] Both Henry IV. and Marie de Medici showed much favour to the Capuchins [5] and several bishops, Richelieu among them, introduced them in their dioceses.[6]

[1] Together with PICOT, I., 45 *seq.*, 159 *seq.*, and PRAT, IV., 59 *seq.*, 67 *seq.*, 87 *seq.*, 91, 95 *seq.*, *cf.* RÄSZ, *Konvertiten*, Bd. III.–V.

[2] See PRAT, II., 672 *seq.*; RÄSZ, III., 270 *seq.*; SERBAT, *Assemblées*, 328 *seq.*, 399 *seq.* The Brief mentioned here addressed to the French clergy respecting converts, is seconded by Paul V.'s *letter to Cardinal Sourdis, of August 5, 1608, in *Epist.*, IV., 93, Papal Secret Archives. *Cf.*, *ibid.*, 316, for the *Brief to Henry IV.

[3] See WERNER, IV., 647. *Cf.* also BREMOND, *loc. cit.*, II., 151 *seq.*, 155 *seq.*, concerning Benoit de Canfeld.

[4] See PICOT, I., 98. *Cf.* also RÄSZ, IV., 338.

[5] *Cf.* POIRSON, *Henri IV.*, III., 749; CHARPENNE, *Hist. des réunions temporaires d'Avignon*, I., Paris, 1886, 247 *seq.*

[6] See HANOTAUX, *Richelieu*, I^2., 94.

The chief strongholds of Calvinism, apart from the very extensive district of Languedoc, were Poitou, Saintonge and Aunis. The Catholic restoration boldly penetrated even into this territory which their opponents claimed for their very own. The Jesuits had made a foundation at Poitiers as early as 1604.[1] At a later date the Capuchin Joseph du Tremblay, who was destined for so much fame, by means of popular missions, did all he could to bring back to the Church the Calvinists of Poitou; his efforts were crowned with considerable success. In 1611 he laid the first stone of a monastery of his Order at Saumur where the Calvinist Academy founded by Du Plessis Mornay constituted a focus of Protestantism.[2] In the following year the Capuchins made foundations at Niort, north of La Rochelle, the chief Calvinist citadel, and at Saint-Maixent, and in 1620 at Thonars.[3] In the South they established themselves at Montpellier in 1609, at Oranges in 1610, at Gap in 1613, at Aigues-Mortes in 1623.[4] Everywhere they preached not only in the churches but in the open as well. Their processions of the Blessed Sacrament, which in most places were something quite unheard of, were soon attended by crowds of worshippers. Numerous conversions rewarded these labours.[5] Everybody admired the devotion to the sick which the Fathers displayed

[1] *Cf.* PRAT, II., 317 *seq.*, and J. DELFOUR, *Les Jésuites à Poitiers*, Paris, 1901.

[2] See FAGNIEZ, *P. Joseph*, I., 288, Paris, 1894. *Cf.* DEDOUVRES, *Le P. Joseph, ses charges, ses prédications de 1604 à 1613*, Angers, 1915.

[3] See MARIÉJOL, VI., 2, 208.

[4] For these establishments see more detailed information in *Cod.* 636, p. 563 *seq.*, 569 *seq.* of the Méjanes Library at Aix (Provence). For the monastery at Montpellier, see the periodical, *La Controverse*, CXXXVI., 396 *seq.*, 407.

[5] See **Description des missions, conversions et autres fruits faits par les Capucins en la province St. Louis appellée de Provence*, in *Cod.* 636, p. 559 *seq.*, of the Méjanes Library, at Aix (Provence). *Cf.* too, MARIÉJOL, VI., 2, 208, who rightly questions the accuracy of the figure of 50,000 converts.

in times of epidemic.[1] It is characteristic of the zeal which animated the Capuchins and Jesuits of France that, notwithstanding that they were overburdened with labours of every kind, they still undertook missionary work in pagan countries.[2]

The general revival which the Church experienced in France, affected the old orders also.[3] True, the reform of these institutions, which had for the most part sunk to a very low level, was a slow process and at times a most difficult one. Thus the reform of the Dominicans, which Sebastian Michaelis had begun at Toulouse, in 1580, and which Paul V. had confirmed, took indeed root in Paris,[4] but all the efforts of the excellent General of the Order, Agostino Galamina, failed to win over the other French convents to this new orientation.[5] The reform of the famous abbey of Montmartre, in Paris, undertaken by Marie de Beauvilliers, met with incredible resistance on the part of the utterly degenerate nuns so that progress was exceedingly slow.[6] The distinguished Marquise de Belle-Isle, Antoinette d'Orléans, who on the death of her husband had entered the convent of the Feuillantes, at Toulouse, and who, through pressure on the part of Paul V., had become Abbess of the Benedictine Convent of Fontevrault, met with so many obstacles in her attempts to

[1] *Cf.* BOUVERIUS, II., 779; PICOT, I., 95; IRENÉE D'AULON, *Nécrologe des Frères min. Capucins de l'anc. prov. d'Aquitaine*, 1582–1790, Carcassonne, 1904.

[2] *Cf.* Vol. XXV., p. 378 *seq.*

[3] Numerous details in PICOT, I., 91 *seq.*, 100 *seq.*, 414 *seq.*, 421 *seq.* *Cf.* also DE MEAUX, *Réforme*, II., 6 *seq.*; *Anal. Francisc.*, I., 359 *seq.* For the reform of the Discalced Augustinian Hermits, furthered by Paul V., see GOUJET, II., 167 *seq.* For the restoration of the ancient discipline in the Benedictine Abbey of St. Symphorian, at Metz, by Karl Hellot, see LAGER, *Die Benediktinerabtei St. Symphorian in Metz*, Brünn, 1892, 34 *seq.*

[4] See PICOT, I., 420.

[5] *Cf.* MORONI, XXVIII., 111, and the *Instruction for the nuncio Corsini of April 4, 1621, Corsini Library, Rome. *Cod.* 472, p. 10 *seq.*

[6] See DE MEAUX, *Réforme*, I., 7 *seq.* *Cf.* BREMOND, II., 442 *seq.*

reform her community, that together with the better-disposed nuns, she withdrew to the Priory of Lencloître from whence she spread her new institute, the strict Congregation of our Lady of Calvary. With the help of the Capuchin, Joseph du Tremblay, she founded, in 1617, a new monastery at Poitiers, in which the rule of St. Benedict was observed in all its primitive rigour. After the premature death of the foundress (1618), Père Joseph completed the work she had begun by effecting a reform in Paris and Angers and by obtaining for it the papal confirmation.[1]

The decree of the Council of Trent, by the terms of which all monasteries directly subject to the Holy See were compelled to form Congregations and to hold General Chapters at regular intervals, proved very advantageous to the Benedictine Order on French soil. The Congregation of St. Vannes, in Lorraine, founded by Didier de la Cour and confirmed by Clement VIII. has already been mentioned.[2] On July 23rd, 1605, Paul V. granted to it all the privileges and faculties enjoyed by the Abbot of Monte Cassino ; at the same time he gave orders for the reform of all the monasteries within the legation of Cardinal Charles of Lorraine. For this purpose the Superior General of the Cassinese Congregation, Lorenzo Lucalberti, was dispatched to Lorraine.[3] Noël Mars, a Benedictine of the ancient abbey of Marmoutier, in Lower Alsace, founded the Congregation of Brittany which was approved by Paul V. in 1606.[4] In the following year the abbey of Saint

[1] *Cf. Vie de la mère Antoinette d'Orléans, fondatrice de la Congrégation de Notre-Dame du Calvaire, par un réligieux feuillant*, publ. avec une introduction par l'abbé Petit, Paris, 1880.

[2] *Cf.* our account, Vol. XXXIII., p. 183.

[3] *Cf.* Haudiquier, *Hist. du vén. Dom Didier de la Cour*, Paris, 1772. *Cf. Hist.-polit. Blätter*, CV., 105, 275 *seq.* The *Brief of Paul V., *Pro reformatione monasteriorum legationis ill. Caroli card. Lotharingiae* " *Ex iniuncto* ", September 27, 1605, is in facsimile in the National Archives, Paris. L. 357.

[4] See Picot, I., 418 ; Schmieder, in the *Studien aus dem Benediktinerorden*, XII., 75 *seq.* ; *Rev. Bénédict.*, XI. (1894), 97 *seq.*

Denis, once famous throughout Europe, put itself at the head of a new Congregation of nine other monasteries. It was approved by Paul V. in 1614.[1] Adverse circumstances, however, chief of which was the abuse of the *commenda*, impeded the work of these Congregations.[2] The difficulties which stood in the way of a reform in the Benedictine Order had been described as early as 1607 in an impressive report of the Visitor of the Province of Aquitania to Cardinal Givry, the protector of the Order, in Rome.[3] The efficiency of the Congregation of Lorraine to which an ever growing number of French monasteries affiliated themselves (St. Augustine, at Limoges, in 1613, St. Faron, near Meaux, St. Junian, at Noailles, St. Pierre of Jumièges in 1615) ; was impeded by one outstanding obstacle—viz. the fact that the French government greatly disliked to see foreign Superiors at the head of French monasteries. In consequence of this the General Chapter of the Congregation of Lorraine, held at Toul in 1618, decreed that the French monasteries should form a Congregation of their own, with its own statutes, Superiors and visitors. The prompt execution of this resolution was mainly due to the influence of the excellent Prior of the Cluniac priory of Paris, Laurent Bénard, who won the support of Louis XIII. and other influential persons for the plan. In this way it became possible to give effect to the decision of the General Chapter of Toul before the end of 1618 in the monastery of Blancsmanteaux, in Paris, which until then had belonged to the Guillaumites.

[1] See *Gallia christ.*, VII., 332 ; FÉLIBIEN, *Hist. de l'abbaye de St.-Denis*, Paris, 1706 ; F. D'AYZAC, *Hist. de l'abbaye de St.-Denis*, 2 vols., Paris, 1861. The *letter of the abbey of St.-Denis, to Cardinal Givry, with the request to ask Paul V. to confirm their reform, dated October 6, 1607, is in *Cod.* 219, p. 199 *seq.*, of the City Library at Metz.

[2] See SCHMIEDER, *loc. cit.*, 74. On the abuse of benefices *cf.* AVENEL, in the *Rev. hist.*, XXXIII., 2 *seq.*

[3] The account " de flebili ac moestissima Benedictini instituti eversione in Galliis ", dated Bordeaux, June 2, 1607, is in Givry's collection of letters in *Cod.* 219, p. 139 of the City Library, Metz.

In order not to offend any of the greater monasteries of France, the new Congregation called itself by the name of St. Maurus, the first disciple of St. Benedict.[1] Didier de la Cour, who died in 1623,[2] lived long enough to see the Maurist Congregation approved by the successor of Paul V. Already at that time it counted among its members Dom Hugh Ménard. That venerable man directed the Maurists to the study of the Christian past, a field in which the Congregation was destined to render imperishable service to scholarship.[3]

Any survey of the renewal of the French Church would be incomplete if it did not include its hierarchy. The episcopate was debarred from taking a leading rôle in that movement inasmuch as in consequence of the abuse of the Concordat on the part of the government, it still counted too many unworthy elements in its ranks, though some improvement had taken place since the reign of Henry IV. During the last years of that prince the French hierarchy had been given several splendid members, among them two friends of Francis de Sales, viz. Pierre Fenouillet, bishop of Montpellier, and Pierre Camus, bishop of Belley. Men of a similiar type were Philippe Cospeau, who was named to the See of Aire in 1607; the Carthusian Bruno Ruade, bishop of Conserans since 1624; and Simon de Marquemont, who became bishop of Lyons in 1612.[4] Jean Bertaut, poet and courtier, who obtained the bishopric of Séez from Henry IV. in 1606, took his duties seriously and became a good bishop.[5]

[1] See BRAUNMÜLLER, in the *Freib. Kirchenlex.*, VIII.², 1059; SCHMIEDER, in the *Studien aus dem Benediktinerorden*, XII., 256 *seq.*; HEIMBUCHER, I., 151. For the reform of the Benedictines of St. Germain-des-Près, at Paris, 1618, see FÉLIBIEN, *Hist. de Paris*, II., 1352.

[2] For Didier's grave see the essay of L. GERMAIN in the *Journal de la Soc. Arch. Lorraine*, XL., 193 *seq.*

[3] For Ménard *cf.* HURTER, *Nomenclator*, I., 477; *Freib. Kirchenlex.*, VIII.², 1243 *seq.*

[4] *Cf.* DE MEAUX, *Luttes*, 377 *seq.*, 379, and *Réforme*, II., 92, 93.

[5] *Cf.* the detailed monograph of G. GRENTE, *Jean Bertaut*, Paris, 1903, 69 *seqq.*

His successor, Jacques Suarez, inherited his spirit.[1] In 1607, the excellent bishop of Narbonne, Louis de Vervins, held a provincial synod in that city, the canons of which proved most beneficial.[2] An extraordinarily fruitful activity had been displayed, since 1607, by the barely twenty-two year old Richelieu in his diocese of Luçon, which he visited in all its parts and whose religious condition he greatly improved by means of missions and sermons and an excellent catechism composed by himself.[3] Like François de la Rochefoucauld, bishop of Senlis since 1610,[4] the bishops of Metz, Cardinal Charles of Lorraine and Cardinal Givry, gave ample proof of their zeal for the reform of the clergy and the religious Orders [5]; Givry was strongly supported by Paul V. in all his efforts.[6] In 1617

[1] See *Gallia christ.*, XI.

[2] *Cf.* PICOT, I., 102.

[3] *Cf.* PERRAUD, *Le card. Richelieu, évêque, théologien* (1882); LACROIX, *Richelieu à Luçon, sa jeunesse, son épiscopat*, Paris, 1890; DE MEAUX, *Réforme*, II., 80 *seq.*; HANOTAUX, *Hist. du card. Richelieu*, I.² (1896), 94 *seq.*, 106 *seq.* In the *Rev. du Bas-Poitou*, IV. (1892), 333 *seq.*, LACROIX tries to prove that Richelieu deceived Pope Paul V., when, in order to obtain the necessary dispensation for his consecration as priest and bishop, owing to his being only in his 21st year, he produced the baptismal certificate of his elder brother, two years older than himself.

[4] See P. ROVERIUS, *De Vita F. de la Rochefoucauld*, Paris, 1645; CARDELLA, VI., 137; *Rev. d. quest. hist.*, XXIII. (1878), 114 *seq.*; G. DE LA ROCHEFOUCAULD, *Le card. Fr. de la Rochefoucauld*, 127 *seq.*, 144 *seq.*, 187 *seq.*, 191 *seq.*

[5] See MEURISSE, *Hist. des évêques de Metz*, Metz, 1634, 640 *seq.*; SCHMIDLIN, 436. *Cf.* Appendix No. 2, the description of the bad condition of the Metz diocese, sent by Givry to Rome in 1609. City Library, Metz, *loc. cit.*

[6] *Cf.* the *Briefs concerning the reform of the Convents in Metz, of November 28, 1608, and June 5, 1610, in *Cod.* 219, p. 376 and 404 of the Town Library, Metz. *Ibid.*, a *Motuproprio, of October 21, 1608, which empowers Cardinal Givry, who was also co-adjutor of Langres, to visit all religious establishments of the diocese. *Cf.* now J. B. KAISER, *Urkunden zur Gesch. des Zisterzienserordens im Anfang des 17. Jahrh.*, in the *Zisterzienser-*

the Dominican, Nicolas Coeffeteau, famous for his literary work, was appointed to the See of Marseilles.[1] Henri and Raimond de la Marthonie were also excellent bishops.[2]

After the death of Henry IV., Rome took every precaution to ensure that only deserving men were appointed to bishoprics. In 1611, the Pope exhorted Marie de Medici to propose for bishoprics such men as conformed to the prescriptions of Canon Law. He pointed out that this was in the interest also of the State.[3] That in this respect there was ground for serious complaint appears from the laments of Ubaldini[4] and from the fact that, in 1614, the clergy demanded the creation of a supreme council to assist the king in the execution of "the most dangerous of all his prerogatives."[5] In a report of 1617, Bentivoglio expressly states that better nominations to episcopal sees were a crying need.[6] These circumstances sufficiently account for the decadence of discipline among the clergy in a number of dioceses. Splendid priests could indeed be found, such as Vincent de Paul, whose labours were crowned with astonishing success first at Clichy, near Paris (in 1612), and subsequently (1617) at Châtillon-les-Dombes, in the diocese of

Chronik, XXIX. (1917). There, on p. 216 *seq.*, is printed the *Brief of Paul V. of March 2, 1606, concerning the nomination of Cardinal Givry as Protector of the Cistercian Order.

[1] *Cf.* CH. URBAIN, *Nicolas Coëffeteau*, Paris, 1894.

[2] As to their activity see AULAGNE, *La réforme catholique du XVII.e siècle dans le diocèse de Limoges*, Paris, 1906.

[3] *Brief of August 17, 1611, *Epist.*, VII. 43, Papal Secret Archives, see Appendix No. 3.

[4] *Cf.* Ubaldini's reports used by PERRENS (II., 2 *seq.*). Villeroi attempted to defend the nomination of unsuitable bishops on account of the circumstances; see Ubaldini's *reports for July 7 and August 5, 1611, Papal Secret Archives, *loc. cit.* ABBÉ OLIVIER DUBOIS, in his letter to Paul V. of September 13, 1610, complained that Rome was frequently too lenient in granting dispensations for age too easily, see *Annales de St. Louis*, X. (1905), 225.

[5] See AVENEL, in the *Rev. hist.*, XXXII., 320 *seq.*

[6] Letter of Bentivoglio, of January 17, 1617, in DE STEFFANI, I., no. 34.

Lyons [1]; Michel le Nobletz, the apostle of Brittany [2]; Bernard Bardon de Brun, at Limoges [3]; the magnificent parish priest of Mattaincourt, Pierre Fourier [4] and lastly, the saintly Adrien Bourdoise.[5] If in many dioceses there was a dearth of men of this calibre, the reason was that the formation of the clergy was grievously neglected.

Notwithstanding that provincial synods had repeatedly decreed the erection of seminaries for priests of the kind prescribed by the Council of Trent, France as yet possessed but a small number of such institutions. This was the result not only of the troubles of the religious and civil wars and other causes, but of the negligence also of many bishops,[6] though in this connection it must be borne in mind that the bishops had the disposal of only about one-half of the benefices in their diocese.[7] This pitiful condition was about to be substantially relieved by the work of a man who could be counted among the most zealous priests of whom France was able to boast at that time.

Pierre de Bérulle [8] was sprung from an ancient noble

[1] *Cf.* Broglie, *Vincent de Paul*, Paris, 1898, 31 *seq.*, 48 *seq.* *Cf. Civ. Catt.*, 1917, IV., 536 *seq.* We shall revert to the activities of St. Vincent de Paul, in the next volume.

[2] See (P. Verjus), *Vie de M. Le Nobletz*, Paris, 1666; Picot, I., 140 *seq.*; Le Gouvello, *Le ven. M. Le Nobletz*, Paris, 1898; Bremond, *Hist. du sentiment relig.*, V. (1920), 82 *seq.*

[3] See Petiot, *Vie de B. Bardon de Brun*, Paris, 1636; Picot, I., 148 *seq.*

[4] *Cf.* about Fourier, our account, Vol. XXXIII., 184. The Congregation of Our Lady founded by Fourier, was confirmed by Paul V. in 1615; see Heimbucher, I., 440 *seq.*

[5] *Cf.* Darche, *Le saint Abbé Bourdoise*, 2 vols., nouv. éd., Paris, 1884. *Cf.*, further, G. Letourneau, *Les saints prêtres français du 17e siècle*, 2 vols., Paris, 1887.

[6] See, on this point, Dudon, in *Études*, CXXXI. (1912), 586 *seq.*

[7] *Cf.* Letourneau, *La mission de J.-J. Olier*, Paris, 1906, 28–9.

[8] For the following, *cf.* Habert, *Vie du card. de Bérulle*, Paris, 1646; Attichy, *De vita card. Berullii*, Paris, 1649; Tabaraud, *Hist. de P. Bérulle*, 2 vols., Paris, 1817; Nourrisson, *Le card.*

family. He was born in the château of Sérilly, in Champagne, in 1575. The plan of his family and that of his father, whom he lost in his early years and who had been counsellor of the Parliament of Paris, was that he should enter the service of the State. However, Bérulle's precocious maturity and deep piety found but little satisfaction in the study of the law. On the other hand he felt wholly in his element when, at the age of twenty, he was able to give himself whole-heartedly to the study of theology at the Sorbonne. Previous to his ordination, which he received in 1599, Bérulle spontaneously withdrew into a convent of Capuchins, for the space of forty days, in order to prepare himself for the reception of the priesthood. The exemplary priest who always wore the soutane—a rare thing in those days—soon found himself in great request as a spiritual guide and ever wider circles took an increasing interest in him. Astonishment was general when he steadfastly refused every post that was offered him, as, for instance, several abbeys and bishoprics to which Henry IV. wished to nominate him, and, finally even the post of tutor to the Dauphin. Bérulle was resolved to labour in obscurity, as a simple priest. That which was nearest his heart was the conversion of the Huguenots. He played a prominent part in the establishment in France of the Carmelite Nuns who devoted their lives to prayer, contemplation and penance. He was to have the happiness of

de Bérulle, Paris, 1856, [3]1866; HOUSSAYE, *N. de Bérulle et les Carmélites de France*, 1575–1611, Paris, 1872; *Ibid.*, *Le Père de Bérulle et l'Oratoire de Jésus*, 1611–1625, Paris, 1874; INGOLD, *Bibl. Oratorienne, Généralats du card. de Bérulle et du P. de Condren. Première Partie du Recueil des Vies de quelques Prêtres de l'Oratoire* de P. CLOYSEAULT, Paris, 1880; *Mémoires domestiques pour servir à l'hist. de l'Oratoire; les Pères qui ont vécu sous le card. de Bérulle*, par L. BATTEREL, publ. par Ingold, Paris, 1902. We have also used the fine essays in the *Correspondant*, 1855, Janvier and Févr. (by NOURRISSON) and in the *Katholik*, XVI. (1875), 248 *seq.*, 344 *seq.*, 469 *seq.*, as well as HEIMBUCHER, II., 347 *seq.* See also LALLEMAND, *Hist. de l'éducation dans l'ancien Oratoire de France*, Paris, 1887, and GOYAU, *Hist. rélig.*, 405 *seq.*

admitting his own mother, a woman of uncommon piety, into the Order.

During a stay in Paris in 1602, Francis de Sales made Bérulle's acquaintance. Ever after the two men remained close friends. Francis frequently sent those who sought his advice to Bérulle; for instance the newly-appointed Bishop of Dol, to whom he wrote: "Bérulle is wholly what I should like to be myself. I have not often found his like." At that time Bérulle already busied himself with the plan of founding a Congregation of secular priests, on the model of that of Philip Neri, with a view to the revival of discipline and learning among the French clergy. Only a delicate consideration for the Jesuits, who had been banned since 1595, restrained him for a time. He feared lest their recall should be deemed superfluous since there was a possibility that it might seem that his own foundation sufficiently provided for the needs of the Church in France. But when, in 1603, the sentence of banishment of the Jesuits was repealed, he judged that he need no longer delay the execution of his plan. His humility, however, made him desirous that someone else should be the head of the new Institute, so he undertook a journey to Annecy, in 1606, to visit Francis de Sales. But the holy bishop could not and would not forsake his flock. On the return journey Bérulle called on César de Bus, at Avignon, but he too, in view of his own foundation, saw himself compelled to decline the offer. Both men, however, urged Bérulle to proceed with his plan and promised their support. On his return to Paris, Bérulle saw himself pressed by the most diverse people to put himself at the head of the undertaking he had conceived and of which there was so great a need. Marie de Medici promised her support and the Marquise de Maignelay besought Bérulle on her knees to make no further difficulties but to undertake the government of the Congregation. When all seemed unavailing, the Marquise had recourse to her brother, Henri de Gondi, bishop of Paris, beseeching him to use his authority. Thereupon Gondi commanded Bérulle, under obedience, to comply with the wishes of so many people. There could be no question of further resistance. Bérulle rented a house in the Faubourg Saint-Jacques and on December 10th, 1611, he took possession with five companions. On the following day they said Mass, in the presence of a few devout women, among them the above-mentioned Marquise and Marie Acarie. Thus was inaugurated, very quietly, the French Oratory whose foundation was hailed with joy by Cardinal Joyeuse, the Jesuit Coton and other outstanding personalities. Authorization by the secular power was promptly obtained. It proved much more difficult to secure the papal approval, for the Cardinals charged with the examination of the plan submitted by Bérulle, raised objections to some points, such as, for instance, the clause that the members of the Oratory were to be subject to the bishops in all things, for in that case any bishop might change the statutes of the Congregation as he pleased. In like manner the stipulation that the Oratorians should not conduct colleges in which the liberal arts were taught was not favourably viewed in Rome. Bérulle was far removed from obstinate insistence on his original plan and submitted in everything to the decision of the Pope.[1] The Constitution by which Paul V. approved the "Congregation of the Oratory of our Lord Jesus Christ" bears the date of May 10th, 1613.[2] It restricts episcopal authority to the pastoral activities of the Oratorians and leaves the prohibition of the conducting of colleges untouched. Bérulle was named Superior of the new Society of secular priests living in community.

The opportuneness of the French Oratory, which Paul V. and Marie de Medici were most anxious to promote,[3] is shown by its rapid spread. As early as 1614, there were foundations at Dieppe and La Rochelle, in 1615 at Orléans and Tours, in

[1] See Ubaldini's report of April 11, 1613, translated in PRAT, III., 548. For the Cardinal's commission *cf.* Borghese's letter of December 6, 1612, in LÄMMER, *Melet.*, 331.

[2] *Bull.*, XII., 205 *seq.*

[3] See Borghese's letter of August 2, 1613, in LÄMMER, *Melet.*, 324.

1616 at Langres, in 1617 at Rouen, Montmorency and Clermont, in 1618 at Riom, Nancy, Troyes and Nevers, in 1619 at Limoges, Saumur, Toulouse and Angers, in 1620 at Joyeuse and Amiens. In 1619 the community of priests of the famous sanctuary of Notre-Dame-des-Grâces, in the diocese of Fréjus, which had received the approval of Clement VIII., as well as a section of the *Doctrinaires*, founded by César de Bus, joined forces with the Oratory.[1] In 1616, Bérulle concluded an agreement with the bishop of Langres, Sebastien Zamet, in consequence of which the Oratorians undertook the direction of his diocesan seminary. Here the beginnings were as humble as at the seminary of St. Magloire, in Paris, which the bishop of the capital, Henri de Gondi, entrusted to Bérulle's Society in 1620.[2] These attempts were of the same kind as the foundation of Adrien Bourdoise, at St. Nicolas du Chardonnet, in Paris. These forerunners of the real Tridentine Seminaries must not be undervalued because of their restricted field; they prepared the ground for the eminently successful work of Bérulle, Eudes, Bourdoise, Vincent de Paul and Olier for the training of good priests.[3]

The Oratory did not cause Bérulle to forget the reformed Spanish Carmelites who came to France in 1604. They spread very rapidly. In 1611, seven years after the foundation of the first Convent in Paris, they had houses at Pontoise, Dijon, Amiens, Tours, Rouen, Bordeaux, and Châlons-sur-Marne. In 1614 they settled at Besançon. By 1620 the number of their convents had risen to thirty-four. The Spanish nuns who had introduced the reform, either died or returned to their own

[1] *Cf.* PERRAUD, *L'Oratoire* [2], 51.

[2] See PRUNEL, "Les premiers Séminaires en France," in *Études*, CXVIII. (1909), 346 *seq.* In Rome, Bérulle's companions with the permission of Louis XIII., undertook the reform of the national establishment of St.-Louis, which had fallen into decay.

[3] *Cf.* LETOURNEAU, *La mission de J.-J. Olier*, Paris, 1906, 34 *seqq.* For St.-Magloire see PRUNEL, *Renaissance cath.*, 54 *seq.* For St.-Nicolas du Chardonnet, see the monograph by SCHOENHER (Paris, 1909).

country, hence the new branch assumed a wholly French character. Its members were recruited from the most diverse social strata. By the side of Madame Acarie's maid, and the daughters of the bourgeoisie, the Order counted a Marquise of Bréauté and the daughter of Marshal Charles de Cossé, duc of Brissac, the same who had opened the gates of Paris to Henry IV. Whereas in former times the convents of nuns had been degraded into being no more than places of refuge for girls without fortune, now only those sought admission who strove for the heights of perfection. Nothing bears more eloquent testimony to the religious fervour of the period than the fact that the strictest of all female Orders was also the most popular.[1] In 1616 the Duchess of Longueville founded another Carmelite convent in Paris to which a third was soon added.[2] The first French Prioress was Madeleine de Fontaines-Marans who, as Mère Madeleine de St. Joseph, exercised a very powerful influence.[3] In 1614, Paul V. appointed Bérulle perpetual Visitor of all the French Carmels. The office occasioned him many annoyances, for some convents demanded to be governed by the discalced reformed Carmelite Fathers.[4] With the encouragement of Paul V., the latter had

[1] See HOUSSAYE, *M. de Bérulle et les Carmélites en France*, 493 *seqq*. DE MEAUX, *Luttes*, 353 *seq*. For the convent at Amiens, see CH. SALMON, *L'Établissement des Carmélites à Amiens*, 1606–1608, Amiens, 1881, and *Études*, LXIX., 413 *seq*. BREMOND (*Hist. litt. du sentiment réligieux en France*, II., 263 *seq*.) ascribes the chief part in the spread of the Reformed Carmelites in France to Jean de Quintandoine de Brétigny, as is noted on his tombstone in Rouen (d. 1634); Jean was the first to translate the writings of St. Teresa into French.

[2] PRUNEL, *Renaissance catholique*, 77.

[3] *Cf*. ERIAU, *Essai sur la vie et les lettres inédites de la ven. Madeleine de St.-Joseph, 1578–1637*, Paris, 1921.

[4] *Cf*. GOUJET, II., 163 *seq*. Originally Paul V. had commissioned the then nuncio to nominate, every three years, a secular priest for the visitation of the French Carmelites; see the Constitution of September 9, 1606, in *Bull*., XI., 352 *seq*.; HOUSSAYE, *loc. cit*., 547 *seqq*.

come to Paris in 1611 [1] and two years later Marie de Medici laid the foundation stone of their new church.[2]

Just as the Church in France received the Carmelites from Spain so did Italy give her the Ursulines, in addition to the Brothers Hospitallers [3] whom Marie de Medici had introduced in the first years of the seventeenth century. It is an inspiring spectacle to see how God had secretly prepared a number of generous souls for a Society whose scope, viz. the instruction and education of young girls—was of supreme importance. The simultaneous rise of these Societies was to shed extraordinary lustre upon the Catholic restoration of France.

The foundation of the first Ursuline convent in France had been laid at l'Isle de Venise, in the comté of Venaissin, during the pontificate of Clement VIII. by a spiritual daughter of the founder of the *Doctrinaires*, César de Bus, namely the devout and gifted Françoise de Bermond.[4] The opening years of the seventeenth century witnessed the establishment of a house at Aix and at Marseilles.[5] Reports of the excellent training which girls were given in these establishments soon spread beyond the boundaries of southern France. In Paris there

[1] *Cf.* the *Briefs to Henry IV. and Cardinal Joyeuse, April 20, 1610, *Epist.*, V., 364, 365, Papal Secret Archives. *Cf.* FÉLIBIEN, *Hist. de Paris*, IV., 55; GOUJET, II., 164.

[2] See DUPLESSY, *Paris réligieux*, Paris, 1900, 338 *seq.* *Cf.* PISANI, *La maison des Carmes à Paris*, Paris, 1895. For the establishment of the Discalced Carmelites at Limoges, 1618, *cf.* *Bull. de la soc. arch. du Limousin*, LVI. (1917–1918), 397 *seq.* The reform of the Calced Carmelites, supported by Clement VIII., had already begun at Rennes in 1604. It was consolidated by the Prior Philip Thibaut, elected in 1608, and the mystic, John of St. Samson; *cf.* *Vie du vén. fr. Jean de St.-Samson par le P. Sernin Marie de St.-André*, Paris, 1881.

[3] See PICOT, I., 101; DE MEAUX, *Réforme*, II., 14 *seq.*; *cf.* MAXIME DU CAMP, *La charité privée à Paris* [3], Paris, 1887, 80; PRUNEL, *Renaissance cath.*, 110 *seq.*; see the same authority for the founding of hospitals by Henry IV. and Louis XIII. (112 *seq.*), and for private philanthropy (118 *seq.*).

[4] *Cf.* our account, Vol. XXXIII, 184.

[5] *Cf.* *Chroniques de l'ordre des Ursulines*, I., Paris, 1676, 316, 352.

was much talk of summoning the "provençal nuns", as they were called, to the capital, especially in the circle of which Madame Acarie was the heart and centre. Her cousin undertook to carry the plan into effect. Madeleine Lhuillier had been married to Claude de Sainte-Beuve at the age of nineteen. Soon after, in the presence of the coffin of her husband, she realized the instability of human happiness and from that moment she devoted herself exclusively to her own sanctification and to the welfare of others.[1] Madame de Sainte-Beuve, as may be seen from her portrait, possessed a truly virile character which commanded the respect of no less a man than Henry IV. himself. When the noble woman manifested to the Jesuit, Lancelot Marin, her desire to undertake some work appropriate to the needs of the times, for the renewal of the religious spirit, the latter mentioned the education of female youth which would be the most effective means of the regeneration of the family and of society. Madame Acarie also was of opinion that the best use her rich cousin could make of her wealth was to found an educational establishment for the management of which none were more suitable than the provençal Ursulines. Madame de Sainte-Beuve, having taken counsel with her confessor, the Jesuit Gontery, agreed with the suggestion and supplied the material means for a foundation in the faubourg Saint-Jacques. The establishment was inaugurated in the spring of 1608, by Françoise de Bermond and one companion who had been called to Paris. The personnel was recruited from those among the young women under Madame Acarie's guidance who had not felt a call to Carmel.

It was also Gontery who suggested that, besides papal approval, they should also pray for the establishment of strict enclosure and the privilege of solemn vows. Madame Acarie did not agree with this suggestion for she had some misgivings

[1] *Cf.* for the following, H. de Leymont, *Madame de St.-Beuve, et les Ursulines de Paris, 1562–1630* [2]; Lyon, 1889 (with a plate of Mad. Lhuillier de Sainte-Beuve); *Vie de Françoise de Bermond par une Ursuline* (1896).

12069

Maryville College
Library
Saint Louis

about departing from the lines laid down by the foundress of the Ursulines, Angela Merici, whom she held in the highest veneration. However, Madame de Sainte-Beuve stuck to the plan of her experienced confessor, a plan which, if properly carried into effect, would put the finishing touches to the original form of the Society. That which clinched the matter was the fact that the Ursulines of Paris, whom the Jesuits Gontery and Coton consulted, decided in favour of the enclosure, though they made a few reservations, by means of which the spirit of the foundress and the particular purpose of the Society were to be secured, especially as regards the education of youth.

The handling of the question at the Curia was undertaken by De Soulfour, a nobleman who subsequently joined the French Oratory. He accompanied Cardinal La Rochefoucauld when the latter journeyed to Rome, to do homage in the name of Louis XIII., in 1610, when he also pressed for the approval of Bérulle's foundation. His task proved by no means a light one for not a few people at the Curia were of opinion that, in view of the troubles and quarrels within the Orders, it would be better to suppress some of them altogether rather than to approve new ones.[1] Another difficulty arose in France itself. The Ursulines of Provence opposed the new plan because they could not see how it could be made to fit in with the intentions of Angela de Merici. In consequence of these objections Françoise de Bermond had to leave Paris and return to Provence without having accomplished anything.

Meanwhile Rome had given its decision. Paul V.'s enthusiasm for the object of the new Institute had silenced every objection.[2] On June 13th, 1612, the Pope had a letter issued from Frascati to Henri de Gondi, bishop of Paris, by which he approved the house founded by Madame Acarie in Paris. The convent was to be subject to the bishop of Paris and governed in his name by three doctors of divinity. The

[1] *Cf.* De Leymont, *loc. cit.*, 189.
[2] See De Leymont, *loc. cit.*, 194.

inmates were authorized to establish strict enclosure and to take solemn vows according to the Rule of St. Augustin. A fourth vow was to be added to the usual three, viz. to devote themselves to the education of young girls as their chief work.[1] To the Ursuline convent founded at Toulouse in 1604, Paul V. likewise granted the privilege of solemn vows.[2] A similiar permission was granted by the Pope, in 1618, to the house founded twelve years earlier at Bordeaux, by Françoise de Cazères with the support of Cardinal Sourdis[3]; to the foundation of Dijon in 1619, and to the six communities which had been established in the archdiocese of Lyons, then governed by De Marquemont, viz. Lyons, Saint-Bonnet, Chaumont, Montbrison-en-Forest, Roanne and Bourg.[4] The papal constitutions for the convents of Bordeaux and Lyons laid down very detailed rules for their internal administration. Especially remarkable are the wise ordinances by which the enclosure is made to harmonize with the chief object of the Institute. The pupils were forbidden to live in the same house as the nuns; in consequence, a special building had to be erected beside the church but connected with the convent whose inmates, though strictly enclosed, would nevertheless be allowed to enter this school building. In view of their duties as teachers, the Ursulines were relieved from the burden of the Canonical Office; in its place they were to recite daily the Little Office of our Lady and the entire rosary of fifteen decades.

Like the convent of Paris, the establishments of Toulouse, Bordeaux and Lyons became mother-houses of extensive Congregations in the course of 1615, 1618 and 1619, for various towns competed with each other in their eagerness to secure such excellent teachers. The Ursulines spread with

[1] Text of Paul V.'s letter, *ibid.*, 403 *seq.*

[2] *Cf.* POYRE, *Chroniques des Réligieuses Ursulines de la Congrégation de Toulouse*, Toulouse, 1680; HEIMBUCHER, I., 517.

[3] *Bull.*, of February 5, 1618, in SALVATORI, 223 *seq.*

[4] Letter to the archbishop of Lyons, April 10, 1619, in *Bull.*, XII., 445 *seq.* The permission for Dijon is of May 23, 1619; see *Chroniques de l'ordre des Ursulines*, I., 165.

extraordinary rapidity over the whole of France ; thus convents arose in 1615 at Abbeville : in 1616 at Pontoise and Amiens : in 1617 at Rennes ; in 1618 at Eu, Laval, Libourne, Poitiers and Saint-Macaire ; in 1619 at Angers, Rouen, Châtillon-sur-Mer, Chaumont, Saumur and Langres ; in 1620 at Ambert, Autun, Brive, Limoges, Macon, Moulins-en-Bourbonnais ; in 1621 at Clermont in Auvergne, at Dinant in Brittany and at Gisors.[1]

Nor did the Ursulines suffer any loss from the fact that yet another teaching Society for young girls was formed at this time, namely the Congregation of Benedictine Nuns of our Lady, founded at Bordeaux by Jeanne de Lestonnac, a niece of Montaigne. The Congregation was approved by Paul V. in 1617.[2]

The Ursulines of Spanish Burgundy differed from their French sisters chiefly in that they only took simple vows and did not accept the enclosure. The first foundation in that province was made at Dôle, by Anne de Xaintonge, in 1606, after almost insuperable difficulties.[3] Filiations were founded in 1615 at Vesoul, in 1617 at Arbois, in 1618 at Saint-Hippolyte-sur-le-Doubs, in 1619 at Besançon and at Pruntrut.

The Burgundian Ursulines were under the special care of the Jesuits. This direction and the measures of prudence prescribed by the Constitutions, especially the ordinance that they were only to go out in twos, were calculated to forestall any abuse of the liberty the Sisters enjoyed. This twofold

[1] See *Chroniques de l'ordre des Ursulines*, I., 138–189 ; *cf.* 475 *seq.* See also, for the Ursulines of Angers, *Mém. de la soc. nat. d'Angers*, 5. series XII. (1900), and RENEAULT, *Les Ursulines de Rouen*, Fécamp, 1919.

[2] See V. MERCIER, *La bienh. Jeanne de Lestonnac*, Poitiers, 1900, and COUZARD, *La bienh. Jeanne de Lestonnac*, Paris, 1904. (*Cf.* the criticism on this work in *Rev. d. quest. hist.*, LXXVII., 312.)

[3] *Cf.* the work of J. MOREY, based on exhaustive research including manuscripts : *Anne de Xainctonge et la Compagnie de St.-Ursule en Bourgogne*, 2 vols., Paris (1891) ; German abridged edition by L. Arens, Freiburg i. Br. 1903. See further A. DE NITRAY, *Une éducatrice du 17e siècle*, Paris, 1919.

guidance proved wholly successful. The Burgundian Ursulines devoted themselves to the religious reform of female youth with no less zeal and success than their French sisters. Thus they too helped towards that efflorescence of Christian life which distinguishes the first half of the seventeenth century. Their successes are to be attributed to the fact that the daughters of Angela Merici, in France and Burgundy, were deeply penetrated by the spirit of the foundress. This spirit was enshrined in the celebrated testament and the moving exhortation of the dying Saint. Therein Angela bequeathed to her Institute a precious inheritance of enlightened experience and motherly love.[1] "In your striving after perfection," she said in her last exhortation, "keep to the ordinary path which the Church points out and which has been smoothed by the feet of so many Saints who have trodden it under the guidance of the Holy Ghost. As for the new opinions in matters of religion which arise at this time, or may yet arise, leave them alone, you have nothing to do with them. But pray and get others to pray that God may not abandon His Church but may reform her according to His good pleasure and as He deems best for us and most conducive to His own glory. In these dangerous times, when so many run to their destruction, you will find no safety except at the foot of the cross. If Jesus is your guide and your teacher, you will be well taught, according to the words of the royal prophet: 'Blessed is the man whom thou shalt instruct, O Lord.'"[2]

In 1618, Paul V. erected into an Order another religious body whose importance was destined to rival that of the Ursulines. This was the Salesian Sisters, or the Sisters of the Visitation of the Blessed Virgin Mary. They owe their origin to the famous bishop of Geneva, Francis de Sales and to the baroness Frances de Chantal. The spirit of the Catholic restoration in the seventeenth century finds so characteristic

[1] The *Testamento* of A. Merici and her *Ricordi* were published by Salvatori (198 *seq.*, 205 *seq.*); good translation in J. Schuler, *Gesch. der hl. A. Merici*, Innsbruck, 1893, 897 *seq.*, 905 *seq.*

[2] *Cf.* Salvatori, 213 *seq.*

an expression in the life and work of these two divinely enlightened souls, especially in that of the bishop of Geneva, that a fuller study is in order.

(3.)

Both as a bishop,[1] and as a founder of an Order, Francis de Sales belongs wholly to the new age. His creation, the Order of the Sisters of the Visitation, bears the imprint, both in its purpose and its peculiar spirituality, of the Catholic restoration: it is wholly devoted to that movement in the seventeenth century, and greatly forwards the new development in the Orders of women in the spirit which the age demands.

The first beginnings of the new Order are connected with the Lenten sermons which Francis preached at Dijon in 1604. On that occasion the Saint became acquainted with the magnificent woman who was destined to become, under his direction, one of the most significant personalities of the period of the Catholic restoration. Jeanne Françoise, daughter of Bénigne Fremyot, president of the tribunal of Dijon, widow of Christophe Rabutin, baron de Chantal, was distinguished not only by the nobility of her mind and the maturity of her judgment, hers was also a nature of truly virile strength, full of determination, decision, endurance and capable of the highest aspirations as well as the tenderest emotions.[2] Her mother died too soon to influence her formation, so she became all the more the image of her father, a nobleman in the fullest sense of the word. During the troubles of the League, when his sense of duty and justice caused him to take the part of the king, he saw his house plundered and he had to listen to the threat that unless he yielded, the head of his son, then a prisoner, would be sent to him. "It is better that the son die innocent than that the father should live in guilt," was his answer.[3] Moreover, he was a convinced

[1] *Cf.* our account, Vol. XXXIII., 416 *seqq.*

[2] Biography by EMILE BOUGAUD, French edit. (4th), Paris, 1866, 2 vols.

[3] *Ibid.*, I., ch. 1.

Catholic; if Henry IV. had not come back to the Church, so he told the king to his face, he would never have raised the cry: "Long live Henry IV." [1] The father's attachment to the Church grew into a passionate love in the daughter. This burning love was no doubt fanned by the troubles of the Huguenot wars which had raged even around her cradle (she was born in 1572) and the consequences of which she could observe in the ruined churches and monasteries which she saw on her journey through the heart of France, on her way to Poitou where she was to rejoin an elder sister for the purpose of completing her education. Not long after, when only sixteen, she cut short the wooing of a Huguenot with the words: "I would rather spend all my life in prison than in the house of a heretic." [1]

In her twentieth year, Frances gave her hand to the twenty-seven year old baron de Chantal. She was now given the opportunity to display, and still further to develop, her considerable administrative talent. The ancestral home of her husband was the manor of Bourbilly, near Semur. The estate had become utterly dilapidated, but she worked it up to such a degree of prosperity that it not only provided for the needs of her household, but also for the large-scale charities of the châtelaine. Her concern for the poor and the sick went to the extent of personal service, so that even then she earned for herself the title of "the holy baroness". [1]

However, her married happiness was short-lived. Baron de Chantal died in 1601, in consequence of a shooting accident. Frances felt the loss most deeply, for she was exceedingly sensitive where family affections were concerned. At a later period, when universally revered as a Saint, she would be so moved on hearing the news of the death of one of her children, as to fall into a swoon. Such was her grief at the death of her husband that she wasted away. She made a vow not to marry again, cut down her wardrobe, reduced her style of living and resolved to give herself wholly to God.

The brilliant days when the châtelaine, beloved by her husband

[1] *Ibid.*, I., ch. I.

and her servants and worshipped by the poor, issued orders and instructions, were now to be followed by seven long years which, no doubt, were of the greatest value as a preparation for her future vocation, but which in the meantime, condemned her to a state of deepest humiliation and abasement. The father of her husband summoned her to his château of Monthelon. She needs must obey for unless she did so, her four children would be disinherited by their grandfather. Now the old baron lived with one of the maids who, in consequence, deemed herself the mistress of the house and took special delight in making the noble lady feel her power by every manner of means. Frances might have freed herself from so humiliating a situation by just informing her father, but in the hope of being able to do something for the soul of her father-in-law, as well as by reason of a desire to daunt her own nature which was of a domineering kind, she resolved to suffer in silence.[1]

In 1604, the bishop of Geneva preached the Lenten sermons at Dijon. President Fremyot invited his daughter to assist at them and by this means these two souls, which were predestined to carry out a joint task, first came in contact with each other. Whilst striving after perfection, Madame de Chantal had become painfully aware of the indispensable need of an experienced and learned guide ; so she entrusted herself unhesitatingly to the direction of the bishop of Geneva who, she felt, had been sent to her by heaven itself. On his part Francis soon perceived that he had to deal with no ordinary woman ; his esteem for her grew steadily and he realized that in her he had found the corner stone of the new Order,[2] the foundation of which he had been studying for some years already.

The era of the Catholic revival had a problem to solve in respect also to the Orders of women. The medieval Orders of

[1] Bougaud, I., ch. iv, v, and viii.

[2] Francis to N. Polliens, May 24, 1610, *Lettres*, IV., 307. For the friendship between the two, see Michael Müller, *Die Freundschaft des hl. Franz von Sales mit der hl. Joh. Franziska von Chantal*, München, 1923.

women were contemplative and their rules laid great stress on bodily austerities. Now there were many persons whose health was unequal to severe fasts and night watches, whilst others were indeed able to appreciate a life consecrated to God and spent in nursing the sick or teaching the young, but a purely contemplative life did not satisfy their need of activity. The traditional forms of the religious life catered for none of these. The great obstacle to any change in this state of affairs lay in the enclosure which seemed practically incompatible with teaching or nursing, but which the Council of Trent had re-imposed, with renewed strictness, on the Orders of women properly so called and which, as a matter of fact, public opinion demanded from all religious communities of women. The expansion of the religious life in the sixteenth century soon led to the formation of communities of women which, whilst leaning, as it were, on Orders of men still in process of development, sought to secure for themselves a share in their external activities. The first results were doubtful. St. Ignatius expressly rejected, from the first, any connection of this kind [1]; with a community of women, which aimed at helping the Barnabites in their pastoral work, bitter experiences had been made—the community saw itself compelled to accept enclosure and thus their external activities were at an end [2]; the Capuchin nuns,[3] like the Theatine nuns whom we first meet in 1618,[4] devoted themselves to contemplation from the beginning. Angela of Merici alone attempted to attract women to the service of the Church without linking them to an Order of men, but her Institute, the Ursulines, was destined to remain in an unfinished state through the whole of the sixteenth century.[5]

A decisive turn came only in the reign of Paul V. French-speaking countries then witnessed the rise of a whole series of

[1] *Cf.* our account, Vol. XII., 51 *seq.*

[2] Heimbucher, II.[2], 287.

[3] Moroni, IX., 201. Cardinal Baronius tried to enlist them in the service of orphans (*ibid.*, 203).

[4] Heimbucher, III.[2], 268 *seq.*

[5] *Cf.* our account, Vol. XI., 525 *seqq.*

female Institutes of an entirely new type. The Carmelites of St. Teresa had come to France in 1604, not without the help of Francis de Sales, the then coadjutor of Geneva,[1] and had been received with enthusiasm: but they were exclusively given to contemplation. In 1607, Paul V. gave his approval to a community devoted to the education of girls, which had been founded in the previous year at Bordeaux by Jeanne Lestonnac.[2] In 1615, Nancy got its Sisters of Christian Doctrine.[3] After 1612, several communities of French Ursulines gradually transformed themselves from isolated associations into Orders properly so-called [4]; in this they were followed, in 1617, by the teaching Sisters whom Pierre Fourier, in 1598, had gathered around him in Lorraine.[5]

The activity of religious Institutes of women, which to-day is so wide spread and so beneficial, has its source in these new foundations. The new Order which honours Saint Francis de Sales as its founder, is an important milestone in the story of their rise and growth.

In the opening paragraphs of the Constitutions of the Order, Francis speaks with exceeding modesty of his creation. He was anxious, he declares, to create a haven of refuge for the many who, though they felt a call to the religious life, did not possess the bodily strength demanded by the exterior austerities of the existing reformed Orders. It should be possible to receive even widows and women of weak health, without, however, excluding those who are strong and in robust health.[6] Now it is precisely this modest aim which

[1] Francis to Clement VIII., November, 1602, *Lettres*, II., 131 *seqq.*; *cf.* 118 note; III., 117 note, 153 note.

[2] *Cf.* above, p. 66.

[3] HEIMBUCHER, III.[2], 543.

[4] *Cf.* above, p. 65 *seq.*

[5] Confirmation was granted by the bishop under Papal authority on May 9, 1617; solemn vows on December 2, 1618. Paul V. had granted leave to receive boarders, on February 1, 1615, and day scholars, on October 6 (HEIMBUCHER, II.[2], 85 *seqq.*).

[6] *Règles de S. Augustin, Constitutions et Direc'oire pour les sœurs réligieuses de la Visitation*, Lyon, 1835, 120.

constitutes the peculiar character of the new Order and which was to be of paramount importance in time to come. Since it was necessary greatly to restrict physical austerity, Francis insisted all the more on the training of the heart in humility, obedience, uprightness, meekness and in that which he considered the basis and stay of everything else, viz. the practice of meditation and contemplation, in favour of which he greatly curtailed the Office said in common. Francis allowed for the spirit of the time which was all for active works of charity; but unlike the majority of the Congregations of the period, his nuns were not to devote themselves to the education of youth, but to the care of the sick and the poor. And since they were to be followers of our Lady, who went into the mountains in order to render service to her cousin Elizabeth, the new Institute was given the name of "The Visitation of St. Mary". For the sake of nursing the sick, Francis was prepared to forego the enclosure which had formed part of his first plan, though this meant that there could be no longer question of an Order strictly so called, but only of a Congregation. The Sisters were to exercise their influence on the outside world by giving private retreats to ladies within their convents. For all that, the Order of the Visitation was from the first mainly contemplative and only two Sisters at a time were to devote themselves to visiting the sick.[1] It may be that the idea of his peculiar creation first came to him when, in 1602, he witnessed in Paris the popularity of the purely contemplative Order of the Spanish Carmelites, but he saw the obstacles which would prevent the general spread of a Rule of such extraordinary strictness.

The original plan of the founder underwent a not inconsiderable alteration when the new Institute was preparing to cross the frontier of France. The archbishop of Lyons, Denis de Marquemont, would not hear of an uncloistered community of women and Francis ended by yielding to the archbishop's pressure. On April 23rd, 1618, Paul V. approved

[1] See A. de Becdelièvre, in *Études*, CXXX. (1912), 821–7; *Saint François de Sales étudié dans ses lettres*, Annecy, 1926.

the Institute of the Visitation as a true Order.[1] By degrees, nursing was replaced by the education of girls in the numerous schools of the Order.[2]

During the founder's lifetime, Madame de Chantal was his right hand and by subsequently putting the finishing touches to the internal structure of the Order, she so completed his work as fully to deserve to be called its co-foundress. She was endowed with just the qualities required if an Order of so novel a complexion was to make headway in the face of a hundred obstacles. At the beginning of 1611 Francis wrote that he was of opinion that God would make of her another St. Paula, Angela, or Catherine of Genoa[3]; it was impossible to find such intelligence and good sense allied with greater humility; when there was question of some holy undertaking she gave proof of a courage which is not usually found in her sex.[4] These remarkable qualities were still further enhanced by the prestige she enjoyed as a lady of the great world and by a charm of manner which had made her the centre of every social gathering at her husband's château.[5]

Madame de Chantal, then, would have possessed all the requisite qualities to begin at once a successful apostolic action in the devout circles, say, of Paris. However, for the time being, Francis left her where she was. All he did was to subject her inner life to a rigorous training. As regards the exterior, he did not demand from her, as he did not demand from anyone else, anything out of the ordinary, or anything that might have annoyed those around her; on the contrary, he bade her strive daily to show greater humility and meekness

[1] BOUGAUD, II., ch. 19. Bellarmine (writing to Francis of Sales on December 29, 1616) advised him to adhere to the original plan (*Lettres*, VII., 418; BELLARMINE'S *Epistulae familiares*, Rome, 1650, 314 *seqq.*). For the foundation of the Visitation at Lyons, *cf. Lettres*, XVI., App. III.

[2] BOUGAUD, II., ch. 29 *seqq.*

[3] *Lettres*, V., 20.

[4] In BOUGAUD, II., ch. 33.

[5] *Ibid.*

towards her father and her father-in-law.[1] Within her own heart she was to avoid all haste, sadness and timidity, as well as everything forced or violent.[2] But she was to strive with all her strength to give herself wholly to God [3]; for whatever is not of God, is nothing, or worse than nothing.[4] Without allowing herself to be perturbed by trials and temptations and without caring whether or no she experienced any delight in serving God,[5] let her do all things for love of God, and deny herself at all times amid the thousand opportunities which daily life creates.[6] From the very first Francis took this matter of self-denial very seriously. Owing to her great love for her husband, Madame de Chantal could scarcely think of the unfortunate nobleman who had been the innocent cause of his death, without an upheaval of her whole interior, and without the horror she had been through at the time of the accident, crushing her heart afresh. An emotion of this kind could hardly be accounted a fault; assuredly it was no more than a natural revulsion over which the will had no control and which was, accordingly, quite blameless. For all that, Francis never ceased to bring pressure to bear upon her until the time came, five years later, when she felt able to make up her mind not only to take up friendly relations with that gentleman, but even to act as godmother to his child.[7] Francis even took advantage of his last meeting with the greatest of his disciples to demand a heavy sacrifice from her. She had not seen her spiritual father for three years so that she naturally longed to consult him on the state of her soul. Francis forbade her to utter a word on the subject—he would only let her speak of business matters.[8] Never, perhaps, did a soul acquire a more virile character as a result

[1] October 14, 1604; *ibid.*, cap. 28 *seq.*
[2] *Lettres*, II., 288, 359.
[3] Early in August, 1606, *ibid.*, III., 200.
[4] January, 1611; *ibid.*, ch. 28.
[5] *Ibid.*, II., 386. (*Lettres* de S. Francis de Sales.)
[6] *Ibid.*, 368.
[7] *Lettres*, III., 67, 122, 357; Bougaud, I., ch. 6.
[8] Bougaud, II., ch. 21.

of the guidance of a director, than Madame de Chantal did at the hands of the gentle Saint of Geneva.

In 1617, when he deemed his willing pupil sufficiently schooled, Francis discussed with her the plan of his new Order. After providing for the education of her children, Madame de Chantal, with five companions, took possession, on June 6th, 1610, of the first small convent of the Visitation, at Annecy.[1] The new Institute speedily assumed vast proportions. At the time of the founder's death, in 1621, the Order counted about thirteen establishments, and about eighty at the time of the death of Madame de Chantal, in 1641.[2] The reputation for holiness which clung to the foundress no less than to Francis de Sales, contributed not a little to this amazing success. Even before Frances' death, her arrival in a town was hailed as an outstanding event: people cut off pieces from her dress in order to keep them as relics.[3]

In the course of the seventeenth century the new Order recruited a considerable number of members from the ranks of the French nobility and, owing to its relations with the highest circles of society, it found itself in a position to exercise upon it no small influence as regards religion. St. Francis' original plan, namely, that of establishing an Institute without either enclosure or solemn vows, was taken up, at a later date, by St. Vincent de Paul, except that he made the work of nursing the sick the real scope of his Society, whereas in Francis' scheme it was only a secondary point. On one occasion Vincent de Paul went so far as to call his foundation "Madame de Chantal's Heritage". After the death of the bishop of Geneva, Vincent had some dealings with her.[4] All the more recent nursing and teaching Orders of women found a prototype in the Constitutions and the Rule of the Visitation in which a man of Francis de Sales' authority lucidly describes the true nature of a perfect Christian life and shows the way that leads to the heights even

[1] *Ibid.*, I., chapters 2, 9, 11, 12.
[2] *Ibid.*, II., 21, 23, 27, 31.
[3] *Ibid.*, II., chapters 21, 22, 30.
[4] *Ibid.*, ch. 25.

without extraordinary austerities.[1] If the constitution of his Order show Francis de Sales as a teacher of religious communities, his other writings make of him a master of asceticism, revered as such by the whole Catholic world. True, his ascetical writings are not his only ones, nor his first.[2] He began as a controversialist, though he did not at first intend for publication the loose sheets in which he discussed various controverted points.[3] Subsequently there came a larger work, on the veneration due to the crucifix, which was also aimed at the Protestants.[4] It was only after his visit to Paris, in 1602, that the Saint took the first step in a field in which he was to reap so rich a harvest. Attracted by his preaching, many persons in the devout circles in Paris, sought his advice and put themselves under his guidance. They were all people in the world. Now Francis soon discovered that there existed no books for the guidance of just such people. He began, therefore, to set down in writing explanations of various points of the spiritual life and these were passed from hand to hand.[5] He also replied by letter to the numerous questions that were put to him. By degrees this correspondence assumed

[1] Even in the East, the Congregation of Melchite nuns of the Visitation of Mary, approved by Clement XIII. in 1762, follows in part, almost literally, the rules of the Visitation nuns. (R. Lübeck, in the *1st Vereinsschrift der Görres-Gesellsch.* [1921], 34.) Francis of Sales had hoped to found a Congregation of men on the lines of the Visitation (*Lettres*, V., 334).

[2] Index of his complete works, in *Œuvres*, I., lxxix. *seqq.*

[3] The first edition of 1672 is mutilated (*Œuvres*, I., cxxx. *seqq.*). One place in which the Pope was called " confirmateur infaillible ", was much discussed during the Vatican Council (*ibid.*, cxiii., cxxxi.).

[4] " Défense de l'Estandard de la Sainte Croix de N.S. Jésus-Christ," Lyon, 1600 (*Œuvres*, II.). *Cf.* Hamon, I., 286, 376; Eug. Ritter, " Recherches sur un ouvrage de Fr. de Sales," in *Bull de l'Institut national Genevois*, XXVI. (1884); Ed. Thamirey, *La méthode d'influence de s. Fr. de Sales*, Paris, 1922. For his polemic explanation of the Creed, see Hamon, I., 284.

[5] *Cf. Lettres*, II., 265, 266, 357, *etc.*

unlooked for dimensions; according to his servant Favre there were few days on which he had not from twenty to twenty-five letters to seal, and we even learn that on a single morning as many as forty or even fifty letters would be lying on his table, all ready for dispatch.[1] It goes without saying that in these letters Francis could not attend to mere style; they had to be rapidly jotted down, at odd moments, whilst "a whole world of quite different affairs", as he himself said,[2] claimed his attention. For all that, there is in these letters, of which many have been preserved,[3] not a trace of haste or carelessness, a fact which proves that the writer is always perfectly master of himself, is always ready, without long deliberation, to draw from the rich store of his knowledge and experience the advice which the situation demands.

When a great mass of counsels and directions had thus accumulated, Francis, at Easter of the year 1607, set himself the task of putting together in a volume all that was more important. This he did, in the first instance, for the benefit of his kinswoman, Madame de Charmoisy.[4] By the summer of 1608, the work was done. The Rector of the Jesuit College

[1] *Lettres*, I., xix.; B. MACKEY, "Saint François de Sales directeur spirituel," in the *Rev. du clergé français*, XXXVII. (1904), 390–402. FR. VINCENT, *Saint Fr. de Sales directeur d'âmes*, Paris, 1924.

[2] "Un monde d'affaires" (*Lettres*, III., 26, 113). "Ce ne sont pas des eaux, ce sont des torrens que les affaires de ce diocèse" (*ibid.*, 139). *Cf. ibid.*, II., 288 ("charge intolérable"), 381, ("pressé de mes affaires"), *etc.*

[3] *Lettres*, I–VIII. The first edition was published under the care of Madame de Chantal. In the course of the seventeenth century the letters appeared in about forty editions (*Lettres*, I., viii. *seqq.*). ÉMILE FAGUET, "Les Lettres spirituelles de s. Fr. de Sales," in the *Revue latine*, III. (1904), 513–540.

[4] Concerning her, see H. BORDEAUX, "La Philothée de s. Fr. de Sales," in the *Correspondant*, CCXXX. (1908), 833–867. *Cf.* also E. RITTER, in the *Revue Savoisienne*, XLIX–L, Annecy, 1908–9.

of Chambéry, Jean Fourier, pressed him to have it printed.[1] Such was the origin of the famous *Introduction to a Devout Life*[2] which obtained a diffusion and an importance in the field of ascetical literature only equalled by the *Imitation of Christ.* Francis himself wrote, in 1620, that the little book had been found very helpful in France, Flanders and England and that the French text had been published more than forty times in various places. By 1656, there existed seventeen translations and to-day there is even a Chinese and an Armenian one.[3] There was not a house of the more cultivated classes, even in Protestant Geneva, in which the little book was not to be found. Marie de Medici sent a copy, encrusted with precious stones, to James I. How widely the *Introduction* was disseminated in England appears from the fact that, with a view to removing a suspicion that he had leanings towards the Catholic religion, Charles I. issued a decree ordering all copies of the book to be seized and burnt. Nevertheless the work retained its popularity with Anglicans.[4]

[1] To De Villars, archbishop of Vienne, February, 1609; to Possevin, December 10, 1609 (*Lettres,* IV., 125, 225). For the second edition he asked Madame de Chantal to send his earlier instructions given by letter (*ibid.,* 131).

[2] *Introduction à la vie dévote,* Lyon, 1609. Copy of the 1619 edition and of the Editio Princeps in *Œuvres,* III., 1–366, and 1–184. Facsimile of the title-page of the 1609 edition is also in A. VINGTRINIER, *Hist. de l'Imprimerie à Lyon,* Lyon, 1894, 300 (*cf.* 341). Later the "Introduction" was also entitled "Philothea" because Francis calls the soul whom he addresses by this name. For the origin of the little book *cf. Œuvres,* III., vi. *seqq.*; FR. VINCENT, *Le travail du style de s. Fr. de Sales d'après les corrections faites sur l'Introduction à la vie dévote,* Paris, 1923 (on 200 pages, similar to those of the 1609 and 1619 editions, 1,037 corrections are found); BREMOND, I. (1916).

[3] *Œuvres,* III., xxvii. On April 26, 1610, Francis writes that it had been reprinted six times in two years (*Lettres,* IV., 292).

[4] *Œuvres,* III., xxviii. *seq.* Fénelon admired especially this trait in Francis, that a man with such profound insight could speak so simply. "Son style naïf montre une simplicité aimable, qui est au-dessus de toutes les grâces de l'esprit profane. Vous

The ascetical principles of the *Introduction* are, of course, nothing new. In the course of his exposition Francis frequently appeals to the acknowledged masters of Catholic theology [1]; in particular the link with the *Exercises* of St. Ignatius of Loyola—which Francis made on several occasions even as a bishop [2]—appears very clearly. What is new is his teaching that these ideals may be realized in the lives of people in the world, amid the rush and noise of the daily task, and in every condition or calling, whereas the existing ascetical writings were intended, for the most part or even exclusively, for persons in religion.

The principles laid down by Francis in his *Introduction* as well as in his spiritual letters are the same as those on which he based his guidance of Madame de Chantal.[3] In order to live wholly for God there is no need to do anything extraordinary or singular; holiness of life consists in the love of God under the impulse of which we do that which is good, fervently, frequently, and readily.[4] Now the love of God consists in doing everything for God,[5] not even excepting

voyez un homme qui, avec une grande pénétration et une parfaite délicatesse pour juger du fond des choses et pour connaître le cœur humain, ne songeoit qu'à parler en bon homme, pour consoler, pour éclairer, pour perfectionner son prochain. Personne ne connoissait mieux que lui la plus haute perfection; mais il se rapetissoit pour les petits et ne dédaignoit jamais rien. Il se faisoit tout à tous, non pour plaire à tous mais pour les gagner tous et pour les gagner à Jésus-Christ et non à soi." (To the Countess of Montberon, January 29, 1700, *Œuvres*, VIII., Paris, 1851, 616.) *Cf.* DELPLANQUE, *St. Fr. de Sales, humaniste et écrivain latin*, Lille, 1907. See also the comments by C. GALASSI PALUZZI in the *Corriere d'Italia* of August 22, 1924, directed against C. RICCI (*Visioni e figure*, Roma, 1924).

[1] *Œuvres*, III., xxxiii. *seqq.*

[2] HAMON, I., 441, 570; *cf.* 449. There is an English adaptation of this biography (Burns Oates and Washbourne).

[3] See present work, p. 74 *seq.*

[4] *Introduction*, I., 1.

[5] *Lettres*, V., 101.

such things as eating and drinking.[1] Hence Christian perfection is compatible with every state of life.[2] Francis demands that everybody should be made to feel its charm and attractiveness; the poor should feel its power by being given more generous alms, the home because it is better looked after, the husband because he receives more loving attention.[3] Where devotion is concerned, pleasant feelings are of no account,[4] it will be all the more solid the less we live according to our personal likes and tastes [5]; and in general we should go forward on the path traced out for us by God without indulging in trivial subtleties, generously and large-heartedly, though with all humility, meekness and interior recollection.[6]

A second ascetical volume, *The Treatise on The Love of God*, completes the instruction of Philotea.[7] In this new treatise he addresses the soul by the name of Theotimus, lest people should think that he only wrote for women.[8] The book owes its origin to the conferences he gave to the Sisters of the Visitation; it is, therefore, addressed to more advanced souls [9]; it even touches on mysticism, though only lightly. For the rest, after some introductory discussion of psychological principles, the book explains the origin and growth of the love of God; how it may be hindered, and what are its symptoms, qualities, advantages and prerogatives.

The significance of these ascetical writings [10] partly lies

[1] *Ibid.*, II., 368.

[2] *Introduction*, I., 3.

[3] *Lettres*, II., 270; *cf.* 345 *seqq.*

[4] *Introduction*, II., 9.

[5] *Lettres*, III., 226.

[6] *Lettres*, III., 392*e*. *Cf.* PIUS XI.'s Encyclical of January 26, 1923, in the *Acta Apost. Sedis*, XV. (1923), 55 *seq.*

[7] "Traicté de l'Amour de Dieu," Lyon, 1616 (*Œuvres*, IV.–V.).

[8] Préface, *Œuvres*, IV., xii.

[9] *Ibid.*, xx.

[10] A brilliant art historian, who died before his time, describes the "Philotea" as "a work full of the wisdom of experience, united with the most delicate psychological counsels by which

in the fact that they were a powerful antidote to the influence which Calvinism might have exercised on Catholics. Basing himself on laws and punishments, Calvin demanded, with appalling rigour, an external moral correctness to which even the lawful aspirations of the heart had to be sacrificed. On the other hand, he had nothing to offer by way of compensation, for in his view these sacrifices have no value in the sight of God, nor have they power to render man intrinsically better since, according to him, grace does not heal man's essential corruption ; all it can do is to cover it up. As against this rigorism, Francis condemns nothing that is naturally good and noble, provided it is sanctified by an interior intention. What he stresses before all else is the discipline of the heart, and as a reward of constant self-denial he promises us a true interior transformation, by which we draw ever nearer to God in this life, only to possess Him in a far superior manner in the next. Calvin crushes man, drives him to despair and ends by stifling in him any desire for ethical improvement. Francis raises him up, gives him courage and opens the road to the heights. The contrast is unconscious, but it is there.[1] In another respect there exists a further unintentional contrast between the two men. Calvin's chief work is concerned with the doctrine of faith ; in the most detailed of all his writings Francis treats of charity. Calvin achieved success, in great part, because he published his principal work in the vernacular.[2] Francis imitated him in

men may awake in their souls a state of beatitude in God, sublimate their lives in the direction of eternal values and within the framework of social life enable them to enjoy that order of feeling which, according to Montaigne, made up abundantly to the Catholic Church of the day for the numbers that had fallen away ". M. Dvořák, *Kunstgeschichte als Geistesgeschichte*, München, 1924, 271 *seq*.

[1] Pierre de Villars, archbishop of Vienne, at once perceived the apologetical value of the " Introduction " ; *cf*. his letter to Francis de Sales of January 25, 1609, in the *Lettres*, IV., 410 ; Desjardins, in *Études*, 5, Serie XII. (1877), 670 *seq*.

[2] *Cf*. F. Brunetière, in the *Revue des Deux Mondes*, October 15, 1900, 907.

this ; in his treatise on charity he too discusses a theological subject in a French of such purity and a language of such grace and sweetness that his place in French literature is assured for all time.[1]

Francis was so safe a guide in the ways of the spiritual life because of the width and precision of his own theological knowledge. Cardinal Du Perron who, with Bellarmine and Stapleton, was the most celebrated controversialist of his time, declared that Francis de Sales was the most learned theologian of the century.[2] Bellarmine too entertained the highest esteem for the learning of the bishop of Geneva. For years the controversy about grace between the Dominicans and the Jesuits had dragged on in Rome without leading to any result. Paul V. sought Francis' advice as to the attitude he ought to adopt in the matter. He passed on the reply of the bishop of Geneva to the Congregation concerned and when the Pope finally came to a decision, it was on the lines suggested by him.[3]

In the writings of the great guide of souls, theological knowledge allies itself with the result of experience gained by contact with souls. When we read him we feel that we are

[1] GODEFROY, *Hist. de la litt. française*, I., 374 ; SAINTE-BEUVE, *Causeries du Lundi*, VII., 220 *seq.* ; A. BAUMGARTNER, *Gesch. der Weltliteratur*, V. (1905), 285 *seqq.* ; RAYMOND, " Fr. de Sales comme écrivain," in the *Mém. de l'Acad. de Savoie*, II. ; A. DELPLANQUE, " S. Fr. de Sales, humaniste et écrivain latin," in the *Mém. et Travaux des facultés cath. de Lille*, fasc. 2, Lille, 1907 ; P. KADEN, *Die Sprache des St. Fr. de Sales* (Diss.), Leipzig, 1908 ; RÉNÉ DOUMIC, in the *Revue des Deux Mondes*, 1894, Mars–Avril, 925–936 (" François de Sales parle la plus pure langue française et la plus moderne," *ibid.*, 928) ; same author, *ibid.*, 1906, October 15, 924–935 ; BREMOND, I., 68 *seq.*, II., 419 *seq.*, 536 *seq.*

[2] *Anal. iuris pontif.*, XVII., 148.

[3] *Ibid.*, 146, 156, 165, 168 ; Anastasio Germonio to Francis, 1607, in *Lettres*, III., 407. *Cf.* Vol. XXV., 240. The controversy was, according to Francis, " di importantissima conseguenza in queste nostre bande afflitte di heresia " (Francis to the Nuncio Costa at Turin, October 12, 1607, *ibid.*, 327 ; HAMON, I., 589 *seq.*).

face to face with real life. What Francis says is not the laboured result of study; the reader feels that on every page he answers difficulties which were really felt by live men and women and that his solutions have stood the test of experience.

In the teaching of the bishop of Geneva, the Catholic Church recognizes her own teaching. At the Vatican Council 452 authorized spokesmen of the Catholic universe moved that he should be given the highest title that a theologian can receive; that is, that he should be claimed a Doctor of the Church.[1] Pius IV. complied with the request.[2]

(4.)

During the reign of Paul V. the Catholic Church experienced in the Spanish Netherlands an efflorescence similar to that which was taking place in France. In those parts the work of restoration and reform, initiated under Sixtus V., had made considerable progress during the pontificate of Clement VIII., thanks to the zeal of the bishops, the regent, archduke Albert, the nuncios and the Jesuits.[3] It was to be Paul V's. good fortune to witness the happy consummation of their combined efforts.

The Holy See was in receipt of regular and accurate information concerning ecclesiastical affairs of the Spanish Catholic Netherlands through the nuncio in Brussels as well as through the legation which the archducal government maintained in Rome from 1600.[4] The nuncio Frangipani, whose arduous

[1] *Acta et decreta ss. Conciliorum recentiorum collectio Lacensis*, VII., Freiburg, 1890, 897. *Cf. Civiltà Catt.*, 10, Series V. (1878), 131.

[2] Decrees of July 19 and November 16, 1877, *Œuvres*, I., xi. *seqq.*, xv. *seqq.*; *Acta S. Sedis*, X. (1877), 362–5, 411–415. Judgment of the Congregation of Rites, *ibid.*, 332–361. *Cf.* DESJARDINS, in *Études*, 5, Series XII. (1877), 305 *seqq.*, 531 *seqq.*, 670 *seqq.*, 807 *seqq.*

[3] *Cf.* our account, Vol. XXIII., p. 400 *seq.*

[4] After the departure of Don Pedro of Toledo, the Auditor of the Rota, Hermann von Ortenberg occupied the embassy of the

labours had been rewarded in September, 1605, with his nomination to the archiepiscopal see of Taranto, was naturally anxious, after so prolonged a sojourn abroad, to devote himself at long last to his diocese. However, archduke Albert, who held Frangipani in high esteem, took steps in Rome with a view to retaining him at Brussels, hence a whole year elapsed before Paul V. yielded to the entreaties of Frangipani.[1] He was succeeded by the Neapolitan Decio Carafa, a sincerely devout man.[2] In his Instruction, dated July 2nd, 1605, the preservation of the Catholic religion, the liberty of the Church and the maintenance of friendly relations with the regents, Albert and Isabella, are singled out as the objectives which he was at all times to aim at.

As regards the religious situation in the Spanish Netherlands, the Instruction remarks that, thanks to the watchfulness of the bishops and the Catholic spirit both of the population and the regents, the future looked most hopeful, notwithstanding that the war with the rebellious provinces was not yet at an end. It must be the nuncio's immediate task to repair the damage inflicted by the war, to restore the destroyed churches, to reform the clergy, more particularly the ancient Orders which were in great need of reform, to establish seminaries and, lastly, to assist the persecuted Catholics of England and Holland.[3]

As early as May, 1607, Carafa was transferred to the Spanish nunciature, but on June 5th, 1607, his successor, Guido Bentivoglio, received similiar instructions.[4] Even before his arrival, events showed that Paul V's. reliance on the bishops of the Netherlands was fully justified,[5] for in June,

Netherlands for a time before it was given to Filips Maes. In April, 1618, John Baptist Vivès succeeded him, see GOEMANS, *Het Belgische Gesantschap*, VI., 10.

[1] See CAUCHIE-MAERE, *Recueil*, xxvii.

[2] See *ibid.*, xxviii.

[3] CAUCHIE-MAERE (*loc. cit.*, 9–26) published the text of the Instruction for Carafa.

[4] See CAUCHIE-MAERE, 27 *seq.* *Cf.* BROM, *Archivalia*, I., 245.

[5] See CAUCHIE-MAERE, 25.

1607, the splendid archbishop of Malines, Matthias van den Hove, convened a provincial council in his metropolitan city, and this meeting was subsequently followed by a number of diocesan synods. The purpose of all these assemblies was the full and universal execution of the reform decrees of the Council of Trent; their observance was assured by the fact that the government gave to the greater number of them force of law.[1] The synod of Malines passed an excellent resolution with regard to the religious teaching of children. Instead of the catechism of Canisius, which was chiefly intended to meet the situation in Germany and which had been in exclusive use until then, a new catechism was to be introduced and adapted to the conditions prevailing in the Spanish Netherlands. The new catechism, whose author was the Jesuit Louis Makeblyde, was published at Antwerp in 1609.[2] Charles Borremeo had been the first to institute "Sunday schools", which were to be held in every parish for the benefit of the children who were at work all the week. Similar classes were now extended to the Spanish Netherlands. Archduke Albert and his wife gave their support to this most beneficial work in an edict of 1608, commanding all civil officials to assist the bishops in forwarding the movement. A synod, held at Antwerp in 1610, made it an obligation for all children between six and fifteen years of age to attend these instructions.[3] Though conflicts between the spiritual and secular powers were not wanting,[4] there was nevertheless complete agreement on essentials. Perfect co-operation obtained where there was question of eliminating the effects

[1] See PIRENNE, IV., 486 *seq.*; DE RAM, *Synodicon Belgicum*, I. *seq.*; MALINES, 1827 *seq.*; PASTURE, *Restauration*, vi. *seq.*, 30 *seq.*

[2] See DE RAM, *loc. cit.*, I., 381; PIRENNE, IV., 489, and now especially PASTURE, *loc. cit.*, 359 *seq.*

[3] PASTURE, *loc. cit.*, 368 *seq.*, where will be found further details on the authorship of the work, which perhaps proceeds from Bishop Henry Cuyck, of Roermond.

[4] *Cf.* the account in detail in PASTURE, *loc. cit.*, 15 *seq.*, 21 *seq.*, 91 *seq.*, 157 *seq.*

of Protestantism and the regeneration of the ecclesiastical and moral life.[1]

One of the most important incidents of Bentivoglio's nunciature was the conclusion, on April 9th, 1609, of a twelve years' truce between archduke Albert and the seditious provinces. Each side now sought to profit by the re-establishment of communications between North and South. The Dutch Calvinists started a fresh propaganda in Flanders and Brabant.[2] However, this drawback was more than counterbalanced by the possibilities for the restoration of orderly ecclesiastical conditions which the cessation of hostilities now offered. It is no exaggeration to say that the tranquillity which followed the armistice of 1609 was a decisive factor in the revival of Catholicism in the Spanish Netherlands.[3] Year by year the Church made immense progress. The churches and monasteries which had been destroyed were rebuilt,[4] and those that had escaped damage were given fresh artistic beauty, in keeping with the taste of the period; above all, and this was of incomparably greater importance, in every sphere of life an intensive religious renewal was set in motion. A number of diocesan synods were held, as in 1609 at Malines, Ghent and Ypres, in 1610 at Antwerp, in 1612 at Hertogenbosch, in 1617 at Cambrai. These assemblies did much for the reform of the secular and regular clergy and for the religious instruction of the people.[5]

Paul V. had a big share in this revival inasmuch as his

[1] See PIRENNE, IV., 456 *seq.*, 466, 491; *Rev. d'hist. ecclés.*, V., 37 *seq.* *Cf.* PASTURE, *Le placard d'hérésie du Décembre*, 1609, and *Mel. d'hist. Charles Moeller*, II., 301.

[2] See PIRENNE, IV., 465 *seq.*, where there is further information on the counter-measures of the Brussels government.

[3] See PASTURE, *Restauration*, 30 *seq.*

[4] *Cf.* P. SAINTENOY, "L'art et la contreréforme sous Albert et Isabelle," in *Bulletin de l'Acad. Roy. l'archéol. de Belgique*, 1919, III., 18.

[5] *Cf.* PASTURE, *loc. cit.*, 31 *seq.*, 69 *seq.*, 198 *seq.*, 272 *seq.*, 280 *seq.*, 344 *seq.* He offers a wealth of details on the best authorities.

nuncios concurred energetically with all that was being done. Moreover, thanks to the obligation which Sixtus V. had laid on all bishops to send in regular reports, the Holy See was in a position to exercise an effective watchfulness over ecclesiastical affairs. The nuncios, above all the shrewd Bentivoglio, were indefatigable. Before all else, they saw to it that only men worthy of the office were appointed to episcopal Sees.[1] In this respect the Catholic restoration benefited enormously by the excellent way in which the secular power used the right of nomination which had been conceded to it at the time of the erection of the new dioceses.[2] When we look into the history of the various dioceses of the Spanish Netherlands, we meet everywhere with none but devoted and conscientious men who never ceased to labour, with the utmost zeal, for the improvement of ecclesiastical conditions. Besides the archbishop of Malines, Matthias van den Hove, who has already been mentioned, the nuncios single out Jean Richardot who died in 1614 as archbishop of Cambrai, Jean Lemire of Antwerp, Gisbert Mais of Hertogenbosch, and Denis Christophori of Bruges.[3] In the diocese of Liège, whose bishops ranked as princes, Paul V. gave strong support to the reforming activity of bishops Ernest and Ferdinand, both scions of the House of Bavaria.[4]

The shrewd Guido Bentivoglio, during the eight years (1607–1615) in which he held the Brussels nunciature, became

[1] See PASTURE, 71 *seq.*, 81 *seq.*, 86 *seq.*, 92. *Cf. ibid.*, 104 *seq.*, on the stimulus to zeal effected by the nuncios' visitations. On the reports of the bishops of the Netherlands in their *ad limina* visits, see PASTURE, in *Bullét. de la Commiss. Roy. d'hist.*, LXXXIII. (1920), 281 *seq.*, 334 *seq.*, 352 *seq.*

[2] See PASTURE, *Restauration*, 11 *seq.*, 24, 155 *seq.*

[3] *Ibid.*, 166 *seq.*

[4] See CHAPEAVILLE, III., 645 *seq.*; *Bull.*, XII., 211 *seq.* For the conferences of priests introduced at Liège by the efforts of the Cologne nuncio, Albergati, in 1613, see MANIGART, *Praxis pastoralis*, III., 551. On the conflict of the Vicar General of Liège with the nuncio of Cologne and the consideration which Rome showed for Ernest, see MERGENTHEIM, I., 201 *seq.*

so acclimatized there that when he was recalled he remarked that he had become half a Fleming.[1] He recorded his observations and experiences in a celebrated report in which he also draws an interesting picture of the state of the Church.[2] In compliance with the intentions of Paul V.[3] he paid great attention to the diocesan seminaries whose organization had been either impeded or completely destroyed in consequence of the disturbed state of the country. The establishment of an institution of this kind in every diocese, which the Council of Trent demanded, met with peculiar difficulties in Spanish Flanders inasmuch as, with the exception of Cambrai, Tournai and Arras, all the other dioceses had but slender revenues. But here also the impetus given by the Provincial Council of Malines in 1607, and by the diocesan synods, brought about a gratifying change.[4] In the dioceses of Bruges and Ypres, Bentivoglio observes, the unity of faith had been completely restored though there were still some hidden Calvinists. The towns of Hertogenbosch and Roermond were wholly Catholic though not the dioceses of the same name. The city of Malines bore an exclusively Catholic stamp, but the same could not be said of Brussels. The bulk of the population of the dioceses of Cambrai, Arras, St. Omer and Valenciennes remained staunchly loyal to the ancient Church.

[1] "Mi son partito di costà quasi più Fiammingo che Italiano," he wrote on April 10, 1616, from Rome to the Dominican Franc. Bivero. *Lettere del card. Bentivoglio*, p.p. Biagioli, Napoli, 1835, 40.

[2] *Relationi*, 142 *seq.* For the abundant MSS. material of the Brussels nunciature of Bentivoglio, contained in the Papal Secret Archives and in the MSS. of the Barberini Library, Rome, and for personal details *cf.* GACHARD, *Le card. Bentivoglio. Sa Nonciature à Bruxelles*, Bruxelles, 1874 ; V.d. ESSEN, in the *Bullét. de la Commiss. Roy. d'hist.*, LXXVIII. (1900), 270 (*cf. ibid.*, 98, the account of the Bentivoglio-acta in Genoa, Ferrara, and in the Bibl. Casatenense, Rome) ; BROM, *Archivalia*, I., 2, 940 ; III., 5 *seq.* ; PASTURE, *Restauration*, xviii. For his departure see CAUCHIE, in the *Mél. P. Fredericq*, 1904, 319 *seq.*

[3] See CAUCHIE-MAERE, *Recueil*, 21.

[4] PASTURE, *Restauration*, 31, 172 *seq.*, 180 *seq.*

Traces of Calvinism still lingered at Tournai and Valenciennes, but both the ecclesiastical and the secular authorities took every precaution with a view to preventing the religious innovators from showing themselves in public.

To the secular clergy of the Spanish Netherlands Bentivoglio gives a good character. He complains of a shortage of priests in Brabant, Flanders, and Gelder, a fact in part explained by the circumstance that in those districts only Flemish-speaking priests could be employed. The French language predominated in the other provinces so that the various dioceses were in a position to lend help to one another. Moreover the religious cleavage between the southern and the northern provinces was not along the racial one between the low-German Flemings and the Gallicized Walloons.

The university of Douai constituted the intellectual centre of the Walloon districts, whilst that of Louvain served the Flemish portion of the people. Bentivoglio notes with satisfaction that the spirit of both universities was strictly Catholic and that the decrees of the Council of Trent were scrupulously observed.[1] The trouble stirred up at Louvain by Baius [2] seemed at an end. The new constitution which the government and Paul V. had given to the university in 1617,[3] was meant to safeguard it against the infiltration of religious innovations. Great lustre was shed upon the university of Louvain at that time by the famous antiquarian Justus Lipsius who, in 1590, unexpectedly resigned his chair at Leiden in order to return to the bosom of the Catholic Church.[4] The university of Douai, which in 1598, had lost the controversialist Thomas Stapleton whom Clement VIII. had deservedly held in high esteem, possessed in the exegetist

[1] *Relationi*, 145 *seq*

[2] *Cf.* our account, Vol. XXI., 186 *seq*.

[3] See *Bull.*, XII., 412 *seq*. *Cf.* BRANTS, *La faculté de droit de Louvain à travers cinq siècles*, Louvain, 1906, 19.

[4] *Cf.* the monographs of GALESLOOT (Bruges, 1877) and AMIEL (Paris, 1884).

William Estius (died 1613) and in Francis Sylvius who succeeded him, scholars of the highest repute.[1]

As regards the secular clergy, Bentivoglio finds that, thanks to the zeal of the bishops, the reform decrees of the Council of Trent had been carried into effect throughout Spanish Flanders. The parochial clergy, he writes, carry out their duties so conscientiously that there is little to be desired.[2] It was otherwise with the regular clergy. Bentivoglio complains in particular that the enclosure was not being enforced in abbeys situated in rural districts. If scandals occurred but seldom, the fact was to be ascribed to the high morality of the people; with some races a naturally sound disposition yields better results than the sternest laws.[3]

Bentivoglio was satisfied with the state of discipline among the Dominicans and the Franciscans Observants. Truly exemplary were the newly reformed Orders, such as the Recollects,[4] introduced under Clement VIII., the discalced Carmelites whom the archducal pair had summoned from Italy,[5] the Ursulines,[6] and lastly, the Capuchins and the Jesuits. "These two Orders," Bentivoglio writes, "have been received in all the larger towns and everywhere they do an immense amount of good." [7]

The rapid spread of the Capuchins,[8] as well as racial contrasts, necessitated the partition of the Province of the

[1] *Cf. Freiburg. Kirchenlexikon*, IV.[2], 930 *seq.*, XI.[2], 1042 *seq.*; HURTER, I., 58 *seq.*, 189 *seq.*, 392 *seq.*

[2] See *Relationi*, 145, 146.

[3] *Ibid.*, 146–7.

[4] See PASTURE, *Restauration*, 301.

[5] *Ibid.*, 113, 305. *Ibid.*, 303 *seq.*, for the reform of the Discalced Carmelites.

[6] *Cf. Chroniques de l'ordre des Ursulines*, Paris, 1676, 203; PIRENNE, IV., 442.

[7] See *Relationi*, 148.

[8] See *Annuarium prov. SS. Trinitatis hollando-belgicae fratr. min. Capucin.*, I., Bruxelles, 1870, 19 *seq.*; PASTURE, *loc. cit.*, 300; *cf.* APPOLLINAIRE DE VALENCE, *Hist. des Capucins de Flandre*, I., Paris, 1878.

Netherlands into a Flemish and a Walloon one. The matter had been discussed already in 1612, and on September 15th, 1615, Paul V. granted the necessary powers. Père Honoré, of Paris, carried out the measure in 1616. To the Flemish Province were assigned the Convents of Antwerp, Alost, Oudenaarde, Brussels, Bruges, Bergues, Courtrai, Furnes, Ghent, Ypres, Louvain, Malines, Menin, Ostend, Hertogenbosch, Termond, Maastricht, and St. Tron. The Walloon Province consisted of the monasteries at Aires, Armentières, Ath, Arras, St. Omer, Béthune, Cambrai, Condé, Dinant, Douai, Enghien, Huy, Lille, Liège, Maubeuge, Malmedy, Mons, Namur, Orchies, Soignies, Tournai and Valenciennes.[1] In the Netherlands the Capuchins, who in 1616 admitted into their Order a member of the illustrious house of Arenberg,[2] devoted themselves, in addition to pastoral work, to visiting prisoners, nursing the sick, caring for the insane, nay, in some towns they even undertook works of public utility such as the organization of fire brigades.[3]

The progress which the Society of Jesus had made in the Spanish Netherlands during the pontificate of Clement VIII. continued during that of Paul V. In view of the ever-growing number of colleges and new members,[4] the General of the Society, Aquaviva, judged it expedient to divide the Province of the Netherlands into two. Very wisely this partition was based on the language frontier. The Flemish-speaking district of the Netherlands and the principality of Liège constituted the Flandro-Belgian Province, whilst the Franco-Belgian

[1] *Annuarium* (see p.91, n.8) I., 21–2; MAZELIN, *Hist. du P. Honoré de Paris*, Paris, 1882, 203 ; PASTURE, *loc. cit.*, 301 ; P. FRÉDÉGAND D'ANVERS, *Étude sur le P. Charles d'Arenberg, frère mineur, 1593–1669*, Paris, 1919, 132 *seqq.* ; A. DE NÖUE, *Étude hist. sur Stavelot et Malmédy*, Liège, 1848, 392 *seq.*

[2] See FRÉDÉGAND D'ANVERS, in the work quoted, note 1, p. 120 *seqq.*

[3] See GOBERT, *Les rues de Liège*, I., 202 ; REMBRY-BARTH, *Hist. de Menin*, I., Bruges, 1881, 285 ; PIRENNE, IV., 515.

[4] 788, according to the *Litt. ann. Soc. Iesu* of 1611, p. 246, as against 448 in the year 1597. *Cf.* PARENT, 63.

Province included the Walloon country to which were likewise added the German parts of Luxemburg. In 1616, the former Province numbered fourteen houses (viz. Antwerp, Bruges, Brussels, Courtrai, Ghent, Ypres, Louvain, Lier, Malines, Roermond, Hertogenbosch, Maastricht, Bergues and Cassel), and the latter fifteen (viz. Douai, St. Omer, Tournai, Liège, Lille, Mons, Valenciennes, Arras, Cambrai, Luxemburg, Namur, Dinant, Hesdin, Aire and Huy).[1] In 1616 the personnel of the Flandro-Belgian Province consisted of 617 members and that of Franco-Belgian of 653.[2] The principal house of the latter was at Douai where there was likewise a Scottish seminary. The houses of probation were at Tournai and Liège. The Flandro-Belgian Province had a college at Louvain as well as a seminary for English students. The houses of probation were at Malines and Lier. In September, 1616, John Berchmans entered at Malines. Together with Stanislaus Kostka and Aloysius Gonzaga, he constitutes the Society's trinity of holy youths.[3] In 1607, a professed house was added to the college of Antwerp. Eight years later a beginning was made with the erection of a new church which was destined to become a magnificent and much-admired building.[4] It consists of three aisles of equal height, in the baroque style, though that particular style has not been systematically followed in its construction. The opinion which prevailed at one time, that the Jesuits made baroque popular because it seemed to them the only ecclesiastical style, is as erroneous as the notion that baroque was a product of the reform movement within the Church.[5] The new art

[1] See IUVENCIUS, P. V. tom. post. 317, 355. *Cf.* PONCELET, *Jésuites en Belgique*, 3 *seq.*, 14 *seq.*; *Anal p. serv. à l'hist. éccles. de la Belgique*, XXXIII. (1907), 278.

[2] See IUVENCIUS, *loc. cit.*, 355.

[3] *Cf.* the monographs of VANDERSPEETEN (Bruxelles, 1868) and F. GOLDIE (London, 1873).

[4] "Templum Iesuitarum stupendum . . . non augustius nec Belgium nec Gallia habet," says GASPAR STEIN, in his **Peregrinus seu peregrinatio terrestris, Cod.* 1751 of the Königsberg Library.

[5] For the reasons given why the baroque style is supposed

would have made headway independently of the movement in question. The Church at no time stood in the way of the changing fashion in the world of arts, hence she would certainly not have impeded the triumphant progress of baroque.[1] Although the Jesuits have indeed erected some important buildings in that style, they were very far from considering it the only one suitable for ecclesiastical edifices. Hence in the churches they erected they everywhere kept to the style of the country, viz. late Gothic,[2] both in western Germany (Münster, Coblenz, Cologne, Molsheim) and in the Spanish Netherlands. This is only another proof of the

to be specifically "Jesuit", see BRAUN, in the *Stimmen aus Maria-Laach*, LXXXVII. (1914), 545 *seq.* Just as there is a tendency to interpret the sumptuousness of baroque churches generally, as intended to give a strong stimulus to the emotions of the masses, without considering at the same time all the other numerous and contributory causes belonging to general culture, this style also has been especially laid at the door of the Jesuits. Many baroque churches of the Catholic Renaissance together with many Jesuit churches do indeed display an excess of decorative ornament. Nevertheless a universal tendency cannot be proved. Moreover, exaggerated decoration, such as that of the Gesù at Rome, as well as of many other Jesuit churches, belongs to a much later date. It is most remarkable that the best authority on these matters, J. BRAUN (*loc. cit.*, 547 *seq.*) demonstrates that the exaggeratedly ornamental Jesuit churches, not only in Germany, the Netherlands, and France, but also in Italy and Spain, constitute a definite minority in relation to the total number of the churches of the Society in those countries. *Cf.* also B. CROCE, *Der Begriff des Barocks und die Gegenreformation*, Zurich, 1926, 29.

[1] See M. FÜRST, in the *Hist.-polit. Blätter*, CLV., 516; J. BRAUN, *Die Kirchenbauten der deutschen Jesuiten*, I., Freiburg, 1908, II., *ibid.*, 1909 (pseudo-Gothic churches in northern Germany are not numerous).

[2] J. BRAUN (*Die Belgischen Jesuitenkirchen*, Freiburg, 1907) shows on quite exhaustive investigation, that almost half of the Belgian Jesuit churches (13), even as late as about the middle of the seventeenth century, were in late-Gothic style. *Cf.* also PARENT, 121 *seq.*

Society's power of adaptability to, and regard for, national peculiarities and historical tradition in all things in which no fundamental principle of the Order was at stake. The Jesuits had no other aim than to build churches that were both beautiful and devotional. But for all their respect for what was indigenous and long-established, they did not reject the claims of the new; the result frequently was a mixture of styles. An accurate examination of existing monuments of the period shows that the style of the Jesuit churches is the one that prevailed at the time in the particular country. Where people built in the Gothic style, they built in Gothic and where the Renaissance or baroque prevailed, they too used the new style.[1]

If in questions of art the authorities allowed the fullest freedom, there was uniformity of method and purpose in all that concerned the cure of souls, the missions and the education of youth. In Spanish Flanders no less than in other countries, the Jesuits devoted themselves with such zeal to the formation of the rising generation, that they were everywhere looked upon as model teachers.[2] Even Protestants admitted the fact.[3] Almost the whole of the nobility and the well-to-do middle classes sent their sons to the schools of the Jesuits, in the firm conviction that "nowhere were they more likely to acquire the literary equipment necessary to a man moving in polite society and one desirous to practise the liberal arts".[4] And since schools were gratuitous, talented

[1] See BRAUN in *Stimmen aus Maria-Laach*, LXXXVII., 548 *seq.*

[2] See PIRENNE, IV., 502. *Cf.* PASTURE, *Restauration*, 311 *seq.*

[3] See v. BUCHELS, *Diarium*, ed. Brom, and L. A. v. LANGERAAD, *Amsterdam*, 1907, 99; PIRENNE, IV., 503.

[4] This is the opinion of PIRENNE (IV., 503), who is not friendly towards the Jesuits. This passage contains further detailed information. The College at Douai numbered in 1600, 400 scholars in arts, 600 in philosophy, 100 in theology; see PONCELET, 17. Besides the Jesuits the Augustinian Hermits also successfully devoted themselves to the education of youth. See PASTURE, *Restauration*, 306. *Cf.* also BETS, *Hist. de Tirlemont*, II., 35 *seq.*

but destitute youths were also able to get their education there. In every college there existed at least four sodalities of our Lady, one for the pupils, a second for the youths, a third for men, and a fourth for young children. These sodalities, or "Guilds" as they were called in Belgium, included an immense number of members who devoted themselves to the most diverse works of mercy; the poor, the sick, the prisoners and the unlearned—all received innumerable tokens of their charity.[1]

As pastors of souls the Jesuits attached supreme importance to preaching and the frequent reception of the sacraments. It is related that at the beginning of the seventeenth century, in the Flandro-Belgian Province, no less than 15,206 sermons were delivered in the course of a single year.[2] The Jesuits showed particular zeal in the teaching of the catechism throughout the Netherlands. This apostolate, which Paul V. did all he could to encourage, was of the simplest kind.[3] They strove to impress the usual prayers and the fundamental truths of the Church as deeply as possible on the children's minds. Teaching was based on the catechism of Canisius which Francis Coster had translated in 1566. In order to arouse interest there were competitions, prizes, theatrical representations and questions and answers set to music and sung in chorus.[4] This method, which had already received the encomiums of Clement VIII., yielded excellent results and the religious and secular authorities encouraged and supported it, with the result that it spread ever more and more. Some colleges conducted as many as thirty or forty children's classes. The confraternity of St. Charles Borromeo, founded

[1] *Cf.* PONCELET, 26 *seq.* The four congregations at Louvain comprised 800 members (*Litt. ann. Soc. Iesu*, 1611, 250). The total in the Flandro-Belgian Province, in 1626, came to 13,727 persons (*Imago primi saeculi*, 774).

[3] See *Imago primi saeculi*, 781.

[3] See *Synopsis*, II., 245.

[4] *Cf.* PERRENS, IV., 506 *seq.* Many details are to be found in *Litt. ann. Soc. Iesu*, 1611, 250 *seq.*; 1613–1614, 287 *seq.*, 342 *seqq.*

in Antwerp in 1618, by one of the Fathers, was soon copied in a great number of towns.[1]

The southern districts of the Netherlands were still exposed to the danger of Calvinist propaganda, hence Paul V. learnt with the greatest joy of the establishment of Jesuit colleges near the frontier. This undertaking was due to the initiative of the nuncio.[2] For the purpose of stemming the flood of Calvinist writings which attacked the Catholic faith in every possible way, Cardinal Bellarmine created a fund the revenue of which was to be applied to the training and supporting of controversialists. Among the scholars who met the Calvinist attack with counter-attack, the Jesuits were in the foremost rank. It is enough to mention Francis Coster (d. 1619), Leonard Lessius (d. 1623), Thomas Saillius (d. 1623), Martin Becanus (d. 1624), Charles Scribianus (d. 1629), Hermann Hugo (d. 1629), Herbert Rosweidus (d. 1629). Together with them, the Franciscan Matthiew Hauzeur also greatly distinguished himself as a controversialist.[3]

The activities of the new Orders as well as the whole movement of religious reaction found strong supporters in the regents Albert and Isabella. By the strength of their faith and the purity of their lives these princes set their subjects a splendid example.[4] The liberality with which they supported the Church could not have been surpassed. Churches, monasteries, seminaries, charitable institutions were either founded, enlarged, adorned or enriched by them. Innumerable are the works of religious art of which they were the originators. Miräus reckons at 300 the number of the churches which were erected under the auspices and by order of the

[1] See PONCELET, 23 *seq.* Here also is the proof that the custom, begun in Tournai in 1645, of celebrating the solemn corporate First Communion of children, was instituted by the Jesuits.

[2] See LÄMMER, *Zur Kirchengesch.*, 84.

[3] See PONCELET, *La Compagnie de Jésus*, 34 ; WERNER, *Gesch. der apolog. Literatur*, IV., 640 *seq.* ; HURTER, I., 161, 245, 293, 295, 347.

[4] See FRÉDÉGAND CALLAEY, in *Bull. de l'Inst. Hist. Belge de Rome*, III. (1924), 40 *seq.*

archducal pair.[1] The numerous yellow and red-tinted baroque churches which are so distinctive a feature of the physiognomy of many Belgian towns, owe their origin to this period. On his return from Rome, 1604, the official architect of the archduke, Wenceslaus Coeberger, built the churches of the Carmelites and the Augustinians in Brussels.[2] In the former, in 1606, the archduke and archduchess had themselves solemnly invested with the scapular. In 1609, Coeberger also built the sanctuary of Montaigu to which Albert and Isabella were wont to withdraw every year for the purpose of making the spiritual exercises for the space of nine days. There they also founded the Rotonda, a place of pilgrimage to this day.[3] In 1609 the office and title of court painter was bestowed on a man of genius, Peter Paul Rubens, who had then just returned from Italy.[4]

One of the archduke Albert's most anxious cares was to make of the churches of his domains worthy shrines for the relics which had escaped the destruction of the churches by the Protestants of Holland and Germany. When the reliquary of St. Albert arrived, the archduke carried it on his own shoulders through the streets of Mons to the church of the Carmelite nuns.[5] Every year, on Maundy Thursday, the archducal pair washed the feet of the poor in the chapel of the palace.

The example of the regents made a powerful impression on the people. All classes were eager to take part in the public processions and in the exercises prescribed for gaining the Indulgences which Paul V. granted repeatedly. Numerous

[1] See MIRAEUS, *De Vita Alberti pii*, Antwerpie, 1612; DE MONTPLEIMCHAMP, *Hist. de l'archiduc Albert*, Bruxelles, 1870, 524 *seq.*, 528 *seq.*, 530 *seq.* *Cf.* PASTURE, *Restauration*, 6 *seq.* See also the life of *Mary Ward*, I., *seq.* 128.

[2] See SCHAYES, *Hist. de l'architecture en Belgique*, IV., 181 *seq.*; SAINTENOY, *loc. cit.*, 26. PARENT, *loc. cit.*

[3] *Cf.* KRONEN, *Marias Heerlykheid en Nederland*, VII., Amsterdam, 191, 1911.

[4] See SAINTENOY, *loc. cit.*, 21.

[5] See PIRENNE, IV., 522 *seq.*

confraternities arose, devotion to the Holy Eucharist grew steadily, as well as devotion to the Mother of God, whose sanctuaries were annually visited by thousands of pilgrims. The most famous among these pilgrimages were those of Hal and Montaigu.[1] Justus Lipsius, a man of immense learning, was so impressed by the sight of the ex-votos in the sanctuary of Hal, which bear witness to the power and the goodness of the Mother of God, that he set himself the task of writing the story of this pilgrimage in classical Latin. This work has been many times reprinted and translated into several languages, German being among them. As the great scholar lay dying in 1606, he asked that the Litany of Loreto be read to him and he declared that his greatest comfort was that he had honoured Mary from the days of his childhood.[2] Like Lipsius, other personages of intellectual or social standing were members of the sodality of our Lady. In the registers of these sodalities, which have come down to us, we find, besides the names of bishops, abbots and nuncios, those of the leading figures of the nobility and the highest authorities, as well as those of artists such as David Teniers, Van Dyck and Rubens.[3] How powerfully the religious revival had got hold of all classes is shown by the fact that a number of devout young women of the burgher families banded themselves together for the purpose of attending to the tidiness and decoration of the churches, teaching the catechism, nursing the sick and burying the dead. The life of people in the world became increasingly impregnated with "that active yet tender piety", the accomplished expression of which is seen in the classical book of St. Francis de Sales, *Introduction to a Devout Life*.[4]

It must have been a great comfort to Paul V. to see how in Spain and Italy and now across the Alps also, in the southern and eastern provinces of the Netherlands, the ancient faith was

[1] See PASTURE, *loc. cit.*, 330 *seq.* *Cf.* A. VAN WEDDINGEN, *Notre-Dame de Montaigu*[3], Bruxelles, 1880.

[2] See the work of KRONEN, quoted above note 3, p. 98.

[3] See PONCELET, 28.

[4] Judgment of PIRENNE (IV., 525).

striking ever deeper roots in the life and thought of the people. If at a later period it was possible to say that "to be a Catholic is part of the Belgian character", the foundations of such a state of things were being laid during those years. Paul V.'s keenness for the furthering and strengthening of the religious restoration in the Spanish Netherlands is clearly seen in the Instructions issued to Bentivoglio's successors. All were instructed to co-operate with the bishops for the elimination of certain abuses which still lingered, such as, especially, the non-observance of the enclosure in monasteries; to prevent the infiltration of Protestant elements, to defend the rights of the Church, to enforce the Tridentine decrees, in a word, to consolidate the work of the reform by every means in their power.[1] The reports of the nuncios as well as other sources bear witness both to the zeal and to the success with which the representatives of the Holy See everywhere promoted the work of the Catholic restoration. In this respect both Bentivoglio and his successor, Gesualdo, deserved well of the Church.[2]

The religious revival in those parts of the Netherlands which had remained Catholic found expression in the arts also. Architecture, painting and sculpture experienced a new efflorescence, in fact their splendour throws lustre upon the whole epoch. The magnificent churches which arose at that time at Antwerp, Bruges, Brussels, Namur, Ghent and Malines call forth admiration even to-day; they display especially a marvellous wealth of decoration, consisting chiefly in marble altars, choir stalls, pulpits, but above all in paintings,[3] for then, as in the fifteenth century, the most

[1] See the Instruction for Ascanio Gesualdo of October 23, 1615, Lucio Morra of June 27, 1617, and Lucio San Severino, of January 2, 1619, in CAUCHIE-MAERE, *Recueil*, 42 *seq.*, 44, 61 *seq.*, 65, 66, 79, 80, 82 *seq.* The Briefs for the nuncios are in BROM, *Archivalia*, I., 247 *seq.*

[2] *Cf.* PASTURE, *Restauration*, 31, 89 *seq.*, 104 *seq.*, 111 *seq.*

[3] *Cf.* DESTRÉE ET MÜLLER DE KETELBOETERE, *L'art Belge au XVIIe siècle*, Louvain, 1910; BRIGGS, *Barockarchitektur* (1914), 196 *seq.*; ROUSSEAU, *La sculpture Belge au XVIIe et XVIIIe siècles*, Bruxelles, 1913.

eminent artists devoted themselves to painting. To the renewed vigour of ecclesiastical life is due the abundance of commissions given to artists ; the wealthy corporations, the ever-growing religious confraternities, the Orders, the Jesuits above all others, but likewise the Dominicans, Franciscans, Augustinians and Carmelites, deemed it a point of honour as well as an indispensable means by which to fan the piety of the people, to provide the house of God with as rich a decoration as possible. Thus the old cathedrals, which had been ravaged by the iconoclasts, as well as the enormous number of new churches built in the peculiar Belgian baroque style, were restored and furnished in most splendid fashion.[1]

However, the greatest as well as the most influential among the artists who put their talent at the service of the Church, Peter Paul Rubens, was not an exclusively religious painter. With astonishing versatility he frequently took his subjects from classical mythology, from history, or himself created allegorico-historical compositions, portraits, genre-paintings, pictures of animals and landscapes. Nevertheless, the number of his religious paintings is extremely great. Rubens was a convinced and practising Catholic. Every morning he heard Mass, before starting work, and his private life was blameless. For all that, from an exaggerated passion for realism, and out of excessive consideration for the wishes of many clients who demanded grossly sensuous representations, in many of his pictures Rubens overstepped those laws of morality which apply also to profane art.[2] Though we pay full homage to his wonderful achievement, it is beyond dispute that in a number of his pictures, the theme of which is taken from the religious sphere, the spiritual or supernatural character is not sufficiently stressed. However frequently he may have

[1] *Cf.* on church architecture, BRIGGS, *loc. cit.*, 194 *seq.*; P. PARENT, *L'architecture des Pays-Bas méridionaux au 16e–18e. siècles*, Paris, 1926, 46 *seq.*, 82 *seq.* ; J. BRAUN, *cf.* above, p. 93, n. 5 ; J. H. PLATENGA, *L'Architecture réligieuse dans l'ancien duché de Brabant*, 1598–1713, La Haye, 1926.

[2] On this aspect of the art of Rubens, *cf.* G. VANZYPE, *P. P. Rubens*, Bruxelles, 1926, 47 *seq.*, 50 *seq.*, 52 *seq.*

painted the Madonna, he never succeeded in doing justice to the deep religious significance of the Mother of God. In like manner many of his figures of Saints fail to come up to what we are entitled to expect from a church painting: they lack all higher inspiration.[1]

In the same way in his many representations of the *Last Judgment*, the religious conception and tone are very much in the background. Like Michelangelo, he conceives the subject exclusively as a penal judgment. He feels himself wholly in his element when he can depict the divine vengeance in the most terrible and awe-inspiring colours. In his picture *Cast into Hell*,[2] which, technically, is of the highest order, the reprobate are, as it were, caught in a whirlwind; they are cast into the dark furnace of the bottomless pit, tumbling head over heels as they fall, screaming, vainly clutching at the empty air. The same theme receives a less violent, or more orderly and academic treatment, in the so-called *Great Last Judgment*[3] for which a German admirer of the master, the Count Palatine of Neuburg, Wolfgang Wilhelm, gave Rubens a commission in the year 1615.[4] Here also there is a mass movement of naked bodies: on the left the ponderous bodies eddy upwards, towards heaven; on the right they fall

[1] See KUHN, III., 903 *seq.*, and KEPPLER, in the *Hist.-polit. Blättern*, XCV., 291 *seq.* J. BURCKHARDT also, in other respects an almost unlimited admirer of the master, says (*Erinnerungen aus Rubens*, 192): "Rubens appears unsatisfactory at all times with regard to the Madonna, not in his style, if we admit that as good, but in relation to spiritual values and to the categories of great art." As a matter of fact SCHNAASE (*Niederländische Briefe*, Stuttgart, 1834, 363) has already pointed out that those forms which appear to us as less devotional, are not due to a lack of religious feeling, but to a different direction of taste and sense of form.

[2] Reproduction in ROSENBERG, no. 87.

[3] Reproduction, *ibid.*, no. 107.

[4] KREITMAIER (in *Repert. für Kunstwissenschaft*, XL. (1917), 247 *seq.*) shows that the picture was painted in 1616, or at latest in the first half of 1617, not at the beginning of 1618, as L. BURCHARD (*Kunstchronik*, N.F., XXIII., 259) surmised.

in tangled knots into hell, where the devil is seen dragging two women into the pit. As in all Rubens' representations of the Last Judgment, here also the unclothed bodies of gross, massive men and women, on which a strong light throws a hard glare, appear for the most part in the foreground and in unseemly attitudes. The impression made by the gigantic canvas commissioned by the Count Palatine of Neuburg, is all the more unpleasant as the figures are above life size. How greatly the views of that period differed from our own, as regards the boundaries of what is objectionable on moral grounds, may be gathered from the fact that the painting was intended for the high altar of the Jesuit church at Neuburg, on the Danube. Only in 1653 was it replaced, "as somewhat unsuitable for the house of God," by another painting,[1] and in 1691 it was taken to Düsseldorf from whence it subsequently went to Munich.

The taste of the period may excuse the transgressions of the boundaries of seemliness in Rubens' scenes of martyrdom in which his passion for realism indulges in an orgy of violence. The maximum of horror of this kind is reached in a picture destined for the high altar of the Jesuit church at Ghent—*The Martyrdom of St. Liévin,* whose excised tongue is held out to a dog which snaps at it. The *Crucifixion of St. Peter* in St. Peter's church, at Cologne, also displays the most horrible realism. In the scene of the martyrdom of St. Liévin the realism is softened by the vision of angels proclaiming from on high the Saint's triumph in heaven.[2]

Numerous as are the works of the greatest master of northern baroque painting which fail to comply with the requirements of an altar-piece, many more are the creations of his brush to which even the most exacting criticism cannot deny a religious character. His *Christ and the Four Penitent*

[1] See BRAUN, *Kirchenbauten der deutschen Jesuiten,* II., 187, note 1. *Cf. Repert. für Kunstwissenschaft,* XL., 249 *seq.* In Dresden there is an autographed sketch, with differences in many respects.

[2] *Cf.* R. VISCHER, *Rubens,* 50; ROOSES, 578 *seq.*, 583 *seq.*; VOLL, *Malerei,* 20 *seq.*

Sinners is a deeply felt piece of work,[1] and his *Apostles* in the Prado Museum of Madrid [2] and his *Ambrose* forbidding the blood-stained emperor Theodosius to enter the door of the basilica,[3] are imposing figures ; and who can behold without emotion his *St. Francis* all aflame with love as he worships Christ crucified ? [4] A genuinely religious atmosphere likewise breathes in the *Assumption of the Blessed Virgin Mary*, the *Carrying of the Cross*,[5] and in a picture destined for the church of the Carmelite nuns of Antwerp, representing St. Teresa prostrate at the feet of Christ and pleading for the release of the Souls in Purgatory which angels are already in the act of assisting out of the flames.[6]

Among the three paintings which Rubens executed for the church of the Franciscans at Antwerp, *The Last Communion of St. Francis of Assissi* is distinguished not only by the glow of its colouring but likewise by a deeply religious conception. In this picture the Flemish master rivals his Italian contemporaries Agostino Caracci and Domenichino who also treated the same theme. The feeling of unbounded faith has rarely been expressed so perfectly, so movingly and so intimately as it is here depicted by Rubens in the attitude of the Saint bowing before the Most Holy Sacrament and in that of his brethren eagerly crowding round him.[7]

Rubens took a prominent part in the decoration of the new

[1] The Pinakothek at Munich, reproduction in ROSENBERG, no. 95. *Cf.* VISCHER, *Rubens*, 41.

[2] See ROSENBERG, no. 10–15.

[3] Vienna Gallery, see ROSENBERG, no. 186.

[4] Liechtenstein Gallery, Vienna ; see ROSENBERG, no. 45.

[5] For the *Assumption of Our Lady*, preserved in the Düsseldorf Gallery, see VISCHER, *Rubens*, 41 ; for the *Carrying of the Cross*, in the Brussels Museum, *cf.* VOLL, *Malerei*, 23 *seq.*

[6] See KEPPLER, *loc. cit.*, 302. *Cf.* ROOSES, 242, where there is a good reproduction.

[7] OLDENBOURG (*Rubens*, 16) considers that this picture, now in the Museum of Antwerp, is the most moving of all the religious pictures of the master. *Cf.* also ROOSES, 225 *seq.*, and BURCKHARDT, *Erinnerungen*, 117.

church of the Jesuit professed house at Antwerp. On March 29th, 1620, he signed a contract by the terms of which he bound himself to provide the sketches for thirty-nine subjects for the vaults of the lateral aisles and the tribunes. These were to be executed by Antony van Dyck and others of his pupils.[1] In 1718 these paintings were destroyed by fire, but three large altar-pieces painted by Rubens previous to 1620 were saved; they are *The Assumption of our Lady*, and the *Miracles of St. Ignatius and St. Francis Xavier*. Rubens took particular delight in labouring for the glorification of these heroes of the Catholic restoration on whom Paul V. had bestowed the honours of our altars. The two paintings are among the most splendid of the master's works. The figure of the great founder and that of his no less glorious disciple stand out powerfully and dominate the whole scene by their impressive dignity and majesty.[2] The feeling of confidence with which the sick and others in need press round and, as it were, mob the Saints, is most happily rendered. In Ignatius the great Flemish master extols the share of the Society of Jesus in the Catholic restoration and in Xavier the powerful impulse which the new Order gave to the spread of the gospel even as far as the extreme Far East. Both pictures were intended for the high altar which they adorned in turns; by reason of the painted architectural features and the colour effects, they constitute a harmonious climax for the interior of the church.

Utterly different in character is the majestic votive picture commissioned in 1630 by the widow of archduke Albert, the Infanta Isabella, for the high altar of the church of St. James on the Coudenberg, at Brussels, a church belonging to the confraternity of the Saint of that name. Though artistically dazzling by reason of the compactness of the composition and the strong, warm tone of the colouring, this canvas does not bear comparison with the infinite charm and strength of the great altar-pieces of the Jesuit church. The

[1] See ROOSES, 237 *seq.*

[2] *Cf.* KUHN, III., 2, 907, and BURCKHARDT, *loc. cit.*, 136, 161.

dazzling splendour of form and colour destroys the religious atmosphere ; religious emotion is indeed movingly depicted in the features of St. Ildephonsus who kisses, with deep emotion, the chasuble which the Mother of God presents to him, but the Madonna lacks the maidenly grace of the Queen of heaven, and as for the female figures around her, they recall far too realistically the court of the regent to create the impression of figures of Saints.[1]

On the other hand another work executed by Rubens to a commission of the archduchess Isabella, namely his sketches for carpets destined for the adornment of the church of the Poor Clares of Madrid,[2] is distinguished by its deeply religious character. Since St. Clare is known for her special devotion to the sacrament of the altar, the theme chosen was the glorification of this mystery. Four sketches deal with the prototypes of the Eucharist ; viz. Melchisedech handing bread and wine to Abraham, the manna in the desert, the sacrifice of the Old Law and Elias fed by an angel. Four other sketches exhibit the witnesses and protagonists of the Catholic teaching on the Eucharist : viz. the Evangelists, the four Doctors of the Latin Church together with Thomas Aquinas, Bonaventure and St. Clare, certain Popes, finally some great men both clerical and lay, especially members of the house of Habsburg.[3] There follow four scenes of triumph which

[1] See Kuhn, III., 2, 907. *Cf.* for the Ildefonso-altar the monograph of G. Glück, in the series, *Meisterwerke in Wien*, Wien, 1921.

[2] See *Descripción de los Tapices de Rubens que se colocan en el claustro del monasterio de las Señoras religiosas descalzas reales*, Madrid, 1881. There are sketches in the Museum at Cambridge, Madrid, and the Louvre ; see Rooses, 462 *seq.* *Cf.* Rosenberg, no. 282–8. There are magnificent large engravings by Schelte a Bolswert, Nic. Lauwers, Adrian and Conrad Lommelin and Joseph Neefs. The explanations of these representations until now have been frequently erroneous, and even W. Rothes (*Monatschrift f. Kunstwissenschaft*, VI. (1913), 448) has not treated the matter quite satisfactorily ; I hope I have hit on the right interpretation.

[3] Reproduction in Rooses, 428.

gave the picture its name. In rich and profound allegories Rubens depicts the triumph of the Eucharistic mystery over paganism, ignorance and wilful blindness and the errors of Luther and Calvin, and, lastly, the triumph of divine love in the Sacrament of the Altar. The first two allegories, which are widely known through excellent engravings, are rightly ranked among the sublimest creations of the master. The victory of the Eucharist over idolatry is symbolized by the interruption of a pagan sacrifice: a luminous angel holding a chalice and host is seen descending from heaven and his apparition troubles and terrifies the priest and his assistant as they prepare to offer sacrifice. A comparison with Raphael's sacrifice of Lystra points to immensely heightened feeling as well as far greater technical resources.

A mighty *Tantum ergo* seems to resound through the *Triumph of the Eucharist over Ignorance and Blindness*. Led by figures symbolizing faith, hope and charity, four horses, the foremost being ridden by a genius with the insignia of the papacy, draw a magnificent triumphal chariot whose wheels crush a writhing devil whilst a pagan in fetters is being driven by the side of it. The Church sits majestically enthroned on the chariot whilst genii hover around her. The wonderful figure, over whose head an angel holds a tiara, has in both hands a monstrance from which flash dazzling rays of light. An eminent connoisseur rightly judges that, as regards artistic effect, none of the numerous allegorical representations of the Church's glory, inspired by the period of Catholic restoration, can stand beside this triumphal picture.[1]

These representations, in which Rubens makes a most eloquent profession of faith in the power and greatness of the mystery of mysteries, bear witness to his truly Catholic sentiments as well as to the deep piety with which he plunges into the contemplation of the Saviour's Passion.[2] His *Pietàs* are most moving. The palm probably belongs to a picture destined to adorn the tomb of a merchant of Antwerp, the central panel of which shows the dead body of Christ lying

[1] See Burckhardt, *Erinnerungen*, 259.

[2] See Rosenberg, XXVIII.

on a stone bench strewn with straw.[1] Mary looks sorrowfully towards heaven as she prepares to cover the pale countenance of her Son with a veil. John supports the body whilst Mary Magdalen looks on, trembling with emotion—" a silent, solemn lament full of tender melancholy." The two wings show St. John the Evangelist looking upwards, towards his eagle, and Mary with her Child whose eyes, expressive of terror, are directed towards the central scene—a hint as ingenious as it is effective that even as a child the God-man foresaw His Passion.[2]

Very characteristic of Rubens are two other pictures of his representing the lament over the dead Christ : in one, now in Vienna, the sorrowful Mother draws a thorn from the head of her dead Son ; in the other, now preserved at Antwerp, she closes His eyes dimmed by death.[3]

Very often Rubens represents the dead Christ upon the cross, either alone or as surrounded by His lieges. He is seen alone in the much copied picture of the Antwerp Gallery. The half-open lips utter the words : " My God, my God, why hast thou forsaken me ? " whilst the half-closed eyes, which, by a supreme effort the dying Man has raised on high, seem to ask a similiar question of heaven. The figure of the crucified of the Pinakothek of Munich also shows Him alone and forsaken on the gibbet : the pale, white body looks ghostly against the gloom of the evening sky.[4]

The last scenes of the drama of Calvary are depicted in the famous altar pieces of Antwerp. The highly dramatic *Raising of the Cross*, which was subsequently transferred to the cathedral, had been painted in 1610 for the church of St. Walburge, at Antwerp. By the enormous display of energy on the part of the herculean executioners who plant their feet against the rock in order to raise the cross, the master sought to give a symbolic expression to the idea that He who was

[1] Hence the name, *Le Christ à la paille* ; Museum of Antwerp, reproduction in ROSENBERG, no. 148.

[2] See KEPPLER, in the *Hist.-polit. Blättern*, XCV., 300.

[3] Reproduction in ROSENBERG, nos. 80 and 81.

[4] See KEPPLER, *loc. cit.*, 301. *Cf.* ROSENBERG, nos. 45 and 46.

nailed to the cross bore the burden of the sins of all mankind.[1] The meek resignation of the Saviour appears in vivid contrast with the roughness and the grim hatred of His tormentors.[2] This incomparably forceful work of art,[3] in which one detects the influence of the manner of Caravaggio, makes an overwhelming impression. Whilst brute force is given full play in this picture, the silent grief of our Lord's friends finds a moving expression in another altar piece also of colossal proportions which now adorns the cathedral of Antwerp: the *Descent from the Cross*, completed in 1612. Two men standing on ladders lean over the cross-beam of the gibbet and so allow the dead body to slip down on a linen sheet. Below, the body is received by John, Joseph of Arimathaea, Nicodemus and the holy women. A dazzling stream of unearthly light falls on the body of the Saviour, which is the centre of the looks, feelings, thoughts and activity of those present. By the admirable compactness of his composition as well as by the happy arrangement of his groups, Rubens surpasses all his predecessors. It is easy to understand that this representation, which glows with the liveliest faith, should have set a fashion for years to come.[4]

These stupendous works, in which Rubens created "for the Netherlands the definitive form of the painted baroque

[1] See WAAGEN, *Kleine Schriften*, Stuttgart, 1875, 253.

[2] See ROOSES, 131 *seq.*; OLDENBOURG, *Rubens*, 73 *seq.*; FROMENTIN, 84 *seq.*

[3] See OLDENBOURG, in the *Jahrbuch der österr. Kunstsamml.*, XXXIV. (1918), 174.

[4] See ROOSES, 166 *seq.*; KEPPLER, *loc. cit.*, 295 *seq.*, who rightly refutes the unjust criticism of CARTIER (*La renaissance italienne et son influence en Europe: Lettres chrétiennes*, Lille, 1880, 364). *Cf.* also WAAGEN, *loc. cit.*, 256; BURCKHARDT, *Erinnerungen*, 115, 132 *seq.*; OLDENBOURG, 8, 88; FROMENTIN, 75 *seq.*; PRINCE GEORGE OF SAXONY (*Die Kunst im slavischen Osten*, Köln, 1919, 29) points out a "Descent from the Cross" of Rubens in the church of St. Nicholas at Kalisz, in Poland. The picture was a gift from the Secretary of State of Sigismund III., Peter Zermoski; a copy is at Arras; see *Kunstchronik N.F.*, XXIII., 271.

altar ",[1] were followed by another masterpiece of religious art, *Christ on the cross between the two thieves*, destined for the high altar of the church of the Recollects at Antwerp.[2] The divine Sufferer's head has sunk on His breast, and He has expired. The thief on His right hand is at his last gasp but looks with confidence towards heaven, whilst the legs of the other robber are being broken and he himself writhes in an agony of despair. Longinus approaches from the right in order to pierce the side of our Lord with his lance. Mary and John turn aside with a shudder whilst the Magdalen, the embodiment of deepest grief, instinctively spreads out her arms as if to ward off the stroke of the lance.

Rubens' productiveness in the field of religious painting was emulated by his numerous pupils whom the master himself had extensively employed in his own creations. An outstanding figure in this crowd is Anton Van Dyck. Van Dyck's artistic temperament differed widely from that of Rubens and he gives proof of a more tender, sensitive, idyllic, and at times, an almost sentimental disposition which reveals itself even in his colouring. Even more than his colouring, the conception of his subjects comes close to that of his Italian contemporaries, such as Domenichino and Reni. His art, like that of his teachers, is the fruit of the Catholic restoration.[3] Anton Van Dyck painted religious subjects for choice, even when he worked without any special purpose and for the sheer love of painting.[4] His numerous Madonnas betray deeper feeling and tenderness than those of Rubens. Like the most famous of these pictures, *The Repose of the Holy*

[1] See Clemen, *Belgische Kunstdenkmäler*, II., München, 1923, 181 *seq.*

[2] The picture known as *Le coup de lance*, is now in the Antwerp Museum (Rosenberg, no. 203). See Keppler, *loc. cit.*, 299 *seq.*; Rooses, 235 *seq.* *Cf.* Burckhardt, *loc. cit.*, 106, 146, who describes the picture as " unique of its kind ".

[3] See W. Rothes, *Die kirchliche Kunst des A. van Dyck*, in the *Wissensch. Beilage der Germania*, 1912, no. 38; by the same also *A. Van Dyck*, München, 1919, 16 *seq.*

[4] See Knackfuss, *A van Dyck*, Bielefeld, 1910, 56.

Family on the Flight to Egypt, now in the picture gallery of Petrograd, his other works bear too many characteristics of genre painting to be ranked as religious pictures.[1] Many of Van Dyck's themes are taken from the lives of the Saints. When only twenty-two he produced a St. Martin sharing his cloak with a beggar—a perfectly mature masterpiece. Later on he repeatedly painted St. Jerome, Mary Magdalen, St. Sebastian and above all St. Francis of Assisi. However, not a few among these paintings, as for instance the *St. Sebastian*, of the Pinakothek of Munich, betray a certain shallowness in the conception of the theme.[2] For the "Confraternity of the unmarried", which the Jesuits directed at Antwerp, he painted the Blessed Hermann Joseph absorbed in prayer at the feet of the Blessed Virgin. The same gravity and the same sincerity of feeling are shown by the picture representing St. Antony contemplating the Child Jesus.[3] As a religious painter Van Dyck is at his best in the works which have for their theme the sufferings of our Lord. His *Lament for Christ* in the Munich Gallery,[4] *The Arrest of Christ*, in the Prado Museum at Madrid,[5] and *The Carrying of the Cross*, in the church of St. Paul at Antwerp,[6] make a profound impression on the beholder. Our Lord shedding His blood upon the cross for the salvation of mankind has been so often and so impressively painted by the master, that it is precisely the mastery of this theme which sums up his creative work in the field of religious art.[7] Van Dyck's representations of the

[1] *Ibid.*, 16 *seq.*

[2] *Ibid.*, 58 *seq.*

[3] *Ibid.*, 58. A copy of the picture now in the Vienna Gallery, is reproduced in SCHAEFFER, 113.

[4] Copy in SCHAEFFER, 28.

[5] Copy *ibid.*, 37. For other pictures of the "Taking of Jesus" see ROTHES, *loc. cit.*

[6] The deathly, weary look of pain with which the Saviour, quite broken beneath the weight of the Cross, looks towards His Mother, is rightly described by ROTHES, *loc. cit.*, as overwhelming.

[7] See ROTHES, *loc. cit.*

crucifixion show no trace of the stormy violence of his master Rubens. He brings home to the beholder the sufferings of Christ by a different method, namely by depicting the heartfelt grief of Mary and other personages. Here, as in all his religious works, Van Dyck gives proof of great warmth and tenderness of feeling.[1]

The most beautiful and most moving of Van Dyck's justly famous large-scale representations of the crucifixion is that in the church of our Lady at Dendermonde. In addition to the Mother of Jesus, who looks up to the cross with unspeakable grief, Mary Magdalen and John are seen on one side, and on the other Longinus and the magnificent figure of St. Francis of Assisi holding the foot of the cross in a loving embrace.[2] The *Crucifixion* in the Museum of Antwerp has been called "a miracle of feeling in colours of utmost impressiveness". All the usual gospel personages are absent, their place being taken by St. Dominic and St. Catherine of Siena. St. Catherine is on her knees and embraces the cross and the feet of the superbly drawn Christ—"one of the most moving representations of a nun in all art." The stone in front of the cross bears the inscription: "That the earth may be light for his father Anton Van Dyck has rolled this stone towards the cross and made a gift of it."[3] The *Crucifixion* in the church of St. Michael, at Ghent, is another admirable composition: it represents the moment when the sponge full of vinegar and myrrh was offered to our Lord.[4]

Van Dyck shows extraordinary skill in the expression of the soul's anguish when, after Christ's body has been taken down from the cross, he depicts the grief of His friends lamenting Him. Some of these scenes are remarkable works of religious art, for instance the two paintings in Paris and

[1] See J. SORENSON, in the *Hist.-polit. Blättern*, CXXIV., 693 *seq.* *Cf.*, too, BURCKHARDT, *Vorträge*, 327.

[2] See WOLTMANN, III., 1, 448; reproduced in SCHAEFFER, 108.

[3] A copy of the picture, now in the Antwerp Museum, is in SCHAEFFER, 106. For other pictures of the Crucifixion by Van Dyck, see ROTHES, *loc. cit.*, and BURCKHARDT, *Vorträge*, 328.

[4] Reproduced in SCHAEFFER, 110.

Munich which represent the sorrowful Mother alone with the dead body of her Son whilst two splendid angels worship Him.[1] In the *Pietà* of the Antwerp Museum, painted for the church of the Béguines in which the artist desired to be buried, the varying intensity of grief of the bystanders is superbly expressed: Mary Magdalen, in tears, kisses the hand of her Lord; John turns a fixed, frightened gaze towards the dead Christ, whereas Mary, in an eloquent gesture, hints at the sea of bitterness which fills her soul at sight of her cruelly misused Child.[2] As art, another *Lament of Christ* ranks even higher. From the Franciscan church at Antwerp the picture came into the museum of the town: it shows Mary leaning against the wall of the Sepulchre and holding on her lap the idealized form of her lifeless Son. In an agony of grief she spreads out both arms whilst St. John, with the forefinger of his left hand, points out to two weeping angels the wound in the left hand of Jesus.[3]

Van Dyck is probably most inspiring when he depicts the Crucified by Himself, alone and forsaken and bleeding to death, suspended between heaven and earth. According to Bellori, Van Dyck painted a picture of this kind for his patron, Cardinal Bentivoglio. The original has been lost but the artist repeated the composition more than once. Imitators and copyists appropriated it so that it is frequently met with.[4] Whilst one representation, now in the museum in Antwerp, depicts the moment when Jesus said, "Father, into thy hands I commend my Spirit!"[5] another fixes the moment described in the Gospel: "There was darkness." The whiteness of the sacred body shines with wonderful luminousness in the gloom which envelops the surrounding country. A crescent moon is seen in the sky; the parchment on which the sentence is written and the loin cloth of our Lord flutter in the wind;

[1] Reproduced by SCHAEFFER, 97, 98.

[2] *Ibid.*, 94.

[3] *Ibid.*, 124 *seq.* *Cf.* SCHNAASE, *Niederländische Briefe*, 280; ROTHES, *loc. cit.*

[4] See SCHAEFFER, 499.

[5] Copy in KNACKFUSS, *loc. cit.*, 41.

the countenance of the divine Sufferer, whose eyelids are stained with blood, inspires tender sympathy and reverence.[1] "In all these pictures," says one of the foremost students of the history of art, "religious pathos and a noble expression of grief attain astonishing heights. We have excellent things of this kind from the school of the Caracci and powerful ones from the Spanish school, but the former leave something to be desired in the colouring and the latter in the purity and finish of form, whereas Van Dyck combines all these qualities. He is, and remains, one of the princes of religious painting." [2] As popular and greatly admired creators of altar-pieces, Rubens and Van Dyck left their mark on the art of the Catholic Netherlands in the seventeenth century, whilst at the same time they rendered valuable service to the cause of the Catholic restoration. No one could escape the enormous impressiveness of their works. Added to preaching and catechizing, their paintings were a powerful help towards the understanding of the dogmas of the Catholic faith. The monumental creations of Rubens had power to enthral every section of the people, even those whose artistic feelings were of a more elementary kind; on the other hand, Van Dyck worked more especially for those circles which would be influenced without the same forcible appeal.

The influence which Rubens chiefly exercised by means of his altar-pieces, which sparkle with light and colour, was not confined to the Netherlands and it was soon felt by the whole of Catholic South Germany. The pupils and successors of the great Master vied with one another in their eagerness to adorn churches with rich altar-pieces, as was done in Italy and Spain. The most recent biographer of Rubens aptly remarks that this great genius was the Catholic painter *par excellence* not only in his own century but in the next also and well into the nineteenth century.[3]

[1] Copy of the picture, now preserved in Munich, in SCHAEFFER, 85.

[2] BURCKHARDT, *Vorträge*, 329.

[3] ROOSES, 182. BURCKHARDT (*Erinnerungen*, 82) says: "It was a wonderful piece of good fortune for Catholicism throughout

The sacred edifices embellished by copies or reproductions of his works must be reckoned by hundreds. And since he himself had most of his creations multiplied by excellent engravers, whom he trained himself, his influence spread even into the Romance countries. Rubens may well be called the greatest of all the painters who put their talent at the service of the Catholic restoration. With his glowing colours and the dramatic power of his compositions, he glorified the Saints of the period, Ignatius, Francis Xavier, Teresa, and proved an effective advocate of the dogmas of the ancient faith which were most fiercely attacked by the religious innovators, viz. Purgatory, the intercession of the Blessed Virgin and the Most Holy Sacrament of the Altar.

The enormous contrast between the Catholic and the Protestant philosophy of life and culture is strikingly brought home to the traveller in the northern parts of the Netherlands, geographically so near, and so much more richly endowed with material wealth, when he visits the sacred edifices which the Gueux stripped bare of their ancient religious ornaments. The effect of these empty churches, with their bare, whitewashed walls, is as depressing as the Calvinist doctrine of predestination. Here one looks in vain for the symphonies in colour of a Rubens or the moving crucifixion scenes of a Van Dyck, which adorn the lavishly furnished, resplendent yet harmoniously coloured churches of the southern Netherlands. Protestantism drove art from the house of God ; the Catholic Church lovingly protected it and gave so many commissions for works of monumental size to the great masters, that even their incredible capacity for work could hardly cope with them. How different, in consequence, was the fate of a Rubens and a Van Dyck from that of Rembrandt and Ruysdels who died in misery ! The difference between Calvinist and Catholic culture is perhaps nowhere more drastically illustrated than it is by the contrast of these churches.

the North, to have an interpreter, so great, gifted and generous, and who was able to feel such enthusiasm for all aspects of religious art."

Though Luther did not go as far as Calvin, his teaching was nevertheless disastrous for the arts. When he rejected all material forms of worship, the veneration of the Saints and the meritoriousness of good works, " he choked the springs of ecclesiastical art in the ideal as well as in the material sense ; he pronounced the death sentence of the religious picture or work of art as far as the churches are concerned, and changed the house of God into a bare, chill assembly-room. Together with alleged abuses he uprooted the whole tree on which, for many centuries, the fairest and sweetest fruits had matured, for the refreshment of millions of way-farers towards their everlasting goal, mankind's fairest achievement rich in infinite revelations." [1]

[1] This is the opinion of J. SAUER, *Reformation und Kunst*, Freiburg, 1919, 4 *seq.*, 9. *Cf.* also DEHIO, in *Archiv. f. Kulturgesch.*, XII. (1914), 1 *seq.*, who shows that besides the obstruction of art caused by the Reformation, it was also forced into profane and realistic channels by the same movement.

CHAPTER II.

THE POSITION OF CATHOLICS IN THE GERMAN DIASPORA, IN THE REPUBLIC OF THE NETHERLANDS, AND IN GREAT BRITAIN AND IRELAND.—THE GUNPOWDER PLOT AND THE OATH OF ALLEGIANCE.—PAUL V. AND JAMES I.'S PLANS FOR A SPANISH MARRIAGE.

(1.)

IT was in North Germany, where so many magnificent cathedrals still recall the memory of a Catholic past, that the storm provoked by the religious innovations, inflicted the most grievous losses to the ancient Church. Like the whole of the North of Europe, this district also came within the jurisdiction of the Cologne nuncio [1] though in the circumstances that dignitary could do but little, for the creation of purely territorial Churches had been done with such thoroughness that no more than faint vestiges seemed to remain of the once flourishing North German Church. The handful of canons and religious who remained true to the ancient faith saw themselves doomed to extinction and the Catholic laity were almost completely deprived of all religious succour, all the more as the Catholic territories, where they might have fulfilled their religious duties, did not lie within easy reach. The most pressing need was to get information on the state of affairs in the North German diaspora.[2] In this way, in 1607, at the

[1] *Cf.* EHSES-MEISTER, *Kölner Nuntiatur*, I. (1895), xliv., II. (1899), xvii. Naturally, the nuncios at the Imperial Court had also to concern themselves often with the ecclesiastical affairs of North Germany. *Cf.* below, ch. IV.

[2] *Diaspora, cf.* I Pet. I., i., German-speaking Catholics use the word to describe small Catholic communities or minorities scattered among Prot. majorities The word is a useful and simple one and it has seemed best to retain it. (Trsl. note.)

instigation of the nuncio Attilio Amalteo, a memorandum was drawn up by a Jesuit on the condition of the Church in North Germany which gives some interesting details on the existing situation.[1] It was an exceedingly gloomy one. As regards the dioceses of Münster and Paderborn, the danger of a triumph for the innovators had been staved off for the time being, but in the two other Westphalian dioceses, Osnabrück and Minden, the position was precarious. At Osnabrück, though the bishops had all been Protestants, the canons, as a body, had remained true to the Catholic faith. The following establishments in the town itself had also been saved for the ancient faith: one monastery of Canons, one convent of Dominicans, two almost empty convents of nuns, a convent of Benedictine nuns on the Gertrudenberg and, elsewhere in the diocese, one Benedictine abbey, one collegiate church of which the choir was in Catholic hands and the nave in Protestant ones, and five convents of nuns. At Minden, in 1607, there were left only five Catholic canons, and in the two collegiate churches of the town the Catholics formed likewise only a minority. One Benedictine monastery as well as a convent of nuns in Minden itself and two convents of nuns in the surrounding country had preserved the faith. In the districts of Brandenburg and Saxony, Catholicism was wholly extinct. In the dioceses of Verden, Halberstadt, Magdeburg, Bremen and Lübeck the new teaching had prevailed almost everywhere and only here and there could there be found an isolated Catholic canon or a religious house. The inmates of some of these—this applies especially to convents of nuns—clung to the ancient faith with wonderful constancy.

[1] The report, originating from *Cod. Ottob.* 2421, of the Vatican Library, was published by SAUERLAND in the *Röm. Quartalschr.*, XIV. (1900), 384 *seq.* For other sources which are unfortunately very rare, see SCHMIDLIN, "Die Anfänge der norddeutschen Diaspora," in the *Akad. Bonifatius-Korrespondenz*, 1910, nos. 4 and 5. *Cf.* also SCHMIDLIN, *Kirchl. Zustände*, 573 *seq.* See also E. SCHWARZ, *Die Lage der Bistümer West- und Norddeutschlands um die Wende des 16. Jahrh.*, in the supplement to the Berlin *Germania*, 1911, no. 4.

Here as elsewhere [1] the monasteries remained centres of Catholic life.[2] A priest trained in the seminary of Braunsberg, Martin Stricker,[3] did much to procure the consolations of religion for the nuns. In 1609 the nuncio of Cologne, Antonio Albergati, who had succeeded Amalteo, appointed this zealous priest as his representative for the diaspora of North Germany[4] in which the greatly shrunken diocese of Hildesheim and Eichsfeld, which the archbishop of Mayence had recovered for Catholicism, constituted as it were two oases in a vast desert. Henceforth Stricker deemed it his life's task to bring spiritual help to the numerous Catholics scattered in those parts, more particularly in Lower Saxony. In 1611, Albergati commissioned the Franciscan Buselius to undertake a visitation of the North German diaspora. Buselius met Stricker in the Benedictine convent at Buxtehude and sent back a glowing account of the latter's piety, learning and zeal for the Catholic cause. Stricker acted, for a time, as Superior of the convent. In 1612, when the Jesuits saw themselves compelled to give up their station at Altona,[5] he undertook to

[1] In Brunswick the convent of S. Ludger held its ground, and its abbot, Conrad vonWerden, a strong Catholic, had re-established the enclosure since 1601 ; see WOKER, *Gesch. der norddeutschen Franziskanermissionen*, 372 *seq*. On the borders of Brunswick a few convents maintained themselves ; see WOKER, *Gesch. der kathol. Kirche in Hannover*, 12 ; SCHMIDLIN, *Anfänge der Diaspora, loc. cit.*, no. 4.

[2] *Cf.* SILLERN, "Hamburgs Beziehungen zum Neukloster bei Buxtehude," in the *Zeitschr. f. hamburgische Geschichte*, IX. (1890), 80, in which are very interesting particulars of all the religious houses in the district of Hamburg.

[3] *Cf.* PIEPER, *Die Propaganda-Kongregation und die nordischen Missionen*, Köln (1886), 26 *seq.*

[4] See *Annuae missionis Hamburgensis a. 1589 ad 1781*, Friburgi Brisg., 1867, 33 *seq.*, and METZLER, *Die Apostol. Vikariate des Nordens*, Paderborn, 1919, 10.

[5] See *Nord-Albingische Studien*, in the *Neues Archiv* of the *Schleswig-Holstein-Lauenburgischen Gesellschaft f. Gesch.*, V., Kiel, 1850, 136.

look after the Catholics at Hamburg.[1] For the support of such as returned to the bosom of the Church the Cologne nuncio, Albergati, formed an association which he attached to the church of the Capuchins in Cologne: this institution received the support of Paul V.[2]

The losses of the Church in South Germany were far less severe than those in the North. However, here also there was a diaspora because the duchy of Württemberg, the marquisates of Ansbach, Baden-Durlach, the county of Hanau-Lichtenberg, the Palatinate, Pfalz-Zweibrücken, by 1613 also Pfalz-Neuburg and a number of cities of empire, had either wholly, or, as regards some cities of empire, only partially gone over to Protestantism. Nevertheless, in many wholly Protestant towns there still existed prebends and houses of the Teutonic Knights of Malta, as, for instance, at Nuremberg, Nördlingen, Frankfort, Strassburg, Heilbronn; in some other towns there still existed collegiate churches of noble ladies, as at Lindau and Buchau. The Catholics still enjoyed the free use of all these churches.[3] The situation of the Catholics of the South German diaspora was also more favourable from another point of view. Unlike their brethren in the North, they were not so completely cut off from all communication with Catholic territories. Plans were discussed as to means by which the Catholic faith might be preserved and even spread in those parts of South Germany. A memorandum addressed to the Holy See contains a number of proposals on the subject, in particular it suggests that what was being done for the religious needs of the faithful in Holland and England, should serve as a model for Germany. The writer, however, does not shut his eyes to the far greater difficulties to be overcome in the latter country, for in the Protestant territories Catholics enjoyed no toleration whatever, so that there no longer existed any considerable groups of Catholics, as was the case in the Netherlands and in England.[4]

[1] See PIEPER, *loc. cit.*, 27 *seq.*

[2] *Cf.* METZLER, *loc. cit.*, 10 *seq.*

[3] See the memoir quoted in foll. note.

[4] *De Missionibus Germanicis*, in DÖLLINGER-REUSCH, *Moralstreitigkeiten*, II., 390 *seq.*; *cf.* I., 662 *seq.*

Every account of conditions in the Republic of the Netherlands confirms the existence there of a considerable Catholic body. Well-informed people even thought that in five out of the seven united Provinces, namely Gelders, Friesland, Overijsel, Groningen and Utrecht, the majority of the population, with characteristic Dutch tenacity, still clung to the Catholic religion.[1] However, the Calvinists were determined not to allow them the free exercise of their religion, as was made clear during the negotiations for a truce with Spain. Paul V. was no less anxious than his predecessors that the opportunity should be seized to secure religious freedom for the Catholics of the Netherlands. On June 5th, 1607, Guido Bentivoglio, the new nuncio of Brussels, was instructed to give his most earnest attention to the matter.[2] That same year Paul V. also appealed to Philip III. who promised to do his best but who met with the most determined opposition.[3] His efforts proved in vain even when he declared his readiness to recognize the sovereignty of the Provinces, on condition that they granted to the Catholics freedom to practice their religion.[4] In view of her very unsound financial condition it was imperative for Spain to yield. Hence, on April 9th, 1609, a twelve years' truce was signed between the rebel provinces and the regent of Belgium, archduke Albert, by which the independence of the Dutch republic was recognized.

Up to the last moment the French envoy made earnest representations to the States General in favour of the rights of the Catholics. He particularly insisted on the fact that they too had borne arms against Spain. In recognition of their conduct all public offices should surely be open to them; in any case, they should be granted that for which the Protestants themselves had fought, namely religious liberty. The States

[1] See PHILIPPSON, *Henrich IV. und Philipp III.*, vol. III., 185.

[2] See CAUCHIE-MAERE, *Recueil*, 34.

[3] *Cf.* the *letter of Philip III. to his Roman ambassador, Marquis de Aytona, dated S. Lorenzo, July 14, 1607. Archives of the Spanish Embassy, Rome, I., 28.

[4] See PHILIPPSON, III., 186 *seq.*

General curtly rejected this proposal; more than that, the French intervention was kept dark; but they promised a measure of moderation.[1] When, at the Pope's request, Henry IV. endeavoured to secure for the Catholics at least the right to worship in private, he was given satisfactory assurances on the point.[2] In this way it became possible for a number of priests to return to the Netherlands.[3] For the time being no severe measures were taken against private Catholic worship.[4] Soon, however, a fresh agitation broke out, which led to another set-back. In 1612, the States General issued several decrees against the activities of Catholic priests and the practice of sending children abroad to Catholic or Jesuit schools.[5] But the ancient Church withstood this fresh outbreak also; its adherents had been chastened by their previous trials and the zealous ministrations of the Jesuits, the Franciscans and other priests had so strengthened them, that their destruction, for which the Calvinists had still hoped in the reign of Gregory XIII., was not to be thought of. Their numbers remained such that a strict application of the laws against them was out of question. In this way at least private worship was rendered possible.[6] An Italian priest,

[1] See BLOK, IV., 143.

[2] *Cf.* the *letter of Borghese to the French nuncio, of November 27, 1609, and February 17, 1610, in LÄMMER, *Zur Kirchengesch.*, 78, 79.

[3] See KNUTTEL, I., 97.

[4] *Cf.* the *report of Marcantonio Correr of 1611 in the *Relazioni Veneziane*, published by BLOK, 87.

[5] See BLOK, IV., 144. *Cf. Fr. Dusseldorpii Annales*, ed. Fruin, 's Gravenhage, 1893, 373, 393, 423, 431.

[6] See BLOK, IV., 144, 152. *Cf.* HUBERT, 101. In a *report, preserved in H. 179, p. 140 *seq.*, of the Ambrosian Library, in Milan. "Media quibus placuit divinae gratiae hoc turbulento statu catholicos Hollandiae septentrionalis in fide ac religione conservare aut aberratos reducere," is reported by a peasant, thirty years of age, who became a priest. "Huius zelo alii sacerdotes incitati easdem et alias derelictas ecclesias coeperunt visitare, populum ad confessionem et s. communionem adhortari caeteraque sacramenta ad salutem necessaria impartiri. Solent

one Vincenzo Laurefici, who visited Amsterdam in 1613, in disguise, and from there journeyed to Haarlem, Leiden, the Hague, Delft, and Flushing, gives us some exceedingly interesting details concerning the moderation of the Dutch authorities in regard to private Catholic worship—a state of affairs which, in the opinion of the Belgian nuncio, Bentivoglio,[1] was due to personal and commercial contacts and interests. "Calvinists, Anabaptists, Lutherans, Anglicans and other sects are all allowed to hold their services in public at Amsterdam. Catholics alone are debarred from such freedom. They are permitted to meet for worship in their own houses, but even there they are forbidden to have either Mass or sermon, though, as a matter of fact, the government does not care what anyone does in his own home. Thus my own host was present, every morning, at Mass which was said secretly in his house. In all the other Provinces many act in the same way. If they are denounced, they, or the priest, has to pay a fine of 200 florins. Priests are fairly numerous everywhere. Though they are well known, they are not molested, unless they draw attention to themselves—for this reason they wear lay attire.[2]

In these circumstances, when Philip Rovenius [3] succeeded

autem sub noctem convocare coetum et primam illius partem insumere concionando, alteram confessiones audiendo, tertiam sacrificando et s. eucharistiam administrando, quartam pueros baptizando et adultos matrimonio coniungendo. . . . Instante luce singuli remeabant ad propria, ut conventus lateret haereticos." Priests used to put in lay readers during their absence, to read the Holy Scriptures on Sundays, they also selected gifted lads and instructed them on points of controversy, so as to enable them to meet the heretics in discussion.

[1] See *Relationi del card. Bentivoglio*, publ. da Erycio Puteano, Colonia, 1632, 152.

[2] See *Archiv f. Kulturgesch.*, I. (1903), 421. *Cf.* too, the instruction for Gesualdo, of 1615, in Cauchie-Maere, *Recueil*, 46, and the Venetian report of 1618, in the *Relaz. Venez.*, ed. Blok, 122.

[3] See v. Lommel in the *Archief v. d. geschied. v. h. aartsbisd. Utrecht*, IV., 32 *seq.*, XIV., 120 *seq.*, 360 *seq.*, XX., 353 *seq.* *Cf.* W. L. Kuif and J. de Jong, *ibid.*, L., 410 *seq.* Rovenius

Sasbold Vosmeer, the Vicar Apostolic of the seven provinces, who died in October, 1614, the Pope could well cherish the hope that Catholicism would maintain itself in Holland. This expectation was all the more justified as no real persecution was to be feared from the regent, Maurice of Orange, who in matters of religion was extremely moderate, not to say indifferent.[1]

Conditions varied greatly from province to province. Where the number of Catholics had become much reduced, as, for instance, in Zeeland, the ministrations of the clergy were rendered exceedingly difficult. No priest was allowed to take up permanent residence in Zeeland. In the county of Holland and in Utrecht, where there still existed a large Catholic population, the penal laws were mildly interpreted and there was a fair number of priests.[2] Owing to the fact that all Church property had been confiscated, the Dutch Catholics themselves had to support their priests, about two hundred in number[3]; the foreign missionaries, Jesuits, Franciscans[4] and Dominicans, received support from abroad. These missionaries received great help from the noble Nicholas Wiggers who, since the reign of Gregory XIII., had repeatedly visited Zeeland, Holland and Friesland, for the purpose of strengthening the scattered Catholics in their faith. Even when, in 1603, he entered the Order of the Observants, at Cologne, he did not forget his persecuted countrymen. In that city, where the Vicar Apostolic also saw himself compelled to reside, a seminary supported by the Catholics of the

only became Titular archbishop of Philippi during the last year of Paul V.'s rule; see C. Friedrich, in the *Zeitschr. f. Missionswiss.*, XI. (1921), 134.

[1] See Blok, IV., 143.

[2] See Bentivoglio, *Relationi*, 152 *seq.*

[3] See the *Relatio* of Rovenius of 1622, in *Archief. v.h. aartsbisd. Utrecht*, XX., 354.

[4] In a *brief to *Ioh. Heynus, commiss. gen. ord. min. de observ. in Belgio*, of November 20, 1607, Paul V. praises his advice on Catholic restoration *apud Batavos*, *Epist.*, III., 283, Papal Secret Archives.

Netherlands, was established for the formation of Dutch priests. To this establishment, to which another was added at Louvain,[1] the Holy See attached the greatest importance.[2] Nearly every year Wiggers visited the old mission stations. On May 23rd, 1611, the nuncio of Cologne, Antonio Albergati, charged him with the visitation of the Netherlands and the adjoining territories, giving him at the same time extensive faculties for the reception of heretics into the Church. Dressed as a layman, Wiggers set out on his arduous journey, one result of which was the decision to entrust to the Franciscans of the Province of Cologne the administration of the previously founded Dutch mission station. The first administrator was Arnold von Witt. From 1613 onwards this man—whom men called the "universal providence", journeyed from place to place, amid great perils, saying Mass and administering the sacraments at night. In 1617 he was joined by Antony Verweg who had been working at Amsterdam, Haarlem and Northern Friesland. In 1621 they were given the assistance of two other Fathers.[3]

The Jesuits also prosecuted their missionary task. By 1606 their numbers had risen from three to six; in 1611 there were fourteen, and in 1622 no less than twenty-two Fathers were at work in the various provinces of the Netherlands. Theirs was an arduous, wandering existence, but their labours were frequently rewarded with splendid results. Thus we read of one Father converting 200 Anabaptists and another 300.[4]

[1] See BENTIVOGLIO, *Relationi*, 153, and *Archief. v.h. aartsbisd. Utrecht*, XX., 355. *Cf. Fr. Dusseldorpii Annales*, ed. Fruin, (1893), 321 *seq.*, 397, 441, 469; *Bijdrag v.d. geschied. v.h. bisd. Haarlem*, I. (1873), 435 *seq.*, VIII. (1880), 1 *seq.*

[2] See DE RAM, in *Annuaire de l'univ. de Louvain*, 1875; *Archief. v.h. aartsbisd. Utrecht*, XXXII. (1907), 382 *seqq.*; *Bijdrag v.h. bisd. Haarlem*, VIII. (1880), 12 *seq.*

[3] See *Hist.-polit. Blätter*, CXXXVI., 812 *seq.*

[4] *Cf.* besides IUVENCIUS, *P. V.* tom. post., 216 *seq.*, and PONCELET, *Jésuites en Belgique*, 33, the special reports in the *Litt. annuae Soc. Iesu*, 1606, p. 393 *seq.*; 1608, p. 657 *seq.*; 1609, p. 257 *seq.*; 1611, p. 335 *seq.*; 1612, p. 387 *seq.*; 1613–

The numerous disputes between the native clergy and the Jesuit missionaries were settled with the help of Paul V.[1] though by no means for good and all. This was all the more regrettable as the situation of the Catholics in the Netherlands remained painful enough. In his report of 1617, Rovenius gives some details of the persecution to which they were subjected. If Catholics do not have their marriages blessed by a preacher, they are looked upon as living in concubinage, and if their children are not christened in a Calvinist church, the parents have to pay a fine. The Jews and Mohammedans are better off in Holland than the Catholics: the Jews have their synagogues, the Mohammedans are free to hold their meetings, Dutch tolerance embraces all sects and heresies—Catholics alone are excluded.[2]

Almost everywhere Catholics were debarred from public offices, and even the privilege of private worship had to be bought with heavy fines.[3] The courage of the Catholics was only equalled by their spirit of self-sacrifice. To raise the sums they had to pay for the privilege of private worship, they refused to appeal to foreign Catholics, for they deemed it a privilege to contribute with their own resources to the preservation of the ancient faith. At Amsterdam, in particular, certain spirited citizens fitted out rooms in private houses, or in warehouses, for the holding of religious services. Thus it came about that to this day certain churches bear the names

1614, p. 331 *seq.* A list of the Superiors of the Jesuits is in **Notizia delle missioni dei PP. Gesuiti nell'Olanda* (*Fondo Gesuit., n.* 1263 of the Vittorio Emanuele Library, Rome); see BLOK, *Verslag van onderzoekingen naar Archivalia in Italië*, 's Gravenhage, 1901, 66. *Cf.*, too, *Archief v.h. aartsbisd. Utrecht*, VI., 8 *seq.* For the missionary journey of P. Joh. Ryser, see ALLARD, *Eene missiereis door Noord-Nederland in de 17e eeuw* (1616–1617), 's Hertogenbosch, 1883.

[1] See BENTIVOGLIO, *Relationi*, 155. *Cf.* CAUCHIE-MAERE, *Recueil*, 47, 67 *seq.*; *Archief v.h. aartsbisd. Utrecht*, XXXII (1907), 412 *seq.*

[2] See the report of ROVENIUS in *Archief v.h. aartsbisd. Utrecht*, XVII., 456; HUBERT, 64.

[3] See ROVENIUS, *loc. cit.*, XX., 356; *cf.* 362.

of old warehouses, for instance," de Krijtberg." A striking picture of the situation of Catholics at Amsterdam at that time is found in an account written in 1617 by the Jesuit, John Ryser, a native of that city. He points out that in that city, now a world emporium, all religions were tolerated; Catholics alone were subjected to penal laws. "Day and night," so he reports, "the 'Schouten' (officials) with their spies are on the alert, with a view to disturbing the assemblies of the faithful. Women, too, are hired whose duty it is to keep an eye on all streets and houses where Catholics live; at times these women go so far as to pretend they are Catholics, in order to facilitate their treason. Quite recently we were compelled to pay 5,000 florins in order to free ourselves from further molestation on the part of the 'Schouten' and to make possible the escape of some priests who were on the point of being arrested. In the course of this year one of our Fathers escaped on no less than ten separate occasions when his pursuers were hot on his heels; but at last his enemies had the satisfaction of venting their rage on the Church furniture which fell into their hands." [1]

The nuncio of Brussels, Bentivoglio, entertained the hope that it was precisely these persecutions that would eventually lead to a great revival of religion in the Netherlands.[2] Another consoling fact was the growing number of conversions [3] which were due in no small measure to the disputes between the Gomarists and the Arminians and of which the Calvinist preachers were the cause. These controversies were still further embittered by political divisions. The regent, Maurice of Orange, was keen on being sole master of the country. He thought it would be to his advantage to league himself with the Gomarists, who were very numerous, and thus to

[1] See H. J. ALLARD, *De St. Franciscus Xaverius-Kerk of de Krijtberg*, Maastricht, 1883, 19 *seq.*

[2] See BENTIVOGLIO, *Relationi*, 155.

[3] See KNUTTEL, I., 83 *seq.*; ALLARD, *loc. cit.*, 23; CAUCHIE MAERE, *Recueil*, 67, 87 *seq.* A college erected in Cologne, by Paul V., for the "eretici convertiti", is mentioned in the *Visite*, LI., p. 22 *seq.* of the Propaganda Archives, Rome.

crush the Arminians as well as the more important republicans. The aged Oldenbarneveldt, on a false accusation that he showed Catholic leanings, was beheaded; the famous Hugo Grotius was thrown into prison. The Synod of Dortrecht proclaimed the Calvinist doctrine of predestination in its most extreme form and deposed 200 preachers who were known to be holding Arminian opinions; others were sent into banishment, among whom were the famous scholars, John Vossius, Caspar Barlæus, and Peter Bertius. The philologist and archeologist Bertius found an asylum in France and it was there that, on July 25th, 1620, he came back to the Catholic Church.[1] Quite apart from the erroneousness of the doctrine proclaimed as a dogma by the Synod of Dortrecht,[2] according to which the grace of God and justification can co-exist with the most shameful crimes, the assembly showed up the inherent weakness of Protestantism. On the other hand "it formally appealed to the promise made by Christ to His Church, that He would be with her until the end of time, whilst according to Protestant assertion He had forsaken her for a thousand years and abandoned her to the grossest errors".[3] The consequences of the victory of the Calvinist extremists at the Synod of Dortrecht were all the more serious for the Dutch Catholics as, with the expiration of the truce between Spain and Holland, (A.D. 1621), a stricter surveillance came in force. A decree of February 26th, 1622, forbade all foreign priests to enter Dutch territory and prohibited the exercise of Catholic worship even in private houses, under threat of heavy fines.[4] Nevertheless, even so, there

[1] See RASZ, IV., 500 *seq.* *Cf.* H. J. ALLARD, *Petrus Bertius*, 's Hertogenbosch, 1870. Macaulay, Fruin, and others rightly condemn the execution of Oldenbarneveldt as a judicial murder. See BLOK, IV., 249.

[2] *Cf.* KAAJAN, *De groote Synode v. Dortrecht, 1618–1619*, Amsterdam, 1918.

[3] This is DÖLLINGER's view (*Kirchengesch.*, 916). *Cf.* POHLE, in the *Freiburg Kirchenlex.*, III.², 1987.

[4] See HUBERT, 66 *seqq.* *Cf.* KNUTTEL, I., 89 *seq.*; CAUCHIE-MAERE, *Recueil*, 114.

appeared no symptom anywhere that the government would attain its end which was nothing less than the uprooting of Catholicism. The Catholics, who, as Oldenbarneveldt assured the British ambassador in 1618, constituted the wealthiest as well as the most sterling section of the population,[1] clung tenaciously to their faith. The persecution which they had to endure was all the more unjust since, as the same Oldenbarneveldt pointed out in his defence, a large section of the Papists had at all times shown themselves true patriots.[2]

(2.)

James I., since 1603 King of England, Scotland and Ireland,[3] fancied himself as a master in the art of governing. The double-dealing, shilly-shallying policy with which he sought to take in the adherents of the old faith as well as those of the new, in the first years of his reign, may, as a matter of fact, have appeared in his eyes as a particularly good exhibition of statecraft. In reality, however, and not least by his attitude towards Catholics, he justified Macaulay's saying that the "Solomon of the North" the "Master of the art of governing" seemed specially predestined to call up everywhere the powers of disruption.[4] The peaceful opening of his reign was rightly considered to be due to his explicit declarations. Hence, when he reopened the war, though there had been no provocation, he drew universal odium on himself by reason of his duplicity,[5] and when he vacillated for a while,

[1] "Het rijkste en deftigste deel der natie," see FRUIN, *Tien jaren uit den tachtigjarigen oorlog*, Haag, 1889, 237.

[2] See FRUIN, *Verspreide geschriften*, III., 342.

[3] He seems to have had a good mind to assume the Imperial title. (A. O. MEYER, in *Quellen u. Forsch. aus ital. Archiven*, X. (1907), 231–7).

[4] "One of those kings whom God seems to send for the express purpose of hastening revolutions" (*Critical and Historical Essays*, II., Leipzig, 1850, 27).

[5] "The King is so odious to all sorts," said Lord Mounteagle to Garnet ("Garnet's Declaration," March 9, 1606, in the *Eng. Hist. Review*, III. (1888), 511).

those able to see below the surface were no longer deceived by his double-dealing. Nevertheless, the Superior of the Jesuits, Henry Garnet, wrote in August, 1605, that he thought he could guarantee in general that the Catholics, trusting the king, or his successors, would persevere in their wonted endurance.[1] As late as October of that year he repeated his statement, at least so far as the better sort of Catholics were concerned,[2] but he now added that it was not possible to answer for individuals whom the tyrannical procedure of harsh officials might well drive to some desperate deed: he hoped that, in his wisdom, the king would prevent such a contingency.

Desperate deeds had in fact been preparing for some time. Daring foolhardiness and reckless violence lay in the blood of the contemporaries of Drake and Hawkins, so that it would have been strange indeed if none of the English Catholics of the period had never asked themselves whether they were really bound in conscience to suffer themselves to be robbed and slain without offering resistance, and whether to meet the violence of the king and Parliament with violence could not be considered as an act of legitimate self-defence.[3] Robert Catesby, a wealthy and distinguished nobleman, who had been heavily fined for being a Catholic, in conversation with Garnet, gave it as his opinion, barely six months after James I.'s accession, that by breaking his word the king had sown the seeds of trouble. The Jesuit replied that the Pope was opposed to violent measures and that his own General, Aquaviva, had communicated to him, in July, an instruction of Clement VIII. to that effect. Garnet begged Catesby and his friend Winter to have nothing to do with a violent coup, were it only that their known relations with the Jesuits

[1] FOLEY, IV., 62.

[2] "I am assured, notwithstanding, that the best sort of Catholics will bear all their losses with patience," (*ibid.*, 63).

[3] "It would be strange if there were not some amongst them who would be driven to meet wrong with violence," is also GARDINER's opinion (I., 234.)

would cause the latter to be suspected of having instigated it. Thereupon Catesby promised to proceed no further.[1]

However, his resolution did not last. Garnet had, at the proper time, informed Catesby and Winter of the two Briefs of Clement VIII., in which the Pope instructed English Catholics to give their support only to a sincerely Catholic pretender to the throne.[2] Catesby now referred to these Briefs. If in midsummer of 1604 it was lawful to do one's best to prevent a non-Catholic from securing the crown, it was surely permissible to try and make him lose it? This reasoning Garnet met with the new papal instruction and once again he successfully stayed Catesby's hand[3]; at four different times, as he subsequently wrote to his General, he had succeeded in preventing a deed of violence.[4]

However Garnet did not delude himself: he knew that he would not be able to restrain for ever the exasperation and despair of men like Catesby. The prestige of the priests was no longer what it had been; it was bound to sink to an even lower level, since, during the disputes at the time of the appointment of an archpriest, a controversy had arisen in their own ranks as to the attitude they should adopt towards the government.[5] The question was freely discussed whether priests, who were for ever concerned with the hereafter and the supernatural, were really the right persons to issue final decisions on the concerns of this world. "Everybody is in despair," Garnet wrote to Rome on May 8th, 1605, "and many Catholics are hostile to the Jesuits; they say that the Jesuits oppose and prevent the use of force in any shape. I dare not attempt to ascertain what their future plans are since the General has forbidden us to meddle with such things."[6] One day, whilst Garnet was at table with Catesby,

[1] Garnet's trial, March 13, 1606, in FOLEY, IV., 157.

[2] See our notes, Vol. XXIV., p. 40.

[3] Garnet's trial, March 14, 1606, in FOLEY, IV., 159.

[4] "Et quidem pro mea parte quater hactenus tumultum impedivi." Garnet to Aquaviva, July 24, 1605, *ibid.*, 61.

[5] *Cf.* our notes, Vol. XXIV., p. 27 *seqq.*

[6] FOLEY, IV., 60.

he spoke of the duty of enduring the persecution with patience. Thereupon Catesby got very angry: "It is principles like these that are responsible for the misfortunes of English Catholics," he exclaimed, "neither priests nor Popes can take away the right to meet wrong with violence."[1] As a matter of fact, at the time of Clement VIII.'s prohibition of all violent measures, many Catholics had taken the liberty to ask whether the Pope could forbid them to defend their lives?[2]

Nonetheless Catesby would have welcomed a word from a priest which might be interpreted as an approval of his scheme. To this end, and without a hint as to his ulterior intention, on June 9th, 1605, Catesby had with Garnet the fateful conversation which the latter was destined to expiate by death at the executioner's hand. Catesby's insidious question was thus formulated: "Supposing that it is lawful, in a given instance, to kill one or more persons, if the attempt on their lives would also cause the death of some innocent persons, would there be any obligation to consider the latter?" Garnet replied that in every just war it was lawful to destroy houses, fortifications, castles without considering the innocent, if it was necessary for victory.[3] When he gave this answer Garnet never dreamt that Catesby could use it

[1] SPILLMANN, IV., 27.

[2] Garnet to Aquaviva, July 24, 1605, in FOLEY, IV., 61.

[3] "Whether, in case it were lawfull to kill a person or persons, it were necessary to regard the innocents which were present lest they also should perish withall. I answered that in all just warres it is practised & held lawfull to beate down houses & walles & castells, notwithstanding innocents were in danger . . ." (Garnet's Declaration, March 9, 1606, published by GARDINER, in the *English Hist. Review*, III. (1888), 510). According to Coke, Garnet's accuser in his trial, Catesby's question had been: "Whether for the good & promotion of the catholic cause against heretics, it be lawful or not among so many nocents to destroy some innocents also." Thus also GARDINER (I., 274). However, Coke could not substantiate his accusation; see LINGARD, VII., 48, note.

to forward his own designs. Before long, however, the Jesuit's suspicion was roused. Consequently, at their next meeting, Garnet supplemented his solution of the case with the statement that the action which would entail the death of the innocent parties must be lawful in itself, and the innocent people in question must not be persons whose lives were necessary to the general good.[1]

Catesby's own actions now convinced Garnet that something was in the air. In conformity with the direction of his General, he made no effort to ascertain what it was, for even mere cognizance of such things was fraught with extreme danger. According to English law he should have denounced Catesby on mere suspicion, but Garnet was anxious to use gentler means at first, and in doing so he had in mind an express papal prohibition of rebellion. In conversation with Lord Mounteagle, Catesby and his associate Francis Tresham, he obtained from all three a formal admission of the fact that an armed rising was hopeless. Thereupon Garnet remarked that this showed how unjust it was to blame the Jesuits if the Catholics did not fight for their rights; as a matter of fact, in view of the circumstances, the only possible course was calm resignation; it was in this sense that he would report to the Pope through his General.[2]

Even before Garnet had time to act on this decision he and Blackwell received, through Aquaviva, a papal command to oppose with the utmost energy any attempt to cause a rising on the part of Catholics. He lost no time in laying the papal document before Catesby. "If the Pope knew what is at stake he would not try to stop me," was Catesby's answer. Garnet then urged that the papal prohibition was a formal command. Catesby replied that he was under no obligation to accept Garnet as interpreter of the Pope's wishes. In that case, Garnet said, let him personally tell the Pope what he was aiming at. Catesby would not hear of this, because of the risk of discovery, but in the end he

[1] Gardiner, in the *English Hist. Review,* III. (1888), 511.
[2] *Ibid.,* 511 *seq.*

promised not to attempt anything until the Pope should have been informed of everything by special messenger. For this mission Garnet then proposed a certain Bainham who was going to Flanders in any case.[1]

Garnet thought he had won the day for nothing would happen before the Pope's decision, and it was not difficult to foresee what this decision would be. For all that, in a report to his General, dated July 24th, 1605, he painted the situation in sombre colours.[2] The Jesuits, he said, would be able to prevent a general rising of Catholics—they still wielded sufficient authority to do that much. But should there be a rising in any part of the country, or should a few hotheads have recourse to violence, it was possible that by degrees all the Catholics would be dragged into the current. A papal prohibition couched in general terms would not be effectual with all Catholics ; the Pope, therefore, should state in detail what may be done and what must be avoided, and enforce his command with a threat of excommunication and other penalties. The letter alludes to Bainham's mission to Rome. Because of the distrust which some felt of the priests, more especially the Jesuits, they had been advised, in order to gain time, to apply to the Pope directly. Bainham's departure was delayed until September and Garnet's reasons for a more severe prohibition of any form of agitation were not found convincing in Rome. The fact was that he could not say all he already knew at that moment about the plot. Twice Catesby had offered to reveal his plans ; twice Garnet declined the dangerous knowledge. At last he learned the secret, *against his will and to his great horror*. Eight noblemen had conceived the plan, on the occasion of the opening of Parliament, on November 5th, to blow up the king and the whole house of Parliament, after which they would provoke a general rising of the whole country, put one of the king's sons on the throne and establish a regency. The Jesuit Greenway had come to know everything, *in confession*,

[1] *Ibid.*, 512 *seq.*

[2] Foley, IV., 61. *Cf.* Garnet's confession, of March 8, 1606, *loc. cit.*, 514.

through Catesby, the organizer and instigator of the plot, and with Catesby's permission and likewise *under the seal of confession*, he had informed Garnet, his Superior, for the purpose of getting his advice. We may well believe Garnet when he assures us that he was never more upset in his whole life and that the knowledge kept him awake at night.[1] There was question here, not only of a monstrous crime, but also of a piece of folly which could only have disastrous consequences for the Catholics of England in general, and for the Jesuits in particular, and he had to keep silence whilst the catastrophe was approaching, *nor could he move a finger to prevent it, for according to Catholic discipline, the seal of confession is utterly inviolable and precludes any use whatever of the secret information thus obtained.*

Thus the fatal fifth of November drew near, a dreadful day, not for the king and the government, but for the Catholics. At an early hour in the morning the awful news spread through the city that an enormous quantity of gunpowder had been discovered under the assembly hall of parliament, in the basement of the building, and that in the night a desperado had been arrested there who was making the final preparations for setting fire to the powder. The plot had been discovered and foiled at the last moment. Horror of the ruthless attempt, detestation of the old religion, the proud conviction that a kindly Providence had watched over the Protestants and taken their part as against the criminal Catholics—such were the feelings which, in the course of the ensuing weeks, grew ever stronger in the Protestant mass of the people. On the night of November 5th, all the bells of the city rang out and the sky was red with the reflection of the bonfires which were lit in every street.[2] Parliament alone seemed but little effected by the general excitement. Though it had only just escaped death, it nevertheless met in that same

[1] "Now I remained in the greatest perplexity that ever I was in my life, & could not sleepe nights. . . . Every day I did offer up all my devotions & Masses, that God . . . would dispose all for the best. . . . (Confession of March 8, 1605, *loc. cit.*, 515).

[2] GARDINER, I., 250 *seq.*, 265.

building from the basement of which it would hardly have been possible to remove by then so enormous a quantity of powder, supposing it to have been there. Coolly, as if nothing had happened, the house discussed various measures in regard to commercial relations with Spain as well as the letter of one of its members who excused his absence by pleading an attack of gout.[1]

The conspirators had fled on the morning of the day and attempted to bring about a rising of the Catholics. Everywhere they preached to deaf ears and all doors were closed to them.[2] On November 8th, they were rounded up at Holbeche. In the affray Catesby and three others were shot dead, the rest, together with their servants, were made prisoners.[3] It would seem that Catesby and those who fell with him at Holbeche, expressed regret for what they had done before they expired.[4] Sentence was pronounced on the survivors on January 27th, amid an immense concourse of people, and on January 31st and February 1st, 1606, they died at the executioner's hand. One of the conspirators, Francis Tresham, had died in prison, on December 22nd. When his associates fled he remained in London and the government treated him with surprising leniency.

During the next few days, following the discovery of the criminal plot, London remained in complete uncertainty as to its details. At the moment only one of the culprits was in the hands of justice, Guy Fawkes, who had been caught at the entrance of the house of Parliament, on the night before the fifth of November. The numerous interrogatories to which he had been subjected had yielded no result of any value, when the government received, from an unknown source, a list of all the conspirators. This list was promptly published, though with the omission of Tresham's name. An account dated November 7th, to which further additions were

[1] *Ibid.*, 285.
[2] "Not a soul was willing to share their fate," (*ibid.*, 261).
[3] *Ibid.*, 257–263.
[4] *Ibid.*, 264.

made two days later, was supposed to give full information to the foreign princes of all that had occurred. For the populace a "True and perfect relation" was published. In March, an address delivered by James I. on November 9th, to the house of Parliament, on the subject of the plot, and the two most important admissions of the conspirators, were put together in a volume which became the famous *King's Book*.[1] According to this information the original plan was to undermine the house of Parliament. To this end a nearby house was rented and, though the conspirators were not used to the rough work of the miner, since they were all gentlemen of rank, they nevertheless set themselves the task of piercing through the foundations of the house and to dig a tunnel. They were already half-way through the thick foundation of the house of Parliament when it suddenly dawned upon the clumsy toilers that their exertions were unnecessary. They could achieve their purpose in a much simpler manner by just hiring the room beneath the assembly hall of Parliament which was used to store coal, wood and other odds and ends. So it was done and thirty-six barrels of gunpowder, about 9,000 pounds in all, were gradually accumulated in the vault.

However, as the date of the execution of the dreadful plot drew near, some of the conspirators became increasingly uneasy at the thought that among so many members of Parliament several Catholic peers would also meet their death. One of Catesby's chief associates, Thomas Percy, was in the service of the [illegible] of Northumberland; Francis Tresham was related by marriage to Lord Stourton and Lord Mounteagle, whilst Lord Montague and the young Earl of Arundel enjoyed the esteem of all their Catholic corregionists.[2] So it came about that one of the conspirators—

[1] The studies of DAVID JARDINE, in the *Criminal Trials*, II., London, 1832, and *A Narrative of the Gunpowder Plot*, London, 1857, are essential to a scientific study of the situation.

[2] GARDINER, I., 246. Mounteagle, moreover, wrote to the king not later than 1605, that he wished to become a Protestant (*ibid.*, 254). He did indeed apostatize later on.

Tresham, without a doubt,[1] wrote a letter to Lord Mounteagle, couched in mysterious phrases, warning him not to take part in the opening of Parliament. Mounteagle communicated the letter to the Earl of Salisbury who, in his turn, showed it to other peers and eventually to the king himself. The cryptic turn of the letter sufficiently hinted that there was question of a murderous attempt to be brought off by means of gunpowder. There followed a search of the house of Parliament, the discovery of the powder hidden under bundles of sticks and piles of wood and, eventually, the arrest of Fawkes.

The three official accounts contain more than one contradiction [2] and, quite apart from this fact, it cannot be denied that they are full of improbabilities. It is difficult to understand how it was possible to remove unnoticed the mass of earth, and the stones of the walls that had to be breached, whilst the tunnel was being dug.[3] When, at a later period, the foundation walls of the house of Parliament were laid bare, there was no sign of the alleged breach. When we are further informed that about four tons of powder, in over thirty casks, were bought and conveyed first to a house on the left bank of the Thames, and from there across the river, to the house they had rented, and from there finally to the house of Parliament, all without attracting attention or

[1] *Ibid.*, 251.

[2] GERARD, in *The Month*, LXXXIII. (1895), 487 *seq.*; XC. (1897), 238 *seq.*, 363. A. JESSOPP, in the *Dictionary of National Biography*, IX., 283, considers that: "In the confused tangle of testimony and contradiction, of confession under torture, hearsay reports and dexterous prevarication on which the story of the Gunpowder Plot is based, it is difficult to unravel the thread of a narrative which is told in so many different ways."

Cf. GERARD for the documents of the Gunpowder Plot, *The Month*, XC. (1897), 356.

[3] The plan of the conspirators, to break through the walls of the foundations, is called even by RANKE (*Engl. Gesch.*, I., 538), "a plan which testifies more to their zeal than to their commonsense, & one which they would hardly have been able to carry out."

suspicion, we do not think the tale a convincing one. As for the story of the letter to Mounteagle, its particulars are so peculiar that it is generally rejected.[1]

It is highly probable that the government had long known all about the conspiracy and that it had purposely allowed it to mature in order to exploit it, at the right moment, for its own purposes.[2] Nevertheless the main features of the traditional account appear to correspond with facts. A plan for the blowing up of Parliament was decided upon [3] and preparations were made for its execution ; how far they got will never be known.[4]

[1] Jardine is of opinion that Mounteagle was informed by Tresham of all the details of the conspiracy, and handed them on to Salisbury ; the letter was, he thinks, a pure forgery of the government, in order to cover the true course of events when the plot was revealed. GARDINER (I., 252 *seq.*) contradicts these statements ; according to him the government received the first news of the conspiracy through the letter ; he thinks Tresham and Mounteagle agreed to frustrate and betray the plot, but in such a way that the conspirators should have time to flee. The letter was designed for this purpose and its wording agreed upon by both before its transmission to Mounteagle.

[2] SALISBURY wrote on November 9, 1605, in his *Despatch* to the ambassador in Spain : " Not but that I had sufficient advertisement, that most of those that now are fled (being all notorious Recusants) with many other of that kind, had a practice in hand for some stirre this Parliament " (in GERARD, *loc. cit.*, LXXXIII. (1895), 491 ; LXXXIV. (1895), 34 *seq.* ; XC. (1897), 357 ; PRAMPAIN, in the *Rev. d. quest. hist.*, XL. (1886), 428 *seq.* Many Catholics were of opinion that Salisbury had been the instigator and secret head of the conspiracy (PRAMPAIN, 429 note).

[3] This transpires from Garnet's trial and confession ; see below, p. 149 *seq.*

[4] The Gunpowder Plot and the question of the credibility of the reports and documents on it, were the subject of a controversy between John Gerard and S. R. Gardiner. *Cf.* J. GERARD, *What was the Gunpowder Plot ?*, London, 1897 ; GARDINER, *What Gunpowder Plot was*, *ibid.*, 1897 ; GERARD, *The Gunpowder Plot and the Gunpowder Plotters. In reply to Professor Gardiner*, *ibid.*, 1897 ; *Thomas Winter's Confession and the Gunpowder Plot*, *ibid.*,

The official reports, the aim of which was to influence public opinion in a certain direction, are adorned with exaggerated and arresting details, with a view to arousing the passions of the populace and exploiting the whole affair so as to serve the designs of the leading politicians. The intention was that the man in the street should be seized with horror and indignation at the mere thought of the sect which was known to shun the light and which was busy undermining the ground beneath the home of the honest citizen, and even beneath the State itself.[1] These accounts were spread not in England alone, they were also dispatched to the ambassadors at foreign courts and translated into different languages and thus they found their way all over Europe.[2] As late as the time of the Titus Oates conspiracy (1679) a new edition of the so-called *King's Book* was published to add fuel to popular excitement.[3]

Catesby's mad attempt came most opportunely for the government. The king's honour was tainted by perjury: for after giving to the adherents of the old religion grounds

1898. Gerard may be said to have demonstrated that the Government had information about the conspiracy, long before the Mounteagle letter, that it exploited the discovered plot most unscrupulously for the annihilation of the Catholics, and that the details of the traditional account sound very unlikely. On the other hand he may have gone too far in attacking the main points of the accepted story. *Cf.* PFÜLF, in the *Stimmen aus Maria-Laach*, LIV. (1899), 41 *seqq.*, 142 *seqq.*, 286 *seqq.*

[1] JARDINE (*Gunpowder Plot*, viii. and 214, in GERARD, *The Month*, LXXXIII. (1895), 12) describes the "True & perfect relation", of the Government as entirely untrustworthy and dishonest, showing that some of the depositions were deliberately falsified; that everything not supported by other documents, must be regarded with suspicion; fables were mingled with undeniable truths, so that the whole account might appear credible, etc., *The Encyclopædia Britannica*, XII. (1910), 720, also states that the "True & perfect relation", is, "a neither true nor complete narrative however, now superseded as an authority."

[2] GERARD, *loc. cit.*, 24.

[3] *Ibid.*, 25.

to hope for toleration, he had cruelly disappointed them. But he would be safe from reproach, the new persecution would be justified and the lingering respect for the ancient Church would be profoundly shaken, if this unfortunate deed could be represented as the act of Catholics and if people could be made to believe it. Salisbury desired the destruction of Catholicism [1]; moreover, up to that moment, he had not been popular, nor was he sure of the favour of his Sovereign.[2] The plot provided him with an occasion to prove to king and people alike how indispensable he was.[3]

A popular proverb of the period, "Property lost, reason lost!" [4] may help us to understand to some extent how the most elementary moral principles came to be lost sight of by men such as Catesby and his associates. An even greater confusion of ideas is revealed in the efforts for the destruction of Catholicism on which the leading English statesmen were now about to enter. All regard for truth and justice was cast aside by them with almost incredible callousness; deliberate lying, cheating, falsification, were deemed legitimate means when there was question of dealing a blow to the greatly hated Church.

In this respect the king himself gave the example. Not long after the discovery of the plot the archpriest Blackwell, in a circular, had condemned the plot in severest terms.[5] On his part the Pope had repeatedly forbidden every form of rebellion or violence.[6] As soon as the attempt became known,

[1] WILLAERT, in *Rev. d'hist. ecclés.*, VIII. (1907), 94.

[2] GERARD, in *The Month*, LXXXIII., 2 *seq.*

[3] *Ibid.*, LXXXIV., 51 *seqq.*

[4] "Qu'il n'y peult avoir seurté tandis que les catholicques seront rudement traittés et qu'on continuera a leur prendre leurs biens, n'estant que trop véritable ce qu'on dict en commung proverbe, que qui perdt son bien, perdt son sens." The regents Albert and Isabella, to their ambassador Hoboken, in London, March 18, 1606, in WILLAERT, *loc. cit.*

[5] He called it "an intolerable, uncharitable, scandalous & desperate fact", "a detestable device" (GERARD, *loc. cit.*).

[6] *Cf.* present work, p. 130.

Paul V., through the French ambassador in London, assured the king that he abhorred and condemned the authors of the dastardly attempt more than any man; if it is proved, as has been mooted, that some of the Jesuits played a part in it, they must be punished with the rest; the Pope's only desire was that the innocent should not be lumped together with the guilty and that the former should not be made to suffer instead of the criminals.[1]

Even before this declaration James I. was well acquainted with the views of the Roman court. For all that, in an address to Parliament, on November 9th, 1605, he threw the responsibility for the plot on the papacy and its teaching. Neither Turks, nor Jews, nor idolaters, the king said, no, not even the pagans of Calicut who worshipped the devil, in a word, no sect of any kind had ever affirmed, on grounds of its own religion, that it was lawful, or, as the Catholics say, meritorious, to kill princes or to work for the subversion of the State. No doubt there were honourable men, even among

[1] LA BODERIE, *Ambassades*, I. (*sine loco*), 1750, 25, in GERARD, *loc. cit.*, 6. A Brief, in BELLESHEIM, *Scotland*, III., 420 *seqq.*; to James I. of July 11, 1606, as follows: As Cardinal & former Protector of the Scotch Catholics, he had seen with joy the son of Mary Stuart, whose relationship to Clement VIII. he knew well, ascend the throne. The expression of his sentiments was delayed by the " nuntius molestissimus coniurationis ", especially as some Catholics were reported to be involved in it. Now that We hear that a Catholic revealed the plot, We congratulate You & beg, " ne innocentibus catholicis regni tui aliena flagitia noceant." He hoped for the return of James to the Church to which all his ancestors had belonged. He was sending Jean Maillane of Lorraine to plead for the Catholics before the king, but he was not to let them know his mission. We desire their obedience. " Non vestra quaerimus, sed vos." He hoped that the king, in view of the great number of religious opinions, would inquire earnestly into the truth, & offered him the assistance of theologians. On the same date Paul V. *wrote to Philip III. of Spain, who had urged the Pope to write to James I.; he informed Philip of the contents of his letter. *Epist.*, II., 75. Papal Secret Archives.

the Popes, who either did not know or did not believe in, the horrible and accursed doctrines of the papacy, that true "mystery of iniquity"[1]; hence not all the papists of past times were to be thought of as excluded from eternal life; but no man who has adopted the principles of that superstition with full knowledge, and who clings to them with obstinate tenacity, may lay claim to be a true Christian or a good citizen.[2] In his letters, James I. spoke even more bitterly: "I learn from his Majesty's messengers," writes John Harrington, "that these attempts were not engineered by a few persons only, but the whole legion of Catholics was called to counsel; the priests soothed their consciences and the Pope granted a general absolution for this splendid undertaking from which so much glory would accrue to God and to His holy religion."[3] Politicians also talked of machinations which proceeded from Rome and from Satan.[4] In February, 1606, Salisbury explained to Hoboken, the Flemish envoy, that the Pope had instigated the plot which was itself but the outcome of Catholic teaching.[5]

In the interrogation of the conspirators the government did its best to obtain evidence of the complicity of the priests.[6]

[1] 2 Thess. ii, 7.

[2] "Quamobrem et Papistas maiores nostros, si qui sub vitae finem in unius Christi crucifixi merito spem fidemque collocarunt, fatemur aeternae vitae factos compotes, et Puritanorum crudelitatem, qui omnes Papistas citra exceptionem ignibus adiudicant, flammis censemus expiandam. . . . At nemo certa cognitione eius superstitionis principia intelligit, iisque constanti fiducia adhaeret, qui veri christiani vel boni civis nomen tueri queat" (IACOBI REGIS, *Opera*, 235).

[3] GERARD, *loc. cit.*, 5.

[4] "Abominable practice of Rome and Satan" (Chichester to Salisbury on receiving notice of the discovery of the plot, in GERARD, *loc. cit.*).

[5] "Entra en long discours sur la dite trahison, disant entre autres propos que le pape estoit autheur d'icelle . . ." (WILLAERT, *loc. cit.*, 91).

[6] "The great object of the Government now was to obtain evidence against the priests (GARDINER, I., 267). *Cf.* LINGARD, VII., 58.

Fawkes was made to undergo torture as early as May 9th,[1] for a long time all efforts were in vain. Eventually he confessed[2] that he had confided his plans to Hugh Owen, but he was not a priest but a soldier.[3] The conspirators, he further confessed, took an oath of secrecy and, with a view to confirming it, received Holy Communion in an adjoining room; he insisted, however, that Gerard was wholly ignorant of the plot.[4] Another conspirator, Thomas Winter, swore that no priest was among the conspirators,[5] whilst a third, Digby, declared that but for the opposition of the priests, trouble would have broken out long ago for the purpose of liberating the Catholics.[6] When Tresham was questioned in his turn, it was soon seen that he knew nothing of the alleged complicity of the priests.[7] So they questioned him on the mission which was sent to Madrid in 1602, for the purpose of securing Spain's help for the Catholics of England. He admitted that the Jesuits, Garnet and Greenway, knew of it, but later on, on his death-bed, he added that Garnet had nothing to do with the discussions.[8] Garnet imagined that the

[1] Gardiner, I., 266.

[2] November 9, 1605 (*ibid.*).

[3] Thus Ranke and rightly; *Engl. Gesch.*, I., 535. *Cf.* Lechat, 143; Prampain, in the *Rév. d. quest. hist.*, XL. (1886), 414; Gerard, in *The Month*, XC. (1897), 559; Willaert, *loc. cit.*, IX. (1908), 57 *seq.*, and the contemporary documents in Lechat, 237 and 239. Gardiner and many others, call Owen a Jesuit; even in the *Calendar of State Papers* he is always designated as "*Father Hugh Owen, the Jesuit*". The English ambassador at Brussels considered Catesby also as a Jesuit (Willaert, *loc. cit.*, VII. (1906), 597).

[4] Gardiner, I., 266; *cf.* 238.

[5] Prampain, *loc. cit.*, 440.

[6] *Ibid.*

[7] "Of their (the priests') connection with the great conspiracy it soon became evident that Tresham knew nothing" (Gardiner, I., 267).

[8] *Ibid.*, 267, 268. He adds (Foley, IV., 189): "that he had not seen him in fourteen years before" (read "sixteen"). That may mean that he had "not seen him during the last sixteen

journey was for the purpose of collecting alms for the English Catholics.[1]

The accused, who were all of gentle birth, stuck to these declarations to the end ; in fact they displayed such courage and constancy that one can only regret that they were not used in the service of a better cause.[2] However, one of their servants, a man of the name of Bates, had been let into the secret and he, on December 4th, was induced to make a deposition against the Jesuit Greenway. We have no means at this date to ascertain the nature of his deposition. In a later statement he pretended that all he meant was that he thought Greenway knew of the affair ; that he regretted his former statement, but trusted God would forgive him, for he had made it not through ill-will but to save his life. On its part the government exhibited a confession of Bates in which he was made to assert that he had discussed the plot with Greenway in confession and that the latter had given it his approval. Father Greenway himself declared, on his salvation, that Bates had never breathed a word about the

years" ; and it was interpreted thus at Garnet's trial without contradiction on the part of the much surprised Garnet (*loc. cit.*). Gardiner takes that view (I., 268 : "that he had neither seen nor heard from him for sixteen years"), and he therefore regards Tresham as a shameless and quite untrustworthy liar. But it may also mean that he had not seen Garnet during the sixteen years previous to 1602. (Garnet came to England in 1586, so that exactly sixteen years had elapsed by 1602) ; ZIMMERMAN accepts this interpretation (in *Katholik*, 1889, II., 276) and PRAMPAIN too (p. 458) ; and this supports Garnet's statement, March 23, 1606 (FOLEY, IV., 163), that he first met Tresham about eighteen years before, but then saw no more of him until between Essex's rising (1601) and the death of the Queen (1603). The context justifies the second interpretation.

[1] Garnet to Anne Vaux, March 2, 1606 ; Conversation with Oldcorne, February 25, 1606, in FOLEY, IV., 84, 150 *seq.* ; T. G. LAW, in the *Dictionary of National Biography*, LXII., 217.

[2] *Cf.* GARDINER, I., 264 : "There was at least nothing mean or selfish about them."

plot, neither in confession nor out of it.[1] In a further statement by Bates, on January 13th, Garnet's name also appears; Bates confessed that after the discovery of the plot and the escape of the conspirators, he took a letter of their's to Garnet.[2] Thus the names of at least three Jesuits were mentioned in the depositions of the witnesses and against two of them there were grounds for suspicion which justified a summons. From this time onward, in official documents, the government spoke as if the complicity of the Pope and the priests were a proven fact about which there could be no controversy.[3] On January 15th, 1606, a proclamation was issued for the arrest of the three Jesuits, Gerard, Greenway and Garnet, as the special instigators of the plot,[4] and though there was no charge against him, Gerard's name headed the list. On January 21st, 1606, Parliament ordered a special service of thanksgiving for its escape.[5] In the preamble of the ordinance "the Jesuits, the Seminarists and the Roman Priests" are described as the instigators of the plot. From that time the following rubric was inserted in the calendar of the *Book of Common Prayer* under November 5th: "Papists' Conspiracy,"[6] and in the official prayers of the day[7] thanks were returned "for the wonderful and mighty salvation" of the royal family, the peers, the clergy and the commons who had been "by popish treachery appointed as sheep to

[1] GERARD, in *The Month*, LXXXIII., 10 *seq.* Gerard tries to establish that before Bates' death, the confession brought forward by the government did not yet exist (p. 12 *seqq.*). GARDINER (I., 243, 270) agrees with Jardine that Greenway's guilt is proven. *Cf.* GERARD, *loc. cit.*, 360 *seq.*

[2] GARDINER, I., 260, 270.

[3] GERARD, in *The Month*, LXXXIII., 15 *seqq.*

[4] It states that it was "plain & evident from the examinations that all three had been peculiarly practisers in the plot, & therefore no less pernicious than the actors & counsellors of the treason." (Cf. LINGARD, VII., 76 *seq.*)

[5] It was observed for 250 years. GARDINER, I., 286.

[6] *Papists Conspiracy.*

[7] A. H. DANIEL, *Codex Liturgicus*, III., Leipzig, 1851, 550–6.

the slaughter, in a most barbarous and savage manner, beyond the examples of former ages ".[1] The indictment on the ground of which the instigators of the plot were tried on January 27th, 1606, does not show any more regard for truth. It asserts that Henry Garnet, Oswald Tesmond (Greenway), John Gerard, and other Jesuits had traitorously met together, and had maliciously, cunningly and traitorously alleged that the king, the peers, the clergy and the Commons were all heretics and excommunicated and had thereby incited the accused and their accomplices, now no longer living, to murder them.[2] The speeches of the attorneys are couched in similiar terms.

The accusations against the Jesuits did not remain unanswered. Gerard had handbills scattered in the streets of London in which he condemned the plot and denied his having had any knowledge of it. In a letter to Salisbury and to members of the Privy Council he likewise protested his innocence.[3] Garnet also wrote in a similiar strain to the Privy Council, on November 30th, 1605.[4] But these protests carried no weight with the masses. The definite charges contained in official documents were bound to prejudice public opinion against the accused. Thus, by means of bold lies, the government successfully got public opinion on its side. When in the course of the sitting of January 27th, one of the accused, Digby, alluded to the promises which the king had made to the Catholics and which he had not kept, Northampton boldly denied that James had ever given such assurances previous to his arrival in England.[5] Salisbury added

[1] *Ibid.*, 552.

[2] *State Trials*, I. (1809), 160, in GERARD, *loc. cit.*, 16.

[3] *Ibid.*, 15.

[4] Printed by FOLEY, IV., 67 *seqq.*

[5] " An assertion which was certainly untrue," says GARDINER, I., 269. Notwithstanding these falsehoods, Northampton did not win the confidence of the Protestants. After he had published his speech at Garnet's trial, it was commonly reported that he had secretly written to Bellarmine, begging him to attach no

that in July, 1603, the king had merely promised the remission of unpaid fines.[1]

Two of the three Jesuits thus publicly accused, viz. Greenway and Gerard, made good their escape over sea. Garnet, their Superior, made no attempt to flee, but lay in hiding in the old castle of Hindlip. There on January 30th, 1606, together with his brother in religion, Oldcorne, he fell into the hands of the pursuivants.

The name of the hated Superior of the Jesuits was known throughout England. His arrest was an event. When he was taken to Whitehall, on February 13th, to be questioned, the streets were thronged with people all eager to see the "provincial", the "Young Pope".[2] The government plan was to exploit their catch in order to brand in his person the whole Jesuit Order, but even more so the whole Catholic Church, and to ruin it in public opinion. In the words of the "True and perfect Relation", the trial was an opportunity "whereby there might be made visible an anatomy of popish doctrine, from whence these treasons have their source and support".[3]

On the very next day after Garnet's arrest the last of the conspirators were executed. The authorities were thus ready to forego the possibility of extorting any further charges against the Jesuit, but they did all they could, by threats and by snares, to entrap him by means of his own statements,

weight to his utterances; he was obliged to speak in this way merely to please the king and the people (*ibid.*, II., 159 *seq.*).

[1] Thereby stating, GARDINER writes, "what he must have known to be untrue" (I., 249).

[2] "There goes a young Pope," i.e. probably "one of the papal brood". Garnet to Anne Vaux, March 2, 1606, in FOLEY, IX., 82.

[3] "When this opportunitie was put into his (Salisbury's) hands, wherby there might be made so visible an anatome of popish doctrine, from whence these treasons have their source & support" (*True & Perfect Relation*, Y. in GERARD, *loc. cit.*, 22). *Cf.* Salisbury, in the law proceedings of March 28, 1606: "Wee shall see such an anatomy of the Popish doctrine, that I trust hereafter it will not have so manie followers" (in FOLEY, IV., 183).

for, as Salisbury wrote, "wee are forced, after soe long a suffering, to run a course more violent than standeth either with the ordinary rules of morall policy, or with the moderation of his Maties (Majesty's) mind." [1] When the interrogatories failed to yield any results, the governor of the prison was instructed to induce Garnet, by pretending interest and sympathy, to enter into epistolary relations with his friends. When his letters also failed to yield anything of consequence, the governor pointed out to Garnet a chink in the door of the next cell, in which Oldcorne was confined; hidden listeners then reported the conversation of the two Jesuits.[2] Garnet and Oldcorne had had ample opportunity, at Hindlip, to exchange views concerning the plot; for all that they dropped several remarks which could be used as pointers at the interrogatories.

A treatise on a question of moral theology, which was found in the house of Tresham, furnished a pretext, in the

[1] Salisbury, to Bruncard, March 3, 1606, in GERARD, *loc. cit.*, 21.

[2] Copies of their depositions in FOLEY, IV., 148–153. Oldcorne's report on these talks of March 25, 1606, *ibid.*, 228–232. Basing himself on one of these conversations (*ibid.*, 149), RANKE affirms (*Engl. Gesch.*, I., 537), that already in the time of Elisabeth, a plan existed for blowing up Parliament, and that Garnet had admitted this to be legitimate. . . . But just at this point, the spies remark that they had not quite understood ("his words *we conceived* tended to this purpose"); this testimony is therefore of no value. Not even Oldcorne himself understood everything clearly (FOLEY, IV., 228). GARNET denied on March 10, 1605 (*Engl. Hist. Review*, III. (1888), 517) that such a plan had existed under Elisabeth. As early as March 3, he writes to Anne Vaux (FOLEY, IV., 108): "M. Catesby did me much wrong, & hath confessed that he tould them that he said he asked me a question in Q. Eliz. time of the powder action, and that I said it was lawful . . . *All which is most untrue.*" According to Fawkes' confession a bag of gunpowder was to have been placed under Elizabeth's bed and set alight in the night (!). GERARD, in *The Month*, LXXXVIII. (1896), 406.

absence of other evidence, to represent Garnet as an arch-rogue to whose deposition no credence could be given. The treatise was on what is called "equivocation", and it bore corrections in Garnet's own hand so that it could be taken as expressing his ideas. A few explanatory remarks on "equivocation" are in order here,[1] for in those days it played a rôle not at Garnet's trial only.

It is related that on one occasion, when St. Athanasius was escaping upstream, his boat was overtaken by the barque of the imperial police. Thereupon the patriarch of Alexandria had his boat turned round and when his pursuers inquired where Athanasius was, he himself replied: "He is not far from here." Everyone will agree that such an answer is not a lie and no fault can be found with it. If we grant this much, we must also admit that a statement is not a lie because it misleads another, even though the mistake is foreseen or permitted by the speaker. The wrongfulness of a lie consists in that the speaker thinks one thing and says another, though he wishes his words to be taken as the true expression of his thought. Now there was no such opposition between St. Athanasius' thought and speech for his words truly represented his thought, though they also bore another meaning which, in fact, was the one in which the police took them; it was the only one they could think of. So we must allow that "equivocations" of this kind are lawful, when there is reasonable ground for their use and if the words can also be taken as a statement of fact.

However, it is necessary to go a step further. The presence of mind which enabled St. Athanasius to answer as he did, is not the gift of everybody and at every moment; there are a hundred cases when, in practice, a secret can only be effectually kept from unauthorized questioners if it is lawful to put them off with a decided "No!" A denial of this kind has always been held to be lawful whenever, in view of the circumstances of time, place, and so forth, it could be taken

[1] *Cf., e.g.*, V. CATHREIN, *Moralphilosophie*, II.[3], Freiburg, 1899, 86–8.

in two senses. If, for instance, a criminal is asked by the judge, previous to any evidence against him, whether he is guilty, he can reply in the negative for in the circumstances his " No " can be taken as meaning that no one can be compelled to be his own accuser and that the accused leaves the onus of proving his guilt to his judges.[1]

Garnet thought he could adopt the latter course at his own trial. To the question whether he had any knowledge of the plot, or whether he conversed with Oldcorne through the chink in the door, he at first replied in a decided negative. But eventually, when driven into a corner, he had to retreat step by step, and to make more than one admission. In an ordinary accused, this would have called forth no surprise, but in a priest it created a painful impression, all the more so as the average Englishman's entire mental outfit would probably lead him to admire a Guy Fawkes who, when arrested, smilingly admitted a deed which, he knew well, would lead to his being quartered, but who scorned every form of trickery or subterfuge. Garnet soon realized his mistake; he now gave an explanation of the line of conduct adopted by him up till then, and since a plain statement of the facts could not hurt anyone, for the conspirators were all dead, he decided, on March 9th, to make a full con-

[1] A certain John Ward, when arrested on January 16, 1606, is said to have attempted to save himself by giving evidence on oath; after his identification by witnesses he explained his oath as follows: he had said he was not a priest, i.e. not a priest of Apollo; that he had never been beyond the seas, i.e. not beyond the Indian seas; that he did not know the witness, i.e. not scientifically; that he had not seen him, i.e. not in the beatific vision (W. H. Frere, *The English Church in the Reigns of Elizabeth and James I.*, London, 1904, 328. This may be a preposterous invention, and certainly such " equivocations " cannot be disinguished from decided lies, for the words used in no way express the intended meaning. For Garnet's remarks about cases when an equivocation is not permissible, see Foley, IV., 190, 192; for Protestant judgments on the lawfulness of equivocations see *The Month,* LXXXIII., 358.

fession.[1] On the following day he added a few complementary details.[2] He admitted that he had a vague knowledge that some violent attempt was preparing, which he did his utmost to prevent, but that the real nature of the plot came to his knowledge solely under the seal of confession. However, Catesby had given him permission to make use even of the knowledge thus acquired.

That the interrogatories had yielded but scant material is shown by the embarrassment of the judges to find, for the final examination on March 28th, 1606, an accusation which would sufficiently compromise Garnet, and in his person, the Catholic Church. They were unwilling to condemn him for being a priest or for keeping the secret of confession, for they wanted him to die as a traitor, amid the execration of the populace.[3] His not having denounced Catesby and thereby handed him over to the executioner, as soon as he came by some vague knowledge of the former's schemes, might seem too slight an offence. In consequence, the indictment formally asserted that on June 9th, Garnet conspired with Catesby to kill the king and the heir to the crown, and that for this purpose he had had powder conveyed under the house of Parliament.[4] It was on June 9th, that Garnet had with Catesby a conversation in which he gave it as his opinion that in a just war it was lawful to kill the guilty even though

[1] Printed by GARDINER, in the *English Hist. Review*, III. (1888), 510–16. The document bears a superscription in Salisbury's hand, "This was forbidden by the king to be given in evidence."

[2] Reproduced by FOLEY, IV., 155 *seqq.*

[3] "It is expedient," wrote Salisbury, March 9, 1606, to the Earl of Mar, "to make it manifest to the world how farre these men's doctrine & practise trencheth into the bowells of treson. And so for ever after stopp the mouths of their calumniation that preach & print our laws to be executed for difference in point of conscience" (in GERARD, *loc. cit.*, 21).

[4] "... (that) hee had conspired with Rob. Catesby ... the death of our sovereigne lord ye king, and of his sonne. ... And for better accomplishment of his dyvellish practice, had caused closely to be conveyed a certaine quantity of powder under the Parliamenthouse" (in FOLEY, IV., 164 *seq.*).

the innocent perished with them.[1] If, when he gave this decision, Garnet knew that Catesby was thinking of an attempt on the life of the king, he would, without any doubt, be an accomplice in the conspiracy, hence some sort of evidence would have to be produced at least for the first part of the indictment.[2]

Evidence in support of the assertion was not to be thought of,[3] but this consideration did not greatly trouble the judges or the people.[4] When there was question of a political crime, the accused could scarcely ever hope for an acquittal in the England of those days. If the government of the time imagined that its tranquillity and security were being undermined by some dark power, its one thought was to destroy the secret plotter at one blow; whether this entailed an infringement of justice or the sacrifice of an innocent life was a secondary consideration. If this applied to any judicial procedure, how much more so in the case of a trial in which the Pope, the Catholic clergy, the seminarists, and the priests could be branded for ever?

Nothing was left undone to make Garnet's condemnation an important political event. The royal commission was made up of the highest officials and peers of the realm, the Lord Mayor of London, the Earls of Nottingham, Suffolk, Worcester, Northampton and Salisbury, the Lord Chief Justice, the first Lord of the Treasury together with Justice Selwyn.[5] There could have been no greater display had there been question of a Roman Cardinal, was Lord Salisbury's comment.[6] Consequently the sitting of March 28th, caused an immense

[1] See present work, p. 132.

[2] GARDINER, I., 277.

[3] Of this knowledge there was no legal proof whatever," says GARDINER (I., 278).

[4] For the system of administrative justice in force in England at the time of Raleigh's trial, see the long and detailed account in GARDINER (Vol. I., Cap. III.): "Change in the view taken of treason" (pp. 124–5); "System of criminal procedure" (pp. 125–6); "The law of treason" (pp. 126–7).

[5] Reprint of the *Arraignment*, in FOLEY, IV., 164.

[6] *Ibid.*, 186.

stir; from all sides people pressed into the Guildhall and the king himself listened to the trial from a secret hiding place. The examination of evidence against the accused and his conviction were a mockery of all justice. The Attorney-General, Edward Coke, who was in the habit of playing the rôle of accuser in every important political trial, and who was none too punctilious in regard to truth,[1] appeared on this occasion also. His marshalling of evidence was extremely weak[2]; he talked of all sorts of things which had nothing to do with the case; when he came to the point on which everything depended,[3] he had nothing to submit except a few probabilities strung together at haphazard.[4] Sallies against the doctrine of equivocation had to fill the gaps.[5] By means of interruptions and exclamations an attempt was made to lessen the effect of Garnet's defence.[6] But most worthy of

[1] GARDINER (I., 127), in describing Raleigh's trial, attributes to Coke not only "habitual violence" in stating the accusation, but also "his usual carelessness" as to the value of evidence: "the charges against the prisoner (Raleigh) were brought forward by Coke, with his usual violence, & with his no less usual carelessness as to the value of the evidence upon which he based his assertions."

[2] The speech is in FOLEY, IV., 165–180.

[3] Namely the conversation with Catesby, of June 9, 1605 (see present work, p. 132 *seq.*).

[4] An accusation often brought forward is to the effect that when Garnet, in the Office of All Saints' day, 1605, made use of the words of the verse: "Auferte gentem perfidam, Credentium de finibus, Ut Christo laudes debitas, Persolvamus alacriter," he interpreted them as a prayer for the extirpation of heresy by means of the gunpowder plot! These lines formed, together with Psalm 78 (79), a prayer for the restoration of Church unity in England and had been indulgenced by the Pope at Cardinal Allen's request; they were therefore certain to have been in frequent use (*Oldcorne*, in FOLEY, IV., 231). The words referred to, from the Office of All Saints', date from the tenth century at the very latest; see CLEM. BLUME, *Analecta hymnica medii aevi*, LI., 151.

[5] FOLEY, IV., 178.

[6] *Ibid.*, 180–190.

condemnation is the fact that the government did not shrink from manifest falsifications of the minutes of the interrogatories. Thus the two conspirators, Fawkes and Winter, had unanimously attested that after binding themselves by oath to secrecy, they received Holy Communion from the hand of Gerard, but added that the priest knew nothing of their oath. When the minutes of the interrogatories were read, this clause was omitted by order of Coke, and in the text of the speech of the Attorney-General, as given by the *True and Perfect Relation*, we read: "At the same time the Jesuit Gerard tendered this oath to Catesby, Percy, Christopher Wright and Thomas Winter, and on another occasion it was tendered by the Jesuit Greenway to Bates and the rest.[1] Garnet's confession of March 9th, which contains the fullest account of his relations with the conspirators, was not read at all, by order of the king,[2] and in the admissions which the jury were allowed to hear, Coke ordered the omission of the passages in which Garnet expresses his disapproval of the plot.[3] However, these are not the only forgeries committed on this occasion.[4]

[1] GERARD, in *The Month*, LXXXIII., 9–10. *This* falsification is condemned by GARDINER also (I., 281).

[2] Present work, p. 152, note 1.

[3] The passages here printed in italics, were suppressed. They occurred in the confession of March 13, 1606 (FOLEY, IV., 157 *seq.*): "About Michaelmas . . . Mr. Catesby told me there would be some stirring, seeing the king kept not promise. *And I greatly misliked it, saying it was against the Pope's express commandment. . . . Therefore I earnestly desired him that he and Mr. Thomas Winter would not join with any such tumults. . . . He assured me he would not. But neither he told, nor I asked any particulars.* Long after this, about Midsummer was twelvemonth, either Mr. Catesby alone, or he & Thos. Winter together, insinuated that they had somewhat in hand, and that they would sure prevail. *I still reproved them: but they entered into no particulars.* Soon after came Mr. Greenwell to me, and told me as much. *I greatly misliked any stirring, and said: etc.*" *Cf.* GERARD, *loc. cit.*, 23 *seq.*; LINGARD, VII., 78 *seq.*

[4] See GERARD, in *The Month*, XC. (1897), 352 *seqq.* (*Cf.*

Even after Garnet had been sentenced, an attempt was made, by means of repeated interrogatories, to extract further information from him.[1] During the last days of his life, the condemned man grievously reproached himself for one point of his conduct ; he now thought that he should have informed the government that he knew that some violent attempt was preparing. In an explanation dated April 4th, 1606, and addressed to the king, he confessed this fault and begged forgiveness.[2] On the other hand he protested, even on the scaffold, that he only knew of the plot through confession.[3]

LXXXVIII. (1896), 400 *seqq.*; FORBES, in *Études*, LXXVI. (1898), 324 *seq.*) For Th. Winter's Confession, see *Thomas Winter's Confession and the Gunpowder Plot*, by JOHN GERARD, London and New York, 1898 ; *cf. The Month*, XCII. (1898), 99–101 ; *Encyclopædia Britannica*, XII. (1910), 729.

[1] Garnet's replies are in FOLEY, IV., 190 *seqq.*

[2] Published by GERARD, in *The Month*, LXXXIII., 349.

[3] Gardiner, too, who is no friend of Garnet's, writes (I., 282) : "On the scaffold he persisted in his denial that he had had any positive information of the plot except in confession, though he allowed . . . that he had had a general & confused knowledge from Catesby. In all probability, this is the exact truth." Gardiner's judgment on Garnet's trial is as follows (I., 277) : "In fact, the scene at Guildhall was a political rather than a judicial spectacle. Neither those who were the principal actors, nor the multitude who thronged every approach to the hall, regarded it as the sole or even as the chief question, whether the old man who stood hopeless but undaunted at the bar, and who, even by his own confession, had been acquainted with the recent conspiracy, had looked upon it with favour or with abhorrence. It was to them rather an opportunity which had at last been gained, of striking a blow against that impalpable system which seemed to meet them at every turn, and which was the more terrible to the imagination because it contained elements with which the sword and the axe were found to be incapable of dealing. . . . The Pope was still too much dreaded to make it possible that fair play should be granted to the supporters of his influence. . . . His power was, to Burghley and Salisbury, a power which was only a little less, and which might any day become greater, than their own. They thought that if they could

It is said that 20,000 spectators witnessed Garnet's execution on May 3rd. The sight of his person inspired reverence, and his dignified manner silenced the jeers of the scoffers; the crowd would not suffer him to be quartered before he was quite dead, and there was no answer when the executioner held up his heart as that of a traitor.[1]

However this mood did not last. In the official account of the execution the government made the ambiguous statement that on the scaffold Garnet had confessed his guilt [2]: this the people naturally construed into an admission of complicity in the gunpowder plot, which he had emphatically denied. Whereas the Catholics, even immediately after the arrest of the conspirators, felt convinced that Salisbury was "playing false", and that the Privy Council "had spun the web in order to entangle these poor gentlemen in its meshes",[3] in Protestant opinion Garnet became, for centuries to come, an arch-conspirator, "the rotten roote of this corrupted tree of treason."[4] Official accounts and the yearly celebration of Guy Fawkes' day, on November 5th, when a caricature of the Pope was dragged through the streets and finally burnt, were effective means by which to keep the Gunpowder plot alive in the memory of the public as "the Jesuits' treason"

get the wolf by the ears, it was the wisest policy, as well as the strictest justice, to hold it fast." JESSOPP (*Dictionary of National Biography*, IX., 283), admits that among the established facts of the history of the Gunpowder Plot this is certain, namely, "that it was not revealed to any Roman priest except under the seal of confession", and that the two Jesuits Garnet & Gerard, who were far too sharp & quick-witted not to see the monstrous stupidity of such an undertaking, shrank from such an atrocity & foreseeing the certainty of its unhappy issue, did their best to prevent it.

[1] In FOLEY, IV., 113–119. *Cf. Relatio martyrii P. Henrici Garneti S.J.*, Chigi Library, Rome, Printed *Miscell.*, vol. 48, no. 3, p. 30–6.

[2] LINGARD, VII., 81.

[3] GERARD, in *The Month*, LXXXIII., 481 *seq.*; PRAMPAIN, *loc. cit.*, 429; FOLEY, IV., 119.

[4] Introductory words of Garnet's trial, in FOLEY, IV., 165.

and the "Popish Conspiracy".[1, 2, 3] In 1606, Vincenzo Giuliani saw in all the streets of London caricatures of the Pope and of Catholic priests.[4] The Gunpowder plot came as a handle for Salisbury to use against various persons that failed to please him. Thus his greatly feared rival, the Earl of Northumberland, lost his liberty, his offices and a large part of his possessions because of his relations with Percy, one of the conspirators.[5] Three Catholic peers were condemned to heavy fines on trivial grounds.[6] Hugh Owen, the officer in the Netherlands, had long ago incurred the displeasure of the government; hence Coke was instructed, in the course of the interrogatories in connection with the plot, to make the heaviest accusations possible against Owen.[7] The attempt seems to have failed badly. True, the printed text of Fawkes' confession of November 17th, 1605, contains an allusion to Owen, but in the original text that particular sentence is missing.[8] Long negotiations now began with the regent of the Netherlands for the extradition of Owen; their issue was that, in 1611, Owen was compelled to leave Flanders.[9] Likewise on the plea of his having had cognizance of the plot, the expulsion from the Netherlands of the Jesuit Baudouin was demanded by the government and acceded to by the regent. Whilst travelling in the Palatinate, Baudouin was

[1] Coke branded it, in his speech for the Prosecution, at Garnet's trial, as "the Jesuits' treson" (*ibid.*, 166).

[2] Present work, p. 146.

[3] Even in the literary controversy which began around Garnet, falsification of evidence was practised at his expense. *Cf.* for Andrews, LINGARD, VII., 546 *seq.*, and for Robert Abbot, *ibid.*, 548, and GERARD, in *The Month*, LXXXVIII., 400, 404, XC., 353.

[4] RODOCANACHI, *Aventures d'un grand Seigneur Italien à travers l'Europe 1606*, Paris (*undated*), 131 *seq.*

[5] LINGARD, VII., 82, 83 *seq.*

[6] *Ibid.*, 82 *seq.*

[7] "You must remember to lay Owen as fowle in this as yow may" (FOLEY, IV., 361; GERARD, *loc. cit.*, LXXXIII., 18).

[8] FOLEY, IV., 397. *Cf.* GERARD, *loc. cit.*, XC., 359 *seq.*

[9] WILLAERT, in the *Rev. d'hist. écclés.*, IX. (1908), 57–61, 736–742.

recognized by the elector Frederic V. who had him taken to England. Though he could not be convicted of complicity, he remained shut up in the Tower for eight years until he was exchanged for an English prisoner of the Roman Inquisition.[1] The elector of the Palatinate made the Gunpowder plot a pretext for a display of his anti-Catholic feelings. By his orders, on the last three Sundays of the year, thanksgiving was "offered in all the churches for deliverance from the blood-thirsty and inhuman attempts of antichrist and the conspiracy of his idolatrous band", and the preachers were instructed to expatiate on the idolatry and blood lust of the Pope.[2]

On account of the Gunpowder plot, Parliament had been adjourned from November 9th, 1605, until January 21st, of the following year.[3] On May 27th, 1606, it passed fresh laws against Catholics. The king had already been warned not to drive those who professed the old religion to despair by inhuman severity. Henry IV. instructed his ambassador to make similiar representations.[4] All was in vain; the government seemed determined to make the best of so favourable an opportunity and to make further acts of desperation impossible by stamping out Catholicism itself. The penalties imposed on Catholics by the new laws covered almost every imaginable situation. Husbands and wives, unless they had been married by a Protestant minister, forfeited every benefit to which he or she might be entitled from the property of the other. If they did not have their children baptized by a Protestant minister, or if they did not have their dead buried in the Protestant cemetery, they were fined £100 in the former case and £20 in the latter. A child sent beyond the sea to be educated was debarred from any inheritance or gift, in favour of the Protestant next-of-kin, until it should return to the national church. A whole series of fresh molestations and fines was devised against those who refused to attend

[1] *Ibid.*, 742 *seq.* = FOLEY, III., 509.

[2] MEYER, *Nuntiaturberichte*, 831; *cf.* 681.

[3] GARDINER, I., 285.

[4] LINGARD, VII., 86. [Edit. of 1902, John Grant, Edinburgh.]

Anglican worship. Without the written permission of four of the nearest magistrates, Catholics could not journey beyond a radius of five miles from their residence; they could not appear at court nor within the boundaries, or within ten miles of the boundaries, of the capital. Whoever did not assist at Anglican worship was incapable of practising surgery or the law and he was treated as if he had been excommunicated formally and by name. His house could be searched, his religious books or objects might be burnt and his horses and arms taken from him at any time, by order of the nearest magistrate. As regards unpaid fines for non-attendance at Church, it was now left open to the king whether to raise the fine of £20 per lunar month, or to confiscate in its place the whole of the movable property, or the immovable property up to two-thirds. Every householder, of whatever religion, receiving Catholic visitors, or keeping Catholic servants, was liable to a fine of £10 per lunar month.[1]

Thus did Parliament reply to the wretched crime of a few men by the enactment of an unjust and barbarous statute,[2] and thousands were to suffer for centuries to come for the insane plans once conceived by a Catesby. Nor was this all.

[1] LINGARD, VII., 87 *seq.*

[2] "It had replied to the miserable crime of a few fanatics by the enactment of an unjust & barbarous statute," says GARDINER (I., 289). That the conspiracy did not originate from the Catholics as a body, and was not approved by them, Gardiner admits elsewhere too: "No candid person can feel surprise that any English Roman Catholic . . . should feel anxious to wipe away the reproach which the plot has brought upon those that share his faith. Not merely were his spiritual predecessors subjected to a persecution borne with the noblest & least self-assertive constancy in consequence of what is now known to all historical students to have been the entirely false charge that the Plot emanated from, or was approved of by the English Roman Catholics as a body, but this false belief prevailed so widely, that it must have hindered, to no slight extent, the spread of that organization, which he regards as having been set forth by divine institution for the salvation of mankind" (GARDINER, *What Gunpowder Plot was*, London, 1897, 2).

The government took pleasure in representing the Gunpowder plot as the fruit of Catholic teaching; hence, lest fresh disastrous floods should spring from such a source, it must. be choked. To this effect a special oath was tendered to the adherents of the old religion, the refusal of which would entail confiscation of property and perpetual imprisonment. Every Catholic had to swear that he believed James I. to be his rightful sovereign, that the Pope had no power to depose him, or to absolve his subjects from their oath of allegiance to him. The juror, therefore, promised loyalty and obedience to his sovereign, without attending to any papal excommunication, to defend him against conspiracies and attempts against his life, and to give information of them; he swore that he rejected the impious, heretical and damnable doctrine that sovereigns excommunicated by the Pope or deprived of their realms could be deposed and put to death by their subjects; that he believed it to be of faith and a dictate of conscience that neither the Pope nor anyone else had power to absolve from this oath; that all this he swore according to the natural meaning of the words, without equivocation; that he promised it from his heart, freely and sincerely, on the faith and loyalty of a Christian.

If we bear in mind the story of the Stuarts from James I. to James II., the formula is not without a smack of tragedy. On the plea of fear for his throne and life, the monarch of England entrenches himself against the ancient Church, yet it was precisely this passion for unlimited independence that led to the deposition and death on the scaffold of James' son, and to the loss of the crown for his whole House under his grandson; it was this that, in the terms of Logan's epigram, opened an era which learnt precisely from the story of Charles I. not to spare sovereigns; an age in which the assassination of princes ended by becoming a sinister epidemic and in which the papacy appeared as the bulwark of law and order. It sounds like a mockery of the wisdom of the British Solomon, when we are told that out of the 500 gentlemen who bled for the cause of his son, no less than 200 came from the ranks of the down-trodden Catholics.[1]

[1] O. KLOPP, *Fall des Hauses Stuart*, I., Wien, 1875, 26.

Owing to its wording, James I.'s oath was a formidable weapon against Catholics. It branded their Church as an enemy of the State and of civilization and provided the further advantage, in case of refusal, of covering religious persecution with a political cloak. It looked as if the times of Nero had come back when the mere fact of being a Christian made a man " an enemy of mankind ". Moreover the formula had been disguised as a snare for the guileless and a wedge by which to split the unity of the Catholics. Every one of its clauses betrays the hand of its author, an apostate priest,[1] who took advantage of his familiarity with things Catholic to cause his former correligionists the worst embarrassment and to sow discord and division in their ranks. It was impossible to take the oath without denying Catholic principles. The very first words of the formula were offensive. They styled James, " Our sovereign lord," that is, in the literal sense of the words, supreme also in things spiritual. At the conclusion it stated that the oath was tendered " by competent and rightful authority ". Now in the oath of allegiance there was question not of temporal things but of affairs of conscience ; hence to attribute to the king full authority in this sphere was practically the same thing as rejecting the Pope and taking a disguised oath of supremacy. As regards the kernel of the formula, the overwhelming majority of theologians of the period maintained the Pope's right to depose princes. Popes and councils, and quite recently Pius V., had claimed it ; and since in the opinion of the Middle Ages, an excommunicated prince could not rule over Christians, deposition was deemed a natural consequence of the Pope's right to exclude from the Church, a right no Catholic could deny. It was not, therefore, lawful for an individual Catholic to decide, on his own authority, between the Gallicans and all the other theologians and thereby to arrogate to himself a power which belonged exclusively to the Church. Still less was he justified in rejecting the universal teaching of theologians as impious, heretical and damnable, if he was not also prepared to maintain that for centuries

[1] The ex-Jesuit Christopher Perkins.

the Church had tolerated an impious and heretical doctrine. Least of all could he concede to a Protestant king the right to decide what was orthodox and what was not, and thus to attribute to him the power to introduce new dogmas into the Church.[1] Even the Gallicans, who denied the Pope's deposing power, could not take the oath, since they did not defend their particular opinions as certain but as merely probable; hence they could not swear that the contrary view was erroneous.[2] Above all, the formula was cunningly made to look perfectly harmless. Nowhere is an uncontroverted dogma or an expressly defined opinion directly attacked. Whatever was calculated to perplex is placed amid propositions which could not be attacked, and is so worded that a moderate explanation did not seem excluded. Thus, for instance, it is not the doctrine that the Pope may depose an excommunicated prince that is styled "impious and heretical", but the claim that the subjects had such a right, and even here there was not simply question of deposition only, but of "deposition and assassination". It was, therefore, doubtful whether the epithets, "impious and heretical," referred to the deposition alone, or to deposition and assassination. Before taking the oath, the juror could take the more moderate view, but once he had sworn it was open to the government to give prominence to the stricter interpretation. This applies also to the clauses which ascribe to the king supreme authority, in fact it is true of the whole formula. Why take the worst meaning as the only possible one? many a one would say to himself. Why attach so much importance to inaccuracies in the wording of the oath? The government knows nothing of theological subtleties; it imagines that it is possible to draw from Catholic dogmas conclusions that might endanger the

[1] *Cf.* HERGENRÖTHER, *Kirch und Staat*, 686 *seqq.*; SERVIÈRE, 12.

[2] This is BOSSUET's opinion: "A Romana sententia abhorrere, perspectis melius rebus, uti nos Franci facimus, erat licitum et bonum; damnare ut haereticam absque Ecclesiae auctoritate, nimium et temerarium videbatur" (*Defensio Declarationis*, cap. 23, in SERVIÈRE, 13).

State and it is in this sense that it demands their rejection. Very well, we will swear just in that sense; we swear to be loyal to the king as our temporal lord, and we also attest on oath that our Catholic faith does not make of us either traitors or regicides.

As a matter of fact differences of opinion on the oath and its lawfulness soon arose among Catholics. Only a few years earlier, thirteen priests from the party of the Appellants, had made an offer to Queen Elizabeth to take an oath which, in many of its clauses, was not unlike the formula of James I.[1] At this time, Blackwell, the archpriest, had among his counsellors priests drawn from the ranks of the Appellants and these exercised considerable influence over him. In a proclamation of July 10th, 1606, the king had reverted to his old plan of banishing the priests, yet at the same time he assured the laymen that he would only consider those as disloyal who, "under plea of zeal really aimed at preaching rebellion and at bringing about the subversion of the Church and society."[2] In his polemical writings, James repeatedly asserts that his formula demands no more than what is demanded by the ordinary loyalty to the king and by civil obedience.[3]

For all that, Blackwell's first thought had been publicly to condemn the oath. On the occasion of a deliberation with three of his ordinary advisers and the Superiors of the Jesuits and the Benedictines, the two religious and one of the secular priests pronounced against the oath whereas the two other secular priests sided with Blackwell. It was decided to consult Rome in the matter and meanwhile to let each individual Catholic decide for himself. Nearly all the laity took the oath but the greater part of the secular clergy and the Jesuits and Benedictines condemned it and refused to take it.[4]

In the meantime Blackwell's agent in Rome, Singleton,

[1] On January 31, 1602; see A. O. MEYER, *England und die kath. Kirche*, 393 *seq.*

[2] GARDINER, II., 15 *seq.*

[3] SERVIÈRE, 14.

[4] *Ibid.*, 15 *seq.*

did all he could to defend the oath, but, as was to be foreseen, he failed to win over a single Cardinal to his view. Nor was the opposition idle. The English Jesuits in Flanders had dispatched two of their number to the eternal City.[1] On the other hand the French ambassador, de Brèves, begged the Pope not to irritate James; in time his own master would no doubt succeed in bringing him round to better sentiments. Paul V. fell in with this view; he even sent one of his chamberlains, the Baron de Magdelène, on a secret visit to London, to congratulate the king on his escape from the Gunpowder plot, to plead on behalf of the Catholics of his realm and to assure him of their loyalty and of the goodwill of the Holy See.[2] The French ambassador in London, Lefèvre de la Boderie, worked in the same sense.[3]

All these efforts having proved in vain, on September 22nd, 1606, a papal Brief was published which, after giving the full text of the oath, went on to declare that there were many things in it which were contrary to the faith and to the welfare of souls, hence it was not lawful to take it. The Pope expressed his conviction that the Catholics of England would courageously prefer the most cruel tortures and death itself to an outrage against God's majesty. In conclusion the Brief exhorts them to preserve concord and charity, as Clement VIII. had exhorted them on October 5th, 1602, on the occasion of the question of the archpriest. Let the Brief of his predecessor be observed literally and without cavilling.[4] This warning refers to the unsuccessful attempt of the party of the Appellant priests, who, through their emissaries Cecil and Champney, sought to obtain from Paul V. what Clement VIII. had refused. The matter was not again to be brought up in future.[5] The papal Brief was sent from Rome

[1] *Ibid.*, 18.

[2] *Ibid.*, 19.

[3] *Ibid.*, 18 *seq.*

[4] Copy of the Brief in JAMES I's controversial works (*Opera*, 113 *seq.*) and in BELLARMINE's reply (*Opera*, V., Venice, 1721, 158 *seq.*).

[5] IUVENCIUS P., IV., I, 13, no. 34, p. 151 *seq.* Both of them

to the Superior of the English Jesuits, Holtby, through whom it came into the hands of Blackwell. However, Blackwell would not publish it: the Brief, he declared, had not been delivered to him with the formalities prescribed by Canon Law and he was surely not bound voluntarily to put the rope round his neck.

The government obtained early information of the Brief. An order was issued for Blackwell's arrest at any cost. On June 24th, 1606, the archpriest fell into the hands of the pursuivants, and with him the whole of the correspondence with Rome.[1] At the residence of the archbishop of Canterbury, Bancroft, he declared before a deputation of bishops and doctors that, notwithstanding the papal Brief, he still believed that the oath was lawful. In that case, Bancroft urged, let him take it! Blackwell did so, appealing at the same time to the explanation of the oath given by the king himself. In a circular of July 7th, 1607, he exhorted the clergy to follow his example and to urge the laity in this sense. Bancroft hastened to make the best of his triumph by broadcasting Blackwell's letter over the whole of England.[2] During thirty years of persecution, the Jesuits wrote in their annual reports,[3] no heavier blow had ever befallen the Church in England.

However, Blackwell's prestige was not such as to render a papal Brief nugatory. As Singleton wrote to Paul V. from Brussels, the interrogatories of the Jesuit, William Wright, a fellow prisoner of Blackwell's in the archiepiscopal palace, greatly helped to open the eyes of many to the real significance of the oath.[4] Others, it is true, sheltered themselves behind the assertion that the Pope had been ill-informed when he published the Brief which represented the views of the Jesuits

had left England at the beginning of May, 1606 (TAUNTON, 366). *Cf.* CARDINAL BORGHESE to the Flemish nuncio, February 20, 1610, in LAEMMER, *Melet.*, 279.

[1] SERVIÈRE, 21.

[2] SERVIÈRE, 22 *seq.*

[3] FOLEY, VII., 982.

[4] SERVIÈRE, 23.

alone.[1] In consequence, on August 22nd, 1607, Paul issued a second Brief in which he protests against such interpretations; his judgment, he wrote, sprang from his own decision, from personal knowledge, and was the fruit of long and mature deliberation.[2] Through Persons and more particularly through Bellarmine, Paul V. sent an earnest exhortation to Blackwell. In his letter, Bellarmine[3] describes the subtle devices by which it was sought to attenuate the formula of the oath as a cunning attempt by which the devil endeavoured to attack, overtly or covertly, the Catholic dogma of the primacy of the Apostolic See; the oath tended, in reality, to put at the head of the Church not the successor of St. Peter but the successor of Henry VIII. It was idle pretence to say that the king's life would be in danger if the Pope wielded in England the authority which he has everywhere. At no time in the Church's history had a Pope ordered the assassination of a prince, or approved the deed when it had been committed. The whole formula, with its mixture of harmless and erroneous assertions, was a reminder of the tricks of Julian the Apostate who ordered the statues of the idols to be placed beside his own, so that a Christian could neither pay, nor refuse to pay, the customary homage to the imperial likeness without being accounted either an idolater, or an enemy of the emperor. Many may be tempted to imagine that in the formula there was question only of trifles and theological subtleties, but where the interests of God are concerned, not a syllable may be sacrificed. Let Blackwell rise from his fall with renewed vigour. In a matter of such gravity he must not rely too much on his own judgment, lest his splendid career should be spoilt by an end which would cause grief to his friends and joy to his enemies.

Blackwell still maintained that Rome had not properly understood the oath of allegiance. In his reply to Bellarmine[4] he explains that, in the received opinion of theologians, the Pope was not the judge of princes, in virtue of his office;

[1] *Ibid.*, 23 *seq.*

[2] *Cf.* p. 165, n. 4.

[3] September 28, 1607, *ibid.*

[4] November 13, 1607, in SERVIÈRE, 27.

only in extraordinary cases could he interfere with their temporal power, and more than this the oath did not affirm. The error of this explanation was soon to be brought home to him. His reply to Bellarmine was intercepted; once more face to face with his judges, the archpriest had to explain his interpretation of the oath. The weakness of the unhappy old man now became apparent. Under the ever-increasing pressure of the judges he ended by signing a document to the effect that the Pope had no power whatever to depose princes, not even when it was question of the needs of the Church and the spread of Christianity. With this new clause, and in this sense, they made him take the oath once more.[1] Blackwell's removal from office could no longer be put off. On February 1st, 1608, a papal decree named George Birkhead as his successor. On August 16th, 1611, Birkhead found himself in the necessity of proclaiming that his predecessor, as well as all priests who had taken the oath, had incurred the penalties of excommunication and suspension. Notwithstanding his subservience to the government, Blackwell did not escape life-long imprisonment—that is, precisely the penalty for the refusal of the oath. He died shortly after his deposition, as Bancroft's prisoner, protesting that he wished to end his life as a true son of the Catholic Church. But he had not submitted to the papal decisions.[2] He boasted of the approval of the Sorbonne; as a matter of fact, several doctors of Paris secretly defended the lawfulness of the oath.[3] Not a few English priests continued to share Blackwell's view, even after publication of the papal decrees. Among them was the Superior of the English Benedictines, Preston, who had at first rejected the oath as unlawful. Under Preston's influence and inspiration, Roger Widdrington wrote in defence of the oath but when his writings were condemned he submitted to the sentence.[4]

[1] *Ibid.*, 28 *seqq.*

[2] *Ibid.*, 30 *seqq.*

[3] *Ubaldini*, June 24, 1608, *ibid.*, note 33.

[4] LÄMMER, *Melet.*, 318 note; FOLEY, VII., 2, 1061; CAUCHIE-MAERE, 171, 238. TAUNTON shows that Widdrington was not merely an *alias*. *Engl. Hist. Review*, XVIII. (1903), 119.

James I. was greatly perturbed by the Briefs of Paul V., notwithstanding Blackwell's pitiful exhibition of weakness. The king still feared a sentence of excommunication, and, in fact, a papal intervention of any kind. It would seem that he had tried to take advantage of previous dealings with the Curia to prevent a papal expression of opinion on the oath. Through the mediation of the Belgian envoy it was hinted in Rome that James was prepared to acknowledge the Pope as the first sovereign in Europe if Paul V. would issue a declaration that it would never be lawful, not even on the plea of religion, for subjects to refuse obedience to their sovereign, or to lay hands on his person. But Rome was not to be taken in; Paul V. briefly answered that the Holy See would never direct Catholics to lay hands on the king.[1]

Thus secret diplomacy had not succeeded in preventing a papal manifestation on the oath of allegiance. Nevertheless, not long after publication of the second Brief, the government felt anxious to effect a reconciliation with Rome. To this end they almost completely dropped the various clauses of the oath. In Ireland, the Earl of Tyrone was suspected of a secret understanding with Spain. Tyrone forestalled the attempt to lure him over to England, with a view to his arrest, by escaping to the continent, together with the Earl of Tyrconel and other noblemen. The news raised great alarm in England; for a moment it was feared that the two earls would return at the head of a new Armada, and the tension became so acute that a general rising of the Catholics of England, Scotland and Ireland was being talked of. Before

[1] "SSmus censuit nihil faciendum, catholicis non mandabitur ab hac S. Sede inferre manus in regem. Fuit etiam dictum, modernum regem Angliae maxime timere, ne in ipsum proferatur excommunicatio" (Inquisition decree of April 20, 1606, printed from a MS. of the Corsini Library, Rome, in the *Anal. Iuris pontif.*, Series 26, Rome–Paris, 1886 *seq.*, 678). All the same, a year later James writes: "quamquam autem inter me et R. Pontificem, alterius videlicet religionis caput, religio ipsa literarum et internuntiorum omne sustulerit commercium" (*Triplici nodo triplex cuneus: Opera*, 113).

the end of October, through the Spanish ambassador, Zúñiga, Salisbury, apparently by order of the king, laid the following proposals before the Pope: not only should his Holiness use the threat of excommunication, in order to prevent the Catholics from rising against the king, he should, on the contrary, command them to defend him with arms in hand. In that eventuality all fines would be remitted and the government would no longer forbid Catholics to have priests in their houses.[1] Rome did not think the proposal worthy of an answer.[2] As late as October, 1608, there prevailed so great a fear of the Irish and the Spaniards, that the Spanish ambassador was assured that Tyrone's pardon and toleration of the Catholic religion were being seriously considered.[3]

In these circumstances it was all-important for the government to nullify the effect of the Pope's condemnation of the oath by representing it as harmless and its condemnation as unjust. Here was a task for theologians. James himself took up his pen in an attempt to refute the two Briefs, and above all Bellarmine's letter to Blackwell.

In vain his ministers pointed out to him that it was not seemly for a crowned head to enter the lists against learned controversialists: James stuck to his resolution. He fancied himself as Europe's first theologian and he was particularly keen to have a tilt at Bellarmine, the most renowned opponent of the new doctrines. In 1607, the king was closeted with his divines, reading and writing for days on end. Even affairs of State had to take second place and only now and again would he indulge in his favourite pastime, the chase.[4] At last, on February 27th, 1608, James was able to send a copy of his work [5] to the French ambassador, together with an assurance

[1] Zúñiga to Philip III., November 10, 1607, in GARDINER, II., 23.

[2] GARDINER, II., 27.

[3] Borghese to the Spanish nuncio, November 11, 1608, *ibid.*, 30.

[4] SERVIÈRE, 34. *Cf.* LINGARD, VII., 95.

[5] "Triplici nodo triplex cuneus, sive apologia pro iuramento fidelitatis, adversus duo brevia Pauli PP. Quinti et epistulam cardinalis Bellarmini ad G. Blackwellum archipresbyterum nuper scriptam," London, 1607 (*Opera*, 112–132).

that it contained nothing for which the Gallican Church did not likewise contend, and the boast that he had given Cardinal Bellarmine a sound thrashing.[1] The book appeared without the author's name but with the royal coat of arms on the title page, and copies were presented to the foreign ambassadors, so that the king's part in its compilation was an open secret. In its pages James repeatedly states that the oath of allegiance demanded no more than civil obedience. He then endeavours to prove from the Scriptures and the Fathers that no human authority has power to release subjects from their duty to their sovereign, even if the prince is an unworthy and criminal personage. Occasionally James does not take the burden of proof very seriously. As against Bellarmine's statement that the Pope had never commissioned any man to murder a prince, he points to the Emperors Henry IV., Frederick Barbarossa, Frederick II., whom fear of papal assassins alone caused to humble themselves before the Popes. For the rest the book shows proof of not a little reading of the Fathers and the Councils.[2] The effect on Catholics was that many accepted the royal explanation of the oath of allegiance and took it.[3] The answer to the royal apology was not long in coming: Persons replied in English, Bellarmine in Latin. Since the king's book bore no author's name, Bellarmine published his refutation under the name of his chaplain, Matteo Torto.[4]

James I. was greatly roused by Bellarmine's reply. His opponent had not only subjected the oath of allegiance to a searching analysis, in consequence of which many Catholics either refused to take it, or retracted it if they had already sworn, but he had also pointed to the king's grave errors

[1] "Le roi m'assura qu'il n'y avait rien dans son livre qui traitât de la foi, ni qui fût contraire à ce que l'Église gallicane a toujours tenu. Il ne parla quasi jamais d'autre chose, montrant de croire qu'il avait donné des étrivières au cardinal Bellarmin," La Boderie, in Servière, 35.

[2] Servière 36–7.

[3] La Boderie, April 24, 1608, *ibid.*, 45.

[4] *Matthaei Torti responsio ad librum inscriptum: Triplici nodo triplex cuneus*, Coloniae Agrippinae, 1608 (*Opera*, V., 155–188).

and mistaken interpretations of texts from the Bible and the Fathers and in the places where James speaks of his own relations with the Catholics, he reproaches him with a distortion of the facts and deliberate falsehood.[1] The royal controversialist was exceedingly angry. Once again he shut himself in with his divines for the purpose of crushing Bellarmine. In vain did his wife beg, and the kings of France and Denmark exhort him to desist from a task which so ill became him. The king of Denmark was told to remember his youth and to blush for his folly at offering advice to a prince so much older and wiser than himself. Nevertheless a few weeks later James deemed it wiser not to give to the public the fruit of his arduous labours.[2] He stopped the sale of the previous book and ordered all the printed copies to be called in, " in order," he said, " to amend the errors which, through the fault of the copyists and printers, had crept into the texts adduced in the arguments." [3] Four bishops toiled many days correcting texts.[4] At length, in February, 1609, the French envoy was able to announce that the king's amended work was in the press and that, enriched with a long preface and an appendix addressed to the rulers of Europe, it would soon see the light. The king had the book so much at heart that, to the great annoyance of the court, notwithstanding the lure of spring and the plague which raged in London, he refused to leave the capital until the printed volume was in his own hands. This time the book appeared under his name.[5] In the preface James repeats his assertion that the oath demanded from Catholics no more than civil obedience,[6] and he adduces a few fresh proofs for his previous assertions. He then endeavours to shift the controversy into

[1] SERVIÈRE, 66; *cf.* 47–65.

[2] LINGARD, VII., 96 *seq.*

[3] SERVIÈRE, 61.

[4] *Ibid.*, 66.

[5] SERVIÈRE, 67. Copy of the preface in *Iacobi I.*, *Opera*, 133–165.

[6] He said it contained nothing but " praeter fidelitatis illius civilisque et temporalis obedientiae professionem, quam ipsa natura omnibus sub regno nascentibus praescribit, etc." (*Opera*, 135; *cf.* 137).

a sphere which had nothing whatever to do with the oath of allegiance. To prove that Bellarmine was politically dangerous, he discusses in detail the Cardinal's teaching on the immunity of the clergy from the secular power, and on the origin of the State [1]; then, in a lengthy profession of faith, he states his views on the motives of faith, the veneration of Saints, relics and images, Purgatory, the authority of bishops and the Pope [2] and ends with a special effort to prove that the Pope is antichrist.[3]

Thus the preface dealt for the most part with things that had nothing to do with the question in dispute. The French envoy gave it as his opinion that the book was the maddest and the most pernicious that had ever been written on such a subject; everybody regretted its publication.[4] Henry IV. advised the Pope to make no reply and even, by his apostolic authority, to forbid any answer whatever.[5] However, in view of the fact that James I. had sent his work to every court, Paul V. was anxious that the refutation also should be read. At his bidding Bellarmine took up his pen once more. To his refutation of the preface [6] he added, this time under his own name, a reprint of his former book against James. At one moment the Pope thought of sending a copy of Bellarmine's refutation to every Christian prince [7]; he desisted eventually in order not to irritate the king uselessly.[8]

[1] *Ibid.*, 137 *seq.*, 157 *seq.*

[2] *Ibid.*, 140–4.

[3] *Ibid.*, 144–156.

[4] "Le plus fou, s'il m'est loisible d'ainsi parler, et le plus pernicieux qui se soit jamais fait sur un tel sujet," LA BODERIE, April 23, 1609, in SERVIÈRE, 89.

[5] SERVIÈRE, 114.

[6] *Opera*, V., 99–154. A copy of the *Apologia* against James, with Bellarmine's notes in the margin, in his own hand, is in *Barb.* 1156, Vatican Library.

[7] *Avviso of September 19, 1609, *Urb.* 1077, Vatican Library.

[8] *Avviso of November 11, 1609, *ibid.* On January 9, 1609 (read 1610), the nuncio Ubaldini at Paris was told: "Per non dare occasione a nuovi irritamenti non voleva N.S. che si publicasse

From the Catholic princes the king earned but scant recognition of his literary labours. In Spain, the British ambassador was advised that it would be better not to present the book to the king—he would certainly refuse to accept it. In Flanders, Savoy, Milan and Florence, the book was also declined [1] James thought, however, that Venice and France

(the book of Bellarmine) da suoi ministri, con tutto ciò, è mente di S.B. che per insegnare detta risposta vera e soda dottrina, non si deve tener per occulta, ma segretamente aiutare la divulgatione, e si lasci correre, se alcuno volesse ristamparla." Library, Stuttgart, MS. 181.

[1] SERVIÈRE, 112. *A warning to the archduke Maximilian of Austria, August 14, 1609, not to accept the English king's pernicious book, in the *Epist.*, V., 74, Papal Secret Archives. *Praise of the Viceroy of Sicily for prohibiting the book, *ibid.* For the refusal of the book in Savoy, see MUTINELLI, III., 290 *seq.*, 375 *seq.* Cardinal Borghese *writes to the nuncio at Rudolph II.'s court, July 11, 1609, telling him to prevent the emperor's accepting the book: "È necessario per ciò dare l'avviso a tempo non solo del tentativo, che si farà per occupare le mani e gli occhi de la Maestà Sua in si infame abominatione, ma di far anco officio con tutto lo spirito, che non sia accettato come prohibito per se stesso et dal Santo Officio espressamente, il che seguirà tra pochi giorni." An enclosed note contains James I.' chief errors: "A theologian may write against the book but his work must be submitted to Rome before printing" (Bibl. Casanatense, Rome, X., VI., 22, p. 34 *seqq.*). To the Swiss nuncio, the bishop of Venafro, August 22, 1609, as follows: "Non essendo ancora pervenuto nè alli mani nè alle orecchie delli Signori catholici d'Elvetia il pernitioso libro del re d'Inghilterra pieno di propositioni heretiche, haverà V.S. facilmente potuto disporre gli animi loro che quando li capitassse o gli fosse offerto, non debbano in alcun modo accettarlo, nel qual proposito N.S. scrive a detti signori l'alligato breve e loda gli uffitii, che in questa materia V.S. ha già fatti insieme col pensiero che ha d'indurre il padre Gretsero Giesuita famoso in materia di confutar eretici ad abbracciare l'impresa di rispondere all'heresie del detto libro, ma dovrà V.S. avvertire che avanti publicare cos'alcuna se ne mandi qua copia" (Stuttgart Library, 181). For the prevention by the nuncio of the book's dissemination in Poland, and for the

would show more interest. In point of fact in the city of the lagoons the Doge at first accepted the book, but at the instance of the Inquisition an edict soon came forth forbidding the printing and selling of James I.' book within the territory of the republic. Thereupon the British envoy, Wotton, judged it helpful to threaten with his departure, but by doing so he embarrassed his master not a little, for when Venice enquired whether London approved the attitude of Wotton, the king, on the one hand, could not very well disavow his representative, nor on the other, forfeit the friendship of the republic. The matter was settled with difficulty but the prohibition of the book, which had given rise to the misunderstanding, remained in force.[1]

In France also the king's book was strictly prohibited. Nevertheless, at the instigation of James, it was secretly translated and printed. Henry IV. similarly forbade Bellarmine's two refutations.[2] This attitude of the French king was due to the rôle of mediator which he had taken up from the outbreak of the quarrel. Of the way in which James I. had tried to make game of the Holy See at the time when he was only king of Scotland, Henry knew nothing, or very little. He was of opinion that, owing to his not being acquainted with conditions in the North, the Pope's manner towards James was too stern, to the harm of English Catholics. Hence, just as he sought to bridle James' anti-Roman ardour, so did he dissuade the Curia from condemning the oath of allegiance and after the condemnation he made no secret of his annoyance.[3] Henry IV. may have been strengthened in his view when Paul V. acknowledged his expostulations with the polite reply that in future, on occasions of this kind, he would first ask the advice of the king of France.[4] James I.'s

refutation issued by the Jesuits in Vilna, see the *reports of Fr. Simonetta to Borghese of November 7 and 21, 1609, State Archives at Massa Carrara.

[1] SERVIÈRE, 112 *seq.*; REIN, 126–134.

[2] SERVIÈRE, 121; PRAT, *Coton*, III., 148–154.

[3] SERVIÈRE, 113 *seq.*

[4] *Ibid.*, 114, note 1.

polemical writings still further confirmed Henry IV. in his opinion. In opposition to Ubaldini's advice, he accepted the book and caused it to be examined by Cardinals du Perron and La Rochefoucauld and the Jesuits Coton and Fronton du Duc. When the examiners gave it as their opinion that James was more moderate in his opinions than other Protestants, Henry conceived the hope that it might be possible to bring the crowned theologian back into the Catholic Church. Once again the nuncio was asked to discuss with the above-mentioned Cardinals and Jesuits appropriate ways and means towards this end. Even Du Perron was of opinion that the Roman theologians were harsh; it would be a good thing to let a Frenchman reply to the king. The nuncio, who was justifiably suspicious of the Gallican ideas of many Frenchmen, suggested that it would be far better to send a theologian to London, for an oral discussion; that Du Perron was the right man for that, and that, in point of fact, the Popes had shown great leniency to James I. The condemnation of the oath of allegiance was unavoidable. However, Du Perron did not go to England. On being sounded on the point, James replied that he would be very glad to listen to a theologian, provided he was not a Cardinal. Paul V. also would not hear of a Cardinal being despatched to a heretical court.[1]

[1] *Ibid.*, 117 *seqq.* For the later literature concerning the oath of allegiance see *ibid.* For Barclay and his controversy with Bellarmine, see *Rev. d. quest. hist.*, LXVIII. (1900), 408; DÖLLINGER-REUSCH, *Moralstreitigkeiten*, I., 538 *seqq.* **Defensio litterarum apostolicarum Pauli V. contra iuramentum Angl. fidelitatis dictum* (directed against a treatise by the English Catholic Howard) in *Cod. Barb.* XXXII., 175, Vatican Library. KASPAR SCHOPP also wrote against James I. (*Forschungen zur deutschen Gesch.*, XI., 428 *seq.*; *Freib. Kirchenlexikon, X.*[2], 2123). Even then opinion in Rome was not very favourable to Schopp: "Di questo huomo credo che V.S. habbia già havuta qualche cognitione. Ma tuttavia è ben che sappia, che fra le altre parti, ch'egli ha, è di cervello assai inquieto, pieno di chimere et di metter in campo ogni giorno nuove cose. Si è mostrato poco ben affetto in diverse occasioni sparlando malamente di questa

Henry IV's. friendly attitude was most opportune for James I.; it enabled him to influence Rome through Paris, with a view to keeping the Pope in suspense as to his real feelings, and, notwithstanding his polemical writings, to restrain him in case he should be inclined to pronounce against him the dreaded sentence of excommunication. To the French envoy the astute monarch explained once again that he was ready to acknowledge the Pope as the first among bishops and the Head of the Church in spiritual things, on condition that Paul V. renounced his claim that he could depose kings. This news was bound promptly to reach Rome by way of Paris.[1] The Pope declared to the French ambassador that if he were to make such a concession he would himself be considered a heretic.[2]

James I. could safely risk the above mentioned information by the round-about way of Paris, though his earlier relations

Corte, con tutto che n'abbia ricevuti molti beneficii et particolarmente da S.Stà, la quale li fa pagare ogni mese etiam in sua assenza da Roma certa provisione. Si è mostrato in oltre mal affetto anco ai P. Gesuiti, i quali sapendo, quando egli sia potente di lingua e di penna, hanno fatto instanza che se ne scriva a V.S. Sarà però bene, che li tenga l'occhio adesso, et procuri d'andarlo moderando." Cardinal Borghese to the Vienna nuncio Melfi, March 28, 1615, Casanatense, Lib., Rome, X., VI., 22, no. 19.

[1] Puysieux to the French ambassador at Rome, De Brèves, July 22, 1609, in *Notices et extraits*, I., 309.

[2] "Lorsque j'ai parlé à sa Sainctеté de ce que le dict roy avait dit à M. de la Boderie, vouloir reconnoistre le Pape pour le premier evesque et chef de l'Église en ce qui est du spirituel, pourvu qu'il se départe de la pretention qu'il a de pouvoir déposer les roys, Elle me dict ne pouvoir faire ceste déclaration qu'elle ne fust au mesme temps Elle-même tenue pour hérétique" (Brèves to Puysieux, August 18, 1609, in SERVIÈRE, 115). *Cf.* GIESELER, *Lehrbuch der Kirchengesch.*, III., 2, Bonn, 1853, 640 *seq.* DÖLLINGER, in his time, accepted this declaration of James I. on its face value and sought to make capital of it against the papacy (*Allgemein, Zeitung*, March 12, 1869, and March 31, 1870, *suppl.* 90, p. 1400). *Cf. Hist.-polit. Blätter*, LXIV. (1869), 322; HERGENRÖTHER, *Kirche u. Staat*, 690.

with the Pope had caused him the greatest embarrassment only a short while ago, for in his first pamphlet Cardinal Bellarmine had revealed the fact that on a previous occasion James had written in friendly fashion to Pope Clement VIII., as well as to Cardinals Aldobrandini and Bellarmine; that he had suggested the nomination of a Scottish Cardinal and that, through his ambassador, he had even hinted at his own return to the Catholic Church.[1] That the letter in question was written in James' name, and with his knowledge and approval, was attested not long after by his own wife Anne.[2] But just as on a previous occasion he had denied having written to the Pope when questioned by Elizabeth, so did he now play a fresh comedy in order to whitewash himself in the eyes of his people. His former private secretary, Lord Balmerino, who happened to be in London at the moment, was summoned before the king and questioned on the subject of the letter. As previously arranged between them, the secretary, falling on his knees, confessed that none other than he himself wrote the letter and laid it before the king together with divers other documents, and that the king signed it together with these documents, without acquainting himself with their contents. Some witnesses were in hiding in another room from which they overheard this avowal.[3] James submitted the whole affair to his Privy Council. "Ye were born strangers to the country where this was done," he wrote to the councillors, "yet are ye no strangers to the king thereof;

[1] "Quibus verbis (Clement VIII.'s in the Briefs of 1600; see Vol. XXIV., 53 *seq.*) non solum Iacobum Scotiae rex non excludebatur, sed includebatur potius, quoniam ministri eius maximam spem fecerant, eum non abhorrere a fide catholica suscipienda, praesertim cum rex ipse ad Pontificem ipsum necnon ad cardinales Aldobrandinum et Bellarminum litteras scripsisset plenas humanitatis, quibus praeter caetera petebat, ut aliquis e gente Scotorum cardinalis S.R.E. crearetur, ut haberet Romae, per quem facilius et tutius cum Pontifice negotia sua tractaret" (*Opera*, V., 166).

[2] A. O. MEYER, in *Quellen und Forschungen*, VII. (1904), 301 *seq.*

[3] GARDINER, II., 31 *seq.*

and ye know, if the king of Scotland prove a knave, the king of England can never be an honest man. Work so, therefore, in this as having interest in your king's reputation." [1] Balmerino pleaded guilty both before the Council and subsequently before a Scottish court at St. Andrew's. He was condemned to death but the king commuted the sentence into imprisonment for life within his own house. The whole pre-arranged plot, as well as Balmerino's condemnation, was looked upon for what it was—a piece of bluff—even in James' lifetime.[2] In his replies to Bellarmine's pamphlet James carefully avoided all reference to his letter to the Pope, but the two letters to Cardinals Aldobrandini and Bellarmine he never attempted to deny.

James I.'s repeated statement in his writings against Bellarmine and on other occasions as well, that the oath of allegiance demanded submission in civil matters only, was accepted by not a few Catholics so that they took the oath as thus interpreted.[3] The Catholic members of the Upper Chamber, of whom there were more than twenty, accepted the condition, with the sole exception of Lord Teynham who, in order to elude an act that would have weighed on his conscience, had recourse to the expedient of not taking his seat on more than one day during each session.[4] In so far

[1] *Ibid.*, 32.

[2] MEYER (*loc. cit.*, 280) is of opinion that the document first published by him (p. 301 *seq.*) makes clear: "1°.—that king James lied when he denied the authorship of his letter to the Pope. 2°.—that he fostered the hopes for his conversion on purpose" GARDINER (II., 31–4) believes in James' innocence; LINGARD (VII., 550) had sufficiently demonstrated the inherent unlikeliness of the whole story.

[3] "Qu'alcuns prestent soubs l'interprétation que le roy leur donne de ce qu'il ne contient rien de ce qui touche le spirituel, quoyque les mots portent visiblement le temporel meslé avecq le spirituel qui tient plusieurs en grande angustie." Thus the secretary of the Flemish ambassador, 1611, in WILLAERT, in the *Rev. d'hist. ecclés.*, VI. (1905), 576.

[4] LINGARD, VII., 98.

as the oath was understood as an oath of civil obedience and not in its literal meaning, it did not, in the opinion of those who took it, imply a denial of Catholic principles. For all that it was and remained a heavy blow for the faithful remainder of the ancient Church. In 1613, the nuncio Bentivoglio wrote that the government had two things in view when it demanded the oath: they wanted a fresh pretext for a more intense persecution of Catholics, and a new wedge with which to split the concord of the Catholic clergy. In both these respects the enemies of the Church achieved considerable success. Many Catholics had been punished with fines and imprisonment for refusing the oath and every day a great number were incurring these penalties. With regard to the clergy, it was true that some priests and religious had been induced to take the oath—when they had gone so far, these men strayed even further from the right path, for they did not hesitate to assert that it was not against the Catholic faith. However, only a very small minority was thus subservient to the government and this minority was recruited from among the least fervent and the least respected. The rest of the clergy, with one accord, opposed the oath, and the bulk of the religious were similarly determined, nay, many among the secular and regular clergy have publicly refuted it with ability and with not a little courage, in view of the fact that they are surrounded by dangers and threats of death.[1]

The oath of allegiance remained James I.'s chief weapon in his war against the ancient Church, though, on the whole, his persecution was less bloody than that of Elizabeth.[2] In the years 1609, 1611, 1613–1615, 1618–1625, no Catholic blood flowed for the sake of the faith; in the other years, sixteen priests and two laymen were executed for the sake of religion. It is generally believed that they could have saved themselves by taking the oath.[3] Though less bloody,

[1] Bentivoglio, *Relationi*, II., 181 *seq.*

[2] *Ibid.*, 182.

[3] Challoner, *Memoirs*, etc., ed. J. H. Pollen, London, 1924, pp. 299, 323, 339, 359 *seq.*; Spillmann, IV., 115–203.

the persecution was not less dangerous; by using milder means it was thought that the remainder of the ancient Church would be destroyed all the more surely, though more slowly.[1] The prisons were crowded with Catholics. In 1622, the number of priests confined in various prisons was reckoned at 400.[2] When in 1606, in order to gain Spain's good will, the victims of the penal laws were set at liberty, the Puritans complained that 4,000 idolaters were now let loose, to pollute the soil purified by the true doctrines of the gospel.[3]

In Yorkshire and the North, so we read in 1607, Catholics were being most cruelly treated: their cattle was driven away, their houses were plundered, their walls pulled down, chests and secret drawers broken open and searched. "On all sides we only hear of violence and severity on the part of the authorities." It was possible to escape ill treatment by taking the oath of allegiance. "The officials of the authorities are not content to plunder; they seize those whom they have robbed, summon them and again let them off on bail. If on the expiration of their bail they present themselves in court, they are thrown into prison unless they pay a heavy ransom; if they fail to appear they are condemned to pay heavy fines. Thus condemnation succeeds condemnation and violence violence. Moreover the minions of the law take more than they are entitled to."[4] In order to squeeze out of the non-jurors all they wanted, it was enough to threaten legal proceedings. From a royal proclamation against these abuses we gather that silver and jewelry were seized without further formality,

[1] "Hora in tempo di questo re si procura principalmente di macerargli quanto più sia possibile con lunghissime prigionie, e di consummare più al vivo, che mai si sia fatto i Cattolici secolari, co'l privargli de beni, cercandosi a questo modo che quelli, e questi vadano a poco a poco, quasi di lenta incurabile infirmità con miserabil fine mancando." BENTIVOGLIO, *loc. cit.*, 182.

[2] LINGARD, VII., 189. *Cf.* the Jesuit's report in FOLEY, VII., 1033.

[3] LINGARD, VII., 190 *seq.*

[4] Jesuit's report of 1607, in FOLEY, VII., 981.

on the pretext that they were serving superstitious purposes or that they belonged to the Jesuits and other priests.[1] Thus the oath became "a mere contrivance for filling the pockets of the courtiers".[2] The Catholics of Yorkshire, by the king's order, suffered much at the hands of the bishop of Bristol. This man was in the habit of first depriving his victims of their flocks and of subsequently allowing them to buy back what was their own, only to seize it once more. In this way it came about that a certain Catholic bought back his own property on seven separate occasions. In the end parliament put a stop to these exactions.[3] The chief instigators of the persecution were the archbishop of Canterbury and the bishop of London.[4]

The assassination of Henry IV. of France brought fresh troubles on the heads of the Catholics of England. An act was passed by Parliament that every Englishman, without exception, must take the oath of allegiance on reaching his 18th year. For the first time also a law was passed in regard to married women who did not attend Protestant worship. They must either receive the sacrament in church or go to prison, unless their husbands redeemed them with a monthly fine of £10.[5] The persecutors of the Catholics were given a fresh opportunity to satisfy their rapacity; "neither pot nor pan, nor bedding, neither rings nor jewels or anything else escapes their rapacity," we read in a letter of the time.[6] Another contemporary letter[7] states that the Catholics hide themselves from their persecutors in holes and caves or flee the country.

[1] LINGARD, VII., 191; Jesuit's report of 1614, FOLEY, VII., 1034.

[2] GARDINER, II., 164.

[3] Jesuit's report for 1608, in FOLEY, VII., 989 *seq.*

[4] *Ibid.*, 989; *cf.* 1017.

[5] LINGARD, VII., 118; GARDINER, II., 72 *seq.* *Cf.* FOLEY, VII., 1008 *seq.*, 1015; WILLAERT, in the *Rev. d'hist. écclés.*, VIII. (1907), 90; LÄMMER, *Melet.*, 288.

[6] From George Lambton, November 2, 1610, in FOLEY, IV., 391.

[7] From Edward Coffin, November 28, 1611, FOLEY, I., 70.

The year 1613 had another surprise in store for Catholics when Edward Coke became Lord Chief Justice. This man's hatred for the ancient Church was sufficiently known to them ever since the trial of Garnet. Coke used his extensive knowledge of English law to dig up all the old enactments against Catholics, many of which had fallen into abeyance, and began to apply them in all their rigour. No marriage was valid unless it had been contracted before a Protestant minister, no baptism was recognized unless it was administered by him, and in consequence of all the fines they had to pay, there remained to the adherents of the old religion less than a third of their income for the support of their household. Even poor people and domestic servants were condemned to fines.[1] "Thank God, at last I have a house from which I cannot be evicted," a poor old man said on his deathbed on hearing that his grave was ready. After the death of his wife, at a time when he had several daughters to support, the poor man had found himself compelled to sell the copper pan on his hearth in order to satisfy his oppressors and for a time, much against his conscience, he had attended the parish church.[2]

On the subject of the oath Coke was unbending. Four times a year the justices of the peace had to send all Catholics of every age and sex before his court in London. Neither sickness nor age or poverty, neither distance nor the inclemency of the season, or sickness of wife and children could be pleaded in excuse. It was said that from one county alone, out of England's fifty, 400 persons were thus summoned.[3] An old woman of eighty having been thus compelled to undertake a journey of over eighty miles, in the depth of winter, refused the oath, had all her property confiscated and saw herself condemned to prison for life.[4] Even when he had taken the

[1] Jesuit's report for 1614, FOLEY, VII., 1036 *seqq.*; UBALDINI to Cardinal Borghese, January 28, 1614, in LÄMMER, *Melet.*, 325 *seq.*

[2] FOLEY, VII., 1038.

[3] *Ibid.*, 1039.

[4] *Ibid.*, 1040.

oath, a Catholic could not feel safe. Coke was well aware that it was only taken outwardly; hence he demanded its renewal four times a year. For many this meant a journey of anything from two hundred to six hundred miles, at all seasons of the year.[1] It is said that up to 1615, no less than 16,000 Catholics were summoned by Coke in connection with the oath.[2] None the less, at the beginning of 1614, James spoke once more of his wish that a general council, convened by the Pope, and at which England would be represented, would re-establish the unity of the Church.[3] But Rome was not to be taken in.[4]

Since several priests, notwithstanding the papal Briefs, declared the oath lawful, many Catholics came to the conclusion that, though the Pope had forbidden it, one might likewise assist at Protestant services [5]; hence Paul V. issued yet another Brief, prohibiting attendance at Anglican services.[6] As a matter of fact the Pope never lost sight of England; he seized every opportunity to help its oppressed Catholics or at least to get persons of influence to exert themselves on their behalf.[7]

[1] *Ibid.*, 1040 *seq.*

[2] Letter from Alexander Fayrecliffe, *ibid.*, 1096.

[3] *Avviso di Londra*, in LÄMMER, *Melet.*, 326 note.

[4] "*Ha letto N.S. l'avviso mandato a V.S. dal suo amico d'Inghilterra intorno al pensiero che mostra havere quel re che si convocasse un concilio generale per il fine avvisuto, ma crede S.S. che sia tutt' arte e da lui si possa sperare molto poco, massime che come ella dice perseguita più che mai li poveri catolici, a favori de' quali è piaciuto a S.B. che V.S. habbia procurato costi, che si ordini all'ambasciadore residente in Londra che interponga i suoi uffitii affinchè non siano tanti angustiati." To the nuncio Ubaldini in Paris, February 27, 1614, Stuttgart Library, *Cod.* 181.

[5] Letter of Richard Blount, July 14, 1606, in FOLEY, I., 64; *cf.* VII., 2, 1003, 1019.

[6] IUVENCIUS P., V., 1, 13, no. 84, p. 187.

[7] This appears from several *Briefs of Paul V. On September 17, 1605, *he praises the viceroy of Sicily, the duke of Feria, for his zeal for the restoration of the faith in England. When he heard that Count François de Vaudemont was travelling to

In 1608 the Pope had a memorandum drawn up on the ways and means by which something could be done for religion in England.[1] The suggestions of its compiler are remarkable for many reasons. It has come home to him that by reason of its geographical situation the island is out of reach of a hostile attack, whilst it is itself in a position to stir up all Europe, as well as the Indies.[2] Hence England is also a danger to religion; a new Calvinistic Church, with an anti-Pope at its head, is in the act of rising there, and both the spiritual and temporal power is in the hands of the king.[3] The danger can no longer be conjured by means of armed intervention by the Catholic king. The very extent of its territories is a handicap for the Spanish world-empire, more than anything else, and the war in Flanders has ended by

England, *he commissioned the archbishop of Nazaret, on August 26, 1607, to send him further information about the position of the English Catholics. A *Brief of April 1, 1608, praises queen Margaret of Navarre for favouring the English Catholics. For the mysterious embassy of Robert Sherley, the Englishman who was overwhelmed with honours at Rome, out of respect for his king and then journeyed on to Philip III., *cf.* the *Brief of October 9, 1609. A *Brief of February 5, 1615, recommends the English Catholics to archduke Albert. *Epist.*, X., 271, Papal Secret Archives.

[1] *Relazione e parere dato al Papa Paolo V. intorno alla religione in Inghilterra, e ai rimedii da usarsi, etc., forse del Padre Generale dei Gesuiti, e probabilmente del P.B. Giustiniani," in *Archiv. Borghese*, 4 Series, n. 47, Papal Secret Archives. The author has consulted in Spain, "più volte," with "persone delle più gravi di Spagna" (p. 139*b*) and also there, with "quelli capitani che vennero con l'Amirante d'Inghilterra in Spagna" (p. 143); this does not fit in with Aquaviva or Giustiniani, but possibly with Persons. The date of the note can be established from the fact that the Hereford rising of 1697 (Foley, IV., 452) is stated on p. 140 to have taken place "l'anno passato".

[2] *"Quelle isole tanto inespugnabili per natura et per il sito loro disposte a inquietare tutta l'Europa et ancora l'Indie" (f. 139).

[3] *Ibid.*, f. 139.

paralysing it altogether.[1] It is even a good thing, the memorandum suggests, that, at the peace, Spain omitted to make religious freedom for English Catholics one of the conditions of the treaty—one that it was easy to secure—for now the Protestants can no longer accuse the Catholics that their conduct is dictated by political considerations for Spain.[2] In view of this accusation it would be a good thing if the victims of English judicial murders were solemnly declared to be true Martyrs who underwent condemnation and death for the sake of religion, not on political grounds.[3] It would seem that the hope of bringing back England as a whole to the Church was pretty well given up. The writer has only two suggestions to make ; the first is to go on sending to England learned and irreproachable priests, both secular and regular. In order to raise the necessary funds for their training, the Pope should urge the Catholic princes to support the seminaries. If, by this means, the old religion revives among the people of England, it may be possible, in the end, to win over the king himself, as was done in France.[4] The second means by which the Catholics of England might be assisted is direct action on the king. One might try to obtain for them the free exercise of their religion at least within the four walls of their own houses.[5] Unlawfully acquired Church property should be left to the ministers and Anglican bishops. The king of France, the grand duke of Tuscany and the other

[1] *" Li molti regni che già possiede gli sono più presto d'impiccio che d'altro " (f. 142) ; " il re cattolico di tal maniera intrigato in quella guerra che non può attendere ad altro " (*ibid.*).

[2] *Ibid.*, f. 139.

[3] " *Pare che adesso sarebbe occasione opportuna di fare la dichiarazione, che molte persone gravi hanno desiderato in altri tempi . . . della causa per la quale moiano li cattolici d'Inghilterra, . . . et si potrebbe deputare doi giorni, uno per li martiri ch'hanno patiti la morte per la fede cattolica et per l'autorità di questa santa Sede sotto il re Henrico ottavo, et l'altro per quelli che sono stati martirizzati per la sua figliuola Elizabetha et di poi celebrando la Chiesa catolica la memoria d'essi " (f. 140).

[4] *Ibid.*

[5] *Ibid.*, f. 141.

princes to whom James, as king of Scotland, had promised his conversion, should press for the fulfilment of the promise, in the same way as the king of Spain has done and is still doing.[1] The princes are bound, under grave sin, to intervene with James I., with a view to making him leave his Catholic subjects in lawful possession of the religion they have inherited, for it was only on this condition, and because they relied on his pledged word, that they had consented to promise him obedience[2]; let the Pope remind the princes of their duty in this matter. After weighing the pros and cons, the writer is of opinion that James I.'s return to the ancient Church is not altogether hopeless[3]; in order to promote it,

[1] " *Et sarà diligenza molt'utile ch'il detto re et il gran duca di Fiorenza et gli altri principi alli quali il re d'Inghilterra, quando era re di Scotia haveva dato parola che si farebbe cattolico, gli ricercassero adesso i compimento di essa, come ha fatto et fa dalla sua parte il re di Spagna " (*ibid.*).

[2] " *che li lasciasse nella giusta possessione della sua antiqua religione et delli suoi antipassati, poi che non consentirono di rendergli obedienza si non con questa condizione et speranza sotto la parola che lui haveva dato a questa S. Sede et ad altri principi (come si è detto) mentre era re di Scotia " (*Ibid.*)

[3] " *Non pare che stiamo fuora di tutta speranza, ch'il re si possa ridurre " (*ibid.*). The future Pope Urban VIII., when nuncio in France, kept the conversion of James always before him as his aim. A correspondent in England, with whom he kept in touch for that purpose, told him nevertheless, " *In quanto all'inclinatione del re, di cui ella mi fa si viva istanza, io non saprei dir cosa fondata sul vero, vedendosi tanta variatione in un momento, che non più presto si prende speranza, ch'egli voglia tornare al grembo della Chiesa, che immantinente si perde. . . . Se ho da dire il vero, ho perso la buona speranza, che io havevo dapoi che domandandone l'opinione sua al primo presidente di Scotia . . . me ne parlò molto liberamente con ferma credenza, che non dovesse succedere il bene che si desidera, fondato principalmente in conoscere l'humore del re, che si presuma di sapere più di quanti santi hanno scritto, e che perciò difficilmente si potrà mai disporre di credere ad altri, e che se alle volte si vedono apparenze in contrario, sono artificii suoi fatti con disegno," *Cod. Barb.*, p. 227 *seq.*, Vatican Library.

he should be assured that the loyalty of his Catholic subjects will not be wanting if he treats them as a king should treat his subjects: if he acts otherwise he would have to fear the Holy See. True, the Pope was "without hands, feet or strength" by reason of the discord among Christian princes,[1] but that was just why every nerve should be strained to re-establish concord between them. The writer then explains in detail how so happy a result might be brought about.[2] He makes more than one reference to the Gunpowder plot; he thinks it was the work of a handful of laymen who would listen to no advice from any priest and that it was provoked, or at least promoted, by the government which carefully saw to it that the chief witnesses should meet a premature end and which, thereupon, against all probability, charged three Jesuits with the crime.[3]

After so many collisions with the Pope, James I.'s matrimonial plans for his children brought him once more in touch with Rome. The king was being pressed on all sides to conclude a family alliance with some reigning Catholic

[1] "*Mentre che lui (James I.) vede (the powerlessness of Spain), et V.S. senza mani, piedi et forze per stare in discordia li principi christiani, delli quelli V.S. se potrebbe agiutare per rifrenare et mettere alla raggione li heretici, quelli d'Inghilterra et il loro re non fanno nè faranno conto della S.V." (f. 142).

[2] *Ibid.*

[3] "*Dio volesse che la indiscretione de'alcuni pochi cattolici secolari (per non pigliar consiglio con chi devevano) trasportati dal sentimento dell'ingiurie esorbitanti fattegli dagli heretici per irritarli a fare qualche disordine, non havesse oscurato questa gloria di patire con titolo della religione. . . . Chi non vede l'ingiustitia . . . in volere estendere la colpa de alcuni pochi al corpo delli cattolici innocenti? per il quale giachè havevano morto a quelli che potevano testificare la verità hanno publicato . . . questa nuova calumnia contra tre religiosi della Compagnia, che non può haver apparentia alcuna di verità (f. 139). E molto probabile, che ci ha havuto qualche partecipatione d'alcuni delli medesimi, si no nel principio, al manco nella prosecutione di questa ultima congiura," of the kind that happened in Babington's conspiracy (f. 140).

house, for among the princes who shared his own Calvinist creed the choice was really too limited ; the petty Lutheran potentates of Germany and the kings of Sweden and Denmark could hardly stand comparison, as regards splendour and wealth, even with the dukes of Savoy and Florence, not to speak of the sovereign houses of Spain, Austria and France. Besides, James viewed himself not a little complacently in the rôle of a great mediator, for by allying himself with a Catholic power, he would be able to initiate a reconciliation between the Catholic and Protestant peoples.[1] His always empty purse would best be served by the rich dowry of a Catholic daughter-in-law.[2] An influential party at Court and one that was still Catholic at heart, headed by the earl of Northampton, seconded these plans ; these men saw in the restoration of the old religion the surest bulwark against puritanism, hence they were anxious for the heir to the crown to marry a Catholic princess.[3]

However, to enable him to form an alliance with a Catholic ruling family the king of England needed the consent of the Pope. He was to have an unpleasant reminder of the fact as early as 1608. At that time James was using his influence in Madrid with a view to the betrothal of his daughter Elizabeth to the nephew of Philip III., the son of the Duke of Savoy. The king of Spain was not unfavourably disposed, but the plan came to nought owing to the objections of Paul V.[4] In 1611, the Duke of Savoy took it up once more ; Elizabeth, he hinted this time, might become a Catholic.[5] However, the discussions led to no better result than did the efforts of even a far more distinguished suitor for Elizabeth's hand, namely the king of Spain himself, a widower since 1611.[6] On February 14th, 1613, with great pomp and amid the

[1] Gardiner, II., 138.

[2] *Ibid.*

[3] *Ibid.*, 137.

[4] Cardinal Millini to Paul V., July 4, 1614, in Gardiner, II., 27.

[5] Gardiner, II., 137.

[6] *Ibid.*, 151.

jubilations of the Protestants, the English princess was married to the leader of the Calvinist party in Germany, Frederick V., elector Palatine, subsequently known as "the Winter King".[1] Though James I. protested—but only after the failure of his efforts for a Spanish alliance—that nothing would persuade him to give his daughter to a Papist,[2] he nevertheless did not relax his efforts to secure a Catholic bride for Henry, the heir to the crown. In 1611, the Duke of Savoy had proposed the marriage of his son with Elizabeth, and that of his daughter with the Prince of Wales.[3] Not long after that, at the instigation of the Spanish envoy, Velasco, James I. thought of betrothing his son, in the first instance, to the Spanish Infanta Anne, then to Anne's sister Mary, then a child of six years old,[4] and finally to a sister of the grand duke of Tuscany. Salisbury, who had been in charge of the negotiations with Florence since 1611, did not fail to make discreet inquiries about the amount of the dowry that might be expected.[5] The grand duke laid the matter before the Pope who declared that he could not sanction the proposal.[6] The duke of Savoy felt fewer scruples than

[1] *Ibid.*, 152, 160 *seq.*

[2] *Ibid.*, 152.

[3] *Ibid.*, 137. "*Instructione per il P. Fra Paolo da Cesena Cappuccino di quello che haverà da trattare col Sigr. Duca di Savoia per impedire il matrimonio del principe di Piemonte con la Principessa d'Inghilterra," August 13, 1619 (*sic!*), in the *Instruzioni politiche sopra varie materie*, Vol. II., *Cod.* 468, f. 456 *seqq.*, Corsini Library, Rome. (*Cf.* LÄMMER, *Zur Kirchengesch.*, 127 *seq.*). The date is wrong as the crown prince of Savoy had already married Christina of France on February 10, 1619. According to SIRI, II., 559, the date of the Instruction is August 13, 1605. *Cf. ibid.*, 585, 712 for the nuncio's efforts in 1611 and 1612.

[4] GARDINER, II., 138 *seq.* Mary was born in 1606.

[5] *Ibid.*, 139 *seq.*

[6] *Ibid.*, 153. "*Summarium rationum, ob quas ill. cardinales a SS. D.N. ad id deputati censuerunt, omnino denegandam esse dispensationem a S. Magno Etruriae duce petitam collocandi in matrimonium unam ex sororibus suis Angliae principi haere-

the Medici, for he saw the advantages of having England for an ally against Spain. He promised a dowry of 700,000 ducats; as for the rest, he declared himself satisfied if the future queen could practise her religion in secret.[1] Marie de Medici, the regent of France, was even less troubled by religious scruples when James I., at the prompting of the duke de Bouillon, proposed to her to marry the Prince of Wales to her daughter Christina, then only six years old. She was prepared to let the child be taken to England in the following year when she would certainly have been brought up as a Protestant.[2]

All these plans were rudely upset by the death, on November 6th, 1612, of prince Henry. Thereupon, James' second son, Charles, was to step into his brother's place, even as the future husband of Christina. In France, in November, 1613, the affair was considered as settled. The more moderate Protestant elements, and the Scottish favourites of the king of England, had been won over to the plan.[3]

However, the friends of Spain at the English Court were not idle. Since 1613 the Spanish ambassador in London was Diego Sarmiento de Acuña, count of Gondomar,[4] a clever diplomat who had been purposely chosen with a view to restraining James from entering into an alliance with France and the Protestant

tico," in *Borghese*, II., 56, 57, p. 292, Papal Secret Archives; *TARQ. PINAORO, "Risolutioni di un politico detto il cattolico scritte l'a. 1612 sopra il corrente dubbio, se N.S. Paolo V. P.M. deve ammettere il matrimonio fra la sorella del gran duca di Toscana e il figlio del re d'Inghilterra eretico e ciò tanto per la ragion di stato quanto di religione, lasciata però la questione teologale a chi tocca," *Urb.*, 860, f. 281–297 (*cf.* 861, f. 360–8), Vatican Library.

[1] GARDINER, II., 153.

[2] *Ibid.*, 154–7.

[3] GARDINER, II., 223 *seq.*

[4] *Ibid.*, 165; F. H. LYON, *Diego de Sarmiento de Acuña, Conde de Gondomar*, Oxford, 1910. *Cf.* WENCESLAO RAMIREZ DE VILLA-URRUTIA, MARQUES DE VILLA-URRUTIA, *La embajada de conde de Gondomar a Inglaterra en 1613*, Madrid, 1913.

Powers.[1] Gondomar gained such an ascendancy over the weak king that soon he came to hold the first place in James' entourage and to make the king his willing tool.[2] Among the royal counsellors Northampton, to whom James' all-powerful favourite, Somerset, was wholly devoted, supported the interests of Spain.[3] Queen Anne also entertained Spanish sympathies, for though she accompanied her husband to Protestant sermons, she never took the Anglican Communion and heard Mass in secret.[4] But when Philip III. made it known that he would never give his hand to a Protestant, the Spanish party in London turned its attention to one of the daughters of the Duke of Savoy.[5]

In the following year, however, the king of Spain tried to resume negotiations.[6] James assured Sarmiento that he would

[1] GARDINER, II., 218.

[2] "No other ambassador, before or since, succeeded so completely in making a tool of an English king" (GARDINER, IV., 335). Paul V., in two Briefs of 1614, praised Sarmiento for his zeal for the Catholic Church in England. *Epist.*, IX., Papal Secret Archives.

[3] GARDINER, II., 218, 225, 247.

[4] *Ibid.*, 225. That Anne was a Catholic is fairly certain; see PLENKERS, in the *Stimmen aus Maria-Laach*, XXXV. (1888), 491 *seqq.*; BELLESHEIM, *Scotland*, III., 348 *seqq.* Meanwhile Paul V. wrote to the nuncio Ubaldini, that no reliance could be placed on Anne as she was very changeable and her husband was becoming increasingly cruel towards the Catholics. (W. BLISS, in the *English Hist. Review*, 1889, 110).

[5] GARDINER, II., 225.

[6] *Ibid.*, 247. *Cf.* FRANCISCO DE JESUS, *El hecho de los tratados del matrimonio pretendido por el principe de Gales con la ser. infante de España Maria, tomado desde sus principios*, ed. S. R. Gardiner (Camden Society), London, 1869; S. R. GARDINER, *Prince Charles & the Spanish Marriage*, London, 1869; LUIGI AREZIO, *L'azione diplomatica del Vaticano nella questione del matrimonio Spagnuolo di Carlo Stuart, principe de Galles (a. 1623)*, Palermo, 1896 (from documents of January 24, to November 1, 1623, at Palermo); LINGARD, VII., 238 *seqq.*; F. KUNX, *Oesterreich und der spanisch-englische Heiratsplan vom Jahre 1623*, Wien,

gladly give up the French marriage provided Philip did not make impossible conditions.[1] Thereupon the envoy advised his master not to insist on the royal heir becoming a Catholic previous to the marriage, nor on the repeal of the anti-Catholic laws; the first of these conditions might cost the king his life; the second was beyond his power without the consent of Parliament. Let him press the king to liberate the priests from prison; not to exact fines, and to refrain from supporting the Protestant powers; then the old religion would once more triumph of its own accord, Protestantism would collapse on the Continent and the king of England would see the necessity of returning to the Church.[2]

Philip III., decided to lay the matter before the Pope. As was to be expected, Paul V.'s decision was unfavourable.[3] He praised the king's first reply to England in which he had stipulated for the heir's conversion to the Catholic faith and informed the king of England that he would never betroth his daughter to a non-Catholic. Philip III. should abide by this decision; unless the royal prince returned to the Church, the Pope could only disapprove and exceedingly abhor such a betrothal [4] since he had successfully maintained, both by written exhortations and by personal envoys, a

1895; A. GINDELY, in *Archiv f. österr. Gesch.*, LXXXIX (1901), 59–76, and in the *Zeitschr. f. allgem. Gesch.*, I (1884), 481–497, 607–629; **Discorso sobre el casamiento que se trata entre el principe de Gales y la ser. Ynfanta de España del conde D. Ant. Xerley dirigido al conde Olivares, Barb.*, 3453, Vatican Library; **Varie scritture che mostrano che la Ynfanta Maria deve darsi in matrimonio al princ. de Gales, Cod. Ottob.* 3077, *ibid.*

[1] GARDINER, II., 252.

[2] *Ibid.*, 255.

[3] Original draft of Paul V.'s letter, printed in BELLESHEIM, II., *seqq.*; the Count of Castro to Philip III., July 14, 1614, in GARDINER, II., 255. *Cf.* an unfavourable opinion of Bellarmine on the Spanish marriage in LE BACHELET, *Auct. Bellarm.*, 541–3.

[4] "Senza la quale non potria S. Santità se non improvare et detestare grandemente questo accasamento" (in BELLESHEIM, *loc. cit.*).

similiar attitude towards other princes. His reasons were many: there was the Church's prohibition of mixed marriages; the scandal for Catholics and the encouragement of the Protestants; the danger to which the faith of a young princess would be exposed through daily intercourse with heretics, more particularly because of certain delicate points in the oath of allegiance which the less instructed might deem irrelevant from the standpoint of orthodoxy.[1] Moreover the children would be brought up in heresy; the consequent intercourse with heretical countries would be fraught with disastrous results; divorce was allowed in England; a very bad example would be set to other Catholic countries. In view of the prevailing conditions in England and the unsatisfactory character of the king, no good result could be expected, hence it was essential that the royal prince should first become a Catholic. The promised concessions were inadequate; the danger of the future queen being drawn into heresy and of her children being brought up as Protestants still subsisted, even if she was permitted to practise her religion in secret and was promised liberty of conscience. A tacit concession of freedom of conscience was worthless because it by no means excluded the possibility that the queen and her children would be driven into the arms of heresy; the mere word of the king was no guarantee of this concession; since he would not explicitly grant religious freedom, he would always be able either to break his promise, or arbitrarily to interpret it. If the tacit concession were equivalent to an express one, he would not confine himself to the former; hence it is clear that he is not honest. To talk of liberty of conscience, without the free exercise of Catholic worship, would not greatly benefit Catholics.

Philip III. refused to be satisfied with this answer. He called a council of theologians and asked for their opinion on James I's proposals, without, however, laying the papal letter before them. The prospect of freedom of conscience for the

[1] "Massime in certi punti sottili che si contengono nel giuramento del Re d'Inghilterra, i quali a chi non è informato non par che tocchino i dogmi della fede" (*ibid.*).

Catholics of England so impressed the meeting that it pronounced in favour of the marriage, subject to the Pope's assent. Thereupon the Privy Council determined the conditions of the match: a change of religion on the part of the heir to the throne was no longer a necessary preliminary, and the remission of the fines by a mere act of grace on the part of the king was approved, on the plea that the Puritans would likewise benefit if the laws were repealed.[1] Meanwhile Paul V. was of opinion that his previous decision was in no way altered by the opinion of the theologians; so he merely pigeon-holed their memorandum. In London and Madrid the exchange of opinions on the marriage pursued an uninterrupted course.[2] Digby, who was in charge of the negotiations at Madrid, bluntly told the king that a Protestant princess was preferable to a Catholic one, notwithstanding the Infanta's rich dowry. A Catholic princess would provoke trouble in the country; Catholics would so increase that stern measures would be needed to repress them. However, if they insisted on a Catholic princess for the heir to the throne, it was, of course, best to look to Spain for there they found the purest royal blood in conjunction with the greatest quantity of the best ducats.[3]

However, at that very time James I. was undecided whether, after all, he should not prefer France to Spain. Just then the French stood high in James' estimation. The famous Spanish theologian, Suarez, had written a refutation of the king's book on the oath of allegiance, and to James' boundless joy, Suarez's book, owing to its incompatibility with Gallican principles, had been burnt in Paris by the hand of the public executioner.[4] So the envoy, Edmondes, was instructed to return to the French capital with fresh proposals for a marriage

[1] GARDINER, II., 256.

[2] GINDELY, in the *Zeitschr. f. allg. Gesch.*, I., 488.

[3] GARDINER, II., 257.

[4] *Cf.* RANCE, in the *Rev. d. quest. hist.*, XXXVII. (1885), 594–608; LÄMMER, *Zur Kirchengesch.*, 88. The French nuncio Ubaldini was commissioned on March 15, 1614, "Quando V.S. senta chè da qualche maligno si parli più del libro del P. Suarez,

settlement, different from those he had made in February However, Marie de Medici had no wish for an alliance with England, so that James needs must turn to Spain once more.[1] Sarmiento thought he might indulge in a little jubilation. If the conditions of the contract in favour of the Catholics are carried out at once, he wrote in December, 1614, and if the Infanta delays her journey to England for a few years, the Catholic religion would have had time to make good progress. Circumstances might be such that the Prince of Wales would be married in Spain and assist at Mass and a sermon in the church of our Lady of Atocha.[2]

At one moment it looked as if Sarmiento had judged the situation aright. Digby set out for Spain and behind his back, Somerset, the king's favourite, also entered into negotiations with Philip III.[3] At the beginning of May, James was acquainted with Spain's conditions. All the children of the future queen were to be baptized Catholics and brought up as such by their mother, and if they wished to remain Catholics that fact was not to be a bar to the succession. All the servants of the Infanta were to be of her faith, and the adherents of the old religion who lived at court were to be assigned a public church, or chapel, to which anyone might have free access; the clergy of that church should be permitted to appear in clerical attire in the open street, and in the meantime the penal laws were to be suspended.[4]

At the moment when these conditions came to his knowledge, James I. was in anything but a friendly mood towards Spain. Because of the remark of a certain Owen, that excommunicated princes might be killed, the naturally timorous monarch lived in constant dread of assassins. He slept in a bed which was protected by a barricade of three other beds;

sarà carissimo che ella con la sua solita accuratezza veda di rimediare con suoi offitii afinchè non ne nasca scandalo ed inconveniente," Stuttgart Library. *Cod.* 181.

[1] Gardiner, II., 314 *seqq.*

[2] *Ibid.*, 316.

[3] *Ibid.*, 316, 321 *seq.*

[4] *Ibid.*, 323 *seq.*

whenever he showed himself in public he was surrounded by a troop of soldiers so that no one could get near him and the whole cortège had to march as fast as possible. James' excited imagination conjured up before his eyes a vision of his own son using the Spanish alliance in order to bring about —with the help of the Catholics—a rebellion against his own father; he already saw himself, as an old man, spending his days behind prison bars or even ending them by the hand of a hired assassin. Hence his fear of getting in closer touch with Spain[1]; hence also the annotations on the back of the document containing the Spanish conditions, which he wrote with his own hand, are for the most part in the negative.[2]

However, this mood did not last. By the end of May the negotiations for a French princess of Wales appeared pretty hopeless, so once again an alliance with the king of Spain appeared in rosiest hues.[3] About the middle of June, 1615, he was prepared, subject to a few minor modifications, to accept the Spanish conditions as a basis for further negotiations.[4] "He was mad with delight," he said, "at having been made the channel of such a communication." "At last," he added, "a prospect was opened of his being able to live and die a professed Catholic, as his ancestors had done before him." Sir Robert Cotton, destined, later on, to become famous as an archæologist, communicated the news to the Spanish envoy by James' command.[5]

In March, 1616, James' envoy, Digby, was back from Madrid. He had succeeded in obtaining some modifications of the conditions. Lerma had agreed that in the marriage settlement nothing should be said of the Catholic baptism and upbringing of the children, nor of a mitigation of the penal laws, and as for the domestic staff of the future queen, the only thing agreed upon was that the king of Spain should select its members.[6] Nevertheless Digby counselled the king

[1] GARDINER, II., 325 *seq.*
[2] *Ibid.*, 324 *seq.*
[3] *Ibid.*, 326.
[4] *Ibid.*, 326.
[5] *Ibid.*, 326 *seq.*
[6] *Ibid.*, 392.

rather to choose a German princess as a future queen, for the king of Spain could do nothing without the Pope's approval, hence he was not in a position to dispose of the hand of his own daughter.[1]

In the course of the year, James made a last attempt to secure the hand of a French princess for his son. Notwithstanding the low level of his exchequer, which induced the king to sell the peerage for gold, his agent, Lord Hay, entered Paris in great state. Legend has it that the horses' silver shoes had been purposely fastened so loosely that they were bound to come off as the cortège trotted along. For all that the English proposals and conditions, chief among which was once more the guarantee of a dowry, were declined by Paris and thus an end was put to the prospect of a French marriage.[2]

With regard to the negotiations with Spain, which had been resumed a few weeks after Digby's return, a preliminary difficulty had to be solved. James had had inquiries made in Madrid whether the Pope would refuse to sanction the marriage *a priori* and in principle, even if he made reasonable concessions? Philip III.'s reply was that it would be an insult to the Pope to ask him whether he would give his sanction to conditions which had not even been laid before him.[3] Nevertheless, through Cardinal Borja, the king of Spain sounded Paul V. who happened to be at Frascati. After a somewhat lengthy delay the answer came, in October, 1616, that the Pope would only give his consent to the match if the Prince of Wales became a Catholic and if English Catholics were granted religious freedom.[4]

In accordance with this decision the Spaniards now strove for a marriage contract with which the Pope could be satisfied. The religion of the heir to the crown must be left to his own choice, hence this point was only lightly touched upon in the discussions between Digby and Luis de Aliaga, the king's confessor. On the other hand, the Spaniards were all the

[1] *Ibid.*, 390.

[2] *Ibid.*, 391–6.

[3] *Ibid.*, 391.

[4] Gindely, *loc. cit.*, 488.

more insistent that, until they came to the age of maturity, the royal children should remain in the care of their mother. As regards English Catholics, Digby was willing to promise toleration, but only a tacit toleration. On the other hand he insisted that Philip III. should pay immediately an advance of half a million ducats on the dowry; to this the Spaniards would not agree.[1]

In 1618 the British agent returned to England. His return was the signal for lengthy discussions of the Privy Council. When Gondomar returned to Spain that year, they were far from having reached a decision, and they were no nearer two years later, when he was back in London. Nevertheless James I. did not fail to impress on the returned traveller how much he had at heart the two million ducats, a fact which caused Gondomar to complain to Buckingham in forceful language. Thereupon James summoned the Spaniard into his presence, assured him that henceforth Catholics might practise their religion, and, with his hand on his breast, swore that no man loved the king of Spain more than he did.[2]

As a matter of fact just then James I. had a special reason to court Spain's friendship. His thoughtless son-in-law, Frederick, Elector Palatine, had accepted the crown of Bohemia at the hands of rebels and was now in danger of losing not only Bohemia, but even his own hereditary State. Spain, by reason of her geographical position in the Netherlands, exercised a real influence over affairs in Germany and could intervene decisively for or against the elector. However the concessions to which James agreed under pressure of circumstances did not yet satisfy Spain. True, he had promised that henceforth no Catholic priest would be executed solely for carrying out his ecclesiastical functions, and that he himself was resolved to extend the utmost consideration to the Catholic recusants.[3] But these promises only implied a modification, not a repeal, of the penal laws, and as for the

[1] *Ibid.*, 490.

[2] *Ibid.*, 490 *seq.*

[3] April 27, 1620; see LINGARD, VII., 239 *seqq.*; GARDINER, III., 346.

Infanta, he had conceded free Catholic worship only within the walls of the palace, but not a public church. Nevertheless, by degrees, opinion in Madrid veered round in favour of James. Gondomar pleaded that the king had given proof of good will and that he had already directed that the penal laws should be suspended; once the Spanish marriage was settled he could be relied upon to do still more. Thereupon the Spanish royal council advised Philip first to obtain from Rome the desired permission for the marriage and then only to demand full religious freedom for Catholics.[1]

Accordingly, at the beginning of 1621, Diego de la Fuente was dispatched from Madrid to Rome, whilst in May George Gage, a Catholic, also came to Rome from London, but Paul V. died before they had had time to get in touch with him and before his successor, Gregory XV. could attend to their proposals, Philip III. also died—March 21st, 1621.[2] It is said that, on his deathbed, he counselled his son and successor to win the imperial crown for the head of the much-wooed Infanta. Six months earlier Philip III. had, in effect, promised the hand of his daughter to the future emperor Ferdinand III.[3] The Infanta's ducats seemed definitely lost to James I.

Though under Paul V. relations with James I. had become very close, they nevertheless failed to exercise on the position of English Catholics the favourable influence that might have been expected and which was even taken for granted, especially in Spain.[4] English Protestants would not hear

[1] GINDELY, *loc. cit.*, 491 *seq.*

[2] GARDINER, IV., 230.

[3] *Ibid.*, 189 *seq.* *Cf.* CAUCHIE-MAERE, *Recueil*, 118.

[4] Annual report of the English Jesuits, 1619, in FOLEY, V., 987. The priest Vincent Laurefici, who visited England in 1613 (*Archiv für Kulturgesch.*, I. (1903), 412) found indeed indulgence for Catholic books at the hands of customs officials; these books could also be bought at the booksellers'; in eating houses, mine host took care to provide for Catholics abstinence food on Fridays and Saturdays. This, however, does not betoken any indulgence on behalf of the government. Though English Catholics attended Catholic worship in the embassy chapels, this was allowed as

of a Spanish marriage and the prospect that they might possibly have a Catholic successor to the throne only added fuel to their hatred for Catholics, and just as the expectation of the marriage of the Prince of Wales with the Spanish princess kept the whole country in suspense, so was the marriage already concluded by his elder sister with the elector Frederick a source of scarcely less trouble. England was overjoyed when Frederick accepted the crown of Bohemia at the hands of rebels. "It is marvellous," we read in an English report of 1619, "what new hopes the disturbances in Bohemia have excited in the minds of the people, and how much is made of the Prince Palatine by all classes. He is regarded as one raised up for the destruction of the Papists, for the advance of the gospel, and the conquest of Rome. These vauntings are used by high and low, the children have songs about them, they enter into every sermon and conversation. False reports of the Prince's achievements add fuel to the fire, and the mischief is that public feeling is daily more and more incensed against Catholics, with a strong desire to oppress them, as though they were opposed to the general interests of the country."[1] Instigated by the Privy Council, local authorities subjected Catholics to fresh acts of violence. Especially was the oath of allegiance insisted upon.[2] Thus at one and the same time Protestants could exult that the Bohemians had deposed their lawful sovereign whilst Catholics were treated as guilty of high treason if they refused to swear that princes could not be deposed. The irony with which history forces the hypocrite to condemn himself out of his own mouth is not always so clear-cut, even under James the double-faced, as it appears in this instance.

an exception and out of respect for the ambassadors. Moreover, in the time of Elizabeth, three weekly abstinence days were kept by Protestants (for the purpose of encouraging the fisheries; see FRERE, 101) and in November, 1606, for example, all who came from Mass at the Belgian Embassy chapel, were arrested. *Cf.* WILLAERT, in the *Rev. d'hist. ecclés.*, VIII. (1907), 82.

[1] Annual report, in FOLEY, V., 987 *seq.*

[2] *Ibid.*, 988, 989.

When the hopes which had been placed on the elector abruptly collapsed at the battle of the Weissen Berg, the anger and embitterment of English Protestants flared up as never before. His death spared Paul V. the spectacle of the further developments of these events.

However threatening, and at times wellnigh desperate, the condition of Catholics under James I. may have appeared, they themselves never lost sight of the internal development of their affairs which had begun under Clement VIII.[1] The efforts to secure a bishop for England were renewed under Paul V.[2] For this purpose, shortly before his death in 1621,

[1] *Cf.* present work, Vol. XXIV., ch. I. *passim.*

[2] Thus in the year 1610 (Foley, VII., 2, 1005, 1018, 1022) and in 1612 (Lämmer, *Melet.*, 319). Maffeo Barberini, the nuncio in France since 1604, supported the nomination of bishops for England: "*Il Generale dei Giesuiti in quell'acerbità di tempi non havendo persona alcuna in Inghilterra, che potesse confortare i suoi religiosi, si raccomandava frequentemente al patrocinio di Maffeo, il quale ricevendo gli avvisi e le lettere, che loro scriveva il medesimo Generale, le faceva poi penetrare in quel regno per mezzo di Gio. Svitto Cattolico e suo corrispondente. Pensò ancora il Nuntio ad un altro ripiego, che fosse atto a porgere aiuto e reggere e consolare quegli afflitti Cattolici e questo sarebbe stato il creare alcuni vescovi in quel regno; onde ne scrisse sensatamente al Papa, con rappresentarli però che dovendosi far questa elettione, si scegliessero soggetti, in cui non potesse cadere sospetto, che fossero per ingerirsi in cose di stato e che non fossero nè del partito de' Gesuiti nè degli appellanti, che erano le due fattioni contrarie poco prima insorte fra i Cattolici di quel regno" (*Nicoletti, Vita di Urbano VIII.*, Barb. 4730, f. 238 *seq.*, Vatican Library). A *letter from the English Benedictines at Douai, of August 18, 1607, to Cardinal Givry, assigns as the reason for this desire for bishops, the quarrels among the clergy. "Cum clerus Anglicanus divisus fuerit per multos annos periculosissima simultate sic ut una pars patribus Iesuitis omnia deferat, altera pars pertinacissime repugnat," therefore unprejudiced men should be chosen as bishops. Rumour mentioned as candidates the President of the Douai Seminary, Th. Worthington; the dean of Courtrai, Wright; the priest Th. Fitzherbert; the layman George Talbot. As for the latter: "omnino ab illis

the archpriest, Harrison, under pretext of asking for a dispensation for the Spanish marriage of the Prince of Wales, dispatched the priest John Bennet, to the Eternal City.[1] The death of Paul V. prevented the settlement of the affair.

An event of importance for the Church in England was the return of the Benedictines to a country which owes its Christianity to their Order. Many natives of England, for the most part pupils of the English seminaries abroad, had become monks in various monasteries. The request that some of their number, on the completion of their studies, might be sent as missionaries to England, was granted by a decree of the Inquisition of December 5th, 1602. This led to a powerful influx of vocations into the Benedictine monasteries in Spain, both from England itself and from the seminary of Valladolid, which was under the direction of the Jesuits. In 1603, in consequence of internal troubles, no less than twenty-five students of the seminary sought admission with the Benedictines.[2] The incident gave rise to some friction between the two Orders which had to be smoothed down by a decree of the Inquisition on December 10th, 1608.[3]

clericis reicitur, qui ad sedem Romanam contra Iesuitas appellarunt." The three former were wholly in favour of the Jesuits (Municipal Library, Metz, MS. 219, p. 157). In the same document are further complaints against the Jesuits: "Haeremus adhuc in iisdem salebris, quoniam per quorundam patrum Iesuitarum consilia nondum obtinuimus facultatem monasterium erigendi, quae sola facultas nobis deest et si adesset a principe, habemus reliqua omnia parata" (*ibid.*, p. 156).

[1] BELLESHEIM, *Scotland*, III., 238 *seqq.*; LINGARD, VII., 240.

[2] CAMM, in *The Month*, XCII. (1898), 374.

[3] Printed in *The English Review*, IV. (1889), 737 *seq.* For the quarrel *cf.* CAMM, *loc. cit.*, 364–377; POLLEN, *ibid.*, XCIV. (1899), 233–248, 348–365; LAW, in *The Engl. Hist. Rev.*, *loc. cit.*, 730–8; LÄMMER, *Melet.*, 278. *Cf.* in the **Lettres et Mémoires du card. Givry*, some letters addressed to him by the Benedictines: The Prior and Community of Douai beg him on June 10, 1607, to take their cloister under his protection (p. 107); on August 28, 1607, they put forward suggestions for putting an end to the strife (p. 156 *seq.*); Letters from the English Benedictine Anselm

There was still living at the time a member of the ancient abbey of Westminster, which had been restored in the reign of Queen Mary, namely Dom Sigebert Buckley, who had lingered in prison during forty years for the sake of the faith. In 1607 a few English monks of the Cassinese Congregation joined him, Paul V. subsequently ratifying all that had been done. In this way all the rights of the former abbey of Westminster passed, through Buckley (d. 1610) to the new body and the connection with the old pre-reformation Benedictines remained unbroken. In 1612 Paul V. approved the confederation of the English Benedictines formed from members of the Spanish and Italian monasteries, and on August 23rd, 1619, he approved the English Missionary Congregation which had come into being at a conference held in Paris under the presidency of the nuncio Bentivoglio. In 1615 there were seventy English members of the Spanish, and twelve of the Cassinese, Congregation. There were many splendid missionary priests among them and not a few gave their lives for the faith.[1] On the Continent they had monasteries at Douai, at Dieulouard in Lorraine, and at Paris,[2] to which others were added at a later date.

The year 1618 also witnessed the restoration of the English Franciscan Province, for in that year John Genning established a convent of Observants at Douai.[3] Henry Garnet had done much for the internal consolidation of the English Jesuit

about the quarrel, Rome, January 25, 1609, etc. (*ibid.*, p. 333 *seq.*); Letter from the Prior of Douai, February 23, 1609, *Cod.* 219 of the Municipal Lib., Metz. *Cf.* CLEM. REYNER, *Apostolatus Benedictorum in Anglia*, Douai, 1626, 242 *seqq.*, and Appendix of documents, 1–40.

[1] P. SCHMIEDER in *Studien u. Mitteil. aus dem Benediktiner-u.-Zisterzienserorden*, XII. (1891), 86–8; E. TAUNTON, *English Black Monks of St. Benedict*, London, 1897; *American Catholic Encyclopædia*, II., 447; POLLEN, in *The Month*, XC. (1897), 581–600.

[2] Founded in 1605, 1606, 1611.

[3] *Annales Minorum continuati a Stanislao Melchiorri de Cereto*, XXV., Quaracchi, 1886, *ad a.* 1618, n. 8, p. 293.

mission. In 1619 it was given the status of a vice-Province and in 1623 that of a Province.[1] Though there is frequent mention of the Jesuits in the last years of Elizabeth, their number was very small. In 1593 there were only eight Jesuits in England. In 1598 there were fourteen at liberty and four in various prisons.[2] The erection of a vice-Province gave the impulse to rapid growth.[3] By 1625 the youthful foundation counted 115 members in Flanders, 152 in England and a total of 366 in 1634, though from that year numbers began to fall off.[4]

Convents of Nuns for English ladies were likewise founded on the Continent.[5] It was precisely in the sphere of female religious associations that an original foundation occurred which was destined to have considerable bearing on the future of these communities: this was when, in 1609, Mary Ward, with a few companions from England, founded a convent in Flanders. The scope of the community, viz. the education of girls, was nothing new; what was original was that with the "English ladies" (as they are called in Germany) the whole organization of the Institute was, for the first time, closely adapted to that scope, chiefly by means of the appointment of a Superior General for the whole Institute, the absence of enclosure and choir and various other details.

The English Seminary in Rome received from Paul V. a fresh confirmation of its privileges [6] and more than once the

[1] FOLEY, VII., 1, lxx. *seqq.* A separate noviciate for the English Jesuits was opened at Watten in Flanders; see WILLAERT in the *Rev. d'hist. ecclés.* IX. (1908), 55. *Cf.* *Paul V. to the bishop of St. Omer, February 17, 1607 (instructing him that the provost's residence at Watten should be given to them), *Epist.*, II., Papal Secret Archives.

[2] FOLEY, VII., 1, lxvi *seq.*

[3] *Cf.* the Jesuit's report for 1619, *ibid.*, V., 988.

[4] *Ibid.*, VII., 1, lxxv. *seqq.*

[5] MORRIS, 2. *Cf.* STEELE, *The Convents of Great Britain*, London, 1902; POLLEN, in *The Month*, XC. (1897), 583; A. PASTURE, in *Annuaire de l'Université cath. de Louvain*, 1913, 449 *seqq.*

[6] September 3, 1607, *Synopsis*, 241.

Pope appealed to princes and magnates on behalf of the English Colleges on the Continent.[1]

(3.)

The Catholics of Scotland were so hard pressed that the French envoy wrote they were even more deserving of pity than their correligionists in England. Thus it was strictly forbidden to let a house to anyone who was merely suspected of being a Catholic. To give lodging to a Papist was to be suspected of heresy. Three citizens of Edinburgh, who had given hospitality to a priest, saw themselves condemned to death, though the sentence was not carried out. John Logan had to expiate the "crime" of having been present at Mass with a fine of £1,000 Scots (£5,000 sterling); others were punished with banishment, and one John Due, who consented to apostatize, had to do penance in sackcloth and ashes for the space of eight days.[2] In 1609, the papal Secretary of State, Cardinal Borghese, was informed that permission to leave Scotland had to be asked of the king, and it was only granted on the traveller promising not to become a Catholic whilst abroad. Catholics leaving the country could only take part of their property and had to leave their children behind; these were then brought up in England, in the Protestant religion. Whosoever was present at Mass, whilst abroad, forfeited his whole property for himself and his heirs, in favour of the crown. The same penalty befell those who were excommunicated by the preachers because of their obstinate adherence to popery.[3]

The death penalty against Catholics was but seldom carried

[1] *Brief to the duke of Lerma, May 7, 1605, to the king of Spain, May 5, 1606; *The Pope recommends the English Seminary at Madrid to the Spanish king in 1611, and *to his confessor, Luis de Aliaga, November 9, 1611 (*Epist.*, VII., Papal Secret Archives). *Cf. Bull.*, XII., 182 *seq.*

[2] BELLESHEIM, Vol. III., p. 401, of Hunter Blair's Engl. transl. (Will. Blackwood, Edinburgh).

[3] Ottavio Mancini to Borghese, April 29, 1609, in BELLESHEIM, II., 470 *seq.*

out in Scotland. An exception was the execution of the Jesuit, John Ogilvie, which was carried out at Glasgow in 1615.[1] By this execution the new bishops, whom James I. had forced upon presbyterian Scotland, hoped to clear themselves of any suspicion that their episcopal office had anything in common with the old religion.[2] Nor were there in Scotland any fines for not attending church. For all that, as a contemporary relates, the persecution was no less severe there.[3] If it had been possible, in Scotland, to buy off the persecution with money, few, if any, among the more distinguished members of the aristocracy would not gladly have given a third of their fortune for the sake of liberty to live openly as Catholics. At present people were made to hope for milder treatment if they attended heretical services ; soon, however, they were pressed to sign an heretical creed ; if they refused, they were punished with confiscation of their property, inprisonment for life, or banishment. In the opinion of the informant, imprisonment was more cruel than death itself ; if they were given the option of an heroic death for the faith, there would not be enough prisons and executioners. Conditions such as these accounted for the apostacy of many and for the prevailing opinion that English Catholics were stauncher in the faith than the Scots. This opinion was an erroneous one for many members of the aristocracy were in exile for the faith, whereas this was not true to the same extent of the nobility of England.

[1] JAMES FORBES, *L'Église catholique en Écosse à la fin du XVIe siècle. Martyre de Jean Ogilvie*, Paris, 1885 ; W. FORBES-LEITH, *Narratives*, 296–316 ; SPILLMANN, in the *Stimmen aus Maria-Laach*, XV. (1878), 1 *seqq.*, 155 *seqq.*, 389 *seqq.*, XVI. (1879), 139 *seqq.*, 242 *seqq.* ; W. E. BROWN, *J. Ogilvie*, London, 1925. *Cf.* Bibl. Casanatense, Rome. *N. 23, p. 354–6 ; *ibid.*, p. 348–354, **Relazione delle cose di Scozia al card. Aldobrandini.*

[2] BELLESHEIM, III., p. 414 *seq.* ; FORBES LEITH, *Narratives*, 296 *seq.*

[3] " Narratio de statu religionis apud Scotos et de rationibus fidei catholicae in magna Britannia restituendae," *Barb.* 2696, Vatican Library, compiled about 1617–1619, according to BELLESHEIM, who quotes a section, III., Appendix No. XIX, p. 497.

On the whole the nobles of Scotland remained Catholics at heart and it was precisely the chief aim of the Protestants to induce them to forsake the ancient faith.[1] On the other hand the writer of the report quoted above chiefly based his hopes for Scotland's return to the Church on the country gentry. The Scottish nobles, he explains, whose country houses are scattered over all the land, enjoy such power and influence, that the common people pay to them almost greater regard than to the king himself; on the other hand, the nobles of the same family stick together and show greater readiness to obey the head of the clan than the sovereign. The cause of the people's attachment to the aristocracy is an economic one. Whereas the English landlord leases his land for a term of fifty years and thereafter has practically no power over either tenant or land, so long as the former regularly pays his rent, the Scottish landlord may evict his tenant at any time; besides he ties him down, beforehand, to all manner of services, especially to military service in the army of his lord. This fact explains how it was possible for the nobles so often to offer armed resistance to their king. Moreover, in Scotland, rent is paid, not in cash, but in kind, the tenant surrendering part of his crops. Thus owner and tenant are incomparably more dependent on each other than they are in England where the rent has to be paid in cash. Hence the English landlord has far more ready money than his Scottish colleague, but the Scottish aristocracy has far greater authority over its dependents than the English, and it never lacks cattle, corn or coal. The compiler of the report, obviously a Scotsman, ends with the suggestion that a beginning should be made with Scotland rather than with England if it was resolved to win back the northern island kingdom to the Catholic faith. Moreover nearly all English harbours are held by government troops who exercise a strict control over all travellers, whereas in Scotland the harbours are in the power of the nearest nobleman.[2]

[1] Bellesheim, III., 402 *seq.*

[2] "Ex his colligitur necessario inchoandum religionis catholicae restitutionem opera Scotorum et non Anglorum, primum

Paul V., during his cardinalate, had been in charge of Scottish affairs. In acknowledging an address of congratulation from the Scots' college at Douai, the Pope declared that, for the above reason, he still cherished a special affection for Scotland,[1] and he proved his interest by recommending the college to archduke Albert.[2] For the rest, neither the above memorandum nor any other pressure succeeded in persuading him to intervene in Scotland. The draft of the special Bull against the oath of allegiance for which a request had come from Scotland, was indeed written but the Bull was never published.[3]

From Ireland also complaints of a fresh "terrible and unheard of blow against Catholics" came to the ears of Paul V. almost as soon as he had succeeded to Peter's throne.[4] On July 4th, 1605, James I. had had an order published which made attendance at Anglican worship compulsory for all and which ordered the forcible expulsion from the country of all priests who would be discovered after December 10th.[5]

The measure, in so far as it concerned the priests, was undoubtedly illegal for no act of Parliament having force of law in Ireland permitted such a penalty. For that reason alone the royal edict was bound to meet with resistance. When the apostate bishop Miler Magrath, convoked in the market-place, to the sound of the bugle, the counsellors and burgesses

ob appulsos et locorum commoditatem, secundo ob nobilium Scotorum authoritatem et vires, tertium ob catholicorum unanimem in coeundo audaciam et voluntatem, quarto ob commeatus opportunitatem et copiam, et denique ob ardentissima vota catholicorum suspirantium ut esse possit auxilium se a persequentium iugo liberandi." *Barb.* 2696, Vatican Library.

1 *Brief to the students of the Scots College at Douai, July 27, 1605, *Epist.*, I., Papal Secret Archives.

2 November 28, 1609, *ibid.*

3 By Bellarmine; see LE BACHELET, *Auct. Bellarm.*, 530.

4 James White, Vicar-Apostolic of Waterford, to Card. Baronius, October 7, 1605, in BELLESHEIM, *Irland*, II., 272 (German text.)

5 GARDINER, I., 391; BELLESHEIM, II., 270, 274.

of Cashel, that they might listen to the proclamation of the edict, not a soul obeyed the summons and every door and window was closed.[1] The expulsion of all priests proved unfeasible. In order to compel people to go to church, recourse had to be had to illegal means, for the law of Ireland did not impose a fine exceeding one shilling for every absence from church. Though for the poor even such a charge was an intolerable burden, the well-to-do were not greatly inconvenienced. Consequently, Chichester, the viceroy, took it on himself to go beyond the law and to impose penalties on his own authority. In October, 1615, he summoned the alderman and the more important burgesses of Dublin into his presence. He had no wish whatever, so he explained, to do violence to their consciences; as a matter of fact, what he wanted them to do was not a matter of conscience at all. All that was asked of them was that, on a given day, and at an appointed time, they should take a seat in church. They would then have to listen to a sermon though they need not agree with its subject matter—the whole thing amounted to no more than a gesture of submission to the law.[2]

However, the Irish were not yet ripe for such moral finessing. Chichester's audience unanimously declared that their conscience would not allow them to do such a thing. The viceroy's answer was an order, on November 13th, for all to be in church on the following Sunday. When none put in appearance, sixteen of their number received a summons to appear before the magistrates, on November 22nd, when one of them lectured them on their duty. Can the king appoint bishops and give them their episcopal power, he argued, and not demand the people's obedience to an authority which he has himself established? Can he order a bishop to give a living to a minister, and at the same time refrain from commanding the parishioners to come to his sermons? Can the

[1] *Ibid.*, 271.

[2] GARDINER, I., 392. For Chichester's policy see A. ZIMMERMANN, in the *Katholik*, 1888, II., 582 *seqq.* *Cf.* MACCAFFREY, in the *Irish Theological Quarterly*, X. (1915), 319 *seqq.*, XI. (1916), 62–75.

king impose on his subjects the duty to serve the State but not that of serving God? The proceedings ended with the submission of one of the sixteen and in the condemnation of nine of their number to a fine of from £50 to £100; all the others were similarly punished.[1] Further acts of violence followed. Before sentence was pronounced the principal peers and burgesses of the country round Dublin presented a petition to the royal Council. They asked for a stay of execution of the royal ordinances until they had had time to bring to the king's notice the unjust proceedings of the Council.[2] Chichester, who had waxed bolder because his first steps against Catholics had yielded an increased attendance at church, threw those who had prompted the petition into prison, though most of them were soon set at liberty after they had prayed for the government's pardon.[3] The fines ordered by the tribunal were not paid and the officials who attempted to collect them found all doors shut against them. In two instances the authorities had the doors opened by force but the consequence was that all Dublin resounded with complaints against such violations of justice.[4]

Nevertheless Chichester, for the time being, went on with the policy he had inaugurated. Juries were selected for the purpose of assessing the value of properties which it was intended to seize instead of the fines that had not been paid. Thereupon the owners, seeing themselves threatened with confiscation of their goods, transferred their property to third persons by means of conveyances ante-dated six months; so great was the general embitterment that the juries did not dare to declare these transactions invalid; on the contrary, they stated that there was nowhere any property for the government to seize, and in the end the Supreme Court had to give a special decision declaring all these fictitious conveyances null and void.[5]

Chichester then took yet another step; he resolved to claim even from those less well off the fine of one shilling for every

[1] GARDINER, I., 393.
[2] *Ibid.*, 393.
[3] *Ibid.*, 394.
[4] *Ibid.*, 394.
[5] *Ibid.*, 395.

absence from church. Four hundred persons received an official summons in Dublin; eighty-eight complied, 149 were sentenced, the rest did not put in an appearance. Similiar proceedings took place in the county of Munster.[1]

Certain subordinate government officials already cherished the hope that Ireland would soon be for the most part Protestant.[2] Chichester knew better. He had his spies all over the country and received early information to the effect that his measures would have already provoked a rising if the horrors of the last civil war were not still vividly present to the minds of all. On the other hand, the viceroy's military effectives—880 foot and 234 cavalry—were far too small to deal with a revolt.[3] So Chichester sought to obtain his end by milder means. On June 3rd, 1603, he wrote to the Privy Council that little could be done with those of the Irish who were of a certain age and fairly prosperous; they should try the young people and the poorer classes. The best prospect of success lay in the education of the young.[4] In the circumstances even the Privy Council in London disapproved the coercive measures that had been applied. On July 3rd, 1616, the Irish Council was called upon to justify its illegal action. It delayed its reply until December 1st: it is a tissue of sophisms and shows the embarrassment of the Irish government.[5] However the English bench, whose opinion had been sought, found the document satisfactory. Even so the authorities in Ireland did not dare to go on with the policy on which they had embarked. On the very day on which the Irish Privy Council wrote its apologia, Chichester stated his own views in a private letter to Salisbury; he declared himself opposed to violent measures and gave it as his opinion

[1] *Ibid.*, 395.
[2] *Ibid.*, 396.
[3] *Ibid.*, 396.
[4] *Ibid.*, 396.
[5] *Ibid.*, 396–8. They even denied that Catholics were in danger of becoming guilty of hypocrisy through the law about attending the established church. For it was the case that God's law commanded attendance at church, and it was impossible to assume that Parliament would order anything contrary to God's law, etc.

that an improvement in the situation could only be looked for from the education of the young. In consequence of a protest by Lord Buttevant against the proceedings in Munster, the English Privy Council on July 26th, 1609, advised a milder treatment of the Catholics of Ireland.[1]

It was precisely in Munster, where Henry Brounker, a decided enemy of Catholicism, was in power, that the persecution was particularly severe. Notwithstanding all exhortations to mildness, priests were being hunted day and night, so we read in a letter of James White to Baronius, written in 1606.[2] One priest who, at the moment of his arrest, made known his profession, was hanged on the spot and three other prisoners were also put to death on the suspicion that they were priests. Fines and terms of imprisonment reduced layfolk to the utmost poverty. The oath of allegiance, which was being enforced in Ireland also, provided a fresh opportunity for cruelty and extortions. In 1607, some priests met in Dublin and reported to the Holy See [3] that a reward of 2,000 florins was offered for the denunciation of a Jesuit and one of a thousand for that of a secular priest. If a servant of a priest fell into the hands of the pursuivants, he was whipped until he revealed his master's hiding-place. Soldiers scoured the whole country for priests and bandits, and when caught they were hanged out of hand, as if the country were under martial law. Lay folk, too, ran the risk of being arbitrarily condemned to death or of having their houses looted. One bishop, one vicar-general, several religious and secular priests and a great number of lay folk languished in prison.[4]

Another calamity befell the Catholics of Ireland when, in 1607, the two powerful earls, Tyrone and Tyrconnel, who owned vast tracts of land in the north of the island, saw themselves forced to flee the country, inasmuch as their emphatic

[1] GARDINER, I., 398 *seq.*

[2] BELLESHEIM, *Irland*, II., 278.

[3] *Ibid.*, 278 *seq.*

[4] *Ibid.*, 279; ZIMMERMANN, *loc. cit.*, 586 *seqq.*

protests against a series of illegalities and the oppression of religion would have brought on them a sentence of imprisonment for life. It would seem that archbishop Lombard of Armagh, who resided in Rome, had led the two earls to hope that the Pope would help them to restore religious liberty in Ireland. True, the nuncio of Brussels, Bentivoglio, pointed out to the two noblemen that such help was beyond the power of the Pope, and Cardinal Borghese subsequently denied that Paul V. had ever given them ground for such expectations. Nevertheless, on the advice of archduke Albert and the Spanish ambassador, they went to Rome where Paul V. gave them a solemn reception, just as Catholics in general had given them a great welcome on their arrival on the Continent. However, the air of Rome did not agree with the men from the North: Tyrconnel died in the Eternal City as early as 1608, and Tyrone in 1616.

The government's own fear and the hope of the Catholics that the two earls would obtain help in Spain for their oppressed countrymen led to a temporary abatement of the persecution immediately after their flight, as well as to a fresh influx of priests.[1] On the other hand, Catholics in Northern Ireland suffered a loss the consequences of which no one could calculate, for with the two fugitives they had lost their mainstay, the formers' possessions being confiscated by the crown and leased to English colonists. Henceforth only those who had taken the oath of supremacy were employed on these extensive estates, or were allowed to acquire some of the land, but neither of these possibilities were open to natives of Ireland.[2] In 1609, archbishop Kearney, of Cashel, wrote to the Holy See as follows: "Day by day colonists come over from England who oppress the Catholics with servitude, fear and terror. Yet hardly one Irishman in a thousand suffers himself to be infected by heresy.[3] It is

[1] BELLESHEIM, II., 286; *cf.* this Vol., p. 169.

[2] BELLESHEIM, II., 280 *seq.* A letter of Chichester of September 17, 1607, about the estates of the two earls, in ZIMMERMANN, *loc. cit.*, 584 *seqq.*

[3] BELLESHEIM, II., 290 *seq.*

calculated that the lands confiscated at divers times by James I. constituted an area of 4,279,000 acres.[1]

Soon after the flight of Tyrconnell, as we learn from archbishop Kearney, the priest-hunters got busy once more.[2] Before returning to his native land, Eugene Matthews, whom Paul V. had appointed to the see of Dublin on May 2nd, 1611, asked for the privilege of the portable altar for Mass inasmuch as all the churches of Ireland had been either ruined or desecrated.[3] In 1617, the government set a price of £500 on the head of archbishop Matthews.[4] Bishop Cornelius O'Devany, a Franciscan, fell into the hands of the government and was publicly executed in 1612.[5] In 1616 the viceroy, Chichester, was indeed recalled, but his successor persecuted the Church with no less violence.[6]

Catholics were not a little excited when in 1613, after a prorogation of twenty-seven years, Lord Chichester once more convoked the Irish Parliament. There were rumours of fresh penal laws. In the Upper House, owing to the presence of Protestant bishops, the enemies of the Catholics were in the majority and in the Lower House the king helped them to secure a like ascendency by creating over thirty new constituencies. In consequence, differences broke out already at the election of the Speaker when the Catholics walked out of the House. Thereupon the viceroy found himself compelled to promise that there would be no fresh penal laws against

[1] *Ibid.*, 290.

[2] *Ibid.*, 291.

[3] *Ibid.*, 292.

[4] *Ibid.*, 292.

[5] *Ibid.*, 294–7; ZIMMERMANN, *loc. cit.*, 590 *seqq.* A *Brief of March 20, 1609 (*Synopsis*, 254), tells of the Jesuits "in regno Iberniae pro conservatione et propagatione fidei catholicae summis cum vitae periculis versantibus nec certum domicilium habentibus". Among the faculties, which the Jesuits could also impart to other priests, is mentioned "recitandi in periculo pro brevario aliquot psalmos memoriter" (*ibid.*, 232).

[6] BELLESHEIM, II., 302 *seqq.* *Cf.* for the sufferings of the Catholics, 1612 *seqq.*; *Spicilegium Ossoriense*, I., 123 *seqq.*, and the annual report of the Jesuits, *ibid.*, 115 *seqq.*

the adherents of the old religion. The Catholics consequently returned to their places in the house and assented to Tyrone and Tyrconnell being declared traitors and to the confiscation of their property by the Crown.[1] The spoliation of Catholics was still further extended by various illegal means.[2]

Paul V. did what he could for the unfortunate island; repeatedly he addressed to the Vicar Apostolic, James White, and to the Irish people, words of comfort and encouragement.[3] Day and night, he said in one of his letters, the fate of Ireland lay heavy on his mind; if he could put an end to the persecution by shedding his own blood, gladly would he do it.[4] On several occasions he recommended the Irish seminaries to the generosity of the Christian princes.[5] On September 22nd,

[1] BELLESHEIM, II., 299–301. *Cf.*, GARDINER, II., 283–303.

[2] *Ibid.*, 302, 303.

[3] *To White, May 19, 1605, and July 10, 1606; *to the nobility, clergy and people of Ireland, February 26, 1607. According to the latter, there were congregations of the Annunciation of Our Lady, at Waterford, Limerick, Kilkenny and "Jaderdensi", to which indulgences were granted. *Epist.*, Papal Secret Archives.

[4] *"Dies noctesque cogitamus. Utinam crudelitatis ardorem ad delendam Ecclesiam Dei in septentrionalibus istis partibus proprio sanguine extinguere possemus." To White, May 19, 1605, *ibid.*

[5] Thus the Seminary of Douai to *general Spinola, February 23, 1607; *to the archduke Albert, September 12, 1608; *to the king of Spain, July 22, 1608, and on the same day, *to the duke of Lerma. *Briefs for the Irish College at Bordeaux were issued on November 11, 1609, to the duke of Joyeuse, and on March 16, 1614, to the king of France. *Briefs of October 10, 1605, and February 21, 1607, to the Spanish king plead for the Irish colleges at Douai and Antwerp, and the latter was assisted by the Irish soldiers out of their pay (*Epist.*, IV. *seq.*, Papal Secret Archives). A *Brief of September 9, 1619, permits that fishermen be allowed to fish on six Sundays, for the support of the Irish College at Seville; see *Synopsis*, 287. Ordination privileges were issued for the Irish Seminaries in Spain on January 24, 1619, *ibid.*, 285. *Cf.* BELLESHEIM, II., 721, 729 *seq.* See also *Bull.*, XII., 204

1606, he condemned the oath of allegiance which was being enforced in Ireland.[1]

For the Irish Seminaries see also L. BERTRAND, *Hist. des Séminaires de Bordeaux* (founded in 1603 by the Irishman McCarthy) *et de Bazas*, Bordeaux, 1894; LAENEN, "Het Iersch college te Antwerpen," in *Bijdragen tot de geschiedenis*, XVII., Antwerpen, 1922, 39–61. The Irish College at Lille was built in 1610 by the Irish Capuchin, Francis Nugety (? Nugent). (Report of December, 1689, in the Archives of Propaganda, Rome.) For the Irish Colleges on the Continent in general, *cf.* BELLESHEIM, II., 218–223, 316–322, 357–361.

[1] *Ibid.*, 278.

CHAPTER III.

RUSSIA AND POLAND—THE END OF THE FALSE DEMETRIUS—CATHOLIC RESTORATION UNDER SIGISMUND III., KING OF POLAND—THE UNION OF THE RUTHENIANS.

(1.)

WHILST Paul V. was as yet only a Cardinal, he had to deal, as a member of the Inquisition, with the case of Demetrius, who claimed to be the son of Ivan IV., and whose conduct gave grounds for a hope of Russia's return to the unity of the Church.[1] Less cautious than the late Clement VIII., the Polish nuncio Rangoni took wholeheartedly the part of the new pretender, who did not stint his promises and of whose genuineness he had no doubt. Since the day on which Demetrius had thrown himself at the feet of Rangoni, he had won the heart of the nuncio. Rangoni set the highest hopes on him, and followed his progress in Russia with keenest attention. Two Jesuits, Fathers Sawicki and Czyrzowski, who acted as chaplains in Demetrius' army, kept him informed of the latter's progress, and the nuncio promptly forwarded their letters to Rome for the information of Paul V.[2]

Though the events in the then but little known East of Europe greatly impressed Paul V., in this affair, as in all else, he did not at once depart from his wonted circumspection. Not many weeks after his election, on June 4th, 1605, the Secretary of State, Cardinal Valenti, requested the Polish nuncio to send in a report, as complete as possible, concerning Demetrius: "the more accurate the report is," Valenti added to the letter in his own hand, "the more it

[1] *Cf.* present work, Vol. XXIV., 143 *seq.*

[2] See PIERLING, in the *Rev. d. quest. hist.*, LVI. (1894), 542.

will please the Pope." At the same time he also asked for a report on the attitude of the King of Poland, and on the state of public opinion in regard to the Russian pretender.[1]

Meanwhile events succeeded each other with bewildering rapidity in Russia. On April 13th, 1605, Czar Boris Godunov died suddenly and his son Feodor was proclaimed his successor in the Kremlin. Whilst the greater number of the provinces recognized Feodor, the bulk of the army supported Demetrius who, on May 25th, began his triumphal march upon Moscow. At the entrance of every village he was welcomed by the inhabitants, who offered to him bread and salt, and his progress was everywhere accompanied by the solemn pealing of church bells. On June 10th Czar Feodor was strangled, and ten days later Demetrius made his solemn entry into the capitol of Russia, amid the acclamations of the populace.[2]

In due time news of these events reached Rome where an accurate report from Rangoni was anxiously awaited. In his impatience Cardinal Valenti instructed him, on July 16th, in cypher, to report at once what should be done in order to strengthen the Catholic leanings which Demetrius had until then manifested, in case the whole empire were to declare in his favour.[3]

In view of the slowness of the means of communication, Paul V. deemed all further delay dangerous, hence, with a haste which was most unusual with him, he gave orders, on July 12th, 1605, for a letter to be sent to Demetrius, congratulating him on his accession to the throne and exhorting him to hold fast to the Catholic faith.[4]

July, 1605, was nearing its close when Rangoni's full account under date of July 2nd, reached Rome at last. On twenty-seven folio sheets all was set down that spoke in favour of

[1] See *ibid.*, p. 343.

[2] See Skribanowitz, *Pseudo-Démétrius*, I., 97 *seq.*, 101 *seq.*, 110 *seq.*

[3] See Pierling, *Rome et Démétrius*, 195.

[4] Turgenjew, *Hist. Russiae Monum.*, II. (1842), n. XXXVII.

Demetrius.[1] Every line shows how cleverly and successfully the pretender had won Rangoni's confidence. The early story and the first emergence of Demetrius are described in the light of the report which Adam Wisniowezki had at one time drawn up for Sigismund III. The further events since 1604, Demetrius' audience with Sigismund III., and the conversion of the pretender to the Catholic Church, Rangoni was able to describe from personal knowledge. As regards his account of Demetrius' successes in Russia, he had made use of the reports which he had received from the Jesuits who were with the army. Opinion in Poland was described by the nuncio as far more favourable than it really was, though he could not disguise the fact that the Senate was divided into two parties, one of which was led by Zamoisky, an opponent of Demetrius, and the other by Zebrzydowski who favoured his cause. Sigismund's attitude towards Demetrius was likewise far too optimistically painted by Rangoni. He even hinted that the king of Poland would lend military assistance to the pretender.

At the end of the lengthy document, the nuncio expresses once more the far too favourable opinion which he had formed of Demetrius, and the prospect which now opened for the union of Russia with Rome and the war against the Turks, through the new czar. The nuncio is full of praise for the lofty character of the pretender, his gifts, his courage, and his devotion to religion. Demetrius, the nuncio reported, had been very gratified when he told him that, by bringing about the reunion of Russia with the Catholic Church, he would win world-wide fame, and that this feat would be recorded for ever by means of a painting to be placed by the side of similar ones in the Vatican.[2]

Rangoni's report of July 23rd, 1605, proved decisive for the Pope's line of conduct. This account of a seemingly well-

[1] The report of Rangoni, long believed to have been lost (see *Rev. d. quest. hist.*, LVI, 543), was found by PIERLING in the Archives of the Inquisition in Rome and published in *La Russie*, III., 431 *seqq.*

[2] Evidently a fresco for the Sala Regia was being thought of.

informed diplomat who had been a witness of the events, but who was both too credulous and an incorrigible optimist, led Paul to think that here was the very ideal of a Christian prince ; that Demetrius would procure for the Church and for Christendom the most splendid triumph, if he was supported as effectively as possible. Consequently, at the beginning of August, a number of measures were taken with a view to encouraging the pretender who seemed to justify such great expectations. Briefs were sent to Sigismund III., to Cardinal Maciejowski, and to the latter's cousin George Mniszek who had great influence with the Polish king. All these personages were exhorted to take advantage of their influence with Demetrius in order to confirm him in his good intentions with regard to the Catholic Church. "We doubt not," the Pope says, "that if Demetrius perseveres in the dispositions in which he has been up till now, he will be able to bring the Muscovites back to the Church inasmuch as that people follows in all things the lead of their rulers."[1] Inspired by his whole-hearted trust in the new czar, Paul V. had also earnestly recommended to him some Carmelite missionaries who were on their way to Persia.[2] More than that, on August 5th there was question of sending Rangoni's nephew, Count Alessandro, to Moscow, and letters accrediting him were drafted.[3] Meanwhile Rangoni had despatched his private secretary, Luigi Pratissoli, on a confidential mission to Moscow, where, on July 31st, 1605, Demetrius had been solemnly crowned as Czar. The letter which Pratissoli was charged to deliver to Demetrius reminded the emperor of his promise to reunite Russia with the Church. The presents for the czar were in keeping with the letter—they were a Latin Bible, a Crucifix, a picture of Our Lady and a Rosary.[4]

Rangoni's confidence seemed justified by the cordial reception of his nephew who reached Moscow in October, 1605.

[1] See TURGENJEW, II., n. XLI, XLII., XLIII.

[2] See *ibid.*, n. XXXVIII.

[3] See *ibid.*, n. LXIV. *Cf.* PIERLING, *La Russie*, III., 220.

[4] See PIERLING, *Rome et Démétrius*, 92 *seq.*, 162 *seq.* ; *La Russie*, III., 220 *seq.*

Provided with presents, he left Moscow again on December 22nd.[1] An intimate of the Czar, John Buczynski, had been previously despatched to the nuncio, to negotiate two affairs which Demetrius had very much at heart, namely the recognition of his imperial title by the king of Poland, and a papal dispensation which would allow Marina, the daughter of George Mniszek who had been married to him by proxy by Cardinal Maciejowski, on November 12th, 1605, to receive Holy Communion from the hand of the schismatical patriarch on the day of her coronation, and to assist at the orthodox service.[2]

As a matter of fact Demetrius had already established direct diplomatic contact with the Pope who, on September 11th, 1605, had congratulated him on his coronation and exhorted him to bring about the reunion of Russia with the Church.[3] The emperor's plenipotentiary was Andrew Lawicki, one of the two Jesuits who had come to Moscow with the imperial army. The Jesuit, who wore the dress of a Russian priest and had grown a beard and long hair, was the bearer of two letters of the emperor to the Pope. In the first, dated November 30th, 1605, Demetrius unfolded a plan for a joint crusade of himself, the emperor and the king of Poland against the Turks; the other, written in December, gave an assurance of protection for the Carmelite missionaries for which the Pope had pleaded. Lawicki was instructed, independently of the war planned against the Turks, to press the Pope with a view to the recognition of his imperial title by the king of Poland and the elevation of Rangoni to the cardinalate.[4] On January 7th, 1606, Marina wrote a submissive letter to the Pope, promising to help in

[1] See PIERLING, *La Russie*, III., 222.

[2] See *ibid.*, *Rome et Démétrius*, 165 *seq.*, 217 *seq.*

[3] See TURGENJEW, II., n. XLIX.

[4] The instruction for Lawicki, of December 18, 1605, in PIERLING, *Rome et Démétrius*, 186 *seq.* *Cf.* also for his mission, TURGENJEW, II., n. LXXVI.; WIELEWICKI, in the *Script. rer. Pol.*, X., 104, 111, 113, 121 *seq.*, 140; PIERLING, *La Russie*, III., 226 *seq.*

the reunion with the Church.[1] This assurance, and still more so the optimistic reports of Cardinal Maciejowski [2] and the communications of the infatuated Lawicki, confirmed Paul V. in his expectation that the Russian autocrat was about to carry out the reunion of his empire with the Church. With a view to making the best use of so favourable an occasion, Lawicki was sent back to Moscow from Rome on April 10th, 1606. He was the bearer of a letter of the same date, in which Paul V. gives unequivocal expression to his hopes. "Since you are all-powerful with your people," the Pope wrote, "command them to acknowledge the Vicar of Christ on earth." [3] In the Pope's letters to Marina's father, and to Marina herself, he recommended the Jesuits to them, especially Lawicki, and exhorted them to see to it that the Protestants got no influence over Demetrius.[4] Lawicki's instructions were concerned with the war against the Turks for which the Pope promised help. For the success of the undertaking, the Pope declared, it was greatly to be desired that Demetrius and Sigismund should sink their differences; for the rest the Pope would do his best to promote the prestige of the Czar.[5] Characteristically enough, Rangoni's cardinalate was passed over in silence. What impression the request had made on the Pope, who was jealous of his independence, may be gauged from the fact that on June 3rd, 1606, Rangoni was recalled from his nunciature.[6]

Nor was there any prospect of Demetrius's prayer for a dispensation for his wife being granted. On that point there already existed an unfavourable decision of the Roman Inquisition, which had been unanimously passed at a sitting of March 2nd, 1600, under the presidency of the Pope himself.[7]

[1] The original of the letter in BORGHESE, II., 449, Papal Secret Archives; see PIERLING, *La Russie*, III., 228.

[2] *Cf.* PIERLING, *ibid.*, 263.

[3] See TURGENJEW, II., n. LXXVI, p. 90.

[4] See PIERLING, *La Russie*, III., 231.

[5] See WIELEWICKI, *loc. cit.*, 122 *seq.*

[6] See PIERLING, *La Russie*, III., 230.

[7] See *ibid.*, 248.

In this instance, as on a former occasion, when there was question of Sigismund III.'s coronation as king of Sweden [1] the Holy See refused to swerve by a hair's breadth from Catholic principles, however great the seeming gain might be. So the prohibition of all participation in a non-Catholic religious service was rigidly upheld.[2]

Lawicki's stay in Rome synchronized with that of Count Alessandro Rangoni at Moscow whither he had gone in the capacity of papal envoy. His reception, and the promises made to him, had so completely won him over to the Czar, that he remained content with a purely passive rôle instead of bringing pressure to bear on Demetrius in the matter of reunion, as the Pope wanted him to do. Rangoni merely noted the Czar's demands.[3] They were as follows: the Pope should send to Moscow a few men who would be able to act as secretaries and chancellors as well as experts in the art of war; he should also help the emperor to establish relations with France and Spain and persuade the rulers of these countries to join him in the war against the Turks.[4] In order to disguise these selfish ambitions, Rangoni was handed, at his departure, a submissive letter of the Czar to Paul V., dated March 5th, 1606, in which Demetrius assured the Pope of his strong attachment to the Pontiff and to the Catholic Church. But of any sort of promise in regard to reunion, which was after all the main point, the letter breathed not a word.[5]

On March 29th, 1609, Alessandro Rangoni met at Mir, near Novogrodek, the bride of the Czar, Marina Mniszek, then on her way to Moscow. Her numerous retinue included, besides her father, five Bernardine Monks and the Jesuit Lawicki who in 1604 had received Demetrius into the Catholic

[1] *Cf.* present work, Vol. XXIV., p. 89 *seqq.*

[2] *Cf.* on this point the Briefs of Paul V. to the English Catholics, on September 22, 1606, and September 22, 1607, see above, p. 165 *seq.*

[3] See SKRIBANOWITZ, *Pseudo-Démétrius*, I., 138, who appositely remarks: "The hammer became an anvil."

[4] See PIERLING, *Rome et Démétrius*, 169 *seq.*

[5] See *ibid.*, 127, 171 *seq.* *Cf.* SKRIBANOWITZ, *Pseudo-Démétrius*, I., 133, 139.

Church. The Jesuit was now to act as the emperor's confessor, supposing that his change of religion was the fruit of genuine conviction.[1] The Pope and the Jesuits, blinded by their optimistic hopes of Russia's return to the Church, took this for granted, for they gave unqualified credence to the numerous favourable reports about Demetrius who seemed to be firmly established on the throne.

In reality the situation was very different. The fresh nuptial blessing of Marina, and her coronation on May 18th, 1606, were performed according to the Greek rite by the schismatical patriarch. However, the imperial couple did not receive Holy Communion.[2] Apart from this detail, there was nothing to show for Demetrius' oft-repeated assurances of his devotion to the Holy See. All he sought was to exploit the friendliness of Paul V. to his own advantage, and all the time he kept putting off the question of reunion with Rome. However, even this intercourse with the Pope was enough to make the orthodox Muscovites exceedingly suspicious of the czar. Not only were they shocked by the presence of the two Jesuits, they were likewise hurt by the fact that several Protestants were in the immediate entourage of the new czar, and that Protestant as well as Catholic services were held in the Kremlin for the benefit of the imperial bodyguard. Discontent was further fanned by Demetrius' marked departure from the sacrosanct old Russian traditions in regard to dress, conduct and ceremonial. Indignation was roused in particular by the czar's love of music at table—a practice abhorred by the orthodox—and by the fact that he ate beef. However, the schismatical clergy were not the only grumblers; everybody was indignant at the conduct of the numerous Poles who had come with Marina and who behaved as if they were in a conquered land. To this must be added the defects which Demetrius betrayed since an unheard-of stroke of good luck

[1] See Skribanowitz, *loc. cit.*, 139. For the reception of Demetrius into the Church by Lawicki, see present work, Vol. XXIV, 143.

[2] *Cf.* Pierling, *La Russie*, III., 304; Skribanowitz, *loc. cit.*, 147.

had raised him to the throne of the czars. Far superior as he was to the Russians as regards ability and culture, he offended them not only by his boundless pride and by the impudence which led him to taunt the nobles with their ignorance, and to exalt the merits of the West to the disparagement of Russia, but also by his prodigality and immoral life.[1]

It was characteristic of Demetrius' presumption that he would heed no warning. Already in February the Jesuit Czyrzowski besought him to be on his guard, inasmuch as a conspiracy was afoot among the popes and the *boyars*, and the people were being roused on the pretext of various innovations.[2] The thoughtlessness of the Czar is shown in a conversation he had with the Jesuit Lawicki shortly before the catastrophe. The latter's report is as follows: "Two days before his death, the Czar sent for me. . . . I found him alone in his bedroom and congratulated him on his coming into his paternal inheritance . . . The Czar thanked me and accepted my presents. He then got out of his chair and we began to walk up and down the room. I turned the conversation to the subject of religion and the various plans of the Czar, this being the reason why my Superiors had sent me to Moscow. . . . Thereupon, Demetrius said he was thinking of erecting a Jesuit college for the purpose of training teachers for the future schools. . . . I took it on myself neither to approve nor to condemn the project. . . . The Czar also spoke of his war plans. He dropped the remark that he was as yet uncertain against whom he would send his army of 100,000 men, whether against the Turks or against someone else. In connection with this he expressed his indignation against the king of Poland for refusing him his proper title. I replied that God's Providence would not permit such an enmity between two powerful rulers. The audience ended after an hour, when Demetrius said he wished to visit his mother."[3]

[1] See PIERLING, *La Russie*, III., 313 seq.; SKRIBANOWITZ, *loc. cit.*, 154.

[2] See PIERLING, *Rome et Démétrius*, 115 *seq.*

[3] See WALIEWICKI, *loc. cit.*, X., 145 *seq.*

At all times autocracy and revolt have dwelt side by side in Russia, for the Slav nature is exceedingly passionate and prone to extremes. Demetrius also was destined to experience this in his own person. On the morning of May 27th, 1606, a revolt broke out which had been skilfully prepared by the ambitious *boyar* Wassilij Schujskij. The Czar was surprised and murdered in the Kremlin. Then the *boyars* rushed into the city, calling the people to arms against the foreign "heathens" who had placed an impostor on the throne. Nearly five hundred Poles fell victims to the popular fury. Mniszek and the two Jesuits managed to escape and subsequently succeeded in reaching their own country. After that day of terror, the horribly mutilated body of Demetrius was summarily buried in unhallowed ground. However, the ghost of the murdered man would not leave the conspirators in peace. The corpse was dug up and burnt, then the ashes were rammed into a cannon and blown to the four winds of heaven. The crown was seized by Wassilij Schujskij, the ringleader of the revolt and the representative of ancient orthodox Russia.[1]

Even to-day the question of the identity of the murdered czar cannot be considered as finally settled, though a small library of books on the "false Demetrius" has gradually accumulated. That the man overthrown with such suddenness had nothing in common with the son of Ivan IV. may be considered as certain. In like manner the official Russian tradition which identified him with Gregory Otrepjew, an escaped monk, has been almost universally abandoned. The only thing certain is the Russian origin of the usurper. Documentary evidence has also completely disposed of the suggestion that the whole intrigue had been engineered by the Pope and the Jesuits. If it is asked whose creature Demetrius was, the most credible opinion is that he was the tool of a party among the *boyars* hostile to Boris.[2]

[1] See PIERLING, *La Russie*, III., 321 *seq.*; SKRIBANOWITZ, *Démétrius*, I., 159 *seq.*

[2] As against KARAMSIN (X., 259), a pupil of Ranke, F. L. NOWAKOWSKI (*De Demetrio I. magno Russiae duce* (Berol., 1840, 62 *seqq.*) maintained with conviction the view that Demetrius

How inadequately informed Western Europe was concerning events in Russia is shown by the contradictory account of the catastrophe which was spread abroad. According to some, Demetrius had escaped; according to others he was dead. The first news reached Rome at the end of August,

was really the son of Ivan IV. At first PIERLING was inclined to this view, though he realized that definite evidence was not forthcoming (*Rome et Démétrius*, xxii.). After Pierling had devoted many years to further research and had secured fresh material, he subjected the question to a new and exacting analysis (*La Russie*, III., 397 *seqq.*). He decided for the view that Demetrius was identical with Gregory Otrepjew. He has adhered to this against WALISZEWSKI (*La crise révolutionnaire*, Paris, 1906); see *Rev. d. quest. hist.*, LXXXI. (1907), 213 *seqq.* Nevertheless he does not disguise the fact that there is no final evidence as to who Demetrius really was. He only feels certain that he was definitely not the son of Ivan IV. R. STÜBE (in a discussion of WALISZEWSKI in the *Beilage zur Allgem. Zeitung*, 1907, no. 199) thinks that the pretender may not have been a deceiver, for he himself felt sure of his pedigree. "He certainly escaped from Russia. Presumably he was somehow connected with the house of Ivan IV., as a bastard. He may have been put forward by a party acting against Boris Godunow, with the help of Poland. But to establish his identity with Prince Demetrius, it would be necessary to prove that the young prince escaped from the massacre in Uglitsch, which actually occurred, & that in his place another boy was murdered. The official reports, after the inquiry, are an incredible tissue of lies. Nevertheless they take it for granted that the Prince lost his life. He is said to have fallen, while at play, upon a knife which cut his throat. Furthermore the body was subsequently buried next to that of Ivan IV. The chief criminal, the subsequent Czar Wassilij Schuiskij, on his accession to the crown, formally declared that Boris Godunow had had the Prince murdered. Everything points to the fact that the murder did take place. What the course of events was must be decided from other reports. Yet there is a quite different tradition, from which it is not impossible to assume that the Prince was rescued. Nevertheless it is almost impossible to distinguish light from darkness in the matter." SKRIBANOWITZ (*Démétrius*, I., 162 *seqq.*) is of opinion that "the

1606 ; a month later it was generally believed that the Czar was dead. Cardinal Borghese wrote these characteristic words at the time : " The unhappy end of Demetrius is a fresh proof of the instability of all things human. May God have mercy on his soul ! " Subsequently further contradictory

subsequent czar Demetrius was without doubt not genuine ". He sums up his view in four points : (1) " Prince Demetrius was killed on May 15, 1591, at Uglič. (2) Gregory Otrepjew escaped from Russia after the usurper, and was at best no more than his assistant. (3) The usurper was of Russian origin, and (4) he was the tool of a *boyar* party working against Boris Godunow." As to the originator of the intrigue, SKRIBANOWITZ considers (I., 178) that : " From Massa & Patterson to Solowjew & Karamsin, many have tried to put the blame on the Jesuits. They say that the S.J. & the Curia behind them, wanted to bring about the long desired union in this way, i.e. to make Moscow dependent on Rome. Only recently has Pierling succeeded in clearing his Order from this grave suspicion." Since the old view that Demetrius had been " chosen by the Jesuits for a great rôle & educated by them for it " (thus WITKOWSKI, in his " *historisch-kritische* " edition of the complete works of SCHILLER, VIII., 149), has not even now ceased to be voiced. I quote the words of PIERLING, in which he sums up the results of his researches (*Rome et Démétrius*, 149–150) :—

" Les historiens qui affirment que Démétrius a été soudoyé soit par le Pape, soit par le nonce Rangoni, soit par les Jésuites, ne peuvent citer aucun document, ni donner aucune preuve qui supporte la critique. Rome et les Jésuites ne sont entrés en rapports avec Démétrius qu'au mois de mars 1604, lorsqu'il passait déjà à la cour de Pologne pour le vrai fils de Jean IV. et qu'il était entouré de ses compatriotes.

" Rome et les Jésuites ont fait des efforts consciencieux pour découvrir la vérité et se sont laissés guider de bonne foi par le roi de Pologne, qu'ils croyaient plus à même de pénétrer le mystère.

" Démétrius a réellement adjuré le schisme et embrassé la foi catholique. Tous ceux qui ont pris part à sa conversion se sont réglés sur des principes de saine théologie et de charité, que l'Église Russe ne saurait mettre en question sans condamner ses procédés envers les Raskolniks.

" Dans les rapports ultérieurs avec Démétrius, Rome n'a cherché

news arrived. Even at the end of 1607, Simonetta, the new Polish nuncio, was assured that Demetrius was alive. The sons of Mniszek, who came to Rome about that time, made a similar declaration.[1]

The death of Demetrius did not put an end to Russia's troubles. Civil war broke out with all its horrors. Another Demetrius arose and advanced as far as Tula, when he was defeated and executed. He was at once succeeded by a third adventurer who claimed to be the real Demetrius. In these circumstances Sigismund III. judged the moment had come

que le bonheur de la Russie, qu'elle voulait éclairer par la lumière de la vérité et faire entrer dans l'alliance européenne contre les Turcs. Les Jésuites sont restés dans les limites de leur vocation, exerçant leur ministère et se montrant prêts à accepter des collèges pour l'instruction de la jeunesse. Démétrius a fait des promesses parfaitement libres et spontanées en faveur de la religion catholique, que les Papes ne pouvaient et ne devaient pas repousser.

" Dans le développement moral de Démétrius il faut distinguer trois périodes : 1.° à Cracovie, il a tout le zèle d'un néophyte et sa piété est exemplaire ; 2.° pendant la campagne, c'est la raison d'État qui prédomine et l'amour de la religion lui est subordonné ; 3.° parvenu au trône et mal entouré, il s'adonne a l'impiété et au désordre en y joignant l'hypocrisie envers le Pape et Sigismond III. Vouloir prouver par le seul fait de ces changements, que la conversion de Démétrius n'a pu être sincère, c'est nier du même coup la mutabilité de la volonté humaine, hélas ! trop souvent constatée.

" Nous nous flattons d'avoir poursuivi dans ce travail une œuvre de conciliation. La part que les Papes ont prise dans l'affaire de Démétrius a toujours été un des principaux griefs historiques de la Russie contre Rome. A la lueur de nos documents, le lecteur impartial aura pu apprécier la sagesse et la prudence du S. Siège et réduire à néant les calomnies élevées contre lui. Un brillant avenir s'ouvrait à la Russie dans la voie que lui indiquaient les Pontifes romains. En y entrant elle aurait échappé a bien des désastres et peutêtre à l'heure qu'il est, aurait-elle été maitresse de l'Orient pacifié par ses efforts, christianisé par ses apôtres."

[1] See PIERLING, in the *Rev. d. quest. hist.*, LVI. (1894), 545 *seq.*; and *La Russie*, III., 330 *seq.*, 347 *seq.*, 357 *seq.*

to settle accounts with Poland's old enemies. He decided on war against the Muscovites. The struggle was to be protracted until 1618. In Rome he represented it as a crusade for the spread of the Catholic faith. Nevertheless his hopes of pecuniary assistance did not materialize at once.[1] Only in 1613, when Paul Wolucki, bishop of Luzk, came to Rome with mission to do homage to the Pope in the king's name, did Paul V. grant 40,000 scudi, on August 10th,[2] and these were subsequently supplemented by another 20,000.[3] The permission to raise money for the purpose from the Polish clergy, which was first granted on June 1st, 1612, was renewed on May 14th, 1613, and again on March 7th, 1614.[4] Nevertheless a real tension arose between Paul V. and Sigismund III. because the Pope persisted in his refusal of the red hat to Rangoni, a favour which the king of Poland greatly desired.

During the struggle with Poland a new dynasty came into power in Russia. The manifesto which, in 1613, announced to the people the elevation to the throne of Michael Romanov, a son of a nephew of Anastasia, the wife of Ivan IV., was full of resentment and contempt for all Latins.[5] Although the new sovereign saw himself forced to buy peace from Sweden in 1617, and a year later from Poland, by ceding territory, the attempt of Sigismund III. to reduce Russia into a Polish province failed in the same way as his efforts to recover his hereditary kingdom of Sweden proved in vain.[6]

[1] See *ibid.*, III., 363 *seq.*

[2] *Cf.* THEINER, *Mon. Pol.*, III., 356 *seq.* The act of homage took place on January 31, 1613; see *Acta Consist.*, *Barb.*, 2926, Vatican Library. For Wolucki's journey to Rome see WALIEWICKI, in the *Script. rer. Pol.*, XIV., 88, and *Anz. der Krakauer Akad.*, 1893, 110.

[3] See notes in BORGHESE, I., 554, p. 10: "Aiuto dato al re di Polonia 60,000 scudi di moneta pagati al depositario generale sotto li 16 Novembre 1614," Papal Secret Archives.

[4] See *Bull.*, XII., 169 *seq.*, 210 *seq.*, 256 *seq.*

[5] See BRÜCKNER, *Gesch. Russlands*, I., Gotha, 1896, 550 *seq.*

[6] *Cf.* DROYSEN, *Gustav Adolf*, I., Leipzig, 1869, 92 *seq.* *Cf. ibid.*, 95, about the Catholic adherents of Sigismund in Sweden. Two

Russian historians exalt the maintenance of national independence. This is both justifiable as well as comprehensible. The same cannot be said of the way in which the separation (from Rome) was prosecuted and enforced by the Romanows during 300 years, for it was only accomplished by the most blameworthy means. One look at the state of the gigantic empire supplies the answer to the question whether it was a good or an ill fortune for the happiness of the Russian people that it was not permitted, as the Pope desired, to become united with the life-giving spiritual forces of the Catholic Church.

(2.)

At the time of the Russian troubles, serious disturbances had also occurred in Poland which, for a time, threatened to interfere with the progress of the Catholic restoration.

The marriage of Sigismund III. with the sister of his first wife, Constance, of the Stirian line of the Hapsburgs, which he contracted in 1605, against the will of the diet, had provoked great resentment in anti-Austrian circles. One section of the nobility felt aggrieved in the matter of the distribution of lucrative offices. The contrast between the cold Scandinavian nature of Sigismund and the mobile character

Jesuits, former students of the Germanicum, had been cruelly executed as late as the time of Charles IX., on the pretext that they had corresponded with Poland; see *Hist. Arkisto XI.*, Helsinginä, 1891, 220. Even under Charles' successor, Gustav Adolf, executions of Catholics took place (*cf.* GFRÖRER, *Gustav Adolf*, 158; CORNELIUS, *Gesch. der schwedischen Kirche nach der Reformation*, Upssala, 1886). Joh. Messenius, the famous historian, was kept a prisoner for his Catholic opinions for twenty years, until his death in 1637; see SCHÜCK, *J. Messenius* (1920). Similar hostility to everything Catholic reigned in Denmark, then belonging to Norway; see A. BRANDRUD, *Klosterlasse. Ei Bidrag til den jesuitiske Propagandas Historie i Norden*, Kristiania, 1895; L. DAAE, in the *Hist. Tidskrift*, III., 3, Kristiania, 1895; For attempts at missionising Denmark itself see also DUHR, II., 2, 75; PIEPER, *Propaganda-Kongregation*, 6 *seq.*

of his Polish subjects became increasingly apparent. A dangerous political opposition arose headed by Nicholas Zebrydowski, the Count Palatine of Cracow, with whom the Polish Protestants and the Ruthenian schismatics allied themselves for the purpose of armed opposition. To this end they had recourse to the so-called *Rokosz*, a form of insurrection which they tried to justify by appealing to the Polish Constitution. The attack on the king was so violent that at the diet of Warsaw, May, 1607, Sigismund saw himself forced to make a number of concessions. The schismatics were granted liberty of worship, whereupon they parted company with the Protestants. The diet declared the continuation of the Rokosz to be high treason and summoned its members to lay down their arms. The proposal was rejected and war ensued. It ended with the victory of the royal troops. In 1608 the Count Palatine of Cracow was forced to surrender. Sigismund thereupon granted a general amnesty.[1] The consequences of the defeat fell, in the first instance, on the Protestants. Owing to the vivacious temperament of the Poles, violent collisions between Protestants and Catholics had occurred before this time. They now became more frequent. Since the Protestants had made the cause of the rebels their own, it was not surprising that the king refused to protect them from the violence of their opponents.[2]

The Papal nuncio, Rangoni, who since the first outbreak of these internal troubles had given strong support to the king, had been replaced in September, 1606, by Francesco

[1] *Cf.* besides ALESS. CILLI, *Storia delle sollevazioni notabili seguite in Poloniagli anni del Signore 1606–8*, Pistoia, 1627 (see for the author of this rare document, CIAMPI, *Notizie di medici, musici, etc., italiani in Polonia*, Lucca, 1830, 49 *seq.*, and CIAMPI, *Bibliografia*, I., 84, 271, 354 *seq.*). *Cf.* also the interesting account of the Jesuit Wielwicki in the *Script. rer. Pol.*, X., 122 *seq.* A collection of political tracts of the time of the Civil War, 1606–8, was published by J. CZUBEK, *Pisma polityczne z czasow rokoszu Zebrzydowskiego, 1606–8*, I., Kraków, 1916.

[2] A detailed account of these events from the Protestant point of view by KRASINSKI, *Gesch. der Reformation in Polen*, 236 *seq.*

Simonetta, bishop of Foligno.[1] The instructions [2] of the new representative of the Holy See were to the effect that he should keep in closest touch with the king and to cultivate good relations with Cardinal Maciejowski, Primate and archbishop of Gnesen; with the Grand Chancellor, Matthias Pstrokónski, the Vice-Chancellor, Stanislaus Miński, with the bishop of Leslau (since 1617 bishop of Cracow), Peter Tylicki, and with the Jesuits. He should press for the rejection of the old demands of the Protestants which they had renewed during the late troubles. These tended to the suppression of appeals to Rome in spiritual affairs, the withholding of the annates from the Curia, and the curtailment of the action of the papal representative at court and in the diet.

As regards the promotion of the Catholic restoration, which Paul V. had pursued with the greatest attention from the beginning of his reign, the instructions contain some interesting directions.

Before all else, the nuncio should work for the establishment everywhere of seminaries for the formation of a capable

[1] See *Epist.*, II., 161 (*cf.* 180), Papal Secret Archives. Simonetta arrived at Cracow on June 20, 1607, Rangoni left on June 29, see *Script. rer. Pol.*, X., 232.

[2] See **Istruzione a Msgr. Simonetta vescovo di Foligno, nunzio in Polonia*, dated November 11, 1606, in *Cod. A. E.*, IX., n. 13, of the Brera Library at Milan. In *Borghese*, I., 311, p. 457 (Papal Secret Archives) the instruction is dated November 16. A Polish translation of the instruction, which is also to be found copied in *Inform. polit.*, X., 721 *seq.*, of the Berlin State Library, in *Relacye Nuncynszow Apost.*, II., 97 *seq.* The *reports of Simonetta 1607–9, in *Borghese*, II., 224, 230, 237, IV., 79, the reports of July, 1609–1610, in the *Nunz. Pol.*, 37A, Papal Secret Archives, and in *Cod. E.*, 34–8, of the Boncompagni Archives, Rome. The *instructions of Cardinal Borghese up to July, 1609, are in *Nunz. Pol.*, 173, *loc. cit.*, for October and November, 1609, in *Barb.*, 5932, and of 1611–1612, in *Barb.* 6575, Vatican Library. *Cf. Anz. der Krakauer Akad.*, 1893, 109 *seq.*, where emphasis is laid on the importance of the reports with regard to the war with Russia.

clergy, as prescribed by the Council of Trent, and for the introduction, in monasteries, of strict discipline. Simonetta's attention is also directed to the establishment in Poland of the more recent and strict Orders, such as the Discalced Carmelites. The nuncio was to take great care that in the appointment of bishops and parish priests, unsuitable persons should be barred. He should encourage the king in his determination to exclude Protestants from public offices. On queen Constance the Pope bestowed the Golden Rose.[1] On the subject of the representation of Catholic interests at the diet, Paul V., on May 1st, 1607, wrote specially to the archbishop of Lemberg, John Zamoiski.[2] On May 19th, 1607, the Pope begged the king's protection for the Jesuits who rendered such signal services to the Catholics, from the attacks which, it was feared, would be made against them at the diet.[3]

The Pope watched with particular satisfaction the work of Cardinal Maciejowski. On August 3rd he praised him for his manly attitude at the diet.[4] In the autumn of 1607 the Cardinal held a provincial synod at Piotrków, which passed several useful measures for the reform of clergy and laity.[5] Efforts for the religious instruction of the people were encouraged by a special Indulgence.[6] The decrees of the synod were confirmed by the Congregation of the Council on April 12th, 1608.[7] In 1611, the Pope praised the zeal with which Cardinal Maciejowski strove to carry out the visitation of his diocese of Gnesen which the Holy See had charged him to undertake.[8] On November 7th, 1609, the Pope had begged

[1] THEINER, III., 294.

[2] **Epist.*, II., 412, Papal Secret Archives.

[3] See THEINER, III., 295.

[4] See **Epist.*, III., 122, *loc. cit.*

[5] See *Concilium Provinciale regni Poloniae, quod Paulo V. Pontifice Bernardus Maciejowski, card. tit. S. Joannis ante portam Latinam, archiep. Gnesnens, eccl. habuit Petricoviae*, A° 1617, Cracoviae, 1617. *Cf.* FABISZA, 204 *seq.*

[6] See FABISZA, 203.

[7] See **Epist.*, III., 264, IV., 161, Papal Secret Archives.

[8] See **Epist.*, IV., 298, Papal Secret Archives.

king Sigismund to assist in the reform of the Polish Premonstratensians.[1] In the following year the Polish sovereign was honoured with the gift of a sword blessed by the Pope.[2]

The king of Poland rendered a distinguished service to the Church in 1611, when, on the occasion of the investiture of the Elector of Brandenburg, John Sigismund, with the duchy of Prussia, he secured for the Catholics of that country better conditions than those under which they had lived until then. The elector was made to guarantee to them freedom of worship and the right of admission to all offices of State and the exercise of the right of patronage. Moreover, John Sigismund bound himself to build in a suburb of Königsberg, within three years, and at his own expense, a Catholic church, and presbytery, and to endow them with an annual income of 1,000 florins. The Elector was accorded the right of presentation of the parish priest, who was to be invested by the bishop of Ermland, under whose jurisdiction he was placed.[3]

Simonetta lived long enough to see these successes of the Catholic cause; his death at Warsaw on January 19th, 1612, put a premature end to his career. The business of the nunciature was carried on for a time by Cesare Baroffio, Simonetta's *uditore*,[4] until the appointment as nuncio of Lelio Ruini, of Bologna, in September, 1612.[5] The new representative of the Holy See was instructed [6] to look on the

[1] **Ibid.*, V., 180.

[2] Brief of February 22, 1610, in THEINER, III., 327.

[3] See DITTRICH, *Gesch. des Katholizismus in Altpreussen*, I., Braunsberg, 1901, 91 *seq.* The conversion of the Elector to Calvinism (1613) was not without one good result, inasmuch as John Sigismund had to show even more tolerance towards his Catholic subjects in order to achieve the support of the king of Poland against the attacks of the Lutherans.

[4] *Reports from BAROFFIO, in *Barb.* 6577, Vatican Library, and in *Cod. E.*, 39, of Boncompagni Archives, Rome.

[5] See the Brief of September 13, 1612, in THEINER, III., 353. Ruini arrived at Cracow on January 14, 1613; see WIELEWICKI, *loc. cit.*, XIV., 95.

[6] **Instruttione per Mgr. Ruini destinato Nuncio da Paolo V.*

establishment of seminaries ordered by Trent, and the reform of the monasteries, as his first task. Like his predecessor, Ruini was exhorted to cultivate good relations with the king, the pious queen, and the Polish episcopate; especially should he do his utmost to keep alive the bishops' zeal for Church reform.

The excellent relations between Sigismund III. and the Holy See, which found expression on the Pope's part in a money contribution towards the war against Russia during Ruini's nunciature, were only strained in some degree, by the unseasonable eagerness with which the king demanded the red hat for Rangoni.[1] Paul V. did not want to see candidates for this high dignity recommended by princes, hence he offered a decided opposition to the king's request. Francesco Diotallevi, who succeeded Ruini in the summer of 1614 [2] was instructed to cut short all expectation in this respect.[3]

al re di Polonia, dated September 26, 1612, in *Cod.* 468, p. 254 *seq.*, of the Corsini Library, Rome, in the *Inform. polit.*, X., 673 *seq.*, of the State Library, Berlin, and in *Ottob.* 1066, p. 614 *seq.*, Vatican Library, also in part in LÄMMER, *Zur Kirchengesch.*, 126 (*cf. Melet.*, 335, note 1); a Polish translation is in *Relacye Nunc. Apost.*, II., 109 *seq.* Ruini's reports of 1612–1613, in *Barb.* 6578, Vatican Library; those of 1614 in *Borghese,* I., 855, Papal Secret Archives.

[1] *Cf.* XXV., 318.

[2] See the *Avviso of July 30, 1614, in the *Studi e docum.*, XV., 278. The letter of recommendation to the Polish king, of September 4, 1614, is in THEINER, III., 358.

[3] "*Instruttione per Mr. Diotallevi, vescovo di S. Angelo, destinato da N.S. per suo Nuntio al re di Polonia,* September 3, 1614, in *Cod.* 6600, p. 439 *seq.*, of the State Library, Vienna; a copy is in *Ottob.*, 2434, p. 829 *seq.*, Vatican Library. RANKE (III.[6], Appendix no. 83) does not give the source. The reports of Diotallevi, the importance of which is rightly noted by LEVINSON (*Polnisch-Preussisches aus der Bibl. Borghesiana* in the Vatican Archives, in the *Zeitschrift der Westpreuss. Geschichtsvereins,* XLVIII., 86) examine in detail the question of the nomination of Rangoni as Cardinal; they are to be found in *Borghese,* II., 221 and 227 for 1615; for 1616, *ibid.*, 219 and 220; for 1617,

The nuncio was likewise to decline a further subsidy. This was done not for lack of goodwill, the Instruction stated, but owing to the financial position of the Holy See. For the rest Diotallevi's instructions were similar to those of his predecessors; the execution of the Tridentine decrees, especially as regards seminaries, the nomination of good bishops and the appointment of good parish priests were particularly emphasized. At the sittings of the diet, the nuncio was to watch lest the slightest concession be made to the Protestants, for even a slender concession to their insatiable appetite would all too easily lead to the worst consequences. Among the personalities with whom the nuncio was instructed to keep in touch the following are singled out on this occasion; besides the king and queen, the heir to the crown, Ladislaus, and among the bishops, Albert Baranowski, Maciejowski's successor at Gnesen, and the bishop of Luzk, Paul Wolucki. During Diotallevi's nunciature (1614–1621), the king's persistent demand of the purple for Rangoni also reacted unfavourably on the relations between Pope and king, inasmuch as for weighty reasons, Paul V. was not inclined to listen to the request.[1] Fortunately this tension did not affect the progress of the Catholic reform. The king's real zeal for the good cause was in no way diminished in consequence, so that Paul V. successor could

ibid., 225 and 227; for 1618, *ibid.*, 185; for 1619, *ibid.*, 235; for 1620, *ibid.*, 231. Papal Secret Archives. Those from December, 1620, to December, 1621, in *Barb.* 6579, Vatican Library. *Cf. Script. rer. Pol.*, XII., 83, and *Anz. der Krakauer Akad.*, 1893, 108. The *instructions of Borghese of 1615, 1616 and 1619 in the Library of S. Paolo fuori le Mura Rome (*cf.* Lämmer, *Melet.*, 336, note 1). The *instructions from January, 1615, to October 28, 1617, are also in Borghese, II., 358, *loc. cit.*; see *Anz. der Krakauer Akad.*, 1894, 26.

[1] See Pierling, III., 39. *Cf.* Theiner, III., 359. When the emperor Ferdinand II., also supported the request of Sigismund III., Paul V. seemed prepared at last to bestow the red hat on Rangoni. See the *Brief to Ferdinand II., of December 19, 1620, in **Epist.*, XVI., 274, Papal Secret Archives. Nevertheless at the nomination on January 11, 1621, Rangoni was passed over.

only thank God from his heart for the change that had been wrought in Poland.[1]

The reports to Rome of Cosmo de Torres, Diotallevi's immediate successor, on the state of the Catholic Church in Poland, gave a most gratifying account of the progress of the Catholic cause in Poland proper and in Mazuria.[2] In 1611 it was calculated that out of a total population of fourteen to fifteen millions, one-fourth belonged to the ancient Church.[3] At a later date the proportion shifted in favour of the Catholics. Catholics were also on the increase in Lithuania. Though there were many schismatics and Protestants there, the power of the latter was weakened owing to their having split up into the most divers sects. In the duchy of Prussia, which was a Polish fief, the majority of the people had adopted partly the Lutheran, partly the Calvinist tenets, but on the occasion of a new enfeoffment, Poland successfully insisted on the construction and upkeep of a Catholic church at Königsberg. The bishopric of Ermland constituted a Catholic oasis in East Prussia and the Jesuits had a flourishing establishment at Braunsberg.[4] At Danzig and Thorn their action was greatly hampered by the relentless hostility of the Protestants. Nevertheless, they were able to found a house at Graudenz, in 1619, and missions at Marienburg (1619) and Bromberg (1621).[5] But in Poland proper the Society of Jesus displayed a wonderful activity. Opposition was not wanting there either, but king Sigismund proved a powerful protector.

[1] *Cf.* **instruttione a Mgr. Torres, arcivescovo d'Adrianopoli, Nuntio designato da N.S. in Polonia*, May 30, 1621, Casanatense Library, Rome, X., V., 15, p. 382.

[2] See *Relayce Nunc. Apost.*, II., 139 *seq.* Minio points out the piety of the Poles in his *report of 1620, see *Notizenblatt zum Archiv f. osterr. Geschichtsquellen*, 1854, 247.

[3] See Gioda, III., 280.

[4] *Cf.* Duhr, I., 179 *seqq.*; II., 1, 375 *seq.*

[5] See *ibid.*, II., 1, 381 *seq.* For the Jesuit mission to Danzig *cf.* also Freytag, in the *Altpreuss. Monatsschrift*, XXVI. (1889), 521 *seq.*, and Levinson, in the *Zeitschrift des Westpreuss. Geschichtsvereins*, XLII.

It was also greatly to the advantage of the Order and the Catholic cause generally, that lucrative posts were only given to Catholics. The higher as well as the lower nobility, who were at all times the mainstay of Protestantism in Poland, returned to the Church in large numbers and the seats in the Senate of Lithuania and Poland were once more almost exclusively held by Catholics.[1] In the royal cities Protestant worship was being increasingly restricted; however, on the estates of the nobles who enjoyed immunity, measures of this kind could not be applied.

The chief means for the revival and expansion of the ancient Church in Torres' eyes was the reform of the secular and regular clergy, and the spread of the new religious Institutes, the Jesuits, the Discalced Carmelites and the Capuchins.[2] The reformed Carmelite nuns and some nursing Brothers also came to Poland during the pontificate of Paul V.[3] To the Pope's great joy Sigismund III. desired also a Capuchin foundation,[4] but the project came to nought. Thus the Jesuits remained the main pillar of the Church and they did great things for her increase in Poland.[5]

The Polish Province which had grown out of the Austrian Province in 1575, had made such progress that in 1608 it had

[1] *Cf.* VÖLKER, *Der Protestantismus in Polen*, Leipzig, 1910, 87, 216.

[2] See *Relayce Nunc. Apost.*, II., 147 *seq.*

[3] See *Script. rer. Pol.*, XIV., 68; FABISZA, 203.

[4] See **Epist.*, XI., 300, Papal Secret Archives.

[5] *Cf.* for what follows, *Litterae Annuae*, for 1605, p. 884 *seq.*; 1606, p. 687 *seq.*; 1607, p. 395 *seq.*; 1608, p. 662 *seq.*; 1609, p. 405 *seqq.*; 1610, p. 402 *seq.*; 1611, p. 589 *seqq.*; 1612, p. 449 *seq.*; 1613–1614, p. 361 *seq.*; I. ARGENTI, *Ad Sigismundum III. de statu Soc. Iesu in prov. Poloniae et Lithuaniae liber*, ed. altera, Ingoldstadii, 1616; J. WIELWICKI, *Historici diarii domus prof. Soc. Iesu Cracoviae, 1600–1629*, in the *Script. rer. Pol.* X., XIV., XVII., Cracoviae, 1886–9; ST. ZALEDKI, *Jesuici w Polsce*, I., II. w IV., 1–3, Kraków, 1904. See also a study by CHOTKOWSKI, *Szkoly jesuickie w Poznazin*, Kraków, 1893; this is important because of the manuscript material used.

to be divided into two, a Polish and a Lithuanian one.[1] A survey of the year 1616 shows that foundations had been made in almost every important town of the realm. The number of members was no less than 795.[2] At Cracow, the ancient city where Poland's kings used to be crowned, they had a novitiate and a professed house. There were colleges at Kalisz, Poznań, Thorn, Yaroslaw, Leopolis, Sandomir, Kamieniec, Lublin and Luzk ; residences were at Przemysl, Rawa, Krasrolrod and Danzig. The most important establishment was that of Poznań. The Order would have liked to see its college in that city erected into a university. Sigismund III. was favourable, but the university of Cracow, fearing its competition, successfully prevented a papal approval of the project.[3]

The heart and centre of the Lithuanian Province was at Vilna. Already Gregory XIII had raised the college to the dignity of a university.[4] The Jesuits had at Vilna a novitiate and a professed house, as well as a second house of probation at Warsaw. In 1616 the Province of Lithuania had colleges at Pułtusk, Plock, Nieświež, Lomźa, Orsza, Połock, Smolensk,

[1] At that time Petrus Fabricus came to be the first Polish Provincial ; before him only Italians, with the exception of one Spaniard, had been appointed. See WIELEWICKI, in the *Script. rer. Pol.*, X., 247, 271. *Cf. Litt. ann.*, 1608, p. 662.

[2] See IUVENCIUS, V., 2, 355.

[3] *Cf.* the paper of L. SCHERMANN, in the *Zeitschr. der Hist. Gesellsch. für die Provinz Posen*, IV., Posen, 1888, 70 *seq.* For the quarrels which afterwards arose between the university of Cracow and the Jesuits, *cf.* WIELEWICKI, in the *Script. rer. Pol.*, XVII. Wielewicki, a Jesuit himself, attributes them to the ill-considered policy of Fr. Lancicius. The conflict damaged the reputation of the Society not a little. That the Jesuits committed serious faults against the Cracow university, appears from the account given with praiseworthy impartiality by the Jesuit ST. ZALESKI, who published a short account of his larger work (1904) mentioned on p. 240, note 5 ; *Jesuici w Polsce. W skróceniu, 5 tomów w zednym, z dwoma mapami*, Kraków, 1908.

[3] *Cf.* present work, Vol. XXIV., 122 *seq.*

Riga and Dorpat. Braunsberg also belonged to the Province of Lithuania.

Of the greatest importance were the flourishing educational establishments of the Jesuits in which the sons of the nobility were educated in a thoroughly Catholic spirit. By this means the functionaries and the higher clergy came to be recruited from among men who were permeated with the spirit of the Catholic reform. Only this new generation could be depended upon to carry out the Tridentine reform decrees.

The Jesuits displayed a no less untiring activity in the pastoral ministry. In this they confined themselves by no means to the towns in which they had residences. On the contrary, they established missions both far and near. They penetrated into the Carpathians and into the Ukraine; they even extended their action beyond the boundaries of Poland, into Silesia and Hungary.[1] In 1615 there was even question of founding a college at Kiew.[2] For many provinces where there was a marked shortage of priests, in particular in Livonia and White Russia, these missions were of incalculable importance.[3]

The Jesuits' successes in the pastoral ministry were no less remarkable than their achievements in the educational sphere. John Argenti, who held a visitation of the Polish and Lithuanian Provinces, was able to report to Sigismund III. in 1615, that a complete change had taken place everywhere in the religious sphere.[4] Besides the return of many heretics to the Church, Argenti lays stress on the renewal of the religious spirit among Catholics, which showed itself in the frequentation of the sacraments. This was due to the zeal with which the Jesuits preached the word of God, not only in Polish, but likewise in German and in Ruthenian, where this was required.[5] The Jesuits bestowed much care on

[1] *Cf. Litt. Ann.*, 1605, p. 884 *seq.*, 886 *seq.*, 891 *seq.*; 1611, p. 635 *seq.*; 1613–1614, p. 459 *seq.*; WIELEWICKI, *loc. cit.*, X., 83 *seq.*, XIV, 87, 106, 189, 203.

[2] See ARGENTI, 31.

[3] *Cf. Litt. ann.*, 1613–1614, p. 461; ARGENTI, 28.

[4] ARGENTI, 37.

[5] *Cf. Litt. ann.*, 1607, p. 472; 1608, p. 705.

catechetical teaching and the explanation of the elements of the faith. They also vied with the other Orders in the care of the sick and the poor and in times of epidemics they showed a devotion which wrung admiration even from their enemies.[1]

In Poland also there were not wanting enemies of the Society of Jesus. The boldness of these was seen already in 1606. Among the many demands which the party of the *Rokosz* presented to Sigismund III. was this, that the Jesuits, inasmuch as they meddled with secular and political affairs, advocated absolutism, opposed all liberal tendencies and urged the subjects to revolt, should be removed at once from court; all non-Polish members should be driven from the country and the houses at Craców, Warsaw, Sandomir, Leopolis, Thorn, Danzig, Połock, Riga and Dorpat should be suppressed.[2] Thereupon, no less a personage than Peter Skarga, the court preacher of Sigismund III., rose up to defend his Order thus threatened and shamefully slandered. To the many services which this splendid man rendered to the Church and to his country, he added a fresh one by his magnificent justification of the Society of Jesus in a sermon preached by him at Wislica, on September 17th, 1606, in presence of the king and a number of Senators. The demand of the *Rokosz* having been rejected by the king and the Senate, Skarga was able to write to Aquaviva that he need have no further anxiety; though their adversaries had not laid down their arms, the position of the Jesuits in Poland was nevertheless assured.[3]

As a matter of fact, in December, 1606, a royal decree ordered the return of the Jesuits who had been driven from Thorn by the Protestant council of the town.[4] The greatness

[1] *Cf.*, *ibid.*, 1605, p. 899 *seq.*; 1606, p. 779; 1607, p. 413; WIELEWICKI, XIV., 112, 153.

[2] See WIELEWICKI, X., 197.

[3] See *ibid.*, 208 *seq.*; BERGA, 256.

[4] See WIELEWICKI, X., 228 *seq.* *Cf.* WERNICKE, *Gesch. Thorns* (1824), 96 *seq.*; E. KESTNER, *Beitr. zur Gesch. der Stadt Thorn* (1882), 225 *seq.* See also LEVINSON, *Polnisch-Preussisches*, in the *Zeitschr. des Westpreuss. Geschichtsvereins*, XLII.

of the change which had come about was seen at the diet of 1607, for that assembly was decisively in favour of the Jesuits and assured the continuation of their work. Notwithstanding all the efforts of their enemies, this decision was again confirmed in 1609 and 1611.[1] However, the old accusations were not silenced. As against the assertion that the Jesuits troubled the peace of the realm, the parish priest Caspar Cichochi showed that the roots of all the troubles lay in the Confederation of Warsaw.[2] Among the writings by which the Jesuits defended themselves, a high place belongs to the report on the state of the Order in Poland and Lithuania which the visitor, John Argenti, addressed to Sigismund III.[3] This document, which was first published in 1615 and disseminated in several editions,[4] refutes in detail the accusations against the Jesuits, especially as regards their alleged meddling with political matters, their stirring up of revolt, and their piling up of wealth. In his Apologia, Argenti also protests against a pamphlet circulated at first in manuscript, and published in 1614 at Cracow, under a false date and indicating a false place of impression. The pamphlet bore the title : "*Monita Secreta Societatis Jesu*—Secret Orders of the Jesuits." He rightly styles this document a monstrous forgery. The author was a Polish ex-Jesuit of the name of Zahorowski, who sought to revenge himself for his dismissal from the Society by publishing this libel. In view of the fact that many people took the satire seriously, Gretser, at the bidding of the General, Muzio Vitelleschi, wrote a refutation which appeared in 1618.[5]

[1] *Cf.*, too, LENGNICH, *Gesch. der Lande Preussen*, V. (1727), 151 *seq.*; WIELEWICKI, X., 245 *seq.*; DUHR, II., 1, 387.

[2] See VÖLKER, *Der Protestantismus in Polen*, 88.

[3] See the title given above, p. 240, note 5.

[4] See SOMMERVOGEL, *Bibliothèque*, I., 536 *seqq.*

[5] For the *Monita Secreta*, rejected also by serious Protestant students, and the replies to them, see DUHR, *Jesuitenfabeln*, 76 *seqq.*, the same, *Gesch. der Jesuiten*, II., 2, 675 *seq.* *Cf.* too, v. AKEN, in the *Préc. hist.*, 1881, 261 *seqq.*, 344 *seqq.*, 432 *seqq.*; *ibid.*, 1890, 83 *seq.*, an essay by SOMMERVOGEL; J. REIBER,

However, at that time the Polish Jesuits were far more grievously affected by many gaps in their ranks caused by death, than by forgeries and pasquinades. One after another the old pioneers died within a short time of each other: first, in 1611, the great Possevino; then, in 1612, Caspar Pętowski and Justus Rabe. These were followed, on September 27th of the same year, by Peter Skarga, and in 1613 by the apostle of Lithuania, Stanislaus Grodziki and in 1615 by Martin Laski.[1] The whole of Poland lamented the death of Skarga.[2] In him the nation lost not only its greatest preacher, but likewise one of its most devoted sons.[3] The Dominican Birkowski, who preached his funeral eulogy, styled him another Elias. As a matter of fact, in his famous sermons at the various diets,[4] before the king and the Polish nobles, this simple religious had exposed, with admirable courage and rare perspicacity, the existing political and social evils, and he predicted, should they be allowed to go on, the ruin of the powerful State: "If you do not amend, the countries united with the kingdom will fall away, and your realm will be conquered. No longer will you have a king of your own blood, on the contrary, you will be driven from your own country to become the objects of the mockery of the enemies whose slaves you will be." In the exhortation to repentance, published in 1610,[5] the "Polish Chrysostom" sums up once more in stirring fashion the warnings he had given to his beloved people. When, two years later, at his repeated request,

Monita secreta, Augsburg, 1902; FR. RODRIGUEZ, *Os Jesuitas e a Monita secreta*, Roma, 1912; BROU, *Les Jésuites de la légende*, I., Paris, 1906, 275 *seq.*; ALBERS, in *Studiën*, 1916, 136 *seq.*

[1] See WIELEWICKI, XIV., 40, 58, 63, 72, 98, 148. For him and other literary men of the Polish Jesuits, see HURTER, I., 174.

[2] *Cf.* present work, Vol. XX., note 2, for the special literature.

[3] See BERGA, 259.

[4] Berga writes of Skarga as a preacher both fully and without partisanship (263–272).

[5] "Invitatio ad poenitentiam incolarum regni Poloniae et Magni ducatus Lituaniae," see ROSENTRETER, in the *Freiburg Kirchenlex.*, XI.[2], 393 *seq.*

he was relieved from the office of court preacher and confessor to Sigismund III., both of which duties he had fulfilled in exemplary fashion during twenty-four years, he retired to Cracow where he soon died at the age of seventy-six. The memory of this man, distinguished as a preacher, a missionary, a writer and a patriot, lives to this day in the memory of the Polish people. His importance at a time when the Church of Poland was in great peril, is comparable to that of Canisius in Germany and that of Coton in France.

Besides Sigismund III., whom Rubens glorifies in one of his paintings as the conqueror of heresy,[1] the Jesuits and the episcopate had a substantial share in the preservation and renewal of the Catholic faith in Poland, for in the nomination of bishops by the king, the nuncios had successfully pressed for the choice of truly religious men. Thus when the primatial See of Gnesen became vacant through the death, in 1608, of Cardinal Maciejowski, it was in turn occupied by the excellent Albert Baranowski, and, at his death in 1615, by Laurence Gembicki.[2] The excellent bishop of Cracow, Peter Tylicki, was succeeded, in 1616, by Martin Szyszkowski, a man of similar character.[3] The following prelates were likewise known for their pastoral zeal: John Zomoiski, of Leopolis, Matthias Pstrokoński, at Przemysl until 1609, then at Wladýslawów (d. 1609), and Paul Wolucki, who laboured in the spirit of the Catholic reform first at Kamieniec, until 1609, then at Luzk, until 1616, and lastly at Leslau. At Luzk he founded a Jesuit College.[4] The bishop of Samogitia,

[1] *Cf. Anz. der Krakauer Akad.*, 1905, 16.

[2] Gembicki held a diocesan synod at Lowicz in 1620 and a provincial synod at Petrikau in 1621. *Cf.* for him and his predecessors, the special literature mentioned in the *Freiburg. Kirchenlexikon*, V.², 764 *seq.*

[3] For P. Tylicki, see WIELEWICKI, XIV., 179, 196 *seq.* M. Szyszkowski had promulgated, since 1621, his "Reformationes generales ad clerum et populum Cracoviens. pertinentes", and had held a synod; see *Frei. Kirchenlex.*, VII.², 1031. For Szyszkowski, *cf.* also BZOVIUS, *Vita Pauli*, V., ch. 33.

[4] See WIELEWICKI, XIV., 7 *seq.*

Melchior Gedroye, brought back to the Church almost the whole of the Lithuanian population of that district.[1]

The significance of the Jesuit Order as well as the religious efflorescence in Poland, found their visible expression in the erection of numerous churches, monasteries and chapels. Foremost among these is the Jesuit church of SS. Peter and Paul at Cracow, erected in 1597, by the art-loving Sigismund III., in the style of the Gesù at Rome, the magnificently gilt dome of which was crowned with a cross in 1619.[2] The construction was superintended first by the Jesuit Giovanni Maria Bernardono, of Como, and after his death by Giovanni Gislenio, of Rome. Specially worthy of attention are the façade of free stone adorned with sculptures and incrusted with marble, and the beautiful forecourt which is shut off from the street by a balustrade adorned with statues of the twelve Apostles. The magnificent church, in which Skarga found a resting place, with its green copper domes, constitutes a characteristic feature of the panorama of the city. In 1610 archbishop John Zamoiski laid the first stone of the Jesuit church there, which, with the help of the Polish aristocracy and especially through the lavish contributions of Elizabeth Gostomska-Siemiawska, became one of the largest of the whole city. The building, probably planned by a Jesuit, with tribunes erected over the aisles, provided room for many thousands of worshippers.[3] At Vilna the Jesuits began by transforming Jagiello's church of St. John and subsequently raised a fine tower by its side. The interior, a model of late Gothic spaciousness, remained untouched. In addition to this—the university church—there arose another Jesuit church, St. Casimir. It was their principal church and was built in the new style. Soon a number of baroque churches rose up in Vilna so that the silhouette of the town reminds one of Salzburg and Würzburg. The Bernardines, who had formed a new Congregation in

[1] See GAMS, 357.

[2] See WIELEWICKI, XIV., 303.

[3] The Church is 41 metres long, 22 m. wide, and 26 m. high; see J. PIOTROWSKI, *Lemberg*, 94.

1580, erected many new churches all over Poland.[1] All are examples of the baroque style which, under the grey skies of the North, evoked the azure dome of Italy's sunlit firmament.

The care with which Paul V. watched over the religious future of Poland showed itself also in his efforts to bring about the union of the Ruthenians with the Roman Church which had been discussed at Brest in 1596. On May 29th, 1605, he confirmed the faculty to consecrate the Ruthenian bishops which his predecessor had granted to Hypatius Pociej, metropolitan of Kiew.[2] In the letter in which Paul V. thanked Pociej for his congratulations on his elevation to the Apostolic See, the Pope paid tribute to the Metropolitan's great zeal in the past and exhorts him in future also to defend, consolidate and extend the union.[3] Pociej's situation was difficult in the extreme; the schismatics were masters of Kiew, so that he was compelled to take up residence at Vilna, and since the former had seized the possessions of his metropolitan See, he retained his diocese of Wladimir.

Realizing these difficulties, the Pope on June 9th, 1606, prayed the Chancellor of Lithuania, Leo Sapieha to do all he could for the metropolitan.[4] In his Instruction, on November, 1606,[5] the new nuncio Simonetta, was directed to do his utmost for the preservation of the union and to co-operate effectively with those who sought to remove the obstacles that stood in its way. After the death of the chief opponent of the union, Prince Ostrožskyj, a turn for the better seemed at hand. His son became a Catholic, introduced the Catholic religion on his estates and founded a convent of Dominicans to provide teachers and preachers of the faith.

[1] Woiwode Nikolaus Zebrzydowski, of Cracow, built the Bernardine Convent and church at Kalwarya in 1603–9. The church is a famous place of pilgrimage.

[2] See BULL., XI., 194 *seq.*

[3] Briefs of December 13, 1605, in THEINER, *Mon. Pol.*, III., 288 *seqq.*

[4] See *ibid.*, 293.

[5] *Cf.* present work, p. 234, note 2.

In 1624 Anna Ostrožska, with whom the line died out, founded a Jesuit College at Ostrog.[1]

Though the most powerful enemy of the union was thus out of the way, the schismatical agitation was not at an end. On January 6th, 1608, the Pope wrote to comfort Pociej.[2] The praise bestowed on that much tried man seems fully deserved, for Pociej laboured unceasingly in the defence of the union, both by the spoken and the written word. The obstacles which he encountered in his demand for judicial recognition of his episcopal office were such that they explain, even if they do not justify, the violence of many of his utterances.[3] It was particularly galling for him that the government for the most part gave him but slender support and that the Polish Latin bishops kept the Uniates at arm's length. It was a particularly bitter disappointment to him that the promise to admit the Ruthenian bishops into the Senate was not fulfilled, though Paul V., in 1611, expressly recalled it to the king's mind.[4]

In consequence of the hostility of the schismatics, Pociej saw his loftiest intentions misjudged and suspected. If he proceeded against the recalcitrants, they lodged exaggerated complaints against his alleged violence. The defeat which they suffered in 1609, in consequence of the measures taken by the king at Vilna, they avenged by attacking and wounding the aged metropolitan in the open street, August 12, 1609.[5] Notwithstanding all the opposition and the dangers which Pociej had to encounter everywhere at Kiew, at Minsk and at Leopolis, whenever he sought to assert his authority,[6] the gallant bishop never relaxed his efforts for the judicial recognition of the union. When he died, July 13th, 1613, he was succeeded by his coadjutor, Wilamin Rutski, who shared his spirit.

Rutski, the scion of an old noble Ruthenian family, had been

[1] *Cf.* Pichler, II., 107 *seq.*

[2] See Theiner, III., 297.

[3] *Cf.* Likowski, 251 *seq.*

[4] Theiner, III., 348.

[5] See Likowski, 255 *seq.*, 257 *seq.*

[6] See *ibid.*, 258.

brought up as a Calvinist but had become a Catholic whilst pursuing his studies at Prague. He completed his education at the Greek College at Rome, under the Jesuits, and after a period of uncertainty entered the Basilian monastery of the Holy Trinity at Vilna, in 1609. There a small but fervent religious family had gathered round the person of Josaphat Kuncewicz, another pupil of the Jesuits and well known for his deep piety, stern asceticism and exhaustive knowledge of the Greek Fathers. The monks' work on behalf of the union drew on them so fierce a persecution on the part of the schismatics that the Basilians of Vilna would have been lost but for the protection of Sigismund III. In 1609 Rutski became archimandrite of the monastery. In 1614 he entrusted the office to his friend Josaphat Kuncewicz [1] who, in the previous year, had erected Basilian monasteries at Byten and Zyrowicz, and who spent all his energy in forwarding the union. In view of the immense influence which Josaphat enjoyed with the Ruthenian people, Rutski, with the consent of the king, raised him in 1617 to the office of coadjutor with right of succession to the nonogenarian bishop of Polozk. On the decease of the bishop, Josaphat took up the task of reforming the sadly neglected diocese. His activity took all forms—visitations, synods, sermons, the composition of a catechism, with the result that at the end of three years almost the whole population of White Russia declared itself in favour of the union.[2]

When Rutski came to Rome in 1615, to give an account of his work as a bishop, he gave the Pope a detailed description of the situation of the Uniates. He explained that the chief weapon of the schismatics was the lie that the union was directed against the Ruthenian rite and served only as a bridge for the introduction of the Latin rite. To cut short this calumny, at Rutski's suggestion, Paul V. published a solemn

[1] *Cf.* A. Guépin, *St. Josaphat, archévêque de Polock*, 2 vols., Poitiers, 1874 ; G. Hofmann, *Roma* (1923) ; Likowski, 263 *seq.*, 303 *seq.* ; G. Hofmann, in *Orientalia Christiana*, I. (Romae, 1923), 297 *seq.* ; III. (1925), 173 *seq.*

[2] See Likowski, 313 *seqq.*

declaration, on December 10th, 1615, in which he emphatically stated that it was not the intention of the Holy See to alter the Ruthenian rite even in the smallest detail, still less to suppress it or to replace it by the Latin rite.[1] At the same time, in view of the great distances, the Pope granted that Ruthenians might receive episcopal consecration from Latins and Latins from Ruthenians. Moreover, the Pope provided four burses for Uniat Ruthenians at the Greek College in Rome.[2] However, this was too slender a help to raise the Ruthenian clergy, whose members had sunk to a low level, and who, owing to the absence of the law of celibacy, were far too much involved in the affairs of everyday life.

In these circumstances, Rutski turned his attention to the ancient and venerable Basilian Order which had been rescued from decadence and filled with fresh vitality by the new archimandrite Josaphat. Foundations similar to those of Byten and Zyrowic were made at Krasnobród and Grodno; the spirit which quickened the monastery of the Holy Trinity of Vilna also penetrated into the ancient houses of Minsk and Novgorod near Vilna. In 1616, a general noviciate for the Order was founded at Byten and placed under the direction of two Jesuits.[3]

In the following year Rutski convened a General Chapter at the castle of Ruta which laid down new rules, adapted to the needs of the time.[4] A protoarchimandrite, elected for life by the members of the Order and approved by the Metropolitan, was to govern the whole Order, appoint or depose local Superiors, hold an annual visitation of all the monasteries and watch over the observance of the reformed Rule. Only the bishops were bound by the law of celibacy. Rutski decreed that henceforth only reformed Basilians were to be raised to the episcopal dignity. At the same time, to forestall every ambition, he made the monks bind themselves

[1] See *Bull.*, XII., 341.

[2] *Ibid.*, 340, 342.

[3] See Likowski, 267.

[4] *Cf. Regole del S.P. Basilio M. ed osservaz. ed instruzioni raccolte da* G. Walamin, Roma, 1854 (*Prop. Fide*).

by vow not to aspire to bishoprics. At first only eight monasteries adopted a reform which was to prove so important for the Ruthenian Church. Seven years later Rutski was able to inform Rome that over twenty monasteries had joined the reform.[1] For the training of the secular clergy, he erected, with the consent of Paul V., two colleges in connection with the Basilian monasteries of Zyrowic, Wladimir and Borun.[2]

All these gratifying developments, as well as the existence of the union, were threatened, in 1620, by a storm of which Cyril Lukaris was the origin. This Cretan, who had been the evil genius of the duke of Ostroźskyj,[3] entertained towards the Catholic Church and the papacy a hatred which was unsurpassed by any of his fellow schismatics or by the Dutch Calvinists with whom he entertained relations. With his accurate knowledge of conditions in Poland, Lukaris understood, perhaps he was the first to do so, the significance of the question of the Cossacks as a means of conjuring up for the kingdom a most serious danger in the political field, as well as helping the schismatical Church, of which he had become the head, to victory over the hated union.[4]

In the spring of the same year, 1620, in which Cyril reached the goal of his ambition, namely the patriarchal see of Constantinople, the patriarch of Jerusalem, Theophanos, on his return journey from Moscow, presented himself at Kiew as his plenipotentiary. The enemies of the union received the high dignitary of the oriental-schismatic Church with enthusiasm. When the astute Greek had sufficiently prepared the ground for his plans, he took, in August, behind closed doors and windows, a step of the utmost significance. On the ground of special powers which he claimed to have received from the Greek Patriarch for the Ruthenian Church, Theophanos pronounced the deposition of Rutski and all the

[1] See Likowski, 268.

[2] *Ibid.*, 269.

[3] *Cf.* our account, Vol. XXIV., p. 136 *seqq.*

[4] Opinion of Smolka, *Die Reussische Welt*, 277. For the previous career of C. Lukaris, whom we shall hear of again in the next volume, see Ph. Meyer in *Herzogs Realenzykl.*, XI.³, 682 *seq.*

Uniate Ruthenian bishops, replaced them by schismatics, viz. one Metropolitan and six suffragans and assigned to them the Sees of the deposed prelates. In taking this step Theophanos looked to the support of the Cossacks of the Ukraine, whose hetmann, Konaševyč-Sahajdačnyi, swore at the consecration of the orthodox bishops, to guard and defend the newly erected schismatical hierarchy with the whole might of his warlike bands.[1]

The alliance between the schismatics and the Cossacks took place at a moment when the Sultan threatened the Polish kingdom with a large army. As a condition of their assistance, the Cossacks demanded the recognition of the schismatical hierarchy by the diet which opened at Warsaw at the beginning of 1621. Besides the two archbishops, Rutski and Josaphat, who hastened in person to Warsaw, the Papal nuncio Diotallevi also rendered signal service in conjuring this peril. Like his predecessor Ruini, Diotallevi had been instructed to do his utmost for the preservation of the union.[2] Though ailing, and notwithstanding the cold of winter, the nuncio hastened to the side of the king, the Latin bishops and the Senators, and to all he made the most pressing representations.[3]

Though the worst was avoided, Sigismund found himself nevertheless in so strained a position that he could not think of proceeding against the schismatics who had violated his royal prerogatives, as he had at first intended. In like manner, in view of the more than lukewarm attitude of the Senators both ecclesiastical and lay, towards the union, the importance of which they failed to realize, the Polish king was compelled to adopt humiliating half-measures and to defer a decision concerning the schismatical bishops.[4] Among these were several energetic men, such as the archimandrite of the famous Cave monastery at Kiew, Job Boretskyj, who

[1] See Likowski, 216 *seq.*, 271 ; Smolka, 277 *seq.*

[2] **Instruction for Diotallevi*, State Library, Vienna, *loc. cit.*

[3] See Likowski, 221, 273 *seq.*

[4] See Smolka, 280 *seq.*

succeeded in winning over a large section of the Ruthenian people. Soon the union saw itself exposed on all sides to grievous attacks which were to reach their climax in the death as a martyr of Josaphat Kuncewicz, the splendid archbishop of Polozk.

CHAPTER IV.

RELATIONS OF PAUL V. WITH THE EMPERORS RUDOLPH II., MATTHIAS AND FERDINAND II—GOOD RESULTS OF THE CATHOLIC RESTORATION IN GERMANY—THE BOHEMIAN REVOLUTION AND THE BEGINNING OF THE THIRTY YEARS WAR.

PAUL V.'s policy with regard to the emperor and the empire differed in no respect from that of Clement VIII. The aims of the Holy See remained the same, viz. assuring the succession of Rudolph in the empire; the support of the emperor in the war against the Turks; the defeat of the Protestant demand for "religious liberty" and the promotion of the Catholic reform and restoration.

All these problems were most closely interconnected, but their solution had been rendered extraordinarily difficult already in the days of Clement VIII. by the disordered mind of the weak-willed emperor whose half-heartedness and indecision produced a highly dangerous situation. The peril became daily more acute owing to the insurrection of the Hungarians whose leader, Stephen Bocskay, did not scruple to ally himself with the hereditary enemy, the Turk.

Whilst bands of insurgents, supported by Turkish flying-columns, repeatedly appeared on the banks of the March and the Drave, and the badly paid imperial army ravaged its own territory, the Austrian aristocracy impatiently pressed its demand for "religious liberty". All this seemed to leave Rudolph unmoved: he remained entirely inactive. This state of affairs induced the archdukes Matthias, Maximilian, Ferdinand of Stiria and his brother, Maximilian Ernest, to swift intervention. On April 30th, 1605, they bound themselves to act as one man on behalf of their House and to make joint representations to the emperor on the dangers that threatened unless provision were speedily made against them. They then betook themselves to Prague, and there obtained from Rudolph II., for his brother Maximilian, full powers for the conduct of the Hungarian war, as well as for the negotiations for an understanding with Bocskay.[1]

The ticklish question of the succession to the empire had only been lightly touched upon at the conference of the archdukes.[2] It was Paul V. who, as the Father of Christendom and the friend of the House of Habsburg, resolved to raise this urgent business which had occupied the Curia for the last twenty years, and to prepare the way for a final settlement. It was clearly recognized, in Rome as well as in Madrid,[3] that a vital interest not only of the House of Habsburg but of the ancient Church also was here at stake, for if Rudolph died, there was the menace of a Protestant imperial vicariate and, eventually, of a Protestant emperor. On June 24th, 1605, Paul V. informed the emperor that the nuncio of Prague, Ferreri, had been commissioned to confer with him on the choice of a king of the Romans. At the same time the Pope asked the chief advisers of Rudolph to assist the nuncio in every way.[4] Already on June 11th, Paul V. had urged Ernest, the Elector of Cologne, to repair to Prague and to press the emperor for a decision on questions in a definite settlement of which Rome saw the only means

[1] *Cf.* GINDELY, I., 71 ; STIEVE, V., 764 ; J. FISCHER, *Der Linzer Tag von* 1695 (Progr.), Feldkirch, 1898. FISCHER proves that it was not the archduke Matthias who was the originator of the diet of Linz, but his brother Maximilian, the then governor of Tirol and the Vorlanden.

[2] *Cf.* FISCHER, *loc. cit.*, 37.

[3] *Cf.* the **Instrucion del Marques de Villena al de Aytona*, dated November 9, 1606, which discusses in detail the dangers which must threaten at the death of the emperor if there were no king of the Romans. Here it is stated : " El negocio de la elecion del Rey de Romanos es oi el mayor i de mas gravidad que pende en el mundo," Archives of Spanish Embassy in Rome, I., 28.

[4] *Cf.* MEYER, *Nuntiaturberichte*, 392, 396 *seq.*

of saving the Church in Germany.[1] The indecision and morbid susceptibility of the emperor, as also his aversion to the regulation of the question of the succession, were at that time greater than ever. However, Paul V.'s pressure was unremitting. On August 22nd, 1605, he wrote again to admonish the emperor not to put off any longer the choice of a king of the Romans. Danger threatened from the plots of the Protestants who had no more ardent wish than to wrest the empire from the House of Austria; the election of a king of the Romans would avert this peril.

A document of similar purport was issued on October 5th, 1605,[2] and a memorandum to the same effect was handed to Rudolph II. by Ferreri at the beginning of November. Against all expectations these admonitions were not ill received by the emperor although, at his audience, the nuncio received only the non-committal answer that the matter would be considered.[3] The Elector Ernest also, from whose visit to Prague Paul V. looked for a clarification of the situation, obtained nothing at his repeated audiences.[4] Ferreri began to despair. On the other hand the Pope persevered in his efforts. A new Brief, dated January 6th, 1606, insisted on a settlement of the affair. Ferreri hesitated to present the document and did so only after repeated orders and censures.[5] Paul V. now clung to the hope that the ecclesiastical Electors would force a decision at the forthcoming Diet of empire.[6]

Together with the settlement of the imperial succession, Paul V. had no less at heart a happy termination of the war against the Turks. To this end, only a fortnight after his

[1] *Ibid.*, 382.

[2] *Ibid.*, 472, 582.

[3] *Ibid.*, 580, 582. On October 5, 1605, Paul V. wrote to the Elector of Mayence in connection with the question of the succession. He had already written to him on the same subject on July 15; *cf.* STIEVE, V., 753.

[4] *Cf.* MEYER, 583 *seq.*, 585, 623, 635–8.

[5] *Cf.* MEYER, 651 *seq.*, 661, 689.

[6] *Ibid.*, 735 *seq.*, 772, 798. *Cf.* STIEVE, V., 857, note.

election, he dispatched his chamberlain, Giacomo Serra, to Hungary, with funds to raise troops.[1] This step was inspired not only by the traditional policy of the Holy See, which aimed at guarding Christendom from the attacks of the infidels, but also by the hope of restraining the emperor from granting concessions in the religious sphere to the Protestants of Austria and Hungary.[2]

It is easy enough to understand how the clamour for freedom of belief and conscience which became ever louder in those countries, had power to alarm the Pope to the utmost, for experience had shown what such a concession entailed for the Catholics. Wherever it had been granted, the sequel was the complete oppression of the Catholics, the deprivation of their churches and possessions and the prohibition of the practice of the Catholic religion.[3] Hence it is not to be wondered at if the Pope and his nuncios condemned with

[1] *Cf.* MEYER, 372, 407, 421, 629 *seq.* According to the report of the *obbedienza* embassy of Lucca, Paul V. had thought of sending a Cardinal to Germany with a view to preventing yet another squandering of his subsidy against the Turks; *cf. Studi e docum.*, XXII., 203.

[2] *Cf.* MEYER, XLVIII.

[3] This fact, which had already been emphasized by contemporaries such as STOBAEUS (see *Epist. ad diversos, Venet.*, 1794, 81, transl. by DUHR, II., 2, 325) is conceded even by a writer as hostile to Catholics as A. KLUCKHOHN (*Zur Vorgeschichte des Dreissigjähr. Krieges*, in the Suppl. to *Allgemeine Zeitung*, 1876, no. 14). How Protestants abhorred the very idea of toleration towards Catholics is shown by the utter rejection of Paul V's. suggestion that one of the many churches and chapels of Nuremberg should be surrendered to the Catholics. For that reason also the diet was not to be held at Nuremberg for "thereby the ordinary man might get the scruple into his head that the Catholic religion cannot be so bad as the preachers make out"; *cf.* CHROUST, X., 85 *seq.*, 298, 424, 740. That Rudolph II. was in any way convinced of the necessity of freedom of conscience or worship, as MEYER (LXVII) supposes, is very doubtful; see *Hist. Zeitschrift*, CXIV, 124 *seq.*

the utmost severity[1] the aspirations of the time towards toleration and withstood them by every available means. However, Paul V. was only partially successful, though the subsidy for the war against the Turks which he and the Spaniards contributed, proved decisive for the rejection, in July, 1605, by the local Diet of Vienna, of religious freedom which the Protestants demanded as the price of their assistance against the Turks.[2] But this relieved the Pope only of part of his anxiety, for the Hungarian rebels also noisily demanded religious freedom, and in view of their close connection with the Porte, much depended on the issue of the Turkish campaign.

The truly pitiful course of the war in Hungary is well known. In the autumn of 1605 the Turks conquered Visegrad and the important town of Gran. The Pope, who at that very time was doing his best to induce the grand duke of Tuscany to lend help to the emperor,[3] was deeply grieved by these losses. His sorrow was further increased when he learnt that the shameful issue of the war was due to the systematic demoralization of the imperial military administration: "Write that we refuse to give further help, for it is clear that all is thrown away," was the sharp remark of the usually calm Paul V. to Ottavio Paravicini, the Cardinal protector of Germany.[4] In his letter of sympathy, dated October 31st, 1605, the Pope spoke to Rudolph in a manner which could not be misunderstood: if there was no improvement, worse was to be expected; as a friend and ally he felt bound to warn him that the bad system must be changed.[5] But of this there was no question: armaments, equipment, and commissariat remained as inadequate as before. In like manner the Pope's attempt to fight the Turk by leaguing together the land and sea forces of Spain, the Italian States,

[1] See MEYER, XLIX.

[2] See MEYER, XL., 434, 442, 446.

[3] *Cf.* the reports in RINIERI, *Clemente VIII. e Sinan Bassa Cicala, Roma*, 1898,125 *seq.*, 187 *seq.*

[4] MEYER, 563.

[5] *Ibid.*, 555 *seq.*

the Catholic parts of Germany and the Slavonic and Croatian princes, failed owing to the indifference of Spain and the opposition of the selfish Venetians.[1]

The total sum spent by the Papal Chamber for Rudolph II.'s Turkish war amounted already then to two million gold scudi; hence the most that Paul V. was still prepared to do at the close of 1605 was a slight delay of the payment of the Papal troops. As a matter of fact in order to re-establish to some extent his financial condition, which was deplorable, he had been obliged, on December 23rd, 1605, to abolish, for the benefit of the income of the Papal chamber, a number of privileges and immunities granted by his predecessors.[2]

Since the emperor was resolved to come to terms with the Hungarian rebels, it was necessary to see to it that the Catholic faith suffered no injury.[3] The danger was great, for the Hungarians demanded not only the confession of Augsburg, but also the Swiss confession, that is Calvinism. The Pope made the most serious representations to the imperial envoy,[4] and in several Briefs besought the archduke Matthias, who was charged with the peace negotiations, not to allow any clause to creep in which would be detrimental to the Church and the true faith.[5]

The Prague nuncio, Ferreri, worked energetically for the same end, and bishop Klesl, whose advice had been sought, urged the necessity of taking this course. He declared, amongst other things, that the queen of England had told the Sultan, through her ambassador, that Calvinism and the Koran did not greatly differ, that, in fact they agreed on most points, and that the Dutch had recently made similar statements at Constantinople. Klesl further pointed out

[1] *Ibid.*, LII. *seq.*, 560.

[2] *Ibid.*, LIV., 611.

[3] See the letter of Cardinal Borghese to Serra, November 19, 1605, in MEYER, 577.

[4] *Cf.* the report in *Archiv des Ver. f. siebenbürgische Landeskunde N.F.*, XIX, (1884), 604 *seq.*

[5] See MEYER, 672, 698. The originals of both Briefs in *Staatsarchiv* at Vienna, *Urkunden*.

that if the Hungarian demands were granted not only would the political consequences be disastrous, but the act would be interpreted as confirming the religious concessions granted in Austria, and other countries would feel encouraged to make similar demands. Lastly he appealed to the coronation oath of the emperor whose person the archduke represented. The emperor had bound himself by a personal oath to maintain and protect the one, universal Church in Hungary and to this end to sacrifice life and goods, if necessary. Therefore let the archduke tell the rebels that it was not in his power to tolerate another religion.[1]

These representations were not without effect. Matthias began by resisting the demands of the rebels, though he ended by allowing himself to be persuaded by the Hungarian magnate, Stephen Illésházy. In this way, after five months of discussion, the fateful peace of Vienna was signed with Hungary on June 23rd, 1606. It expressly revoked Rudolph's supplementary article of 1604 concerning the fresh confirmation of decrees published by previous kings in favour of the Church and, though Calvinism was not mentioned, it also granted freedom to practise their religion to the Estates of Hungary, that is, to the magnates, the nobles, the free cities, and the boroughs immediately subject to the king, though no prejudice was to accrue to the Catholic Church, and her clergy were not to be interfered with.[2]

Whilst the negotiations were still pending, the nuncio of Prague, Ferreri, had urged the emperor that, with a view to saving his conscience, he should except from confirmation, when ratifying the agreement, whatever was against religion.[3] In the end Ferreri even went so far as to threaten to break

[1] See HAMMER, *Klesl*, II., *Beil* no. 186.

[2] See KATONA, XXVIII., 545 *seq*. *Cf*. STIEVE, V., 804, note 3, and GEZA LENCZ, *Der Aufstand Boskays und der Wiener Friede* (in Hungarian), DEBRECZEN, 1917, whose account, however, is not altogether unexceptionable (*cf*. *Wiener Zeitschr. f. Gesch*., I., 624), for as STEINACKER justly remarks (*Hist. Zeitschr*., CXXVII., 116 *seq*.) his presentment of facts is one-sided.

[3] MEYER, 691.

off diplomatic relations if the opposite were to take place. However, this sharp procedure, which was bound to lead to the gravest complications, was not approved by the Holy See.[1] When Rudolph, after much hesitation, allowed himself to be persuaded to sign the peace of Vienna, on August 6th, 1606, he had recourse to a subterfuge, for in a secret document he protested that he had acted under compulsion and that he did not consider himself bound by the articles which conflicted with his oath as a Catholic king.[2] However, even so the peace of Vienna was a heavy blow to the Church, for the prosecution of the Catholic restoration in Hungary was now no longer to be thought of.[3]

The emperor had obviously sought to attenuate the consequences of the peace of Vienna, out of consideration for the Pope who, notwithstanding his financial straits, decided, in 1606 to grant yet another subsidy of no less than 130,000 scudi for the war against the Turks.[4] However, this sacrifice was also made in vain. The peace of Vienna was succeeded by an agreement with the Porte, concluded on November 11th, 1606, at Komorn, a place where the river Zsitva enters the Danube. Paul V. himself had ended by counselling an agreement for at this time the Pope was fully taken up with his struggle with mighty Venice.[5] On the Turkish side, the scales in favour of an agreement were heavily weighted by the peril which threatened from Persia, with whose ruler Paul V. had had relations in 1605.[6] In view of the emperor's lofty conception of his dignity, he must have deeply felt the

[1] *Ibid.*, 692, 711.

[2] See SCHMIDT, *Gesch. der Deutschen*, VIII., 159. The fable dished up by HUBER (*Der Jesuitenorden*, 137) of the advice of a Jesuit in this matter is also rejected by STIEVE (V., 808, n. 2.).

[3] MEYER, LVII., 787.

[4] *Ibid.*, LIV.

[5] *Cf.* STIEVE, V., 810, 828.

[6] *Cf.* **Relazione del negotiato fatto da un padre Carmelitano scalzo mandato da Paolo V. al Re di Persia l'a. 1605 per unire i principi cattolici contro il Turco* (in Spanish), Cod. 35, B. 9, p. 96–101, Bibl. Corsini, Rome, *cf.* Vol. XXV., p. 363 *seqq.* of this work.

humiliation of the unfavourable peace treaty with the Hungarian rebels and the Turks. He was by no means minded to acquiesce for ever, though for a long time he was unable to come to a decision. However, from the summer of 1607 onwards he was not afraid to infringe the peace of Vienna and he gave unmistakable proofs of his intention to renew the war against the Turks. The necessary money for a struggle against the Turks, on which Paul V. was once more keen [1] and for which he was willing to grant a subsidy,[2] was to be provided by the Diet of Ratisbon.

To the great annoyance of the Protestants, Rudolph appointed the rigidly Catholic archduke Ferdinand to represent him at that assembly. On October 3rd, 1607, Paul V. informed the emperor that the archbishop of Capua, Antonio Caetani, who in June had succeeded Ferreri as nuncio at Prague, was delegated to represent the Holy See at the Diet.[3] Briefs were handed to Caetani for the Catholic princes

[1] As soon as the compromise with Venice had been arranged Paul V. resumed his efforts with a view to fighting the Turks; *cf.* the reports of Mantuanese envoy from Rome of April 7, May 19, and July 21, 1607, Gonzaga Archives at Mantua.

[2] See STIEVE, V., 841. On Paul V.'s support of the fleet of Ferdinand I. of Tuscany and the Order of St. Stephen, in their enterprises against the Turks, see LE BRET, VIII., 467 *seq.*; REUMONT, *Toskana*, I., 351 *seq.*; JORGA, III., 393 *seq.*; UZIELLI, *Cenni s. imprese scient. maritt. e coloniali di Ferdinando I.*, Firenze, 1901 (publ. Nozze). *Cf.* also the letter to ALY GIAMPULAT, *princip. et protect. regni Syriae*, dated February 2, 1607, praising him for resisting the Turkish tyranny and for liberating the people of that country, *Epist.*, III., 375, Papal Secret Archives.

[3] *Brief to Rudolph II., dated 1607, *V. Non. Oct.*, *Epist.*, III., 227, *ibid.* The Instruction for Caetani, dated October 20, 1607, in EGLOFFSTEIN, 114 *seq.*; on Caetani's arrival in Prague, see STIEVE, V., 481, n. 3. The statement that the Pope had at first been inclined to send Cardinal Carlo Madruzzo to the Diet as legate (*cf. Instrucion del Marq. de Villena al de Aytona*, dated November 9, 1606, Archives of Spanish Embassy in Rome, I., 28) is incorrect. In the *Brief to Philip III. of September 22, 1606, the Pope says that in order to hasten the election of a king of

of empire which, besides accrediting himself, contained an exhortation to oppose the Protestant designs, to interest themselves in the spread of the Catholic faith, and above all to secure the restitution of the confiscated monasteries and other Church property. The emperor, who was informed of the existence of these letters, imagined that they dealt with the question of the succession—a matter which was odious to him—but Caetani was able to allay his suspicion at once.[1]

Rudolph II. was strongly opposed to Caetani's presence at Ratisbon for he feared that the Protestants, who were already greatly annoyed by the nomination of the archduke Ferdinand as his personal representative, would be still further incensed by the nuncio's presence. The imperial counsellors urged Caetani not to go to Ratisbon. They pointed out that the Diet was convened solely for the purpose of raising money for the Turkish war and that it was not customary for nuncios to be present at such assemblies in the absence of the emperor; the nuncio would do better service to religion if he remained with the emperor at Prague.[2] In the circumstances Paul V. decided to cancel the mission he had given to Caetani: he did so in a Brief of November 24th, 1607, which Caetani communicated to the emperor. At the same time Caetani presented a memorial in which the emperor was exhorted not to grant to Protestant administrators of dioceses any indult or privilege unfavourable to the Church, not to admit to the Diet the administrator of Magdeburg and all other usurpers and not to interfere any longer with the rights of Catholics in respect of Church property. In a covering letter the nuncio added that though the Pope

the Romans, he would send a prudent person to Germany, as the king recommends, but a Cardinal only after the diet should have been convoked. *Epist.*, II., 199, Papal Secret Archives.

[1] STIEVE, V., 903, and PIEPER, " Der Augustiner F. Milensio," in *Römish. Quartalschr.*, V. (1891), 58, n. 1. A general survey of Caetani's nunciature may be found in *Vita del card. Ant. Caetani di Msgr. Christoforo Caetani vesc. di Foligno*, Barb. 6030, p. 21, Vatican Library.

[2] PIEPER, *loc. cit.*, 59, n. 1.

had agreed that he should stay away from the Diet, he had commanded him to repair to Ratisbon and to carry out his first instructions in the eventuality of the emperor refusing to give complete satisfaction on the above-mentioned questions. Therefore let the emperor forthwith give precise instructions to the archduke Ferdinand. On his part Caetani dispatched his *uditore* to Ratisbon with the task of explaining more fully the Pope's wishes to the archduke.[1]

In addition to these precautions for the safety of the interests of the Church, Caetani deemed it necessary to send a confidential messenger to Ratisbon with mission to report on the proceedings of the Diet. He intended to entrust the task to his *uditore,* but Rome feared to offend the emperor.[2] In the end Caetani's choice fell on the Neapolitan Augustinian Friar, Felice Milensio, who had been engaged, since 1602, in the visitation of the German and Bohemian monasteries of his Order.[3] Since the emperor was resolved himself to see to the interests of religion, it was said in Milensio's instructions, the Pope wished the nuncio to remain at Prague. He had, however, instructed him to send a confidential representative to Ratisbon whose task it would be to keep him and Cardinal Borghese informed of what took place at the Diet. As for himself he must show the greatest caution and reserve and treat with the archduke through the latter's confessor, Father Miller: only a very few people must know of his presence.[4] Milensio's duty as a mere reporter was not extended by Rome during the whole course of the Diet; only on one occasion, on March 8th, 1608, was he commissioned to deliver Briefs to the archduke and to the bishop of Ratisbon, and to encourage the Catholic commissaries and prelates in their determination not to consent to any decision prejudicial to the Catholic religion. During the

[1] STIEVE, V., 897, 903 *seq.*; PIEPER, 59.

[2] STIEVE, VI., 108.

[3] PIEPER, 61, 151 *seq.* On Milensio *cf.* OSSINGER, *Bibl. August., Ingolstadii,* 1768, 590 *seq.* See also WIEDEMANN, II., 189, and BERTOLOTTI, in the *Bibliofilo* of Bologna (1885), no. 10–11.

[4] See EGLOFFSTEIN, 110; PIEPER, 152.

Diet, Milensio confined his activity strictly within these limits. At Ratisbon he lived at the monastery of his Order, hence only a very few people were aware of his presence and he exercised no influence whatever on the discussions.[1]

[1] This is made quite clear by Milensio's reports which were first published by PIEPER (153 *seq.*) from the originals in the Papal Secret Archives, as well as by the directions sent to him by the secretariate of State, which are also preserved there (the latter are also in MSS. 181 of the *Stadtbibl.* of Stuttgart). RANKE (*Päpste*, II.[6], 270 *seq.*, III., 102 *seq.*) based his assertion of the opposite (" this nameless Augustinian friar defeated, at the decisive moment, an imperial concession which would probably have satisfied the Protestants ") on a report of Milensio (*Ragguaglio della dieta imperiale fatta in Ratisbona, etc.*) ; RANKE does not indicate his source but it is evident that he used Barb. 5137. Though Ranke acknowledges that this report " was drawn up many years later ", he did not subject it to a critical examination. This was first done by GINDELY (*Rudolf II.*, Bd. I., 163, note) when he came to the conclusion that Milensio attributes to himself more than he was entitled to. Gindely's proof is a negative one in that he demonstrates that neither he, nor Hammer or Hurter, in their researches on the year 1608, discovered anything in the Vienna *Staatsarchiv* which would bear out Milensio's report ; as a matter of fact the very opposite is shown by the correspondence of archduke Ferdinand with his mother during the Diet of Ratisbon (full text in HURTER, *Ferdinand II.*, Bd. V.) ; and Ferdinand's silence in the detailed report of April 28, 1608, which does not mention the matter, is decisive. In the subsequent editions of his history of the Popes, Ranke ignored this important correction ; in his book, *Zur Deutschen Geschichte*, he repeats (p. 165) Milensio's assertion and remarks as against Gindely, though without mentioning him, that " so definite a testimony as that of Milensio could not be shaken by the arguments adduced against it ". STIEVE (*Ursprung des Dreissigjähr. Krieges*, 238, note 3, and EGLOFFSTEIN (97 *seqq.*) took the side of Gindely. PIEPER (*loc. cit.*, 57 *seq.*), basing himself on Milensio's correspondence, which has been preserved in its entirety, has finally clinched the matter against Ranke (*cf.* STIEVE), VI., 156, 243 *seq.*). Pieper shows that Milensio was not a papal *chargé d'affaires*, as Ranke assumes, that the account of the imaginative Neapolitan

Wholly against the intentions of Rudolph II., and to the great distress of Paul V.,[1] religious strife soon began to occupy the foreground at Ratisbon. The fact was intimately connected with an occurrence of little significance in itself but which had greatly roused Protestant resentment, namely the putting under the ban of empire of the small Suabian town of Donauwörth.[2]

Donauwörth was one of those towns in which, in accordance with the agreement of Augsburg, Catholics and Lutherans were to preserve their rights and to live in peace and tranquillity whilst both parties followed their own religion and customs. However, there, as everywhere else, tolerable relations between the two confessions did not last for as soon as the Protestants had secured a majority in the council, that body, regardless of the peace settlement, began to oppress the Catholics in every possible way. Not only were they excluded from all public offices, they were even denied the public practice of their religion. With what harshness the authorities proceeded is shown by the fact that when one of the townswomen was dying in hospital, she was denied the last consolations of the Catholic religion. The complaints of the ordinary, the bishop of Augsburg, and, at a later date, those of the Catholic Estates at the Diet of 1594, had not led to an improvement, but rather to a further deterioration in the state of affairs. The Catholics, who had melted down to a mere handful, would have been utterly crushed at Donauwörth had they not found support in the nearby Benedictine

of his decisive intervention is a fable and that the account of the *Ragguaglio* (printed by EGLOFFSTEIN, 105 *seq.*), to which Ranke attached so much importance, " in view of the many errors contained in it is of no value whatever for historical research."

[1] *Cf.* *the directions to Milensio of March 1 and 8, 1608, Papal Secret Archives.

[2] *Cf.* for what follows, LOSSEN, *Die Reichstadt Donauwörth und Herzog Maximilian*, Munich, 1866; STIEVE, *Der Ursprung des Dreissigjährig. Krieges*, 1. Buch, München, 1875; JANSSEN-PASTOR, V., 292 *seq.*; DUHR, II., 2, 334 *seq.* See also STRENGER, *Verfassung und Verwaltung der Reichstadt Donauwörth* (1909).

monastery of *Heilig Kreuz*. When the monks, most of whom had been pupils of the Jesuits of Dillingen, wished to revive the public processions, with cross and banners, which had long been in abeyance, the Council forbade the function. The bishop of Augsburg, Heinrich von Knäringen, protested to the imperial court council against this and other curtailments of the privileges of the Catholics of Donauwörth. The only result of a decree issued by that body for the protection of the Catholic religion was that, in April 1606, a Rogation procession which had started from the monastery of *Heilig Kreuz*, was assaulted and scattered by the populace at the instigation of the preachers.

The Council refused to punish the sacriligious attack, in the course of which a crucifix had been thrown to the ground, and ended by offering to the crown council the excuse that they were no longer masters of the fanatical populace. In consequence of this admission the emperor, without heeding the authorities of the Suabian League, in March, 1607, instructed the archduke Maximilian of Bavaria to protect the Catholics of Donauwörth from further vexations. When the commissaries of the duke were threatened in their own persons, the ban was pronounced upon Donauwörth which had been threatened for a long time because of the violation of the religious and territorial peace, and since the measure proved inadequate by itself, it was put into execution in December, 1607, by means of Bavarian troops. On December 17th the soldiery occupied the town from which the preachers and most of the ringleaders had already fled. Maximilian at once gave orders for the ecclesiastical restoration, summoned some Jesuits and restored to the Catholics the parish church abandoned by the preachers. But for the rest he proceeded with great caution.[1]

In a letter to the Pope, Maximilian expressed the hope that by the prompt execution of the ban against Donauwörth the prestige of the emperor had been not a little enhanced and that the Catholic religion had been given " a considerable

[1] *Cf.* STIEVE, *loc. cit.*, 216 *seq.*, 448 *seq.*, and DUHR, II., 2, 335.

impulse and help ", a fact which would prove " comfortable and profitable " in other places also.[1] These hopes, which Paul V. shared,[2] were not fulfilled. The proceedings against Donauwörth benefited neither the Catholic religion nor the imperial prestige, on the contrary, they turned to the advantage of the revolutionary party of the Palatinate.

The Diet had scarcely been opened on January 12, 1608, when the most sensational rumours began to circulate. The Pope, it was rumoured, had 10,000 men under arms who, under the leadership of Jesuits disguised as officers, were about to march into the empire; that the king of Spain had secretly set aside 100,000 ducats and was now enrolling soldiers; that the duke of Bavaria also had 15,000 men in readiness; that a cruel sea of blood was about to burst upon the hapless followers of the gospel.[3] In view of the deep impression which the proceedings against Donauwörth had created, rumours of this kind were readily believed, all the more so as the Protestants thought archduke Ferdinand capable of the worst, ever since he had made a prompt and decisive use of the right of reform and had carried out the ecclesiastical restoration in his territory. In these circumstances the disagreement which had existed until then between the

[1] See WOLF, II., 255. *Cf.* STIEVE, *loc. cit.*, *Quellenbericht*, 80.

[2] See the *letter of Cardinal Paravicini to Rudolph II., dated Rome, January 12, 1608, in which we read : " Mandò il duca di Baviera quà relatione a S.S$^{\underline{tà}}$ del seguito di Dannevert et il suo agente la pubblicò poi alli altri, et è stata di grandissima allegrezza et consolatione ; S.S$^{\underline{tà}}$ ne giubilava, et il Collegio ancora, come cosa di gran conseguenza per la religione cattolica et per il magior rispetto, che habbiano da portare li heretici per l'avenire ; io oltre a tutte queste cause ne rendo grazie al Signore con vero affetto et me ne rallegro con V.M$^{\underline{tà}}$ humilmente perchè vedo che tanto più sarà riverita e stimata la M$^{\underline{tà}}$ S. quanto che mostrarà riosa sua risolutione contra ribelli de Dio et suoi " (State Archives at Vienna, MS. n. 595, t. XII., 39). *Cf.* also Paul V.'s laudatory *Brief to Maximilian I. of January 10, 1608, *Epist.*, V., Papal Secret Archives.

[3] See JANSSEN-PASTOR, V., 304 *seq.*

Lutheran States of the empire and the Calvinists of the Palatinate sank into the background: the latter became the leaders of the Protestants.

What this meant was seen at the Diet of Ratisbon, to the horror of Paul V.[1] Even the Elector of Saxony now made his promise of help against the Turks dependent on satisfaction being given to Protestant claims. The religious peace should be both confirmed and amplified, in the sense that the Catholics renounced all Church property of which they had been robbed since 1555. The Catholic Electors were willing to agree to this so long as the opponents would give a guarantee that thereafter they would not infringe the settlement. This the Elector Palatine refused: in the future also Protestants were to have a free hand to confiscate Church property.

Any right-minded man was bound to ask himself what advantage could the Catholics derive from any agreement if their opponents could declare in one breath: What we have taken from you, that we keep, and what we may be able to take from you, in the future, that we shall take.[2] On the motion of archduke Ferdinand, the Catholic members of the Council of Princes, to whom the ecclesiastical Electors now joined themselves, decided that the religious peace should be ratified with the addition of the following clause: Whatever has been appropriated by either party in defiance of this agreement, must be restored. The implied threat failed of its purpose, hence, in view of the emperor's precarious position, the archduke proposed a compromise, on March 16th, 1608. It consisted in a renewal of the religious peace without the proposed clause, but its omission was not to prejudice anyone. But even such large concessions to the demands of the Protestant minority failed to satisfy the people of the Palatinate; they demanded the express suppression of the proposed reservation. This would have gravely prejudiced

[1] *Cf.* the *Instruction to Milensio of March 29, April 5, 19, 26, and May 3, 1608, Papal Secret Archives.

[2] Opinion of GINDELY (*Rudolf*, II., Vol. I., 159 *seq.*).

Catholic interests.[1] For fear lest the Diet should get completely off the track, the Elector of Saxony was unwilling to drive the opposition to extremes. However, the archduke Matthias' revolt against the emperor encouraged the party of the Palatinate to break up the Diet at the end of April by their own withdrawal from it.

When the last vital organ of the constitution of the empire had thus been paralysed[2] the plan of a Protestant separate league became a reality; this Henry IV. of France had proposed and worked for during the last ten years. On May 15th and 16th, 1608, at Ahausen, a village of Ansbach, the Elector Palatine, the duke of Württemberg, the Palatine of Neuburg, the rulers of Baden-Durlach, Brandenburg-Ansbach, and Kulmbach, formed a league, ostensibly for the sole purpose of defending the "evangelical" faith, but in reality with a view to defending by force of arms all that had been illegally acquired since the religious peace of Augsburg, as well as all further demands of the Protestants.[3]

That which the Protestant Estates of Empire undertook against the constitution of the Empire was likewise attempted, on a smaller scale, by the Estates of the Austrian Crown lands who, under the cloak of the new gospel, in reality worked for the establishment of oligarchic, aristocratic republics. When a few dozen princes and counts in Germany had imposed their unlimited domination on the consciences of the people of their territories, all in the name of "the liberty of the gospel", and had thereby even won a rich booty of Church property, a few hundred heads of aristocratic houses in Austria, Hungary, and Bohemia were anxious to imitate so alluring an example. Everywhere, of course, the cry was solely for freedom of conscience and protection against religious compulsion, but the real aim was to subtract the subjects from the authority of the Church and to hand

[1] See RITTER, *Briefe u. Akten*, II., 227 *seq.* *Cf. Hist. Zeitschr.*, LXXVI., 75 *seq.*

[2] *Cf.* DÖBERL, *Gesch. Bayerns*, I.[3] (1916), 535.

[3] See JANSSEN-PASTOR, V., 336 *seq.* *Cf.* KLOPP, *Dreissigjähr. Krieg.*, I., 49 *seq.*; GINDELY, *Rudolf*, II., I., 140.

them over to the arbitrary domination of the heads of aristocratic Houses. "Real liberty of conscience presupposed social conditions such as did not exist in the seventeenth century."[1] Moreover in those days, when Church and State were closely linked together, no ruler in Europe could be sure of his throne if his subjects gave up the Catholic faith. Wherever the ancient dynasties had remained faithful to the Church the religious innovations invariably took the form of political revolutions. This was especially the case in the various Austrian territories.[2] There the leaders were in very close contact with the anti-imperial party of the empire, especially with the Elector of the Palatinate, Frederic IV., a notorious drunkard, and with the intriguer, Christian of Anhalt-Bernburg. With a view to the complete oppression of the Catholics, these "heads and leaders" of the revolutionary party in the empire, cast their nets in every direction, from Paris to Venice and Constantinople. And in order that nothing might be wanting to misfortune, a dissension now broke out in the House of Habsburg which threatened the very existence of the dynasty.

Already in April, 1606, the archdukes, in a secret family council, had declared Rudolph II. incapable to govern "by reason of a certain malady of the mind", and they had chosen Matthias as head of the House. Two years later, the latter, who nursed a profound personal resentment against the emperor, took the desperate decision of leaguing himself with the almost wholly Protestant Estates of the various territories in order to put an end to the misrule of the head of the empire by means of a revolutionary rising. He began by making sure of the support of Hungary and Austria at the Diet of Pressburg. The recalcitrants were compelled by threats to join with the others.[3] The Moravian magnates who were openly aiming at an unlimited aristocratic government, joined the movement which Rudolph II. met only with half measures. About the middle of April, 1608, Matthias,

[1] GINDELY rightly emphasizes this (*loc. cit.*, 307).

[2] See *ibid.*

[3] See *Mon. Hung. dipl.*, III., 252.

who was increasingly becoming a mere tool of the heads of the Calvinist party—viz. the Hungarian Illésházy, the Austrian Tschernembl and the Moravian Zierotin—advanced from Hungary against Prague at the head of a considerable army recruited from the Hungarian and Austrian Estates, in order to force a decision between himself and his brother. Christian of Anhalt was already hoping that the last hour of the House of Habsburg, which he hated with a deadly hatred, had struck. His plan [1] was for the Electors—Spain and the Pope being excluded—to undertake to mediate between the two hostile brothers. The Estates of Hungary and Austria were to be guaranteed full religious freedom for any subject "whosoever he may be"; Matthias was to have the government of Hungary and Austria, but in Bohemia the emperor was to appoint his brother Maximilian as his lieutenant. From the dissension which was sure to arise between Matthias and Maximilian, as a result of such an arrangement, Anhalt hoped for complications which would be bound to bring about the downfall of the House of Austria.[2]

However, the execution of these plans proved impossible. The mediation was undertaken not by the Electors but by the representatives of precisely those Powers which Anhalt wished to see excluded, viz. the envoy of Philip III., San Clemente, and the papal nuncio, Caetani. The negotiations proved exceedingly arduous but neither the Spanish envoy nor the papal nuncio allowed themselves to be discouraged.[3] That which decided the issue was the fact that the Bohemian Estates refused to join the rebels. Rudolph won them over by meeting their political aspirations, by postponing the settlement of ecclesiastical questions until a new Diet which

[1] Ritter, *loc. cit.*, I., 687 *seq.*

[2] On the *terminus fatalis domus Austriacae* see Gindely, *loc. cit.*, 210. According to a *letter of the prince of Anhalt to the Elector Palatine, July 29, 1609, Tschernembl too thought that in view of the incapacity of Rudolph II. and Matthias, the *terminus fatalis domus Austriacae* had arrived. Archives at Bernburg. Reg., VI., B. 4, p. 24.

[3] See Gindely, *loc. cit.*, 211; Huber, IV., 506 *seq.*

was to be held in November, and by promising religious freedom until the time when that assembly should meet. The agreement concluded on June 25th, 1608, at Lieben, gave Matthias only half a victory. Rudolph ceded to him Hungary, Austria, and Moravia, but retained Bohemia, Silesia, and Lausitz, of which Matthias only secured the eventual succession.

Such was the situation at the moment of the arrival in Prague of Cardinal Giangarzia Millini who had been appointed legate to the emperor at a consistory held on May 5th, 1608.[1] The Pope, who was most reluctant to meddle with political questions, had been obliged to take this step because the strife between the two Habsburg brothers threatened to inflict grievous injury on the Church.[2] All the written exhortations of the Pope [3] and the efforts of his nuncio having yielded no result, a member of the Sacred College, who had been tried in several diplomatic missions, was now to attempt to mediate between the two brothers. That his task would be fraught with the greatest difficulties was very well realized in Rome.[4]

[1] See **Acta consist.* (of the vice-chancellor), Barb. 2926, Vatican Library. The faculties for Millini in *Bull.*, XI., 477 *seq.*

[2] GINDELY, *loc. cit.*, 250. On March 1, 1608, the Provincial of the Jesuits had written from Vienna to Cardinal Borghese: *Le cose qui sono in cativissimo termine poichè da quello si può congetturare non potrano terminarsi senza grandissima ruina del Christianismo. The Pope must put an end to the brothers' quarrel, BORGHESE, II., 163, Papal Secret Archives.

[3] See **Epist.*, III., *ibid.*

[4] The *Avvertimenti dati al card. Millini*, dated May 12, 1608, as published by M. KOCH in the *Denkschriften der Wiener Akademie* (I., 2, Vienna, 1850, 14*k seqq.*) are so incomplete, so full of mistakes, and so erroneously explained that one can only wonder how such nonsense came to be printed by a learned body. The mistakes of Koch, who obviously was ignorant of the very elements of Italian, are discussed by PIEPER in a publication on the occasion of the jubilee of the German *Campo Santo* in Rome (Freiburg, 1897), 264 *seqq.* In the same work there is an authentic reprint (p. 267 *seq.*) of the Instruction from *Nunziat. di Germania*, XVIII.

One great difficulty came at once from the emperor himself, for he surmised, and rightly so, that Millini was also charged to press for the choice of a king of the Romans and that the Pope, however much he condemned Matthias' revolt, would not unconditionally take the emperor's side.[1] So he sought to prevent Millini's mission, alleging that if a special envoy of the Pope were to arrive now, a suspicion would be created that there was question of a league against the Protestant Estates of the empire.[2] For this reason, on June 6, 1608, Rudolph dispatched a messenger to the Cardinal in the person of Matthias Renzi, with mission to beg him to delay his journey long enough to enable the Pope to send him fresh instructions.[3]

Cardinal Millini had only left Rome on May 20th, 1608. The cause of the delay had been the Pope's wish to await the report of the Prague nuncio who had gone to see the emperor.[4] Meanwhile Millini dispatched before him an Augustinian, one Peter Mander, of Neuhausen, who was well acquainted with Austrian conditions.[5] On May 31st

(Papal Secret Archives). A copy of the *Avvertimenti* is in the Stadtbibl. of Stuttgart, MS. 181.

[1] *Cf.* Stieve, VI., 372, 398.

[2] *Ibid.*, 403.

[3] See the letter of Rudolph II. to Cardinal Millini, June 4, 1608, in Pieper, *loc. cit.*, 265, n. 1.

[4] See Cardinal Paravicini's report to the emperor in Stieve, VI., 372, n. 2. *Cf.* the *Instruction to Millini, of May 17, 1608 (Papal Secret Archives).

[5] *Cf. Relatione di me Pietro Mandero di Neuhausen mandato di Roma la 17 Maggio 1608 e dell' operato in Germania, Bohemia, Austria, Ungaria sin alli 2 Settembre che tornai d'Innsbruck per Roma dove son gionto li 12 detto*, Borghese, I., 28, p. 19 *seq.* (Papal Secret Archives). In this diffuse report, addressed to Paul V., Mander describes his journey, his transactions and his impressions. He reached Innsbruck on May 27; from there he journeyed to Linz viâ Ratisbon (July 1); on July 4 he was at Prague which he left on August 14 to go to Vienna. On August 6 he arrived at Salzburg, having come from Vienna, and on August 14 he was back at Innsbruck.

Millini was at Bologna; on June 9th he had reached Trent.[1] There he waited for the answer of Paul V. This was to the effect that the Pope and the Congregation for German affairs judged that the misgivings of the emperor were groundless, hence he was to start for Prague without any more ado.[2] Thereupon the Cardinal set out at once with a small retinue. He reached Prague as early as the evening of July 9th.[3] The emperor, who was failing more and more both in mind and body,[4] gave unmistakable tokens of his displeasure at the arrival of the legate. He put off the reception of the papal representative for the space of three days—in fact he would have preferred not to receive him at all. When at last he granted him an audience, in the afternoon of July 12th,

[1] See the original *Letters of Millini on his journey in *Borghese*, II., 154 (Papal Secret Archives). According to them, Millini was at Bologna on May 31 (from there he wrote: "Io ho risoluto di menar meco in Germania con licenza di suo generale fr. Baldassare Bolognetti dell' Ord. de Servi, padre di molte lettere et integrità," who also enjoyed the esteem of the Pope), on June 4 in Mantua, on June 9 at Trent.

[2] See the Instruction of June 21 in PIEPER, *loc. cit.*, 265, n. 2. The Brief to Rudolph II., dated June 21, 1608, here mentioned ("necessario progrediendum ulterius legat. apost. cum jam Oenipontem pervenerit nec amplius esse locum revocationis") in the *Epist.*, IV., 16, Papal Secret Archives. The discussions of the German Congregation are mentioned in *Avviso of June 18, 1608, Vatican Library.

[3] On June 28, 1608, Millini writes from Ala (Hall near Innsbruck) where he took ship on the Inn; see *Borghese*, II., 154, Papal Secret Archives. On his arrival at Prague see STIEVE, VI., 434, n. 2, where, however, a reference is omitted to a report of Gaspar Paluzzi from Prague, dated July 14, 1609, printed in SAGGIATORE, III., 5 (1846), 140.

[4] "*Attende alla alchemia più che mai," Mander reports, "di giorno in giorno va calando di sanità et crescendo in malinconia": he cannot write all he hears. At the conclusion of his report Mander paints in darkest colours the intellectual and moral decadence of the emperor. *Borghese*, I., 28, Papal Secret Archives.

he did it with as little grace as possible. He barely walked half-way across the hall to meet the Cardinal legate. Those in the ante-room observed that when the emperor uncovered his head, he greeted the Cardinal with only a slight bow, whereas Millini made a profound obeisance.[1] The audience lasted barely a quarter of an hour.

The task of the legate, who found himself in the rôle of an unwanted mentor, was only seemingly eased by the compromise between the two warring brothers of which Millini had received news on his way to Prague, for though the treaty of Lieben had averted the peril of open war between Rudolph II. and Matthias, tolerable relations between the two had not been established. In view of Rudolph's character it was not to be expected that he would ever forget that his brother had robbed him of the greater part of his territories. To this must be added that the treaty did not stay the revolutionary movement which had broken out in the Estates. Both brothers had to expect that, as their reward, the Estates would demand far-reaching concessions, both political and religious. The Cardinal legate clearly discerned the germs of further disorders and grave dangers for the Church which lurked in the treaty of Lieben.[2] In compliance with his instructions he began by advising the emperor to cultivate good relations with Matthias and to resist the demands which the Protestants were sure to make.[3] The ticklish question of the imperial succession he put off until the end of the audience.

[1] See the reports in STIEVE, VI., 434 *seq.*, 439. The legate reports in his first letter to Borghese, dated July 14, 1608, on the emperor's unwillingness to give him an audience and the sad state of the court (*Borghese*, II., 163, p. 11, Papal Secret Archives). To this must be added three more letters of the same date (p. 7 *seq.*, 9 *seq.*, 34 *seq.*) of which GINDELY used only the one dealing with the election of a king, after a copy in the Archives of Simancas (*Rudolf II.*, Vol. I., 252 *seq.*); PIEPER, *loc. cit.*, 275, first gave the more important passages of the other letters.

[2] *Cf.* Millini's Relatione in PIEPER, 273. [3] PIEPER, 272.

To the first two points the emperor's answer, according to the legate's report of July 14th, 1608, was spoken in so low a voice that Millini could scarcely understand him.[1] Rudolph thanked the Pope for showing so much solicitude to act as mediator in the quarrel with his brother who had behaved very badly. The conduct of Matthias had encouraged the Bohemians to demand religious freedom; but he was determined to protect the Catholic religion in the future as he had done in the past; as for particular measures he intended to take, he would inform the legate of them later on. In support of his urgent request that the emperor would not put off any longer a decision in the matter of the imperial succession, Millini pointed to the dangers which threatened the welfare of the House of Habsburg and of religion itself if this affair was further shirked. If the emperor were to die to-day without an heir, the empire would become the plaything of the heretics; they would be joined not only by their foreign sympathizers, but by all the enemies of the House of Austria, and it could scarcely be doubted that in view of the division of the Electors into a Catholic and a Protestant party, the result of the election of a successor would not be to the advantage of the Habsburgs.

During these representations the emperor did not seek to disguise how much allusion to this question annoyed him, for the humiliation which Matthias had so recently inflicted on him had still further complicated it. His answer was spoken in an even lower tone than before, so that Millini had to approach as close to him as possible in order to hear him. Rudolph explained that he had made up his mind to take up seriously the question of the election of a king of the Romans—which had been so often discussed, when he was prevented by recent events: for the rest the real

[2] In view of the letter of Vischere to Fleckhammer of July 12, 1608, published by STIEVE (VI., 434 *seq.*), the reliability of which is attested by its origin and intrinsic probability, it is not unlikely that Millini failed to understand all the emperor said. *Cf.* PIEPER, 275, n.

decision lay with the Electors; he would inform the legate of his further decisions.

Millini replied that a great ruler should surely think more of the welfare of religion, the State, and his own dynasty than of his personal grievances, all the more so as everything depended on the emperor's personal decision, for he would not find it difficult to get the Electors to fall in with his views. Rudolph made no reply to these representations and put an end to the audience. In his report of the conversation which Millini dispatched to Rome on July 14th, 1608, he relates that Rudolph told his private secretary, Barvitius,[1] that the Cardinal was quite right when he exhorted him to think only of the welfare of Christendom, but that his resentment against his brother was still too great. Subsequently Millini made further unsuccessful attempts to induce the emperor, through his counsellors, to make up his mind in the matter of a king of the Romans, for the monarch was more unapproachable than ever. In view of existing conditions Millini doubted not that only Matthias could succeed to the empire, but that the emperor would never, of his own accord, take a step in that direction, unless he had reason to fear the worst, viz. his own deposition; but the Cardinal thought that it would be too big a risk to give to this fear a greater semblance of certainty.[2]

At the same time Millini worked zealously upon the imperial counsellors and others in order to make sure that, at the forthcoming Diet, no religious liberty should be conceded to the Bohemian Estates.[3] In the midst of his efforts he was alarmed by information that the Silesians made similar demands and threatened to secede from Matthias. Millini thereupon addressed to the emperor a counter-remonstrance

[1] The nuncio A. Caetani, in a report to Cardinal Borghese, of July 14, 1608 (*Borghese*, II., 163, p. 14, Papal Secret Archives), describes Barvitius as *ministro timido e pieno d'infiniti rispetti*. *Cf.* in this connection MEYER, *Nuntiaturberichte*, LXX. *seq.*

[2] See Millini's report of July 14, 1608, translated by GINDELY, I., 253.

[3] See Millini's report of July 14, translated by Gindely.

in writing which, he was told, successfully prevented Rudolph at the last moment from making a concession of this kind.[1]

In the meantime, the new envoy of Philip III., Baltasar de Zúñiga, had arrived in Prague. The emperor was very indignant at his appearance on the scene and kept him waiting for an audience even longer than the legate.[2] It goes without saying that in the question of the succession Zúñiga fared no better than Millini. The envoy, who had not seen the emperor for two years, found him much altered. He agreed with Millini and Caetani that the unhappy monarch had not long to live.[3] Nevertheless Millini took endless trouble with a view to bringing about a reconciliation between Rudolph and Matthias, and to prevent concessions being made to the Protestants. In this last respect he thought he had achieved some success.[4]

On August 18th, 1608, Millini had another audience with

[1] See Millini's reports of July 18 and 21, 1608, in PIEPER, 276, n. 1.

[2] *" Zúñiga arrived three days ago. Egli sta aspettando di havere la prima audienza et prevedendo quanto havrà da penare per la seconda, ha risoluto di trattare in questa de negotio et particolarmente del principale dell' elettione del Re de Romani " (report of Mellini on July 28, 1608, *Borghese*, II., 163, Papal Secret Archives). On August 4, 1608, Millini *reports that he has not yet had his second audience and the Spanish envoy not yet his first. " L'aspettar li par molto duro. Si dorme profondamente in tutte le risolutioni." A *second report of August 4 states: Pensano alcuni per ottimo rimedio che S. M[tà] armi vedendo che sono armati gl'heretici. . . . L'imperatore va pensando di fuggirsene." A third *letter of August 4 reports: S. M[tà] parla di volersi ritirare. Non crede il Nuntio (A. Caetani che S. M[tà] sia per far mai tal risolutione " (*ibid.*).

[3] See Zúñiga's letter of August 9, 1608, in STIEVE, VI., 460, and Millini's report of August 11, 1608, Papal Secret Archives.

[4] *Cf.* Millini's *reports of August 4 and the two *letters of August 11, 1608. In the second of these he says: " Continua S. M[tà], per quanto dice ne la resolutione di non concedere cosa alcuna pregiudiciale a la s. religione," Papal Secret Archives, *loc. cit.*

the emperor. He thanked him for his intention firmly to resist the Protestants and then turned the conversation once more to the question of the election of a king of the Romans. In doing so the legate put the religious interests in the foreground and once more counselled a reconciliation with Matthias. The emperor's answer was brief, very low, and scarcely audible. He would treat with the Electors, convene a Diet in the near future and settle the affair as soon as possible. The words of his Majesty, Millini said in his report, could not have been more gratifying ; but similar assurances have been given often, and as far as my knowledge of this court goes, no hope can be based on them.[1] A third audience on August 25th, 1608, in which Millini took his farewell, yielded nothing new.[2]

On the very next day the Cardinal Legate left the capital of Bohemia. At the last moment the emperor honoured him with the gift of valuable presents.[3] He went on to Vienna in order to inform archduke Matthias how matters stood with regard to the question of the succession, to exhort him to make his peace with Rudolph II., and to restrain him from making any concessions in matters of religion which would injure the Catholic Church.[4] On the last point he thought he could hope for a measure of success inasmuch as Mander had reported very favourably on Matthias' Catholic sentiments.[5]

Millini reached Vienna on September 3rd and there awaited Matthias' return from Moravia. Matthias had given a general promise to the Diet of that country that no one should be

[1] See Millini's four reports of August 18, 1608, *Borghese*, II., 163, p. 158 *seq.*, Papal Secret Archives., from which PIEPER extracted the answer of Rudolph II.

[2] See Millini's *report of July 25, 1608, Papal Secret Archives, *loc. cit.*

[3] See STIEVE, VI., 463, n. 3.

[4] See Instruction to Millini dated July 25, 1608, in PIEPER, 265, n. 3.

[5] He was *religioso cattolico* and went to Mass daily ; *cf.* Mander's *report in *Borghese*, I., 28, p. 57*b*, Papal Secret Archives.

persecuted for his religion, but on the other hand, he had refused to grant unconditional freedom of conscience.[1] Millini exhorted Matthias to show a like firmness against the Estates of Austria and Hungary. Warnings of this kind were very necessary. In Upper Austria, under the influence of Tschernembl, a Calvinist as energetic as he was ambitious, the Estates sought to establish the principle that previous to the oath of loyalty, sovereignty lay with the regional administration. Accordingly the free practice of the Protestant religion, as it had existed under Maximilian II., was re-established and on August 31st Protestant worship was inaugurated at Linz, Steyr and Gmunden. In Lower Austria only one of the gentlemen, one Adam Geyer, of Inzersdorf, near Vienna, had the courage to follow this example. At Millini's suggestion, Matthias had the church closed and Geyer arrested. Thereupon the Protestant Estates left Vienna, betook themselves to Horn and prepared to extort by armed force their demand for freedom of religion. The Catholic Estates broke with those of Horn and did homage to Matthias.[2] Matthias was not strong enough to crush the men of Horn, so he sought to isolate them by coming to terms with the Hungarians.

Matthias succeeded in getting himself elected king of Hungary, whereupon, on November 19th, 1608, he was crowned by the archbishop of Gran, Cardinal Forgács. But he was made to pay a heavy price for his triumph ; not only was his political power confined within such narrow boundaries as to make him but the shadow of a king, in the religious sphere also the weak prince made concessions against which the bishops, pressed by Paul V., lodged a protest. Besides the noble and royal free cities all the other towns and villages were granted religious liberty. The Jesuits were debarred

[1] See CHLUMECKY, I., 516 *seq.*

[2] See HUBER, IV., 518 *seq.* He recounts Millini's intervention in his *Relatione* in PIEPER, *loc. cit.*, 278. Millini left Vienna on September 12 (see STIEVE, VI., 463, n. 1) ; his reception in the consistory in Rome took place on November 8, 1608 ; *cf.* **Acta Consist., Barb.*, 2926, Papal Secret Archives.

from the ownership of immovable possessions, and the previous safeguards of the Catholics were simply brushed aside.[1]

Paul V. had never really trusted Matthias. When therefore on August 22nd, 1608, he begged the Pope to support his election as king of the Romans, the latter replied on September 6th by merely referring to the report which Matthias was to receive from Millini; at the same time he admonished him to make no concessions to the Estates which would be detrimental to the Catholic religion.[2] Already on August 23rd, at the suggestion of Klesl,[3] the Pope had despatched the bishop of Melfi, Placido de Marra, who was in Mellini's suite, to Matthias with mission to congratulate the archduke on his nomination as king of Hungary, and to admonish him to make no concessions to the Protestants that would injure the Catholic religion.[4] The anxiety with which the Pope watched developments in Austria and Hungary is shown by the fact that on August 27th he proclaimed a jubilee in order to implore the divine assistance.[5] He still hoped that on the question of religion Matthias would pursue the policy of refusal which he had followed in Austria. For this reason he commissioned de Marra to congratulate the arch-

[1] See HUBER, IV., 529 *seq.* On Paul V' exhortation to the Hungarian bishops, see HERGENRÖTHER, III., 671, n. 1.

[2] See STIEVE, VI., 458, n. 1.

[3] On August 4, 1608, Millini wrote from Prague to Cardinal Borghese, transmitting a letter of Klesl's in which the latter insisted on the necessity of sending a special nuncio to Matthias. Millini seizes the opportunity to draw attention to de Marra on whom he bestows great praise. *Borghese*, II., 163, Papal Secret Archives.

[4] See the *Instructions of the Secretary of State to P. de Marra of August 23 and 26, 1608, MSS. 181 of *Stadtbibl.* at Stuttgart. On the Briefs see STIEVE, VI., 464, n. 1. *Cf.* also the Relation of Millini in PIEPER, *loc. cit.*, 279. The *inventory of the nunciatures in Barb. 4141 (Vatican Library) describes de Marra as *Huomo di dolce tratto.*

[5] See **Acta Consist.*, *loc. cit.*; the suggestion of the Jubilee in Millini's *letter of August 4, 1608, Papal Secret Archives.

duke on his having secured the crown of Hungary.[1] But when the protests of Cardinal Forgács against the concessions granted to the Protestants by Matthias reached Rome,[2] soon to be followed by the news of the expulsion of the Jesuits,[3] the Pope felt justified in having refused the subsidy which he had asked for, and for which Spain had also warmly pleaded, to enable him to repress the Protestants by force. Paul V.'s reply at the time had been that he would only grant such a subsidy if a league were formed including Matthias, the emperor and all the Catholic princes of Germany. The Pope's reserve sprang by no means, as has been suggested, from ill-advised economy, still less from avarice, but from a clear and accurate observation of the situation. A subsidy of money could only yield fruit if unity among the Catholic princes gave some hope that the measures taken had some prospects of success. A distribution of money to this prince and to that would only scatter and diminish the resources of the Holy See without achieving anything. The experience which the Holy See had had with the big sums granted to Rudolph II. militated against money being given to so inconstant and weak a ruler as Matthias.[4] Nevertheless, how much allowance

[1] See the Instruction to de Marra of November 15, 1608, in the *Denkschrift der Wiener Akad.*, I., 2, Vienna, 1850, 145.

[2] *Cf.* the *letter of Cardinal Forgács to Paul V., dated Posonii, 1608, November 1, *Borghese*, II., 163, p. 352; *ibid.*, p. 353, *a letter of the Cardinal to Paul V., dat. Posonii, 1608, December 5: *Liquefacta est anima.* To the Pope's exhortation that he should do something to meet the Church's losses in Hungary, the Cardinal replies: "Nunquam Vest Stas credat, quales Ungari, antea ab ubere s. matris ecclesiae lactati, catholica pietate celebres, ubi venena haeresum hauserunt, evaserint, quanto furore ad destructionem religionis catholicae, ad diripiendum praedandumque patrimonium Christi," Papal Secret Archives.

[3] Cardinal Forgács announced this to the Pope in a *letter dated Tyrnaviae, 1608, December 30, in which he says: "Inter has dictae Ungariae tempestates obruta propemodum haec ecclesia nostra catholica," *ibid.*, 355.

[4] This is the opinion of CHLUMECKY, who is none too friendly to the papacy (*Zierotin*, I., 564).

was made in Rome for Matthias' difficult position in Hungary is shown by the fact that Paul V. was extremely moderate in the expression of his displeasure; he took into account the circumstance that, in substance, only the existing state of affairs had been sanctioned.[1]

But things were very different when Matthias, after much hesitation, and in order to safeguard his sovereignty, granted to the Estates of Horn, in March, 1609, much more than Maximilian II. had at one time conceded, so much so that, as the bishops pointed out at once in their protest, the Catholic religion was bound to perish.[2]

This time Paul V. addressed to Matthias a Brief of severe blame.[3] When the king wished to fulfil his Easter duty, bishop Klesl declared that he could not be admitted to the sacraments since all those who had taken a share in this affair had incurred the excommunication pronounced by the Bull *In Coena Domini*. Thereupon the scruples which the king had already previously felt in consequence of his conduct awakened anew, and with such force that he sought absolution in Rome.

To obtain it those counsellors who had advised Matthias to yield were compelled publicly to declare that the articles which had been granted were erroneous and null, and to pray the king to revoke them at the first opportunity.[4]

The successes of the Protestant party in the countries which had seceded from the emperor had an immediate and powerful

[1] See GINDELY, *Rudolf* II., Vol. L., 308.

[2] See HURTER, *Ferdinand* II., Vol. VI., 186 *seq.*; HUBER, LV., 541 *seq.*; *cf.* BIBL. in *Jahrbuch des Verb. f. Landeskunde von Nieder. Österreich*, 1903, 28 *seq.*, and in *Archiv f. österr. Gesch.*, CIX., 433.

[3] Text of *letter dated April 4, 1609, in Appendix No. 1 (Papal Secret Archives).

[4] See report of Bodenius to Maximilian I., dated April 23, 1609 (*Reichsarchiv* at Munich) used by CHLUMECKY, I., 561–2, and Klesl's letter to Zúñiga in GINDELY, I., 308, note. On the legal question *cf.* the memorial of Bellarmine of 1608 in *Le Bachelet, Bellarmin avant son cardinalat*, 595 *seq.*

repercussion on the Bohemian Estates. A contemporary aptly sums up the situation when he says that it was intended at Prague to stage " a Bohemian Horn ". The movement was controlled by the spiritual head of the " Union of Brethren ", Wencelaus Budowec of Budowa. The aim of this eloquent and energetic man, who was thoroughly steeped in the teaching of Calvinistic statecraft, was the establishment of an unlimited Czecho-Protestant aristocratic government on the ruins of the ancient Church and the royal throne. This plan was opposed, in conjunction with the Papal nuncio Caetani and the Spanish envoy Zúñiga, by the archbishop of Prague, Karl von Lamberg, by the high chancellor Popel of Lobkowic, by William Slawata and Jaroslaw of Martinitz. The emperor, broken in mind and body and thinking only of revenging himself against Matthias, was unable to arrive at a decision.

The struggle lasted from January till July and during its progress the majority of the Estates, which were composed of Lutherans and Bohemian Brethren, did not shrink from threats of open secession. In the end nothing was left to the emperor but the alternative between abdication in favour of his brother or unconditional acceptance of the Protestant demands. In his hatred for Matthias he was all the more willing to choose the latter course as his allegiance to the Catholic faith had wavered for a long time.

On July 9th, 1609, Rudolph II. gave his sanction to that " sheet of parchment which was to set half the world on fire ", the so-called " Letter of Majesty ". This was followed by a compromise, sanctioned by the emperor, between the Catholic and the Protestant Estates, which went still further. Both documents granted full liberty to all the inhabitants of Bohemia, irrespective of class, to embrace the Bohemian Confession of 1575, which is a mixture of Hussite, Lutheran and Calvinistic doctrines. The " Letter of Majesty " granted the right to build churches only to the three upper Estates, viz. the nobles, the knights and the royal Estates; the " Compromise " extended it also to the inhabitants of the royal domains. In view of the fact that the Protestants included the ecclesiastical domains among these, a point which the Catholics contested, further disputes were inevitable.[1]

At Rome it was fully realized that since Rudolph II. had failed to obtain even now from the Protestant Estates the disbandment of their troops, his authority was almost completely undermined.[2]

He soon saw himself under the necessity of issuing a "Letter of Majesty" to the Silesians, the Bohemians' allies, which granted to the subjects the right to build churches in even more emphatic terms than had been done in the "letter" to the Bohemians.[3]

Through the weakness and indecision of the two Habsburg brothers of Prague and Vienna, who were also mortal enemies, Protestantism had made enormous strides in the Austrian territories where archduke Ferdinand alone still upheld the unity of the faith. The reaction on ecclesiastical conditions in the empire was inevitable. Since the formation, there, of the Protestant *Separate League*, the so-called "Union"—the decision of Germany's destiny rested on the point of the sword. The *Union* was bound to provoke a Catholic defence organization, viz. the *League.*

It is in the nature of the defensive to be less quick to act than the offensive. Thus the Catholic League has a long pre-history. The plan of a vast Catholic defensive association against the aggressive Protestant party had been frequently discussed ever since the first impulse had been given towards a Catholic restoration; but the most varied causes, chief among them being the jealousy between Bavaria and Austria and the timidity of the ecclesiastical Princes, had hitherto nullified all efforts, though the Protestants already represented

[1] GINDELY, *Gesch. der Erteilung des Böhm. Majestätsbriefes*, Prague, 1868, and *Rudolf*, II., Vol. I., 309 *seq.*; CHLUMECKY, *Zierotin*, I., 575 *seq.*; JANSSEN-PASTOR, V., 615 *seq.*; HUBER, IV., 544 *seq.*; KRÖSS, in *Zeitschrift f. kath. Theol.*, XXXI., 474 *seq.*

[2] See Borghese's letter to the nuncio at Prague, dated August 8, 1609, in LÄMMER, *Zur Kirchengesch.*, 82.

[3] See GRÜNHAGEN, II., 140 *seq.*

it as an accomplished fact and made capital out of it for controversial purposes.[1]

Soon after Paul V.'s election, in June, 1605, the nuncio at the imperial court had been instructed, in view of the situation in Germany, which was fraught with danger for the Church, to press for the formation, in the hereditary States of the Habsburgs, of a league of the ecclesiastical and other good Catholic princes.[2] In July, 1605, the nuncio of Gran, Girolamo Porzia, suggested to Maximilian I., duke of Bavaria, the formation of a Catholic Defence League. The duke, who at that moment was fully taken up with the ordering of his own internal affairs, observed as always, a cautious reserve ; in fact he did not take the hint.[3] But the events of Donauwörth [4] brought about a change in his policy [5] for he now clearly perceived that the Protestants aimed at the destruction of the Church and the subversion of the empire.[6] In his own resolute and energetic way, Maximilian decided on strong counter-measures. In June, 1607, he caused representations to be made to the Elector of Cologne on the need of a Catholic defence league. The weakness of Rudolph II., the dissolution of the Diet of Ratisbon through the machinations of the party of the Elector Palatine, and, lastly, the quarrel between the two Habsburg brothers,

[1] Cardinal Otto Truchsess, 1561–2, was the first to point to the necessity of a Catholic federation in the empire ; in 1569 Albrecht IX. of Bavaria planned an extension of the league of Landsberg (see RIEZLER, IV., 587 *seq.*). The new impulse which came from the papal legate Madruzzo in 1582 (see our notes in Vol. XX., 271 *seqq.*) led to the plans for a federation of William V. which were, however, doomed to failure owing to the jealousy between Bavaria and Austria ; *cf.* RITTER, II., 13 *seq.* For later developments see BURGER, *Ligapolitik Joh. Schweikarts* (1908), 11 *seq.*

[2] See MEYER, *Nuntiaturberichte*, 396.

[3] See STIEVE, V., 781 *seq.*

[4] See above, p. 267 *seq.*

[5] For what follows see RIEZLER, V., 60, who gives the literature on the subject.

[6] DÖBERL, *Gesch. Bayerns*, I., 536.

drove the duke of Bavaria ever further. Without heeding the emperor, who was quite unfit to rule, non-Austrian Catholic Germany was to be united in a defensive league. To remove every appearance of selfish views, Maximilian thought of leaving the initiative to the three ecclesiastical Electors as to the most distinguished as well as the most threatened Catholic Estates. However, fear of their Protestant neighbours caused these to hesitate ; their eyes were only opened when the " Union " became an accomplished fact. In July, 1608, they declared their approval in principle of a counter-league and even agreed on details. Subsequently they adopted a waiting policy [1] so that six months went by before the foundation stone of the Catholic League could be laid. That which eventually clinched the matter was the attack by the Elector Palatine on the possessions of the bishop of Spire, in April, 1609. Under the impression which this attack made on the minds of the ecclesiastical Estates, an alliance was signed at Munich, on June 10th, 1609, between Bavaria, the bishops of Würzburg, Constance, Augsburg, Ratisbon, the archduke Leopold in his capacity as bishop of Passau and Strassburg, the Provost of Ellwangen and the abbot of Kempten.

[illegible] alliance, subsequently styled " The League ", was to [illegible] one purpose, viz. the defence and preservation of the Catholic religion, and the protection of religious peace and the laws of the empire.[2] The misgivings of the three Electors of the Rhineland, on account of the exclusion of Austria, were finally overcome. Under pressure of the peril threatening their dioceses by reason of the burning question of the succession of Jülich,[3] they joined the League on August 30th, 1609, and on this occasion, in addition to the duke of Bavaria, the Elector of Mayence was likewise appointed supreme head of the League.

[1] *Cf.* BÜRGER, *loc. cit.*, 16 *seq.*

[2] See DÖBERL, *loc. cit.* *Cf.* HEFELE, *Der Würzburger Fürstbischof Julius Echter von Mespelbrunn und die Liga*, Würzburg, 1912, 31 *seq.*

[3] See BÜRGER, *loc. cit.*, 18 *seq.*, 21 *seq.*, 24 *seq.*

Just as the Union leaned on France, so did the League seek the support of Spain and the Pope. Here also Maximilian appears as the moving and guiding force. In a secret memorial of June, 1608, on the subject of a Catholic federation, Maximilian insisted on the necessity of support by the Holy See with the legate Millini who was expected at Munich about that time.[1] In the autumn the duke had some confidential discussions, through his envoy, Forstenhauser, with the nuncio of Prague, Caetani, on the question of a papal subsidy for the League. In November Paul V. replied that it was necessary to ascertain first whether the Protestants had really decided to form a general league against the Catholics, otherwise it would not be advisable to form a Catholic league, because this would only force the opponents to federate themselves and to rouse other Powers as well. This view, which events showed to have been erroneous, so annoyed Maximilian that he ordered the negotiations with Caetani to be broken off.[2] In the following year, however, immediately before the formation of the League, he renewed his attempt, but this time, on June 22nd, 1609, he wrote a pressing letter direct to the Pope himself. He suggested that the Pope, and, at his instigation, the king of Spain, the grand duke of Tuscany and other foreign princes should assist the German Catholics either with money or with troops.[3] Meanwhile there arrived at Munich the famous Capuchin, Lorenzo da Brindisi, whom Zúñiga, the Spanish ambassador, with the concurrence of the nuncio Caetani, charged with a special mission to Madrid. Maximilian handed him a memorial for Philip III. in which he begged for the latter's support of the German Catholics. The courier who was to take the letter of June 22nd to Rome, was entrusted with a second letter for the Pope, dated June 25th, which prayed His

[1] See STIEVE, VI., 418 *seq.*

[2] See WOLF, II., 464, note; STIEVE, VI., 418 *seq.*, 475 *seq.*, 489 *seq.*

[3] See CORNELIUS, in *Münchner Hist. Jahrb.*, 1865–6, 162 *seq.* *Cf.* STIEVE, VI., 711 *seq.*

Holiness to give his support to the Capuchin's entreaties with Philip III. Paul V. answered by return, on July 3rd, 1609, that he had at once done his utmost to second Maximilian's request with Philip III., and that on his own part he would do all he could.[1]

After the three ecclesiastical Electors had given their adhesion to the League, on August 30th, a deputation was sent, in November, 1609, to the Pope and to the Italian princes, with mission to secure their assistance. Maximilian despatched his counsellor, Giulio Cesare Crivelli, to Rome for the same purpose. The negotiations seemed at first to hold some promise, for Paul V. evinced the greatest interest in the League and gave repeated assurances that he meant to help, not only with money, but with troops also. The Pope was particularly strengthened in this view by Cardinal Bellarmine, who offered to put at his disposal part of his own revenues should it be necessary.[2]

Nevertheless, the envoys of the League were unable to conclude a definite pact, and after a three month's stay they had to depart with no more than general assurances. This surprising attitude of Paul V. is explained, not only by his consideration for the House of Austria,[3] but likewise by the clever opposition of the French ambassador, Brèves, who, as soon as the Pope showed signs of willingness to support the League, always knew how to turn him from his purpose by his insinuations.[4] Paul V. imagined that he ought to show the greatest consideration for the powerful French ruler, and he feared lest a too open support of the League, which was

[1] See Stieve, VI., 719 *seq.*; *cf.* Cornelius, *loc. cit.*, 163.

[2] See Mayr, VII., 53, 157 *seq.*, 181 *seq.*, 215, 260, 264 *seq.*, 356 *seq.*, 361 *seq.*, 369 *seq.*, 371, 392, 403 *seq.*; VIII., 24, 201 *seq.*, 414 *seq.*

[3] See *ibid.*, VII., 317 *seq.*, VIII., 343, note. Riezler (V., 70) is of opinion that a contributory cause may have been the fact that "Paul V. was completely taken up with his struggle with Venice"; but when he wrote thus he overlooked the fact that the quarrel with Venice had been settled already in April, 1607.

[4] See Gindely, *Rudolf II.*, vol. II., 64 *seq.*

allied with Spain, should lead to strained relations with France. Moreover, he was little inclined to reinforce still further the Spanish preponderance, which was already great enough in itself, and which, in Italy, made itself heavily felt by the Holy See.

To this must be added the fact that the exceedingly cautious Pontiff was afraid, as he had been in the contemporary question of Jülich-Cleve, to take any step in the matter of the League which might lead to a war between Catholics and Protestants. A risk of this kind he deemed far too dangerous in view of the relative strength of the parties at that moment. However much his personal sympathies may have been with the League, he was nevertheless unwilling to cause a war in Germany for the sake of religion. If, however, things should come to that extremity, then, so he openly declared to the French ambassador in January, 1610, he would give his support to the League.[1]

The assassination of Henry IV. removed the danger of war on a big scale, but in its place, in consequence of the acts of violence of the people of the Union in the dioceses of central Germany, there was a threat of a collision with the League. It was greatly to the disadvantage of the League that it had not given a different turn to its relations with Austria. Like Spain, the Pope made his support of the League dependent on Austria being given the supreme direction of the federation. Thereupon Maximilian threatened to withdraw from it, a threat which led Spain to moderate its former demands. On August 14th, 1610, an agreement was reached by which Philip III. bound himself to make a monthly payment of 30,000 ducats on the sole condition that archduke Ferdinand was to be no more than vice-protector, with the title of co-director of the League, and its chief in the place of the king, and that he would take part in all the deliberations on those terms. At the same time the nuncio of Prague promised in the name of the Pope an annual contribution of 66,000 scudi to the

[1] See *Letters and Acts*, III., 499; HILTEBRANDT, in *Quellen u. Forsch. des preuss. Instituts*, XV., 347 *seq.*, 353 *seq.*

chest of the League for as long as it would have to be under arms for the defence of Catholicism.[1]

The warlike preparations of Maximilian[2] and his allies alarmed the members of the Union to such a degree that they lost heart. On October 24th a compromise was reached between them and the League by the terms of which both parties laid down their arms. Meanwhile the discord between the two brothers, Rudolph and Matthias was not at an end. Like all the other friends of the House of Habsburg, Paul V. saw in this quarrel one of the chief sources of every misfortune and a constant danger to the interests of the Church. In order to re-establish tolerable relations between the two disputants it was decided to take up once more the plan of a meeting of all the archdukes which had been suggested from the first, but which had failed owing to the mistrust of Rudolph. More than anyone else Klesl, Matthias' first counsellor, advocated the idea of restoring peace within the House of Habsburg by this means.[3]

In the hope of inducing his brother to restore the lands which he had taken from him, Rudolph II. allowed himself, in January, 1610, to be persuaded by the Elector of Cologne to convene a meeting of this kind. The congress did eventually come together, but not as a family council, as Matthias wished, but as an assembly of princes. In September, 1610, a com-

[1] See GINDELY, *loc. cit.*, 68 *seq.*; MAYR, VIII., 528 (*cf.* 24, note 2).

[2] In a Brief of March 29, 1610 (original in *Staatsarchiv*, Munich, transl. in *Darmstädter Allg. Kirchenzeitung*, XLVII. (1868), no. 37), Paul V. had exhorted the bishops and abbots of Bavaria to furnish horses and men to Maximilian for his war against the heretics, at the same time as Maximilian received absolution for any censures he might have incurred whilst taking measures towards this end. In the eventuality of war with the Union, Maximilian prayed that the Capuchin Laurence of Brindisi might be with his army, a request which the Pope granted on October 10, 1610. The Brief quoted by MAYR (VIII., 569) has long been in print.

[3] See KERSCHBAUMER, *Klesl*, 163.

promise between Rudolph and Matthias was arrived at.[1] In view of the emperor's inconstancy and the powerful efforts of the Protestants to fan the discord anew, Rome feared from the first for the stability of the compromise; hence the bishop of Sarzana, Giovan Battista Salvago,[2] who had been appointed to succeed Caetani as nuncio at Prague in November, 1610, was instructed to watch with the utmost care that the enemies of the Church and the House of Habsburg did not rekindle the domestic quarrel; to this end he should secure the assistance of the nuncio at Vienna and the Spanish envoy.[3]

That the fears of the Holy See that the reconciliation between the two brothers was only an apparent one were but too well founded, was soon seen. Filled with bitter resentment against Matthias, Rudolph was forging desperate plans with the ambitious archduke Leopold who had arrived in Prague with a view to recovering his lost power. In this enterprise

[1] See GINDELY, *Rudolf II.*, Vol. II., 127 *seq.*; MAYR, VIII., 125 *seq.*, 598.

[2] See the *Brief of November 12, 1610, to Rudolph II., *Epist.*, VI., 184, Papal Secret Archives.

[3] *" Ma perchè i medesimi heretici et altri mali affetti alla casa d'Austria procureranno per loro interesse di disunire con nove arti gli animi di queste M^tà^ et indurle a nuove scissure, appartenera a V.S. stare vigilantissimo per la sua parte acciò che s'impedischino tutti li tentativi di ridurre le cose a discordie peggiori delle prime in che deverà anco invigilare Monsig^re^ Nuntio in Vienna et insieme con V.S. Don Baldassar de Zunica, ambasciator cattolico in Praga, desiderando il suo re che la riconciliatione sudetta sia stabile per i buoni effetti che ne possono seguire a beneficio dell'Imperio, della casa d'Austria e della religione cattolica in Germania (*Instruttione a Msgr. vescovo di Sarzana*, etc., of October 23, 1610. *Cod.* 468, p. 215 of Corsini Library, Rome; other copies of the Instruction in *Ottob.*, 1066, p. 178 *seq.*, Vatican Library, and in *Nunziat. div.*, 240, p. 43 *seq.*, Papal Secret Archives). Salvaggo's *reports of 1611, in Vat. 9611–9615; those of 1612, in Barb. 6915, Vatican Library. The instruction of the Secretary of State to him from 1610–1612 in Barb. 5928, *ibid.*

he was to have the help of the Passau troops which had been unemployed since the pitiful issue of Leopold's campaign against Jülich. The appearance of these troops in Bohemia precipitated the catastrophe. Heedless of the warnings of the papal nuncio, Giovan Battista Salvago, and those of the Spanish envoy, Zúñiga, archduke Leopold laid aside the clerical garb and assumed the supreme command of these undisciplined bands. When they reached Prague, Rudolph, whose appalling hatred for his brother was described with surprising accuracy by his alchemist, Hauser,[1] openly took their side. After their withdrawal Matthias, for whose protection against Rudolph the Bohemian Estates had prayed, appeared at the head of an army. On March 24th, 1611, he made his solemn entrance into Prague; on May 23rd he received the Bohemian crown which the helpless emperor had had to resign. For a last time the mortally offended man hoped to regain what he had lost. To overthrow his brother he was willing to ask for the help of the bitterest enemies of his House, the Protestant Union. By his death, on January 20th, 1612, he was spared further humiliations and disappointments.[2]

It was with great anxiety and "boundless grief" that Paul V. saw the quarrel between the two brothers flare up anew. In vain he had sought to "calm the storm", and to induce Rudolph II., as well as the archdukes Matthias and Leopold, to conclude an amicable arrangement. The mentally enfeebled emperor was under the delusion that the Pope was his worst enemy, whereas the truth was that Paul V. did all he could to bring about a compromise, and when the fall of the unhappy monarch could be arrested no longer, he had sought to soften the blow through the intervention of his nuncios, Salvago and de Marra.[3] When the Pope was informed

[1] See MAYR, IX., 517 *seq.*

[2] See GINDELY, *loc. cit.*, II., 164 *seq.*, 195 *seq.*, 279 *seq.*, 291 *seq.*, 310 *seq.*, 326 *seq.*

[3] *Cf.* MAYR, IX., 99, 208 *seq.*, 308; GINDELY, II., 196; BOHM, *Landtagsverhandl.*, XV., 73, 84, 226 *seq.*, 228, 490, 545, 614 *seq.*, 635, 706, 751, 755 *seq.*, 757 *seq.* On the high value of the nuncia-

of Rudolph's death he paid tribute to his memory at the consistory of February 6th, 1612,[1] and since news arrived at the same time that the emperor had made his confession before the end came, the usual obsequies were held for him on the following day in the Sistine Chapel, in the presence of Paul V. Later on, however, the Pope learnt with sorrow that Rudolph had refused to make his confession and had died unrepentant. Consequently the Prague nuncio was instructed to keep the impenitence of the mentally stricken monarch as secret as possible. The secret was kept so successfully that only the most recent research has brought to light the true state of things.[2]

The death of Rudolph II. brought about once more in Germany, for the first time in a hundred years, the dangerous condition of an interregnum [3] during which the Electors of the Palatinate and Saxony, who were both Protestants, assumed the administration of the empire in the capacity of Vicars. It was natural that this circumstance should give rise to grave anxiety in Rome lest fresh injury should be done to Catholic interests ; hence Paul V., as early as February 4th, 1612, directed his nuncios to do their utmost to speed up the

ture reports of that year for the history of Bohemia *cf.* Novak, in *Mitteil. des böhm. Landesarchivs*, I.

[1] See **Acta consist.*, Barb. 2926, Vatican Library.

[2] See Cardinal Borghese's letter to the Prague nuncio, dated Rome, February 11, 1612, in *Nunziat. div.*, 8, p. 463*b seq.*, given by Turba in *Archiv f. österr. Gesch.*, LXXXVI. (1899), 357, note 1. Chroust (X., 243 *seq.*), in discussing the question whether or no the emperor made his confession, has overlooked decisive evidence ; this suffices even without the reports of the Prague nunciature (which have not been found until now) on the last months of Rudolph II.'s life. *Cf.* also the attestation of the Mantuan envoy in Luzio, *L'Archivio Gonzaga*, II., 97. On the funeral solemnities in the Sistine chapel, see *Avviso of February 8, 1612, Vatican Library, and on those in the *Anima*, see Schmidlin, 451 ; on those in the *Campo Santo*, De Waal, *Campo Santo*, 165 *seq.*

[3] *Cf.* Mander's report in *Borghese*, I., 28, p. 44*b*, Papal Secret Archives.

election.[1] In a consistory of February 6th, 1612, public prayers for a happy issue of the imperial election were ordered.[2] So great was the Pope's anxiety that he decided to send a legate to the ecclesiastical Electors,[3] though there were already six representatives of the Holy See on German soil, viz. Giovan Battista Salvago at Prague, Placido de Marra with king Matthias, Pietro Antonio da Ponte at Graz, Antonio Albergati at Cologne, Antonio Diaz at Salzburg, and Guido Bentivoglio at Brussels. A suitable person for this legation was found in Ottavio Mirto Frangipani who was familiar with existing conditions through having held the nunciatures of Cologne and Brussels. Salvago, who had been consulted, sent a detailed report on the situation from Prague, under date of February 27th, 1612. He began by pointing out that, to his knowledge, no legate had ever been sent to an imperial election, and he stated with emphasis that the occasion rather demanded a nuncio. A legate would not accomplish more than one of the ordinary representatives of the Holy See. Nor would he be able to appear as became his dignity, for, according to the *Golden Bull*, the Electors were permitted to bring only small retinues with them to Frankfort, and there were several Protestants among them.[4] To a subsequent question of the Cologne nuncio to the Elector of Mayence, the latter replied that were it only for the suspicion to which the mission of a legate would give rise in the mind of the heterodox Electors, such a step was not advisable.[5] Thereupon Rome dropped the matter.[6]

[1] *Cf.* CHROUST, X., 277 *seq.*

[2] See *Avviso of February 11, 1612, Vatican Library. On the prayers offered at the *Anima* see SCHMIDLIN, 451.

[3] See the dissertation *Se il Papa debba mandare o no persona in Germania a procurare d'un Imperatore Cattolico, se debba mandare un cardinale legato o pure nuntio et a chi persona più opportuna commettere questo carico*, in Cod. 6621, p. 725 *seq.*, of the Staatsbibl., Vienna.

[4] See *Salvago's report of February 27, 1612, Corsini Library, Rome, 35, B. 6, p. 270.

[5] CHROUST, X., 280.

[6] The examination of the consistorial acts, which is mentioned in an undated *Avviso, probably of February (Vatican Library),

The Pope, consequently, sought to influence the Electors through his nuncios, his principal agent being the nuncio of Cologne, Antonio Albergati. In 1611, Albergati had been instructed to press for the election of a king of the Romans. On February 8th, 1612, he presented a Brief to that effect, dated December 16th, 1611,[1] to the Elector of Mayence, Johann Schweikhart, at Ashaffenburg. He told the latter, in confidence, that the Pope no longer favoured the election of Matthias inasmuch as the latter's dependence on the Protestant Estates had shown that his election would not be to the advantage of Catholic interests. At the same time the nuncio cautiously hinted at the election of archduke Albert. The Elector's reply was no less cautious, though, as a matter of fact, he fully agreed with the suggestion and had already won the Elector of Saxony for the election of Albert.[2]

Rudolph's death had created an entirely new situation. There was no longer question of electing a king of the Romans but an emperor. Notwithstanding the opposition of the ecclesiastical Electors, Matthias' prospects were good : Spain and France likewise supported his candidature. The Elector Palatine worked energetically on his behalf, moving heaven and earth to prevent Albert's election.[3] The attitude of Rome was greatly influenced by the fact that Albert's elevation threatened not only to provoke a dispute in the House of Habsburg, but also to trouble once more the good relations between Spain and France, a fact which could not fail grievously to injure Catholic interests. In consequence of this Paul V., on the death of Rudolph II., reverted to his first plan of supporting Matthias' candidature.[4] He worked in

is no doubt connected with the discussions on the question of the dispatch of a legate.

[1] The original of the *Brief to the Elector of Mayence, of December, 1611, is kept in the Staatsarchiv of Vienna, *cf.* CHROUST, X., 296, n. 1.

[2] See the protocol in CHROUST, X., 294 *seq.*

[3] L. WILZ, *Die Wahl des Kaisers Matthias*, Leipzig, 1911, 62 *seq.*

[4] See the report of Mander von Neuhausen, dated February 4, 1612, Rome, in CHROUST, X., 278 *seq.*

this sense everywhere, even with Albert at Brussels.[1] His first care was to speed up the election for only thus could those of the Palatinate be prevented from exploiting the interregnum. Briefs were sent in all directions, pressing for a speedy and a good election.[2] On February 25th, Paul V. wrote to the Elector of Mayence that the existing condition of Germany during the interregnum left him no peace; he could never lose sight of the dangers for the Catholic Church and the empire which would be still further increased by any delay of the election; hence he urged him and his ecclesiastical fellow princes to hasten it as much as possible.[3] The death of the Elector of Cologne, Ernest, which occurred on February 17th, 1612, greatly grieved Paul V., for he had set great hopes on him for the imperial election.[4] By the middle of March diplomatic circles in Rome considered Matthias' election as good as assured.[5] On May 4th a fresh exhortation to make haste was addressed to the Elector of Mayence. In a covering letter the nuncio, Marra, spoke of the Pope's great anxiety for the speedy election and elevation of a candidate who would have at heart the honour of the empire and the protection of the Church.[6] This letter also expressed anxiety lest the Protestant Electors should endeavour to alter the traditional form of the oath, as they had done at Rudolph II.'s election, in the sense that the Pope would be styled the "lieutenant" of the Roman emperor. A further letter, dated June 1st, 1612, instructs the Elector of Mayence to get the emperor to

[1] *Cf. Bijdragen tot de geschiedenis v. Brabant*, VII. (1908), 508.

[2] *Cf.* the letter to the nuncio in Venice of February 11, 1612, in LÄMMER, *Melet.*, 310 *seq.*

[3] CHROUST, X., 352 *seq.* The nuncio whom Chroust describes as "bishop of Vigiliae" without further explanation, is Antonio Albergati who had been bishop of Bisceglia (Vigilia) since 1609.

[4] See the *dispatch of Tommaso Contarini, dated March 3, 1612, in CL., VII., Cod. MXIII. of the Library of St Mark at Venice.

[5] See the *letter of Mgr. Aurelio Recordati, dated Rome, March 14, 1612, Gonzaga Archives at Mantua.

[6] See CHROUST, X., 500 *seq.*

abrogate all decrees detrimental to the Catholic cause.[1] Hopes of this kind were in vain inasmuch as the election of Matthias, on June 13th, 1612, was the fruit of a compromise between Catholics and Protestants. The decisive factor was that, to the joy of the members of the Union and the astonishment of the ecclesiastical Electors, the Elector of Saxony went over to Matthias ; thus they too could but join the majority.[2] Hence they were merely polite when they wrote to the Pope that nothing but the influence of His Holiness could have induced them to vote for Matthias.[3] But they were right when

[1] *Ibid.*, 513 *seq.*

[2] See WILZ, *loc. cit.*, 91 *seq.*

[3] The text of the report drawn up immediately after the election by the ecclesiastical Electors is in CHROUST, X., 544 *seq.*, according to a rough draft of the *Staatsarchiv* of Vienna ; but Chroust overlooks the fact that the piece had already been published in a German translation based upon Cod. 851, p. 65 *seq.* of the Corsini library, Rome, by SCHMID, in *Hist. Jahrbücher*, VI., 195 *seq.* The demands of the ecclesiastical Electors, for the realization of which the Pope was requested to press the newly elected monarch, are as follows : (1) Before all else he was to use his authority in order to compel the enemies of the Catholic Church to restore the Church property they had seized. (2) The emperor must not himself take a measure, or sanction, or permit one, which would in any way injure the rights, statutes, customs, goods and revenues of the Church. (3) He must revoke, by an authentic document, any promises he may have made, either freely or under compulsion, which would be prejudicial either to religion in general or to some particular church. (4) Within a year, without delay or tergiversation, he must consent to have a king of the Romans elected. (5) Should it be necessary to take arms in self-defence, the emperor should favour, support, and defend the Catholic party with his imperial majesty. (6) That which has been done until now for the common good by the Electors or in their name, the emperor should not misinterpret nor take any special proceedings against any of their number, under any pretext whatsoever. (7) Let him throw the mantle of brotherly affection over the conduct of the archduke Leopold and not make it a pretext for any action against his person, his possessions or his subjects. . . . Should some step have been

they pointed out that, at the election, the ecclesiastical Electors had overcome some great dangers which threatened the Church, for when the terms of the election were settled, they had successfully prevented the changes favourable to the Protestants which the Palatine and Brandenburg had sought to introduce.[1] On the very day of his elevation the emperor wrote a most deferential letter to the Pope. He expressed the hope that he would have his Holiness' further support and announced the early dispatch of an embassy of homage.[2]

At Rome the news of the election of the emperor was received with the usual demonstrations of joy. It was generally believed that Matthias was sincerely Catholic-minded.[3] Even Paul V. showed no sign of the anxiety which Matthias' policy of compromise had formerly aroused in him. His letter of congratulation, dated June 23, 1612, bears witness to this attitude.[4] A month later Marra was appointed nuncio at the imperial court.[5] He was to insist that the papal confirmation of the election must formally be asked for, and that in its address the embassy should use the word obedience (*obedientia*). As regards the oath, Paul V. would be satisfied if the formula of Frankfort was sent in. The emperor's secretary, Barvitius, declared to the nuncio that there was no documentary evidence in the imperial chancellery that confirmation had ever been asked for. As regards the profession

decided upon, let him revoke it and restore everything to the *statu quo*. (8) Let him in general, do his very utmost to promote the glory of God, the exaltation of the Church and her peace and tranquillity. When the nuncio handed in Paul V.'s reply, dated June 23, 1612, in CHROUST, X., 546, note), he expressed the wish of the Pope to have a copy of the coronation oath sent to him, a request which met with immediate compliance (*ibid.*).

[1] See WILZ, *loc. cit.*, 76 *seq.*

[2] See SCHMID, in *Hist. Jahrb.*, VI., 194 *seq.*

[3] See the *report of Msgr. Aurelio Recordati, dated Rome, June 23, 1612, Gonzaga Archives at Mantua. *Cf.* also *Bijdragen tot de geschied. v. Brabant*, VII. (1908), 508.

[4] See **Epist.*, VIII., 24, Papal Secret Archives.

[5] *Brief of July 21, 1612, *Epist.*, VIII., 62, *ibid.*

of obedience, Matthias would allow himself to be styled a most obedient son of His Holiness and of the Church.[1] A promise was also given that copies of the instrument of the election and the oath would be sent in. With these promises Paul V. declared himself content.[2]

The imperial mission of homage set out in November, 1612. It was headed by the excellent bishop of Bamberg, Johann Gottfried von Aschhausen.[3] The bishop was commissioned by the League to do his best to get an extension of the subsidy granted in 1610 for the support of the Catholic alliance at the level of 20,000 ducats.[4] He reached Rome shortly before Christmas and was received with the usual honours. The bishop lodged at the palace of Cardinal Madruzzo. He was welcomed there by the Secretary of State, Cardinal Borghese, accompanied by seven other Cardinals, who then escorted him into the presence of the Pope. Aschhausen presented his credentials which, like the address, substantially conformed to the model of Maximilian II.[5] When the copies of the instruments of the election and the emperor's oath had been examined, the Pope, in a consistory of January 7th, 1613, made to the Cardinals appropriate communications and confirmed the election.[6] On the following day, in the Sala

[1] Obedientissimus (instead of observantissimus) filius Suae S^tis^ sanctaeque matris Ecclesiae ; see SCHMID, *loc. cit.*, 197.

[2] *Ibid.*

[3] *Cf.* besides HÄUTLE, *Des Bamberger Fürstbischofs J. Gottfried von Aschhausen Gesandschaftsreise nach Rom und Italien 1612 u. 1613* (*Bibl. des Stuttg. Lit. Vereins*, Vol. 155), Tübingen, 1881, also ZWIEDINECK, in *Archiv f. österr. Gesch.*, LVIII., 1888 *seq.* ; CHROUST, X., 750 ; SCHMIDLIN, 451 *seq.*

[4] CHROUST, X., 736 *seq.*

[5] See *Archiv f. österr. Gesch.*, LVIII., 190 *seq.* ; SCHMID in *Hist. Jahrb.*, VI., 197. On the arrival of Aschhausen, see *Studien aus dem Benediktinerorden*, IV., 2, 154 *seq.* ; *Avviso of December 22, 1612, Vatican Library. *Cf.* SCHMIDLIN, 451, n. 6, though there the date of the arrival is wrongly given as December 30, and the *report of Msgr. Aurelio Recordati, dated Rome, December 22, 1612, Gonzaga Archives, Mantua.

[6] See **Acta consist.*, 2926, Vatican Library.

Regia, the bishop of Bamberg made a solemn act of obedience. The function was carried out in the usual way. Fenzoni, the *uditore* of Cardinal Borghese, proposed to Aschhausen the drawing up of a Bull of confirmation, and in so doing he appealed to the evidence of the Secretary of Briefs, Scipione Cobelluzio, who testified that it was an ancient custom to draw up such Bulls. Aschhausen replied that they had never been accepted, but promised to report the matter to the emperor.[1]

(2.)

Though only fifty-five years old, the emperor Matthias was a decrepit old man. Now that he had at last reached the goal of his ambitions, the easy-going and genial old gentleman wished before all else to enjoy his exalted dignity and to be troubled as little as possible with affairs of state. Consequently power fell into the hands of his counsellors, the most distinguished of whom was Melchior Klesl.[2]

Born in 1553, this gifted man, whose father was a Protestant master baker of Vienna, returned to the Catholic Church during his student years. His ability, application and irreproachable conduct won for him rapid promotion. In 1579 he was Provost of the Chapter of St. Stephen at Vienna

[1] See **Acta consist., loc. cit.*, and SCHMID, *loc. cit.*, 197 *seq.*

[2] The story of Klesl has still to be written. The large work of HAMMER is only valuable as a collection of documents and even as such it is by no means complete. The very meritorious monograph of KERSCHBAUMER is not critical enough and since its publication in 1865 as well as since the publication of the very valuable article by RITTER in the *Allg. Deutschen Biogr.*, XVI., much new material has been brought to light on the person of Klesl, particularly in the letters and acts published by the *Hist. Kommission* of Munich. But much material still lies in the Austrian and Roman archives. The former would help towards an appreciation of Klesl's influence in the internal government of Austria under Matthias; from the latter, Professor DENGEL is about to publish fresh information, more particularly on Klesl's trial.

and chancellor of the University; in 1581 he was vicar-general of the bishop of Passau for the part of the diocese situate in Lower Austria; in 1588 he became bishop of Wiener–Neustadt; in 1590 chairman of the religious commission for Lower Austria, and in 1598 he was raised to the see of Vienna. In all these posts he showed great activity, defended the liberty of the Church against the Commission dealing with the convents, and fought Protestantism with such determination that he could rightly be styled the leader of the Catholic restoration in Lower Austria. From the time of his taking up the government of the small diocese of Vienna, Klesl got into ever closer relations with archduke Matthias, then lieutenant of Lower Austria and Hungary and completely won his confidence. From that time onwards he also intervened increasingly in political affairs.

How keenly Klesl at first fought for the aims of the Catholic restoration and reform is shown by a memorandum drawn up by him in 1596 for the bishop of Passau, in which he utterly condemned every form of temporizing, yielding and accommodation.[1] In 1604, in a memorial which the archduke Matthias presented to the emperor as his own composition, he demanded that the assurances which Maximilian II. had made to the Protestants should be revoked.[2] In 1606 and 1608 he begged of Matthias, in most earnest fashion, not to make concessions of any kind to those who had left the Church.[3] How strongly Klesl still maintained this standpoint in 1609 is shown by his bold action at Easter of that year, when Matthias had yielded to the rebels of Horn.[4] Nevertheless not only through Maximilian, duke of Bavaria,[5] but likewise through the nuncios, who very likely felt hurt by Klesl's

[1] See HAMMER, *Urk.*, 131. *Cf.* KERSCHBAUMER, 79 *seq.*

[2] In so doing Klesl pointed to Ferdinand as to a "living example"; see KHEVENHULLER, V., 2781 *seq.*; HUBER, IV., 355 *seq.*

[3] See the opinions in HAMMER, *Urk.*, 186 and 240. *Cf.* HAMMER, II., 95; STIEVE, V., 803 *seq.*, 907 *seq.*

[4] *Cf.* above, p. 285.

[5] *Cf.* HAMMER, *Urk.*, 266.

somewhat sharp and brusque manner, reports reached Rome which were anything but favourable to him. In the Instruction of May, 1607, for the papal nuncio, Caetani, Klesl's excellent work on behalf of the Church is indeed recognized, but he is also represented as self-willed and presumptuous and as not having opposed with the zeal one expected from him, the concessions which were granted to the Protestants on the occasion of the peace treaty lately concluded with the Hungarians.[1] In the autumn of 1608, Klesl himself felt that the Pope did not hold the best opinion of him.[2] In the spring of 1609 the nuncio of Graz reported the rumour that Klesl had had a hand in the concessions made to the Protestants.[3] In August the nuncio of Vienna drew the Curia's attention to the fact that, though he had been named a bishop a good while ago, he had not yet been consecrated.[4] Thereupon the nuncio was instructed to urge the consecration; for all that Klesl put it off for several years longer.[5] When, in October, 1609, the nuncio reported to Cardinal Borghese a communication he had from Klesl, to the effect that Matthias was thinking of asking for his elevation to the cardinalate, he added the remark that this communication had not been made without clever calculation, for the idea was that it should be passed on to Rome.[6] Yet in July, 1610, the same nuncio was compelled to admit that Klesl was the only defender of the Church in those parts.[7] A Brief of Paul V. of May, 1611, praised Klesl's efforts in defence of the

[1] See the passage in the Instruction in KERSCHBAUMER, 213. *Cf.* also our data, Vol. XXIII., p. 313, on Klesl's disputes with the Jesuits.

[2] See Borghese's letter to de Marra, of October 29, 1608, in the *Denkschr. der Wiener Akad.*, I., 2, Vienna, 1850, 145.

[3] Report of April 11, 1609, in KERSCHBAUMER, 142.

[4] Report of August 22, 1609, *ibid.*, 213, n. 2.

[5] Letter dated July 10, 1610, *ibid.*, 217. On Klesl and the Catholic restoration in Vienna see *Gesch. der Stadt Wien*, IV., 125 *seq.*

[6] Report of October 31, 1609, in HAMMER, *Urk.*, 260.

[7] *Cf.* KERSCHBAUMER, 203.

Catholic religion. A Brief of August 1st in the same year is to the same effect, except for a warning to steadfastness against the attempts of the Protestants.[1] The letters of Cardinal Borghese to the nuncio of Vienna in June and July, 1611, concerning Klesl's equivocal attitude towards the Protestants, are much more explicit; there we read that it was regrettable that such a man should have so much influence; may God's grace enlighten him.[2] The hostility to which Klesl found himself exposed on many sides led him, towards the end of 1609, to entertain the idea of retiring from the political arena. Twice, in fact, viz. in 1610 and 1611, he asked to be released, but Matthias was unwilling to lose a trusty favourite and a counsellor who had become indispensable. Nor did he have cause to regret his action, for Klesl rendered him exceedingly valuable service at the time of his elevation to the kingdom of Bohemia and to the imperial throne.[3]

The more Matthias, now raised to the most exalted dignity, got entangled in a labyrinth of difficulties, the less able was he to do without the help of Klesl. As president of the Privy Council the indefatigable and ambitious man became "the emperor's manager" and his veritable *factotum* during the whole of his reign. His influence was all the greater as he was able to supply considerable sums to a man who was for ever in need of money. If, on occasion, Klesl would profess to be no more than a humble and faithful servant of his master, he was at times imprudent enough to boast that Matthias owed him everything and that he had helped him to his crowns. In a satirical dialogue of the time on existing political conditions, we read that Klesl was universally styled the "vice-emperor", and that though he was indeed a "Papist" he knew how to trim his sails according to the wind and that he had one foot in each camp.[4]

Judgments of this kind became intelligible in view of the

[1] See HAMMER, *Urk.*, 309, 343. *Cf.* KERSCHBAUMER, 211.

[2] See KERSCHBAUMER, 214, n. 2.

[3] See *ibid.*, 143 *seq.*, 173 *seq.*, 180 *seq.*, 185 *seq.*

[4] See JANSSEN-PASTOR, V., 679 *seq.*

change which had come over Klesl since the coldly calculating politician in him had pushed the prince of the Church into the background. He who had until now sternly rejected every form of temporizing and compromising in religious matters, now, under pressure of the grave weakening of the Catholic and monarchical principle, caused by the quarrel of the two Habsburg brothers, weakly advocated a policy of accommodation by which he hoped to save the authority of the House of Austria. Now as before, it is true, he resisted the demands of the Protestants in the Austrian hereditary States and promoted the Catholic reform movement there, but the aim of his imperial policy was to win over the Protestants, by means of concessions, to the common cause and by reconstructing the Catholic League, to subject it to his imperial master. How far Klesl was prepared to yield is shown by his conduct in the most important of all the questions then pending between Catholics and Protestants —the question, namely, of the imperial dioceses which the latter had illegally seized. To the demand of the Protestant administrator of the archbishopric of Magdeburg for investiture, or a corresponding indult, as well as the grant of a seat and a vote at the Diet, Klesl was so far willing to accede as to consider the grant of an indult for a few years, subject to certain conditions.[1] This meant nothing else but the temporary legalizing of the robbery of Church property and a breach in the ecclesiastical *Reservation* which was so closely linked to the religious peace of Augsburg.

The earliest as well as the most decided opponent of these plans of Klesl's was duke Maximilian of Bavaria who took the field against him on the occasion of the Diet convened at Ratisbon for the summer of 1613. He rejected every concession to the Protestant administrators of dioceses, whether it consisted in an indult of investiture or in the grant of a seat and vote at the Diet which was so frequently demanded ; for these men could not be considered as having any legal right. If the Protestant administrators of dioceses were given

[1] *Cf.* RITTER, II., 380.

seat and vote at the Diet, Maximilian insisted, the Protestants would have in the council of princes the majority they already possessed in the councils of the cities, and would not fail to use it for the complete oppression of the Catholics.[1] Maximilian was equally opposed to any change in the constitution of the Catholic Defence League which was his very own creation and of the leadership of which he would allow no one to deprive him. It was to be expected that the duke of Bavaria would seek to make his influence felt in Rome on these questions as against the designs of Klesl.[2]

Already then, as later on, it was said that Paul V., together with the Jesuits and the Catholic Estates of empire, were determined to abrogate the religious peace of Augsburg and to open a war of extermination against the adherents of the new faith. There never was question of this.[3] However strongly the Holy See, the Jesuits and the rest of the Catholic polemists protested in point of fact, against the numerous violations of the rights of the Church which were implied in the religious settlement of Augsburg, they never questioned the validity of the agreement as a political and civil treaty of peace. It is true that the Holy See had not positively sanctioned the agreement of 1555, but tolerated it in practice as the less of two evils.[4] For the same reason Paul V.

[1] See WOLF, III., 340 *seq.*

[2] *Cf.* CHROUST, XI., 20 *seq.*

[3] "The opinion is commonly held," says STIEVE (*Abhandl.*, 175 *seq.*) "that since the rise of the movement of restoration the Estates of empire felt increasingly inclined to revoke the religious peace and to destroy Protestantism altogether; that the Jesuits in particular agitated in this sense and that the thirty years' war broke out because they and their sympathizers thought that the right moment had come to carry out the long cherished plan. However, this opinion mainly sprang from the imagination of contemporary Protestants, by which historians have allowed themselves to be influenced up to our own days because they were in ignorance of the *Acts* of the Catholic Estates."

[4] See JANSSEN-PASTOR, V., 457 *seq.*, 471 *seq.* *Cf.* DUHR, II., 1, 456 *seq.*

even went a step further when he counselled its maintenance. Repeatedly, especially in the years 1610 and 1611, he expressed himself in the sense that "in these times, which were already sufficiently troubled and difficult, the religious and the civil peace should not be jeopardized, nor should any cause or occasion be given for open war and rebellion within the holy empire".[1] For the year 1612 we have several proofs that Paul V. directed the electors to preserve the religious peace.[2] Nothing was further from the circumspect and cautious Pontiff than a desire to provoke warlike complications, for he was well aware that the Catholics were the weaker party in the empire, so that it would have been most imprudent to tamper with the religious peace of Augsburg. The Pope shrank from the responsibility of giving the signal for the outbreak of a war of the issue of which he was afraid. This, and consideration for the House of Habsburg, were the decisive factors in the attitude of reserve which the Pope adopted towards the League. However much he approved of a Catholic Defence League as such, he gave it his support hesitatingly and cautiously,[3] and in 1611 he roundly declared he would not contribute a penny if the Catholics were to undertake anything against the Protestants which would be at variance with the religious peace.[4] However, this peace should have been observed not alone by the Catholics but likewise by the Protestants. For this reason the Pope condemned those concessions which broke the ecclesiastical Reservation[5]; hence also

[1] See MAYR, VII., 340, and CHROUST, IX., 312 ("Dixit nuncius quod Sua Sanctitas cupiat religionem augustanae confessionis et talia compactata illassa et si quid contra statuatur, quod non velit contribuere praemissa"). MERKLE (in the *Allg. Zeitung*, 1905, Beil., n. 4) proposes to read *promissa* instead of *praemissa*.

[2] See CHROUST, X., 299, n. 1, and 419.

[3] See above, p. 290.

[4] See CHROUST, IX., 79.

[5] Already the nuncio Caetani had opposed, in the name of Paul V., the grant of an Indult of investiture or of the regalia to the Protestant administrator of Magdeburg. His successor, de Marra, received orders to pursue the same policy. In his

he utterly condemned Klesl's policy of compromise. Cardinal Carlo Madruzzo, who was appointed apostolic legate for the Diet of Ratisbon,[1] was directed in his instruction of March, 1613, to exert himself to the utmost so as to prevent the grave damage to the Catholic cause which was bound to arise from such a policy. In this Instruction Klesl's policy is subjected

*Instruction, dated October 23, 1610, we read: "In questo proposito si dice che Regali o indulti non si devono concedere da S.M^tà^ ad alcuno, se prima non è confirmato dalla Sede Apost., et ogni volta che senza la detta confirmatione si tratterà di queste materie, V.S. doverà contradire atteso che questi tali dimandano simili concessioni dall'Imperatore per potere fondare con titulo colorato le violenze loro, imperochè in virtù di Regali gli eletti acquistano giurisdizione nei sudditi, voto e sessione nelle diete e collatione de canonicati, la qual collatione appartiene a N.S^re^ conforme ai concordati di Germania et ne è fino oggi in possesso non solo ne'vescovati cattolici, ma anco ne gli usurpati dell'heretici come Brema, Brandeburgh, Alberstadio et simili, et poichè V.S. sa che senza confirmatione di qua i vescovi eletti non sono vescovi, deve stare molto attenta, che non abbiano luogo nelle diete imperiali e non si introduca, come si studia d'introdurre che gli heretici sieno non meno che i Cattolici capaci della dignità et beneficii ecclesiastici contro loro costitutione della pace stabilita l'anno [15]55, in Augusta (Cod. 468 of the Corsini Library, Rome). As against Ranke's contentions it must be borne in mind that there was not merely question of Church property but of the uprooting of the Catholic faith in the imperial dioceses.

[1] C. Madruzzo had been appointed legate to the diet of Ratisbon at the consistory of February 25, 1613; see **Acta consist.*, Barb. 2926, Vatican Library. The Pope announced Madruzzo's appointment to the emperor in a *Brief of April 3, 1613; see *Epist.*, VIII., 307, Papal Secret Archives. *Ibid.*, 327, to the German abbots on Madruzzo's mission, April 3 (*cf.* BONELLI, III., 467 *seq.*). The Brief of the same date to Klesl in HAMMER, *Urk.*, 395. Cardinal Madruzzo went to Ratisbon, accompanied by his nephew, Giovanni Gaudenzio, and with a suite of 200 persons: see the **Vita* of the Cardinal in Cod. Mazzetti, LX. of the city Library of Trent. Paul V. assigned to the Cardinal the Capuchin Giacinto as his theologian; see *Venanzio da Lago Santo, il P. Giacinto*, Milano, 1886, 74. On the auditor of the Rota, Giov. Batt. Rimboldi,

to the severest criticism. The emperor's counsellors, it says, think of political conditions and the advantage of the moment rather than of the glory of God, the preservation of the Catholic religion and the true welfare of the State. From worldly motives and through thinking only of the present moment, they devise various political schemes which they then seek to force upon other Catholics. They flatter themselves that by so doing they deprive the Catholics of nothing, whilst they satisfy their opponents, and thus assure the longed for peace. Anyone who sees deeper, the Instruction goes on, knows from experience that no one has done more grievous harm to all Catholics and to the Catholic religion than those politicians who want to stand well with all parties. Hence, at the coming Diet, the legate's duty will be to oppose

who was also at the Diet, see *Bijdragen tot de geschiedenis v. Brabant*, VI. (1904), 277. From the *Letters of Madruzzo to Cardinal Borghese, partly found in the *Registro del negotio della legatione Imperiale 1613* (*Barb.* 5912, Vatican Library) we learn that he received his first Instruction on the *negotii publici* at Trent, on April 29, 1613; then another on the *feudi d'Asti* and yet a third about Salzburg, on May 6. On May 20 the Cardinal expresses his satisfaction that P. Giacinto had been given to him as his theologian. Madruzzo left Trent on June 20. On the 23rd he writes from Brixen; on the 28th from Hall; on 29th from Kufstein (discussion with archduke Maximilian who is unable to set out before August 22). On July 8 he reports from Ratisbon that he had met P. Giacinto at Landshut and that he had told him there was great danger that the indult would be granted to the administrator of Magdeburg. On the further information of the Father that the duke of Bavaria intended to put in an appearance at the Diet only towards the end of August, he had written to the duke a *lettera efficace* praying him to be present when the emperor should arrive, *poichè i pericoli più importanti s'hanno a temere degli heretici nell-ingresso della dieta.* On July 9 Madruzzo also urged the archbishop of Salzburg to be present at the arrival of the emperor. The Cardinal had reached Ratisbon on July 5; see **Relatione della dieta Imperiale data dal card. Madruzzo legato a 6 Novembre 1613*, BORGHESE, I., 115–116. Papal Secret Archives.

by every means the plans of Klesl which consider only the passing moment, and which, though seemingly acceptable, are in reality most injurious. The legate should get the Catholics to oppose a united resistance.[1] On the Catholic side no one bestirred himself more than Maximilian of Bavaria. He besought the emperor, the nuncio Marra [2] and the legate Madruzzo, not to yield in the matter of the grant of an indult to the administrator of Magdeburg. Were they to yield on this point they would never be able to answer for it to the Pope whose still existing rights in Germany would be most grievously injured, nor to the Catholics who would be threatened with the direst disaster.[3] When the nuncio ascertained that some Catholic Estates took up a completely negative attitude on the matter, he set down all the arguments against it in a memorial addressed to the emperor.[4] At one time Klesl hoped to win over to his view the Elector of Mayence, and even the legate himself, to whom he tried to represent the whole thing as a purely political question and one in which no danger lurked for religion. But Madruzzo was not to be taken in.[5] He replied to Klesl, on July 24th,

[1] CHROUST (XI., 177 *seq.*) gives a German translation of the Instruction from a copy in the *Staatsarchiv*, Munich. Another copy, also undated, in Ottob. 1066, p. 257 *seq.*, Vatican Library. A third copy of the Instruction is in the Bibl. Nationale of Paris, MSS. espagnols, 441, I., p. 256 *seq.* *Ibid.*, p. 248 *seq.*, 252 *seq.*, further *Instructions for Madruzzo of April 13 and 27, the first dealing with the affairs of Salzburg.

[2] See CHROUST, XI., 506, note.

[3] See *ibid.*, 499, note.

[4] See *ibid.*, 490.

[5] Madruzzo reports in his *Relatione : " Il negotio del indulto si era in pericolo per concedere all'intruso Magdeburgense sotto alcune concessioni che parevano di prima faccia admissibili et avvantaggiose che venivano per tali stimate da Msgr. Cleselio. . . . Furono perciò le predette conditioni addotte dal medesimo Monsignor considerate et accortosi che sub mele latebat venenum perchè concedendosi qualunque indulto benchè conditionato si veniva ad approvare un heretico intruso per legitimo e davasi occasione ad altri di pretendere il medesimo con grave et irreparabile danno de cattolici." Papal Secret Archives.

that the grant of an indult of investiture to the Protestant administrator of Magdeburg was contrary to Canon Law, to the laws of empire, and in particular, to the religious peace, and that it would encourage Protestants to seize yet more bishoprics and monasteries and other Church property. He could not sanction concessions of this kind, all the more as on this point the Pope had marked down a clear line of conduct for him.[1] When the indult, against the grant of which Madruzzo worked with all his might,[2] was eventually refused, Klesl made futile efforts to soothe the Catholics who were still irritated against him. From Bavaria he had to listen to bitter reproaches; but what was of far greater importance was that the annoyance of the Catholics brought about a revulsion of feeling against the whole imperial policy of moderation. That policy failed utterly at the Diet of Ratisbon,[3] for, notwithstanding all the advances on the

[1] See Chroust, XI., 506, note.

[2] See his explanation in the **Relatione* just quoted.

[3] At the diet Madruzzo strove before all else for unity among the Catholics; it was he too who urged the Catholic Estates to urge their grievances; see his above quoted **Relatione* in which these further details about the legate's activities are found: "Nella causa d'Alberstadio non ha mancato il card. Legato di affaticarsi molto, si perchè venghi levato il decreto fatto già da quel capitolo pregiuditiale a cattolici, come perchè quella chiesa cada in sogetto cattolico, et in questo effetto ha non solo inviato un breve di Nro. Sigre a quel decano promesso espresso, ma accompagnatolo ancora con ogni conveniente e caldo uffitio. . . . Non ha lasciato intentato alcun offitio per far levare la concessione estorta dalli Stati di Slesia sotto l'Imperatore passato, non solo per ordine espresso di S.Stà ma ancora sollecitato dal sigr. arciduca Carlo, et con tutto che più volte habbia rinovato l'instanza, nondimeno non ha per questo potuto ottenere altro che una buona volontà di Sua Maestà. Perchè venghino soppressi i libri famosi pestiferi pubblicati contra la Stà Sede et la Chiesa cattolica, non ha mancato destramente di rappresentare quanto ha stimato bene, ma per esser le cose di Germania confuse, et sotto il dominio di diversi principi, non vede che si possa darvi quel compenso che sarebbe necessario per assicurare la Christi-

imperial side, an agreement could not even be reached with the Calvinist party of the Palatinate. With the declaration, which was a mockery of every principle of constitutional law and right, that they refused to bow to majority decisions, not only in matters of religion, but in all other questions also, the Calvinist party formally refused obedience to the constitutions of the empire. The party finally protested against a decision of the Diet of empire granting a subsidy of thirty months for the war against the Turks which had been passed by the Estates which still remained loyal to the emperor and which, besides the Catholics, included Saxony and Darmstadt from the Lutheran party.[1] The Palatine Calvinist party could dare to behave thus because, through the Union's alliances with England (April 7th, 1612) and Holland (May 6th, 1613) they had strong foreign support.[2] How blinded Klesl must have been when he hoped to bring about a compromise with such a people!

Paul had left Klesl in no uncertainty as to how much he condemned his policy of compromise. Cardinal Madruzzo was commissioned to inform him that the Pope did not merely disapprove any concession in the matter of the Protestant administrator of Magdeburg, but that he forbade it in virtue of his supreme authority: Klesl's arguments were futile nor could questions of religion be handled according to the principles of *raison d'état*.[3] When Klesl attempted

anità da veneno così pestifero." On the discovery of a case of plague in the household of the Elector of Cologne, the latter left the Diet; his action was imitated, on October 9, by the Elector of Mayence who, however, left his commissary at Ratisbon; "et il suo esempio seguì poi alli 12 l'illustr. legato con poco gusto di S.M[tà]," the nuncio Marra says in his **Relatione della Dieta Imperiale di Ratisbona dell'a 1613*, in BORGHESE, I., 115–116, p. 25*b*, Papal Secret Archives.

[1] See RITTER, II., 382 *seq*. *Cf*. K. A. MENZEL, VI., 49 *seq*., 53; HUBER, V., 48 *seq*.; JANSSEN-PASTOR, V., 694 *seq*.

[2] *Cf*. RANKE, *Zur deutsch. Gesch*., 231. RITTER, II., 361, 491.

[3] See Borghese's *letter of August 10, 1613, Cod. X., VI., 22, n. 11, Bibl. Casanatense, Rome, in part given by KERSCHBAUMER, 215.

to plead the concessions of former emperors, he was told through Cardinal Borghese, that these clearly proved the exact opposite inasmuch as every concession hitherto granted had done extraordinary harm to religion ; if worse were not to follow all further concessions must be avoided as much as possible.[1] Out of regard for the person of the influential minister, Paul V. allowed him almost at the same date to retain all the benefices he had held until then, viz. the dioceses of Vienna and Wiener-Neustadt, the post of provost of the Chapter of St. Stephen at Vienna, and the parish of Oberhollabrunn.[2]

Whilst the agreement with the Protestants, at which Klesl had aimed, was thus utterly wrecked, his plan for a reconstruction of the League which was directed against the growing influence of Bavaria and which had the support of Schweikart, the Elector of Mayence, made a great step forward at a League meeting of the time, for on that occasion it definitely came under the influence of the emperor.[3]

Paul V., in his anxiety to avoid offending either the emperor or the League,[4] had always viewed with displeasure Austria's exclusion from the Catholic federation, and as early as 1609, at the request of the Spanish ambassador, he had taken steps for the admission of the Habsburgs into the League.[5] His efforts to settle the disputes between Maximilian and the Elector of Mayence, Schweikart, had, however, been

[1] See Borghese's *letter of September 7, 1613, in part *ibid.*, 215. *Cf.* also CHROUST, XI., 786.

[2] *Brief of August 31, 1613, in HAMMER, *Urk.*, 399. *Cf.*, *ibid.*, 397, the Brief of July 13, 1613 ; also *Borghese's letter to the nuncio of Vienna, of July 20, 1613, which points out that the Brief was composed "nella più favorevole forma ch'è stata possibile et si è ordinato che passi ogni cosa gratis," Cod. X., VI., 22, n. 22, Bibl. Casanatense, Rome.

[3] See RIEZLER, V., 108 *seq.* ; DÖBERL, I., 541.

[4] See the report of J. G. ASCHHAUSEN, in CHROUST, XI., 51.

[5] See the *report of the marquis de Aytona to Philip III., dated Rome, April 26, 1609, original in arch. at Simancas, 990/20.

in vain.[1] How greatly the Pope regretted this discord was seen at the beginning of 1613, in the discussions with the archbishop of Bamberg, Johann Gottfried von Aschhausen, who had come to Rome to do homage in the emperor's name. Notwithstanding the intrigues of the Austrian party, the envoy obtained a promise from Paul V. that he would continue, and that for a period of three years, the subsidy which he had previously guaranteed.[2] However, the suspicion spread by the same party, to the effect that Maximilian had other views than the safeguarding of religion and the interests of the emperor, continued to make a strong impression upon the Pope and the Roman Cardinals.

In October, 1613, before he had learnt of the reconstruction of the League at its latest assembly, Paul V. had informed the Count of Collalto, whom the emperor had dispatched to Rome, that he was prepared to co-operate in any effort which would induce the Catholic League to obey the emperor and which would guarantee that the subsidy he had promised to it would be spent on the war against the Turks.[3] On the part of Rome, therefore, Klesl had nothing to fear as regards the League, except that it did not approve the eligibility of Protestants for membership which had been agreed to at its last meeting. Eventually he succeeded in completely conciliating the Pope. In pursuance of his policy of conciliation, and notwithstanding his failure at the Diet of Ratisbon, he now began to make propaganda for it in Rome. His letter of September 1st, 1614, to Cardinal Borghese shows how cleverly he proceeded: "If I were in Rome," he wrote, "and could describe the situation in Germany, His Holiness and the Sacred College would be far better informed. The nuncios are often mistaken for they have no access to State secrets". For the rest he was ready to

[1] See CHROUST, X., No. 11; BURGER, *Ligapolitik*, 71; SETTERL, *Die Ligapolitik des Bamberger Fürstbischofs J.G. von Aschhausen*, Bamberg, 1915, 72, 136.

[2] On Aschhausen's negotiations with Paul V. in January and February, 1613, see SETTERL, *loc. cit.*, 72 *seq.*, 78.

[3] See CHROUST, XI., 811, 989.

do the will of His Holiness in all things, as he had repeatedly declared.[1]

These assurances, however, were belied by Klesl's attitude with regard to the appointment of a successor to Matthias, a question which was coming more and more into the foreground, since the emperor had no children. The uncertainty of the succession gravely jeopardized not only the interests of the House of Habsburg and those of the empire, but the welfare also of the Catholic Church, for the Union was planning, not only the exclusion of the Habsburgs, but the utter extirpation of the Catholics of Germany, even if the whole constitution of the empire were to crumble in the process.[2] Consequently, ever since the day of the emperor's election, Paul V., the Austrian archdukes and, subsequently to the Diet of Ratisbon the ecclesiastical Electors also, had insisted on some decisive measure with regard to the succession. All the above-named had in view, as their candidate for the Habsburg Hereditary States as well as for the empire, the archduke Ferdinand who was head of the line of Stiria and in the flower of his age. The papal nuncio favoured this candidature, which was not only strongly opposed by most of the Protestants, but, to the painful surprise of many, by Spain also, for the reason that Philip III. imagined that he had some hereditary claims to Bohemia and Hungary.[3] A further delay was caused by Klesl's insistence on the necessity of first concluding an agreement —a "Composition", that is—between the religious parties which opposed each other with such bitter hostility, an issue which he hoped to arrive at through his diplomatic skill and his little tricks.[4] However, he lacked the necessary resolution which might have caused his policy of conciliation

[1] See Kerschbaumer, 216.

[2] See Janssen-Pastor, V., 734.

[3] *Cf.* Gindely, *Dreissigjähr. Krieg,* I., 7 *seq.*; A. Wahl, *Kompositions-u. Sukzessionsbestrebungen unter Kaiser Matthias, 1613–1615,* Bonn, 1895.

[4] *Cf.* J. Müller, in *Ergänzungsband zu den Mitt. des österr. Inst.,* V., 619.

to triumph; nor did he wholly belong to any one party. Hence, in view of his hesitation and indecision, it was inevitable that sooner or later he should lose control of events.[1]

Archduke Maximilian, in his great anxiety for the future of the House of Habsburg, insisted with the utmost determination on a prompt settlement of the succession. The slackness with which Klesl proceeded in this all-important affair roused him to fierce indignation, so much so that he accused him of being actuated by the lowest motives. More and more the idea took root in the fiery archduke's mind that Klesl was a traitor and an enemy of the dynasty. There can be no doubt that Maximilian went too far in his interpretation of the very tortuous paths and the somewhat obscure policy of Klesl. Not a few of Klesl's arguments for a delay of a settlement of the succession were not without solid grounds. Thus it was sound reasoning when he insisted on the necessity of first arriving at an understanding with Spain, and of preparing the ground in Germany and Bohemia.[2]

It would be difficult to prove that Klesl's slackness in so important a matter, which his habitual energy makes all the more astounding, had its roots in a traitorous disposition of mind. Nor does it seem just to imagine that he allowed himself to be prompted by the fear that an early settlement of the succession would rob him of the unlimited influence which up till then he had exercised over the emperor Matthias. It would rather seem that, from patriotic motives, Klesl wanted an agreement between the various parties to take

[1] See W. MEIER, *Kompositions-u. Sukzessionsverhandlungen unter Kaiser Matthias während der Jahre 1615–1618*, Bonn, 1895 (Continuation of A. WAHL's work, also of 1895, on the period 1613–1615), p. 66 *seq.*

[2] See HUBER, V., 89 *seq.* W. MEIER, in the above-mentioned work, also reproaches Klesl with "utter selfishness, which made him fear a too early election of a successor and a wish to concentrate in his own hands the management of all the business of the hereditary lands as well as those of the empire, a task to which his capacity for work, and as regards the latter, his competence, were inadequate".

precedence over all else, an attitude that does credit rather to his heart than to his political sense.[1]

Already in 1614 Rome had failed to find in Klesl's attitude to the question of the succession the necessary clarity, and had warned him not to yield in the matter of granting a vote to the Protestant administrator of the diocese of Magdeburg, for no evil may be done for the sake of a good result.[2]

In July, 1614, and in June, 1615, Paul V. had urged the ecclesiastical Electors to hasten the election of a king of the Romans.[3] In August, 1615, through the nuncio, he exhorted Klesl, now that peace had been made with the Turks and affairs had been settled in Bohemia, to add to his fame by settling the question of the succession.[4] A Brief to the same purport was despatched to the ecclesiastical Electors on October 27th, 1615.[5]

Whilst the number of the opponents of Klesl, whose blunt and rough manner hurt many and whose tongue spared no one, grew even at the imperial court, the weak and indolent Matthias remained unshaken in his confidence in him. To this circumstance Klesl owed it that, though the gravest accusations and the worst suspicions had been voiced against him in his capacity as leader of the imperial policy, especially by archduke Maximilian, Paul V., in a consistory of April 11th, 1616, proclaimed his elevation to the cardinalate

[1] *Cf.* J. MÜLLER, *loc. cit.*, 605 *seq.* C. MAGINI (*La guerra de' eretici in Germania*, Siena, 1907) sees in Klesl (p. 23) a real traitor to the House of Habsburg. In arriving at this judgment he attaches great weight to the impartial statement of Cardinal Medici.

[2] See Borghese's *letter to the nuncio of Vienna of September 20, 1614, Bibl. Casanatense, Rome, *loc. cit.*, n. 35 (*non sunt facienda mala, ut inde veniant bona*).

[3] See the hitherto unknown *Briefs of July 12, 1614, and June 28, 1615, *Epist.*, X. and XI., Papal Secret Archives (*cf.* Appendix, Nos. 4 and 6).

[4] See the *Instruction to the nuncio, dated August 19, 1615 (Papal Secret Archives). In part, in KERSCHBAUMER, 250.

[5] See *text in Appendix, No. 7; Papal Secret Archives.

which, at the emperor's intervention, had already taken place in secret on December 2nd, 1615.[1] The chamberlain Ludovico Ridolfi was charged with the presentation of the red biretta; he also brought the Golden Rose to the empress.[2] In the same consistory Klesl was given the office of Protector of Germany.[3]

Thus did the son of the Viennese baker attain the highest degree of ecclesiastical honours. He had now reached the peak of his fortune and occupied a position similar to that once held by Wolsey in England and, later on, by Richelieu in France. As in the case of those two men so in him also, the Statesman overshadowed the Churchman. The letter he wrote to the emperor as soon as his elevation was made public, is characteristic evidence of this change: "Early this morning," he wrote on April 20th, 1616, "the Rome courier brought me letters of congratulation from Cardinal Borghese and many other Cardinals in as much as their Lord had proclaimed me a Cardinal on the 11th April. God knows that this gives me no pleasure. But in order to conform with your Majesty's will, and because the evil tongues of wicked people drive me to it, it has to be; for it is impossible for a Roman emperor to show greater favour to a Churchman. But your Majesty's favour, affection, and true confidence are worth more to me than the papacy itself." [4]

Paul V. had charged Ridolfi to urge Klesl by word of mouth in the matter of the succession. This anxiety for a speedy settlement of the question also found expression in a Brief dated May 6th, 1616, of which Ridolfi was the bearer.[5] On

[1] See Vol. XXV., p. 337.

[2] See Paul V. *Brief to the emperor Matthias of April 27, 1616, *Epist.*, XV., Papal Secret Archives. *Cf.* Ridolfi's letter of April 30, 1616, in Hammer, *Urk.*, 630.

[3] See **Acta consist.*, Barb. 2926, Vatican Library.

[4] Hammer, *Urk.*, 624. In other letters of the same period Klesl writes in a very different strain: *cf.* Janssen-Pastor, 702, note 2.

[5] See *text of this piece in Appendix No. 8. It is missing in Hammer, Papal Secret Archives.

the same day similar Briefs were likewise dispatched to the ecclesiastical Electors.[1]

On June 19th, 1616, Klesl wrote to the Pope in answer to the Brief of May 6th, and the message of Ridolfi. "Though the whole College of Cardinals," he writes, "especially those named by Paul V., were greatly beholden to the Pope, none were more so than he himself, whom His Holiness had singled out from among all men for so great an honour, and on whom his fatherly affection had bestowed so many graces and favours. There was not a man living who was more anxious to live and die according to the wishes and desires of the Pope than himself, seeing that he had more grounds for it than any other man." Klesl then goes on to state, in emphatic terms, his wish to satisfy the Pope in the question of the succession. There follows an exhaustive account of the various stages of the affair. He ends by saying that as much as in him lay, and as far as the parties would follow his lead, he would work day and night in order to satisfy the Pope. But as long as Spain refused to desist from its demands, little could be hoped for, inasmuch as the emperor would never go against Philip III., since such action would upset the whole House of Habsburg. "There is, therefore, no other remedy," he says in conclusion, "but your Holiness' personal authority and intervention. But there is no time to lose, for the emperor is old and often ailing. Your Holiness will gather from this report where the difficulty lies, and what it is that ties my hands; hence I am not to blame. But if I get the necessary support I shall not fail, with God's grace, to do my best in order to fulfil your Holiness' will." [2]

This letter crossed a Brief of June 25th,[3] which once more urged the speeding up of the business. At the same time

[1] See *Epist.*, XI., 264, *ibid.*

[2] See HAMMER, *Urk.*, 647.

[3] This *piece also is missing in HAMMER; it is in *Epist.*, XII., 18, Papal Secret Archives. The Brief of June 11, 1616, alluded to by HURTER (VII., 50, note 128) is not addressed to Klesl, as that writer thinks.

the Pope wrote to Maximilian.[1] On December 16th, 1616, Paul V. sent yet another exhortation to the emperor and to Klesl.[2] Despite the Pope's insistence, Klesl nevertheless set to work in this question of the succession with almost pedantic caution and easy-going deliberation.[3] Again and again he insisted that his efforts for the election of a king of the Romans would yield no result without the compromise—the so-called "Composition"—with the Protestants.[4] The irritation, not to say the despair, of the impetuous Maximilian was steadily growing. In the autumn he dispatched to Klesl Eustace von Westernach, Knight-Commander of the Teutonic Order, with instructions roundly to tell the Cardinal that he must set to work and execute what he promised by word of mouth and in writing, even on his eternal salvation; if he refused, the archduke would be compelled to look on him as the worst enemy, nay, as the destroyer of the House of Habsburg, and to take every possible means to defend it against such a danger.[5]

Until then Klesl had shown himself a master in the art of evading a solution of the question of the succession. It was a heavy blow for him when, in the spring of 1617, an agreement with Spain became a certainty.[6] By this means the archdukes Maximilian and Ferdinand thought they would force the cunning fox from his last hiding-place. When Klesl attempted further evasion they threatened to remove him by force. On his part the Spanish ambassador told the Cardinal that he would complain to the Pope. At last Klesl saw himself

[1] The Brief, dated *XV. Cal. Julii* (June 17, 1616), is in the *Epist.*, XII., 5, Papal Secret Archives.

[2] See text in Appendix Nos. 9 and 10.

[3] Opinion of KERSCHBAUMER, who is very partial to Klesl.

[4] *Cf.* W. MEIER, *Kompositions-u. Sukzessionsverhandlungen unter Kaiser Matthias während der Jahre 1615–1618*, Bonn, 1895.

[5] See HURTER, VII., 59 *seq.*

[6] See *ibid.*, 74: GINDELY, *Dreissigjähr. Krieg.*, I., 53 *seq.* RANKE's presentment, *Zur deutschen Gesch.*, 248, is in part erroneous. Ferdinand's secret obligation there mentioned is dated January 31, not June, 1617.

compelled to yield, at least to the extent of convoking the Bohemian Diet for August, 1617. The two archdukes had made up their minds to seize Klesl by force should he fail to abide by this time limit which was still further reduced when the emperor fell seriously ill at the end of April, 1617. In consequence Klesl was forced to give his consent to the convocation of the Bohemian Estates for June 5th.[1] The emperor's proposal was to the effect, that in view of his approaching old age as well as the renunciation of his brothers Maximilian and Albert, the succession in Bohemia should be settled in such wise that his adopted son, the archduke Ferdinand, should be "accepted (not elected), proclaimed and crowned". When the Protestant opposition had been sufficiently intimidated, Ferdinand was almost unanimously accepted as king of Bohemia on June 6th. Paul V. hailed the event with the greatest joy.[2] Ferdinand, having promised to ratify, after the emperor's death, the rights and privileges of Bohemia, among which was the "Letter of Majesty", was crowned on June 19th.[3] Shortly before these events Paul V. had once more pressed Klesl in the matter of the succession in the empire.[4] The affair was carried a step further when, at the beginning of August, the emperor journeyed to Dresden, to visit the Elector of Saxony, Johann Georg, in company with Ferdinand, his brother Maximilian and Klesl. On this occasion the Elector promised to attend, anywhere and at any time, a Diet of the Electors to be convoked by Matthias, and to take part in the election of a king of the Romans.[5] Candlemas-day, 1618, was agreed upon as the date of the Diet. Klesl had succeeded in getting the "Composition", or compromise with the Protestants, placed

[1] GINDELY, *loc. cit.*, 55 *seq.*

[2] *Cf.* *the Brief of June 22, 1617, to the emperor Matthias, *Epist.*, XIII., 32, Papal Secret Archives.

[3] GINDELY, I., 159 *seq.*

[4] See *Briefs to Klesl, May 13 and 21, 1617, in *Epist.*, XII., 289 and 293, Papal Secret Archives; not given by HAMMER.

[5] GINDELY, I., 189 *seq.*

on the agenda of the Diet, for the Cardinal clung to his idea of the necessity of concessions to the latter.

That Klesl was chiefly guided by political consideration and gave but little evidence of having any solid principles where religious questions were concerned, is shown by his efforts to bring about a marriage between the archduke Ferdinand and the Protestant widow of the former Elector of Saxony. The Cardinal, who in this matter also acted merely as a politician, hoped to win the support of the Protestants as soon as it became known that the princess was free to follow her religion at court and to have her preacher with her. However, a man like Ferdinand was not to be won over by a scheme which did not square with the laws of the Church and which would endanger his life's work—the Catholic restoration in Stiria.[1]

The election of Ferdinand as king of Bohemia was a heavy blow for the Elector Palatine, Frederick V., who, in his suit for the hand of the daughter of the king of England, had spoken of the crown of Wenceslaus as his own future possession.[2] The Union now decided that at any rate Ferdinand, whom the Protestants detested because of his strict Catholic attitude in Central Austria, should not ascend the imperial throne; in their desperation they even went the length of inviting their bitterest opponent, viz. Maximilian of Bavaria, to accept that dignity. However, at Munich this was seen to be "A Calvinist trap" the aim of which was to stir up enmity between Bavaria and Austria and the Catholic Powers, and, by delaying the election of Ferdinand, which could scarcely be prevented, to secure a long imperial vicariate for the Palatine.[3] In the spring of 1618, Ferdinand's chances were favourable. The meeting of the electoral Diet seemed assured and his election, for which five votes had been made sure of, could not be prevented even by the Palatine and Brandenburg, when all of a sudden new difficulties arose. Curiously enough they originated at the court. Their

[1] Gindely, I., 183 *seq.*; Ritter, II., 444.

[2] Gindely, I., 186.

[3] See Riezler, V., 118 *seq.*; Döberl, I.[3], 544.

author was Klesl, the man of " impenetrable craft ", of which the Vienna nuncio had spoken already in 1610.[1]

Once again Klesl showed himself a master in the art of temporizing and of postponing a decision. In view of a declaration of the Elector of Brandenburg, the Diet of princes convoked at Ratisbon for Candlemas-day was postponed till May 28th. Then it was given out that the travelling expenses of the emperor to Ratisbon must first be provided by means of a Spanish subsidy. For a while discussions on this point sank into the background in consequence of the meeting of the Hungarian Diet, at which, as a sequel to a compromise between the government and the Estates, Peter Pázmány, since May 16th, 1616, archbishop of Gran and primate, secured, on May 16th, 1618, the proclamation of Ferdinand as king of Hungary.[2] Meanwhile, Klesl, despite Paul V.'s earnest warnings,[3] went on intriguing against the princes' Diet, and in so doing, he did not shrink from deceit. That the Cardinal, as was maintained by archduke Maximilian and by many people in Bavaria, was actually a traitor and in collusion with the Hungarian opposition, is neither likely, nor has any proof been discovered up to the present time.[4] But it is a fact that, by his intrigues, he succeeded in delaying the opening of the electoral Diet for which the archduke Maximilian was pressing with the utmost zeal, long enough to make its assembly impossible owing to the outbreak of revolution in Bohemia. Ferdinand and Maximilian were now obliged to concentrate their attention on the preservation of the crown of Bohemia rather than on obtaining that of Germany.[5]

In view of the fact that even in regard to the Bohemian rebels Klesl stood for a policy of temporizing, and thus

[1] See KERSCHBAUMER, 390, note 1.

[2] GINDELY, I., 184 *seq.*, 203 *seq.*; FRAKNOI, I., 299 *seq.*, 623 *seq.*

[3] See the Brief of February 10, 1618, in HAMMER, *Urk.*, 826. In his reply of April 30, 1618 (*ibid.*, 846) Klesl asserts that the letter only came into his hands on April 25, which is very surprising and cannot be correct.

[4] GINDELY, I., 229–231.

[5] *Ibid.*, 236.

rendered joint energetic action impossible, Ferdinand and Maximilian decided to put a stop to the "impenetrable intrigues" of the Cardinal-minister by having him arrested and taken into the Tyrol, on July 20th, 1618.[1] In Rome such an issue had been feared for some time. In April the Pope had adjured Klesl not to put off any longer the opening of the Diet of the Electors inasmuch as the delay might lead to the worst consequences for his own person.[2]

In a secret consistory of August 6th, 1618, Paul V. communicated to the Cardinals the report of the Vienna nuncio on the arrest of Klesl, at the same time expressing his regret that violent hands should have been laid on a Cardinal and a bishop in his own residence. A commission of Cardinals was appointed to devise on the measures to be taken in this matter.[3] Obviously the injury done to the dignity of a Cardinal could not be condoned, but neither could king Ferdinand be offended, for on him all Catholic hopes were centred. In consequence Paul V. proceeded with great caution and mildness.[4] He acknowledged the report of the emperor Matthias in a Brief of August 13th in which he refers the emperor to an oral message of the nuncio. A no less carefully worded Brief addressed to Ferdinand and Maximilian was to the same effect.[5] The nuncio demanded that the archdukes should seek absolution of the censures they had

[1] Kerschbaumer, 280 *seq.*; Klopp, I., 273 *seq.*; Duhr, II., 2, 215 *seq.*

[2] Kerschbaumer, 255.

[3] See *Acta consist.* in Kerschbaumer, 300. The letters of the archdukes were read at a consistory on August 20 (see **Acta consist.*, Barb. 2926, Vatican Library). Bellarmine was also a member of the Cardinalitial Congregation; see his report in Le Bachelet, *Auct. Bellarm.*, 540 *seq.* Cardinal Giustiniani, also a member of the commission, was the recipient of the **Ragionamento di Tarquinio Pinaoro sopra la rettentione del card. Cleselio,* dated Rome, August 25, 1618, *Coll. Cam.*, 44, p. 257 *seq.*, *Staatsbibl.* of Munich and *Vat.* 6344, p. 221 *seq.*, Vatican Library.

[4] *Cf.* Siri, IV., 530.

[5] Briefs in Hammer, *Urk.*, 906, 907.

incurred by arresting Klesl and to state their grievances against him.[1] When this demand elicited no reply, Fabrizio Verospi was dispatched to Vienna as nuncio extraordinary, in February, 1619. He was also charged to hear what Klesl had to say.[2] Thereupon Ferdinand yielded. He not only sought absolution from the censures, he also handed over Klesl to the papal envoy. Under the most stringent safeguards, Verospi escorted the Cardinal to the monastery of St. Georgenberg near Schwaz, in the Tyrol, where he was kept in close confinement.[3] Klesl, nevertheless, felt greatly relieved. In a letter of October 7th, 1619, he thanked the Pope for sending Verospi and surrendered himself wholly to the will of His Holiness.[4]

(3.)

Whilst in consequence of the quarrel between the Habsburg brothers the Catholic cause suffered heavy losses in Austria and several dioceses in North Germany were likewise lost to the Church, in other parts of the empire the Catholic restoration was able to register considerable successes which promised to compensate the Church for the loss of several extensive territories.[5] One splendid triumph for the ancient Church was the profession of the Catholic faith, first privately in July, 1613, and publicly in the following year, of the Count Palatine Wolfgang Wilhelm von Neuburg.[6] Paul V. had

[1] Kerschbaumer, 302.

[2] *Ibid.*

[3] *Ibid.*, 302 *seq.* Ferdinand's absolution from censures, dated October 25, 1619, in *Bull.*, XII., 455 *seq.*

[4] See Hammer, *Urk.*, 929.

[5] In 1611 G. Botero reckoned the number of *Cattolici professi* in Germany at seven millions out of a total population of 27 millions ; in Italy, including the islands, at 10 millions ; in Spain, at 8½ millions ; in France, at 12½ millions ; see Gioda, *Botero*, III., 278.

[6] *Cf.* in addition to the literature mentioned in Janssen-Pastor, V., 710, also Sperl, *Gesch. der Gegenreformation in den pfalz-*

encouraged the intentions of the Neuburger with the grant of ecclesiastical revenues.[1] After his reception, he expressed his thanks and obligation to Maximilian I. for his share in the conversion, at the same time as he granted the necessary dispensation, owing to kinship, for the marriage of the convert with Magdalen, the sister of the duke of Bavaria.[2] As early as January, 1614, the Pope instructed the nuncio of Cologne to confer with Wolfgang Wilhelm on the subject of the Catholic restoration in his territory.[3] The latter, at the death of his father, availed himself of his right of reform, slowly at first, but later on with increasing determination. In 1617, the Catholic faith was proclaimed as the religion of the country and the activities of all preachers were terminated.[4] Already at the close of 1613 the first Jesuits had been called to Neuburg, and before long the grammar school and the court church were handed over to them.[5] Owing to the shortage of priests, the Jesuits, to whom Paul V. assigned, in 1617, the monastery of Eschenbrunn which the Protestants had seized, and the Capuchins, had to do most of the work of the restoration of the Catholic religion in all the remaining districts of the territory of Pfalz-Neuburg. To this end they employed the means then universally in use: a general invitation to come back to the Church, adequate instruction, and, as a last remedy in regard to the obstinate, expulsion from the country.[6] The conversion of the

sulzbachischen und hipoltsteinischen Landen, I., Rothenburg, 1889, 9 *seq.*, and RIEZLER, V., 96 *seq.* The report sent to Rome on the conversion of Wolfgang Wilhelm in WOLF, III., 497 *seq.*

[1] See KIEWNING, *Nuntiaturberichte*, II., 290.

[2] See WOLF, III., 535 *seq.*

[3] *Brief to Wolfgang Wilhelm of January 31, 1614, in the *Epist.*, IX., 233, Papal Secret Archives. *Ibid.*, 164, the *Brief of December 13, 1613, on the conversion.

[4] See MENZEL, VI., 68 *seq.*; RIEZLER, V., 101; *cf.* the report on the state of his diocese by the bishop of Augsburg for the year 1616 in MERKLE's *Archiv*, I. (1848), 555 *seq.*

[5] See DUHR, II., 1, 239 *seq.*

[6] See LIPOWSKY, *Gesch. der Landstände von Pfalz-Neuberg* (1827); DUHR, II., 1, 239; II., 2, 236 *seq.* On the difficulties

Count Palatine, Wolfgang Wilhelm, was all the more important for the repression of Protestantism in the empire, inasmuch as he drove a wedge into the Union and prevented the duchies of the Lower Rhine from passing completely into the hands of the Protestants.[1] The Protestant attempt to destroy the ancient Church in the territory of the Lower Rhine had failed.

It was of no less consequence for North-Western Germany that, at the death of the Elector of Cologne, Ernest (February 17th, 1612) he was succeeded by his nephew, the strictly Catholic-minded Ferdinand of Bavaria, at Cologne in March, and at Münster in April. It was due to the prudence and energy of this man that the restoration of religious unity, which his predecessor had begun, was completed in the diocese of Münster. Where Protestantism had struck deeper roots obstinate resistance was, of course, not wanting, but in many localities, where the majority of the people were sunk in ignorance rather than in heresy, it was not difficult to bring whole parishes back to the Church. Owing to the scarcity of good priests, men, that is, of irreproachable conduct, it proved much more difficult to bring about the internal restoration of the Church which was being pursued at the same time. In addition to his vicar-general, Johann Hartmann, a man full of circumspection and a former pupil at the Germanicum, Ferdinand had chiefly recourse to the services of the Jesuits whose school at Münster was gaining an increasing influence in the more cultivated circles. Like the Jesuits, the Capuchins, who had come to Münster in 1612, also enjoyed the bishop's support. In the following year

with which Wolfgang Wilhelm had to contend in his endeavours to introduce Catholicism in Neuberg, see SCHNITZER, in *Jahresber. des Hist. Ver. Dillingen*, XXVIII., 117 *seq.*

[1] See DÖBERL, I., 539; KELLER, III., 74 *seq.*; DUHR, II., 1, 81 *seq.*; *the Brief of November 21, 1620, in which Paul V. exhorts Wolfgang Wilhelm to protect the interests of the Church in Jülich (original in *Staatsarchiv*, Munich) is translated in the *Allg. Darmstädter Kirchenzeitung*, XLVII. (1868), no. 37.

Ferdinand also founded at Münster a convent of the Franciscans of the strict observance.[1]

In Paderborn also it was of supreme consequence that, with the help of Paul V., it had become possible, in 1612, to give to the aged Dietrich von Fürstenberg, in the person of Ferdinand, a coadjutor who had both the power and the will successfully to carry through the Catholic restoration without heeding the protests of his Protestant neighbours.[2] Fürstenberg, who had hoped that his nephew would be chosen, had needed repeated warnings from the Pope [3] before he became reconciled with Ferdinand's appointment. But once the election had become an accomplished fact he passed, in conjunction with his coadjutor, all the necessary measures for carrying out the Catholic reform and restoration. In this respect great services were rendered by the Capuchins who had come to Paderborn in 1612, and even more so by the Jesuits who were indefatigable in their efforts to revive the Catholic spirit by means of sermons, devotions, processions and confraternities.[4] The school of philosophy and

[1] See KELLER, III., 279 *seq.*, 287 *seq.*, 302 *seq.*, 323 *seq.*; DUHR, II., 1, 52, 56 *seq.* *Schafmeister, Herzog Ferdinand von Bayern u. Erzbischof von Köln als Fürstbischof von Münster* (1612 to 1650), Haselünne, 1912, 70 *seq.* In his capacity as administrator of the monastery of Berchtesgaden, Ferdinand bestirred himself there also as a reformer; see LINSENMAYER, in the *Forsch. zur Gesch. Bayerns*, VIII., 117 *seq.* On J. HARTMANN, see TIBUS, *Weihbischöfe von Münster*, 144 *seq.* On the valuable writing desk which Ferdinand ordered for Cardinal Borghese in 1612, see *Zeitschrift f. Schwaben*, VIII., 10 *seq.*

[2] See KELLER, III., 611 *seq.*, 618 *seq.*, 644 *seq.*, 646 *seq.*, 652 *seq.* *Cf.* LEINEWEBER, in the *Zeitschr. f. Gesch. Westfalens*, LXVII., 200.

[3] See KELLER, III., 653 *seq.*, 666, 686 *seq.* The Brief of July 23, 1611, which is here given in part only, has long ago been published in its entirety, *Bull.*, XII., 7 *seq.*

[4] *Cf.* RICHTER, *Gesch. der Paderborner Jesuiten*, I., 107 *seq.* and *Festschrift zur Feier des 300 jährigen Jubiläums des Gymnasium Theodosianum in Paderborn*, 1912, 42 *seqq*; KELLER, III., 627. A Chronicle of the Capuchins of Paderborn, begun in 1612, is preserved, in MSS., at the Capuchin convent of Dieburg in Hessen; *Liber annal. conv. Capuc. Paderb.*

theology founded by Dietrich at Paderborn in 1614, and enriched with the usual privileges by Paul V.,[1] was opened two years later and entrusted to the Jesuits. It was destined to become an intellectual centre and a seed plot of the Catholic faith for the diocese, as well as a strong point from which apostles could sally forth to reconquer the surrounding territories.[2]

In the archdiocese of Cologne also the Jesuits and the Capuchins were the chief agents of the Catholic reform. A proof of the Elector Ferdinand's support of the Jesuits at Cologne may be seen in the magnificent church of the Assumption, an edifice still completely on Gothic lines, of which the nuncio Albergati laid the foundation stone in 1618.[3] The city council of Cologne gave powerful support to the Catholic cause generally [4] and to the Jesuits in particular, for its members realized that their work had not only a religious value, but a social and civic one as well.[5] In 1613 a few Jesuits of Cologne went to Essen. At Neuss, in 1615, Ferdinand assigned to them the Franciscan convent, but in this matter he proceeded with so much violence that Paul V. had to rebuke him. In like manner the seminary of Cologne, erected in 1615, for the establishment of which the Pope had already urgently pressed in 1611, was confided by the Elector

[1] See *Bull.*, XII., 299 *seq.*

[2] See KELLER, III., 627. *Cf.* RICHTER, I., 127 *seq.*, 202 *seq.*; FREISEN, *Die Universität Paderborn*, I., 3 *seq.*, 12 *seq.*; DUHR, II., 1, 586 *seq.*

[3] *Cf.* BRAUN, *Kirchenbauten*, I., 64 *seq.*; *Stimmen aus Maria Laach*, 1909, I., 282 *seq.*; CLEMEN, *Kunstdenkmäler der Rheinprovinz*, II., Cologne (1911), 125 *seq.*

[4] To the congratulations of the council, Paul V. *replied on September 25, 1605, praising them for their support of the university of Cologne "hisce calamitosis temporibus tam necessarium opus"; you will best serve the interests of religion, "si vestri homines ut instituantur curaveritis," *Epist.*, I., 219, Papal Secret Archives.

[5] See DUHR, II., 1, 20 *seq.*; *cf.* A. MÜLLER, *Die Kölner Bürger-Sodalität, 1608–1908*, Paderborn, 1909.

to the sons of St. Ignatius.[1] At the suggestion of Paul V. the Capuchins came to Cologne in 1611; in 1615 they made a foundation at Essen, and in 1618 another at Bonn.[2]

The Catholic reform was in some measure hindered in consequence of the conflicts which Ferdinand had had with the nuncio Coriolano Garzadoro being repeated under his successor, Attilio Amalteo.[3] Antonio Albergati, who succeeded Amalteo in 1610,[4] also had many difficulties with the archiepiscopal curia. Nevertheless during his eleven years' tenure of the nunciature, he was able to display so fruitful an activity that the rapid and vigorous rise of Catholic life in the archdiocese of Cologne was in a large part due to him.[5] Albergati's friend, the indefatigable Franciscan Nicholas Wiggers, like-

[1] See Duhr, II., 1, 23, 106 *seq.*, 644 *seq.* The nuncio Albergati had been commissioned by Paul V., in a *Brief dated May 21, 1611, to press the archbishop to found a seminary at Cologne. *Epist.*, XV., Papal Secret Archives.

[2] See Binterim-Mooren, *Die alte und neue Erzdiözese Köln*, I., 125 *seq.*; Clemen, *Kunstdenkmäler der Rheinprovinz*, III., Bonn (1905), 120 *seq.* In 1614 Paul V. laboured for the introduction of the Carmelites in Cologne; see *Brief to the senate, *Epist.*, IX., 2, Papal Secret Archives.

[3] See Unkel, "Der erste Kölner Nuntiaturstreit," in *Hist Jahrb.*, XVI., 786 *seq.* A. Amalteo had been appointed nuncio on September 1, 1606 (**Epist.*, II., Papal Secret Archives). His *Instruction, dated September 3, 1606 (in Ottob. 2415, II., 294 *seq.*, Vatican Library) shows how very much the Pope had at heart the progress of the Catholic restoration. Paul V.'s confirmation of the archbishop's decrees for the reform of the religious Orders in Cologne, dated June 6, 1607, in *Bull.*, XI., 424 *seq.* Amalteo's reports of 1606–1610 in *Barb.*, LXIV., 22–5, Vatican Library.

[4] On April 26 (**Epist.*, II., Papal Secret Archives); *cf. ibid.*, *the credentials to the archbishop of Mayence, of May 27, 1610.

[5] See Unkel, *loc. cit.*, 791. Albergati's *Instruction, dated Rome, May 12, 1610, in *Ottob.*, 2476, p. 415 *seq.*, Vatican Library. Hess has published (*Urkunden des Pfarrarchivs von St. Severin*, Köln, 1901) the ordinances of archbishop Ferdinand of 1615 and 1620 for the execution of the decrees of Trent in the parish of St. Severin.

wise accomplished a vast amount of good; he established at Cologne the confraternity of the Blessed Sacrament which was confirmed by Paul V. in 1611.[1]

In 1611 the Protestants caused a rising in the wealthy and powerful imperial city of Aix-la-Chapelle. They stormed the Jesuit college. The Catholic population found itself in such straits that, in 1612, the Elector Ferdinand appealed to the Pope on their behalf. A complete revulsion occurred in 1614 when Spinola the Spanish general enforced the penalties inflicted by the emperor and restored the Catholic city council. By this means the old imperial city was saved for the Church. In 1615 the Jesuits began the erection there of a new college, and soon after, that of a fair-sized church.[2] The Capuchins had been accommodated in the old monastery of St. Servatius.[3]

In the diocese of Trèves Lothar von Metternich pursued with undiminished zeal his work for ecclesiastical regeneration. Outstanding features of his activity were his visitation of parishes,[4] the reform of the Benedictine abbey of St. Maximin,[5] and the Capuchin foundation at Trèves.[6] As "founder and a most lavish benefactor of the Capuchin Fathers",[7] the Elector laid the foundation, in 1617, of their church there. His help enabled them at a later date to found

[1] See *Freib. Kirchenlex.*, XII.[2], 1572.

[2] *Cf.* NOPPIUS, *Aachener Chronik*, II. (1632), 217 *seq.*; MEYER, *Aachensche Gesch.*, I. (1781), 549 *seq.*; PELTZER, in *Zeitschr. des Aachener Geschichtsvereins*, XXV. (1903), 198 *seq.*; CLASSEN, *ibid.*, XXVIII.; WESSLING, *Konfessionelle Unruhen in Aachen* (1905); FRITZ, *Das Aachener Jesuitengymnasium, Aachen*, 1906, 37 *seq.*; DUHR, II., 1, 76 *seq.* On the church of the Jesuits at Aachen see besides BRAUN, I., 105, also SCHEINS, *Gesch. der Jesuitenkirche in Aachen* (1884).

[3] See PICK, *Aus Aachens Vergangenheit*, Aachen, 1895, 77 *seq.*

[4] *Cf.* A. SCHÜLLER, *Pfarrvisitationen in der Diözese Trier*, 1609, *seq.*, in *Trierischen Archiv*, XVI. (1910).

[5] See *Studien aus dem Benediktinerorden*, XVI. (1895), 193 *seq.*, 280 *seq.*

[6] See MARX, *Gesch. des Erzstiftes Trier*, II., Trier, 1862, 385 *seq.*

[7] Metternich is thus described on a sandstone tablet found in

a house also at Cochem, on the Moselle.[1] Paul V. did not fail to support Metternich's efforts for the reform.[2] He styled him the pattern of a bishop.[3]

As regards Church reform, the Elector of Mayence, Johann Schweikart, was completely in line with the Council of Trent. The reform, which ended by triumphing over very great difficulties, found expression in the Church ordinance of 1615 and its supplementary articles of 1617.[4] At this time the property of the Catholic Church in the archdiocese was fairly secure. At the very outset of Paul V.'s pontificate Schweikart had successfully carried out the Catholic restoration in the domain of Königstein.[5] The Pope repeatedly praised his zeal in special Briefs.[6] But it was only by degrees

1908, near the city theatre of Trèves, which gives the date of the laying of the foundation stone as June 2, 1617.

[1] See the periodical *Pastor Bonus*, 1900, 85.

[2] See the *Brief to the canons of Trèves, asking them to support the visitation then being held by the nuncio; dated August 4, 1612, in the *Epist.*, VIII., 77, Papal Secret Archives. In a *letter of 1612 Santeul writes to Cardinal Givry, bishop of Metz: "Monsieur l'archévêsque de Trèves recognoissant le grand besoing que son diocèse et ceulx de ses suffragants ont d'un concile provincial pour remedier aux grands abus qui s'y commettent, il le desiroit intimer. Mais par ce qu'il craint que messieurs de Metz, Verdun et Toul ne refusent de s'y trouver comme pretendants avoir quelque exemption ou pour ne l'oser faire sans en avoir la permession du roy, il en a escrit a Ms. le nonce lequel vous supplie luy mander," etc. The last provincial council of Trèves had been held in 1549. Cod. 219, p. 487, of Stadtbibl. of Metz.

[3] See the *Instruction for A. Amalteo quoted above, p. 332, n. 3.

[4] See A. L. Veit, *Kirche u. Kirchenreform in der Erzdiözese Mainz in Zeitalter der Glaubensspaltung und der beginnenden tridentinischen Reformation* (*Erl. und Erg. zu Janssens Gesch. des deutschen Volkes*, von L. Frh. v. Pastor, X., 3), Freiburg, 1920, 35 *seq.*, 93 *seq.* *Cf.* also *Katholik*, 1850, I., 227 *seq.*

[5] See Schmidt, *Kathol. Restauration*, 98 *seq.*

[6] A *Brief of August 5, 1605, praises Schweikart's zeal on behalf of the Jesuits on the Eichsfeld. **Epist.*, I., 114, Papal

that he overcame the difficulties he had to encounter when he undertook to bring back to the Catholic Church the various localities of the county of Rieneck which were the joint property of the Elector of Mayence and the lord of Hanau.[1] Even more arduous was the Catholic restoration of the Eichsfeld, partly owing to its distance from the archiepiscopal residence; but there also the goal was eventually reached by means of frequent visitations, the appointment of sound Catholic officials, and through the Jesuits, who had a college and a school at Heiligenstadt.[2] In other parts also of the diocese Schweikart made use of the Jesuits for the internal strengthening of the ancient Church. At Mayence he built a large school for them; in 1612 he established them in his winter residence at Aschaffenburg, and at Erfurt he protected the Fathers from hostile attacks.[3] The Elector enabled the Capuchins to found a convent at Mayence in 1612, and another at Aschaffenburg in 1620.[4]

Paul V. resolved to take advantage of a rising at Frankfort on the Main, and the fear of the impending imperial punishment, to recover for the Church a town which had for the most part gone over to Protestantism. With this purpose in mind he requested, in 1615, the Elector of Mayence, who had been appointed imperial commissary for the purpose of

Secret Archives. *Ibid.*, II., 503, a general *laudatory Brief of 1616. *Cf.* also the expressions of praise in the *Instruction for the nuncio to Cologne, A. Amalteo (September 3, 1606), in *Ottob.*, 2415, p. 300, Vatican Library.

[1] SCHMIDT, *loc. cit.*, 108 *seq.*

[2] KNIEB, *Reformation und Gegenreformation auf dem Eichsfeld*, 266 *seq.*; SCHMIDLIN, *Zustände*, 476.

[3] DUHR, II., 1148 *seq.*; II., 2, 685 *seq.*

[4] See ROCCO DA CESINALE, I., 375 *seq.*, and the "Festschrift": *Die Kapuziner in Mainz*, 1901, 8 *seq.*; *a Relatio eccles. Mogunt.* (about 1620), published by FALK, in *Röm. Quartalschr.*, XXI., 140 *seq.* In 1620 the Capuchins likewise obtained the pilgrimage place of Nothgottes in the Rheingau; see D. DIEFENBACH, in the *Kölnische Volkszeitung*, 1903, no. 898, and P. KILIAN (MULLER), *Die Aufhebung der Wallfahrt Nothgottes*, Mayence, 1907.

quelling the rising, to take steps that the practice of the Catholic religion, which had been unduly circumscribed, should enjoy complete freedom and that the Jesuits should be allowed to open a college in the city.[1] The Pope also wished to make it possible for the Capuchins to make a foundation in the old imperial city.[2] The Jesuits did not succeed in establishing themselves at Frankfort and the Capuchins were only able to do so in 1626. With regard to the convocation of a provincial council by the archbishop of Mayence, the Holy See, in view of the troubled times, requested the Cologne nuncio, in 1609, to send in a report.[3] In 1614 Albergati was instructed to hold visitations at Mayence, Cologne and Bamberg.[4]

The newly-appointed bishop of Spire, Philip Christoph von Sötern, was early pressed by Paul V. to reform his cathedral chapter.[5] Subsequently he supported Sötern's labours in the cause of the restoration with so much energy that the bishop was able to write that the Pope's memory would remain for ever in benediction in the diocese.[6] In 1606 the zealous bishop of Worms, Wilhelm von Effern, called a few Jesuits into his diocese. The Cologne nuncio

[1] See the Brief of November 25, 1615, in *Archiv. f. Frankfurts Gesch.*, VI. (1854), 128. Paul V.' letter to Schweikart: **Breve credent. in nunt. de catholicis in Frankfurt,* dated August 31, 1612, refers to previous efforts on the part of the Pope (*Epist.*, VIII., 95, Papal Secret Archives).

[2] See the Brief to Schweikart **Breve credent. in nunt. de erigendo monast. Capuccinor. Francofurti,* dated July 24, 1615, *Epist.*, XI., 33, Papal Secret Archives.

[3] See Borghese's letter in LÄMMER, *Zur Kirchengesch.*, 81.

[4] Albergati's faculties in *Bull.*, XII., 278 *seq.* *Cf.* the *Brief to the chapter of Mayence of October 18, 1614; the *Briefs to the archbishops of Mayence and Cologne and the bishop of Bamberg of January 10, 1615, in *Epist.*, XV., *ibid.*, XVI., a *Brief to the archbishop of Cologne dated August 9, 1619, begging him to support Albergati's efforts for the reform of the Carmelites of the city and province of Cologne, Papal Secret Archives.

[5] *Brief of December 11, 1610, *ibid.*, VI., 232.

[6] SCHMIDLIN, 453.

praised their work and protected them against the violent attacks which they had to encounter.[1] Johann Friedrich von Schwalbach, who had been elected abbot of Fulda in 1606, enjoyed the strong support of Paul V. in his plans for a reform.[2] In 1608 an extremely laudatory Brief was sent to the aged, highly deserving bishop of Würzburg, Julius Echter von Mespelbrunn.[3] In the following year the Pope commissioned him to watch over the interests of the Church on the occasion of the election of a bishop for the vacant see of Bamberg.[4] Owing to the fact that duke Maximilian also gave his attention to the matter, and with the help of the dean of the chapter, Johann Christoph von Neustetter, a former pupil of the Germanicum,[5] the choice fell, on July 23rd, 1609, on the excellent Johann Gottfried von Aschhausen.

The new bishop of Bamberg undertook at once, with burning zeal, the internal as well as the external renewal of his diocese which had been utterly neglected by his unworthy predecessor, Gebsattel,[6] so that already in 1610 [7] Paul V. sent him an expression of his highest satisfaction. In the spring of 1611, Johann Gottfried ordered a general visitation

[1] See DUHR, II., 1, 174 *seq.* To the literature indicated by him must be added a paper in *Archiv f. hess. Gesch.*, II., 3, 473 *seqq.*

[2] *Cf.* the *Briefs to the abbot of Fulda of March 15, 1608, October 17, 1609, October 22, 1611, and March 7, 1619, in the *Epist.*, III., 430, VI, 58, VII, 147, XIV, 54, Papal Secret Archives. On the splendid parish priest of Salmünster, Joh. Haal (1603–1609), see RICHTER, *Quellen zur Gesch. der Abtei Fulda*, IV. (1907), 45 *seq.*

[3] *Brief of May 9, 1608, *Epist.*, III., 494, Papal Secret Archives.

[4] *Brief of August 1, 1609, *Epist.*, III., 494; original in the catalogue of the auction of *Kubasta*, Vienna, 1899, no. 655.

[5] *Cf.* STEINHUBER, 12, 384.

[6] *Cf.* JOH. WEBER, *Joh. Gottfried von Aschhausen, Fürstbischof von Bamberg*, Würzburg, 1889; LOOSHORN, V. (1903), 391 *seq.*; SCHMIDLIN, *Zustände*, 155 *seq.*; RIEDLER, in *Bericht des Hist. Vereins von Bamberg*, LX., 57 *seq.*, LXI., 2 *seq.*

[7] SCHMIDLIN, 155, note 1.

of the diocese which was carried out with great circumspection under the personal supervision of Friedrich Forner, his vicar-general. In the same year the bishop called the Jesuits to Bamberg.[1] On the occasion of his journey to Rome, as imperial envoy for the purpose of doing homage to the Pope (at the close of 1612), he seized the opportunity to give an account of his diocese. As efficacious remedies against prevailing evils he mentioned the following: the celebration of diocesan synods, the revival of rural deaneries and the establishment of confraternities of the Blessed Sacrament and the Blessed Virgin. All these ideals Johann Gottfried carried into effect. Himself the pattern of what a priest ought to be, he gave to his court an almost monastic character. He personally visited a large part of his diocese, built several churches, one large hospital and a seminary for poor students. As the Rhenish Jesuit Provincial reported to the Pope in 1615,[2] ecclesiastical conditions in the diocese of Bamberg had undergone a complete transformation. When on September 13th, 1617, Julius Echter closed his tired eyes, Johann Gottfried was put at the head of the diocese of Würzburg also. He presided over both dioceses until 1622, and during that time he reformed the Benedictine monasteries in them.[3]

In 1612 the splendid bishop of Eichstätt, Konrad von Gemmingen, was given a successor of like character. In the teeth of the opposition of the cathedral chapter, he summoned the Jesuits to Eichstätt. They took charge of the seminary and, together with the Capuchins, zealously devoted themselves also to pastoral work outside the city.[4]

The diocese of Ratisbon also underwent a complete renewal

[1] See Duhr, II., 1, 164 *seq.*

[2] See Schmidlin, 351 *seq.*

[3] See Weber, *Aschhausen*, 56 *seq.*, 70. The faculty granted by Paul V. to the nuncio Albergati to hold a visitation of the diocese of Bamberg, in *Bull.*, XII., 417 *seq.*

[4] Besides Duhr, II., 1236 *seq.*, *cf.* the excellent essay which my friend provost J. G. Suttner (died 1888) devoted to bishop Wetterstein in the *Kathol. Blättern aus Franken*, 1852, nos. 17–28.

at the hands of the excellent bishop Wolfgang von Hausen (1600-1613) who zealously visited his diocese and arranged for missions to be given by Jesuits and Capuchins. He was no less keen on the improvement of public worship than on the reform of the monasteries. His successor, Albert, Freiherr von Törring, continued his work in the same spirit.[1]

Among the promoters of the Catholic restoration mention must be made of archduke Leopold who, though he allowed political questions to distract him from his pastoral duties, nevertheless did much for Church reform during the time he occupied the see of Passau, and later on also at Strassburg. For the purpose of maintaining ecclesiastical discipline, he instituted a diocesan council in both bishoprics. At Passau he encouraged a Capuchin foundation and built a magnificent college for the Jesuits.[2] His activity in the diocese of Strassburg was repeatedly acknowledged by Paul V. Later on, when he neglected his ecclesiastical duties for the pursuit of politics, he was sharply reprimanded in a Papal Brief.[3] Subsequently Leopold applied himself exclusively to the government of his dioceses and from that time onwards Paul V. had every reason to be satisfied with his work. In 1614 the archduke ordered a general visitation which led to a sensible improvement in the religious condition of Alsace.[4] In 1614 the Jesuits were given a college at Hagenau and in 1615 a residence at Schlettstatt.[5] Above all Leopold furthered the principal Jesuit establishment at Molsheim.

[1] See LIPF, *Gesch. der Bischöfe von Regensburg*, 216 *seq.*; SCHMIDLIN, 115 *seq.* Paul V.'s *Brief to W. v. Hausen, with the *facultas reformandi monast. S. Jacobi Scotorum* is dated May 8, 1615, *Epist.*, X., 343, Papal Secret Archives.

[2] SCHMIDLIN, 205 *seq.*; SCHÖLLER, *Bischöfe von Passau* (1844), 206 *seq.*

[3] SCHÖLLER, 411–412, note.

[4] See *ibid.*, 412 *seq.* A study by Professor SCHMIDLIN on the Catholic restoration in Alsace, to appear in *Erl. und Erg. zu Janssens Gesch. des deutsch. Volkes*, will supply further information on this subject.

[5] DUHR, II., 1, 190 *seq.*

The church adjoining the college, which was consecrated in 1618, is a splendid proof of his liberality; next to the Jesuit church in Cologne it is the largest and most important Gothic edifice of the seventeenth century on German soil.[1] Simultaneously with the consecration of this imposing edifice, the college, with Paul V.'s consent, was given the status of an academy.[2]

In the extensive diocese of Constance the devout bishop Johann Georg von Hallweil had energetically striven, in the first years of the seventeenth century, to raise ecclesiastical discipline, but his reign was too brief (1601–1603) to enable him to remove the numerous abuses which had crept in under his predecessor.[3] This was the task which the noble Jakob

[1] *Cf.* Braun, *Kirchenbauten der deutschen Jesuiten*, I., 49 *seq.*; Polaczek, *Denkmale der Baukunst im Elsass* (1906), 94 *seq.*

[2] Duhr, II., 1, 188 *seq.*, 592. In 1618, when archduke Leopold, at the death of the Grand-master, Maximilian, became regent of the Tyrol and the Vorlanden, he promoted there also the ecclesiastical renewal. We shall have to say more about this in the next volume for only a very small fraction of it falls into the pontificate of Paul V.; but the introduction of the Jesuits at Freiburg im Breisgau, due to Leopold, still falls into the reign of the Borghese Pope; *cf.* Duhr, II., 1, 268 *seq.*

[3] On the bad conditions there, *cf.* the protocols of visitations in the *Zeitschr. f. die Gesch. des Oberrheins*, XXV., 129 *seq.*, XXVIII., 489 *seqq.* Against the widely spread concubinage J. Lorichius, in particular, raised his voice (see on this splendid scholar Ehses, *Festschrift des Campo Santo* (1897), 242), *Contra incontinentiam et concubinatum clericorum lectiones Iod, Lorichii, theol. doct. et prof. in acad. Brisg*, a treatise beginning with these words: "In foeda, ignominiosa ac damanabili vitiorum seu peccatorum colluvie nullum est quo se nostri ordinis viri, proh dolor, frequentius, obstinatius, detestabilius, polluant quam incontinentia." C. 1–5 treat *de damnis incontinentiae*; c. 6, *de causis*; c. 7, *de remediis incontinentiae*; c. 8, *diluuntur argumenta concubinariorum obstinatorum* (Cod. 262 of the Freiburg University Library). In the same volume a treatise by Lorichius: *De templis christianorum* (1598) with an Appendix *de abusibus spectaculorum in festo Corporis Christi.*

Fugger set himself. He was elected on January 27th, 1604, and his reforming zeal was repeatedly encouraged by Paul V.[1] He clearly saw that the spread of heresy could only be stopped by means of a thorough reform of the clergy, hence in the autumn of 1609, he held a diocesan synod the statutes of which were put into the hands of the clergy, in book form, in the following year. Here excellent rules were laid down for the pastoral ministry, preaching, catechizing, and clerical life generally. The synod divided the diocese into four districts each of which, in addition to the deans, was to have its own visitor who, as well as the deans themselves, was to be subject to two visitors general residing at Constance. The bishop took a personal share in the work of visitation and he was assisted by his coadjutor, Jakob Mirgel, a former pupil of the Germanicum.[2]

Owing to the fact that most of the monasteries of the old Orders had lost sight of their original purpose—Weingarten alone, under its excellent abbot, Georg Wegelin, forming an exception—the new reformed Orders stepped into the breach in the diocese of Constance also. To the college which the Jesuits already possessed at Constance another was added in 1620, at Freiburg in Breisgau. Bishop Fugger favoured the Jesuits wherever he could, but he had perhaps even closer relations with the Capuchins in whose church at Constance he chose his last resting place. During his reign the number of Capuchin convents in the different parts of the diocese rose to twenty-one. Jesuits and Capuchins distinguished themselves especially during the plague of 1611, when they devoted themselves with the utmost zeal, day and night, to the bodily and spiritual welfare of the sick.[3]

It is strange that so zealous a bishop as Fugger was in all Church matters, should have refused to comply with the duty

[1] *Cf.*, on what follows, the excellent monograph of Holl: *Fürstbischof Jakob Fugger von Konstanz* (1604–1626), Freiburg, 1898.

[2] See Holl, 117, 133 *seq.*, 189 *seq.* Schmidlin, 379 *seq.*

[3] Holl, 98 *seq.*, 112.

of personally reporting in Rome. The Swiss nuncio, Ladislao d'Aquino, suspected that this was due to national antipathy towards the Italians. It may have been so; but a no less weighty reason was the heavy expense of such a journey and the dangers which an absence of some length entailed for the diocese in such troublous times. For the rest Fugger repeatedly sent delegates to report in his place, and Rome refrained from blaming his conduct.[1]

The Curia found itself greatly embarrassed when the long-standing quarrel of the hot-headed archbishop of Salzburg, Wolfgang Dietrich von Raitenau, with Maximilian of Bavaria, became so acute that in the autumn of 1613 the duke overthrew his opponent by violent measures.[2] The excitement caused in Rome by Maximilian's action was at first very great. The older Cardinals were for stern measures against the duke of Bavaria who, nevertheless, found a keen defender in the person of Cardinal Millini.[3] On Millini's proposal, Antonio Diaz was dispatched to Salzburg as nuncio extraordinary, with mission to inquire into the affair, the first reports of which had borne a strong party colour. Diaz prevailed on Maximilian to hand over to him the captive bishop, but he himself treated him with the utmost harshness, compelled him on March 7th, 1612, to resign his see, and forthwith had him taken back to prison. Whilst in prison Raitenau wrote a detailed account of the harsh treatment he had been subjected to, declared that the accusations of his enemies, with the exception of his unlawful liaison with Salome Alt, were calumnies, complained bitterly of Diaz, and demanded a fresh inquiry by the bishops of Seckau and Lavant. However the document was intercepted and given to the

[1] HOLL, 126 *seq.*; SCHMIDLIN, 387 *seq.*

[2] *Cf.* for what follows the well documented work of F. MARTIN, *Des Erzbischofs Wolf Dietrich letzte Lebensjahre*, in *Mitteil. der Gesellsch. f. Salzburger Landeskunde*, L. (1910), 157 *seqq.* See also F. MARTIN's monograph of *Wolf Dietrich von Raitenau*, Vienna, 1925.

[3] *Cf.* MEMMOLI, *Vita del card. Millino*, Roma, 1644, 28 *seq.*

nuncio.[1] Before his departure, the latter handed over the prisoner to Mark Sittich von Hohenems who had been elected archbishop in the meantime. Though the brothers of Wolf Dietrich strove desperately to get him set at liberty, all their efforts failed owing to the opposition of Mark Sittich who feared for his position and who, contrary to what had been agreed, detained his unhappy predecessor in strict confinement at Hohensalzburg until the day of his death, January 16th, 1617.

The archbishop began his reign with a general visitation which brought to light deplorable conditions among the clergy.[2] Improvement was bound to be slow, and Mark Sittich, who proceeded with great harshness, obtained no more than an outward conversion of the Protestants in the archdiocese. The latter were particularly numerous in the Pongau.[3] With a view to carrying out the Tridentine decrees, Mark Sittich published, in 1616, a number of excellent ordinances and, in order to make stricter vigilance over the clergy practicable, he divided the archidiaconate of Salzburg into seven deaneries. The archbishop himself set a good example to the clergy for he said Mass almost daily and preached frequently. He also sought to strengthen the spiritual life by the introduction of the Forty Hours' Prayer and the Roman Rite, by the establishment of numerous confraternities, by favouring the Capuchins and by means of pilgrimages and processions. For the formation of good priests Mark Sittich built a college which, later on, in keeping with his plan, developed into a university and was entrusted to the Benedictines.[4] Thus from the ecclesiastical standpoint, Mark Sittich was the very antithesis of his predecessor though he resembled him in his love of magnificence and building

[1] See ZAUNER, *Chronik von Zalzburg*, VII., 204 *seq.* *Cf.* MARTIN, *Letzte Lebensjahre*, 188.

[2] SCHMIDLIN, 91.

[3] See WOLF, *Geschichtl. Bilder aus Österreich*, I. (1878), 187 *seq.*; LOSERTH, in *Mitteil. des österr. Instituts*, XIX., 676 *seq.*

[4] See WIDMANN, III., 263 *seqq.* *Cf. Studien aus dem Benediktinerorden*, XI., 64 *seq.*; *Zeitschr. f. kath. Theol.*, 1910, 614 *seq.*

on the big scale ; to the latter passion the castle and park of Heilbrunn and the cathedral of Salzburg owe their origin. This magnificent church, which at the time of Raitenau's fall was hardly begun, and of which Mark Sittich laid the foundation stone for a second time in 1614, was now built, not as a rotunda, as had been planned by the celebrated pupil of Palladio, Vincenzo Scamozzi, but with a nave, on the model of the Gesù in Rome. The mighty structure erected by the Lombard, Santino Solari, which is wholly instinct with the spirit of the Roman baroque, was roofed in by the time of Sittich's death in 1619, and the façade had reached half its height.[1] To Sittich, who found his last resting place in the cathedral, belongs the glory of having created Germany's most remarkable sacred edifice of the first half of the seventeenth century.[2] Probably the most important and most deserving bishop of Germany of that period was, besides Johann Gottfried von Aschhausen of Bamberg and the aged Echter von Mespelbrunn, the bishop of Augsburg, Henry V. von Knöringen. Richly endowed, energetic, deeply pious, conscientious, an indefatigable worker and burning with zeal for the Catholic cause, Henry devoted all his energy to establishing religious unity in his vast diocese and recalling clergy and people alike to discipline and order. He started his work of restoration in the second year of his reign by publishing a strong mandate on the subject of religion, and his efforts culminated in the reform decrees promulgated at the diocesan synod of 1610. He went on building on the foundation thus laid, by regular visitations of the parishes and by numerous ordinances for the secular and regular clergy and the people. In all this he was effectively assisted by the Jesuits, the Capuchins and the Franciscans, to all of whom he was a generous benefactor.

[1] See TIETZE, in *Österr. Kunsttopographie*, IX. (1912), 1 *seqq.* ; WIDMANN, III., 362 *seqq.* ; MÜHLMANN, *Der Dom zu Salzburg*, Vienna, 1925 ; J. WEINGARTNER, in the periodical, *Das neue Reich*, VIII. (1925), no. 10.

[2] Opinion of WACKERNAGEL, *Die Baukunst des 17. und 18. Jahrhunderts in den germanischen Ländern.*, 44.

The bishop, who had made his studies with the Jesuits of Dillingen, is the founder of their university in that town. He also contributed to the erection of a new church, which in its lay-out and structure resembles the church of St. Michael at Munich. He consecrated it in 1617. In 1614 he had established a Tridentine seminary and confided its direction to the Jesuits. The statutes breathe the same spirit as those of the papal seminary of Dillingen.[1] The praise which Paul V., in 1612, bestowed on his pastoral solicitude [2] was all the more deserved as he had proved the first and most loyal supporter of Maximilian in the latter's efforts for the formation of the Catholic Defence League.

Maximilian I., the greatest of all Bavaria's rulers, had the defence of Catholic interests in the empire quite as much at heart as the promotion of the Catholic reform in his own territory. For this Paul V. rewarded him with valuable privileges, heaped ecclesiastical dignities and revenues upon his brother Ferdinand, and overlooked many things in the internal ecclesiastical policy of the duke. However much, as a practical politician, he may have studied his own advantage, Maximilian's Catholic sentiments nevertheless sprang from a most genuine conviction. In his recommendation to his son he states that the first and noblest duty of a ruler is to promote the glory of God, the Catholic religion, and the salvation of the souls of the subjects whom God has committed to him and for whom he will have to give an account at the last day. Maximilian's ecclesiastical policy, which was both detailed and comprehensive, was dictated

[1] J. SPINDLER devotes an excellent monograph to Heinrich von Knöringen, in the *Jahrb. des Hist. Vereins Dillingen*, XXIV. (1911), 1–138. *Cf.* SPECHT, *Gesch. der Universität Dillingen* (1902); LOCHNER, *Die Jesuitenkirche in Dillingen*, Stuttgart, 1895; BRAUN, *Jesuitenkirchen*, II., 133 *seq.*; DUHR, II., 1, 288 *seq.*, 570 *seq.* See ROTTENKOLLER, in *Allgäuer Geschichtsfreund* on the visitations held by the prince abbot of Kempten, Heinrich von Ulm, whom Paul V., on the occasion of his confirmation, on March 3, 1608, exhorted to see to the preservation of the faith within his domain.

[2] Brief of November 24, 1612, in STEICHELE, *Beiträge*, I., 324 *seq.*

by his lively sense of duty. The purpose for which he strove, namely the preservation of the unity of the faith and the promotion of the religious and moral life of his subjects was, in the main, fully realized. On the other hand the duke was on dangerous ground when he enforced compliance with the laws of the Church by police measures and even appointed special spies to that effect. It was also a serious matter that Maximilian claimed for the State sovereign rights in Church matters which went far beyond the concessions of the Concordat, and when he at times seriously encroached on the jurisdiction of the bishops. If here there is question of very debatable government measures, Maximilian's merits in respect to the moral improvement of a sadly neglected clergy and people stand out all the more conspicuously. In this respect the most important measure was the introduction all over the country of a systematic teaching of religion for which the excellent catechisms of Canisius were used.[1]

The duke himself set his subjects the very best example. In contrast to the repulsive spectacle presented by most Protestant princely courts of the time, the conduct of the court of Munich was exemplary. It reacted on the capital, of which it has been said that it sheltered, at that time, one of the most strictly moral populations of Christendom.[2]

The religious life, of which the congregations of our Lady and splendid processions were characteristic manifestations, was fostered with indefatigable zeal by the Jesuits. Their colleges at Ingolstadt and Munich reached the apex of their splendour at that time.[3] The Capuchins devoted themselves to the great mass of the population. They, like the Jesuits, stood in close relation with the court. The Jesuit Buslidius was the duke's confessor.[4] The duke also held in high regard

[1] See STIEVE, *Das kirchliche Polizeiregiment in Vayern unter Maximilian*, I., Munich, 1876; *Zeitschr. f. Kirchenrecht*, XIII., 375 *seq.*; XIV., 63 *seq.*; RIEZLER, VI., 242 *seq.*; DÖBERL, I., 489 *seq.*, 492 *seq.*

[2] Opinion of RIEZLER (VI., 253).

[3] DUHR, II., 1, 202 *seq.*, 204 *seq.*.

[4] DUHR, *Jesuiten an den Fürstenhofen*, 137.

the Capuchin Lorenzo of Brindisi, who rendered valuable service to him in matters connected with the League. More than once the duke served Lorenzo's mass.[1] Yet another Capuchin, Giacinto of Casale, was destined to play an important rôle in the life of Maximilian. This remarkable man, together with Lorenzo of Brindisi,[2] had been appointed a missioner in Germany by Paul V. He laboured there in 1606 and 1607 and thus came into relations with the imperial House of Habsburg. In 1613 he was again despatched to Germany in the suite of the Cardinal legate, Madruzzo, when he made the acquaintance of Maximilian and introduced the Capuchins at Ratisbon.[3] The latter had already settled at Rosenheim in 1606. Maximilian founded a convent for them at Landshut in 1610, and at Straubing in 1614. Other convents were founded at Würzburg in 1615, and at Günzburg in 1616.[4] In 1609 a convent of the Jesuit Sisters founded by Mary Ward for the education of girls was established at Munich. They eventually became known as "the English Ladies".[5]

The old Orders also awoke to a new life. In 1617 Paul V. appealed to Maximilian with regard to the reform of the Bavarian Augustinians.[6] In 1620, on the initiative of the Holy See, the Bavarian Franciscans were subjected to a

[1] *Cf.* BON. DE COCALLIO et ERARDO DA RADKERSBURGO, *Vita del b. Lorenzo da Brindisi*, Roma, 1783; STIEVE, *Briefe u. Akten*, VI.; MAYR, *Briefe u. Akten*, VII. and VIII.

[2] See the papal faculties for Lorenzo, dated May 12 and 28, 1606, in *Bull. Capuc.*, I., 51.

[3] See *Venanzio da Lago Santo*, 74; W. GOETZ, *P. Hyacinth*, in the *Hist. Zeitschr.*, CIX., 103 *seq.* GOETZ justly laments the absence of all references to sources in Venanzio, but he himself has overlooked one of the most important of them all, viz. the *Bull. Capuc.*, III., 238–289.

[4] See EBERL, 46 *seq.*, 49 *seq.*, 51 *seq.*

[5] See REIMBUCHER, II., 316.

[6] *Brief of February 12, 1617, *Epist.*, XV., Papal Secret Archives.

thorough reform.[1] In a Brief of February 23rd, 1620, to Maximilian, the Pope expressed his satisfaction at the result.[2]

In the Tyrol also the religious life underwent a renewal similar to that which had taken place in Bavaria. Here also besides the prince bishops of Brixen and Trent, Andreas von Spaur and Carlo Madruzzo,[3] it was the ruling prince, Maximilian, Grand-master of the Teutonic Order, who assured the triumph of the Catholic reform and restoration.[4] All the reports that reached Rome about Maximilian's life and dispositions could but justify the highest hopes. The Augustinian, Mander, who visited him in 1608, described him as the true ideal of a Catholic prince.[5] Such praise was not undeserved. Though many a measure of Maximilian's may not have been compatible with the letter of Canon Law, there can be no doubt that he strove for the best both for the Church and for his subjects.[6] Hence Paul V. repeatedly praised the Grand-master's zeal for the progress of religion in his territory.[7] As in Bavaria, so in the Tyrol, the encroachments of the State on the sphere of the Church, which were largely the result of circumstances, were attenuated by the devout sense of the prince who did not content himself with the enjoyment of the dignity and the revenues of a Grand-master but who lived accordingly, and even composed a prayer-book.[8]

[1] See MINGES, *Gesch. der Franziskaner in Bayern* (1896), 106 *seq.* *Cf.* LINS, *Gesch. der bayr. Franziskanerprovinz 1620–1802*, Munich, 1926.

[2] **Epist.*, XVI., 246, *loc. cit.*

[3] See further on p. 351.

[4] *Cf.* for what follows the exhaustive presentment by HIRN, *Maximilian I.*, 212 to 340.

[5] *Della natura et qualità del ser. Massimiliano*, in Mander's report quoted above, p. 275, n. 5, BORGHESE, I., 28, p. 67, Papal Secret Archives.

[6] This is rightly emphasized by FR. M. STRAGANZ, in his essay on Maximilian (*Tirol. Stimmen*, 1918, no. 247).

[7] *See the Briefs of December, 1609, and March 4, 1613 (*Epist.*, V., 232, VIII., 248, Papal Secret Archives), of which the latter deals with the establishment of the Capuchins at Meran.

[8] HIRN, *Maximilian*, I., 216.

A remarkable characteristic of Maximilian, and one altogether singular in view of the acute religious feeling of the time, was a certain toleration towards heretics. Thus, in the year before his death, he appointed an anabaptist as his surgeon. He also protested against a decree of the synod of Brixen which would have forbidden the sick to call in a physician who did not profess Catholicism.[1] Hence in dealing with heretics Maximilian would use external pressure only as a secondary means. Solid instruction and the example of good priests he considered to be the noblest, as well as the most effective means, for bringing about a Catholic renewal. His rule, so far as the Tyrol is concerned, proved decisive as regards that revival. The change in the clergy is shown by the reports of visitations which took place regularly after the reform synod of 1603. Year by year these documents bear witness to increasing improvement. Among the people that spirit now asserted itself to which the Tyrol owes its world-wide reputation as a staunch Catholic country. On all sides churches and chapels were either being erected or restored; the Easter Sepulchre, the crib at Christmas came into use in churches and private houses; after 1615 the custom spread of ringing a second bell after the evening *Angelus* to summon the people to pray for the departed; attendance at sermons and catechetical instructions and participation in confraternities, pilgrimages and processions became general; the recitation of the rosary established itself as a household practice; and the reception of the sacraments increased.[2]

The newly reformed Orders took a prominent part in this transformation. Maximilian's biographers justly praise the Jesuits for their incredible zeal in the sphere of education as well as in the pastoral ministry.[3] The higher education was almost exclusively in their hands. The Grand-master built a fine Grammar school for the fathers at Innsbruck, and heaped all manner of favours on the college. He likewise

[1] HIRN, I., 338.

[2] *Ibid.*, 255 *seq.*, 272 *seq.*, 308.

[3] *Ibid.*, 307. On the work of the Jesuits in the Valley of the Adige, in 1614, see KROPF, VIII., n. 618.

made every effort to settle the Society at Hagenau, Ensisheim, Freiburg in Breisgau and at Trent.[1] The widow of archduke Ferdinand, Anna Catharina, received sympathetic support from Paul V. for her religious foundations in the capital of the Tyrol. Close to the convent of the Servite Nuns she erected the so-called " Regelhaus ". Thither she withdrew in company with her younger daughter, in order to live the life of the Servite Tertiaries under the name of Anna Juliana. In 1614, she founded a monastery of Servite Friars in the new part of the town of Innsbruck. In recent years a suitable monument has been erected over her tomb in the church of the convent. In 1621, the Innsbruck Servites took charge of the famous place of pilgrimage of Waldrast. From the Tyrol they spread over almost all the crown lands of the Habsburg Hereditary States and from there they penetrated as far as the Rhine. Three Provinces of the Order, with nearly thirty monasteries, sprang from the foundation of the pious archduchess.[2]

Maximilian kept up such close relations with the Capuchins of Innsbruck that he almost looked upon himself as one of them. His energy and liberality enabled him, notwithstanding all kinds of difficulties, to found a Capuchin convent at Meran, in 1616. There the Fathers took complete charge of religious instruction ; they also introduced the Good-Friday night procession, which had been established at Brixen in 1609, and which was soon imitated in other places. In conjunction with the bishop of Chur, Johann Flugi von Aspermont, Maximilian charged the Capuchins with the care of the people of the Vintschgau whose faith was in danger.[3] Maximilian likewise lent help at the foundation of the Capuchin convent of Neumarkt, in the valley of the Adige.[4] At Ala the Order had already established itself in 1606.

Notwithstanding the numerous religious communities which

[1] Duhr, II., 1, 210 *seq.* ; II., 2, 237, 289.

[2] See besides Hirn, I., 304 *seq.*, also Heimbucher, I., 476, and the literature mentioned by him.

[3] See Agapit Hohenegger, *Das Kapuzinerkloster zu Meran*, Innsbruck, 1889.

[4] See Eberl, 64 *seq.*

established themselves in these various places, other localities also suffered from a crying need of priests ; thus, for instance, in 1607 Bruneck had as yet no priest of its own. This state of affairs moved Spaur, bishop of Brixen, in 1607 to found a seminary for priests.[1] In 1618 the bishop of Trent, Carlo Madruzzo, in whose diocese the dearth of priests was likewise keenly felt, confided his recently restored seminary to the Somaschi whom he had summoned from Pavia, and at a later date he also called the Capuchins into his episcopal city.[2] The bishop of Brixen repeatedly begged for good priests from the papal seminaries of Rome, Dillingen and Graz. Paul V. showed himself a generous supporter of these and similar institutions. German ecclesiastical history records with gratitude the regular subsidies granted by him to the seminaries of Braunsberg, Fulda, Prague, Vienna and Olmütz.[3] Paul V.'s aims in regard to Germany are defined in the Instruction of the nuncio Caetani, under date October 20th, 1607 ; viz. publication of the reform decrees of Trent by the bishops or by provincial councils, such as had been held in 1569 at Salzburg and Liège ; restoration of clerical discipline, chiefly by means of visitations and the granting of benefices to worthy candidates only ; the training of such men in the seminaries ; removal of abuses in cathedral chapters ; observance of the concordat ; abolition of pluralism ; removal of Protestants from the courts of Catholic princes ; prohibition for the subjects of bishops (prince-bishops) to send their children to non-Catholic schools ; assiduous teaching of religion to the people.[4] Though so comprehensive a pro-

[1] *Cf.* the monograph by FREISEISEN, Brixen, 1908.

[2] The Somaschans were given the church of St. Maria Maddalena, the Capuchins Santa Croce ; see **Cod. Mazzetti*, LX., 22 *seq.*, of *Stadtbibl. Trier*. On Madruzzo's efforts, which only bore fruit at a later period, to get the Jesuits to Trent, see PROBST, *Gesch. der Gymnasien in Tirol*, Innsbruck, 1858, 105 *seq.* *Cf* **Ambraser Akten*, VI., 60, in *Landesregierungsarchiv*, at Innsbruck.

[3] *Cf.* the information in Costaguti's notes in Appendix No. 14, Costaguti Archives, in Rome.

[4] See EGLOFFSTEIN, *Reichstag zu Regensburg*, 114 *seq.*

gramme was not by any means everywhere carried out in its fullness, one may nevertheless say, on looking back, that during the reign of the Borghese Pope, very considerable progress was realized in respect of the ecclesiastical and religious renewal of Germany.[1]

(4.)

Whereas within the empire the government of the emperor Matthias showed a willingness for wide concessions to the Protestants, in Bohemia, on the contrary, it endeavoured to protect the ancient Church from the encroachments of the religious innovators. In the dispute on the interpretation of the "Letter of Majesty" and the "Compromise" of 1609, the government withstood the Protestants and promoted, slowly but consecutively, the Catholic reform and restoration,[2]

[1] Already in 1613 Paul V. received gratifying information on this subject in the following letter written by a member of Madruzzo's suite: "... Si desidera principalmente che Monsignore rappresenti alla Santità Sua per particolare consolatione lo stato buono de' prelati et clero di Germania, il quale è molto diverso da quello che altre volte fu osservato nella dieta di Augusta e nell' altra di Ratisbona, poichè, non solo nell' habito esteriore, ma nell'interiore ancora si è visto un grande acquisto in pochi anni, havendo i prelati celebrato spessissimo et communicate le famiglie loro con molta edificatione di tutti. Onde in così buona congiuntura non si stima difficile il ridurli ad una riforma et disporli alle visite et alle funtioni sinodali, si come alcuni di loro, coi quali n'ha trattato il cardinale Legato, se ne sono mostrati desiderosi. Et quando si risolvesse Sua Beat^ne^ a così sant' opera, bisogneria pensare a deputare persona intelligente et destra e che habbia qualche cognitione delle cose di Germania et passar in oltre offitio con Sua Maestà Cesarea che volesse farvi assistere commissarii delle medesime conditioni, et se cadesse l'elettione in persona ecclesiastica, si potrebbe sperare maggiore satisfattione et frutto. Di Trento li 6 di novembre 1613, in BORGHESE, I., 115–16, p. 9*b*, Papal Secret Archives.

[2] *Cf.* for what follows GINDELY, I., 59 *seq.*, 124 *seq.*, 237 *seq.*; KLOPP, I., 246 *seq.*; HUBER, V., 54 *seq.*, 84 *seq.*, 101 *seq.*; RITTER, II., 393 *seq.*, 453 *seq.* On the legal question see, besides Ritter's

which had also the fervent support of the excellent archbishop of Prague, Johann Lohelius,[1] the provost of Leitmeritz, Johann Sixt von Lerchenfels,[2] the Jesuits and the Capuchins.[3] The stronger the Catholic defence became the more violent also became the Protestant attack. Wherever the adherents of the ancient faith were in a minority, as, for instance, at Braunan, they saw themselves exposed to insults and rowdy demonstrations of every kind, so that many families migrated elsewhere.[4] The Protestants grew bolder because a small but resolute party of nobles, led by count Heinrich Matthias

remarks in Reusch's *Theol. Literaturblatt*, 1870, 865, also SWOBODA, "Die Kirchenschliessung zu Klostergrab und Braunau," in the *Innsbr. Zeitschr. f. kath. Theol.*, X., 396 *seq.*; DUHR, *Jesuitenfabeln*,[4] 167 *seq.*; KNOLL, in the *Mitteil des Vereins. f. Gesch. der Deutschen in Böhmen*, XLV. (1907), 48 *seq.* The actual facts are excellently discussed by L. WINTERA, who bases himself on the evidence of the archives, in his *Gesch. der protest., Bewegung in Braunau*, Prague, 1894 (reprint from the *Mitteil. des Vereins f. Gesch. der Deutschen in Böhmen* XXXI. and XXXII.), and *Braunau und der Dreissigjährige Krieg*[2], Warnsdorf, 1905. The view here opposed is the oft-asserted claim that the closing of the Protestant church in Braunau was the immediate cause of the thirty years' war. Wintera proves beyond dispute that the assertion which is even repeated by GINDELY (I., 75), is untenable, since the Protestant church in Braunau was closed neither in 1614 nor in 1618, whereas the frequently mentioned Protestant church at Klostergrab was pulled down by the Protestants themselves.

[1] *Cf.* FRIND, *Gesch. der Bischöfe u. Erzbischöfe von Prag*, 200 *seq.*; GINDELY, *Gegenreformation in Böhmen*, 86; SCHMIDLIN, *Zustände*, 159 *seq.*, *cf. ibid.*, 178 *seq.*, on the successful work for Catholic restoration by the bishop of Olmütz, Cardinal Dietrichstein, whom Paul V. eulogized repeatedly.

[2] *Cf.* SCHLENZ, in *Mitteil des Vereins f. Gesch. der Deutschen in Böhmen*, XLVIII., 384 *seq.*, XLIX., 1 *seq.*, 153 *seq.*

[3] For the Jesuits, see KRÖSS, *Gesch. der böhm. Provinz der Gesellschaft Jesu*, I., Vienna, 1910, and *Zeitschr. f. kath. Theol.*, XX., 186 *seq.* On the Capuchins see *Mitteil. des Vereins f. Gesch. der Deutschen in Böhmen*, XLVII. (1909), 248 *seq.*

[4] *Cf.* WINTERA, *Braunau*, 17 *seq.*, 33.

von Thurn, stood by them and they also enjoyed the support of the Calvinists of the empire.[1] This assistance was prompted less by religious motives than by political ones, for Thurn and his followers, as well as the German Calvinists, aimed before all else at the downfall of the House of Habsburg.

In view of the Bohemian disputes, the calculated vagueness of Rudolph II.'s religious legislation was simply disastrous. When at the end of 1617 and the beginning of 1618, both the government and the archbishop of Prague showed a determination to put an end to the propaganda of the heretics by the way in which they tackled the question of the erection of a Protestant church at Braunau and Klostergrab, which had remained undecided for six years, Thurn and his confederates saw their aim, viz. the setting up of a Calvinistic aristocratic republic, seriously threatened; hence they judged they could wait no longer. The count's scheme was to drive the Estates to a step which must necessarily lead to open revolt.[2] Thus came about, on May 23rd, 1618, the murderous attempt on the Catholic lieutenants of the emperor Matthias known as the defenestration of Prague—(Prager Fenstersturz) —an attempt which failed as such but which fully accomplished its purpose, which was to create an irreparable breach. The Protestants of Silesia and Austria at once showed their sympathy with the outbreak in Bohemia. The head of the Union, the Calvinist Elector Palatine, Frederick V., judged the moment favourable for seizing the crown of St. Wenceslaus and for turning the Bohemian rising into the starting point of a great war of annihilation against the House of Habsburg. To this end allies were sought even abroad, but owing to France and England adopting a policy of neutrality, the Dutch States General thus left to themselves could do nothing. Negotiations with the ambitious Carlo Emmanuele, duke of Savoy, who had long meditated the destruction of the

[1] *Ibid.*, 24 *seq.*

[2] That the defenestration was a premeditated act is also admitted by F. MACHÁČEK, who studies the occurrence in the most recent number of *Ceský Casopis hist.*, XIV., 197 *seq.*, 297 *seq.*, 436 *seq.*

Habsburg-Spanish Power, yielded at first no result.[1] For all that, the action of the rebels had gravely jeopardized Catholic interests. What their aims were was quickly shown by the expulsion of the archbishop of Prague and the abbot of Braunau, and that of the Jesuits from Bohemia and Moravia.[2] Thus, from the very outset, the struggle took on the character of a war of religion.[3] Consequently, despite the adverse state of his finances, Paul V. granted the emperor Matthias' request, which had the very warm support of Cardinal Borja, for a monthly war subsidy of 10,000 florins for a period of six months.[4] Even more important was the action of Paul V. when he used his influence with Louis XIII. to prevent the French government from exploiting the revolt in Bohemia to the emperor's disadvantage.[5]

With the death of the emperor Matthias, on March 20th, 1619, the last barrier fell before the Bohemian rebels and their friends.[6] Ferdinand's declaration, by which he bound himself to maintain all privileges and prescriptions of former kings, hence also the "Letter of Majesty", was answered by Thurn's invasion of Moravia: the revolt spread rapidly. Because of the declaration, the Estates of Upper Austria and the Protestants of Lower Austria refused to do homage to

[1] *Cf.* ERDMANNSDÖRFER, *Karl Emmanuel,* 131 *seq.*, 152 *seq.*

[2] *Cf.* PESCHECK, I., 340 *seq.*; KRÓSS, I., 907 *seq.*; DUHR, III., 9 *seq.*, 393; II., 2, 687 *seq.*; an *Apologia pro Societ. Iesu ex Boemia proscripta,* 1618, in CL., VII., Cod. 1221 of the Library of St. Mark, Venice.

[3] *Cf. Vorschlag zur successiven Ausrottung der römisch-katholischen Religion in Deutschland und an andern Orten de anno 1618,* in LÜNIG, I., 977 *seq.* This document was composed shortly after the defenestration of Prague.

[4] Besides GINDELY, II., 397, see the report of L. Ridolfi, from Rome, July 7, 1618, in SCHNITZER, 154, note 1. *Cf.* v. ZWIEDINECK-SÜDENHORST, *Politik Venedigs,* I., 42, 275.

[5] *Cf.* BENTIVOGLIO, *Nunziatura,* III., 132, 137, and GINDELY, I., 359.

[6] *Cf.* the report of the envoys of Lucca in A. PELLEGRINI, *Relaz. inedite di ambasciatori Lucchesi alla corte di Vienna,* Lucca, 1902, 25.

Ferdinand. At the beginning of June, Thurn stood before Vienna. He was too late, however, to take the city and the successes of Buquoy and Ferdinand's defence measures [1] compelled him to beat a hasty retreat into Bohemia. Thereupon Ferdinand, with quick decision, hastened to Frankfort to secure the imperial crown. The party of the Palatine did its utmost to prevent it or at least to obtain a prorogation of the day of the election which had been fixed for July 20th.

How much depended on prompt action was quickly recognized in Rome also. Hence on April 6th, 1619, Paul V. wrote to the ecclesiastical Electors urging them to speed up the imperial election.[2] He repeated his request in August [3] and at the same requested the Elector of Mayence to take immediate counsel with the newly elected emperor on the means of defending the severely threatened Church of Germany.[4] The Pope's piety had prompted him before this to have recourse to prayer. Public prayers were recited in Rome. On April 23rd Paul prayed at the tomb of St. Peter for help for Germany.[5] Great was his joy, therefore, when, on August 28th, news reached Rome that Ferdinand had been elected Roman emperor of the German nation. When he announced the event to the Cardinals he said that the extra-

[1] See HUBER, V., 126. On the part played by the soldiers of Florence in the defence of Vienna, see now G. BANDINI, *Un episodio mediceo della guerra dei trenta anni*, Firenze, 1901, and C. MAGINI, *La guerra de' trent'anni in Germania dal 23 Maggio 1618 all' 11 Giugno 1619 secondo i documenti Fiorentini*, Siena, 1907, 47–55.

[2] See the *Briefs to the Electors of Mayence, Cologne, and Trèves of April 6, 1619, in *Epist.*, XII., 73, Papal Secret Archives. On August 8, 1619, the Pope announced in a consistory the death of the emperor Matthias and expressed his hope for a good election; see **Act. consist.*, Barb. 2926, Vatican Library.

[3] See the *Briefs to the Electors of Mayence, Cologne, and Trèves of August 23, 1619, exhorting them to make a good and speedy election, *Epist.*, XIV–XV., 215, Papal Secret Archives.

[4] *Brief of August 24, 1619, *ibid.*, 19.

[5] **Pregando Dio per la quiete delli correnti motivi di Germania*, Avviso of April 27, 1619, Vatican Library.

ordinary piety of the emperor elect and his outstanding devotion to the Apostolic See, justified the highest hopes for the Catholic Church.[1] In a Brief to Philip III. of Spain, the Pope also gave vent to his satisfaction.[2] The long letter of congratulation which he wrote to the new emperor was couched in the most cordial terms.[3] On the same day the Pope held a service of thanksgiving for the happy issue of the election in the Pauline chapel of the Quirinal, in presence of the Cardinals. Cardinal Borghese,[4] as protector of Germany, was the celebrant of the Mass. The German colony celebrated the event with loud demonstrations of joy.[5]

However, the immediate future brought to the emperor days of heavy anxiety. His election was scarcely an accomplished fact when news reached Frankfort that the Estates of Bohemia had formally deposed him " as a pupil of the Jesuits and an arch-enemy of the religion of the gospel ",

[1] See **Acta consist., loc. cit.* Already in his first *Brief to archduke Ferdinand, on June 23, 1605, Paul V. praised his Catholic zeal (*Epist.*, I., 16, Papal Secret Archives). In a Brief of November 22, 1605, the Pope assured the widowed archduchess Mary of his affection for her son and for her House ; see *Steierische Geschichtsblatter*, I., Graz, 1880, 89 *seq.* In 1617 Paul V. presented archduke Ferdinand with two precious reliquaries ; *cf.* GRAUS, *Die zwei Reliquienschreine in Dom zu Graz*, Graz, 1882. The archducal court was constantly and closely in touch with Rome through the nuncios ; *cf.* in this connection the details given by STARZER, in the *Mitteil. des Hist. Vereins f. Steiermark*, XLI., (1893), 119 *seq.*, and BIAUDET, 184 *seq.* See also LOSERTH, in *Fontes rer. Austr.*, LX., 461 *seq.*, and especially LANG, *Beitr. zur Kirchengesch. der Steirmark* (*Veröffentlichungen der Hist. Landeskommission f. Steiermark*, XVIII.), Graz, 1903, where there is a portrait of the nuncio of Graz, Erasmo Paravicini, whom DUHR (II., 2, 696) describes as a pessimist.

[2] *Brief to Philip III., of Spain, of September 9, 1619, *Epist.*, XIV.–XV., 230, Papal Secret Archives.

[3] *Brief to *Ferdinandus in Imperat. elect.* of September 11, 1619, *ibid.*

[4] See *Avviso of September 11, 1619, Vatican Library.

[5] SCHMIDLIN, 452.

and that they had chosen the Elector Palatine, Frederick V., as King of Bohemia.[1] Ferdinand's position grew rapidly more and more critical; the representatives of the territories adjacent to Bohemia approved his deposition; in Moravia a regular persecution of Catholics set in and the Protestants of Upper Hungary threw in their lot with the grand-duke of Transylvania, Bethlen Gábor, who, relying on the help of the Turks, and supported by the Protestants of Austria, was advancing on Vienna at the head of an army.[2]

Beset as he was by so many dangers, Ferdinand had early looked for allies. Besides the assistance of the king of Spain,[3] it was of the utmost consequence for the emperor that Maximilian of Bavaria, fully realizing that the existence of the Danubian State of the Habsburgs as well as the future of the Catholic Church in the empire were at stake, decided to go to the assistance of Ferdinand.[4] The decision was taken in October, 1619, during the emperor's stay at Munich on his return journey from Frankfort. In the covenant into which they entered on that occasion, the emperor guaranteed to Maximilian the absolute and supreme direction of the League which had become disintegrated in 1616, but which now rose to a new life. Ferdinand further promised to the duke of Bavaria, in return for military aid, full compensation for his expenses and for any losses of men or goods that he might incur, by means of the cession of Austrian territory. An oral agreement also held out to Maximilian the prospect

[1] See LUNDORP, I., 712 *seq.*

[2] HUBER, V., 142 *seq.* On the persecution of the Catholics in Moravia, *cf.* the chronicle of the city of Olmütz for the years 1619 and 1620, in the publications of the *Mährisch-Schlesische Gesellsch.*, 1851, where there is further information about the inhuman tortures with which Canon Johannes Sarkander was put to death. See also *Hist.-polit. Blätter*, XXI., 215 *seq.*, and *Freib. Kirchenlex.*, X.^{2}, 1718 *seq.*

[3] GINDELY, II., 66 *seq.*, 368 *seq.*, 401 *seq.*; HURTER, VIII., 264 *seq.*

[4] RIEZLER, V., 124 *seq.*, 368 *seq.*, 401 *seq.*; GINDELY, II., 381 *seq.*

of the Palatinate.[1] With his wonted decision Maximilian at once saw to the necessary military and financial preparations for the struggle. This he did at two assemblies of the League at Würzburg, in December, 1619, and February, 1620. The rejuvenated League included, from among the ecclesiastical Estates, the occupants of the three Rhenish archbishoprics, Mayence, Trèves and Cologne, likewise, the dioceses of Bamberg, Würzburg, Worms, Spire, Strassburg, Eichstätt, Salzburg, Augsburg, Hildesheim, Paderborn, Münster, Liège, Constance, Freising and Passau; the abbeys of Fulda, Ellwangen, Salmansweiler and Odenheim, and four Swabian prelates, and among the secular Estates, besides Bavaria, Pfalz-Neuburg, Leuchtenberg, the imperial city of Aix-la-Chapelle, and Burgundy. Meanwhile Bavarian diplomats were busily engaged in Paris, Madrid and Rome in raising troops or money.[2]

Already in December, 1618, Paul V. had spontaneously promised to the League a subsidy of 200,000 florins, payable within three years, as well as the revenue of ecclesiastical tithes. Not long after, when Cardinal Borja requested the Pope, in the name of the king of Spain, to raise the monthly subsidy which he had granted to emperor Matthias, Paul V. declared that in view of his adverse financial position he was unable to do this and he clung to this decision even though the Cardinal gave full vent to his impetuous temperament to his face. When Borja referred to the treasure of the Church which lay in the vaults of the castle of St. Angelo and which could be touched when there was question of an emergency of this kind, Paul V. replied that the present case was not one in which these monies could be touched.[3] These and other expressions of opinion [4] show that Rome considerably under-

[1] DÖBERL, I., 547 *seq.*

[2] DÖBERL, I., 549.

[3] GINDELY, II., 397 *seq.*

[4] *Cf.* the *Briefs to Mayence of May 2 and July 20, 1619, *Epist.*, XIV.–XV., 88, and 196, Papal Secret Archives. On July 4, 1619, Paul V. wrote to the bishops of Würzburg and Augsburg urging them to bring about a confederation of the

estimated the gravity of the situation.[1] However, Maximilian and Ferdinand did not weary of imploring the Pope's help with so much insistence, that before long the Curia grew so seriously alarmed about the future [2] that it was decided to drop a plan for a big enterprise against the Turks which had been contemplated at the beginning of 1618.[3]

Catholic princes, *ibid.* The Brussels nuncio was instructed, on June 2, 1619, to urge Albert and Isabella to support the ecclesiastical Electors; see CAUCHIE-MAERE, *Recueil.* 98.

[1] See RIEZLER, V., 126.

[2] *Cf.* WOLF, IV., 175, note; GINDELY, II., 399. *Cf.* *the Briefs to Mayence of October 18 and 26 and to Cologne of December 27, 1619, *Epist.*, XIV.–XV., 265, 268, 336, Papal Secret Archives. What hopes the Pope set on Maximilian are made clear in the Briefs addressed to him on November 22, December 13, and 31, 1619 (originals in *Staatsarchiv*, Munich), translated in the *Darmstädter Allg. Kirchenzeitung*, XLVII. (1868), no. 37, though the *Brief of October 30, 1619, is missing here; *Epist.* XIV.–XV., Papal Secret Archives. *Cf.* also WOLF, IV., 354, note, and HURTER, VIII., 194 (Brief to Mayence of December 21, 1619).

[3] See JORGA, III., 342 *seq.* Paul V.'s lively realization of the duty of defending Christendom against the Turks is shown in the classical expositions of Mocenigo (107 *seq.*). At the beginning of 1818 the Pope was still busily engaged on a scheme for a great league against the Turks even though he doubted the possibility of its realization; see BENTIVOGLIO, *Nunziatura*, II., 246, 263, 294, 322, and the *Brief of February 3, 1618, to Ferdinand II., *Epist.*, XV., 264, Papal Secret Archives. *Cf.* KLOPP, I., 236 *seq.*; FAGNIEZ, *Le Père Joseph et Richelieu, le projet de croisade* (1616–1625), in the *Rev. d. quest. hist.*, XLVI. (1889), 461 *seq.*; FAGNIEZ, *P. Joseph*, I., 135 *seq.*, 152 *seq.* There exist innumerable writings about Paul V.'s action with regard to the war against the Turks. Besides that of Marcello Marchesi (see MEYER, 366, note 2; it is also found in the Bibl. Nationale, Paris; see M. D'AYALA, *Bibliogr. milit.*, Torino, 1848, 39) and GIROLAMO VECCHIETTI (print. in *Beccar.*, XI., 176 *seq.*), also *Relazione del Conto Rob. Shirley Inglese, ambasc. del re di Persia a Paolo V. circa la lega contro il Turco* (1609), in *Ottob.*, 2682, p. 168 *seq.*, Vatican Library, and *Raggionamento di Tarquinio*

The emperor also prayed for help from Rome. At the beginning of October, 1619, Ferdinand dispatched Freiherr Max von Trauttmansdorff to Rome to represent to the Pope the difficulty and danger of his position. The attack of the Calvinists, the envoy explained, was directed against the Church ; they openly proclaimed that as soon as they should have defeated the Catholics in Germany, they would turn against Italy, to put an end to the papacy. For these reasons he prayed that Paul V. would grant him, for the duration of the war, a monthly subsidy of 100,000 florins instead of the 10,000 he had contributed until then and that he would also grant him a loan of 1,000,000 kronen from the treasury in the castle of St. Angelo. Trauttmansdorff was further bidden to press the Pope to induce the Italian princes to lend help and to call into being a league of all the Catholic princes of Europe. The envoy was instructed to proceed in all these questions according to the advice of Cardinal Borja, the Protector of Germany and in the eventuality of Paul V. taking up a negative attitude, he was to ask to be heard by the College of Cardinals. Lastly Trauttmansdorff was instructed to ask the Pope whether, in view of the desperate state of affairs, it would not be permissible to depart slightly from the strictness of the law and to grant to the Austrian Estates the "right of reform" in order to withdraw them from their alliance with the rebels and so to save the Catholics of that country from utter extinction.[1]

In the audience of an hour and a half which Trauttmansdorff had with the Pope on his arrival, the latter declared that as Supreme Head of the Church he could not give his assent to a concession of that kind, but that he would exercise discretion in the matter. As for raising the monthly subsidy from 10,000 to 100,000 florins, Paul V. answered that his

Pinaoro intorno agli apparati di guerra marittima e terrestre che fa il Turco contro all'Italia, Urb. 1492, p. 37 *seq.*, *ibid.*

[1] See HURTER, VIII., 130 *seq.*, who, like SCHNITZER, 155, has overlooked the fact that the whole Instruction has long been in print in HAEBERLIN and SENKENBERG in *Neuere Teutsche Reichsgeschichte,* XXIV., Halle, 1793, xlviii *seq.*

debts amounted to 18,000,000 scudi. Though the expenses for the maintenance of the court had been considerably cut down, the usual alms nevertheless demanded 120,000 scudi annually, and he had promised 200,000 to the League. The treasure in St. Angelo, according to existing laws, he could only touch in the eventuality of the Pontifical States being directly threatened, nor was it so considerable as people imagined. To bring about a union of the Catholic princes, particularly those of Spain, France and Poland in a vast League, would demand lengthy preliminary negotiations; for the rest, if the emperor requested her help, Spain would do as much as if she belonged to a league; as for France, she thought she was doing a great deal if she remained neutral, and from her it would hardly be possible to get anything more.[1]

Though Trauttmansdorff failed in his immediate purpose, he had hopes for the future. On his advice, on December 24th, 1619, Ferdinand made another appeal to the Pope and in so doing he was able to point to the renewed threat to his capital on the part of the rebels.[2] Thereupon the Pope decided, at the beginning of 1620, besides proclaiming a universal jubilee to obtain God's help "against the enemies of the Catholic faith in Germany"[3] to levy, for a period of three years, a tenth on all ecclesiastical benefices in Italy, which was calculated to yield a sum of 200,000 scudi, and to double the monthly subsidy of 10,000 scudi as from March.[4] On

[1] See HURTER, VIII., 256 *seq.*; *Hist.-polit. Blätter*, XXXI., 281 *seq.*; SCHNITZER, 155 *seq.*

[2] HURTER, VIII., 258.

[3] See **Acta consist.*, for June 13, 1620, Vatican Library. *Cf.* the *Avvisi of January 21, 1620, "Sunday, publication of the Jubilee Bull; to-day opening of the Jubilee; the Pope, accompanied by all the Cardinals and prelates, went from S. Maria degli Angeli to S. Maria Maggiore)" and February 5, 1620 ("affissa in publico l'estensione del giubileo per tutta questa settimana a quelli che non havessero potuto nelle due settimane preced."), *ibid.*

[4] See HURTER, VIII., 259. The proclamation of the tenth was not made by a Brief of July 13, 1620, as one might be led

February 7th, 1620, Paul V. informed the emperor that the nuncios in Spain and France had received appropriate instructions with regard to promoting a general league, though these were to be kept as secret as possible. Meanwhile, the Pope prayed, let the emperor apply himself with all his might to beating down the insurrection.[1]

At the very time when Paul V. was being thus pressed for help by Ferdinand II., baron Giulio Cesare Crivelli and the dean of the chapter of Augsburg, Zacharias von Furtenbach, arrived in Rome on April 11th, 1620, as envoys of Maximilian and the League, for a like purpose.[2] Although Paul V. saw in the League one of the chief means for the preservation of the Catholic religion in Germany[3] and placed great hopes on the duke of Bavaria, since he had thrown in his lot with

to think from HURTER (*loc. cit.*), but by a Bull of January 13, 1620; see *Bull.*, XII., 459 *seq.*

[1] *Brief of February 7, 1620, original in *Staatsarchiv* of Vienna. *Ibid.*, a *Brief of July 18, 1620, in which Paul V. makes excuses for his inability to send any subsidies notwithstanding the bad news from Transylvania and Hungary. On the act of obedience by Ferdinand II. through prince Paolo Savelli, who had been specially dispatched for this purpose and who made his entrance into Rome on May 1, 1620 (see ORBAAN, *Documenti*, 32 *seq.*), *cf.* besides ZWIEDINECK, in his paper on the embassies of homage of the German emperors in *Archiv f. österr. Gesch.*, LVIII., 196 *seq.*, also SCHMID, in *Hist. Jahrb.*, VI., 199 *seq.* The dates missing both here and in Zwiedineck, are gathered from the **Acta consist.* of Vatican Library. According to them the confirmation of Ferdinand's election took place on May 4 and the *obedienza* on May 5, 1620. The Bull. of confirmation is dated May 5, 1620; see *Bull.*, XII., 467 *seq.*; *ibid.*, 472 *seq.*, under date of June 4, 1620, an indult for Ferdinand *nominandi ad beneficia primo vacatura* (*primariae preces*). Paul V.'s *letter of thanks to Ferdinand II. of May 7, 1620, in the *Epist.*, XV.–XVI., 67, Papal Secret Archives.

[2] The Instruction for the envoys is dated February 20, 1620; see WOLF, IV., 353, and HURTER, VIII., 202. *Cf.* SCHNITZER, 157; RIEZLER, V., 141.

[3] See BENTIVOGLIO, *Nunziatura*, III., 256.

the emperor,[1] his financial situation, and the fact that he had just promised to double the subsidy guaranteed to Ferdinand II., made it exceedingly difficult for the Pope to listen to this new request. He therefore sought to gain time by making the grant of help dependent on the opening of hostilities.[2] In the end the representatives of the League succeeded in obtaining from the Pope a subsidy which far exceeded that promised to the emperor. This was owing to an assurance of considerable sums which the king of Spain had given to Ferdinand II. Crivelli was given 100,000 scudi, the result of the tenth imposed on twelve religious Orders of men and which the court of Vienna had confidently hoped to get. Finally the Pope gave leave to all German bishops to impose a tenth on all benefices, a tax which was expected to yield 1,500,000 florins. It was the Pope's intention that the big sums granted to the League should likewise benefit the emperor. This was realized at least indirectly in that the League exerted itself to the upmost for its own safety as well as for the cause of Ferdinand.[3]

To these considerable subsidies of the Pope [4] must also be

[1] See above, p. 360, note 2.

[2] This greatly annoyed Maximilian ; see WOLF, IV., 355 *seq.*

[3] See besides HURTER, VIII., 259, especially SCHNITZER, 157 *seq.* and *Jahrbuch des Hist. Vereins Dilligen*, XXVIII., 10. The Bull. on the taxation of the Orders of men in *Bull. Casin.*, I., 297 *seq.* The Bull on the *Impositio decimae in Germania pro religionis defensione ab omnibus eccles. uno tantum anno persolvendae*, of July 31, 1620, in *Bull.*, XII., 478 *seq.* In the anonymous dissertation **Se dalla Sede Ap$^{\underline{ca}}$ debba mandarsi prelato et qual sia più a proposito per assistere nelli conventi, compositioni, accomodomenti et speditioni militari della sacra lega cattolica di Germania* (Cod. X., VI., 30, p. 142 *seq.*, of the Lib. Casanatense, Rome), the Spaniard, Antonio Diaz, who had been nuncio extraordinary at Salzburg, is recommended for this delicate post. Concerning the League we read here : *la qual si può dirsi essere l'unico mezzo di salvare la Germania.*

[4] *Cf.* SIRI, V., 168 *seq.* HURTER's opinion is very just (VIII., 260 *seq.*) : " If we consider the sums which the Popes spent on the uninterrupted wars against the Turks ; and if we also

added the very great help which his nuncios gave in Madrid and in Paris, and that with such success that both Spain and France held out the prospect of military assistance against the insurgents.

What had Frederick V. and his friends to oppose to these forces? The most disastrous thing of all for them was the pitiable attitude of the Union, rich in words but poor in deeds; its hesitation made it so much easier for the Dutch States General and for cautious James I. of England to refuse immediate help. The republic of St. Mark also met the rebellious Bohemians' urgent requests for help with a refusal.[1] It was a no less heavy blow to them that the hope of joint support by all Protestants was dashed by the irreconcilable opposition between Calvinists and Lutherans. Satisfactory reassurances with regard to the retention of confiscated Church property and the pledge of the Lausitz won over even the Elector of Saxony, Johann Georg, to the support of the emperor. The negotiations on these questions had

bear in mind that already at the time of Sixtus V. less than 180,000 scudi flowed into the Apostolic Chamber, the grants made both to the League and to the emperor must still appear considerable, though it is not to be wondered at if they did not always flow as regularly as the needs of the recipient demanded." The sums actually paid cannot be accurately indicated owing to the discrepancies in the various accounts. According to Götz ("Die Kriegskosten Bayerns," in *Forsch. zur Gesch. Bayerns*, XII., 114) the Pope's contribution in 1620 amounted to 98,385 florins, whereas Spain only gave 57,520 florins. According to *Costaguti* (Appendix No. 14), the emperor received 228,000 scudi. According to a note in Borghese, I., 554, p. 11, the *aiuto dato al Imperatore et alla lega l'anni 1619–1620*, amounted to 156,115 scudi, to which must be added the *denari delle sei decime et quello che hanno contribuito le 11 congregationi et regolari* (Papal Secret Archives). The latter amounted to 100,000 scudi; see *Miscell. di Clemente*, XI., 213, p. 182 (*ibid.*).

[1] See v. Zwiedineck-Südenhorst, *Politik Venedigs*, I., 101 *seq.*; on the motives for Venice's attitude, see *Hist. polit. Blätter*, XCIV., 368 *seq.*

been conducted by the landgrave Louis V. of Hessen-Darmstadt who had fallen out with the Calvinist line of Kassel. During a visit to Rome, in March, 1619, the prudent conduct of Paul V. had not indeed won Louis back to the ancient faith, as many Protestants feared, but it had nevertheless freed him from the worst prejudices against the papacy.[1] Thus Frederick V. was mainly thrown upon the Calvinist grand-duke of Transylvania, Bethlen Gábor, who, in August 25th, 1620, had had himself elected rival king of Hungary, and upon the Turks and the Bohemians. In Bohemia, however, very bad conditions prevailed in every respect, especially militarily and financially, and these deteriorated still further owing to the mistakes of the personally incompetent king who was totally ignorant of the language and customs of the country. Already in December, 1619, on the advice of his court preacher Scultetus, Frederick V. had abandoned the cathedral of St. Vitus, at Prague, a sanctuary adorned with the art of two centuries, to the Calvinist iconoclasts.[2] By his subsequent measures for the establishment of the reformed confession, he incurred the odium not only of the Catholics but also that of the Utraquists and the Lutherans of the empire. The feudal aristocracy of Bohemia, which had provoked the insurrection, saw its hopes unfulfilled and grumbled at seeing the most important posts going to foreigners.[3]

Heedless of the perils threatening from outside and the anarchical conditions which had made headway in Prague itself, the pleasure-loving Palatine spent the winter in riotous living.[4] His fate was decided on the day on which the

[1] *Cf.*, in addition to K. A. MENZEL, VI., 442, a paper by BAUR on the journey of the landgrave Louis V., in *Archiv. f. hess. Gesch.*, IV., 2, Darmstadt, 1845, 19 *seq.*

[2] *Cf.* SCHLENZ, in *Mitteilungen des Vereins f. Gesch. der Deutschen in Böhmen*, LVIII. (1920), 155 *seq.*

[3] RITTER, III., 73 *seq.*, 81 *seq.*

[4] *Solstitialis rex* is the name already given him by L. PAPPUS, the *Tacitus* of the Thirty Years' War, in his *Epitome rer. Germanic.*, ed. L. Arndts., I., Vienna, 1856, 160.

shrewd duke of Bavaria succeeded in severing the Union from him. The French government rendered substantial service at this juncture. At the close of 1619, the emperor dispatched count Wradislav von Fürstenberg to France to beg for armed assistance against a danger that threatened all princes, in view of the republican tendencies of the Calvinists.[1]

At the moment, not only the fate of the House of Habsburg, but that of the ancient Church depended, in large measure, on the attitude adopted by France. In the final decision, which turned out to be in favour of the Catholic cause, the papal nuncio Bentivoglio saw a true miracle and a manifest intervention of Providence. In conjunction with the confessor of Louis XIII., the Jesuit Arnould and the Catholic party, he had done his utmost to win over the son of Henry IV. It is true that armed help such as Spain gave, was not guaranteed, but France nevertheless declared her opposition to the Bohemian pretender. Letters were written to the princely members of the Union, with a view to inducing them to leave that body, and a great embassy was dispatched to Germany to make propaganda for the cause of the emperor. The Calvinists were not prepared for a blow of this kind and from such a quarter.[2] The embassy, which was headed by the duke of Angoulême, intimidated the Union to such an extent that by an agreement with the League signed at Ulm on July 3rd, 1620, it completely broke with Bohemia. Thus was a brilliant victory won before a shot was fired and Frederick defeated even before battle was joined. With his rear thus guarded, Maximilian was able, at the end of July, to proceed against the rebels in Austria, to compel them to do homage, and from thence to set out on his march against Bohemia. The army, whose principal standard was decorated with a picture of the Blessed Virgin Mary, included among

[1] SIRI, V., 66 *seq.* *Cf. Mercure Français*, IX., 342 *seq.*

[2] SIRI, V., 86 *seq.*; GINDELY, III., 3 *seq.*; KLOPP, I., 532 *seq.*; HANOTAUX, in *Rev. d. deux Mondes*, 1902, VII., 28 *seq.* On BENTIVOGLIO's work see his *Nunziatura*, IV., 22, 60, 66, 86, 90, 134, 198, 218, 296.

other princely personages the young duke Virginio Orsini, of Rome.[1] A number of Jesuits and Capuchins and the Spanish Carmelite Dominic a Jesu Maria accompanied the army as chaplains.[2]

In the autumn of 1620 destruction threatened the rebels from three sides. Whilst the Spanish-Netherlandish army under Spinola invaded the Palatinate and the Elector of Saxony penetrated into the Lausitz, the armies of the emperor and the League advanced jointly against Bohemia. On November 8th a decisive battle was fought on the Weissenberg, West of Prague. The decision of the war council to attack the fortified positions of the Bohemians was, to a great extent, the result of the eloquence of Dominic a Jesu Maria whom everybody venerated as a Saint. Exhibiting an image of the Blessed Virgin Mary, which the Calvinists had mutilated, he spoke in burning accents in support of Maximilian's and Tilly's proposal to attack at once, promising the protection of all the Saints whose octave was being kept that day.[3] Within an hour the defeat of the rebels was complete and Frederick V. in full flight.

[1] *Cf.* *Avviso of February 12, 1620, Vatican Library.

[2] Reizler, V., 151, and *Abhandl. der. Münchner Akad.*, XXIII., 1, 105 *seq.* *Cf.* Duhr, II., 2, 302 *seq.*

[3] The influence exercised by Fr. Dominic a Jesu Maria on the council of war which Krebs, in his otherwise excellent work, *Die Schlacht am Weissen Berge*, rejects as a fable, is established as a fact by the testimony of Maximilian I. himself; see Gindely, in *Archiv f. österr. Gesch.*, LXV., 1 (1883), 137 *seq.* *Cf.* also Riezler, in *Sitzungsber. der Münchner Akad., Phil.-hist. Kl.*, 1897, 423 *seq.* On November 28, 1620, the Florentine envoy, Altoviti, reports from Vienna: "È stata una segnalata vittoria qual s'attribuisce a Dio et alla giustizia della causa come è dovere et multa parte ve n'hanno l'esortazioni d'un padre degli Scalzi di vita esemplarissima, che assiste a Baviera, il qual confortò mentre si stava in ambiguità la battaglia et assicurò la vittoria." (State Archives of Florence). Dr. Anschutz, of Munich, possesses a portrait of Fr. Dominic a Jesu Maria by Rubens; see *Münchner Jahrb. f. bild. Kunst*, XI., 58; Oldenbourg, *Rubens*, 140 *seq.*

Immediately after the battle, even before Prague had opened its gates, the handful of Catholics still remaining in the city hastened out into the camp in order to congratulate the duke of Bavaria and Buquoy and to beg them to occupy Prague and restore the old religion. "Such was their joy that some of them spent the whole of the following night in prayer." When the army entered the town, the Catholics almost fought among themselves as to who should be the first to greet the duke of Bavaria. Whereas only a short while ago the Catholic faith was regarded as the religion of the lowest classes and one that a nobleman should be ashamed to belong to, many Calvinists and Lutherans now walked about with a Breviary or a rosary in their hands, or sought safety in some convent, both for their persons and their goods. The preachers lay in hiding; they no longer dared openly to stand up for their tenets [1]; on the contrary, by abject submissiveness to the authorities, they sought to obliterate the memory of their share in the rebellion. The pastor of the church of the Tein and administrator of the "lower consistory", Dikastus, who had crowned the winter king, now declared him an enemy of the country and prayed for the emperor's victory, and these sentiments he expressed in all his sermons.[2]

Not only in Prague but elsewhere also the victory of the Weissen Berg was rightly interpreted as a victory of the old religion and a defeat of Protestantism. As a matter of fact, here there was question not merely of preserving the Bohemian crown for Ferdinand, but also of the future of the Catholic Church in the territories of the Habsburgs and in the empire.[3]

How keenly the Catholic party realized the decisive significance of the war in Bohemia was evidenced by the public prayers which had been ordered all over Germany at the opening of the campaign, and by the fervour with which the people took part in them. At Augsburg all the churches were frequented by such crowds, and the devotion

[1] CARAFA, *Comment.*, 105–6.

[2] GINDELY, *Gegenreformation*, 105.

[3] DÖBERL, I., 552.

of the worshippers was so great, that the Protestants were struck with astonishment. In the Society of Jesus several thousand Masses and many prayers were offered every week for a happy issue of the war.[1] If the whole Catholic world thus celebrated the downfall of "the Calvinist monarchy" in Bohemia,[2] joy was particularly great in Rome. Maximilian, who had contributed more than anyone else to the triumph, announced it to Paul V. by a special courier who arrived in the Eternal City on December 1st, 1620: "I myself came indeed and saw, but God conquered," wrote the noble duke.[3]

Paul V. who, on January 24th, 1620, had headed, on foot, a procession of intercession from St. Maria sopra Minerva to the German national church,[4] had followed the Bavarian duke's progress with tense interest.[5] He fully realized that the defeat of the Bohemian rebels meant "an incalculable weakening of the power of the Protestants in Germany".[6] As soon as the first news was confirmed by the arrival of Maximilian's courier, Paul hastened to his favourite church of Sta. Maria Maggiore where he prayed for a whole hour before the miraculous picture of the Cappella Paolina, giving thanks to God for so signal a victory which could not fail to prove of the utmost advantage to the Catholic religion in Germany.[7]

[1] REIFFENBERG, 514, 525.

[2] *Cf.* besides CARAFA, 110, also *Hist.-polit. Blätter*, XXXI., 829, *Script. rer. Pol.*, XVII., 33, 36, and on the celebration in Vienna, GINDELY, III., 359.

[3] See ADLZREITER, 79.

[4] SCHMIDLIN, 452.

[5] In a *Brief of September 16, 1620, to Fr. Dominic a Jesu Maria, he gave expression to his satisfaction at the conquest of Linz, *Epist.*, XV.–XVI., 200, Papal Secret Archives.

[6] This is RITTER's opinion in his review of GINDELY's "Gesch. des Dreissigjährigen Krieges," in the *Allg. Zeitung*, 1879, Beil., no. 85.

[7] **Dopo la qual nuova*, the Pope hastened to S. Maria Maggiore, *dove stette nella capella della Madonna circa un buon' hora ringratiando di vittoria così segnalata e di tante buone consequenze per*

The public thanksgiving was fixed for December 3rd. Notwithstanding the unfavourable weather the Pope again took part in the procession from the Minerva to the Anima. There the joyful psalm *Exaudiat te Dominus* was sung, prayers were recited and at the conclusion, Paul V. said the Mass of thanksgiving at the high altar, in the presence of all the Cardinals, even those being present who might have been excused either by age or infirmities, of all the prelates and officials of the court, the governor of the city, the envoys of the emperor and those of France, Venice and Savoy. At the conclusion of the ceremony the Pope granted a plenary Indulgence. At night a *feu de joie* was fired from the castle of St. Angelo and the houses of ambassadors and Cardinals were illuminated.[1]

The date of December 3rd likewise appears on the letters of congratulation addressed to Maximilian [2] and to the emperor. In these the Pope points out the importance of the victory for the spread of the Catholic faith. "Even as the rebellion of Bohemia," the Pope writes, "was at one time a source of many troubles in Germany, so will the subjugation of the Bohemians bring back the other insurgents to obedience." [3] In another letter to the emperor, dated December 19th, 1620, the Pope said he could not find words with which to express his joy.[4] At the same time, through the imperial envoy,

la religione cattolica. Avviso of December 2, 1620, Vatican Library.

[1] See *Avviso of December 5, 1620, Vatican Library. *Cf.* SCHMIDLIN, 452.

[2] *Epist.*, XV.–XVI., 259 (Papal Secret Archives), printed in ADLZREITER, *Annal.*, III., 84 *seq.*, and after a copy in DUDIK, *Drei Urkunden aus der Vallicella zu Rom*, Munich, 1857, 9 *seq.*; here also the letter of Maximilian to Cardinal Borghese, dated Prague, November 13, 1610.

[3] See SCHNITZER, 160.

[4] **Epist.*, XV.–XVI., 275. *Ibid.*, 273, also a laudatory *Brief of the same date to Buquoy for his share in the victory (Papal Secret Archives). A *report of Savelli, dated January 9, 1621, shows Paul V.'s great concern for the emperor.

Prince Savelli, he urged Ferdinand to exploit his success to the utmost, to the advantage of the Catholic religion. This aim he should keep before his eyes during the forthcoming discussions at Prague with the dukes of Bavaria and Saxony. In view of the fact that the Elector Johann Georg had shown signs of an inclination to return to the Church, Ferdinand should do his best to encourage him. If difficulties arose because of confiscated Church property, the Pope would try to find ways and means to overcome them. As regards the Palatinate, he was wholly in favour of its being bestowed on the duke of Bavaria.[1] A suggestion of Paul V. that advantage should be taken of Spinola's successes in the Palatinate, Ferdinand II. deemed inopportune and he refused to act on it,[2] so that, for the time being, the Catholic restoration was limited to the localities conquered by the Spanish General.[3]

There is an element of tragedy in the fact that Paul V., whose iron constitution had been equal, until then, to every exertion,[4] should suddenly feel his strength waning at the moment when he had reached the climax of his pontificate. Towards the end of 1620, in his sixty-ninth year, the infirmities of age made themselves felt,[5] though this did not hinder him

[1] See HURTER, IX., 157; SCHNITZER, 160–1; Cardinal Bellarmine had already written to Maximilian in September, 1620, on the subject of the Elector of Saxony's return to the Church, a task in which Fr. Dominic a Jesu Maria should assist; see *Bellarmini Epist. famil.*, Romae, 1650, 384, 386.

[2] The passage in question, in Carafa's *Instruction of April 12, 1621 (Bibl. Corsini, Rome, 38, A 11) was first published by RANKE (III.[6], App. No. 96).

[3] The Franciscans returned to Kreuznach at that time and did much for the Catholic restoration, see *Pastor Bonus*, XV., 367 *seq.*

[4] *" Il cui corso d'anni fu così felice che non hebbe mai un dolor di testa o altro male che gli facesse tralasciare funtione alcuna," says Cardinal Orsini in his report entitled *Conclave per la morte di Paolo V.*, Barb. 4676, p. 1, Vatican Library.

[5] According to NICOLETTI (*Vita d'Urbano VIII.*, I., 539, Vatican Library) Paul V. suffered from senile gangrene. To Ranke's

from carrying out the duties of his office. On January 11th, 1621, he created a number of cardinals,[1] and on the 16th he imposed the red hat on five of the new members of the Sacred College.[2]

Now, as before, the Pope paid frequent visits to the churches both within and without the city; thus he visited St. Sebastian's on January 20th, and on the 21st St. Agnes' without the walls.[3] On the occasion of the latter visit he suffered a slight stroke. He sought to allay the anxiety of his suite by holding himself erect by sheer will-power,[4] but a fresh stroke which he suffered on Sunday, the 24th, whilst saying Mass, led to his death four days later.[5] At the

assertion (II.,[6] 296), made without any proof to support it, that Paul V. had a stroke during the procession at the celebration of the battle of the Weissenberg, *Gröne* (II., 390) contradicts the evidence of the well-informed Bzovius (c. 57). Nevertheless the statement has been repeatedly made, by Schnitzer also (161). There is no confirmation in the *Avvisi and other sources. When recording the death at the Quirinal of Paul V., on January 28, 1620, the **Acta consist.* says: "Qui ante exitum superioris anni vexari morbo ceperat, cum illum videretur negligere et functionibus adesset et populo se praeberet videndum, subito veterno gravi correptus post dies quattuor interiit" (Barb. 2926, Vatican Library). On January 28, 1621, Cardinal Borghese wrote to Ferdinand II. that his uncle, the Pope, had died *doppo una breve indispositione di pochi giorni* (*Staatsarchiv*, Vienna).

[1] See Vol. XXV., p. 339.

[2] See **Acta consist.*, Vatican Library. The *Avviso of January 13, 1621, announces that the Pope had attended *alle divotioni di S. Maria Maggiore*, S. Croce in *Gerusalemme et S. Giovanni Laterano*, Vatican Library.

[3] See Bzovius, c. 57. An *Avviso of January 20, 1621, gives the information that on the Sunday Paul V. went from the Quirinal to the Vatican and from there to St. Peter's, where he held a *capella* on the feast of St. Peter's Chair, Vatican Library.

[4] See Agost. Mascardi, **Scrittura intorno all'elettione in s. pontifice del card. Ludovisio*, Cod. C. 20 of Boncompagni Archives, Rome. *Cf. Conclavi*, I., 378.

[5] The *Avviso of January 30, 1621, reports that on the evening of the 25th Paul V. "cominciò ad esser travagliato da humori

obsequies Gasparo Palloni pronounced the funeral oration.[1] The mortal remains of the Pope were temporarily laid to rest in St. Peter's.[2] A year later they were transferred, at the expense of Cardinal Scipio Borghese, to the magnificent Cappella Paolina in St. Maria Maggiore[3] where Paul V. had

soporifici o vero lethargo, onde subito li furno applicati diversi rimedii di bottoni di fuoco, vessicatorii et simili con che la natura si è alquanto rihavuta sendo subito state poste l'orationi delle 40 hore in molti luoghi pii della città ". On the 28th " su le 23 hore rese lo spirito et la sera fu portato a S. Pietro et corpo esposto al luogo dell'adoratione e già il collegio ha cominciato le solite esequie " (Vatican Library). *Cf.* also the *report of Fabrizio Aragona of January 27, 1621, Gonzaga Archives at Mantua. Aragona gives some details about the death in a *report of January 30, 1621, *ibid.* See also GATTICUS, I., 457. On Paul V.'s physicians, *cf.* HAESER, II.[3], 123.

[1] See *Avviso of February 10, 1621, Vatican Library. Gasparo Palloni was secretary of secret Briefs. In the **Elogii delli Pontifici Romani in ottava rima composte da Giacinto Gigli Romano* we read :—

" Porta il tempio di Pietro il nome in fronte
Del Quinto Paolo, e l' suo splendor dimostra
L'Esquilie e l'Quirinale e l'nobile Fonte
Che con l'antica maestà ben giostra.
La pace e la giustizia ognun' racconte
E l'abbondanza data al età nostra."

Cod. Sessor., 359, p. 126*b*, Bibl. Vittorio Emmanuele, Rome. ACCARISIUS (*Vita Gregorii*, XV., 1, 2, c. 14, says of Paul V. : " Cuius in morte haec passim ab omnibus ferebantur, Paulum V. singulari iustitia populum rexisse, opportunaque omni moderatione enascentes bellorum faces compressisse, quae causa deinde fuit, ut urbem toto sui principatus tempore frugum ubertate exhilarare potuerit " . . . (Cod. B. 7 of Boncompagni Archives, Rome).

[2] *" Sepolto in una nichia della navata incontro alla Capella Gregoriana." Avviso of February 3, 1621, Vatican Library.

[3] *Racconto della trasportatione del corpo di Paolo V. a S. Maria Maggiore con l'orazione recitata nelle sue esequie di Lelio Guidiccioni*, Roma, 1623.

erected a sepulchral monument for himself in his own lifetime.

There was universal recognition in Rome of the unwearying zeal and activity of the Borghese Pope, of his spotless moral conduct, his strict justice, his splendid care for the provisioning of Rome and the magnificent buildings with which he had enriched the City. But the long pontificate of fifteen years and eight months had none the less given rise, in the widest circles, to a desire for a change. This wish was all the stronger as the favours and the liberality of the Pope had been almost wholly limited to his own family. The whole world, says Cardinal Orsini, was weary of the amiable but empty promises of the Pope's nephew, Cardinal Borghese, and dislike for the latter had still further increased since the last promotion of Cardinals.[1] The radiance which the victory of the Weissenberg shed on the last days of Paul V. came as a compensation for the many anxieties which the situation in Germany had caused him during his long pontificate. There was nothing the Borghese Pope feared so much as the issue of an armed conflict between the Catholics and the Protestants of Germany, for since the unsatisfactory termination of his own struggle with Venice he had grown exceedingly timorous. He displayed the greatest caution and did his utmost to avoid a collision of this kind, and only reluctantly did he consent to support the emperor and the League. When the course of events compelled him to intervene, an almost miraculous concatenation of events brought about a complete change in a short time. Splendid vistas opened for the Catholic restoration which Paul V. had always systematically promoted, according as he was able, in Germany as much as in France, the Netherlands, Switzerland and Poland. His sepulchral monument was already completed, hence the most important and most pregnant event of his pontificate could no longer be recorded on it. The reliefs and inscriptions of the monument pay a just tribute to Paul V.'s labours on behalf of peace, for by

[1] See CARD. ORSINI, "Conclave per la morte di Paolo V.," in Barb. 4676, p. 2 *seq.*, Vatican Library.

the neutrality which he successfully observed between the Habsburg and the Bourbons he rendered a permanent service to Catholic interests. Very appropriately also the inscriptions praise Paul V.'s solicitude for the Church and its temporal possessions, for his share in safeguarding Hungary against the Turks and for the works of art with which he enriched eternal Rome.

CHAPTER V.

PAUL V. AS A PATRON OF THE ARTS—COMPLETION OF ST. PETER'S—THE PAULINE CHAPEL IN S. MARIA MAGGIORE—THE PALACE OF THE QUIRINAL—STREETS AND FOUNTAINS—THE BORGHESE PALACE AND VILLA—TRANSFORMATION OF THE ETERNAL CITY.

Fond of building as few of his predecessors had been, and a true Roman, Paul V. was the right man to continue, on a large and magnificent scale, the Popes' traditional patronage of the arts. "The Holy Father," so we read in an ambassador's letter of September 23rd, 1605, "meditates building-plans such as befit a prince who to the highest spiritual power unites also the temporal."[1]

Like Sixtus V., Paul V. thought before all else of the completion of St. Peter's. This gigantic work, whose dome was looked upon as one of the world's wonders, was at the very heart of all his artistic interests during the whole of his long reign.[2]

Whatever concerned the *fabbrica di San Pietro* had hitherto been dealt with by a college of prelates which Clement VIII.

[1] See the *report of FR. M. VIALARDO, dat. Rome, September 23, 1605.

[2] A pamphlet probably composed by Paul de Angelis from material in c. 42 of BZOVIUS, **Magnificentia Pauli V. Pont. Max. seu publicae utilitatis et splendoris opera a Paulo V. P.M. vel in urbe vel alibi instituta,* says: "Publica urbana opera maximo operum illo concludens quod inter orbis terrae miracula non immerito connumerandum multi censuerunt, id est d. Petri Vaticani templum, quod quanquam a solo Paulo pontifice extructum nequaquam sit, cum in eo pontifices amplius septemdecem a Julio II. usque ad Paulum V. vires pecuniasque contulerint, unius tamen Pauli iussu impensisque constructa eius templi pars cum reliquis ab omnibus retro pontificibus extructis partibus merito conferri potest." *Barb.*, 2353, Vatican Library.

had reorganized—the *Congregazione della Rev. Fabbrica de San Pietro.* Paul V. confirmed these arrangements and appointed as additional members the following Cardinals, Giovanni Evangelista Pallotta, Bernardo Giustiniani, Francesco Maria de' Monti, Pompeo Arigoni, Alfonso Visconti, Bartolomeo Cesi, Pietro Paulo Crescenzi and Jacopo Serra. On the demise of Visconti (September 19th, 1608) Maffeo Barberini took his place and when Arigoni died (April 4th, 1616) Marcello Lante succeeded him.[1] Giovanni Fontana and Carlo Maderno were retained as architects.[2] Born at Capolago, in the Canton Tessin, Maderno had come to the Eternal City before Sixtus V.'s time and had worked for a time with his uncle. In 1603, he had created the lovely façade of St. Susanna, but now tasks of the highest importance were about to be entrusted to him as to the most talented of all contemporary architects.[3]

At the beginning of Paul V.'s pontificate, there still stood untouched a considerable portion of the nave of the Constantinian basilica. It was separated from the new church by a wall put up by Paul III.[4] There likewise remained the extensive buildings situate in front of the basilica. The forecourt, flanked on the right by the house of the archpriest and on the right by the benediction loggia of three bays and the old belfry,[5] formed an oblong square which had originally

[1] See Grimaldi's *account in Barb. 2733, p. 34, Vatican Library, partly printed by EHRLE, *Veduta Maggi-Mascardi,* 10, note 4, where, however, the number of Cardinals is wrongly given as eleven. Grimaldi gives a biography of Pallotta in *Miscellanea Arm.,* 7, t. 45, p. 188 *seqq.,* Vatican Library.

[2] See ORBAAN, *Abbruch von Alt-St. Peter,* 4 *seq.,* 35. On Maderno *cf.* the details given by BERTOLOTTI, in *Bollet. d. Suizz. ital.,* VII., 109 *seq.*

[3] Opinion of WÖLFFLIN (316).

[4] Reproduction in *Grimaldi,* *Barb. 2733, p. 116, together with the entrance gate bearing the inscription, *Paulus III., P.M.,* Vatican Library.

[5] The belfry rose on the spot where now stands the colossal statue of St. Paul, by the steps of the new basilica. The metal cock which crowned the top is preserved in the sacristy of Pius VI.

been surrounded by porticoes of Corinthian columns. The lateral porticos, however, had had to make room for other buildings—those on the left for the oratory of the confraternity of the Blessed Sacrament built under Gregory XIII., and the house of the Cappella Giulia and the lower ministers of the church, and those on the right for the spacious palace of Innocent VIII.[1] In the middle of this square, at a small distance from the façade of the present basilica, stood the fountain (cantharus) erected either by Constantine or by his son Constantius, under a small dome supported by eight columns and surmounted by a colossal bronze cone which was believed to have been taken from the mausoleum of Hadrian. From this court the eye contemplated the façade of old St. Peter's, resplendent with gold and vivid colours and completely covered with mosaics which had been restored in the sixteenth century, and crowned, in the centre, by a figure of Christ enthroned and giving His blessing. To this image millions of devout pilgrims had gazed up during the centuries. Internally the five-aisled basilica, with its forest of precious columns, was adorned with a wealth of altars, shrines and monuments of Popes and other ecclesiastical and secular dignitaries of every century. The roof consisted of open woodwork. The walls of the central nave, from the architrave upwards, displayed both in colour and in mosaic, scenes from Holy Scripture and the portraits of all the Popes.

It is easy to understand Paul V.'s hesitation to lay hands on a basilica so venerable by reason of the memories of a history of more than a thousand years, and endowed with so immense a wealth of sacred shrines and precious monuments. On the other hand, the juxtaposition of two utterly heterogeneous buildings, the curious effect of which may be observed in the sketches of Marten van Heemskerk,[2] could not be tolerated for ever. To this must be added the ruinous condition, already ascertained at the time of Nicholas V.

[1] See GRISAR, *Anal.*, I., 488, 505 *seq.*, and *tav.* 11–12. Better reproductions of the design of Grimaldi-Tasselli, in PASTOR, *Rom.*, 19, and in ORBAAN, *Abbruch*, 12 *seq.*

[2] See PASTOR, *Rom.*, 21, 24; ORBAAN, *Abbruch*, 3, 29 *seq.*

and Julius V., of the fourth century basilica,[1] a condition of which Paul V. himself speaks in some of his inscriptions as a notorious fact.[2] A most trustworthy contemporary, Jacopo Grimaldi, attests that the paintings on the South wall were almost unrecognizable owing to the crust of dust which stuck to them, whilst the opposite wall was leaning inwards.[3] Elsewhere also, even in the woodwork of the open roof, many damaged places were apparent.[4] An earthquake could not have failed to turn the whole church into a heap of ruins. An alarming occurrence came as a further warning to make haste. During a severe storm, in September, 1605, a huge marble block fell from a window near the altar of the Madonna della Colonna. Mass was being said at that altar at the time so that it seemed a miracle that no one was hurt.[5] Cardinal Pallotta, the archpriest of St. Peter's, pointed to this occurrence in the consistory of September 26th, 1605, in which he reported on the dilapidated condition of the basilica, basing himself on the reports of the experts. As a sequel to a decision by the cardinalitial commission of September 17th,[6] the Pope resolved to demolish the remaining part of the old basilica. At the same time he decreed that the various monuments and the relics of the Saints should be removed and preserved with the greatest care.[7] These injunctions were no doubt prompted by the strong opposition raised by the learned historian of the Church, Cardinal Baronius, against the demolition of a building which enshrined so many sacred and inspiring monuments of the

[1] See our account, Vol. II., p. 179 *seq.*; VI., 471 *seq.*

[2] See FORCELLA, VI., 121.

[3] See MÜNTZ, *Les arts*, I., 118, also other places in ORBAAN, *Abbruch*, 2, note 3.

[4] See Avviso of March 4, 1606, in ORBAAN, *Abbruch*, 47.

[5] See Pallotta's account of the occurrence in GRIMALDI, Barb. 2733, Vatican Library.

[6] See Avviso in ORBAAN, *Abbruch*, 35. MIGNANTI (II., 53) erroneously speaks of a consistorial decision.

[7] The all too brief account of the *Acta consist.* in ORBAAN, *Abbruch*, 35.

history of the papacy.[1] To Cardinal Pallotta was allotted the task of superintending the work of demolition.[2]

Sestilio Mazucca, bishop of Alessano and Paolo Bizoni, both canons of St. Peter's, received pressing recommendations from Paul V. to watch over the monuments of the venerable sanctuary and to see to it that everything was accurately preserved for posterity by means of pictures and written accounts, especially the Lady Chapel of John VII., at the entrance to the basilica, which was entirely covered with mosaics, the ciborium with Veronica's handkerchief, the mosaics of Gregory XI. on the façade and other ancient monuments. On the occasion of the translation of the sacred bodies and relics of Saints, protocols were to be drawn up

[1] "Actum in senatu de veteris Vaticanae basilicae demolitione utque ad normam et architecturam Michaelis Angeli Bonarotae, eminentissimi quondam ingenii et egregii molitionum opificis reduceretur, sicut magno Julio placuerat omnibus assentientibus; nam necessitas exprimebatur, prout volebant Pallotta et Arigonius in gratiam Maderni tantum opus foedare ausi. Baronius acriter et religiose repugnavit, et sapientes ac pii parietum illorum miserebantur, illos esse memorantes, quos magnus Constantinus excelsissimae pietatis vel egesta humeris effossaque manu humo construxerat in honorem principis Apostolorum, quos Theodosius magnus, Honorius, Valentinianus, quos Caroli, Ludovici, Othones aliique Caesares et Summi Divorum nutantes firmarant, quos tot reges, antistites, duces praesulesque spectavissent, in queis depictae imagines quae defunctis ob veritatem testimonium exhibuerant; proclinatis capitibus spectabantur altaria illa verenda, in quibus sanctissimi viri et omni praecinio celebratissimi litarant, sanctimoniam ac religionem spirantia, illi lateres, illae columnae, illa marmora tot sanctorum vestigiis calcata, sepulchrales moles veterum Divorum ac Caesarum tumuli ac reliquiae tantae molis proruendae, in miserationem, tristitiam ac gemitum animos omnium converterant: et ea tunc basilica manibus nostris excindebatur" (*Hist. Pauli Aemilii Santorii*, 1, 14, Barb. 2580, p. 2, Vatican Library). Hence ORBAAN is mistaken when he says (*Abbruch*, 1) "that no party among the contemporaries defended the preservation of the edifice".

[2] See *Acta consist.*, *loc. cit.*

and graves were only to be opened in presence of the clergy of the basilica. The bishop of Alessano was charged to superintend everything.[1]

It must be regarded as a piece of particularly good fortune that in Jacopo Grimaldi (died January 7th, 1623) canon and keeper of the archives of the Chapter of St. Peter's, a man was found who thoroughly understood the past and who also possessed extensive technical knowledge. He made accurate drawings and sketches of the various monuments doomed to destruction.[2]

The plan of the work of demolition, as drawn up in the architect's office, probably under Maderno's direction, comprised three tasks: viz. the opening of the Popes' graves and other sepulchral monuments as well as the reliquaries, and the

[1] The **Iussio Pauli V. canonicis basilicae S. Petri vivae vocis oraculo de veteribus templi Vaticani memoriis servandis* of October 30, 1605, is textually given by GRIMALDI, Barb. 2733, p. 112*b*, Vatican Library.

[2] The notes of Grimaldi, which unfortunately have not yet been published in their entirety and which are one of the chief sources for the study of the history of the basilica of the Prince of the Apostles, have been examined by MÜNTZ, in *Bibl. de Rome*, I., 235 *seqq.*, and in *Mel. d'archéol.*, VIII., 119 *seqq.*, and by KIRSCH, in *Röm. Quartalschrift*, II., 114 *seq.* Both writers were acquainted with the following MSS. of them: (1) Archives of St. Peter's, *Cod.* G. 13; (2) Vatican Library, Barb. 2732 and 2733 (with many drawings in colour); (3) Corsini Library, Rome, Cod. 276 (copy). To this must be added a codex of Grimaldi formerly kept in Papal Secret Archives, and now in Vatican Library, *Miscell. Arm.* 7, t. 45. BONANNI already gave some of Grimaldi's notes (*Numismata templi Vatic.*, 82 *seqq.*) and after him especially MÜNTZ and ORBAAN; but, as KIRSCH remarks, *loc. cit.*, they were but little used by some of the more recent historians of the basilica. The detailed account of MIGNANTI, II., 54 *seqq.*, must surely be based on these sources though he gives no references. GRISAR (*Anal.*, I., 484 *seqq.*) was the first to draw attention to the valuable collection of drawings of old St. Peter's by Domenico Tasselli, enriched with notes by Grimaldi and executed under his direction. They are kept in the Archives of St. Peter's.

translation of their contents ; then the demolition itself, in which every precaution was to be taken against a possible catastrophe ; thirdly, the preservation of all those objects which, out of reverence, were to be housed in the crypt—the so-called Vatican Grottos—or which were to be utilized in one way or another in the new structure.[1]

As soon as the demolition had been decided upon, the work began.[2] On September 28th, Cardinal Pallotta transferred the Blessed Sacrament in solemn procession, accompanied by all the clergy of the basilica, into the new building where it was placed in the Cappella Gregoriana. Next the altar of the Apostles SS. Simon and Jude was deprived of its consecration with the ceremonies prescribed by the ritual ; the relics it had contained were translated into the new church, after which the altar was taken down. On October 11th, the tomb of Boniface VIII. was opened and on the 20th that of Boniface IV., close to the adjoining altar. The following day witnessed the taking up of the bodies of SS. Processus and Martinianus. On October 30th, Paul V. inspected the work of demolition of the altars and ordered the erection of new ones so that the number of the seven privileged altars might be preserved.[3]

On December 29th, 1605, the mortal remains of St. Gregory the Great were taken up with special solemnity, and on January 8th, 1606, they were translated into the Cappella Clementina. The same month also witnessed the demolition of the altar under which rested the bones of Leo IX., and that of the altar of the Holy Cross under which Paul I. had laid the body of St. Petronilla, in the year 757. Great pomp marked the translation of all these relics [4] ; similar solemnity was observed on January 26th, at the translation of Veronica's

[1] See ORBAAN, *Abbruch*, 8.

[2] For what follows *cf.* the careful *notes of GRIMALDI, *loc. cit.*, and the accounts and notices of the Avvisi published by ORBAAN (*Abbruch*, 33 *seq.*).

[3] See *GRIMALDI, Barb. 2733, p. 15, Vatican Library ; ORBAAN, *Documenti*, 63 *seq.* ; *cf.* BARBIER DE MONTAULT, II., 418, 423.

[4] *Cf.* KIRSCH, in *Festgabe für Schlecht*, 1917, 181 *seq.*

handkerchief, the head of St. Andrew and the holy lance. These relics were temporarily kept, for greater safety, in the last room of the Chapter archives.[1] So many graves had now been opened in the floor that it became necessary to remove the earth to the rapidly growing rubbish heap near the Porta Angelica.[2]

On February 8th, 1606, the dismantling of the roof began and on February 16th the great marble cross of the façade was taken down. Work proceeded with the utmost speed; the Pope came down in person to urge the workmen to make haste. These visits convinced him of the decay of the venerable old basilica whose collapse had been predicted for the year 1609. The work proceeded with feverish rapidity—the labourers toiled even at night, by candle light.[3]

The demolition of the walls began on March 29th; their utter dilapidation now became apparent. The cause of this condition was subsequently ascertained; the South wall and the columns that supported it, had been erected on the remains of Nero's race-course which were unable to bear indefinitely so heavy a weight.[4]

In July, 1606, a committee was appointed which also included Jacopo Grimaldi. It was charged by the cardinalitial commission with the task of seeing to the preservation of the monuments of the Popes situate in the lateral aisles and in the central nave of the basilica.[5] The grave of Innocent VIII. was opened on September 5th, after which the bones of Nicholas V., Urban VI., Innocent VII. and IX., Marcellus II. and Hadrian IV. were similarly raised and translated.[6]

[1] See ORBAAN, *Abbruch*, 54.

[2] *Ibid.*, 8.

[3] *Ibid.*, 43, 46 *seq.*

[4] See GRIMALDI, Barb. 2733, p. 205*b*–206*b*, Vatican Library; MIGNANTI, II., 69; ORBAAN, *Documenti*, 70 *seq.* *Cf.* HÜLSEN, *Il Circo di Nerone*, in the *Miscell. Ceriani, Milano*, 1910, 258 *seqq.*

[5] *Cf.* MÜNTZ, in the *Bibl. de Rome*, I., 250 *seq.*; ORBAAN, *Documenti*, 67 *seq.*, 71.

[6] See GRIMALDI, Barb. 2733, p. 178 *seqq.*, *loc. cit.*

In May, 1607, the body of Leo the Great was found. Subsequently the remains of the second, third and fourth Leo were likewise found; they were all enclosed in a magnificent marble sarcophagus. Paul V. came down on May 30th to venerate the relics of his holy predecessors.[1]

Meanwhile the discussions of the commission of Cardinals on the completion of the new building had also been concluded. They had last nearly two years.[2] This is not at all surprising, for the commission had to solve some exceedingly knotty problems, such as the joining up of the new façade with the Vatican palace and the plan of the façade and the benediction loggia, and opinions were greatly divided. Some were of opinion that the plans of Bramante and Michelangelo should be strictly adhered to, according to which the façade would be immediately connected with the new building, but others were in favour of adding a nave to the rotunda. Nearly every architect of mark whom Italy then possessed was invited to send in plans, before all others Flaminio Ponzio, Carlo Maderno and Giovanni Fontana; then Girolamo Rainaldi, Niccolò Braconio, Ottavio Turriani, all residents in Rome. Among outsiders, Domenico Fontana, of Naples, Giovanni Antonio Dosio, the painter Ludovico Cigoli of Florence, and many others were likewise consulted.[3]

During the reign of Gregory XIII., Tiberio Alfarano had counselled the erection of a nave and in that of Sixtus V., Domenico Fontana had drawn up a plan allowing for a nave divided into three aisles, its breadth equalling the width of the pillars supporting the dome, which would have produced the effect of a vestibule leading up to the rotunda. Fontana still retained Michelangelo's façade.[4] However, on the

[1] See MIGNANTI, II., 64 *seq.*; ORBAAN, *Abbruch*, 59 *seq.*; *Documenti*, 81.

[2] See GRIMALDI, in EHRLE, *Veduta Maggi-Mascardi*, 10, note 5.

[3] See *ibid.*, CIGOLI's plan for the façade published in *I disegni d. Galleria degli Uffizi*, 2 series, *Portafoglio* 1, Firenze, 1913, *tav.* 4; in reduced size in MUÑOZ, *Roma barocca*, 52.

[4] The ground plan of D. Fontana is preserved in the collection of hand drawings of the Uffizi, reproduced in BONANNI, *Historia*,

occasion of the consecration of the high altar, in 1595, under Clement VIII., the papal Master of Ceremonies, Giovanni Paolo Mucanzio, pointed out that the rotunda, as planned by Bramante and Michelangelo, departed too much from the traditional idea of a church which was supposed to represent the body of Christ on the cross and that it was ill adapted to ecclesiastical functions.[1] A further argument was also urged; it almost amounted to a sacrilege if the whole of the ground covered by the old basilica were not included in the new one.

But the opposite view also found staunch advocates. We still possess two detailed reports of Gian Paolo Maggi and Paolo Rughesi, both determined opponents of a nave. In pleading for the retention of Michelangelo's rotunda, Gian Paolo Maggi stressed above all else the fact that here the great master had conceived something so beautiful and so perfect in every respect, that any alteration would spoil, nay, destroy its artistic value.[2] Paolo Rughesi defended the retention of Michelangelo's rotunda no less warmly; the whole world admired it as something unique; the addition of a nave would cost enormous sums, probably half as much as had already been spent; it would prevent a full view of the dome and destroy the light effects. If they wished to add anything, let them create a vast forecourt which would thus include all the hallowed space covered by the old basilica. In this way space would be provided for the holding of processions

table 27, p. 103. *Cf.* Wölfflin, *Renaissance u. Barock*, 4th edit., by H. Rose, Munich, 1926, 313 *seq.*

[1] See Cerrati, *Tib. Alpharani de basil. Vatic. structura liber* 24, n. 2. On the medieval symbolism which was at that time experiencing a revival in consequence of the study of scholasticism, see Schlosser, *Materialien zur Quellenkunde*, IV., 36, and Wölfflin, *loc. cit.*, 311 *seq.*

[2] *Consideratione sopra la pianta di Giov. Paolo Maggi architetto fatta per la fabrica di S. Pietro in Vaticano et Sacro Palazzo*, Barb. 4344, p. 18 *seq.*, Vatican Library. Extracts in Ehrle, *Roma al tempo di Urbano VIII.*, Rome, 1915, 9 *seq.*

and the reading of Bulls of excommunication and other important documents.[1]

Of all the architects consulted, Carlo Maderno was the most ardent advocate of the abandonment of the plan of a Greek cross in favour of lengthening the fourth arm of the cross into a nave. Only in this way, he insisted, would the hallowed site of the old basilica be preserved from profanation and those spaces be created, the absence of which in Michelangelo's plan the cardinalitial Congregation had criticized from the beginning, namely, a choir for the canons, a sacristy, a baptistery, a spacious vestibule and a loggia for the ceremony of the papal blessing.[2]

In view of the importance of the solemn functions at which the Pope officiates as head of a Church which embraces all peoples and countries, a good solution of the problem of space by lengthening Michelangelo's rotunda into a nave, was bound to weigh decisively in the scales.[3] It was chiefly for this reason, without doubt, that not only Cardinals Pallotta, Arigoni and Cesi,[4] but the Pope himself, were all inclined to support Maderno's idea.

Paul V. refused to swerve from this decision even when it was opposed by a man of such artistic feeling as Cardinal Maffeo Barberini. Herrera's life of Urban VIII. alone gives some account of the discussions of that time, in the course of

[1] The *Consideratione* of P. Rughesi completely in CERRATI, 203 *seqq*. *Ibid*., 48, fig. 3, a plan for the lengthening of St. Peter's in keeping with the memorandum, in the Archives of the Chapter of the basilica.

[2] *Cf*. the letter of Maderno to Paul V., dated May 30, 1613, in BONANNI, *Numismata templi Vatic*., 104–5, in BOTTARI-TICOZZI, *Lett*., VI., 44, and again in ORBAAN, *Abbruch*, 125 *seq*.

[3] This is the opinion of BRINCKMANN (*Baukunst*, 1920) and WÖLFFLIN (*loc. cit*., 312 *seq*.).

[4] This appears from the *report of Paolo Emilio Santori, quoted above, p. 381, n. 1. HERRERA (**Memorie intorno la vita d'Urbano VIII*.) says: "C. Maderno era portato dalli cardinali Cesi et Arigone . . .; lo favorivano perchè serviva loro nelle fabriche," Barb. 4901, p. 49, Vatican Library.

which the Cardinal suggested that the missing choir of the canons should be put into a crypt near the Confession.[1] One can only rejoice that the Pope refused to entertain such a project.

On March 8th, 1607, in presence of the architects of St. Peter's and the Governor of Rome, the work was begun on the foundations for the extension of the basilica, under the present chapel of the Blessed Sacrament.[2] Work was pushed on so rapidly that already on May 7th, after he had said Mass in the Cappella Gregoriana, Cardinal Pallotta was able to perform the solemn laying of the foundation stone which the Pope had previously blessed at the Quirinal.[3] In the meantime, Giuseppe Bianchi had completed a model in wood of Maderno's plan which showed every detail of the scheme. On September 15th, the Pope came to St. Peter's from the Quirinal, to study the model. He was extraordinarily pleased with it and gave orders for the completion of the vestibule within six years; at the same time he supplied the sums required to meet the considerable cost of the work.[4]

It is wholly in keeping with the spirit of the baroque age that Paul V. commanded that work should begin with the façade, for this was deemed the most important part. On November 5th, 1607, work was begun on the foundations of the façade and the portico, to the joy of the pilgrims and the Romans who had begun to despair of St. Peter's ever being completed.[5] February 10th, 1608, was fixed for the laying of the first stone of the façade. The Pope blessed it after his Mass in the Quirinal and on the same day it was fixed in the foundation with appropriate ceremony.[6] Soon after, on *Laetare*

[1] See **Memorie intorno la vita d'Urbano VIII. cavate dall'orig. di Msgr. Herrera, Barb.*, p. 47*b seq.* (Vatican Library), see Appendix No. 12.

[2] See ORBAAN, *Abbruch*, 57.

[3] GRIMALDI, Barb. 2733, p. 190, Vatican Library; BONANNI, *Numismata*, 83.

[4] See ORBAAN, *loc. cit.*, 57, 63 *seq.*

[5] *Ibid.*, 65 *seq.*

[6] See GRIMALDI, in BONANNI, *loc. cit.*, 83.

Sunday (March 16th) the Pope bestowed the Golden Rose on the basilica of the Prince of the Apostles.[1]

So far no final decision had been arrived at as to whether Maderno's plan for St. Peter's should be carried out also in respect to its breadth, in consequence of the inability of the commission of Cardinals to agree; but unanimity was hoped for as soon as Cardinal Arigoni should have arrived in Rome. The decisive meeting took place on June 16th, 1608. The result was communicated to the Pope on the following day. Maderno's plan had prevailed at last.[2]

On June 15th, 1608, the first travertine block of the new façade appeared above ground; all the bells of St. Peter's were rung to hail the event. People recalled to mind that on the same day Sixtus V. had begun the completion of the dome.[3]

Demolition and new construction now intermingled more than ever. On November 13th, 1608, the graves of Pius II., Pius III., and Julius III. were opened.[4] The Pope had at first thought of transferring the great marble monuments of the two Piccolomini Popes to the new St. Peter's,[5] but eventually, in 1614, they were taken to St. Andrea della Valle.[6] At the beginning of 1609, work began on the demolition, in front of the slowly rising façade, of the great

[1] See GRIMALDI, Barb. 2733, p. 214, Vatican Library.

[2] See ORBAAN, *loc. cit.*, 67. A copper medal of Paul V. of 1609 still shows St. Peter's as a rotunda; on a small silver medal, without date, the façade of Maderno is seen with the corner tower; see D. FREY, *Bramante Studien*, 118 *seq.*

[3] See GRIMALDI, Barb. 2733, p. 215, Vatican Library.

[4] GRIMALDI, in MÜNTZ, *Les arts à la cour des Papes Innocent VIII., Alexander VI., Pius III.*, Paris, 1898, 277 *seq.*

[5] See the *Brief to Sienna of June 1, 1606, in which Paul V. says: "Senam semper valde dileximus, nam ab ea oriundi." *Epist.*, II., Papal Secret Archives, original in State Archives, Siena, *Cassa della Lupa*.

[6] CERRATI, 85. The bishop of Suana, Metello Bichi, wrote from Rome to Lelio Piccolomini, on March 27, 1610, that the Theatines had taken fresh steps to obtain the monuments of Pius II. and Pius III., *B.V.*, 8, p. 106, of Siena Library.

palace of Innocent VIII. which had housed the Rota and other administrative offices. Nearly three hundred labourers were continuously at work. Cart after cart of tufa was arriving from the quarries near Porta Portese and whole forests of wood were dragged to the site for the scaffolding. Such masses of travertine from the quarries of Tivoli were landed near St. Angelo, that the road from Santo Spirito to St. Peter's had to be repaired.[1]

In the floor of the old church the remains of Nero's racecourse and numerous graves were laid bare, among the latter the tomb of the German Pope, Gregory V., on January 15th, 1609.[2] When the summer heat set in, the workmen were protected by a huge tent. In July the construction of the portico was so far advanced that the clamps for the travertine facing could be inserted. On the twenty-fourth of that month, the Pope inspected the work. He also studied with admiration an antique sarcophagus bearing representations of the rape of Helen, which had been brought to light in the course of the excavations. Three days later, Paul V. repeated his visit in order to look at some newly discovered graves; on August 31st, the Persian envoy, who had visited the Vatican the day before, came to St. Peter's where the organ restored by Giuseppe Bianchi was played in his honour. On September 19th, the Pope again stood in admiration before the rapidly rising façade.[3]

Soon nothing remained of the old church except Sixtus IV.'s choir. On November 15th, 1609, Mario Altieri celebrated the last Mass in it. On the following day the altar was deprived of its consecration and its demolition begun. Parts of Perugino's paintings, which adorned the sanctuary, were given to Cardinals Borghese and Montalto. The magnificent bronze monument of Sixtus IV., beneath which Julius II. likewise reposed, was removed for safety to the sacristy in 1610, as well as Michelangelo's Pietà which Gregory XIII.

[1] See ORBAAN, *Abbruch*, 14 *seq*.
[2] See CERRATI, 84; ORBAAN, *Documenti*, 136.
[3] ORBAAN, *Abbruch*, 75 *seq*.

had placed in the choir of Sixtus IV.: both were subsequently destined to adorn the new basilica of St. Peter.[1]

As the demolition of the buildings which still stood in front of the new façade approached, Paul V., as at every other decisive moment, arrived on the site on July 27th, 1610. He was received by Cardinals Pallotta and Cesi and other members of the *fabbrica*. On this occasion he ordered that Giotto's mosaic, known as the *Navicella*, which Cardinal Giacomo Gaetano Stefaneschi had had executed at the end of the thirteenth century, should be taken down with every precaution from the archpriest's palace adjoining the forecourt. The Pope at the same time gave orders for the demolition of the aforesaid palace and the benediction loggia. He confirmed this order on August 30th and once more urged all concerned to speed up the construction of the façade.[2]

The columns of the benediction loggia were set aside by the Pope for the adornment of the *Acqua Paola*, but he had to pay the *fabbrica*, like everyone else who obtained fragments of the old basilica.[3]

The taking down of Giotto's famous mosaic of the *Navicella* began on October 20th; after a none too successful restoration by Matteo Provenzale it was placed near the entrance to the Vatican, in 1618.[4] October, 1610, witnessed the opening of the grave of the Emperor Otto II. and the beginning of the demolition of the belfry, the remains of which collapsed of themselves.[5]

Work on St. Peter's was pushed forward with greater ardour than ever. More than seven hundred workmen were employed day and night in filling in the foundations, piling

[1] *Ibid.*, 78 *seq.*, 82.

[2] *Ibid.*, 86, 88. *Cf.* G. CASCIOLI, *La Navicella di Giotto a S. Pietro in Vaticano*, Roma, 1916. See also VENTURI, *La Navicella*, in *L'Arte*, XXV. (1922).

[3] ORBAAN, *Abbruch*, 15, 56.

[4] See CASCIOLI, *loc. cit.*, 17. *Cf.* ZIMMERMANN, *Giotto*, I., 390 *seq.*, and MUÑOZ, "I ristauri della Navicella di Giotto," in *Bollet. d'Arte*, IV. (1925), 433 *seq.*

[5] CERRATI, 111 *seq.*; ORBAAN, *Abbruch*, 26, 92, 95.

up blocks of travertine, and demolishing the old façade. At the beginning of 1611, all that remained of the old church was a heap of stones.[1] This feverish activity went on also during the following years so that the immense building advanced with giant strides towards its completion.

About Lady-day, 1612, the mosaics of the great dome, which had been executed from the cartoons of Cesare d'Arpino, were completed amid the jubilation of the artists who had been at work on them since 1598[2] and on 29th of the same month the façade also could be considered as completed.[3] Already in May, Cardinal Cesi had given a commission for the thirteen colossal statues (Christ, John the Baptist and eleven Apostles) which were to be placed on its upper balustrade; however, this fresh adornment could only be unveiled two years later.[4] The cardinalitial commission took care to have plaster models erected on the balustrade, by way of trial, so as to make sure that they were of the right proportions. In like manner, the Congregation had submitted to it a model of the huge papal coat of arms for the façade as well as the design of the inscription which it was to bear.[5] The inscription was thus worded: In honour of the Prince of the Apostles Paul V., Sovereign Pontiff, of the Roman family

[1] ORBAAN, *loc. cit.*, 18.

[2] *A. 1612 in vigilia Annunciationis beatae Virginis absolvitur opus musivum tubi Vaticani inchoatum a 1598 magno tunc pictorum plausu et clamoribus in laetitiae signum ardui et laboriosi operis. S. Johannes Evangelista et Lucas a Io. de Vecchis a Burgo Sepulcri, S. Matthaeus et Marcus a Cesare Nebula Urbevet., Angeli in triangulis Evangelistarum a Christoph. Pomerancio, caetera omnia ipsius tubi a Iosepho Arpinate egregiis pictoribus acta sunt," says GRIMALDI, Barb. 2733, p. 246*b*, Vatican Library. *Cf.* ORBAAN, *Abbruch*, 120. The cartoons for the Apostles are in the refectory of the abbey of Monte Cassino.

[3] GRIMALDI, in ORBAAN, *loc. cit.*, 112.

[4] ORBAAN, 112 *seq.*, 132.

[5] *Ibid.*, 22. The marble for the coat of arms was taken from the Forum of Nerva; this is one of the few instances of ancient material being used for the new construction.

of Borghese, in the seventh year of his reign. (*In honorem Principis Apostolorum Paulus V. Borghesius Romanus Pont. Max. Anno Domini MDCXII Pont. VII.*)

The considerable sums of money which the Pope once more contributed,[1] showed how much he had at heart the completion of the basilica. On September 2nd, 1612, after a fresh inspection of the façade, he gave definite instructions for the erection of a belfry on either side.[2] These corner structures, designed by Maderno, were mainly intended to bring into relief the longitudinal arm, to make it stand out at least when beheld from the piazza of St. Peter's and so to eliminate, as regards the external appearance, the disturbing disproportion between the rotunda and the nave. The towers are indispensable if we are to grasp the artistic purpose of the master, for only by their means " is the grouping of the structure made clear, the silhouette enlivened, the dome artistically pushed back, the breadth attenuated, the preponderance of the attic diminished and a new artistic harmony generated ".[3]

Notwithstanding that work went on day and night [4] the

[1] Not 200,000 scudi, as indicated by the Avviso of July 7, 1612 (ORBAAN, *loc. cit.*, 111), but 100,000; see Appendix No. 13 (Papal Secret Archives). The sum of 600,000 scudi which the last prince of Bisignano had left to the Pope, was assigned by him to the *fabbrica* of St. Peter's in November, 1610; see ORBAAN, *loc. cit.*, 96. In 1608 Paul V. set aside 10,000 scudi of the Spanish Cruzada for St. Peter's (*Bull.*, XI., 557 *seq.*; *cf.* 610 *seq.*). The ever growing expenses for St. Peter's were repeatedly pointed out in the instructions given to the nuncio at Naples, Guigl. Bastoni, who was urged to find funds, as, for instance, in the letters of January 18, February 1, April 4, and July 18, 1608. MS. in *Stadtbibl.*, Stuttgart. See also POLLAK, " Akten zur Gesch. der Peterskirche," in *Jahrb. der preuss. Kunstsamml.*, XXXVI., *Beiheft* 78 *seq.*, and *Studi e docum.*, XV., 278.

[2] ORBAAN, *Abbruch*, 114.

[3] See GURLITT, *Barockstil*, 338, where there is also a view of St. Peter's with the towers planned by Maderno.

[4] This is mentioned by Grimaldi in his report, *De Fundamento campanilis Vaticani ad meridiem inchoati 1 Aug, 1618, Miscell., loc. cit.*, p. 165, Papal Secret Archives.

towers did not rise above the attics in Maderno's lifetime.[1] It was nevertheless granted to him to bring the gigantic work of the nave to completion within a relatively short time. In the summer of 1613, the structure had reached the spring of the arches of the chapels[2]; a year later, when Giovanni Fontana died,[3] the wooden framework of the vaulting already spanned the central nave. In September, 1614, at a sitting of the cardinalitial Congregation, Maderno promised to complete the whole colossal tunnel vault within a year.[4] Not only was the promise kept, but the time limit was even considerably shortened. Jacopo Grimaldi attests that the inner side of the wonderful, richly gilt tunnel vault, the caissons of which were decorated with roses, was completed by November 22nd, and the outer side by December 12th, 1614. The ringing of bells and the thunder of cannon from the castle of St. Angelo celebrated the achievement.[5] In February, 1615, a start could be made with the removal of the wall erected by Paul III., which still separated the two buildings; with it fell the last bit of old St. Peter's.[6] On Palm Sunday, April 12th, it was possible, for the first time, to behold the whole length of the greatest and most magnificent church of the Eternal City,[7] which reflects in unique fashion the

[1] In his letter to Paul V. of May 30, 1613, Maderno speaks "degli altissimi campanili de quali al presente si fanno li fondamenti" (BONANNI, *Numismata templi Vatic.*, 85); in a letter to Cardinal Barberini of June 30, 1613, he reports that the right tower "è alto sino alli primi capitelli" (POLLAK, "Künstlerbriefe," in *Jahrb. der preuss. Kunstsamml.*, XXXVI. (1913), 28). The left tower was begun in 1618; see ORBAAN, *Documenti*, 254. Accounts for work on the foundations of the South tower of the façade in POLLAK, *Akten*, 100 *seq.* *Cf.* also DE WAAL, *Campo Santo*, 156 *seq.*

[2] See letter of June 30, 1613, quoted in preceding note.

[3] See *Diario* in *Studi e documenti*, XV., 278.

[4] ORBAAN, *Abbruch*, 133–4.

[5] GRIMALDI, Barb. 2733, p. 247, Vatican Library. *Cf.* ORBAAN, *loc. cit.*, 136.

[6] See the account in POLLAK, *Akten*, 105.

[7] See GRIMALDI, in ORBAAN, *loc. cit.*, 139.

world power of the Church now renewed by the Catholic reformation. With justifiable pride the Romans gazed at the wonderful work which a Pope, whose cradle had stood in their city, had at last brought to completion. The inscription within the basilica, which records the fact, gives the year 1615 [1]; however, the work was only completely terminated in 1617, when new steps were laid down and the statues of the Princes of the Apostles dating from the time of Pius II., were re erected by their side.[2]

It needed a personality like Paul V. to call into being, within a space of ten years, such gigantic creations. But not alone the name of Paul V., but that also of Maderno is linked for all time with the most colossal building of Christendom. Yet the architect's work has been rewarded with more blame than praise.[3] However, he does not bear alone the responsibility for the departure from Michelangelo's plan; that burden is shared by the Congregation of Cardinals and by Paul V. That which decided it was the exigencies of the liturgy and ecclesiastical tradition.

After all the blame so long heaped upon Maderno's head, his work has been more justly appraised in recent times. Unprejudiced critics recognize that he solved with great ability the exceedingly difficult problem set to him.[4] It is, of course, regrettable that in consequence of the addition of the nave, the dome is not completely visible from outside,

[1] See BONANNI, *Numismata*, 86, where there is also mention of the subsequent alteration of the inscription by Urban VIII.

[2] See the inscription in FORCELLA, VI., 143.

[3] MILIZIA styled Maderno "il più gran reo di lesa architettura!"

[4] See especially GURLITT, *Barockstil*, 333 *seq.*; M. G. ZIMMERMANN, *Kunstgesch. des Barock, Rokoko und der Neuzeit*, Bielefeld, 1903, 24 *seq.*; MUÑOZ, *Roma Barocca*, 64 *seqq.*; the same, C. MADERNO, Roma, 10 *seqq.*; BRINCKMANN (*Die Baukunst des 17. und 18. Jahrhunderts*, I., Berlin, 51) says that "Maderno solved the problem of space not only as well as he could, but as well as it was possible to solve it at all." *Cf.* also RIEGL, *Barockkunst*, 136 *seq.*

except from a distance,[1] and that within the building the full majesty of the edifice is not revealed as soon as one enters. But Maderno did his best to remedy these unavoidable defects by introducing variety as well as movement into the vast structure. The piercing of the tunnel vault by great upper windows—an attempt none too happy in itself—has resulted in an illumination which greatly contributes to the effect of the interior; in conformity with the principle applied at the Gesù, the moderately illuminated anterior part of the nave is followed by a dark section which stands in sharpest contrast with the flood of radiant light which falls in streams from the dome into the central space and so redoubles the impressiveness of Michelangelo's masterpiece.

The façade comes in for most blame, and to a large extent deservedly so. Three hundred and fifty-seven feet broad and one hundred and forty feet high, it is adorned with eight magnificent columns, four pilasters, six half-pilasters of the Corinthian order, and surmounted by a balustrade. To appraise it aright it is necessary to bear in mind the belfries planned for the two corners, the absence of which causes the attics to appear excessively heavy and increases the contrast between the division into two storeys with an intermediary half-storey and the colossal masses. However, here Maderno was in a tight corner for he had to allow for a benediction loggia which Michelangelo had left out of his plan.[2]

[1] Cardinal Barberini had already made this objection to Maderno; see Maderno's letter of August 10, 1613, in POLLAK, *Künstlerbriefe*, 28 *seq.*; also HERRERA, in his *Life of Urban VIII.* (see above, p. 388, note 1), who says: "Stando il cardinale in Bologna, Carlo Maderno gli mandò la stampa grande del disegno di San Pietro, dove sopra la facciata si fa veder tutta la cuppola grande. Gli rispose che quel disegno era falsissimo, perchè da nessuna parte del piano, diceva, si può vedere tanta cuppola quanta in esso si vuole, nè anche da luoghi alti come da Montecavallo, e che egli per questo era falsario publicando un disegno falso," Barb. 4901, p. 49*b*, Vatican Library.

[2] See BERGNER, *Barockes Rom.*, 46. For a criticism of the façade also BRINCKMANN, *loc. cit.*, I., 65; ROSE, *Spätbarock*, 88, and

The portico is universally recognized as a masterpiece. It is 468 feet in length, 50 feet wide and 66 feet in height. Five entrances lead into it just as the same number of doors give access from it into the basilica. The three largest outer entrances are each adorned with four antique columns; the two columns of the central gate, of pavonazzetto and African breccia, formerly stood at the entrance to the principal nave of the old basilica. Two antique columns of pavonazzetto were likewise set apart to adorn three of the doors leading from the porch into the church. For the main entrance, the bronze doors of old St. Peter's made by Filarete, in the reign of Eugene IV., were used, though it was necessary to add to them at top and bottom. On the wall, between the doors that bear his name, Paul V. caused to be affixed three venerable inscriptions from old St. Peter's: viz. the Jubilee Bull of Boniface VIII., Charlemagne's funeral inscription for Hadrian I., and an act of donation of the year 720 for the upkeep of the lamps at the tomb of the Prince of Apostles.[1]

Owing to its imposing majesty and magnificent perspective the portico is one of the most solemn and inspiring architectural creations of modern times. It forms a worthy preparation for the interior of St. Peter's. No modern building in Rome equals it.[2]

The splendid stucco ornamentations with which the vault of the portico, like that of the nave, was decorated, according to the drawings of Giovan Battista Ricci, of Novara—dull

RIEGL, *Barockkunst*, 138 *seq.*, who points out that in this instance Maderno was faced with the most arduous problem with which modern church-building has ever been confronted. WÖLFFLIN, after enumerating all the defects of the façade, ends by saying that, when all is said, Maderno " has preserved from Michelangelo's plan all that was best, namely its vastness, that is, just as much as it was possible to save under the circumstances," 9, p. 322). See even now, MUÑOZ, *S. Pietro*, 28 *seq.*, and D. FREY, *L'architettura barocca*, Roma, 1927, 20 *seq.*

[1] *Cf.* CERRATI, 117.

[2] See EBE, *Spät-Renaissance*, I. (1886), 320; ZIMMERMANN, *loc. cit.*, 25.

gold on a white ground—show, besides arabesques and other ornamentations, the coat-of-arms of the Borghese Pope and scenes from the lives of the Apostles.[1] In the tunnel vaulting of the nave, the coat-of-arms of Paul V., made in mosaic by Marcello Provenzale, was similarly affixed.[2] The pictorial decoration of the great benediction loggia situate above the portico, which the Pope intended to entrust to Lanfranco, was not carried out in consequence of the dilatoriness of the Congregation *della Fabbrica*.[3]

In addition to the mosaics of the dome, the completion of which is due to the Borghese Pope and in which his coat-of-arms appears once more, the basilica of St. Peter also owes to him the *Confessio* and the Grottos.

There are two kinds of grottos: the *grotte vecchie*, a name which designates the crypt constructed in 1594 by Clement VIII., between the old and the new floor, and the *grotte nuove*, which consist of the crypt properly so called and already adorned by the Aldobrandini Pope, of a corridor in the shape of a horse shoe and of several other chapels. Into these underground vaults Paul V., between 1606 and 1617, transferred the most important monuments of Popes, Cardinals and Bishops, as well as various altars, ciboria, statues, mosaics and inscriptions of old St. Peter's. As early

[1] See MIGNANTI, II., 83. Illustrations of *Stucchi* of the *Portico di S. Pietro* in MUÑOZ, M. FERABOSCO, in *Vita d'Arte*, IV. (1911), 98, 99, and in RICCI, *Architettura barocca in Italia*, Bergamo, 1912, 60. P. M. FELINI (*Trattato nuovo*, ed. 1615) writes (p. 15): "La volta del restante del tempio è già fatta insieme con tutto il corpo delle cappelle da ciascun lato restandovi hora solamente da intonacare le muraglie con aggiungervi tutti gli ornamenti." *Cf.* also POLLAK, *Akten*, 106, 117. On the magnificent stucco work carried out between 1620–1, by Martino Ferrabosco in the chapels of the choir and the Blessed Sacrament, see G. BELTRAMI, in *L'Arte*, XXIX. (1926), 31, 34 *seq.*

[2] See BAGLIONE, 350; FORCELLA, VI., 141. At the time of the restoration under Pius VI., the coat of arms was replaced by that of the latter Pope.

[3] See BELLORI, II., 108.

as 1618, Francesco Maria Torrigio composed a guide for pilgrims and visitors through this underground city of the dead which contains more historic monuments than any other cemetery in the world.[1] Torrigio gives some account, unfortunately only a brief one, of excavations carried out in 1615 near the *Confessio*.[2] The entrance to the crypt, to which women were at one time only admitted on Whit Monday, was near the Colonna Santa where the altar of St. Helen stands to-day.[3]

In the case of the greater number of the pieces transferred into the grottos, their meaning and the year of their translation were fixed by means of inscription. Inscriptions drew attention to objects of special interest, as, for instance, to the polyandrium marked with the monogram of Christ, in which were collected all the bones found in the course of the excavations then in progress.[4] Unfortunately not by any means all the monuments of the old basilica were saved. Not a few pieces, some of them valuable ones, came into the churches of Rome [5] or were even sent away, for instance to Poli, Assisi, Florence and other places. Quite recently some valuable relics of old St. Peter's were discovered in the small town of Bauco (Boville Ernica) which the bishop of the place, Giovan Battista Simoncelli, had secured for the adornment of his oratory. The altar of the chapel is surmounted

[1] F. M. Torrigio, *Le sacre gotte Vaticane*, Viterbo, 1618, and since then many times reprinted in augmented editions. *Cf.* also Dionysius, *Sacrarum Vatic. Basil. Cryptarum monumenta, ed. alt. Romae 1828* (*App. auctor. St. Sarto et I. Settele*, Romae, 1840); Barbier de Montault, *Les Souterrains de St. Pierre à Rome*, Rome, 1866; Dufresne, *Les Cryptes Vaticanes*, Rome, 1902, and the charming essay of E. Steinmann, in *Pilgerfahrten in Italien*, 4, Leipzig, 1922, 320 *seq.*

[2] See De Rossi, *Inscript. christ.*, II., 1, 235 *seq.*, and Leitzmann, *Petrus und Paulus in Rom.*, Bonn, 1915, 142 *seq.*

[3] Forcella, VI., 144.

[4] *Cf.* K. M. Kaufmann, in *Katholik*, 1901, II., 322.

[5] Part of the mosaic, "The Adoration of the Magi," of the Lady chapel of John VII. (*cf.* above, p. 387) is kept in the sacristy of St. Maria in Cosmedin.

by a large mosaic medallion designed by Giotto and representing the half-bust of an angel, which was part of the *Navicella*. Other relics also of the Constantinian basilica, such as a cross of porphyry, a large bas-relief and two marble statues of the Princes of the Apostles were secured by bishop Simoncelli for the adornment of his domestic chapel.[1]

However much one must regret such a dispersion, so much has been safely bestowed in the hallowed gloom of the grottos, especially of the great monuments of the fifteenth century, even though it may be scattered and fragmentary, that these may well be styled the most splendid museum of the early Renaissance. Paul V.'s merit in connection with this museum can only be fully appraised when one considers the indifference and lack of reverence with which, under Julius II., Bramante, "in the full consciousness of his own creative genius," dealt with the monuments of antiquity.[2] It will always remain a remarkable thing that a Pope of the baroque epoch gave proof of more understanding and reverence for them than the leading lights of the Renaissance at its height, who mercilessly buried even valuable pieces in the foundations.[3] True, it is most regrettable that even under Paul V. the necessary caution and care were not brought to the task of removing the monuments from old St. Peter's into the grottos, but this

[1] See Muñoz, in *Bollet. d'arte*, V., 161 *seqq.*, VI., 239 *seqq.*, VII., 264 *seqq.*; Orbaan, *Abbruch*, 49, 61, 66; Cerrati, 20, 109; *Arte christiana*, 1916, 116 *seq.*; Lanciani, *Wanderings through ancient Roman Churches*, Boston, 1924, 106 *seq.* On the great mosaic representing Mary interceding with God on behalf of men, which had been over the Holy Door and which Paul V. presented to the Florentine Antonio Ricci (bishop of Arezzo since 1612) which he in turn gave to the church of St. Mark in Florence, see L. Ferretti, in the periodical *Roma Aeterna*, VI. (1926), 232 *seq.* The museum of the German Campo Santo also preserves relics of the old Confessio and two front pieces of sarcophagi which came to light when the floor of St. Peter's was restored. They had been simply turned round and used as paving-stones.

[2] See Steinmann, *loc. cit.*, 323. *Cf.* our data, Vol. VI, 477 *seqq.*

[3] See Escher, *Barock*, 17. *Cf. Röm. Quartalschr.*, 1911, 165.

can be explained by the fact that the protection and care of monuments are the achievement of a much later epoch.[1]

In view of the fact that the underground chapel near the tomb of the Apostles could not be opened to the general public, Paul V., for the purpose of facilitating approach to the shrine [2] resolved, in 1611, to build a *Confessio* [3] before the high altar, under the dome, which would communicate immediately with that chapel, as had been done at the Lateran and in the Sistine chapel of St. Mary Major. Martino Ferabosco and Carlo Maderno submitted plans for the scheme. The Pope chose that of Maderno in which the sunken chapel was not circular but in the shape of a horse shoe.[4]

An open balustrade of coloured marble encloses the holy spot to which one descends from the church by a double staircase of white marble. Below, the central niche (the *Confessio* properly so called) which is embellished with an ancient mosaic of Christ, is closed by a perforated bronze door adorned with scenes from the martyrdom of the Princes of the Apostles as well as their busts; behind this door there is yet another door of the same metal made under Innocent III. Above the niche, on a tablet of black marble, we read the following inscription :—

> *Sacra B. Petri Confessio a Paulo Papa V. eius servo exornata Ann. Dom. MDCXV. Pontif. XI.*

The pavement with the great papal altar forms the roof of the niche. The vault of the niche is adorned with three frescos of Giovan Battista Ricci representing the oratory of Pope Anacletus I., Pope Silvester I.'s altar of St. Peter, and Paul V. in prayer before the new *Confessio.* In the inscription, the Pope exalts the power of the intercession of the Princes

[1] Recently some of the monuments in the grottos have been transferred to the new museum of St. Peter; see *Guida del Museo di S. Pietro* (1925).

[2] See the *Avviso* in ORBAAN, *Documenti*, 184.

[3] On the name *Confessio* see BARBIER DE MONTAULT, *Œuvres*, XI., 311.

[4] See BONANNI, *Numismata templi Vatic.*, 123 *seq.*

of the Apostles, which he and his predecessors had so often experienced.[1]

On either side of the central niche are two precious alabaster columns whilst the adjoining niches are adorned with the gilt bronze statues of SS. Peter and Paul. For the pavement and the walls of the *Confessio* everything possible was done in order to give splendour to the holy spot. Wherever one looks, an abundance of precious, many-coloured marbles meets the eye ; the large coat-of-arms of the Borghese Pope shines against the sides, and the background, between the alabaster columns, shows the keys and cross of Peter. To the right and the left, iron gates admit to the new grottos, the roof of which is adorned with stucco decorations. In 1618 and 1619, Giovan Battista Ricci executed frescos on the walls depicting favours granted by St. Peter to people who had recourse to him.[2]

To the lamps which had burnt at the tomb of St. Peter from time immemorial and which still further enhance the solemnity of the spot, Paul V. added a seven-branched silver candlestick weighing seventy pounds.[3]

The cost of the decoration of the *Confessio*, of which the principal elements were only completed by Christmas, 1615, amounted to 12,000 scudi. The bronze statues of the Princes of the Apostles, the work of Ambrogio Bonvicino, were only put up on October 16th, 1616, whilst the bronze door of the niche, the work of a pupil of Sebastiano Torrigiano, was fixed on February 17th, 1617.[4]

[1] FORCELLA, VI., 142.

[2] *Cf.* besides the details given by GRIMALDI, I., Miscell. A., VII., 145, p. 162 *seq.*, Vatican Library) and TORRIGIO (*Grotte*, 23 *seqq.*), the still but little known work of D'ACHILLE, *I sepolchri dei Romani Pontefici*, Roma, 1867, 22 *seq.*, who gives a better description of the Confession than any other writer. Reproductions in COSTAGUTI, *Architettura di S. Pietro*, Roma, 1620 (new edit. 1684), *tav.* 26.

[3] See TORRIGIO, 23.

[4] *Ibid.*, 23–4. That by 1615 the decoration was practically finished appears from the inscription (*ibid.*, 24) and the *Avviso* in ORBAAN, *Documenti*, 239.

The memory of Paul V. is kept alive by yet another great church in the Eternal City. The Pope cherished a special devotion to the Mother of God. Whilst still attached to the church of St. Mary Major he had had an opportunity, day by day, to watch the progress of the sumptuous chapel of Sixtus V. As soon as he himself was raised to the supreme dignity, he resolved, as early as June 6th, 1605, to create a counterpart to the Sistine chapel in the left transept of the basilica.[1] It was to be the shrine of the greatly revered picture of the Madonna ascribed to St. Luke, which had been carried in solemn procession through the streets of Rome already in the days of St. Gregory the Great whilst the plague was raging [2]; there also he wished to prepare a tomb both for his predecessor Clement VIII. and for himself.

At the beginning of August, 1605, the Pope himself laid the first stone of the building for which a plan had been drawn up by his domestic architect, the Lombard Flaminio Ponzio.[3] As in the chapel of Sixtus V., the dome rises from a short Greek cross, but all else is on a broader and more massive scale. Here also two smaller chapels flank the entrance on either side. They are dedicated to the two heroes of the Church canonized by Paul V., Charles Borromeo and Francesca Romana. The lateral walls were to receive the two sepulchral monuments, the altar, however, was not placed in the middle but against the back wall. No less than 150,000 scudi were set apart for the church—for the proportions of the chapel are those of a church,[4] but by the autumn of 1618, twice that amount had been spent.[5] The Pope took the

[1] See the *Avviso* in ORBAAN, *loc. cit.*, 49. RIEGL's data in his edition of the *Vita* of Bernini by Baldinucci are erroneous (Vienna, 1912, p. 21).

[2] *Cf.* FR. DE CONTI FABI MONTANI, *Dell'antica immagine di Maria santiss. nella basilica Liberiana,* Roma, 1861 ; WILPERT, *Mosaiken,* II., 1134 *seq.*

[3] See *Avviso* in ORBAAN, *loc. cit.*, 57. *Cf.* BAGLIONE, 135, LAVAGNINO E MOSCHINO, *S. Maria Maggiore*, 77 *seq.*

[4] See *Avviso* in ORBAAN, 58 ; *cf.* 60, 64.

[5] *Cf* Appendix No. 13*a*, Papal Secret Archives.

greatest interest in the building. From the start he closely followed the work which was under the direction of Giovan Battista Crescenzi [1] and he assured himself of its progress by repeated visits.[2]

By 1611 the shell was finished,[3] but the internal decoration took still a long time to complete. The Pope's wish to say Mass in the chapel on Ascension Day, 1611, could not be realized.[4] Much time was taken up in executing the metal work [5] and in procuring the various kinds of precious marbles. To this end not only were the ancient monuments of Rome and its neighbourhood ransacked, but, as we learn from the account books, marble was also procured from Ravenna, from Lake Garda, and even from Sicily, Sardinia and Corsica.[6] Lucca furnished precious jasper columns.[7] Their fluting was decorated with metal. This new kind of decoration which, as the contemporaries admiringly relate, had remained unknown even to the ancients,[8] was a discovery of the Roman Pompeo Targone whom Paul V. had summoned from Flanders.[9] The Pope took so much interest in everything that on one occasion he even paid a visit to Targone's workshop. Nicolas Cordier, who carved four statues for the chapel, was likewise honoured by a visit of Paul V.[10]

On January 27th, 1613, with much solemnity, St. Luke's picture was transferred to the sumptuous altar of the new

[1] See BAGLIONE, 367.

[2] See *Avvisi*, in ORBAAN, 75, 120, 176, 180, 184, 203, 204.

[3] The inscriptions on the floor, in the lantern of the dome and on the outside of the chapel give the year 1611.

[4] See *Avviso* in ORBAAN, 183.

[5] *Cf.* the *Avviso, ibid.*, 205.

[6] See the accounts, *ibid.*, 186 note.

[7] See the *letter of thanks to Lucca, dated 1609 *XVII. Cal. Febr.*, *Epist.*, IV., 296, Papal Secret Archives. *Ibid.*, VI., 377, a *letter of thanks to the same effect to the *Princeps Castilionis*, dated 1611 *Prid. Cal. Maii.*

[8] See the *Avviso*, in ORBAAN, 204.

[9] See BAGLIONE, 330.

[10] See the *Avviso* in ORBAAN, 193, and BAGLIONE, 116.

chapel,[1] but the Pope had to wait until the feast of Our Lady's Nativity (September 8th) for the happiness of saying Mass at the new altar.[2] Even then the rich decoration around the image was not yet completed; it was only unveiled at the beginning of December, 1616.[3] A whole crowd of poets sang the praises of the new sanctuary in the most exuberant language.[4]

It is characteristic of the taste of the period that Baglione, in his *Lives of Artists*, should say that in the opinion of most people the chapel of Paul V. far surpassed that of Sixtus V.[5] No doubt in the chapel of the Borghese Pope the colour scheme is far more brilliant, the decoration richer and more precious, yet one gets the impression that the general effect suffers from an excess of good things. Above all, the high altar, executed by Pompeo Targone to a design of the Roman Girolamo Rainaldi, displays a superabundance of dazzling splendour [6] and its ornamentation in gold forms a brilliant

[1] See *Diarium* of FR. ALALEONE in ORBAAN, 12. *Cf.* SEVERANO, *Sette Chiese*, I., 710. See also the *notice of GIUSEPPE MARIA BARGI in Arch. of St. Mary Major, in Rome.

[2] ORBAAN, 13.

[3] *Avviso* of December 7, 1616, *ibid.*, 246.

[4] CIACONIUS, IV., 391, names most of these poets. *Cf.* *BORGHESE, IV., 100, Papal Secret Archives, and *Vat. 6785, p. 185*b* *seqq.*, Vatican Library.

[5] BAGLIONE, 94.

[6] See *ibid.*, 326–7, 330. Detailed descriptions both of the altar and of the whole chapel have been given by the following: BRUNELLI, *De ampliss. aede in basil. S. Mariae Mai. aedificata*, Romae, 1613; A. VITTORELLI, *Gloriose memorie della B.V. Madre di Dio . . . nella Cappella Borghesia*, Roma, 1616, 52 *seqq.*; PAULUS DE ANGELIS, *Basil. S. Mariae Mai. de Urbe descriptio et delineatio*, Romae, 1621; GERARDI, *La Basilica Liberiana*, Roma, 1839; SEVERANO, I., 701 *seq.*; PANCIROLI, *Tesori nascosti* (1615), 254 *seqq.*; L. PORTELLI, *Descrizione della Borghesiana Cappella*, Roma, 1849; FELLI, *Guida alla Cappella Borghese in S. Maria Maggiore*, Roma, 1893; TACCONE GALLUCCI, *S. Maria Maggiore*, Roma, 1911, 123; LAVAGNINO E MOSCHINI, *loc. cit.*, *Evelyn's Diary* (p. 103) describes the Capella Borghese as beyond all imagination glorious and beyond description.

contrast to the background of brown marble. Plinths of green Sicilian marble, covered with precious agate, support four mighty jasper columns of the colour of blood with ledges in their fluting and composite capitals of gilt bronze. Between the pillars the image of the Madonna, supported by five angels and surmounted by a dove, the symbol of the Holy Ghost, is seen in a small niche set with amethysts and other precious stones, against a background of lapis lazuli. The niche is generally kept closed. Both this decoration as well as the two large and three small angels on the pinnacle are of gilt bronze; they were cast by the Roman Domenico Ferrerio to the design of Camillo Mariani of Vicenza.[1] The same workshop was responsible for the bronze relief of the pinnacle, designed by Stefano Maderno,[2] representing the miracle of the snow to which legend attributes the origin of the basilica.[3]

The niches by the two sides of the altar were filled with large marble statues; on the right that of St. John the Evangelist, by Camillo Mariani, on the left that of St. Joseph, by Ambrogio Bonvicino.[4] Along the lateral walls rise the huge marble monuments of Clement VIII. and Paul V. They are so exactly copied from those in the Sistine chapel that here Clement VIII. is seated just as Pius V. is seated there, whilst the attitude of Paul V. reproduces that of the kneeling Sixtus V. Both statues were erected in December, 1611.[5]

The reliefs of these two mural sepulchres refer to the achievements of the dead men. The upper part of Clement VIII.'s monument represents the conclusion of peace between France and Spain; it is the work of Ippolito Buzzi; also the canonization of SS. Raymond and Hyacinth,

[1] See BAGLIONE, 114.

[2] *Ibid.*, 345.

[3] Reproduction of altar in MUÑOZ, *Roma Barocca*, 58; *ibid.*, 59, the dome and p. 60, a view of the interior of the chapel. See also MAGNI, *Il barocco a Roma*, I., *tav.* 88–9.

[4] See BAGLIONE, 114, 171.

[5] See ORBAAN, *Documenti*, 195.

by Antonio Balsoldo, and, in the centre, the Pope's coronation —a work remarkable for its naturalism. It is due to the chisel of Pietro Bernini.[1] The reliefs by the side of the central niche which is occupied by the statue of Clement VIII., by Silla da Viggiù, celebrate the conquest of Ferrara and the part played in the Turkish war in Hungary by Gian Francisco Aldobrandini — the former is the work of Ambrogio Bonvicino, the latter that of Camillo Mariani.[2]

The upper part of the central relief on Paul V.'s tomb also represents his coronation, whilst the lateral reliefs recall the canonization of St. Frances of Rome and St. Charles Borromeo and the reception of some Asiatic envoys. The reliefs about the statue of the Pope perpetuate the memory of the support he gave to Rudolph II. in his war against the Turks and the construction of the citadel of Ferrara.[3]

The statues of Paul V. and Clement VIII. are both the work of Silla da Viggiù, whilst Stefano Maderno is responsible for the reliefs representing the Pope's coronation and his support of Rudolph II. The remaining reliefs are the work of Giovan Antonio Valsoldo, Cristoforo Stati, Ambrogio Bonvicino and Francesco Mochi. To these artists from upper Italy must be added the highly gifted Nicolà Cordieri (Cordier), a Lorrainer, who carved the beautiful statues for the niches near the monuments; they represent Aaron and St. Bernard near Clement VIII.'s tomb and David and St. Denis near that of Paul V.[4]

[1] See FRASCHETTI, 4–5, and especially SOBOTKA, in *L'Arte*, XII. (1909), 416 *seqq.* *Cf.* BALDINUCCI, *Bernini*, ed. RIEGL (1902), 27.

[2] The inscriptions in CIACONIUS, IV., 271. Criticism of relief in MUÑOZ, *Roma barocca*, 60.

[3] Inscriptions in CIACONIUS, IV., 387. The relief of the reception of the envoys is reproduced in MUÑOZ, *loc. cit.*, 67.

[4] Nomi de Scultori [delle statue di S. Maria Maggiore]: David, Aron, Santo Bernardo e Sto Dionisio sono opere del Franciosino [Cordier]; see BAGLIONE, 115 *seq.* San Giovanni del Vicentino [Camillo Mariani]; San Gioseppe del'Amroscino [Bonvicino]; le

It is worthy of notice that the female caryatids [1] on both monuments are draped. Here we have a proof that Paul V.'s decree of 1603, in his capacity as Cardinal Vicar, in regard to the application of the strict injunctions of the Council of Trent concerning pictorial representations in churches, was then operative. As a matter of fact the decree was published anew in 1610 and 1619.[2]

The marble decoration of the chapel, which is closed by a magnificent grate of gilt bronze,[3] was completed by paintings and gilt stucco ornamentation on the ceiling: here a pupil of Prospero Bresciani, the Milanese Ambrogio Bonvicino, Cristoforo and Francesco Stati and Prospero Ferrucei [4] have executed some noble work.[5]

The Mother of God is the theme of all the paintings; their

due statue delli Papi del Silla; l'Incoronatione della S^{tà} V^{ra} del Butio [BAGLIONE, 341]; la Canonizatione del Valsoldo; l'Imbasciaria del Braccianese [Christoforo Stati; see BAGLIONE, 162]; il Soccorso del'Imperatore del Maderno; la Fortificatione di Ferrara del'Ambroscino [BONVICINO, see BAGLIONE, 305, who mentions yet other works]; la Pace del Butio; la Canonizatione del Valsoldo; la Ricuperatione di Ferrara del'Ambroscino; la Presa di Strigonia del Mochi (BORGHESE, II., 27–8, p. 115, Papal Secret Archives). For payments see BERTOLOTTI, *Art. Lomb.*, II., 113 *seqq.*; ORBAAN, *Documenti*, 96, note, 296 *seq.*, and in *Bollet. d. Suizz. ital.*, VII., 161. See also BRINKMANN, *Barocksculptur*, II., 217 *seq.*

[1] *Cf.* SOBOTKA, *P. Bernini*, in *L'Arte*, XII. (1909), 417, and MUÑOZ, *La scultura barocca a Roma, V.: Le tombe Papali*, Milano, 1918, 6.

[2] *Editto del card. vic. gen. Millini* of August 24, 1619. *Bandi*, V., 7, p. 6, Papal Secret Archives. The Avvisi (ORBAAN, *Documenti*, 181) speak of a renewal of the decree in 1610. An unsuitable picture by Caravaggio was removed from St. Peter's and presented to Cardinal Borghese; see VENTURI, *Cat. d. Gall.*, BORGHESE, 106.

[3] Reproduction in JOZZI, *Storia di S. Maria Maggiore*, Roma, 1904, *tav.* 9–10.

[4] See RICCI, *Architettura barocca*, 67.

[5] See BAGLIONE, 171.

artistic value is very unequal.[1] Ludovico Cigoli's frescos in the dome, representing Mary's glory in heaven, are the weakest [2]; much better are the frescos of D'Arpino; the figures of the four prophets, Isaias, Jeremias, Ezechiel and Daniel, with which he adorned the pendentives of the dome, are distinguished by gravity and grandeur. The fresco in the principal lunette above the altar, which shows St. Gregory Thaumaturgus, is an able piece of work,[3] and yet, how far from the frescos of Guido Reni whom D'Arpino himself is said to have summoned to Rome as a counterpoise to the naturalistic tendency of Caravaggio! [4]

In the right-hand lunette, divided by a window, above the monument of Clement VIII., Guido Reni glorifies two miracles: at Mary's prayers an angel restores to St. John Damascene [5] his amputated right hand and St. Ildephonsus is rewarded for his defence of the Mother of God by the gift, at her hand, of a chasuble. In the left lunette, above the monument of Paul V., the gifted pupil of the Caracci perpetuates the confidence which two captains, viz. the emperor Heraclius in his struggle with the Persians, and Narses, Italy's deliverer from the Goths, placed in the protection of the Queen of heaven. The circle of the arches on both sides of the lunettes Reni likewise decorated with pictures of Fathers of the Church and Saints, as well as the

[1] The scheme of the pictures, obviously the work of theologians, among them probably Andrea Vittorelli (*cf.* his paper dedicated to Paul V., quoted on p. 405, n. 6) and Baronius (see CALENZIO, 993 *seqq.*) appears from the inscriptions given in the descriptions mentioned above, p. 405, n. 6. An Avviso of January 15, 1611 (in ORBAAN, *Documenti*, 183–4) states that Paul V. had engaged the services of D'Arpino, Baglione, Cigoli and Giov. Alberti for the decoration of the Cappella Paolina; however, there is proof of payments not only to Cigoli but likewise to G. Reni from the year 1611; see BERTOLOTTI, *Art. Bolognesi*, 141.

[2] See BAGLIONE, 154. Payment to CIGOLI, 1610, in BERTOLOTTI, *loc. cit.*, *ibid.*, also for G. RENI.

[3] See VOSS, II., 586. *Cf.* THIEME, VI., 310.

[4] *Cf.* the opinion of MANCINI, *Viaggio*, ed. Schudt, 77.

[5] Not John Chrysostom, as v. BÖHM (Reni) has it.

vaulting of the arches themselves. On the epistle side the Holy Ghost is seen, on the gospel side God the Father to whom the great founders of Orders, Francis and Dominic—both magnificent figures and full of expression—offer supplication.[1]

Though they are not seen in a good light, Guido Reni's frescos—which well deserved to be celebrated in a poem by Maffeo Barberini, the future Urban VIII.[2]—constitute the most beautiful and valuable ornament of the Cappella Paolina, as the new sanctuary was named, after its founder, and which, like the chapel of Sixtus V., gives an idea of the great magnificence of the churches of the period of the Catholic restoration. Paul V. gave proof of true artistic understanding when he refused to be deprived of Reni's co-operation in the pictorial decoration of his chapel. The irritable master—it is related—having fallen out with the Pope's treasurer, dropped his work and returned post haste to Bologna, his native town, where, in San Domenico, he painted the half-dome of the mortuary chapel of St. Dominic, the founder of the Dominicans, and, in 1616, created a monumental work of deep religious conception in the great Pietà with the five Patron Saints of Bologna (SS. Petronius, Dominic, Francis of Assisi, Proculus and Charles Borromeo). Paul V., however, would not rest until he had succeeded in persuading the artist to come back to Rome.[3]

Besides the above-mentioned painters, Lanfranco[4] and Domenico Passignano were also employed by Paul V. at S. Maria Maggiore. Passignano adorned both the *small* sacristy of the Pauline chapel and the *great* sacristy which the Pope had newly erected—the most beautiful of all Roman sacristies[5]—with frescos from the life of Our Lady.[6]

[1] See PASSERI, 72 *seqq.* A good copy of St. Francis in MUÑOZ, *Roma barocca,* 61. [2] See *Poemata Urbani,* VIII., p. 194.

[3] See MALVASIA, *Vite,* II. (1841), 14 *seq.*; O. POLLAK, *Künstlerbriefe,* in *Jahrb. der preuss. Kunstsamml.,* XXXIV. (1913), 43.

[4] BELLORI, II., 108.

[5] G. V. IMPERIALE thus described it as early as 1609; see *Atti Ligure,* XXIX., 67.

[6] BAGLIONE, 95, 332; FELLI, *loc. cit.,* 89 *seqq.*; VOSS, II., 402. (with reproduction). *Cf.* LAVAGNINO E MOSCHINI, *loc. cit.,* 97 *seq.*

The Pope seemed unable to do enough for the glorification of the heavenly Queen. In 1613, news was spread that the magnificent column of white marble which still stood on the site of the basilica erected by Maxentius—the so-called temple of Peace—was to be erected in front of the main entrance of St. Mary Major.[1] To Carlo Maderno was entrusted the execution of a task which was far from easy, in view of the technical resources of the time.[2] Maderno followed the course already adopted by Fontana for the erection of the obelisk of Sixtus V. In October the gigantic column was laid low; in April, 1614, it was successfully re-erected in its new position.[3] The Pope crowned it with a bronze statue of the Most Blessed Virgin. The sculptor Guillaume Berthelot had been summoned from Paris for the purpose of making a model of the statue; the casting was carried out by two Romans, Domenico Ferrerio and Orazio Censore.[4]

The statue, richly gilt, was erected on July 18th, 1614.[5] The inscription affixed to the pedestal, which bears the Borghese coat-of-arms in bronze,[6] shows that Paul V.'s action was inspired by the same thought as that which had prompted Sixtus V.: a monument of paganism was to serve Christian worship; for this reason an exorcism was first pronounced over the column, as had been done on a former occasion, over the obelisks.[7]

To the munificence of Paul V. the church of Our Lady on

[1] Avviso in ORBAAN, *Documenti*, 210.

[2] BAGLIONE, 95, 308. *Cf.* BERTOLOTTI, *Art. Lomb.*, II., 213, and *Art. Suizz.*, Bellinzona, 1886, 34.

[3] See the Avvisi in ORBAAN, *loc. cit.*, 212, 217–18.

[4] BAGLIONE, 325, 338–9; BERTOLOTTI, *Art. Bologn.*, 188.

[5] See *Alaleone*, in ORBAAN, 13 (*cf.* 223). On the cost see FEA, *Miscell. filolog.*, II. (1839), 12.

[6] FORCELLA, XIII., 130–1.

[7] See the *Diarium P. Alaleonis* under date July 18, 1614, Vatican Library. RANKE (III.[6], 50) failed to understand the Pope's intention; he also wrongly asserts that "at that time the basilica of Maxentius was still in a fair state of preservation"; see HOFLER, in the *Annali di scienze relig.*, VI. (1838), 413.

the Esquiline also owes a big new bell [1] and a house for the canons who serve it.[2] The Lady altar of the Pauline chapel was endowed with rich indulgences [3] and for the worthy discharge of the divine service, chaplaincies were erected which were to be in the gift of the Borghese family.[4] The members of that family were to find their lasting resting place in the crypt of the chapel.[5] In token of their gratitude for all the benefits lavished on the Liberian basilica, the canons erected a large bronze statue of the Pope; it is the work of Paolo San Quirico and was put up in the new sacristy in 1621.[6]

Other Roman churches also testify to the munificence and the passion for building of Paul V., in which he was emulated by his Cardinals, especially by his art-loving nephew, Scipio Borghese.

Shortly after his election, Paul V. remembered his former titular church of St. Crisogono in the Trastevere. At his prompting, Cardinal Scipio Borghese had the venerable old basilica adorned with paintings, a new high altar, and a ceiling

On a *Madrigale di Giov. Batt. Basile per la colonna drizzata nel Esquilino da Paolo V.*, see ADEMOLLO, *La bell' Adriana*, Città di Castello, 1888, 244, note 1. A poem of *Gregorius Portius Anconitanus, De Columna in Exqiliis erecta ac Deiparae Virg. a Paulo V. dicata,* in Barb. 1825, Vatican Library.

[1] See *Magnificentia Pauli V.*, Barb. 2353, *ibid.*; CIACONIUS, IV., 380; BERTOLOTTI, *Art. Bologn.*, 187.

[2] BAGLIONE, 95. An inscription mentions 1605 as the year of the construction.

[3] FORCELLA, XI., 61, 63.

[4] See *Bull.*, XII., 315 *seq.* In accordance with the decrees of the new Codex juris Canonici prince Scipio Borghese freely renounced the patronage on July 22, 1924, in favour of Pope Pius XI., a deed which the latter confirmed by a Brief of August 5, 1925. The Pope left the use of the chapel to the Chapter whilst retaining the right of ownership for the Holy See.

[5] *Cf.* AMAYDEN-BERTINI, *Storia delle famiglie Romane*, I., Roma, 1910, 174, 176.

[6] BAGLIONE, 323; ORBAAN, *Documenti*, 259; BRINCKMANN, *Barockskulptur*, II., 217. The inscription in FORCELLA, XI., 64; copy in MUÑOZ, *Roma barocca*, 68.

decorated with richly gilt carvings. The new façade, designed by Gianbattista Soria, was only completed after the Pope's death.[1] The Pope likewise gave the first impulse to the restoration of St. Gregory's on the Coelian hill. Soria was commissioned by Scipio Borghese to build the flight of steps which lead up to the church, the forecourt and the noble façade which also was only completed under Urban VIII.[2]

In the chapels east of S. Gregorio, on which Cardinal Baronius had bestowed his solicitude,[3] Scipio Borghese continued the work of the learned historian of the Church when, after his death on June 30th, 1607, he succeeded him as commendatory abbot. In the middle chapel, that of St. Andrew, the cardinal had executed in 1608 the two famous frescos in which Domenichino and Guido Reni competed for the palm.[4] To the right of the entrance, Domenichino painted the martyrdom of St. Andrew who, stripped and tied with ropes to a bench, is about to be scourged by the rough executioners; in well arranged groups, deeply moved spectators stand around the realistic scene of horror. Reni's corresponding picture on the left shows the Saint on his way to the place of execution, to which he gave a beautiful rural background. It is a more refined and deeply felt painting. Nothing could be more profoundly moving than the figure of the aged Saint, surrounded by his executioners, falling upon his knees to thank God for the grace of martyrdom as soon as he beholds on a hill-top the cross on which he is to die.[5]

[1] BAGLIONE, 97; PANCIROLI, *Tes. nasc.* (1625), 601 (SOFFITO, 1620); FORCELLA, II., 186 (Inscriptions of 1623 and 1626).

[2] BAGLIONE, 97; FORCELLA, II., 129 (Inscription of 1633); A. GIBELLI, *Mem. stor. d. chiesa dei ss. Andrea e Gregorio al clivo di Scauro*, Siena, 1888, 31 *seq.*

[3] See our data in Vol. XXIV., p. 518.

[4] FORCELLA, II., 124; ORBAAN, *Documenti*, 124; PASSERI, 15 *seqq.*, 64.

[5] See PHILIPPI, *Kunst der Nachblüte in Italien und Spanien*, Leipzig, 1900, 74; BÖHN, *G. Reni*, 56; SCHMERBER, *Ital. Malerei* (1906), 12; FRIEDLÄNDER, *N. Poussin* (1914), 18; SERRA,

Unfortunately both frescos have been very much restored. In the apse of the chapel of St. Silvia, the colouring of the graceful concert of angels over whose joyous group the heavenly Father spreads His hands from on high in a gesture of blessing, is almost completely destroyed. This glorification of Church music, instinct with the spirit and beauty of Melozzo da Forlì, was painted by Guido in 1609, also by commission of Cardinal Scipio.[1] To this Prince of the Church, possessed of so much understanding of art, are likewise due the roofs of the chapels, the beauty of which lies in their simplicity.

Not alone here, but at St. Sebastian's outside the Walls also, Scipio Borghese's name appears repeatedly. The Cardinal entrusted the restoration of this sanctuary, which had become ruinous, to Flaminio Ponzio, and, after the latter's death, to Jan van Santen. He completely modernized the church; unfortunately in the course of the work many ancient remains of great value were destroyed.[2] The same happened when, in 1620, Cardinal Millini undertook the restoration of the venerable old church of SS. Quattro Coronati, on the Coelian.[3] Cardinal Torres restored

Domenichino, 26 *seqq.*; Voss, *Malerei*, 193, 507. Sauer justly remarks in *Kraus' Kunstgesch.*, II., 2, 790: "As against parallel representations of Domenichino which are distinguished by the harmonious arrangement of the figures, their greater clarity of outline and extraordinary beauty, Reni's pictures exhibit a finer and more imposing characterization as well as a remarkable feeling for landscape motifs."

[1] Forcella, II., 124; Böhn, *G. Reni*, 13, 56; Muñoz, *loc. cit.*, 269 *seqq.*; Moschini, *S. Gregorio al Celio*, Roma, 12.

[2] Baglione, 135, 175 (*cf.* 115 on works of Cordier); Forcella, XII., 151 *seq.*; *Katholik*, 1915, fasc. 15, p. 299, 304; *Civ. Catt.*, 1919, III., 146 *seqq.* In April, 1608, Paul V. inspected the work carried out by Scipio Borghese at St. Paul's outside the walls; *cf.* Orbaan, *Documenti*, 100; *cf.* Totti, 117.

[3] Forcella, VIII., 292; Memmoli, *Vita, chiesa e reliquie dei SS. Quattro Coronati*, Roma, 1628, and *Vita del card. Millini*, Roma, 1644; Muñoz, *Il ristauro d. chiesa dei S.S. Quattro Coronati*, Roma, 1914, 52 *seq.*, 77 *seqq.*

S. Pancrazio before the Gate of the same name [1]; Cardinal Lena, S. Giorgio in Velabro,[2] and Cardinal Lancellotti, S. Simeone.[3]

In 1617, the richly gilt ceiling of S. Maria in Trastevere, the gift of Cardinal Aldobrandini, was unveiled. It had been designed by Domenichino. An oil painting by the master, in the centre of the ceiling, represents Mary's Assumption.[4] For the same Cardinal, Domenichino painted the "Communion of St. Jerome" a picture famous throughout the world which is now in the Vatican gallery. St. Ephrem gives the holy Viaticum to the dying Saint. Its virtue revives for the last time the former energy of the old man. This picture "in which by the side of human frailty the greatness of God appears growing into infinitude" adorned at one time the high altar of S. Girolamo della Carità.[5]

In St. Agnes' outside the Walls, Leo XI., when still a Cardinal, had done much for the restoration and adornment of the church. Cardinal Sfondrato continued the work with all the more zeal as in its course the relics of the titular Saint and those of St. Emerentiana, had been found. Paul V. had a large silver reliquary made, and he himself officiated when the shrine was placed beneath the high altar. Nicolas Cordier was commissioned by Sfondrato to make the statue of St. Agnes which stands above the high altar of oriental alabaster.[6]

[1] ORBAAN, *Documenti*, 79; FORCELLA, VI., 371, 383.

[2] FORCELLA, XI., 385.

[3] TOTTI, 252.

[4] BAGLIONE, 383; BELLORI, II., 48, 49; PASSERI, 21; ORBAAN, *loc. cit.*, 252; SCHMERBER, *Ital. Malerie*, 13; SERRA, *Domenichino*, 58; RICCI, *Baukunst*, 59; Reni's picture has been replaced by a copy.

[5] PASSERI, 16 *seq.*; ORBAAN, 227; SERRA, *loc. cit.*, 42 *seqq*; THIEME, IX., 401; VOSS, *Malerei*, 450.

[6] BAGLIONE, 97; ORBAAN, 64; CIACONIUS, IV., 384; C. CECCHETTI, *S. Agnese fuori le Mura*, 15; FORCELLA, XI., 351 *seq.*; *Magnificentia Pauli V.*, Barb. 2353, Vatican Library. *Cf.* Paul V.'s register of expenses in Appendix, n. 13a, Papal Secret Archives.

Paul V. likewise carried out restorations and embellishments in the basilica of the Lateran,[1] Sant'Angelo in Pescaria,[2] S. Marta,[3] Santi Quirico e Giulitta,[4] San Niccolo de' Lorenesi [5] and San Sisto on the Via Appia.[6] The convent of St. Magdalen, for penitents, on the Corso, was rebuilt at the Pope's expense.[7] Paul V. also contributed to the erection of the convent of Santa Susanna.[8]

Work on the great new churches went on throughout the pontificate of the Borghese Pope. Cardinal Montalto was especially keen on completing Sant Andrea della Valle on which he spent considerable sums of money. At the time of the Pope's death Maderno's magnificent dome of that church, the most beautiful after that of St. Peter's, was nearly completed.[9] In the years 1611–1614, the tribune and the high altar of Santa Maria della Pace underwent alterations and the ceiling of the tribune was adorned with

During the restoration of 1901 (see *Röm. Quartalschr.*, XVI., 58) the silver coffin, 4 feet long and nearly 1½ feet in height and breadth, was rediscovered by Mgr. Wilpert. The front and back are adorned with the rich coat-of-arms of Paul V. and the top with a crown and two crossed palms, all gilt, even the inscription.

[1] See LAUER, 639; ORBAAN, 125; the sacristy possesses a bust of Paul V. by Cordier; see BAGLIONE, 96.

[2] ORBAAN, 332.

[3] FORCELLA, VIII., 297.

[4] See PLATNER-BUNSEN, III., 2, 237; ORBAAN, 298; Inventario, 31; FORCELLA, VIII., 297.

[5] ORBAAN, 336, note.

[6] Paul V.'s coat-of-arms are on the portal and the ceiling; see ANGELI, *Chiese*, 564.

[7] BAGLIONE, 97; ORBAAN, *Documenti*, 252; FORCELLA, XII., 467. *Cf.*, in Appendix, No. 13, Register of expenses of Paul V., Papal Secret Archives.

[8] ORBAAN, 297; FORCELLA, IX., 537.

[9] ORBAAN, 107, 119, 193 *seqq.*, 216; PASSERI, 135; BONI, *S. Andrea della Valle* (1907), 10. *Cf.* REYMOND, *De Michelange à Tiepolo*, Paris, 1912, 147.

paintings by Francesco Albani.[1] Between 1616–1617, Domenichino painted his scenes from the legend of St. Cecilia for San Luigi de' Francesi.[2] In 1620, Faustolo Rughesi completed the façade of the church of the Oratorians, Santa Maria della Vallicella, to the designs of Martino Longhi.[3] In 1608, Rubens had adorned the high altar of this church with three magnificent pictures.[4]

New churches were still rising. Thus in 1605, Giovanni Guerra, of Modena, began Sant'Andrea delle Fratte.[5] The same year witnessed the consecration of the national church of the Lombards, del Santo Sudario,[6] and in 1612 the foundation stone was laid of the church of the Barnabites, San Carlo ai Catinari.[7] The plan of this perfectly homogeneous building was drawn up by Rosato Rosati[8] after motifs from Bramante's plan for St. Peter's. The interior, a Greek cross with a lofty cupola, makes a powerful impression by reason of its spaciousness. In 1612, Cardinal Paolo Emilio Sfondrato laid the first stone of the new national church of the Lombards, San Carlo al Corso,[9] the construction of which was supervised by Onorio Longhi, and, when he died (1619), by his son Martino.[10] The plan differs substantially from that of the Gesù: the wide central nave is flanked by two lateral aisles so that, in consequence, the transepts also are wider and a spacious ambulatory

[1] FORCELLA, V., 487; THIEME, I., 174.

[2] THIEME, IX., 401.

[3] GURLITT, *Barock*, 192.

[4] See ROSENBERG, in *Zeitschr. f. bild. Kunst.*, 1896, 111 *seq.*, and OLDENBOURG, in *Jahrb. der preuss. Kunstsamml.*, XXXVII. (1916), 278 *seq.*; Rubens lived in the Via della Croce; see BERTOLOTTI, *Art. Belgi*, 25; *cf. Buonarotti*, 3, series III., 34 *seq.*

[5] GURLITT, *loc. cit.*, 364.

[6] ORBAAN, 49.

[7] ORBAAN, 194, 201; PREMOLI, *Posa della prima pietra della chiesa di S. Carlo a'Catinari*, Roma, 1912.

[8] BAGLIONE, V., 331.

[9] ORBAAN, 195, 199. *Cf.* FORCELLA, V., 331.

[10] BAGLIONE, 157. *Cf.* inscription in Forcella, V., 352.

surrounds the semi-circular main choir. Paul V. contributed to the building fund. By 1614, part of the nave was completed.[1] A small church of St. Charles arose near Quattro Fontane, in 1612, in honour of the recently canonized Saint. Cardinal Bandini helped the building.[2] In 1612, San Salvatore in Cacaberis underwent alterations and was thereafter known by the name of Santa Maria del Pianto.[3] A year earlier, San Niccolò de Calcarario had undergone a similar process.[4] In 1618, the new chapel near the Monte di Pietà was opened.[5] In 1615, through the liberality of Cardinal Sfondrato, the church of St. Frances of Rome, near the Forum, received a richly gilt ceiling and a new façade, designed by Carlo Lombardo of Arezzo, the first façade in Rome to have pilasters.[6]

In 1614, the Trinitarians erected a small church, dedicated to Francesca Romana, in the Via Sistina.[7] In 1615, the people of Lucca resolved to build a church and hospital on the Lungara[8]; the church of the confraternity of Santa Maria del Suffragio arose in 1616, in the Via Giulia[9]; in 1617, Santa Maria Liberatrice, in the Forum, underwent a process of alteration and rebuilding at the hands of Onorio Longhi,[10] and San Dionisio delle Quattro Fontane was erected in 1619.[11]

Splendid chapels were likewise erected in the Pope's summer palace on the Quirinal[12] which, in view of the fact that the

[1] See B. Nogara, *S. Ambrogio e S. Carlo al Corso*, 7 *seq.*

[2] Orbaan, 203. *Cf.* Hempel, *Borromini*, Vienna, 1924, 33.

[3] Armellini, *Chiese*², 570; *La Chiesa di S. Maria del Pianto*, Roma, 1907.

[4] Armellini, *Chiese*, 493.

[5] Tamilia, *Il s. Monte di Pietà di Roma*, Roma, 1900, 104.

[6] Orbaan, 231; P. Lugano, *S. Maria Nova*, Roma (1923), text accompanying reproduction no. 3; *cf.* Brinckmann, 66.

[7] Armellini, *Chiese*, 304.

[8] Orbaan, 235.

[9] Armellini, 358.

[10] Baglione, 156; Gurlitt, *Barock*, 202.

[11] Titi, 284; Armellini, 187.

[12] There exists no monograph of the Quirinal. The account of M. de Benedetti (*I Palazzi e Ville Reali d'Italia*, I., Firenze,

Vatican was very much exposed to malaria, was more and more frequently chosen by the Pope for his residence during the hot season.[1] In May, 1605, Paul V. gave orders for the prosecution of the constructions which his predecessor had begun. At the same time he ordered the erection of a spacious chapel to enable him to carry out there, with the Cardinals, all the solemn functions, during the hot season.[2] The work was directed by the Lombard Flaminio Ponzio and, after his early death, by Carlo Maderno [3] who, since the completion of St. Peter's, had become the most famous artist of Rome. He drew up the plans for the great chapel and the new portal of the Quirinal.[4]

To gain space for the enlargement of the Quirinal palace, it became necessary to pull down the small church of San Saturnino and to acquire the adjoining summer residence of the Benedictines.[5] In course of time a small Capuchin church

1911) is inadequate. Until 1897 the main portal of the palace, beneath the balcony, was surmounted by the arms of Paul V. which were removed under pretext of repairs and replaced by those of Savoy. The inscription on the Via XX. Settembre was also destroyed (FORCELLA, XIII., 159). In the Sala Paolina the cross of Savoy has been stuck over the large coat of arms of Paul V. in the middle of the room! It was, however, impossible to remove every trace of the former owners of the palace, which was forcibly seized on October 8, 1870, by General Alf. La Marmora, for in that case it would have been necessary to destroy the magnificent ceilings on which the papal arms are everywhere the main decorative motif. Paul V.'s inscriptions in the Quirinal are found in their entirety in CIACONIUS, IV., 393.

[1] *Cf.* CELLI, 280 *seq.*, 352 *seq.*, 355 *seq.*, 361.

[2] ORBAAN, *Documenti*, 73.

[3] BAGLIONE, 95, 135, 308. On PONZIO's death, see GROSSI-GONDI, *Ville Tusc.*, 105; on his charming little house in the Via Alessandrina (No. 7) now doomed to be demolished, see ORBAAN, 207, note. *Cf.* also *Repert. f. Kunstwissenschaft*, XXXVII., 40.

[4] MUÑOZ, *Maderno*, 14.

[5] ORBAAN, 86, 94, 98; *cf.* 231; see also *Studi e docum.*, XV., 289; *Moroni*, L., 233.

and many houses had to make room for the new building.[1] The Pope often visited it and never failed to urge everyone concerned to make haste.[2] In 1609, it was said that 200,000 scudi were to be spent on the work.[3] To secure tranquillity during the summer sojourn, orders were given that work on the Quirinal should be done only in winter, and on the Vatican in summer.[4] For the laying out of a more commodious approach to the Quirinal, which had been contemplated since 1610, more houses had to be bought.[5] Medals of the years 1611 and 1612 record the extension of the palace,[6] in the great hall of which it was possible to hold a consistory, by August, 1611.[7] However, the work was only comparatively completed by 1618. The cost amounted to 364,142 scudi.[8]

The new residence on the Quirinal was worthy, in the words of a contemporary, of a sovereign whose dominion spread over the whole world.[9] The main portal, facing the piazza of the Quirinal, which, according to its inscription, was completed in 1615,[10] must certainly be attributed to Ponzio.[11] It was adorned with two columns of cipollin marble and the statues of the Apostles Peter and Paul by Guillaume Berthelot and Stefano Maderno[12]; between them stood the Madonna with

[1] ORBAAN, 139.

[2] *Ibid.*, 134, 136, 159, 180, 182, 184, 187.

[3] *Ibid.*, 132.

[4] *Ibid.*

[5] *Ibid.*, 168, 189; *cf.* 297.

[6] BONANNI, II., 509. *Cf.* inscriptions in FORCELLA, XIII., 157 *seq.*; P. M. FELINI, *Trattato nuovo di cose mem. di Roma* (1610), 218; *Hora Paolo V. attende a finire il Palazzo et corregere l'architettura ove peccava.*

[7] See *Alaleone* in ORBAAN, 10.

[8] See the register of Paul V.'s expenses in Appendix 13, Papal Secret Archives.

[9] BAGLIONE, 308.

[10] FORCELLA, XIII., 159, no. 298.

[11] BRICARELLI, in *Civ. Catt.*, 1918, II., 426.

[12] BAGLIONE, 339, 345; BERTOLOTTI, *Art. Francesi* (1886), 163; THIEME, III., 492. Reproduction in M. DE BENEDETTI.

the Child by Pompeo Ferrucei, which was subsequently used by Bernini to crown the benediction loggia built by him.[1]

The gems of the palace are the gorgeous rooms facing the Via Pia of which the one was to serve for secular, the other for religious festivities.

The Sala Paolina [2] vied with the Sala Clementina in the Vatican both in size and splendour, and like the latter it provided accommodation for the Swiss Guard. The floor is of many-coloured marbles. The richly gilt, magnificent wooden ceiling exhibits three times a huge coat-of-arms of the Borghese Pope whose heraldic animals, the eagle and the dragon, appear repeatedly as a decorative motif.[3] A painted frieze with allegorical figures and biblical scenes runs along beneath the ceiling. This richly coloured and sumptuous decoration [4] was the work of Giovanni Lanfranco,[5] Carlo Saraceni, Agostino Tassi and Orazio Gentileschi.[6] Over the great entrance door of the Cappella Paolina, Paul V. placed Taddeo Landini's marble relief which was not in a good light in the Cappella Gregoriana.[7]

The scene "Christ washing the feet of the disciples" was most appropriate in the palace of the Popes who style themselves the servants of the servants of God. The pinnacle above the relief is adorned with two angels holding the papal coat-

[1] BAGLIONE, 347; BRICARELLI, *loc. cit.*

[2] Reproduced in M. DE BENEDETTI, 25, and RICCI, *Baukunst*, 193.

[3] Reproduced in M. DE BENEDETTI, 31.

[4] *Cf.* POSSE, in *Jahrb. der preuss Kunstsamml.*, XL., 136 *seq.*

[5] Copy in M. DE BENEDETTI, 29, and VOSS, *Malerei*, 95 (*cf.* 450). Also BAGLIONE, 146 *seq.*; PASSERI, 106, 131; BELLORI, II., 107.

[6] TITI (305) only mentions A. Tassi and Gentileschi, but BAGLIONE and other sources establish the part of Lanfranco and Saraceni. In the *Mandati delle fabriche* there are payments, from August, 1611, onwards to A. Tassi, C. Saraceni and Giov. Lanfranco (State Archives, Rome). *Cf.* also BERTOLOTTI, *A. Tassi*, 27.

[7] Copy in M. DE BENEDETTI, 33.

of-arms; the one on the right is the work of Pietro Bernini, the one on the left that of Guillaume Berthelot.[1]

The Cappella Paolina, which in size and appearance resembles the Sistine in the Vatican, is justly famous[2] especially for its ceiling of gilt stucco which, according to the account books, was designed and carried out by Martino Ferabosco, between 1616–1618.[3] The magnificent work in which religious subjects (in the centre an angel holds a monstrance) alternate with the arms of Paul V., is an excellent example of the transition from the cinque-cento to pure baroque. In the corners of the vault views of Paul V.'s chief constructions are shown in gilt stucco reliefs.[4] The sanctuary was divided from the body of the building by eight columns of Pietra Santa. These rose from white marble pedestals and carried an entablature on which stood eight candelabra of gilt metal. The singers were accommodated in a special tribune.[5] On the feast of the conversion of St. Paul, January 25th, 1617, the Pope himself consecrated the new shrine of the Mother of God for whom he cherished so tender a devotion.[6] Whereas former Popes were accustomed to date the Bulls and Briefs issued from the Quirinal either as from this hill or as from " near S. Marco ", Paul V., in 1614, began

[1] BAGLIONE, 305, 339. MUÑOZ, in the *Vita d'Arte*, IV., (1909), 447; SOBOTKA, P. Bernini, in *L'Arte*, XII. (1909), 419, 422. Paul V.'s coat of arms in the centre of the ceiling was pasted over after the confiscation of the Quirinal by the Italian government and the frieze has been disfigured by the arms of the Italian towns.

[2] TOTTI, 276.

[3] MUÑOZ, " M. Ferabosco," in the *Vita d'Arte*, IV., (1909), 93 *seqq.*, 97, with excellent reproductions. *Cf.* also RICCI, *Baukunst*, 61, 62; MAGNI, *Il barocco*, II., 67; G. BELTRAMI, in *L'Arte*, 1926, 28 *seq.* The Cappella Paolina, first plundered by the French in 1798, served until 1923—it may seem incredible yet it is a fact—as a lumber-room of the royal palace!

[4] MUÑOZ, *loc. cit.*, 97.

[5] MORONI, VIII., 139.

[6] See *Alaleone* in ORBAAN, 15. The inscriptions in FORCELLA, XIII., 160 *seq.* indicate the year 1616.

to date them as from "near Saint Mary Major".[1] Each of the three great patriarchal basilicas now had its respective palace.

Since the Cappella Paolina was only meant for the greater solemnities, Paul V. had another chapel prepared, on the West side of the palace, facing the garden, which, though much smaller, was just as sumptuously decorated. This chapel of the Annunciata, erected in 1610, forms a Greek cross surmounted by a cupola.[2] The most famous artist of the time, Guido Reni, was commissioned to decorate the sacred edifice. He had already painted for the Pope "The Descent of the Holy Ghost", the "Transfiguration" and the "Ascension", and for Cardinal Scipio Borghese three scenes from the life of Samson.[3] To these he added the famous "Annunciation", which Paul V. destined for the marble altar of his private chapel.[4] In the chapel itself Guido Reni depicted, on the arc of triumph, God the Father surrounded by angels; in the cupola, the Assumption of the most holy Virgin, in the corners, Moses, David, Solomon, and Daniel; in the lunettes, scenes from the life of Our Lady, in a genre-like manner, and on the arches, on the inner side of the pilasters, the ancestors of Mary. Besides Guido Reni, Francesco Albani also worked in the chapel; his best known picture is "Mary's presentation in the Temple".[5]

For the Cardinals and prelates living at the palace, Paul V. erected the Cappella del Presepio which was also richly decorated with stucco and frescos. The altar piece showed the adoration of the shepherds; it was flanked by a representation

[1] See Moroni, L., 234.

[2] See the inscription in Forcella, XIII., 158.

[3] Passeri, 69 *seqq.* *Cf.* Bertolotti, *Art. Bologn.*, 140.

[4] Reproduction in M. de Benedetti, 38.

[5] See Titi, 310 and 481, and Sobotka, *G. Reni*, in the periodical *Daheim*, 1913. Final payment to G. Reni in 1612, for the paintings in the Cappella di Monte Cavallo, in Bertolotti, *Art. Bologn.*, 142. *Cf.* M. de Benedetti, 40. Three distichs "de picturis Guidonis Rheni in aedibus Quirinalibus card. Burghesii," in Vat. 6967, p. 215, Vatican Library.

of the slaughter of the Innocents and the adoration of the Magi. The dome was adorned with angels in glory and the lunettes with the four evangelists.[1] Yet another chapel was fitted up beneath the Pauline chapel[2]; it was no doubt here that Baldassare Croce executed the frescos mentioned by Baglione.[3] Other painters, such as Pasquale Cati and Antonio Caracci, were also employed in decoration work in the various rooms of the palace.[4]

Paul V. paid particular attention to the garden of the Quirinal for which Cement VIII. had already done much but which owes to him its finished beauty and its rounding off as a complete whole.[5] An engraving by Giovanni Maggi, of 1612, gives a vivid picture of the state of this place of recreation at that time, with its fountains, water jets, flower beds, orange trees and three small groves in the part facing the Via Pia.[6] Paul V., who took special delight in the palace, derived no less pleasure from the garden,[7] from which the visitor enjoys one of the most magnificent views of Rome.

Several poets vied with one another in exalting all that the Borghese Pope had accomplished on the Quirinal Hill.[8] It

[1] MORONI, IX., 161.

[2] *Ibid.*

[3] BAGLIONE, 299, and TITI, 311.

[4] BAGLIONE, 113, 151. *Cf.* VENUTI, *Roma moderna*, Rome, 1767, 234.

[5] See Avviso, in ORBAAN, *Documenti*, 146.

[6] See L. DAMI, "Il giardino del Quirinale," in *Bollet. d'arte*, 1919, 113 *seqq.* (with copy of plan). *Cf.* MORONI, L., 234; A. KAUFMANN, *Der Gartenbau im Mittelalter*, Berlin, 1892, 55; HÜLSEN, *Antikengarten*, Heidelberg, 1917, VIII., 90; GUIDI, *Fontane*, 30; L. DAMI, *Il giardino Italiano*, Milano, 1924, 41; COLASANTI, *Fontane*, 181.

[7] See Avviso of June 26, 1610, in Staatsarchiv, Vienna.

[8] See the poem, *Mons Quirinalis Nicolai Tassi*," dedicated to Paul V., in Barb. 1951, Vatican Library. *Cf. Horti Quirinales Pontificii* by ALEX. DONATI, S.J., in *Parnassus Soc. Jesu*, I., Francofurti, 1654, 152 *seqq.*, and the poem *De colle Quirinali*, in BORGHESE, II., 27–8, p. 68, Papal Secret Archives. An epigram by Silos in FEA, *Notizie sui conclavi*, 71.

was thought that here the famous Villa Medici was left far behind.[1] The extensions of the Quirinal destined to accommodate the Court were chiefly towards the old city.[2] Hence it was there also that the new building of the Dataria arose in 1611. Its construction was necessitated by the demolition of the palace of Pope Innocent VIII.[3]

In the Vatican, Paul V. also carried out several works of restoration and embellishment, in particular the frieze in the hall of consistories was beautifully decorated with landscapes.[4] Part of the old palace of Innocent VIII., facing St. Peter's, still remained, together with its entrance gate. But in view of the fact that this remainder as it were crushed the new façade of St. Peter's, and was not in harmony with the adjoining palace, Paul V., in 1617 [5] reduced the entrance and eliminated the irregularity by the construction of a corridor destined for the Swiss Guard, the external wall of which was adorned with a fountain and the mosaic of the Navicella.[6] The so-called *Porta di Bronzo* with its lovely marble columns, by which one enters the Vatican to this day, represents the last remnant of the palace of Innocent VIII. Paul V.'s additions, his coat-of-arms and the inscription,[7]

[1] Thus G. V. Imperiale, 1609; see *Atti Ligure*, XXIX., 63.

[2] See the inscriptions in *Magnificentia Pauli V., loc. cit.*, Vatican Library.

[3] Baglione, 95. The inscription in Moroni, XXIX., 112. *Cf.* Ehrle, *Veduta Maggi-Mascardi*, 12. The Rota and the Camera Apostolica which had likewise been housed in the palace of Innocent VIII. were transferred by Paul V. into the new Vatican Palace.

[4] See Bzovius, c. 42; Chattard, II., 167; Costaguti, in Appendix 14, in Costaguti Archives, Rome. To this day numerous coats-of-arms and inscriptions bear witness to the work of Paul V.; see Ciaconius, IV., 393 *seq.*; Forcella, VI., 123 *seqq.* Over the death chamber of Leo XIII. one reads: "Paulus P.M.V." and a frieze painted *al fresco* is also to be seen in the ante-room of the Secretary of State on the first floor.

[5] Orbaan, *Documenti*, 25 *seq.*

[6] Totti, 19; Ehrle, *Veduta Maggi-Mascardi* (1615), 15.

[7] Forcella, VI., 146.

have disappeared, but there still remains, in the centre, the image of the Mother of God with the two Princes of the Apostles which had been executed in mosaic to a design of Giuseppe Cesare d'Arpino.[1] To this day the bronze door shows the Borghese coat-of-arms. However, a tower-like structure, with a clock and a graceful, open belfry surmounted by a cross, at one time erected by Paul V., were removed at a later period.[2] The whole scheme was carried out between 1616–1617, after the plans of Martino Ferabosco, assisted by Giovanni Vasanzio.[3] The Vatican was given another monumental entrance behind St. Peter's [4]; it is known to all Rome pilgrims as the present day entrance to the archives, the library and the museum.

New offices were prepared in the Vatican for the Apostolic Secretariate.[5] The rooms of the Pope and those of his nephews were embellished with paintings among which those by Guido Reni were the most admired.[6]

Two new rooms were added to the Vatican library. The Pope had the adjoining corridors embellished with decorative paintings, whilst the pictures of his buildings and other important events of his reign, were to be seen in the lunettes.[7] Additions to the library in the form of valuable manuscripts and the assignment of new revenues are here perpetuated by means of inscriptions.[8]

A newly constructed staircase enabled the Pope freely to

[1] BERTOLOTTI, *Art. subalp.*, 200 *seq.*

[2] See reproduction in EHRLE, *loc. cit.*, 14.

[3] BAGLIONE, 96, 176 ; G. B. COSTAGUTI, *Architettura di S. Pietro*, Roma, 1620 ; *tav.* 12 and 30 ; EGGER, *Rom. Veduten*, I., 26–7 ; ID., *Architekt. Handzeichnungen*, table 21–3 ; MUÑOZ, in the *Vita d'Arte*, IV. (1909), 86 ; VOSS, in *Jahrb. der preuss. Kunstsamml.*, XLIII., 2 *seq.*

[4] INVENTARIO, 313.

[5] FORCELLA, VI., 125.

[6] See TAJA, 95 *seqq.*, 279 *seqq.*

[7] These representations, which TAJA (456 *seqq.*) describes in detail, have not all been preserved ; *cf.* FORCELLA, VI., 127 *seq.*

[8] FORCELLA, VI., 124 ; BARBIER DE MONTAULT, II., 181 *seq.*

enter the Vatican gardens.[1] By his order Carlo Maderno built there three magnificent fountains: the small *Fontana degli Specchi*, surrounded by water jets, and the great *Fontana delle Torri*, so called because it is flanked by two towers, and lastly the extraordinarily picturesque *Fontana dello Scoglio* (the cliff fountain), which consists of three rocky caves built round a semi-circular basin and surmounted by an eagle.[2] The spectacle of the water tumbling all over the piled up rockery is described by Bzovius as unique.[3] In 1609, the court of the Belvedere was also adorned with a large fountain for which use was made of an enormous basin which Julius II. had removed from the baths of Titus.[4] Other fountains besides these were erected in the Vatican.[5] Paul V. also commissioned Maderno to restore the graceful fountain near Bramante's steps, called *La Galera*, because the basin carried a ship dressed all over.[6] In September 1611, the Pope purposely came from the Quirinal to the Vatican to judge for himself of the impression created by the waters of the fountain in the court of the Belvedere which had been carried thither by the new conduit of the *Acqua Paola*.[7]

Acqua Paola was the name given in honour of its restorer to the ancient aqueduct of the emperor Trajan which carried the water collected near the lake of Bracciano as far as the Trastevere. The *Acqua Trajana* had become utterly

[1] EHRLE, *Veduta Maggi-Mascardi*, 16, 17, 19.

[2] BONANNI, *Numismata*, 174 *seq*. The inscription in FORCELLA, VI., 126. FALDA, *Giardini*, *tav*. 3 and 4; FORCELLA, VI., 125; GUIDI, *Fontane*, 34 and *tav*. VIII. *Cf*. BARBIER DE MONTAULT, II., 85; WÖLFFLIN, *Renaissance u. Barock*, 174 *seq*.; L. DAMI, *Il giardino italiano*, 37; COLASANTI, *Fontane*, 185, 188.

[3] BZOVIUS, c. 42.

[4] FALDA, *Fontane*, I. (1669), 4 *seq*. The inscription in FORCELLA, VI., 126. *Cf*. STEINMANN, *Sixtin. Kapelle*, II., 56, note 2. EHRLE, *loc. cit.*, 18; COLASANTI, *Fontane*, 180.

[5] BAGLIONE, 96, 176; GUIDI, 34, 40. *Cf*. FORCELLA, VI., 189; EHRLE, 16, 17.

[6] MUÑOZ, *Maderno*, 14; COLASANTI, *Fontane*, 183.

[7] ORBAAN. *Documenti*, 193.

dilapidated. As early as November, 1605, Paul V. conceived the project of repairing it,[1] though work only began in 1607,[2] under the supervision of two eminent architects, Giovanni Fontana and Pompeo Targone.[3] In August, 1608, the Pope bought the springs which were the property of Virginio Orsini, duke of Bracciano.[4] It soon became evident that the restoration would demand sums far larger than those the experts had foreseen, for most of the ancient arches could not be put to any use.[5]

Since here there was question of a work of public utility, the Pope was justified in demanding the co-operation of the Roman municipality[6]; he was, nevertheless, obliged to contribute 400,000 scudi of his own,[7] which were only

[1] *Ibid.*, 65.

[2] *Ibid.*, 80 *seqq.* *Cf.* **Editti*, V., 51, p. 47: "Editto sopra li appalti de lavori da farsi per la condotta dell'acque di Bracciano a Roma," date February 15, 1608; p. 48: "Prorogatione dell'offerte alli lavori di Bracciano," February 29, 1608; p. 49: "Editto contro quelli che hanno guastato li condotti vecchi dell'acque di Bracciano," March 1, 1608 (*cf.* ORBAAN, 99); p. 50: Editto per gli scarpellini," March 6, 1608; p. 107: "Editto contro quelli che non hanno fatto fare li ristauri alle loro fonti," June 5, 1608; further edicts addressed to Galeazzo Sanvitale, arcivesc. di Bari e chierico di Camera, Aless. Monti et Paolo Millini deputati sopra l'opera de'condotti dell'Acqua Paola, of August 31, 1609, May 6, 1610, September 3, 1611; p. 54–6*b*: "Pauli P.V erectio congregationis ac deputationis officialium super Aquae Paulae et illius Aqueductis curae et administratione," November 29, 1612 (in *Bull.*, XII., 185 *seq.*, dated September 13, 1612); p. 57 *seqq.*: edicts of the commission, dated May 23, 1614, and September 23, 1616, Papal Secret Archives. *Cf.* FEA, 143 *seq.*; ORBAAN, 99, note 1.

[3] BAGLIONE, 96, 131; ORBAAN, 80, on *Targone*. GURLITT (213) and GUIDI (*Fontane*, 68) suppose that C. Maderno also participated in the work.

[4] See FEA, *Storia delle Acque*, Roma, 1832, 41, 135 *seqq.*

[5] ORBAAN, 140, 168.

[6] *Ibid.*, 82 *seqq.*

[7] See Appendix No. 13, Papal Secret Archives.

partially recovered from the sale of the water—200 scudi the uncia—owing to the fact that the Pope largely renounced his claim to compensation.[1]

The conduit, in part underground, is extolled by a contemporary as an undertaking comparable to the works of the imperial epoch.[2] The poet Tarquinius Gallutius wrote a poem in praise of the blessing which Paul V. had conferred upon his native city,[3] and medals were struck in commemoration of the event.[4]

In 1611, the first trial of the new aqueduct was made near S. Pietro in Montorio.[5] A little above this church, at a spot where the spectator gets one of the finest views of the city and the hills, Paul V., in 1612, caused Giovanni Fontana and Carlo Maderno to construct in travertine the splendid water castle of the Fontana dell' Acqua Paola of whose charm Göthe and Platen have left inimitable descriptions. The inscription states that the Pope had brought the water from the excellent springs near the lake of Bracciano, over a distance of thirty-five miglias (about 50 km.) by repairing the ancient aqueduct and adding a new conduit.[6] The

[1] FEA, *loc. cit.*, 41, 45. *A memorial of Pompeo Targone *sopra i profitti da cavarsi dell'acqua di Bracciano* in Barb., p. 43 *seqq.*, Vatican Library.

[2] "Aquae penuria tota Transtiberina regio mirum in modum laborabat; opus ergo molis immensae Paulus aggressus incredibilem aquae copiam ex agro Braccianensi deductam et quinti et trigesimo milliario, partim subterraneo specu, partim arcuato opere in summum Janiculum perduxit. Rem profecto Caesarum opibus comparabilem." *Magnificentia Pauli V.*, Barb. 2353, Vatican Library.

[3] **Tarquinii Gallutii carmen de novo fonte ex agro Sabatino in urbem a Paulo V. P.M. corrivato, Vat.* 5557, Vatican Library.

[4] See ARTIOLI in the work mentioned on p. 430, note 4, pp. 9 and 10. Paul V.'s inscriptions on the aqueduct in CIACONIUS, IV., 394. Reproduction of the *Arco dell'Acquedotto d. Acqua Paola* in the Villa Pamfili with an inscription of the year 1609, in MAGNI, *Il barocco*, II., Turin, 1911, 22.

[5] ORBAAN, 191.

[6] FEA, *loc. cit.*, 42; FORCELLA, XII., 107. Both inscriptions on the aqueduct outside Porta S. Pancrazio in FORCELLA, XIII., 63.

decorative structure of monumental proportions, with six granite columns of the Ionian order standing on a lofty base, is the first of Rome's fountains in which a huge volume of water gushes forth with a roaring noise and in a cloud of spray. The granite columns, which derive from old St. Peter's, form a framework for three large, semi-circular vaulted niches and for two small niches at the sides. The pediment is surmounted by a colossal inscription and the whole is finished off by Paul V.'s coat-of-arms supported by two angels, above which rises a cross. The corners are adorned with the heraldic animals of the Borghese, the eagle and the dragon. Originally the water fell in rushing cascades from the three central niches into as many basins in which huge dragons spat up powerful jets of water.[1] These heraldic animals were removed under Alexander VIII. and replaced by a large basin of white marble.[2]

The new aqueduct was intended, in the first instance, to relieve the shortage of water in the Trastevere and the Borgo, but by means of leaden pipes laid across the Ponte Sisto, the water was also made to serve the districts on the other side of the Tiber. Hence, between 1612–1613, Paul V. commanded Giovanni Fontana and Jan van Santen to erect, at the spot where the Via Giulia joins the Ponte Sisto, and adjoining the home of the poor erected by Sixtus V., a second arch, on the model of a triumphal arch, but with only one niche. The water falls from above into a first basin from which it rushes into a lower one in which two dragons shoot up water jets that cross each other.[3]

[1] The water spat forth by the dragons beneath the small arcades also flowed into separate basins.

[2] Moroni, XXV., 172. The original aspect of the *Aqua Paola* in Artioli on page 25 of the monograph quoted in the next note. For a discussion of the work see Gurlitt, 213 *seq.*; Riegl, 131; Guidi, 24, 69.

[3] See Baglione, 96, 131; Bonanni, II., 536, Orbaan, 212, and especially R. Artioli, *Il Fontane di Ponte Sisto in Roma*, Roma, 1899, 14 *seqq.*, 30 *seqq.*, 46 *seqq.*, with reproduction of the structure which was unfortunately demolished in 1879 and re-erected in 1897–8, though in a somewhat altered form, in the Piazza di Ponte Sisto on the other side of the Tiber.

The restoration and extension of Hadrian's aqueduct, the upkeep and administration of which was entrusted to a special Congregation under the presidency of Cardinal Borghese,[1] made it possible to provide water for the many new fountains with which Paul V. enriched his residence. The most beautiful of them all adorns the piazza of St. Peter's beside the Vatican.[2] Here Maderno has created a work of magnificent simplicity which splendidly realizes a bold conception. In a pyramid about 25 feet high, the water is shot upwards in powerful jets; then, hitting the mushroom-like body of the spout, it falls back into a gracefully shaped granite shell from which it overflows into the octagonal basin. The mass of water powerfully shot upwards only to glide down from basin to basin, like an enfolding veil, imparts to the whole work its fascination and materially helps to give life to the piazza.[3] "From the topmost point," Fontana writes, "the waters rise in thick masses into the air; then they rush down like rivers from the shells into the basins, with such a roar that they call forth the greatest admiration. The mass of water appears even more magnificent when powerful winds sweep it beyond the basins so that it spreads like clouds on which the sun paints the colours of the rainbow: such a spectacle provokes wonder and admiration." [4]

[1] *Cf.* Constitution of September 13, 1612, in FEA, *Acque*, 141 *seq.*

[2] BAGLIONE, 96; FALDA, I., 3; BONANNI, *Numismata*, 161; GUIDI, *Fontane*, 65 *seqq.*

[3] *Cf.* DURM, *Renaissance in Italien*, 375; H. SEMPER, *Monumentalbrunnen*, in the *Zeitschr. des. bayr. Kunstgewerbevereins*, 1891, 57; MACKOWSKY, "Röm. Brunnen," in *Museum*, III., 35; RIEGL, 142; "In the rhythmic gradation of basins, cups and shaft," Voss writes (*Jahrb. der preuss. Kunstsamml.*, XXXI., 104), "this fountain is probably unique of its kind." *Cf.* also WEISBACH, *Die Kunst des Barock in Italien*, Berlin, 1924, 30 *seq.*; good reproductions in FRIEDLÄNDER, *Römische Barockbrunnen*, Leipzig, 1922, 6, and in COLASANTI, *Fontane*, 189. *Cf.* INVENTARIO, 322.

[4] FONTANA, *Il tempio Vaticano*, Roma, 1694, 199. *Cf.* the poem of GIROLAMO PRETI, in his *Poesie*, Perugia, 1632, 57.

In 1614, the Pope commissioned Carlo Maderno to erect two more isolated fountains, in the centre of the Piazza Scossa Cavalli and the Piazza di Castello.[1] To these must be added a number of small, graceful fountains built into walls, as in the Borgo, in the Via de' Banchi and the Lungara, as well as a fountain in the convent of San Francesco a Ripa.[2] The piazza of S. Maria Maggiore [3] and that of the Lateran, were also adorned with fountains.[4] A fountain was erected in the Via Cernaia, "for the thirsty country people and the dust-covered carriers." [5]

The Pope's solicitude extended itself also to the Jews who lacked good water in the Ghetto; they were given a fountain in the piazza of the synagogue; its decoration includes, in addition to the customary dragon, the seven-branched candlestick.[6]

To Paul V. the Romans also owe the restoration of the salubrious well of the *Acqua Acetosa,* and the baths of the *Acqua Santa,* near the Via Appia Nuova.[7]

Not content with having given to the Eternal City her foaming fountains and her gushing wells which constitute an embellishment as attractive and distinctive as it is useful, Paul V. also improved the network of Rome's streets, by

[1] Baglione, 96; Orbaan, 215. The fountain in the Piazza Scossa Cavalli in Falda, *Fontane di Roma,* I (1669), 30, and Colasanti, 187; the fountain in Piazza di Castello was destroyed by the revolution of 1849. See Moroni, LI., 135. *Cf.* Fea, *Acque,* 45.

[2] See **Magnificentia Pauli V., loc. cit.,* Vatican Library; Inventario, 302; Forcella, XIII., 107; H. Semper, *loc. cit.,* 65 *seq.*; Guidi, *Fontane,* 28. *Cf.* reproductions in Ricci, *Archit. barocca in Italia,* 266; Friedländer, *loc. cit.,* 16; *Architetture minori in Italia,* I., Rome, Turin, 1926, 163.

[3] Orbaan, 230. *Cf.* Falda, *Fontane,* I., 9; Inventario, 343; Colasanti, 191 *seq.*

[4] See *Bull.,* XII., 257 *seq.*; Falda, I., 10; *cf.* Inventario, 15.

[5] Inventario, 339.

[6] Forcella, XIII., 109.

[7] Orbaan, 215; Forcella, XIII., 108.

paving existing roadways and creating new ones.[1] The Trastevere, thanks to the work done there, developed in a most gratifying degree.[2] By the correction of the street from San Benedetto towards San Francesco a Ripa and beyond, towards the Porta Portese, the Pope wished to foster devotion towards the Poverello of Assisi and at the same time create a better perspective.[3] Religious as well as æsthetic motives prompted the drawing of a rectilineal street between the newly erected column of the Madonna in front of St. Mary Major and the Lateran,[4] thereby creating a beautiful perspective which gladdens the eye to this day. The via della Scrofa underwent improvements because the envoys who came in by the Porta del Popolo, rode over it as they went to the Vatican.[5] The Pope took extraordinary trouble to create better roads of approach to the Quirinal; but he saw to it that the owners of expropriated houses were given a just compensation.[6] The street leading towards San Giuseppe a Capo le Case also owes its origin to Paul V.[7] The difficult ascent of the Aventine was likewise corrected.[8] The City's well-being was also served by the maintenance of the aqueducts[9] and public fountains,[10] the establishment

[1] Bzovius, c. 42; L. Allatius, **De aedificiis Pauli V.* (*cf.* p. 434, note 3): *Via a foro Boario ad amphitheatrum Vespasiani et aliae lapidibus stratae. Via a Porta Flumentana* (sic!) *ad pontem Milvium aliaeque dilapidantur* (Vatican Library). *Cf.* also Orbaan, 57.

[2] Baglione, 96; Orbaan, 101.

[3] Bzovius, c. 42; *cf.* Totti, 58, 63.

[4] Orbaan, 212.

[5] *Ibid.*, 173. Forcella, XIII., 89; L. Allatius, *loc. cit.*

[6] Orbaan, 140, 172, 188 *seqq.*, 195, 214; Forcella, XIII., 88; *Inventario*, 51, and Allatius' dissertation mentioned in note 1.

[7] Orbaan, 253.

[8] See *L. Allatius' dissertation, note 1.

[9] Bzovius, c. 42; Fea, *Acque*, 106–110. *Cf.* also *Bull.*, XI., 437 *seq.*

[10] See **Editto che Piazza Navona e le fonte pubbliche si conservino nette* of June 15, 1607, in the *Editti*, V., 74, p. 157, Papal Secret Archives.

of a special timber-yard near the harbour of Ripetta,[1] the restoration of the bridge of the Quattro Capi [2] and the bridges of the Anio,[3] the cleaning and improvement of the sewers,[4] the removal of the filthy stalls near the Portico of the Pantheon [5] and the enlargement of the grain stores.[6]

The difficult problem of the correction of the Tiber, which had left its banks anew on January 25th, 1606, caused the Pope much anxiety.[7] Discussions on the subject began in February, 1606,[8] and a number of memorials with old and new suggestions, were sent in.[9] Maderno and Ponzio gave their opinion on one of these schemes which had been submitted by Giovanni Paolo Maggi.[10] Not alone the difficulty of the task, but the enormous cost and the Roman engineers' jealousy of Pompeo Targone, also proved serious hindrances.[11] Fresh inundations at the end of December,

[1] BAGLIONE, 96; ORBAAN, 216, 222, 223.

[2] FORCELLA, XIII., 55.

[3] *Pontes Salarius et Mammolus in Anione nutantes reficiuntur. Alii item ponticuli.* L. ALLATIUS, **De aedificiis Pauli V. curatore aquarum ac viarum Laelio Biscia,* in Barb. 3060[8]., Vatican Library.

[4] L. ALLATIUS, **De aedificiis, Pauli V., loc. cit.*; BZOVIUS, c. 42.

[5] *L. ALLATIUS, *loc. cit.*

[6] BZOVIUS, c. 42; **Magnificentia Pauli V., loc. cit.*, Vatican Library. *ALLATIUS, *loc. cit. Cf.* ORBAAN, 137, 158; FORCELLA, XIII., 177 *seq.*; INVENTARIO, 339, 349 *seq.* Paul V. executed some small repairs of the city walls (see NIBBY, *Le mura di Roma*, Rome, 1820, 355) on the Villa Giulia (ORBAAN, 97, 99). Inscription about restoration of the Capitol in CIACONIUS, IV., 396. An inscription of Paul V.' now in the garden of the Castle St. Angelo, also refers to some work of restoration.

[7] Inscription in FORCELLA, XIII., 220.

[8] ORBAAN, 69 *seqq.*, 72.

[9] Two such *memorials in Borghese, II., 27–28, p. 235 *seqq.*, 240 *seq.*, Papal Secret Archives.

[10] See **Cod.* H., II, 43, of Chigi Library, Rome, p. 166 *seqq.*: *Proposta fatta da Giov. Fontana,* May 14, 1606; p. 168 *seq.*: *Proposta di Giov. Paolo Maggi. Cf.* EHRLE, *Pianta di Maggi-Maupin-Losi,* Rome, 9; 5, 9.

[11] ORBAAN, 87, 92.

1607, and in the beginning of 1608 [1] demonstrated the urgency of the work, but once again the high cost and the opposition of the Romans to further taxation prevented anything being done.[2] For the time being an attempt was made to stem the evil by forbidding to build on the banks of the Tiber and to throw rubbish into the stream, and by dredging its bed. After 1610 this was all that was done except that an effort was made at one moment to alter the course of some of the tributary rivers, a work for which a Spanish architect was called in.[3]

In an inscription of 1611, which may be seen to this day on the outer wall of San Francisco a Ripa, the Senate and people of Rome recount how Paul V. had adorned the Eternal City with new churches and other buildings; how he had provided the Trastevere with a plentiful supply of water, made it healthier and more prosperous, and enriched it with new streets; how he had repaired the Ponte Fabricio and provided it with steps leading down to the edge of the stream.[4] There still exists a number of similar inscriptions recording Paul V.'s works of public utility, though many of them have disappeared, as may be gathered from a comparison with old collections.[5]

The contemporaries cannot sufficiently praise, in verse and prose, that which Paul V. did for Rome.[6] "All over the city," we read in a contemporary biography of the Pope, "he has lowered the hills; where there were corners and twists in the streets, he opened wide vistas, laid out extensive squares,

[1] *Ibid.*, 7, 88.

[2] *Ibid.*, 112, 118, 120. *Cf.* **Relatione del negotiato del popolo Romano circa il negotio di trovar denari per la reparatione del Tevere*, in Borghese II., 27–8, p. 220 *seqq.*, Papal Secret Archives.

[3] ORBAAN, 121, 144. *Cf.* BZOVIUS, c. 42.

[4] FORCELLA, LV.; INVENTARIO, 270.

[5] The complete collection in **Magnificentia Pauli V. seu publicae utilitatis et splendoris opera*, Barb. 2335, Vatican Library.

[6] *Ibid.* and the **Vita Pauli V.* mentioned in next footnote. Also FRANCESCO DELLA VALLE, Le nuove fabbriche di Roma sotto Paolo V., in the *Lirici marinisti*, ed. B. Croce, Bari, 1910, 44.

and further enhanced their beauty by the erection of new buildings; the water which he brought into the town is no longer subject to the whim of a pipe, it bursts forth like a stream. The splendour of his palaces is contrasted and emulated by the gardens laid out by him. The interior of his private chapels sparkle with gold and silver; they are not so much adorned, as filled, with jewels." The biographer concludes on a note of that admiration for the splendid and the colossal which characterizes the period: "The public chapels rise like basilicas, the basilicas like temples, the temples like mountains of marble." [1]

How extensive were the alterations and new constructions of the Borghese Pope may be gathered from a letter of Bentivoglio. When, in 1616, he returned to Rome from Flanders where he had lived since 1607, the Cardinal not only found the entire court altered, but the city itself completely transformed in its buildings and streets.[2] The Pope's passion for building [3] had communicated itself to the cardinals, the nobles and the private citizens, so that the city had grown in size and the general prosperity had risen to an extraordinary degree.[4] The population grew steadily. At the beginning of Paul V.'s reign, Rome numbered 99,647 inhabitants; in the year of his death there were 118,356.[5]

The Venetian envoys who came to Rome in 1621, to do

[1] **Vita Pauli V.* (Barb. 2670, p. 8^{b}, 9^{a}, Vatican Library). German translation in RANKE, III.[6] Latin text in MAES, *Villa Borghese*, Rome, 1885, 58.

[2] BENTIVOGLIO, *Lettere*, ed. Biagiolio, I., 59.

[3] *Cf.* Avviso, in ORBAAN, 183.

[4] BZOVIUS, c. 42. *Cf.* TOMASSETTI, IV., 415, and above, vol. XXV., p. 76, n. 2.

[5] See above, vol. XXV., p. 74, n. 3. As regards the composition of the population of Rome, ample materials, until now almost wholly untouched, are found in the parish archives of the city which have now all been collected in the *Archivio generale del Vicariato di Roma*, which, thanks to the solicitude of Pope Pius XI., has found a home in the left wing of the colonnade of St. Peter's. For the parishes see *Studi e docum.*, XII., 197 *seq.*

homage to Gregory XV., could scarcely find words with which to describe the splendour of the papal residence. Paul V had adorned it with marvels, they write, which challenge those of the ancients. These works of art and the palace itself, they justly remark, constitute an incomparable whole.[1] How much the city, over which lay the spell of the centuries, still bore that unique, soul-stirring character which it only lost in the seventies of the nineteenth century, appears from the views, plans and descriptions of the city dating from that period.

In the "views", the remains of antiquity play a most important rôle. The artists of the seventeenth century reproduced them with greater realism than their predecessors. In this respect the *vedutas* of Alò Giovannoli, 146 sheets of which were published between 1615–1619, together with a plan of the city, are justly famous. Though roughly executed they are nevertheless most accurately drawn so that they constitute a real treasure-house of information on the monuments of Rome at the time of Paul V.[2] This was followed up, in 1618, by a series of copper plate reproductions, by the Roman Giovanni Maggi, of the buildings and ruins of Rome. This work is entirely devoted to the antiquities, with the exception of views of the Castle St. Angelo, the island of the Tiber and S. Stefano Rotondo.[3] In the same year this artist also published a set of views of the chief fountains of Rome.[4] To him we likewise owe the magnificent copper plates in which he perpetuated, in 1612, the splendour of

[1] BAROZZI-BERCHET, *Relazioni*, I., Rome, 119 *seq.*

[2] *Roma antica di Alo Giovannoli*, 10, 15–19. *Cf.* BARTOLI, *Cento vedute di Roma antica*, Firenze, 1911, 31.

[3] *Aedificiorum et ruinarum Romae ex antiquis atque hodiernis monumentis . . . incisus et delineatus a Io. Maggio Romano . . . Ioseph de Rubeis Mediolanensis D.D.* 1618 (CICOGNARA, IV., 3768), in the *Staatsbibl.* of Munich—the only complete copy. *Cf.* BARTOLI, *loc. cit.*, 32; EHRLE, *La pianta di Roma Maggi-Maupin-Losi*, Rome, 1915, 14, where there is also some information about the author.

[4] *Le Fontane di Roma* (1618), *cf. Repert f. Kunstwiss.*, 1909, 406, and the periodical *Capitolium*, 1926, 356.

the new Quirinal palace,[1] and in 1615 that of St. Peter's and the Vatican.[2]

Paul V.'s activity in the sphere of art prompted the publication of monographs on St. Mary Major [3] and St. Peter's.[4] In 1615, the Servite Pietro Martire Felini, published his treatise on the marvels of the Eternal City. This book, which marks a further development of the Guide to Rome of Franzini published in the years 1588 and 1600, was likewise printed by the house of Franzini, by then the leading firm in the production of Guide Books. In the preface of his pioneer publication, the author justly criticizes the inaccuracies that disfigured the previous Guide Books. He adopted the material collected by his predecessors and gave it a new shape which was destined to become classical. Interest in monuments, which until then had been sporadic, comes definitely to the surface in his book which, by its numerous new data rendered all the old guides obsolete.[5]

Giulio Mancini, a native of Siena, who worked for a number of years as a physician at the hospital of Santo Spirito, produced an entirely original work.[6] His *Viaggio di Roma*, begun under Paul V. and completed in 1626, is utterly different from the usual Rome guides, though the writer confines his

[1] This print, of which there exist only a few copies (see *Cat. of the printed Maps, Plans and Charts in the British Museum*, II., London, 1882, 3556) is to be republished and explained by Mgr. St. Le Grelle from the plate preserved in the archives of St. Mary Major.

[2] See Ehrle, *La grande veduta Maggi-Mascardi del Tempio e del Palazzo Vaticano*, Rome, 1914.

[3] Vittorelli (1616) and de Angelis (1621).

[4] G. B. Costaguti (*Maggiordomo di Paolo V.*), *Architettura d. basilica di S. Pietro con tavole da Martino Ferrabosco*, 1620 (a very rare edition). A new edition, of 1684, was dedicated to Innocent XI.

[5] See Schudt, *Mancini*, 30 *seq.*, 121. A very summary Guide through Rome, of 1613, to enable the visitor to see the chief places of interest in three days, is mentioned in the travel notes of bishop von Aschhausen, referred to on p. 440.

[6] Schudt, 8 *seq.*, 10 *seq.*

attention to paintings. This work, which has only recently become known, constitutes a source of the first rank for the history of art and one in every way unique by reason of the abundance of the material examined. Mancini's chief interest lies in the churches of which he describes nearly a hundred, whereas the palaces, about fifteen in number, and the villas, are very much kept in the background. Mancini is the first writer to neglect completely, in his description of churches, that on which other Guides had until then laid the greatest stress, namely, the relics, Indulgences, and legendary accounts of their foundation, in order to concentrate exclusively on their monuments, and in so doing, he confines himself to paintings, in keeping with the limits he had laid down for himself. But here he supplies an astonishing amount of information though in concisest form. Whereas previous Guides concern themselves exclusively with "more recent painters", that is, with the art of the Renaissance, starting with Giotto, he includes many of the more important monuments of early Christian and medieval art. The number of works described by him and the artists mentioned by name, is so considerable, that he surpasses all his predecessors. For the first time an attempt is made in these pages to give a survey of all existing works of art. Mancini is so reliable an authority that although a number of mistakes have crept into his book, most of his data stand the test of modern criticism.[1]

How greatly Mancini, who observed with the eye of the sensitive connoisseur and who sought exact information, excelled his contemporaries is best seen by a comparison with the descriptions supplied by Rome pilgrims of the period. One is astonished to see how little the greatness and beauty of the Eternal City was appreciated both by Italians and non-Italians. A classical proof of the fact is furnished by the travel notes of Gian Vincenzo Imperiale, of 1609,[2] on the

[1] SCHUDT, 38 *seq.*, to whom we owe a masterly edition of the *Viaggio di Roma.*

[2] Published by A. G. BARRILI, in the *Atti Ligure di stor. patria,* XXIX., 62 *seqq.*

one hand, and, on the other, by the account of the journey of the prince-bishop of Bamberg, Johann Gottfried von Aschhausen, 1612–13, drawn up by his travelling companions.[1] A much higher standard is attained in the still unpublished travel notes of Dr. Kaspar Stein, a physician of Königsberg, who, though by no means an unconditional admirer of Italy, was nevertheless powerfully impressed by this "paradise".[2] What most surprised him in Rome was the vast number of churches (over a hundred) and the excellent hospitals and hospices. He praises the wonderful attention which the poor and the sick received in them, whether Romans or strangers. He also mentions the numerous orphanages.[3]

[1] *Des Bamberger Fürstbischofs Joh. Gottfried von Aschhausen Gesandtschaftsreise nach Italien und Rom. 1612 und 1613*, publ. by CHR. HÄUTLE, Tübingen, 1881. *Cf.* NOACK, *Deutsches Leben in Rom.*, Stuttgart, 1907, 19 *seq.* The notes of GUARINONI, who went to Rome in 1613, in the *Zeitschr. des Innsbrucker Ferdinandeums, 3 Folge*, XXIII. (1878), 77 *seq.* Of AG. GELENIUS, who was in Rome in 1619, we only have a description of his return journey; see *Hist. Annalen für den Niederrhein*, XXIII., 7 *seq.* The notes of an Englishman who visited Rome in 1622 are also very jejune; see *Papers of the British School*, VI. (1913), 482 *seq.*

[2] **Peregrinus sive peregrinatio terrestris et coelestis a Casparo Stein Regiomontano, Borusso, medicinae licentiato et historico scriptus*, MS. No. 1751 of Königsberg Library. Dr. Stein (*cf.* on him *Acta Borussica*, I., 195) here characterizes the Italians as revengeful and envious and remarks among other things that *multae vigiliae, ieiunia et dies festi non sine molestia celebrantur*; he also complains of the charlatans and begging friars and, like Nicolai, of the plague of fleas in Italy; food cooked in oil did not agree with him, but he nevertheless says that *Italia ob amoenitatem orbis paradisus vocatur.* The insecurity, of which other travellers complain (see the periodical *Roma*, 1926, 244 *seq.*) is not alluded to by Stein. Yet another North German traveller's notes may here be referred to: **Journal d'un voyage à Rome de Johann Georgius a Born, gentilhomme Brandenburgue*, 1609, in *Ottob.*, 2659, Vatican Library.

[3] *"Hospitalia et xenodochia tanta magnificentia extructa, ut inter recentia urbis Romae monumenta nihil fere praedicationis dignius, in qua inquilini et peregrini pauperes ac infirmi recipiuntur

Among the sights of the city, Dr. Stein assigns the first place to the new St. Peter's in the sacristy of which, besides the gifts formerly presented by Henry VIII. of England and the king of Portugal to Gregory XIII., he greatly admired those which the duke of Tuscany had recently bestowed on Paul V. In the Vatican, besides the Sala Regia, the frescos of Raphael and Michelangelo and the collection of antique statues, the traveller from Königsberg likewise admired the Pope's private apartments decorated with royal magnificence, and the garden which, he says, was famous throughout the world. The Swiss Guard, according to Stein, was usually 200, and at times 300 men strong. In the summer palace of the Quirinal the traveller was able to visit all the rooms ; he describes the splendour of their furniture,[1] nor does he forget to add that, after the election of the emperor Ferdinand II., Paul V. himself said the Mass of thanksgiving in the Cappella Paolina. In the garden of the Quirinal, Stein, as on a previous occasion Heinrich Schickhardt, the companion of the duke of Württemberg, was struck by the clever hydraulic works, especially by the hydraulic organ and by the aquatic practical jokes which would give the guileless visitor an unexpected soaking. In his description of the Castle of St. Angelo, he mentions the magnificent display of fireworks which took place there on the great feasts, such as Easter, Pentecost, Corpus Christi and St. Michael.

et a medicis, chirurgis, pharmacopoecis et ministris ordinariis magna diligentia curantur." *S. Spirito*, he says, has 200,000 *coroni* of annual income. Among national hospices he mentions : (1) *Anima* (*Belgorum et Germanorum*), (2) *S. Luigi* (*Gallorum*), (3) *S. Jacopo* (*Hispan.*), (4) *S. Toma* (*Anglorum*), (5) *S. Pietro* (*Ungaror.*), (6) *S. Brigitta* (*Svecor.*), (7) *S. Andrea* (*prope Argentinam Flandror.*), (8) *S. Giov. Battista prope rip. Tib.* (*Genuen.*). On S. Spirito see also the above quoted travel journal of the bishop of Bamberg, J. G. von Aschhausen, p. 104.

[1] *" Cubiculum pontificis hybernum cum lecto et culcitris ex byssino rubro aureo fulgente. Cubiculum pontificis aestivum cum lecto et culcitris ex byssino albo et molli, auro et argenteo artificiose intertexto et speculo magno pellucidissimo."

The Königsberg physician saw the Pope on his way to the Villa Borghese, when he travelled in a sedan-chair covered with red silk and drawn by two mules. The solemn cortège, at whose approach everybody fell on their knees, made a deep impression on him too. The Cardinals, of whom nearly forty were then in Rome, seemed like kings to Stein.

Besides the churches, Dr. Stein did not fail to visit the palaces. He examined all the principal ones, especially the newly erected Palazzo Mattei,[1] the palazzo Farnese with the gigantic statue of the Farnese bull which happened to be boarded off just then, and the two Borghese palaces of whose artistic treasures he writes with enthusiasm. The stranger from the North was particularly delighted with the magnificence of the gardens attached to the villas. He singles out, in particular, the villa of Sixtus V., that of the grand-duke of Tuscany on the Pincio, where the youth of Rome was wont to play in those days, the gardens of the Farnese on the Palatine and, lastly, the new Villa Borghese. Stein also visited the Catacombs on the Via Appia. Here a monk acted as his guide, but everywhere else he had for guide a certain Johann Hoch, of Lucerne, with whom he had fallen in at the Sword Inn: *Albergo della Spada*, at which, as well as the old *Albergo dell'Orso*, most Germans were wont to put up at that time.[2]

We can best realize the immense building activity which marked the reign of Paul V., by comparing two great contemporary plans of the city which have been preserved to this day. The one, by the Florentine Antonio Tempesta, dates from the year 1601[3]; the other is the work of Matthäus Greuter, of Strassburg, and dates from the year 1618.[4]

[1] On the palace built by Maderno between 1595–1610 for Asdrubale Mattei, see Muñoz, *Maderno*, 7.

[2] On the inns of Rome at that time see Orbaan, 88 *seqq.*

[3] This plan is to be published by Cardinal Ehrle.

[4] *Disegno nuovo di Roma moderna . . . disegnata et data in luce da Matteo Greuter tedesco nell'anno* 1618 (see Hülsen, in *Arch. Rom.*, XXXVIII., 81 *seqq.*), published by Orbaan, *Documenti, tav.* IV–VII; *cf. ibid.*, p. CXV *seqq.*

Greuter's perspective plan of Rome, which served as a model for Falda's masterpiece, gives, as it were, an account of the stupendous activity of Paul V., which reached its climax in the completion of St. Peter's. "The considerable aggrandizement of Rome," Greuter writes, "by means of so many and such large buildings, especially by the construction, now nearly completed, of St. Peter's, and that of the magnificent Chapel of Paul V. at S. Maria Maggiore, the levelling of the hills and their enrichment with commodious dwellings, the laying out of new streets near the Quirinal, Via Felice (Sistina), Capo le Case, Arco de'Patani, in the quarter de' Monti, in the Suburra, in the Borgo, in the Trastevere and in many other places, as well as the many new churches, have prompted me to undertake this work, in order to place the new Rome before the eyes of the world. Since this City rose anew, so to speak, under Paul V., it gives me particular satisfaction that my work sees the light during the reign of that Pope."

Greuter's plan of Rome, the artistic finish of which is most pleasing, is dedicated to Cardinal Medici. It shows the Eternal City at a moment when the efflorescence of a characteristically Roman art, due to the Borghese pontificate, had begun to assume definite form. The plan exhibits, on the upper left hand margin, together with the arms of Paul V., the figure of Rome, flanked by the Prince of the Apostles, whilst the lower, right-hand margin shows the seven principal churches. The Strassburg artist has succeeded in fixing with greatest accuracy and with fine artistic feeling the image of Rome as transformed by Paul V., with its churches, its palaces, most of them two-storied, its houses, squares and fountains. One gets a bird's-eye view of the labyrinth of Rome's streets and alleys where History sits at every corner with well-covered tablets in her hand. One sees how the sinuous course of the Tiber was framed by numerous, picturesque houses which have all been sacrificed to the correction of the river banks, and one observes how many remains from the times of the old Romans—the aqueducts, the temple of Minerva Medica, the *amphitheatrum castrense*, the baths of Diocletian and Caracalla, were then in a far better state of preservation than they are to-day. One specially attractive feature of a former Rome, the breath of the rural Campagna wafted into the city from all sides, is most admirably suggested by Greuter's plan.

Many exceedingly picturesque features enliven the plan, as for instance the mills at anchor near San Giovanni de' Fiorentini and near the island of San Bartolomeo, and the charming garden of the palazzo Bentivoglio (Mazarin-Rospigliosi), and similar striking details. Behind St. Peter's may be seen the yard for the work of demolition of the old basilica and the construction of the new, the stacks of materials near Santa Marta and the still smoking lime kilns of the *fabbrica* of St. Peter's. Greuter shows the basilica of St. Peter completed, the great palaces of the Borghese also finished and the Villa Borghese in its original aspect.

The Borghese palace, in the low-lying part of the field of Mars, had been built by Martino Longhi for Cardinal Deza. After the death of that prince of the Church, Cardinal Camillo Borghese bought it, in February, 1605, for the sum of 42,000 scudi.[1] When shortly afterwards he became Pope, Paul V. bestowed it on his brothers and had it completed by Flaminio Ponzio and Maderno, on a truly Roman scale.[2]

[1] BAGLIONE, 68; *Arch. Rom.*, XXXIII., 299.

[2] BAGLIONE, 135, 308; ORBAAN, 66, 70, 174. Work was still in progress in 1610; see FELINI, *Trattato nuovo delle cose mem. di Roma* (1610). In 1613 Paul V. presented the palace with its magnificent appointments to Marcantonio Borghese, prince of Sulmona, the eldest son of his brother Giambattista. In July, 1614, the Pope dined in the *Stanze nove* of the palace; see the DIARIO in *Studi e docum.*, XV., 276. On the palace see INVENTARIO, 81; LETAROUILLY, *Édif.*, II., 175 *seq.*; MAGNI, *Il barocco a Roma*, II., Turin, 1911, 17 *seq.*; GURLITT, 197; RIEGL, 144; BERGNER, 27 *seq.*; ROSE, *Spätbarock*, 165 *seq.*, 189 *seq.* The mementos of the time of Paul V., which were enshrined in the palace, were sold by auction and scattered to the winds at the time of the financial crash of the house of Borghese in 1892. Majolicas from the Sala di Bagno went into the Castle St. Angelo. Six gold reliefs with scenes from ancient mythology forming part of a jewelbox of the Borghese collection, and which tradition

Longhi had created the courtyard, magnificent in its severity, encircled on the ground and the first floor with a portico, the arcades of which are supported by close on a hundred antique granite columns. Ponzio, who was the family architect of the Borghese, nearly doubled the size of the palace by lengthening it in the direction of the Ripetto.[1] In this way it acquired an irregular shape, the ground plan of which was not unlike a piano—hence it came to be popularly called *il clavicembalo Borghese.*[2]

has it that Paul V. had had executed in his youth by Benvenuto Cellini, came into the Kaiser-Friedrich Museum of Berlin; see *Kunstchronik*, XVI. (1904–5), 301.

[1] The Ripetta is rounded off by an exceptionally picturesque corner façade with an ornamental balcony and a hanging garden designed by Carlo Rainaldi in 1690 (see HEMPEL, *Rainaldi*, 95 *seq.*). The magnificent view which one formerly enjoyed from this beautifully conceived building on the green plain on the other side of the Tiber, with St. Peter's, surpassed even the famous vista of the garden through the open arcades at the back of the court. To this was added a third, most original view: To prolong the line which cuts the suite of rooms on the ground floor of the opposite wing, a labyrinth of small rooms was built which continued over the Ripetta street in the direction of the Tiber as a kind of tunnel under a neighbouring building; in it a number of thin jets of water were continually crossing each other. A fountain which sent up a powerful jet of water closed up this vista. All this, when seen through a suite of several rooms, made a fairy-like spectacle, all the more so as the play of the water jets was still further enhanced by the green of the trees on the other side of the Tiber. See *Seb. Brunner, Italien*, II., 155. *Cf.* GURLITT, 205.

[2] *Cf.* the Roman proverb quoted by BROSSE (*Reisen*, II., 412):

"Il cembalo di Borghese
Il Dado di Farnese
Il Portone di Carboniani
E la Scala dei Gaetani
Sono i quattro maravigli Romani."

"The cymbal of the Borghese
The dice of the Farnese
The gate of the Carboniani
The stairs of the Gaetani
Are the four marvels of Rome."

The exterior of the Borghese palace, with its long façade, presents a severe and sober appearance [1]; the decoration of the portal and the windows is sternly restricted; but when the visitor enters the splendid courts surrounded by rows of columns and from there goes up the broad stairs to the upper rooms, he feels that he enters a building which can stand comparison with many a royal castle. The rooms, decorated with frescos and stucco,[2] with the Borghese arms on the ceiling, have a spaciousness such as is only found in Rome; thus the State room could easily accommodate a small house.[3]

So as to be within easy reach of the Pope during the latter's stay at the Vatican, Cardinal Scipio Borghese bought from the Campeggi the palace which Bramante had erected for Cardinal Adriano Castellesi, in the Borgo. From there a wooden passage was erected to link up with the corridor which connects the Castle of St. Angelo with the Vatican.[4] However, it was also necessary for the Cardinal nephew to be by the side of the Pope during the Pontiff's stay at the Quirinal, in the hot season. Hence Flaminio Ponzio, and after his death, Jan van Santen and Maderno were commissioned by Scipio Borghese to construct for him, facing the papal residence, a new palace, complete with garden and *casino*, or summer house. This work entailed the removal of the ruins of the baths of Constantine and those of Aurelius' temple of the Sun.[5]

[1] According to the Avvisi, in ORBAAN, 117, 124, the Pope was by no means satisfied with the building.

[2] The frieze of several rooms was painted by the Capuchin Cosimo of Venice; see BAGLIONE, 161.

[3] A library was also begun in the palace and the space before it widened; see ORBAAN, 173, 175, 181; *cf.* 255; inspection of the *Pitture et paramenti nuovi* in the palace by the Pope (August 1, 1618).

[4] See ORBAAN, 145, 178.

[5] BAGLIONE, 135, 176, 308; EISLER, in *Burlington Magazine*, VII. (1905), 313 *seq.*; JORDAN-HÜLSEN, *Topographie von Rom.*, I., 3, 439.

The third Borghese palace in Rome, which was bought in 1621 from Cardinal Bentivoglio, and at a later period passed into the hands of Mazarin, until it finally became the property of the Rospigliosi, was richly adorned with frescos. Lodovico Cigoli, Antonio Tempesta, Paul Bril and Guido Reni, were all engaged on the work. Their creations, such as the statues and fountains of the garden, with its myrtles, hyacinths and narcissi, were extolled by the poet Gregorius Portius.[1] In the graceful garden house, the entrance to which is adorned with four antique pillars—two of them of rosso antico, the only ones of the kind in Rome—Guido Reni painted, in 1609, his masterpiece, the world-renowned, highly poetical "Aurora". The goddess advances scattering flowers before the chariot of the sun god which is surrounded by the dancing hours; four dappled horses draw the chariot over which hovers winged Hesperus, torch in hand. Far below the first streaks of dawn fall upon the still slumbering earth.[2] An exacting critic has given it as his opinion that this wonderful fresco is the most perfect Italian picture of the last two centuries.[3] Guido's "Aurora" retains all its fame. The "incomparable charm of the picture is largely due to its warm colour of gold".[4] Close by, Guido was busy carrying out yet another commission of Scipio, in a small

[1] *Horti Quirinalis ill. card^lis Burghesii carmen Grogorii Portii Anconitani*, original in *Borghese*, IV., 50, Papal Secret Archives, beginning thus:—

"O decus et sydus sacri venerande senatus
Scipio Burghesie gentis et urbis honor."

Cf. Vat. Lat. 6967, f. 215 (Vatican Library): **De picturis Guidonis Rheni in aedibus Quirinalibus cardinalis Burghesii*:—

"Ut trahit, ut retinet defixaque lumina fallit
Quod Rhenus celso fornice pinxit opus!
Pictorem celebras, haeres immotus et anceps,
Ambigis an scultor sit vel uterque simul.
Sculpta putas quae picta vides: sic undique pulchre
Prominet eximia perlitus arte color."

[2] BAGLIONE, 154, 297, 315; PASSERI, 68; BÖHN, 6.

[3] BURCKHARDT, *Cicerone*, II.[2], 770.

[4] BÖHN, 61 *seq.*

loggia, on the frieze of which Antonio Tempesta painted the triumph of Love and Fame, according to Petrarch's well-known poem. Paul Bril filled the lunettes with landscapes representing the four seasons; he also gave a most graceful decoration to the ceiling; the spectator beholds an arbour thickly festooned with vine branches and enlivened by all manner of creatures—birds, butterflies, bees and rich, luscious bunches of grapes. The charming *putti* who also give life to the bower, are by Guido Reni—they display all the grace of the Master.[1] Another garden house, which was sacrificed when the Via Nazionale was widened, contained a cycle of frescos with four scenes from the story of Amor and Psyche which Cigoli executed in the year of his death—1613. These frescos, to which Francesco Bracciolini refers in the introduction to his *Psiche,* where he ascribes to Cigoli the credit of having inspired the poet, were transferred to the gallery on the Capitol. For a long time they were erroneously described as the work of Annibale Caracci.[2] These frescos were only part of the decoration of Cardinal Scipio Borghese's palaces; he also lavishly enriched them with paintings by old and new masters, antique and modern statues, bronzes, gobelins, majolicas and other smaller works of art.[3]

Not for a long time had Rome seen so sensitive and so liberal a patron of the Arts as this papal nephew. He was no less enthusiastic for music [4] than he was for the plastic arts. Like the Pope who, in 1609, bought the famous collection of statues of the sculptor Tommaso della Porta,[5] the nephew collected, both unwearyingly and with exquisite taste, all

[1] MAYER, *Brill,* 46 *seq.,* 51 *seq.*; EISLER, "An unknown fresco work by G. Reni," in *Burlington Magazine,* VII. (1905), 313 *seqq.*

[2] BAGLIONE, 154; A. SACCHETTI SASSETTI, in *L'Arte,* XVI. (1913), 307 *seq.* In another *loggietta nel giardino* Orazio Gentileschi painted the nine Muses; BAGLIONE, 359.

[3] Avviso in ORBAAN, 244.

[4] *Cf.* HABERL'S *Jahrb. für Musik,* 1887, 72. Paul V. also was extremely fond of music. ORBAAN, *Documenti,* LIII.

[5] *Cf.* *the deed of purchase of October 2, 1609, with the catalogue of statues, in *Borghese,* II., 517, Papal Secret Archives.

over Italy, works of art which reached him from all sides, either as gifts or as purchases.[1] He had excavations made both within and without the city. From Paris and Brussels he obtained, with the assistance of the nuncios, a number of valuable gobelins [2] which were considered as the essential foundations of a sumptuous, truly princely decoration of a house. Mosaics, among them the picture of his uncle, were made for him by Marcello Provenzale.[3] Besides Christian and classical antiques,[4] the Cardinal was above all bent on acquiring valuable pictures, so much so that his gallery rivalled that of the emperor Rudolph II. Among his pictures were works by masters of the first rank. Great was the joy of the art-loving prelate when he succeeded, in 1608, in acquiring for his collection the "Burial of Christ" which Raphael had painted in his twenty-fifth year for Atalante Baglioni, at San Francesco in Perugia.[5] This picture became henceforth the jewel of his collection in which one also admired a "St. John" by Raphael, a Madonna by Fra Bartolomeo, Domenichini's "Sibyl of Cumae" and "Diana's Chase", "The Burning of Troy", by Barocci, a "Roma" by D'Arpino, a "Nativity of Christ" by Salviati, a "Judith"

[1] A *Brief for the benefit of Borghese (undated) contains an absolution "a censuris et poenis incursis ob acquisitionem statuarum pretiosarum et columnarum marmor. et operum divers. insign. tam sculpt. quam pictuar. ad ornamentum palatinorum et villarum suarum tam urbis quam extra cum facultate alias acquirendi absque licentiae requisitione," *Arm.* 42, t. 57, p. 25, and 108, Papal Secret Archives.

[2] See BENTIVOGLIO, *Lettere*, I. *passim*. *Cf.* MÜNTZ, *La tapisserie en Italie*, I., 38; ORBAAN, 203; BROM, *Archivalia*, III., 5; *Mededeelingen v. h. Nederlandsch. Hist. Institut te Rome*, I. (1921), 141 *seq.*, III. (1923), 209 *seq.*; IV. (1925), 137 *seq.*

[3] BAGLIONE, 350; the mosaic portrait of Paul V. is in the Galleria Borghese; it bears the inscription, *Paulus P.M.A. 1621.*

[4] See BOSIO, *Roma Sotterranea*, 287.

[5] On the peculiar manner with which Borghese proceeded in his passion for collecting objects of art, a manner that is incomprehensible to us to-day, see J. SAUER, *Wie Raffaels "Grablegung" in den Besitz der Borghese kam*, Rome, 1924.

by Baglioni, a "David with the head of Goliath" by Caravaggio, Titian's "Venus recumbent", as well as pictures by Cigoli, Lavinio Fontana, Pordenone, Paolo Veronese, Passignano and Bril. The enthusiastic art collector overlooked the fact that representations of Venus were hardly suitable for the rooms of a Cardinal. Scipio Borghese admired these scenes inspired by ancient mythology with the unembarrassed enjoyment of the man of the Renaissance. Among modern sculptures, his collection included works by Cordier, Berthelot, Prospero Bresciano, Guidotti and the young Bernini. Mention is also made of a piece by Michelangelo.[1]

These treasures, which he loved to show to distinguished visitors, as, for instance, in 1613 to the ambassador of the emperor,[2] the Cardinal distributed between his Roman palaces; a large part also went to his country house outside the Porta Pinciana and some he took to his villa amid the hills of Frascati.

In the Tusculum of antiquity Paul V. had begun by buying for his nephew the villa of Cardinal Galli, and there he resided during the summer months between 1607–1614. In 1613, he acquired, together with the possessions of duke Gian Angelo Altemps, the Villa Mondragone, and to this he soon after-

[1] List in ORBAAN, 110–115. *Cf.* also VENTURI, *Note sulla Galleria Borghese, in L'Arte,* XII. (1909), 31 *seqq.*; the poem mentioned by ORBAAN is not by Fantuzzi but by Scipione Francucci: *La galleria del ill. Scipione card. Borghese cantata,* 1613 (*Borghese,* IV., 102, Papal Secret Archives, original text). VENTURI mentions an impression of it at Arezzo, 1647. In Manilli's description (60 *seqq.*; see below, p. 450, n. 7) it is not clear what the Borghese acquired after the death of Scipione. Purchases of statues are mentioned in the following Avvisi in ORBAAN: 90, 155, 190. Notwithstanding Borghese's passion for collecting, many antique pieces went abroad now as before, especially to Florence; see BERTOLOTTI, *Esportazioni di oggetti di belle arti nella Toscana,* in the *Riv. Europea,* 1877, II., 717 *seqq.*

[2] ORBAAN, 207.

wards added the Villa Taverna.[1] In view of the fact that from 1614 until the end of his life, the Pope resided for a considerable period at the Villa Mondragone, both in spring and in the autumn, it became necessary considerably to enlarge and embellish that country house.[2] It was thus that the immense terrace came to be built, as well as the great fountain, with three basins supported underneath by four dragons and above by four eagles.[3] The alterations at the Villa Mondragone were directed by Jan van Santen,[4] a native of the Netherlands, who since the death, in 1613, of Ponzio, had become architect of the pontifical palaces.[5] To him also fell the task of erecting the garden house of the town villa which Cardinal Scipio planned for himself on the North side, just outside the gates of Rome. In 1606,[6] he began buying the hilly stretch of country between the Porta Flaminia and the Porta Pinciana on which subsequently arose the garden house and the park of three miles circumference. Succeeding centuries have so profoundly altered this estate that its primitive aspect can only be visualized by means of old prints and travellers' descriptions.[7]

[1] GROSSI-GONDI, *Le Ville Tusculane* (1901), 89 *seqq.*; *cf.* TOMASSETTI, IV., 447, 449.

[2] GROSSI-GONDI, 93 *seqq.*, 100.

[3] COLASANTI, *Fontane*, 157.

[4] Grossi-Gondi has proved this from the accounts (105 *seqq.*). It was only under Urban VIII. that Carlo Rainaldi made the magnificent main portal (*ibid.*, 107 *seqq.*).

[5] BAGLIONE, 175; *cf.* ORBAAN, 310. July 27, 1613, first, February 19, 1621, last payment to Jan van Santen (see BERTOLOTTI, *Artisti Belgi ed Olandesi* (1880), 38 *seqq.*), who appears in 1611 as *architetto delle fontane*; see ORBAAN, *Bescheiden in Italië*, I., 66.

[6] ORBAAN, 75.

[7] For what follows see *The Diary of John Evelyn* (1644), 106; JACOMO MANILLI, *Villa Borghese fuori di porta Pincia descritta da J.M.*, Roma, 1650 (detailed description *da servire alla curiosità de' forastieri e particolarmente de' signori oltramontani, divotissimi, per così dire, delle antichità nostre*); D. MONTELATICI, *Villa Borghese*, Roma, 1700; KEYSSLER, *Reisen*, II., 118 *seq.*; MORONI, C., 214 *seqq.*; FALDA, *Giardini*, see COLASANTI, *Fontane*, 194 *seq.*;

The park, laid out by Domenico Savino and Girolamo Rainaldi, included about three-fifths of the present shady recreation ground known to every visitor to Rome. Entirely enclosed by a double wall, it was adorned with pyramids, summer houses and towers, so that, when seen from a distance, it presented the appearance "of a small town in itself".[1]

The main entrance, "a gunshot" north of the Porta Pinciana, the cardinal adorned with his own and the Pope's coat-of-arms and the inscription *Villa Burghesia*.[2] By it one

L. Vicchi, *Villa Borghese nella storia e nelle tradizioni del popolo Romano*, Roma, 1885; Justi, *Winckelmann*, II.[2], 19 *seq.*; Durm, *Renaissance in Italien*, 214 *seq.*; Rodani, *B. Cenci*, Rome, 1899, 53 *seqq.*; Bergner, in *Zeitschr. f. bild. Kunst., N.F.*, XXV. (1914), 15 *seq.*; A. Venturi, *Il Museo e la Galeria Borghese, con 157 illustrazioni*, Bergamo, 1906; M. Gothein, I., 346 *seq.*; O. v. Gerstfeldt u. E. Steinmann, *Pilgerfahrten in Italien*,[4] Leipzig, 1922, 344 *seq.*; E. v. Kerkhoff, *Oud Italiansche Villa's*, Rotterdam, 1923, XL. *seq.*, 46 *seq.* Cardinal Borghese had yet another villa which the Pope visited on several occasions (see *Alaleone* in Orbaan, 18, 29), namely Cecchignola, situated most picturesquely on the Acqua Ferentina but which remained incomplete and which in its present state of desolation is almost completely forgotten. The last Pope to make repeated stays there was Leo XII.

[1] This was Evelyn's impression when he visited the villa on November 17, 1644 (*Diary*, 106). Totti had already expressed himself in similar terms (*Roma moderna* (1638), 341.

[2] This entrance still remains but is always closed (reproduction in Rusconi, 87). The present approach near the Porta Pinciana stands on ground subsequently acquired. The part near Porta del Popolo, where the villa Giustiniani stood, was only bought at the beginning of the nineteenth century by prince Camillo Borghese. As early as the eighteenth century prince Marcantonio had altered the old park "into an English park showing strong classical tendencies" and so changed the original character as to make it almost unrecognizable. It was then that the Giardino del Lago, the Hippodrome, the medieval castle, etc., were built; the summer house was also altered in 1782. In 1902 the family sold the whole estate to the Italian government which gave it to the city of Rome for a public park.

entered the first section of the villa, the so-called Giardino Boscareccio.[1] At the end of a long, gently rising and shady avenue of elm trees, the visitor beheld a fountain in a rocky cave surmounted by an eagle and flanked by four lofty plane trees.[2] This entrance way, by the side of which ran three lateral walks, was crossed, in the middle, by the main avenue to which again corresponded two lateral ones. Only at the crossing did one get the first glimpse of the garden house of the Villa.

The Giardino Boscareccio was divided into square bosquets surrounded by hedges and planted with laurels, cypresses, planes, pines and oaks. On both sides of the main alley, at the points where it crossed the lateral alleys, plain yet beautiful fountains were erected in circular spaces and surrounded with circular seats and a great many statues: the whole of Olympus was represented here.[3] Near the enclosure wall, but completely hidden, a small round temple of the Doric order rose above an ivy-clad cave which served as a wine cellar. In the summer heat this temple was used as a dining room, as, for instance in July, 1614, on the occasion of the Spanish ambassador's visit to the villa.[4]

Behind the garden house the second section of the villa, nearly as large as the first, which it rivalled with its babbling fountains and its statues, stretched away in an eastern direction. In the centre stood an obelisk surmounted by the Borghese eagle. In the southern section stood a building with stables, coach-houses and rooms for the domestic staff. The northern enclosure wall was decorated like a stage and its columns, statues of gods, and ancient inscriptions presented a

[1] The old division is already given in the earliest guide book, that of MANILLI (p. 2). *Cf.* the plan engraved by Simone Felice in FALDA, *Giardini*, 16, and on a smaller scale in GOTHEIN, I., 345.

[2] This spot is now occupied by the beautiful fountain of the sea horses.

[3] MANILLI, 11; GUIDI, 33. The fountains still remain; reproductions in FRIEDLÄNDER, 3.

[4] See Avviso in ORBAAN, 223.

most picturesque spectacle.[1] In the centre, on a marble tablet, the visitor read the much discussed inscription: "Whoever thou art, so long as thou art a free man, fear not here the bonds of the laws! Go where thou wilt, ask whatever thou desirest, go away whenever thou wishest. More is here provided for the stranger than for the owner. In this golden age, which holds the promise of universal security, the master of the house wishes to lay no iron laws upon the well-bred. Let seemly enjoyment be the guest's only law. But let him who with malice aforethought offends against the golden law of urbanity fear lest the irate custodian burn for him the sacred emblems of hospitality."[2] From two windows one had a view of the adjoining open hunting grounds which, owing to the fact that they had been left in their natural state, constituted a most effective contrast to these lavishly ornamental pleasure grounds.

The third section of the villa consisted of a large animal preserve. Here meadow land, valleys and forest-clad hills joined together all the beauties of a natural landscape and a

[1] Still standing, though in a ruinous condition.

[2] For the correct text, which was already wrongly given by MANILLI (159) and more recently by GOTHEIN (I., 350), and which disappeared in 1848, see VICCHI (288), who rejects the idea that the villa was open to the public at that time. This view has been recently defended by MAES (*La questione di Villa Borghese*, Roma, 1885. *Cf.* also *Il diritto del popolo Romano sulla Villa Borghese*, Roma, 1885). The documents here given speak in favour of Maes' view. It is certain that at first admission was granted to strangers, even to foreigners. But when a visitor from a country north of the Alps had been shocked by some of the pictures to be seen at the summer house, Paul V. forbade admission to it. RECORDATI reports this on December 8, 1612, in the following terms: "De ordini santissimi s'è dato ordine al guardarobba di Borghese che non mostri più il casino di Borghese a persona veruna, perchè un Fiamengo ch'ha veduto certe pitture dentro un puoco lascive, onde ha detto cose da fuoco, che resapute dal Papa ha dato questa commissione," Gonzaga Archives, Mantua.

southern vegetation. All over the varied ground and harmonizing with it, there were scattered special small shelters for ostriches, peacocks, tortoises, a lake with two tiny islands and enlivened by swans, ducks and other aquatic creatures, thickets for deer and doe, cages for a lion and a leopard which a merchant of Tunis had presented to the Cardinal together with two camels.[1] There were also to be found bird-decoys, small summer-houses, tiny ornamental gardens and fountains. The eye was charmed by a shady wood of majestic pines, long alleys of ilexes and elms, groups of decorative cypresses, evergreen hedges of rare shrubs, broad-leaved fig trees and miniature vineyards. In the direction of the *muro torto* a garden was laid out with rare flowers, fruit trees, fountains and statues. A fairly large garden house adjoined it. This part was approached from the first by a gateway bearing the Borghese arms surmounted by two dragons and an eagle. A long alley of ilexes opened here. The other gateway, towards the *muro torto*, though much altered, remains to this day.

This magnificent park, in which nature and art joined forces and by which Scipio Borghese and the Pope, who provided the funds, vied, as genuine Romans, with their forefathers, soon became the theme of the poets' songs,[2] was described by all travellers,[3] and admired as one of the world's wonders.[4] It constituted a worthy setting for Jan van Santen's

[1] See ORBAAN, 269 *seq.*; K. Stein mentions, besides the camel, *alia animalia ac res varae ex India et America aliisque orbis terrarum partibus nuper allatae, loc. cit.*, Königsberg Library.

[2] See the poem of F. FRANCUCCI, referred to above, p. 450, note 1; L. LEPOREO, *Villa Borghese* (*cf.* Appendix No. 11); A. BRIGENTIUS, *Villa Burghesia*, Romae, 1716.

[3] See especially the above quoted travel notes of K. Stein, of the year 1619 (p. 440, n. 2), Library of Königsberg.

[4] TOTTI, *Roma moderna* (1638), 341 *seq.*; P. ROSSINI, *Il Mercurio errante II.* (1704), 91; EVELYN (1644) calls the villa a paradise.

garden house,[1] a typical baroque building [2] which was not intended for a dwelling place, but solely as a resort where the Cardinal could retire, mostly for short periods, for the purpose of recreation or to receive his visitors.

A picture by Johann Wilhelm Baur (1610–1640), shows the original appearance of the subsequently greatly altered two-storied house, the centre of which was adorned with two towers.[3] Here one sees with what ingenuity the Dutch master turned the front of the house into a stone tablet, which one had never done reading [4]: the niches are occupied by great ancient statues, the wall space is systematically covered with a mass of antique fragments, so as completely to hide the heavy structural lines of the building; busts of emperors alternate with reliefs, architectural fragments, festoons, garlands and inscriptions.

Baur's picture also shows the busy life of which the spacious, quadrangular court in front of the garden house was the

[1] BAGLIONE, 97, 176, and BERTOLOTTI, *Artisti Suizz.*, 58. The Flemish master's name was not Hans von Xanten, as stated by BERGNER (37), nor Zans, as given by GROSSI-GONDI (106), but Jan van Santen; he was a native of Utrecht, and is mentioned, after 1596, in the Deeds of the archives of the Campo Santo al Vaticano. In 1606 he was camerlengo of the confraternity there; see HOOGEWERFF, *Nederlandsche Schilders in Italië*, Utrecht, 1912, 261. The first payment to him is dated July, 1613, the last April, 1621, in BERTOLOTTI, *Artisti Belgi et Oland*, 38 *seq.*; the engravings mentioned above (p. 437, n. 3) of the *aedif. et ruinar. Romae* are dedicated *Ioanni van Santeen Flandro Ultraiect., Pauli V. architecto.* For an exhaustive account of his life and work *cf.* HOOGEWERFF, "Een Nederlandsch 'Monument' te Rome en zijn boumeester Jan van Santen," in *Bullet. van den Ned. Oudheidk. Bond*, 1914, 205 *seqq.* The artist died on August 25, 1621.

[2] WÖLFFLIN, *Renaissance und Barock*, 1587.

[3] The picture (see catalogue Venturi, 221) with other paintings by Baur (Quirinal, Capitol, etc.) adorns the Galleria Borghese; reproduction in MUÑOZ, *Roma barocca*, 73. On *J. Baur* see THIEME, III., 89.

[4] JUSTI, *Winckelmann*, II.², 19.

scene. The drive is framed by a splendid travertine parapet with seats, at the crossings pedestals support antique statues, the lower ones being skilfully made to serve as fountains. In the somewhat smaller court, at the back of the house, there are splendid hermæ [1] and antique statues surrounded by laurel and oleander bushes; the centre is occupied by the basin of a fountain with a statue of Narcissus.

In keeping with the usual custom, small gardens (*giardini segreti*) were laid out on either side of the house, in which the fragrance of orange blossom mingled with that of rare flowers and plants. Bentivoglio had procured the tulips from Holland.[2] The North garden is adorned with two aviaries richly decorated with statues, busts and stucco,[3] similar to those in the Farnese gardens on the Palatine. On the pedestals of the statues and everywhere else the dragon of the Borghese appears as a decorative motif.

A beautiful vestibule leads into the interior of the house. Here three doors open into the great central reception hall; by the side of it are two smaller rooms; at the back there is a gallery connected with two rooms, a large and a small one.[4] By a modest winding staircase the visitor reaches the upper storey which is similarly divided. Here also all the rooms are inter-connected, spacious, and designed from the beginning for the display of valuable works of art and, accordingly, richly adorned, especially the gallery, which is a masterpiece of marble incrustation.[5] To this must be added bright-hued frescos on the ceilings and in the loggia of the upper storey by Lanfranco.[6] The contemporaries cannot find words to express

[1] Reproduction in RUSCONI, 77, and FERRARI, *Lo stucco nell'arte ital.*, 101 *seq.*

[2] See HENSEN, in the *Mededeelingen v. h. Nederl. Hist. Institut. te Rome*, III. (1923), 205 *seq.*

[3] Reproduced in RUSCONI, 73, 77.

[4] GURLITT, 99; ROSE, *Spätbarock*, 141 *seq.*, 177, 188.

[5] BURCKHARDT, *Cicerone*, II.[4], 277; HOOGEWERFF, *Een Nederlandsch Monument*, 225.

[6] PASSERI, 131; BELLORI, II., 122; MANILLI, 95; *Jahrb. der preuss. Kunstsamml.*, XL., 144; ROSE, 215.

their admiration of the art treasures preserved in the garden house.[1] The antique pieces, in part displayed in niches, the pillars of oriental alabaster and other kinds of valuable stone adorned with statuettes, the tables of porphyry and Florentine mosaics of semi-precious stones, were rivalled by a number of expensive and valuable pictures, among them being works by Raphael, Michelangelo, Titian, Pordenone, Pomarancio, D'Arpino and Palma Vecchio.[2] Mention is also made of an ingenious musical instrument, a rare set of chessmen and a surprise chair which held fast the person who sat in it.[3]

Not content with the masterpieces of ancient sculpture (the "Wrestler" of Agasias of Ephesus,[4] the dying Seneca, a Venus and a Hermaphrodite), Cardinal Borghese had a scene from Virgil carved in marble by Pietro Bernini and his son Lorenzo. The group represents Aeneas rescuing his aged father Anchises, who holds his domestic gods (*Penates*) in his hands, from the sea of flames which devour Troy. The genius of the young artist which here still appears fettered by the mannerism of his father, reached its full development in the statue of "David with the sling" which was finished in 1619. Even more famous than this work, which was exposed in the South lateral corridor of the ground floor, is another and later group which also owes its origin to a commission of Scipio Borghese. It represents Daphne, pursued by Apollo, metamorphosed into a laurel tree, in such wise that her feet grow into the ground as roots and laurel leaves sprout from the

[1] The first accurate description was given by the *guardaroba* of the villa, MANILLI (53–115).

[2] *Cf.* in Appendix No. 11 the poem of L. LEPOREO, Papal Secret Archives.

[3] K. STEIN, besides the four antique statues, mentions also "*instrumentum musicum artificiosissimum; ludus scaccarum rarissimus; mensae marmoreae pretiosissimae; sella admirabilis, quae insidentes ita concludit, ut se movere non possint*" (Library of Königsberg). *Cf.* EVELYN'S *Diary, loc. cit.*

[4] Now in the Louvre, Paris.

hair of her head and from the hands which she rings in her mortal anguish.[1]

Pope and Cardinal frequently sought an escape from the tumult of affairs among these works of art. They found refreshment in the summer house and the garden which, in the words of an English traveller, had not their equal in the whole world.[2] The Eternal City, with its never ceasing traffic, seemed far away, for one could neither see nor hear it. From the windows one could look out over the green park into the silent campagna and contemplate the incomparable ring of blue mountains, from jagged Soracte to the lofty chain of the Apennines and the smiling Alban hills.

Lorenzo Bernini has immortalized his patron in two wonderful portrait busts. Baldinucci tells a charming anecdote in connection with the work. He relates that before the first bust was completed the artist discovered, on the forehead and temples, a disfiguring vein in the marble which gave the countenance an unpleasing expression. Bernini, who wanted above all things to gratify his noble patron, decided to make a new bust, which he completed within a fortnight of feverish work. When the Cardinal came to the studio, Bernini began by showing him the first bust, at the sight of which Scipio Borghese only hid his disappointment with difficulty. His pleasure was all the greater when Bernini uncovered the second bust. All the same, from the artistic point of view and notwithstanding the flaw in the marble, the first bust is by far the most successful and the most characteristic. Here Scipio Borghese appears extraordinarily life-like, in all the vigour of his mature manhood, his countenance expressive of energy and enterprise and radiating joy in the possession of his art treasures, so much so that the beholder almost imagines

[1] BALDINUCCI, *Bernini*, 63 *seq.*, 67 *seq.*, 73 *seq.* *Cf.* MUÑOZ, *Roma barocca*, 76 *seq.* VENTURI, in *L'Arte*, XII., 50, has ascertained the date of the "David" by means of a payment to the artist. On the position of David see MANILLI, 61 ; *ibid.*, 69, on the groups of the Aeneas and Daphne in the *terza stanza* of the ground floor.

[2] See *Pap. of the British School*, VI. (1913), 485.

he lives and breathes—the bust is an instantaneous photograph in marble.[1]

After many wanderings, both busts have once more found in the summer house a most appropriate home. In conjunction with Bernini's [2] small bust of Paul V., they remind the visitor that the Cardinal's patronage of the arts attained its climax in the sumptuous villa outside the Porta del Popolo, in the same way as that of the Pope in the completion of the basilica of St. Peter. Whilst the art lover admires these masterpieces, they remind the historian that nepotism which, from the ecclesiastical standpoint was so blameworthy, substantially helped to uphold the best tradition of the Renaissance, viz. the fostering of the arts.

No other family, perhaps, has left so many splendid and lasting monuments of itself in Rome, as the Borghese: churches, chapels, palaces, aqueducts, fountains, streets, villas and gardens loudly proclaim what the Borghese have done for the arts and for the common good. The Pope and his nephew deemed it one of their most weighty duties to embellish the Eternal City. They acted thus, as true Romans, not only for the good of their native city, but they likewise sought to shed still greater lustre upon the papacy.[3] Their names, like those of Julius II. and Sixtus V., are written for all time in letters of gold in the annals of art and civilization.

[1] BALDINUCCI, *Bernini*, ed. Riegl, 56 *seqq.*; MUÑOZ, *Roma barocca*, 87 *seq.* According to the accounts of January, 1633, referred to by Fraschetti, both busts were made to an order of Urban VIII., in which case Baldinucci's anecdote is disposed of.

[2] See vol. XXV, 44, n. 3

[3] *Cf.* the remarks of GIOVANNI TOMMASI, in his *Tractatus de cardinalibus* (Cod., X., VI., 18, Bibl. Casanatense, Rome), quoted by MAES, *Villa Borghese*, 59 *seq.* "Paul V.," says ESCHER (*Barock*, 16), "by reason of his energy and determination, was the right man to reshape Rome in the spirit of Julius II. and Sixtus V.; as a matter of fact not only did he endeavour to vie with the latter, he even sought to surpass him by the number, greatness and magnificence of his undertakings."

APPENDIX

OF

UNPUBLISHED DOCUMENTS

AND

EXTRACTS FROM ARCHIVES

APPENDIX

1. Pope Paul V. to Matthias, King of Hungary.[1]

Rome, April 4th, 1609.

Carissimo in Christo filio Nostro Matthiae Ungariae regi illustri.
Paulus Papa V.

Carissime in Christo fili Noster, salutem et apostolicam benedictionem. Gravissima animi molestia affecti sumus ex his quae accepimus de compositione inter Maiestatem Tuam et Austriae haereticos nuper facta. Dolemus enim vehementer id tanto cum divini honoris et catholicae religionis atque communis boni detrimento transactum fuisse, et Tua etiam causa valde dolemus, qui de Tua tranquillitate atque honore, ut patrem amantissimum decet, semper solliciti, videmus quam timere debeas Dei iram, cuius misericordiam propitiam Tibi reddere iugiter studuimus. Fili carissime, Deus est per quem reges regnant et hominum cogitationes vanae sunt. Divinum igitur auxilium nobis concilienus inprimis oportet, et humana consilia, quae alio respiciunt, perniciem afferunt, non securitatem; sed hoc assequi non potest, quicunque Dei honorem negligit et apparentis fallacisque commoditatis rationem illi praeponit. Nos quidem versamur in magna afflictione et venerabilis frater Placidus episcopus Melphiensis Apostolicus Nuncius Noster significabit Maiestati Tuae Nostram hanc vehementem sollicitudinem multaque simul ad negocium pertinentia Tibi renunciabit, cui fidem consuetam adhibeas cupimus. Dirigat Dominus cogitationes et opera Tua in beneplacito suo, et Nos Maiestati Tuae apostolicam benedictionem Nostram tribuimus.

Datum Romae apud Sanctum Petrum sub annulo piscatoris pridie nonas Aprilis MDCIX., pontificatus Nostri anno quarto.

Petrus Stroza.

[*Arm.* 44, t. 4, n. 384, Papal Secret Archives.]

[1] See above, p. 285.

2. A Memorial to Pope Paul V. on the State of the Diocese of Metz.[1]

[End of 1609.]

Beatissimo Padre.

La chiesa di Metz, della quale hoggidì si trova vescovo il cardinale di Givry, è insigne e principale in quei contorni, posta ai confini di Lorena, Germania e Flandria, ha qualche infettione di heresia e se ne può sperare bene si sarà aiutata da chi deve. Ma il clero di quella è molto corrotto et tutto camina al peggio sendo in possesso di usar della lubricità della carne li ecclesiastici et in specie il capitolo et canonici della cathedrale con pretensione che il vescovo non possa supra di loro havere iurisdittione alcuna, et havendo detto cardinale et vescovo dato principio a voler correggere et emendare tal inconveniente, detto capitolo et canonici si sono opposti et con cavilationi et appellationi vanno turbando ogni cosa, onde si vede che si V. S. motu proprio non provede a tal inconveniente col dare Breve delegatorio amplissimo di correggere, punire et castigare simil corrutela in buona forma procedendo avanti ad ogni atto rigoroso tanto nelle cause comminciate et pendenti quanto in quelle che a suo tempo si comminceranno auctoritate apostolica al detto cardinale vescovo commandandoli di impiegarsi in tal funtione, si vede che detta chiesa corre pericolo di roinare in tutto, poichè dalla vita del clero nasce lo scandalo publico, si contrastano i catholici, li heretici pigliano piede et tutti insieme tendono a tal ruina si come el medesimo et per l'istesse cause ruinò già del trenta sei la chiesa di Geneva, come si vede con tanto danno essere sucesso, et quella di Bisanzone archivescovato camina a gran passo al medesimo, si Vostra Beatitudine non provede ; et chi acenna questo è molto bene informato et è stato poco fa sul luogo et basti che si sia scarricato la coscienza col sommo pastor della Chiesa.

[*Cod.* 219, p. 379 *seq.*, Stadtbibl. at Metz.]

3. Pope Paul V. to Marie de Medici, Queen of France.[2]

Rome, August 17th, 1611.

Carissimae in Christo filiae Nostrae Mariae Francorum reginae christianissimae regenti.

Paulus Papa quintus.

Carissima in Christo filia Nostra, salutem et apostolicam benedictionem. Universalis Ecclesiae cura humilitati Nostrae

[1] See above, p. 54. [2] See above, p. 55.

divina dispensatione commissa exigit a Nobis, ut quantum praestare possumus, singularum ecclesiarum statui et conservationi iuxta apostolicam disciplinam prospiciamus. Ideo mentis oculos intenta cogitatione ad omnes christiani orbis partes circumferimus diligentique investigatione vineam Domini et operarios culturae illius praepositos ubique locorum, quatenus permissum est, lustrare atque recognoscere sedulo curamus, piorum atque prudentum virorum fidem atque diligentiam in hoc tam gravi negocio adhibentes. Et vero non leve solatium Nobis attulerunt, quae de statu multarum atque insignium ecclesiarum in amplissimo florentissimoque Galliarum regno accepimus, in quibus episcopi, zelo Dei et gregis sibi commissi caritate incensi, ministerium suum adimplere ex apostolico praecepto student. Quo nomine Maiestati Tuae plurimum gratulamur, cum nihil sit quod aeque conducat ad regni felicem facilemque gubernationem ac sacerdotii probitas. Duo enim sunt, carissima in Christo filia, quibus regia auctoritas maxime fulcitur: divina nempe gratia et subiectorum obedientia; utraque sacerdotalis virtus et bonitas praestat. Haec propitium regi reddit divinum auxilium assiduitate precum et puritate sacrificiorum, haec populos divino timore instruit, legibus obtemperare assuefacit; facile enim leges observant, qui, ne in Deum peccent, non solum iniquas operationes, sed pravas quoque cogitationes vitant. Sic enim de timore Domini scriptum legimus, quod dilectio illius custodia legum est. Contra verum, ubi, sacerdotum socordia atque negligentia, pretiosus iste thesaurus omnium virtutum amittitur, cuncta ruunt, nec tantum ecclesiasticus ordo, sed totius regni quies atque tranquillitas confunditur. Experimentis nimis frequentibus res comprobata est. Propterea in eligendis episcopis maxima cura atque diligentia est adhibenda, debent enim doctrina scientiaque rerum divinarum atque prudentia esse veluti sal, quo caeteri sacerdotes condiantur, eisque exemplo integritatis suae vitae et caritatis ardore lucem praeferre, ut per semitam rectam Deo servientes et animarum saluti consulentes gradiantur. Quare Maiestatem Tuam hortamur atque paternae caritatis affectu admonemus, ut pro Tuo pietatis zelo, quem summum esse cognoscimus, satagas, quotiescunque occasio tulerit, ut alicui ecclesiae in Galliarum regno novus episcopus sit praeficiendus, is Nobis proponatur, qui zelum, prudentiam, doctrinam, caritatem, eam demum virtutis atque probitatis commendationem habeat, quam sacri canones in sacerdotibus ad tantum munus digne assumendis exigunt. Mandavimus venerabili fratri Roberto episcopo Montispolitiani Nuncio Nostro Apostolico, ut plura adhuc in hoc gravissimo negocio Maiestati Tuae exponeret. Illi consuetam fidem adhiberi abs Te cupimus. Deum oramus, continua Te protectione custodiat, et Maiestati Tuae peramanter benedicimus.

Datum Romae apud Sanctum Marcum sub annulo piscatoris XVI. calendas Septembris MDCXI., pontificatus Nostri anno septimo.

[*Arm.* 44, t. 7, n. 43, Papal Secret Archives.]

4. Pope Paul V. to Ferdinand, Elector and Archbishop of Cologne.[1]

Rome, July 12th, 1614.

Venerabili fratri Ferdinando archiepiscopo Coloniensi, sacri Romani imperii principi electori.
Paulus Papa quintus.

Venerabilis frater, salutem et apostolicam benedictionem. Neque fraternitati Tuae pluribus exponamus necesse est sollicitudinem Nostram de regis Romanorum electione quamprimum facienda, ut hoc obstaculo irrita reddamus studia illorum, qui ex filiorum Nostrorum discordia vires acquirunt in detrimentum Ecclesiae sanctae catholicae. Nam periculum, quod ab eius dilatione imminet, et Nostrum de communi quiete zelum non ignoras. Itaque longa oratione minime utemur, ut Tibi persuadeamus, quam gratum Nobis praestiteris officium, si, ut confidimus atque postulamus, dabis operam, ut electio ista maturetur. Nam ab anxietate animi, qua Nos sublevabis, ut Tibi renunciabit venerabilis frater Antonius episcopus Vigiliensis Noster Apostolicus Nuncius, satis hoc intelligere poteris. Qui Noster Nuncius habet a Nobis in mandatis, ut de hoc negocio Tecum sedulo agat Nostroque nomine Te efficaciter requirat, ut quibuscunque modis ac rationibus, quae opportuniores Tibi videbuntur, studeas accelerare hanc electionem, ac simul certiorem Te faciat de fiducia, quam habemus in Tua singulari prudentia, et quam Nobis polliceamur de Tua in Nos observantia atque studiosa voluntate. Illi igitur fidem

[1] See above, p. 319.

in omnibus indubitatam adhibebis et Nos benedictionem Nostram apostolicam fraternitati Tuae peramanter impartimur.

Datum ut supra [apud Sanctam Mariam Maiorem sub annulo piscatoris IV. idus Iulii MDCXIV., pontificatus Nostri anno decimo].

Petrus Stroza.

[*Arm.* 45, t. 10, n. 57, Papal Secret Archives.]

5. Pope Paul V. to Louis XIII., King of France.[1]

Rome, January 22nd, 1615.

Carissimo in Christo filio Nostro Ludovico Francorum regi christianissimo.

Paulus Papa quintus.

Carissime in Christo fili Noster, salutem et apostolicam benedictionem. Occasione conventus causa status nuper habiti retulisse ad Maiestatem Tuam accepimus praelatos et ordinem universum ecclesiasticum amplissimi istius regni Tui quam gravibus necessitatibus, quam multis incommodis ac perturbationibus eorum ecclesiae sint implicitae, atque generatim clerus omnis in Gallia, et insuper quam expediret, ut sacrosancti concilii Tridentini decreta istic reciperentur. Etsi facile Nobis persuadeamus, confisi in Tua ingenita pietate, religione optimaque voluntate, fore ut iustas hac de causa postulationes ordinis ecclesiastici regni Tui non modo humaniter audias, sed benigne quoque exaudias, tamen voluimus, zelo officii Nostri pastoralis commoti, quo indemnitati studere debemus cunctarum ecclesiarum, atque paterno affectu, quo propitiam Maiestati Tuae magis semper cupimus reddere divinam bonitatem, revocare Tibi in mentem Nostris hisce litteris obligationem, qua teneris ob innumera beneficia a misericordiarum patre Deo accepta Ecclesiae sanctae suae utilitatem curare, Christianissimorum regum maiorum Tuorum laudabilissimo exemplo, tueri ac defendere. Etenim, si Ecclesiae eiusque auctoritati faveris, ut confidimus, sperare poteris regiam Tuam auctoritatem praesidio divinae gratiae maius semper incrementum accepturam esse, ut optamus. Venerabilis frater Robertus episcopus Montispolitiani Nuncius Noster Apostolicus adhuc uberius aget mandato Nostro cum Maiestate Tua de hoc negocio, et quam Nobis cordi sit, qui

[1] See above, p. 32.

pariter Nostrum desiderium de Tua vera felicitate et quam ex animo oremus pro Te divinam clementiam, Tibi significabit, cui consuetam fidem in omnibus adhiberi abs Te cupimus, et ex intimis Nostrae paternae caritatis visceribus benedictionem Nostram apostolicam Maiestati Tuae impartimur.

Datum Romae apud Sanctam Mariam Maiorem sub annulo piscatoris XI. calendas Februarii MDCXV., pontificatus Nostri anno decimo.

Petrus Stroza.

[*Arm.* 45, t. 10, n. 252, Papal Secret Archives.]

6. Pope Paul V. to Archbishop Schweikart, Elector of Mayence.[1]

Rome, June 28th, 1615.

Venerabili fratri Ioanni Suicardo archiepiscopo Moguntino sacri Romani imperii principi electori.
Paulus Papa quintus.

Venerabilis frater, salutem et apostolicam benedictionem. Eadem animi sollicitudine de communi christianae reipublicae tranquillitate, potissimum autem de Germaniae utilitate atque commodo, ut alias fraternitati Tuae significavimus, vehementer cupimus maturationem electionis regis Romanorum, eoque vehementius, quo magis in dies apparet ex dilatione illius necessitas perfectionis huius tam gravis negocii. Cum autem tantopere confidamus in Tua prudentia atque auctoritate, ut optime nosti, mandamus venerabili fratri Antonio episcopo Vigiliensi Nuncio Nostro Apostolico, ut denuo Tibi exponat Nostrum hoc tam necessarium desiderium et quae opportuna existimemus, ut commodius et celerius perficiatur, sicut praesens rerum Germanicarum status maxime exigere videtur Nuncio igitur Nostro Apostolico eandem plane fidem adhibebis, quam Nobis haberes, si Te alloqueremur. Dirigat Dominus cogitationes et opera Tua in eius sancto beneplacito Tuosque pastorales labores aura suae sanctae gratiae clementer sublevet.

Datum Romae apud Sanctam Mariam Maiorem sub annulo piscatoris IV. cal. Iulii MDCXV., pontificatus Nostri anno undecimo.

[*Arm.* 45, t. 11, n. 8, Papal Secret Archives.]

[1] See above, p. 319.

7. POPE PAUL V. TO ARCHBISHOP SCHWEIKART, ELECTOR OF MAYENCE.[1]

Rome, October 27th, 1615.

Venerabili fratri Ioanni Suicardo archiepiscopo Moguntino sacri Romani imperii principi electori.
Paulus Papa quintus.

Venerabilis frater, salutem et apostolicam benedictionem. Hactenus fraternitati Tuae perspectam esse sollicitudinem Nostram scimus de maturanda electione regis Romanorum, neque dubitamus eam Tibi maxime cordi esse, conscii prudentiae et pietatis Tuae, qua semper communis pacis et quietis conservationem studuisti instaurationi catholicae religionis et imperii bono. Nihilomius facere non possumus, quin, etsi minime dubii de Tua voluntate, iterum Te efficacissime hortemur, ut studia conatusque Tuos in hoc gravissimo negocio iteres, et si fieri potest etiam augeas. Dilatio quippe huius electionis nimis periculosa est, ut nosti, et Nos communi utilitati prospicere sedulo debemus. Minime Te Nostris exhortationibus egere plane novimus ; verum iterum Tibi confirmamus tanto arctiori vinculo caritatem Nostram Tibi obstricturum, quanto magis celeriter Nostrum animum hac sollicitudine levabis, perfectione huius desideratissimi negocii. Exaudiat Dominus petitiones Tuas et omne Tuum consilium confirmet.

Datum Romae apud Sanctum Petrum sub annulo piscatoris pridie calendas Novembris MDCXV., pontificatus Nostri anno undecimo.

[*Arm*. 45, t. 11, n. 118, Papal Secret Archives.]

8. POPE PAUL V. TO CARDINAL KLESL.[2]

Rome, May 6th, 1616.

Dilecto filio Nostro Melchiori S. R. E. presbytero cardinali Cleselio nuncupato.
Paulus Papa quintus.

Dilecte fili Noster, salutem et apostolicam benedictionem. Quam necessaria sit conservationi cum Romani imperii tum catholicae religionis regis Romanorum electio, prudentiam

[1] See above, p. 319.
[2] See above, p. 320.

Tuam non latet, imo vero nemo hoc fortasse melius intelligit, qui tantopere praestas rerum Germanicarum peritia atque experimento. Propterea haud necessarium existimamus, ut enitamur declaratione huius necessitatis Tibi suadere, ut ad communem imperii Romani et catholicae religionis utilitatem studeas adiuvare accelerationem huius electionis. Verum, cum absolutio huius gravissimi negocii potissimum pendeat a voluntate Caesaris, Tuque apud ipsum spectatae Tuae in eum fidei ac eximiae prudentiae merito, gratia et auctoritate maxime polleas, efficaciter petere a Te voluimus, ut sedulo serioque electioni regis Romanorum faveas, ita ut quam primum, sicut omnes boni desiderant et reipublicae tranquillitas maxime exigit et Nos ad Dei gloriam et Ecclesiae sanctae catholicae tutelam maxime cupimus, absolvatur. Satis Tibi declarare non possumus, quantopere Tibi devincturus sis occasione hac Nostram paternam caritatem. Sed ex gravitate sollicitudinis, qua Nos sublevabis, facile coniicere poteris, qui pro singulari prudentia Tua optime intelligis, quam anxie curare debeamus hanc electionem vel hac potissimum una da causa, ne haereticorum vires et audacia magis augeantur pari cum detrimento Ecclesiae catholicae, Romani imperii et augustae Austriacae familiae Nobis tantopere dilectae. Omnipotens ac misericors Deus Te in suo sancto servitio confortare et conservare dignetur, et Nos Tibi peramanter benedicimus.

Datum ut supra [Romae apud S. Mariam Maiorem sub annulo piscatoris pridie nonas Maii MDCXVI., pontificatus Nostri anno undecimo].

[*Arm.* 45, t. 11, n. 263, Papal Secret Archives.]

9. Pope Paul V. to the Emperor Matthias.[1]

Rome, December 16th, 1616.

Carissimo in Christo filio Nostro Matthiae Hungariae et Bohemiae regi illustri in Rom. imperatorem electo.
Paulus Papa quintus.

Carissime in Christo fili Noster, salutem et apostolicam benedictionem. Paternae caritatis zelo, quo de tranquillitate ac pace christianae reipublicae solliciti sumus, cogimur

[1] See above, p. 322.

renovare petitiones adhortationesque, quibus toties iam a Maiestate Tua efficacissime postulavimus absolutionem gravissimi negocii successionis. Ea Nobis hactenus renunciata fuerunt de propensa ad hoc voluntate Tua, ut firmam spem concepissemus desiderati solatii. Valde quidem afficit animum Nostrum haec sollicitudo, carissime fili ; nam tametsi diuturnam speremus et precemur Maiestati Tuae vitam, nihilominus ambiguitas haec tam nostris est periculosa quam adversariis opportuna : quod nemo melius Te novit. Igitur ut uno eodemque tempore, una eademque re communi utilitati, peculiari augustae familiae Tuae bono eximiaeque Tuae prudentiae laudi ac propriae Nostrae consolationi consulas, a Te etiam atque etiam petimus, sicut uberius frater Vitalianus archiepiscopus Adrianopolitanus Noster Apostolicus Nuncius Tibi significabit, et Maiestati Tuae ex intimis Nostrae caritatis visceribus benedictionem Nostram apostolicam impartimur.

Datum Romae apud Sanctam Mariam Maiorem sub annulo piscatoris XVII. calendas Ianuarii MDCXVI., pontificatus Nostri anno duodecimo.

[*Arm.* 45, t. 11, n. 183, Papal Secret Archives.]

10. Paul V. to Cardinal Klesl.[1]

Rome, December 16th, 1616.

Dilecto filio Nostro Melchiori S. R. E. card. Cleselio nuncupato.
Paulus Papa quintus.

Dilecte fili Noster, salutem et apostolicam benedictionem. Conquiescebamus ea spe, quam excitaverant in Nobis absolutionis gravissimi negocii successioni litterae Tuae prudenter et accurate ad Nos iamdudum scriptae. Sed cum imperfectum adhuc illud videamus, multo sane maiori animi molestia atque sollicitudine afficimur, tantoque magis, quanto de voluntate deque diligentia Tua minus dubitare possumus. De impedimentis itaque atque difficultatibus dubii, sed de Tua auctoritate et gratia apud Caesarem certi, ad quem hac de causa sane quam efficaciter scribimus, significare Tibi non modo Nostris hisce litteris, sed per venerabilem quoque fratrem Vitalianum archiepiscopum Adrianopolitanum sollicitudinem Nostram voluimus atque etiam enixe a Te petere, ut omnibus

[1] See above, p. 322.

rationibus ac modis, qui praestanti prudentiae Tuae opportuniores videbuntur, velis Nos a cura tam gravi, qua diu noctuque premimur, sublevare et una communi christianae reipublicae bono et catholicae religionis conservationi prospicere. Diligimus Te quidem ex animo, sed Noster paternus in Te amor plurimum augebitur ex solatio, quod Nobis pollicemur ex opera Tua, sicut latius Tibi Noster Apostolicus Nuncius exponet, quem non secus ac Nos loquentes audies, et Nos cum omni caritatis affectu Nostram Tibi apostolicam benedictionem impartimur.

Datum ut supra [Romae apud Sanctam Mariam Maiorem sub annulo piscatoris XVII. calendas Ianuarii MDCXVI., pontificatus Nostri anno duodecimo].

[*Arm.* 45, t. 11, n. 184, Papal Secret Archives.]

11. Poem of Ludovico Leporeo on the Villa Borghese.[1]

Villa Borghese
cantata da Lodovico Leporeo
all'ill^{mo} et rev^{mo} sig^{r} card. padrone.

Sestina 1^{a}.

O famose di Pindo habitatrici,
Meco cangiate le magioni antiche,
E venite a goder de più felici
Selve, prati, antri, fonti e piagge apriche ;
Tutte accorrete a vagheggiare il sito
De la Borghese Villa, ove io v'invito.

7^{a}.

Scipion di nome e d'animo Romano,
Illustrator del fosco secol nostro,
Che l'alto impero ha della Chiesa in mano
Non men splendente di valor che d'ostro,
Degnissimo che 'l mondo honori et ami
E semideo de' porporati il chiami.

. . . .

[1] See above, p. 458.

65ª.

Illustri statue e lucide colonne
Splendono intorno gli angoli leggiadri
E di famosi eroi, d'eroiche donne
Sono i bei volti effigiati in quadri :
Hor qui mirate imagini più belle
Che mai pingesse col pennello Apelle

66ª.

Delle città la gigantessa altera
In ampio quadro par che parli e dica :
Hoggi rinasco a degnità primiera.
Hoggi racquisto la mia gloria antica,
Mentre novo Scipion mi rinovella,
Risorgo più che pria famosa e bella.

67ª.

Cedan le penne e cedano gl'inchiostri
D'almi poeti e nobili oratori,
O sien d'antichi o pur de' tempi nostri,
E i vaghi altrui pennelli e bei colori
Ch'illuminar od ombreggiar simile
Indarno s'affatica ogn'altro stile.

68ª.

Opra mirate qui del gran Titiano,
Dell'opre sue la più famosa e diva
Che figurò con maestrevol mano
De l'humanato Dio l'imagin viva,
Fanciullo testè nato in grembo a quella
Che sola madre e vergine s'appella.

69ª.

L'impicciolito Creator del mondo
Sotto mortali e tenerelle membra,
Agli occhi altrui severo, altrui giocondo,
Tanto l'arte potè, dubbio rassembra,
E tal splendor dai lumi suoi traluce
Che ad adorar sua Deità n'induce.

70[a].

Quivi la bella madre il suo bel figlio,
Che per noi partorì, dimostra in seno,
A lei simile, candido e vermiglio,
D'ogni giocondità del ciel ripieno;
Vergin beata e madre semidea
Che col beato suo fanciul ne bea.

71[a].

Ma, s'io non erro, voi voi sete Muse,
Le vergini antichissime Sibille,
Che del presente alto mistero infuse
Lo prediceste già mille anni e mille,
Onde tropp'oltre sorvolò mia penna,
Se questa vi spiegò, l'altre v'accenna.

72[a].

Emuli di Titian la coppia egregia,
Pordenon, Buonaroti e Raffaello,
Per cui l'andato secolo si pregia
Colorir con angelico pennello
Sacrate istorie quei, questi profane,
Che colman di stupor le menti humane.

73[a].

Qui pure esercitaro i lor pennelli
Pasignan, Pomarancio, Arpino e Palma,
De la moderna età viventi Apelli,
Nè dir saprei chi la vittoria impalma;
Ditelo voi, vergini saggie e vaghe,
Qual di quell'opre sia che più v'appaghe.

74[a].

Con vago e distint'ordine ristretti
Per artificio inimitabil rari
Mirate in angustissimi quadretti
Spatiose campagne, immensi mari;
Qui l'ampia varietà de la natura
Similissima a lei l'arte figura.

[*Borghese*, I., 425, pp. 1–2, 12[b]–13[b], Papal Secret Archives.]

12. Pope Paul V. and the Church of St. Peter.[1]

. . . Papa Paolo faceva obiettione che Michelangelo non haveva fatto sacristia. Rispondeva egli[2] che nel vano di due lumache grandi si potevano cavar due sacristie, lasciandovi due altre lumache delle quattro che vi sono, e che vicino alla tribuna erano due stanze capaci con altre di sopra che potevano servire a questo effetto, e che in Fiorenza nella chiesa principale sono anco due sacristie, ciascuna di mediocre capacità. Diceva di più Papa Paolo che nel disegno di Michelangelo mancava il coro per li canonici. Rispondeva egli che il coro si poteva fare sotto, attorno alli corpi delli Apostoli, dove hoggi è la Confessione, dando ad esso lume da più bande, ma particolarmente dalla faccia orientale dell'altare grande, che si poteva vacar sotto per questo effetto, aggiuntandovi però altrettanto verso oriente [sic], per fare che relassi [sic] in mezzo della cuppola, come hebbe pensiero Michelangelo. Soggiunse di più Papa Paolo, che mancava il campanile; rispose egli che vi erano quattro campanili bellissimi, cioè le quattro cupole picciole che circondano la cuppola grande. Finalmente disse che era inconveniente che restasse scoperta parte alcuna della chiesa di prima, il che sarebbe . . .[3] col disegno di Michelangelo; rispose che ne anco questo seguiva, perchè il sudetto Michelangelo faceva il portico avanti overo antetempio, come hoggi si vede nella chiesa della Ritonda, il quale veniva a coprire il luogo di detta chiesa vecchia. Sopra la parte di mezzo del tempio di Michelangelo si poteva cavar spatio sufficiente con bella ringhiera per le benedittioni et il Papa sarebbe stato sotto il portico et una buona parte del popolo, e l'altro, che non capiva dentro ad esso, sarebbe rimasto fuori: cosa che dava grandezza. Disse a Papa Paolo che un altro Papa haverebbe demolito il nuovo disegno del Maderno per restituire quello di Michelangelo. Rispose Paolo quinto che vi haverebbe fatto tale spesa attorno che ogni Papa haverebbe pensato a demolirlo. Quando vello [sic] attaccorno la nave fatta dal Maderno alla fabrica di Michelangelo, si vidde che quella era più alta di molti palmi della volta e nel pavimento era più depressa. Papa Paolo entrò in collera grande contra il Maderno; ma il card. Barberino lo difese, dicendo che non era sua la colpa, che in tal luogo

[1] See above, p. 388.
[2] Cardinal Barberini.
[3] Here there is a gap in the MSS.

facesse un coro . . .[1] et in un altro una sacristia di altezza e grandezza tale che per ubedire queste fabriche lo havevano portato a quello inconveniente ; soggiunse come si poteva in qualche modo rappezzare che non facesse si brutta volta, cioè nella volta cornici e nel pavimento scalini che facessero unione il più che si poteva con il restante. Dolendosi il medesimo Paolo che Michelangelo havea fatto una gran gofferia, con porre l'altare delli Apostoli non in mezzo della cuppola, rispose che, se questo era errore, non era di Michelangelo, ma di Bramante che haveva fatto li fondamenti e parte dell'alzato ; ma che non era errore, perchè secondo il disegno di Michelangelo all'altare delli Apostoli ne va aggiunto altretanto dalla banda di oriente e così il tutto resta in mezzo e da quattro lati delle tribune fa . . .[1] di quadrato. Portò una volta Carlo Maderno un modello di un pezzo di colonna col capitello che doveva farsi nella facciata di San Pietro, il quale, mostrando di essere di ordine Ionico per le volute, haveva nel mezzo il fiore dell'acanto che appartiene solo all'ordine Corintio. Dimandò il card. Barberino con che regola haveva fatto quel capitello. Rispose Carlo che l'haveva cavato da quel maestro ch'egli tanto stimava, cioè da Michelangelo nel palazzo di Campidoglio, ma che in luogo di maschera haveva fatto il fiore. Replicò il cardinale che haveva fatto male, perchè il fiore è solo dell'ordine Corintio, e che in cambio di maschera, per esser chiesa, si poteva fare un cherubino e si fece in alcune ; in altre volsero porre il fiore. Carlo Maderno era portato dalli card^{li} Cesi et Avignone, senza haver essi intelligenza proportionata al mestiero, nè essi sapevano di architettura, ma lo favorivano perchè serviva loro nelle fabriche.

Memorie intorno la vita d'Urbano VIII. cavate dall'originale di Msgr. Herrera.

[*Barb.* 4901, pp. 47^{b}–49^{b}, Vatican Library.]

13. From the Register of Expenses of Pope Paul V.[2]

Denari che N^{ro} Sig^{re} ha dato contanti alla fabrica
di San Pietro.

A dì . . .[1] febraro 1612 scudi 100 000, retratti in più somma de luoghi del Monte delle Lumiere,

[1] Here there is a gap in the MSS.

[2] See above pp. 393, 403, 415, 416, 420, 428.

luoghi 258⅓ del Monte Novennale e luoghi 300 della Fede	sc.	100 000.—
A dì . . .[1] maggio 1614 sc. 50 241.66, retratti da luoghi 420 del Monte della Fede	sc.	50 241.66
A dì 23 ottobre 1614 sc. 70 800, retratti da luoghi 600 del Monte della Fede	sc.	70 800.—
A dì . . .[1] luglio 1618 sc. 70 467 moneta havuti dal re di Francia per la concordia fatta con S. M[tà] per li Monti che haveva in Roma la già Lionora Concina, compresovi li frutti decorsi per tutto aprile 1618	sc.	70 467.—
	sc.	291 508.66

Cappella e sacristia di Sta Maria Maggiore con la colonna.

Nella fabrica della cappella che la Santità di N. S[re] Papa Paolo V. ha fatta in Sta Maria Maggiore, compresavi la sacristia di detta cappella, le cappellette due di S. Carlo et Sta Francesca, dentro a detta cappella l'altare fatto di metallo e pietre dure et il nicchio dove si è messa la santissima Madonna, et li depositi, statue e pitture, come anco la sacristia grande della chiesa con il coro, che sta congionto a detta sacristia, si trova che si è speso in muratori, scarpellini, pittori, scultori, ferraro, ottonaro et altri, dal principio di detta fabrica per tutto l'ultimo d'ottobre 1618	sc.	306 987.76
E più si è speso nella colonna, che N. S[re] ha fatto drizzare sopra la piazza della chiesa di Sta Maria Maggiore, come si vede nel conto a parte tenuto per la detta colonna	sc.	13 232.41
	sc.	320 220.17

Le sudette spese sono oltre l'argentaria et altri addobamenti et mobili di bellezza e valore grandissimo.

[1] Gap in the MSS.

Palazzo Vaticano.

Nel palazzo di S. Pietro, trovato da N. S[re], quando fu assonto al pontificato, in stato che haveva di bisogno di riparatione necessaria in molti luoghi et tutto conquassato per le due sede vacanti precedenti, vi ha speso in accomodare il portone vecchio di esso Palazzo dentro e fuori, il cortile del teatro, levar terra, far chiaviche, fortificare, coprire et restaurare la galaria [sic] Gregoriana, le stanze et soffitte nell'appartamento nuovo, li forni e tutte le case contigue ad essi, li fenili, stalle et il torron grande della lanterna, il muro della spaliera de' Merlangoli, il muro del giardino di Paolo III., le stanze della stampa, con il bastione sotto la galleria scoperta verso il giardino de' Merlangoli, la galleria bianca coperta e sua volta, rimesse delle carozze, granari, stanze della biada, munitione della legna, galinaro, scale del giardino, delle statue, corritoro scoperto sopra il corritoro longo, stanze della sacristia, armaria, condotti dell'Acqua vecchia de S[to] Antonio, le fontane e palazzina di Pio IV., stanze del Maestro del S[o] Palazzo, fatto di nuovo le stanze et portone sopra la Panattaria con le scale, terrapieno et salita a cordoni, stradone che va alla stampa, molti muri del giardino, dov'erano fatti condotti di S. Antonio a diverse fontane dell'Acqua Paola per tutto il giardino, le stanze dell'archivio a canto della libraria, accomodato le stanze per la Rota, la Segretaria de brevi, li statiolini per l'inverno, e risarcito il Palazzo per li danni fatti nelle dette due sede vacanti passate, ristaurato la guardia delli cavalli leggieri, Svizzari, campanile di Sta Maria Maggiore, vigna di Papa Giulio, e fatto li condotti e fontane per Borgo, in tutto sc. 200 613.50

Nel porton nuovo con la fortificatione et accomodamento delle facciate contigue ad esso, si è speso sc. 33 997.38

sc. 234 610.88

Monte Cavallo.

Nella fabrica di Monte Cavallo, cioè nelle quattro stanze contigue al Palazzo vecchio, nella sala e scale, Dataria, cucine e nel Palazzo di Verselli, nel giardino, stalle, strade, piazza et anche nel riquadramento di detto palazzo di Montecavallo con la capella, che N^ro^ S^re^ ha fatto fare in esso Palazzo, si trova essersi speso in muratori, scarpellini, falegnami, ferrari, stagnari, pittori, vetrari et altri artisti, dal principio di detta fabrica a tutto l'ottobre 1618 sc.	330 370.24
E più sc. 14 000 pagati al sig^r^ Roberto Primi, il quale ne diede credito alla Camera in un conto a parte per pagarne il prezzo delle case che si presero alla salita di Montecavallo e son retratti de Monti Novennali eretti da maggio 1611 sopra l'avanzo che si fece quando s'estinse li luoghi 350 del Monte delle Galere sc.	14 000.—
E più sc. 13 920, che importa luoghi 130 del Monte della Fede a sc. 156 per luogo, dati al sig^r^ Bernardino Maffei per il prezzo del suo Palazzo dove si è messa la Dataria sc.	13 920.—
E più sc. 3300 che importa luoghi 33 del Monte della Pace del Giustiniani a sc. 100 per luogo, dati, cioè sc. 2300. a Francesco Moroni Bergamasco per il prezzo di una casa posta nella salita di Monte Cavallo e sc. 1000 al sig^r^ Tiberio Lancilotto per il canone che haveva sopra detta casa sc.	3 300.—
E più sc. 2552, che importa il prezzo de luoghi 22 del Monte della Fede a sc. 116 assignati alla capella dei sig^ri^ Lancelotti in San Giovanni Laterno in loco delle due case poste nella salita di Montecavallo destinato per detta capella sc.	2 552.—
sc.	364 142.24

Acqua Paola.

Nella fabrica delli condotto dell'Acqua Paola, ch'è stata condotta da Bracciano alla mostra

vicina a S. Pietro Montorio, si trova essersi speso per mezo del Banco di S^{to} Spirito sc. 152 532.11, ritratti de luoghi $1416\frac{2}{3}$ del Monte di S. Spirito con alcuni frutti decorsi sc.	152 532.11
E più sc. 198 944.50 per mezo dell'istesso Banco di S. Spirito, retratto de luoghi 1772 del Monte della Carne, con alcuni frutti decorsi sc.	198 944.50
E più sc. 25 000 pagati a D. Virginio Orsino per l'acqua che s'è havuta da lui e per tutti li danni patiti da S. E. nello stato di Bracciano per li condotti di detta Acqua sc.	25 000.—
E più sc. 20 000 per luoghi 200 dell'istesso Monte di S^{to} Spirito eretti quando si ridusse detto Monte, li frutti de quali servirono per dote e mantenimento delli condotti di detta Acqua sc.	20 000.—
sc.	396 476.61

Convertite.

Aiuto dato alle monache convertite per ristaurare il loro convento che per accidente s'abbrugiò, sc. 12 000, retratti da luoghi 100 del Monte di S. Bonaventura eretti a questo effetto sopra l'avanzo della ridutione del Monte Pio sc.	12 000.—

Sant'Agnese.

Nella tribuna et altare di Sta Agnese, opera di muro e scarpelle s'è speso sc.	1 440.47
Per la cassa d'argento sc.	3 440.35
sc.	4 880.82

Debito lasciato da N. S^{re} Papa Paolo V., dedutto l'estintioni fatte de danari lasciati contanti alla sua morte scudi un milione ottanta tre mila duecento cinquanta sc.	1 083 250.85
E più nelli Monti del Popolo Romano scudi diciassette milla e cento sc.	17 100.—
sc.	1 100 350.85

Sommario dell'esito di P. Paolo V.

Denari dati all' Abbundanza	sc.	744 054.60
Spesi al porto di Civita Vecchia	sc.	78 042.17
Nella palificata di Fiumicino	sc.	80 291.—
Nel porto d'Ancona	sc.	15 050.52
Aiuti dati a principi	sc.	335 029.54
Fortezza di Ferrara	sc.	560 874.—
Cappella di Sta Maria Maggiore	sc.	320 220.17
Fabrica della chiesa di S. Pietro	sc.	291 508.66
Palazzo Vaticano	sc.	234 610.88
Palazzo di Monte Cavallo	sc.	364 142.24
Acqua Paola	sc.	396 475.61
Aiuto delle Convertite	sc.	12 000.—
Nella tribuna e cassa di Sta Agnese	sc.	4 800.—
	sc.	3 437 099.39

Questo è l'esito delle cose straordinarie del tempo dalla felice memoria di N[ro] S[re] Papa Paolo V., oltre le spese fatte nel tempo delli rumori di Venetia, de' quali non s'è fatto mentione in questo libro.

Come anco delli mobili che detto Paolo V. fece fare per servitio delli palazzi di S. Pietro e di Monte Cavallo, che ascendono a scudi cinquantamila.

[*Borghese*, I., 554 and *Biblioteca Pia*, 265, p. 64[b] *seq.*, Papal Secret Archives.]

14. Biographies of Paul V. and the Notes of Giovan Battista Costaguti.

Soon after the death of Paul V. the Polish Dominican Abraham Bzovius [1] composed a biography of the Pope which he dedicated to Urban VIII.[2] His work is based on good sources, both written and oral, and supplies much valuable information as well as a number of important official documents. Bzovius was under great obligation to Paul V., hence

[1] *Cf.* Hurter, *Nomenclator*, I., 338 *seq.*

[2] Paulus V. Burghesius P.O.M.F. Abrahami Bzovii Poloni S.T., magistri, Ord. Praed. Romae, 1626, with the motto: In memoria aeterna erit justus, ab auditione mala non timebit. Psalm CXI.

his gratitude has influenced his pen to such an extent that in places his biography becomes a sheer panegyric.[1]

The same feature characterizes an anonymous publication : *Pauli V. Pont. Max. Vita compendio scripta* (Barb. 2670, Vatican Library), to which RANKE (III.[6], 99) refers briefly, though without drawing from it to any considerable extent.

In 1765 there was published at Amsterdam an anonymous *Histoire de Paul V.* (in two volumes), the author of which was the Abbé Cl. P. Goujet, a keen adherent of the party of the *Appellants* (*cf.* REUSCH, *Index*, II., 768). Goujet seems to have been in no way shocked by the Pope's nepotism. His party spirit caused him to be interested in quite another matter, and he makes no mystery of its nature : this was, opposition to the Jesuits who had just been expelled from France, opposition also to all *prétentions ultramontaines* and to Molinism (*cf.* vol. xxv., p. 249, note 1). Nevertheless he quotes a number of useful passages which he extracted from the reports of Savary de Brèves, Henry IV.'s envoy in Rome, now preserved in the Bibliothèque Nationale of Paris, though these must be used with caution. PERRENS, in the *Revue hist.*, LXXIV., 242 *seq.*, points out Goujet's partisanship, but, as has been explained in the *Hist. Zeitschr.*, XXXI., 95, Perrens himself makes the mistake of relying, for his characterization of Paul V., on the unfair and frequently self-contradictory reports of so intolerant a Gallican as Brèves. Of incomparably greater value are the notes of GIOVAN BATTISTA COSTAGUTI, which were not even meant for publication. They are based all through on his own personal observation for which, as Bzovius remarks (c. 42), he was well placed owing to his office of " Forriere maggiore " and eventually of " Maggiordomo " of Paul V.[2] The title of these notes is

[1] *Cf.* especially chapters 20 and 56 on the nephews and the comparison with other Popes in chapter 59.

[2] According to MORONI (XLI., 263) he held this post from 1618 to 1621. To complete Moroni's data we may add that, according to the original documents of the Costaguti Archives, Giov. Battista was named a Protonotary on July 19, 1608, having received the first Tonsure on July 17. In December, 1614, he became a Canon of St. Mary Major ; see *Studi e docum.*, XV., 284. Here he is already styled *maestro di casa del Papa*. See also RENAZZI, *Maggiordomi Pontifici*, Roma, 1785, 112 ; also in Costaguti Archives a document on "Allogio preparato per commandamento di Paolo V. per la venuta a Roma dell'Altezza di Mantova da G. B. Costaguta foriere maggiore di S.S. nel mese di Dicembre 1618 ".

as follows: *Alcune attioni di Paolo V. raccolte da Giovan Battista Costaguta* (sic !) *suo maggiordomo e foriere maggiore di quello e pervenuto a sua notitia o per haverle trattate o per haverle S.S^{tà} con lui conferite.* I had the good fortune to find them in the year 1904 in the private archives of the Costaguti family; so far they have not been used at all by historians (Cod. No. 11).

Costaguti praises the good intentions of Paul V. as regards the Papal State, viz. the upholding of justice and the establishment of public tranquillity, his solicitude for the welfare of the people, security of the State from external attacks, and lastly, the improvement and embellishment of his residence, Rome. His work is divided into four chapters or parts. It is not easy to give a concise account of the contents for there is but little sequence in the entries. Costaguti is exceedingly sparing of chronological data. It is clear that his work is a first draft which he intended to retouch at a later date. The writer is chiefly interested in matters of finance on which all four sections furnish us with valuable information. The first part consists mainly of a survey of the Pope's activities with special reference to his expenditure. The second section begins with a memorial: *Donde nasca il mancamento della Sede Apostolica.* There follow data on the Pope's buildings. The latter are discussed in even greater detail in the third and most important section. In this part the author speaks also of the subsidies to Catholic princes. The fourth part deals with embassies sent to Paul V., indicates the personnel of some of the Congregation established by him and once more gives some information on expenditure, the most interesting being details of the expenditure on St. Peter's and other constructions of the Pope.[1] Some of the most important passages I herewith quote textually:—

[Chapter I.]

Abondanza.

Hebbe a cuore l'Abondanza, e nel suo stato mai si patì di vittoaglie, ne di prezzo eccessivo, come è successo ne luoghi convicini.

[1] Vol. XXV. pp. 49 *seqq.*, 53, 78, 86 *seqq.*, 96, 99 *seqq.*, 104, 105, 109, 110, 275. Vol. XXVI., 351, 365.

Ha provista di roba anco di fuori dello stato, quando è occorso il bisogno senza guardare ne a spesa, ne ad interesse.

Per mantenimento delle vittoaglie ha fabricato granari e farinari, dove faceva conservare molta quantità di grano e farina. E la farina particolarmente contro la malitia de fornari et inondatione del fiume.

Ha procurato l'accrescimento dell'arte del campo, e dati privilegi agli agricoltori tanto di Roma quanto di Corneto.

All'Abondanza di Roma ha lasciato grosso corpo di denari.

Deputò una Congregatione di prelati per il governo di essa, e volse che si facesse in Palazzo contigua alle sue stanze per potervi intervenire a suo piacere o sentire de vicino quello che in essa si discorreva e li pareri d'ognuno de congregati.

Le risolutioni faceva annotare a un libro et a Sua Santità se ne mandava copia et in margine annotava quello approvava, reprovava, raccordava o commandava si havesse ad esseguire.

Da principio hebbe pensiero, che l'Abondanza consistesse principalmente nel fare le pagnotte grosse. Questa opinione era fomentata da alcuni della Congregatione o fosse per aderire alla volontà del principe o perchè così credevano et essendo state alcune bone raccolte agiutarono questa opinione.

Cominciò poi la terra a non rendere il frutto così abondante. Li mercati perciò a lasciare di sementare, poichè non potevano dare il grano al prezzo, che era necessario al fornaro per fare il peso del pane, come voleva il prefetto dell'Annona. Li fornari facevano pane cattivo per poterne cavare il denaro e pagare il prezzo del grano a quei mercanti che restavano.

Il principe rimetteva di borsa in far venire i grani di fuori a grave prezzo per potere supplire al mancamento di quello che non nasceva nel territorio di Roma.

Da questo disordine volse Sua Santità che nella Congregatione si facesse discorso di quello si havesse da fare. E li pareri furono diversi, quali si dettero in iscritto a Sua Santità e si notorno nel libro delle resolutioni. Fu il cardinale Serra di parere, che si mantenesse il pane grosso. Monsignor Rucellai prefetto dell'Annona disse, che li dava l'animo di mantenere il pane al peso, che si trovava, se così commandava Sua Santità. Il Commissario della Camera et il Costaguta affermorno, che si dovea calare il peso, valendo più al popolo il pane di manco peso e buono, che grosso e cattivo, e che oltre al servitio del popolo era utile del principe, che non vi rimetteva di borsa, e si sariano mantenuti i mercanti, che haveriano potuto lavorar il terreno.

In ogni modo era tanto il zelo di Sua Santità verso li poveri, che volse seguitare il parere di lasciare il pane di peso grave. Ma verso la fine dell'anno accortosi del pan cattivo, che si faceva et accertatosene con mandarlo a comprare da parafranieri, e da alcune false accuse, che vennero dati contro i mercanti de grani che le cose violenti non sono durabili, fece dal Costaguta fare discorso di quello le paresse circa il modo di governar l'Abondanza. Glielo detti in scritto l'anno 1613.[1] E nell'anni seguenti si governò conforme alle stagioni con gran facilità. E quando le raccolte eran triste, come fu l'anno 1617, con la quantità do grani che teneva ne granari, havea tempo di fare le provisioni di fuori, si come fece di gran somma, e quello che perdeva ne grani forastieri in tempo di strettezza, lo guadagnava in quelli che haveva già provisti ne tempi di larghezza.

Mantenimento dello stato.

Sapeva Sua Santità lo stato ricuperato da Giulio II. a santa Chiesa, la prohibitione di non alienarlo fatta da Pio V. e 'l tesoro messo in Castello da Sisto V. Ma non giudicando Sua Santità bastanti queste provisioni lo ha assicurato :

Con fortezze.

Finì quella di Ferrara cominciata da Clemente VIII., risarcì quelle del mare Adriatico, quelle del Mar Tirreno e fabricò nove torri per scoperta dell'incursioni de Corsari. Volse, che fussero munite d'armi e di vittoaglie.

Con l'armi.

Fece due armarie in Roma, in Castel S. Angelo l'una, e l'altra in Vaticano. Una in Ancona, una in Bologna, et una in Ferrara, et fondere molte artiglierie.

E volse, che dal Costaguta si procurassero inventari di tutte l'armi offensive e difensive, che sono nell'armerie, fortezze, città, terre e luoghi dello stato provisti da Sua Santità e da

[1] The *Discorso di G. B. Costaguta sopra il governo dell'Abbondanza di Roma data alla s. mem. di Paolo V. l'anno 1614 (*sic* !) is kept in Costaguti Archives in Rome.

suoi predecessori. De quali fu fatto libro, e lasciato l'esemplare in Camera non più per l'adietro usato.

Introdusse in Tivoli la fabrica d'ogni sorte d'armi offensive e difensive per la soldatesca non più stata per l'adietro in altro luogo del stato ecclesiastico.

Con le militie.

Instituì le militie a piede et a cavallo per tutto lo stato, le fece armare a certo numero, e le nobilitò con privilegi, sapendo che non basta al principe haver li popoli ben affetti, se in tempo di bisogno non sono armati ed essercitati.

Con denari.

There follows a general survey of activity in this sphere.

Conservatione delle Scritture.

Per conservatione delle scritture della Sede Apostolica ha fatto nel Vaticano archivii, perchè non siano strabalzate, come per li tempi passati. Levò però la stampa del Palazzo Vaticano, ancorchè utile, quando se li fosse atteso, acciochè li poco amorevoli della Sede Apostolica non potessero far comento sopra i libri stampati con qualche errore o per inavertenza del stampatore o poca cura del correttore.

Accrebbe la libraria di stanze e di libri e la ornò.

Roma.

A Roma città dominante e sua patria hebbe amore particolare ne tralasciò cosa che potesse credere utile alla città o particolari.

Agiutò la povertà, quelli non atti a lavorare con l'elemosine manuali, nelle quali si distribuiva grossa somma a monasteri, luoghi pii, persone vergognose, povere zitelle, che o si monacavano o si maritavano, poveri infermi et altri d'ogni sorte. A quelli che erano atti a lavorare dava il modo di guadagnare con le fabriche, che ha fatto principalmente per trattenimento de poveri della città, che in conseguenza hanno causato bellezza ad essa città, commodo a Pontefici et honore al Signore Idio et alla sua santissima Madre. Ha però fatta condurre l'Acqua Paola, fabricato il Palazzo di Monte Cavallo con la cappella, ristaurato il Palazzo Vaticano, fornita la chiesa di S. Pietro con la loggia della benedittione et Confessione, la cappella di Santa Maria Maggiore e sacristia, la sacristia di detta chiesa, eretta la colonna che stava al tempio della Pace avanti a detta chiesa, et a Santa Agnese fatto il ciborio sopra l'altare et in esso altare riposti li corpi di detta Santa e di santa Emerenziana in una cassa d'argento, ristaurato il monasterio delle Convertite, et altro. Quali fabriche et elemosine, che mantenevano molta quantità di persone, hanno dato occasione d'augumento alla città. . . .

[Chapter II.]

Porti e strade fatte e raccomodate.

Porto di Fano.
Porto di Civitavecchia.
Porto d'Ancona.
Ponte di Ciprano et altri accomodati e risarciti.
La bocca della Fiumara di Roma.
La strada di Campagna per Napoli . . .

Fabriche in servitio dell'Abondanza.

Granari a Termini oltre un farinaio. Un cortile grande per commodità d'asciugar i grani, che fossero in qualche modo offesi.

Fontana per commodità delli bestiami, che portano il grano.

Accomodato il Palazzo di S. Giovanni Laterano a uso di granaro.

Risarciti li granari di Ripa Grande.

Fatto granaro nel Palazzo Vaticano per servitio del Palazzo e di Borgo . . .

[Chapter III.]

Fabriche per servitio dello stato.

Fortezza di Ferrara.

Torre di Badino appresso Terracina. Torri di Valdalga e Marangone appresso a Civitavecchia.

Ristaurato la fortezza e città d'Ancona e la Santa Casa et altri luoghi maritimi tanto del Mar Adriatico come dal Mar Tirreno . . .

Fabrica dell'armi in Tivoli.

Sua Santità dette molti privilegi a quest'arte con facoltà d'estraere fuor del stato la roba fabricata, e dette intentione, avviata che fosse la fabrica, di prohibire l'introdurre nel stato simili opere forestiere . . .

Elemosine

continoate e fatte fare dalla santa memoria di Paolo V.

A sette collegi oltramontani [1] e case de poveri, e sono l'infrascritte :

Il Collegio di Braunsperga, Fulda, Velna, Praga, Vienna [2] . . ., Olmus e . . .,[2] Case de proveri di Fulda e Praga	sc.	11 190
Collegio di Remes in Francia	sc.	2 100
Collegio delli Inglesi in Roma	sc.	600
Collegio de Maroniti di Roma	sc.	600
Collegio di Scio	sc.	520
Al P. Generale de Gesuiti per sovvenitione della missione di Costantinopoli	sc.	600
Al detto per sovvenitione d'alcuni padri che sono in Altena	sc.	100
Alla Casa del Rifugio di Roma	sc.	1 000
Al Collegio Scozzese di Roma	sc.	600
Penitentieri di S. Pietro	sc.	1 000
Penitentieri di S. Giovanni Laterano	sc.	160
Alle Scuole Pie	sc.	200
Alla Dottrina Christiana	sc.	200
Alle coltre delle Catedrali	sc.	500
Vestiti d'infedeli che venivano al santissimo battesimo	sc.	3 000
Alla Santissima Nuntiata per il maritaggio delle zitelle sc. 1500 d'oro per	sc.	1 950
Al Confalone per il maritaggio delle zitelle sc. 300 d'oro per	sc.	390

All'elemosiniero publico e segreto per distribuir a luoghi pii, a poveri religiosi, e zitelle che si monacavano o maritavano. Pelegrini et oltramontani, che

[1] *Cf.* the *Tabella per le paghe da farsi dal depositario della Camera in 1619. *Cod.* 362, p. 16 of Archivio di Propaganda, in Rome.

[2] Name illegible.

venivano a Roma. Poveri vergognosi, et infermi della Città e simili sc. 42 000

Al decano de parafrenieri per dar a poveri mendichi ogn'anno in Camera sc. 1 000

A luoghi pii per lo stato sc. 5 000

Elemosine di Palazzo, cioè in Campo Santo pane e vino due giorni la settimana a 1000 poveri. Si dava a mangiare a 27 poveri ogni giorno. Elemosine a diversi luoghi pii di Roma una volta la settimana. Alla casa delli Indiani e loro interprete e capellano. All'ospedale di Santa Marta quello bisogna. Alli prigioni. A molte persone nobili venute in povertà. A molti venuti alla fede. Il tutto si calcola possa importare sc. 10 000

sc. 82,710

Oltre alle sudette se ne facevano
Dal Datario.
Da Monsignor Tesoriere.
Da tribunali.
Da doganieri per l'esentione.
Dalli appaltatori di sale in sale.
Da Sua Santità di sua mano.

Acqua Paola.

L'Acqua Paola condotta da Bracciano fa capo in due luoghi, cioè nel Janicolo a S. Pietro Montorio e nel Vaticano in Belvedere.

Da S. Pietro Montorio si riparte a Ponte Sisto, a Savelli, a Orsini, in Trastevere et altri luoghi. Da Belvedere si riparte dentro al Palazzo alli torrioni, a piede alle scale, dentro al giardino, alla fontana Isolata, alla Musaica, alla Palazzina, alle statue d'Innocentio, alla Cleopatra, alla Peschiera grande, sopra la Galleria, alla Vignola, alla libraria, nel teatro, alla Panattaria, alli Svizzeri, Fuor del Palazzo : sotto il Porticale di S. Pietro, nella Piazza di S. Pictro, alla Piazza del signor cardinale Borghese, alla Traspontina vecchia, per Borgo novo, per Borgo vecchio, a S. Spirito per l'ospedale, per Borgo-S. Spirito, alla Lungara et altri luoghi.

Il condurre l'acqua e far cisterne publiche è peso del principe a spese de popoli, che ne sentono il benefitio, la necessità dell'acqua è cosa naturale et il popolo e particolamente i poveri la possono havere solo per mezzo delli acquedotti e cisterne publiche, non havendo essi ne modo ne commodità di farne. Che in Trastevere e Borgo, per quali luoghi è stata condotta principalmente quest'acqua ve ne fosse bisogno, si vede chiaramente, e già vi fu condotta l'Acqua Felice dalla santa memoria di Clemente VIII., che poi per la rottura del Ponte Santa Maria non potè continuare. È utile perchè cresce la città d'habitatori per la commodità dell'acqua e li datii publici.

Monte Cavallo.

Aperta et indolcita la strada. Allargata la piazza. Fabricata la guardia de cavalli a Vercelli, le stalle per il Palazzo con le commodità delle fontane. Comprò il Palazzo della Dataria. Et attaccato al Palazzo molta quantità di case per la commodità della Corte con cortili grandi. Il giardino nobilitato di fontane e di piante, fabricato nella galleria del Palazzo un salotto con due camerini, capella et altre commodità per l'inverno ottime.

Verso il giardino.

Fabricar le scale ample, alte e chiare, un salone con due sale. Quattro stanze, et una capella privata belle et ornate di pitture con altre commodità sopra. Riquadrato il cortile e selciato.

Verso strada Pia.

Una sala con sei stanze belle. Un salone con la capella nobilissima per funtioni publiche. Sotto stanze nobili per li tribunali della Ruota e Camera e per li ministri della capella. Sopra molte commodità per la famiglia.

È stato necessario fabricare questo palazzo per havere il principe luogo, dove ritirarsi massime l'estate per fuggire la mal aria del Vaticano, conforme all'esempio degli antecessori, che molti sono anche andati fuor di Roma. E da Gregorio XIII. ultimamente fu preso questo luogo, dove per serie continoata hanno habitato tutti i Papi, ma con molto incommodo loro e della famiglia e di tutta la Corte, danno di molte migliaia di scudi alla Camera per le pigioni delle case che si pagavano e roba che si strapazzava in portarla e riportarla da un luogo all'altro, gridi d'habitatori convicini, ch'erano cacciati di casa, lamenti de padroni di esse case, che non trovavano a locarle, e che da cortigiani gli erano lasciate in cattivi termini, e che era più la spesa che facevano in accomodarle, che il provento di esse pigioni.

Palazzo Vaticano.

Accomodato il portone vecchio di esso Palazzo dentro e fuori. Il cortile del Teatro. Levata terra. Fatte chiaviche. Fortificata, coperta e ristaurata la galeria Gregoriana. Le stanze e soffitte dell'appartamento nuovo. Li forni e tutte le case contigue ad essi. Le fenili, stalle. Il torron grande della lanterna. Il muro della spalliera de Melangoli. Il muro del giardino di Paolo III. Le stanze della stampa con il bastone sotto la galeria scoperta, e sua volta. Rimesse delle carrozze, granari, stanze della biada. Munitione della legna. Gallinaro, scale del giardino delle statue. Corritore scoperto sopra il corritore longo. Stanze della sacristia. Armeria. Condotti dell'Acqua vecchia di S. Antonio. Le fontane e palazzina di Pio IV., stanze del Maestro del Sacro Palazzo. Fatte di novo le stanze, e portone sopra la panataria con le scale, terrapieno e salita a cordone. Stradone, che va alla stampa. Molti muri del giardino, dove erano fratte. Condotti di S. Antonio, e diverse fontane del l'Acqua Paolo per tutto il giardino. Le stanze dell'Archivio acanto alla libraria. Accomodato nel palazzo novo la Dataria con tutti gli offitiali. Dato luogo alli registri di tutti gli offitii della Corte, le stanze per la Ruota. La Segreteria de brevi. Li stanziolini per l'inverno. Risarcito il Palazzo per li danni fatti nelle due sedi vacanti passate. Ristaurata la guardia de cavalli legieri et svizzeri. Li bastioni di Borgo. In Castello molti luoghi. Il Corridore che dal Palazzo Vaticano va in Castello. Rifatto l'albero di Castello abbrugiato dalla saetta.

Due sono state le necessità di fabricare in questo palazzo. L'una causata dall'antichità di esso Palazzo che in questo tempo era venuto a termine d'haver bisogno di molto risarcimento essendovi in esso molte parti, che minacciavano rovina, oltre il ristauramento de danni, che furono fatti grandi nelle due sedi vacanti antecedenti. La seconda causata dall'haver atterrata molta parte di esso Palazzo per dar luogo alla fabrica della Chiesa di S. Pietro, che è bisognato risarcire quella parte che è restata e trovar nuovo luogo alla Dataria, Camera, Ruota et altri offitii della Corte necessarii et utili per grandezza della Sede Apostolica.

Chiesa di S. Pietro.

La Chiesa di S. Pietro fornita. Il porticale. La loggia della benedittione. La sacristia. Il choro. La Confessione di S. Pietro con pietre belle, statue di metallo indorato di molto valore. Una lampada d'argento bella per l'artifitio, e di valore per il peso. Entrata per il mantenimento de lumi e per la custodia di essi.

Questa fabrica era in stato di manifesta ruina, come fu considerato da molti architetti. Da Nostro Signore col consiglio del sacro Collegio de cardinali in un concistoro segreto fu risoluto, che si buttasse a terra e quanto prima si rifacesse, e con molta ragione essendovi quel santo corpo, che tutto il mondo riverisce, capo di santa Chiesa, e dal quale Roma riceve gloria e la Sede Apostolica veneratione.

Per dar luogo a questa fabrica fu necessario buttar a terra gran parte del Palazzo ad essa contiguo, dove eran stanze e molte commodità per li Pontifici, loro corte e famiglia. E dovendo Giov. Battista Costaguta come forier maggiore trovarli nuovo luogo, fece fare la pianta del restante Palazzo con tutte le parti adiacenti, inclusa la detta basilica et essendole parsa oltre al suo bisogno cosa curiosa, essortò Martino Ferrabosco valente architetto a far l'intagliare in rame, et insieme l'alzata, prospetto et altre parti della basilica vecchia e nova, e darla al mondo si per memoria di esse, come per gusto delli intelligenti della professione.

Accettò volentieri l'impresa et in vita di esso Paolo V. havendone finite alcune tavole li furono mostrate. E vistole Sua Santità lodò talmente l'opera, che commandò si attendesse alla fine, e che le tavole si facessero vestite d'historia. Fu però chiamato Ferrante Carlo scelto fra primi letterati della Corte et eminente in ogni professione, et a questo effetto gli furono assegnate stanze in Palazzo vicino alla libraria e provisto il suo bisogno, acciò potesse con più facilità attendere all'opera.[1]

[1] See above, p. 426, n. 2.

Santa Maria Maggiore.

Da fondamenti fatta la sacristia per li canonici et altra per li beneficiati con palazzo per habitatione de canonici e ministri della chiesa, stanze per far il Capitolo et il choro per uso del clero.

Ristaurato il tetto del sudetto palazzo abbrugiato per inavvertenza di un ministro, che dormiva in una stanza sotto a esso tetto.

Accomodato il campanile tocco due volte dalla saetta e copertolo di piombo.

Rifatta la campana grossa.

Drizzata la colonna, levata dal tempio della Pace e messavi sopra la Madonna Santissima col putto in braccio in metallo indorato. Condotta l'acqua alla detta colonna et alla guglia situata dall'altra parte di essa chiesa. Aperte molte strade. Da fondamenti eretta la nobilissima capella ornata di marmi bellissimi con statue di marmo et in essa postovi il deposito di Clemente e sue imprese. Il telaro dell'altare di essa capella ornato di diaspro con colonne e basi dell'istesso, e sopra di esso angeli di tutto rilievo di metallo indorato. La luce del quadro di esso altare, di lapislazaro con angiolini di mezzo rilievo di metallo indorato et il telari in faccia alla santissima imagine di amatista con un altro telaro a torno pieno di diverse gioie. Il legno, dov'è dipinta la santissima imagine, è posto dentro a una cassa di metallo in un solo pezzo indorato, coperto con ornamento d'argento con oro, adornata con una bellissima collana, e corona di gioie diverse legate in oro et argento, et una croce d'oro con belli diamanti con catena d'oro.

Contigoa alla capella ha fabricata la sacristia per servitio di essa molto bella con abitatione per il sacristano e protettore pro tempore.

Ha ornata detta capella e sacristia, e così quella de canonici di molto belle e vaghe pitture, descritte in libro da Andrea Vittorelli l'anno 1616. Per servitio di questa capella Sua Santità a fatto una molto bella, ricca e vaga supellettile. Sei candelieri e croce d'argento per l'altar maggiore di vago lavoro e molto peso. Due torchieroni grandi pure d'argento, et una lampada, et altre simili d'ottone.

Per le capellette candalieri, croce e lampada d'argento, oltre quelle d'ottone per li giorni ordinarii. Teste molto grandi.

Apostoli in statue di rilevo, reliquiari belli. Vasi per fiori tutti d'argento.

Di questi vasi ve ne sono anco d'ottone e di christallo ornati d'argento.

Molti calici con loro patene. Profumieri grandi. Ostensori, bacili d'oro, e di essi due con gioie, piviali, tonicelle, paramenti d'altare di ricamo d'oro, di damasco con trine d'oro et altri in gran quantità.

Biancheria per tutto il bisogno in gran copia e con lavori belli assai. Tutto quello, che è necessario per la consacratione de vescovi, tanto per il consacrato, quanto per il consacrante.

Data entrata per mantenere i ministri, la fabrica e la supellettile.

I canonici di detta basilica per gratitudine di animo di tanti benefitii fatti a detta chiesa, gli hanno eretta una statua maggiore del naturale di metallo.

Sua Santità era particolarmente divoto della santissima Vergine e da lei riconosceva ogni sua grandezza e bene.

Altre fabriche pie.

A Santa Agnese ha fatto il ciborio. Una cassa d'argento, dove è stato riposto il corpo di essa Santa e di sant'Emerenziana.

Alla fabrica del monasterio delle Convertite abrugiato casualmente ha dato grosso agiuto.

Al Seminario Romano comprò il palazzo.

A Frascati ha fatta la chiesa de Camaldoli, da Sua Santità introdotti a quel luogo.

Fabriche publiche.

A Ripa Grande le scale per commodità del scarico delle barche. A Ripetta luogo capace per le legna, che publicamente si vendono.

Aperte strade a S. Francesco in Trastevere.

Allargata e ridrizzata la strada a Ponte quattro capi.

Alla Scrofa et altre intorno a Monte Cavallo selciata la strada del Popolo sino a Ponte Molle . . .

[Chapter IV.]

Congregationi instituite da Paolo V.

Congregatione per la militia.

Signor cardinale De Cesis.
Monsignor Cappone tesoriere generale [1] e poi cardinale.
Signor Mario Farnese luogotenente generale.
Monsignor Malvasia chierico di Camera.
Monsignor [Giulio] Monterentio commissario della Camera.[2]
Giovan Battista Costaguta.

Congregatione del saldo de conti.

Monsignor Cappone tesoriere generale.
Monsignor Malvasia chierico di Camera.
Monsignor Monterentio commissario della Camera.
Giovan Battista Costaguta.

Antonio Fracasso Fantino Benzi Matteo Pini Giov. Carlo Claratio	computisti della Camera.

Congregatione delle fabriche.

Monsignor Cappone tesoriere generale.
Giovan Battista Costaguta.
Giov. Angelo Formento.
Flaminio Ponsi architetto di Sua Santità.
Carlo Maderno architetto della fabbrica di S. Pietro.

Congregatione dell'Abondanza.

Monsignor Serra tesoriere generale e poi cardinale.[3]
Monsignor [Girolamo] Serlupi chierico di Camera e presidente della Grascia.
Monsignor Rucellai chierico di Camera e prefetto dell'Annona.
Signor Ortensio de Rossi commissario della Camera.
Giov. Battista Costaguta.

[1] See above, vol. XXV., 54.
[2] Cf. Moroni, XCIX., 140.
[3] Above, XXV., p. 333.

Congregatione per l'interessi della Camera.

Monsignor Patritio tesoriere generale.
Signor Ortensio de Rossi commissario della Camera.
Giov. Battista Costaguta.

Fabriche in Roma e per il stato.

Fortezza di Ferrara c[a]	sc.	600 000
Porto di Civitavecchia	sc.	82 000
Fiumicino c[a]	sc.	62 000
Investiti nel Monte delle Communità seconda erettione per mantenimento di essa c[a]	sc.	18 000
Laghetto in Castel Gandolfo c[a]	sc.	3 600
Porto d'Ancona	sc.	15 000
Palazzo Vaticano	sc.	240 000
Monte Cavallo c[a]	sc.	365 000
Acqua Paola c[a]	sc.	400 000
Granari di Termini	sc.	25 000
	sc.	1 810 600

Fabrica di S. Pietro.

Ha donato per servitio di dessa fabrica : A dì . . . Febraro 1612 sc. 100[m], ritratti in più somma da luoghi 300 del Monte delle Lumiere. Luoghi 258⅓ del Monte Novenale e luoghi 300 della Fede eretti sopra li detti 2000 delli pescivendoli di Roma. E scudi 3000 dell'avanzo della reduttione del Monte Sisto	sc.	100 000
A dì . . . Maggio 1614 sc. 50241, ritratti da luoghi 420 del Monte della Fede eretti sopra l'avanzo della riduttione del Monte della Fede	sc.	50 241
A dì 23 Ottobre 1614 sc. 70 800, ritratti da luoghi 600 del Monte della Fede eretti sopra l'apalto del Banco di Pescaria	sc.	70 800
A dì . . . Luglio 1618 sc. 70 467 moneta, havuti dal re di Francia per la concordia fatta con Sua Maestà per li Monti, che doveva in Roma la già Leonora Concina compresivi li frutti decorsi per tutto Aprile 1618	sc.	70 467
	sc.	291 508

Li sudetti Monti sono compresi nel debito fatto da esso Paolo V. di sopra descritto.

Entrate donate da Paolo V. alla fabrica di S. Pietro oltre alla retroscritta somma de denari.

In Napoli.

Gabella del grano a rotolo detti 7243, tari 2 e grani 7.
Gabella de frutti et agrumi detti 5096, tari 1 e grani 9.
Gabella del 2º grano a rotolo detti 4999, tari 4 e grani 18.

In Portogallo.

Assegnamento sopra la Crociata di Portogallo detti 10ᵐ de reais, sc. 500 ogn'anno . . .

Fabriche de luoghi pii.

A Santa Maria Maggiore in fabrica cª	sc.	330 000
Nella capella in mobili cª	sc.	50 000
Alle convertite cª	sc.	12 000
Palazzo comprà per il Seminario Romano cª	sc.	18 300
Santa Agnese cª	sc.	5 000
A Frascati a Camaldoli cª	sc.	6 000
	sc.	421 300

Agiuto dato a' principi.

All'imperator Rodolpho l'anno 1606 circa	sc.	130 000
Al re di Polonia l'anno 1613 cª	sc.	40 000
Al principe di Nemburgh l'anno 1614 cª	sc.	10 000
All'imperator Ferdinando fiorini 380ᵐ che sono in cª	sc.	228 000
	sc.	408 000

Alla lega di Germania li denari cavati dalle decime del clero d'Italia.

INDEX OF NAMES IN VOL. XXVI.

Printed in Great Britain by Stephen Austin & Sons, Ltd., Hertford.